The HTML Sourcebook
Second Edition

A Complete Guide to HTML 3.0

Ian S. Graham

Wiley Computer Publishing

John Wiley & Sons, Inc.

New York • Chichester • Brisbane • Toronto • Singapore

Publisher: Katherine Schowalter
Editor: Philip M. Sutherland
Assistant Editor: Allison Roarty
Managing Editor: Mark Hayden
Text Design & Composition: Benchmark Productions, Inc.

Library of Congress Cataloging-in-Publication Data:
ISBN 0-471-14242-5

Printed in the United States of America

10   9   8   7   6   5   4   3

CONTENTS ▰▰▰

In the introduction to the first edition of this book, I stated that the World Wide Web had "taken the Internet by storm." At the time I hoped this was appropriate, but felt in my heart that I was probably overstating things, if only a little. In retrospect, it was a gross understatement. Over the past year the Web has grown far beyond everyone's expectations (well, perhaps not Marc Andreessen's!), to become one of the core new technologies of the 1990s. Hundreds if not thousands of companies now offer Web-based products, and the trickle of products available in late 1994 has grown, by late 1995, into a torrent. Purely Web-based companies such as Netscape Communications are now market-valued in the billions of dollars—and Netscape did not even exist a year ago. This is not "a storm," but a tidal wave of epic proportions.

What we are seeing is not just the birth of a new technology, but the springing into existence of a whole new paradigm of culture and communication. This is because the World Wide Web model makes distributing and accessing any form of digital data easy and inexpensive for anyone—company or consumer—with profound implications for business, culture, and society. Thus it is no surprise that seemingly "everyone" is now buying or downloading the latest in Web tools and is madly learning how to build pages, so that they too can join this new electronic world.

A tool may be easy to use, but usually requires skill and training to be used well. This is certainly true of the tools involved in preparing and distributing information via HyperText documents and Internet HyperText servers. Preparing well-designed, useful, and reliable Web resources requires an in-depth understanding of how the tools that deliver these resources work and how to use them *well*. The intention of this book, as of the first edition, is to help you develop this understanding. In essence, there are three tools or concepts that you need to know:

1. *Uniform Resource Locators*, or *URLs*, which is the scheme by which Internet resources are addressed in the WWW.

2. *The HyperText Transfer Protocol (HTTP)* and HTTP *client-server* interactions. HTTP servers are designed specifically to distribute HyperText documents, and you must know how they work if you are to take advantage of their powerful features.

3. The *HyperText Markup Language*, or *HTML*. This is the markup language with which World Wide Web HyperText documents are written and is what allows you to create HyperText links, fill-in forms, and clickable images. Writing good HTML documents involves both technical issues (proper construction of the HTML document) and design issues (ensuring the information content is clearly presented to the user).

The goal of this book is to explain these three main concepts and to give you the tools you need to develop your own high-quality World Wide Web products. The remainder of this preface looks briefly at these three components and explains their basic features, and then outlines the organization of the book.

UNIFORM RESOURCE LOCATORS

Uniform Resource Locators, or URLs, are a naming scheme for specifying how and where to find any Internet server resource, such as from Gopher, FTP, or WAIS servers. For example, the URL that references the file *macweb.zip* in the directory */pub/web/browsers* on the anonymous FTP server *ftp.bozo.net* is simply:

```
ftp://ftp.bozo.net/pub/web/browsers/macweb.zip
```

WWW HyperText documents use URLs to reference other HyperText resources.

THE HYPERTEXT TRANSFER PROTOCOL

The *HyperText Transfer Protocol*, or HTTP, is a new Internet protocol designed expressly for the rapid distribution of HyperText documents. Like other Internet tools such as FTP, WAIS, and Gopher, HTTP is a *client-server* protocol. In the client-server model a *client* program, running on the user's machine, sends a message requesting service to a *server* program running on another machine on the Internet. The server responds to the request by sending a message back to the client. In exchanging these messages, the client and server use a well understood *protocol*. FTP, WAIS, and Gopher are other examples of Internet client-server protocols, all of which are accessible to a World Wide Web browser. However, the HTTP protocol is designed expressly for HyperText document delivery, so most of your communication will be with HTTP servers.

At the simplest level, HTTP servers act much like anonymous FTP servers, delivering up files when clients request them. However, HTTP servers support additional important features:

- the ability to return to the client not just files but also information generated by programs running on the serve
- the ability to take data sent from the client and pass this information on to other programs on the server for further processing

The special server-side programs that implement these features are called *gateway* programs, as they usually act as a gateway between the HTTP server and other local resources, such as databases. Just as an FTP server can access many files, an HTTP server can access many different gateway programs; in both cases you specify which (file or program) resource you want through a URL.

The interaction between the server and these gateway programs is governed by the *Common Gateway Interface (CGI)* specifications. Using the CGI specifications, a programmer can easily write simple programs or scripts to process user queries, interrogate databases, make images that respond to mouse clicks, and so on.

THE HYPERTEXT MARKUP LANGUAGE

The *HyperText Markup Language*, or HTML, is the language used to prepare HyperText documents. These are the documents you distribute on the World Wide Web and are what your human clients actually see. HTML contains commands, called *tags*, to mark text as headings, paragraphs, lists, quotations, and so on. It also has tags for including images within the documents, for including fill-in forms that accept user input, and, most importantly, for including HyperText links connecting the document being read to other documents or Internet resources such as WAIS databases and anonymous FTP sites. It is this last feature that allows the user to click on a string of highlighted text and access a new document, an image, or a movie file from a computer thousands of miles away. And how does the HTML document specify where this new document is? Through a URL, which is included in the HTML markup instructions and which is used by the user's browser to find the designated resource.

What resources can URLs point to? They can be other HTML documents, pictures, sound files, movie files, or even database search engines located anywhere on the Internet. They can be accessed from HTTP servers or from FTP, Gopher, WAIS, or other servers. The URL is an immensely flexible scheme, and in combination with HTML yields an incredibly powerful package for preparing a web of HyperText documents linked to each other and to Internet resources around the world. This image of interlinked resources is in fact the vision that gave rise to the name World Wide Web.

OVERVIEW OF THE BOOK

This book is an introduction to HTML, URLs, HTTP, and the CGI interface, and to the design and preparation of resources for delivery via the World Wide Web. It begins with the HTML language. Almost every resource that you prepare will be presented through an HTML document, so that your HTML presentation is your "face" to the world. It is crucial that you know how to write proper HTML and that you understand the design issues involved in creating good documents if you are to make a lasting impression on your audience and present your information clearly and concisely. It won't matter if the Internet resources you make available are the best in the world if your presentation of them is badly designed, frustratingly slow, or difficult to follow.

HTML is also an obvious place to start. You can write simple HTML documents and view them with a WWW browser such as **Mosaic, Netscape,** or **lynx** without having to worry about CGI programs, HTTP servers, and other advanced features. You can also easily include in your documents URLs pointing to server resources around the world, and get used to how the system works: browsers understand HTML *HyperText anchors* and the URLs they contain and have built-in software to talk to Internet servers using the proper protocols. You can accomplish a lot just by creating a few pages of HTML.

Chapter 1 is an elementary introduction to HTML and to the design issues involved in preparing HTML documents. This nontechnical chapter combines a brief overview of HTML with some aspects of the document design process. The details of the HTML language and more sophisticated client-server issues are left to later chapters. Chapter 1 should give you a feel for how HTML documents work and are designed, with the details of the language coming later.

Design issues are very important in developing good World Wide Web presentations. HTML documents, are not like text documents and are not like traditional HyperText presentations, since they are limited by the varied capabilities of browsers and by the speed with which documents can be transported across the Internet. Chapter 2 discusses what this means in practice, and gives guidelines for avoiding major HTML authoring mistakes. In most cases this is done using examples, with the important issues being presented in point form, so that you can easily extract the main points on first reading.

At the same time, designing an HTML document *collection* is more than just writing pages—the design of a collection is critically important, and involves design issues that are not always apparent from the point of view of a single page. Chapter 3 looks in detail at the issues surrounding document collection design, and will help you through the process of designing a real document "web."

One point that is emphasized in Chapters 1, 2, and everywhere else in the book, is the importance of using correct HTML markup constructions when you create your HTML documents. Although HTML is a relatively straightforward language, there are many important rules specifying where tags can be placed. Ensuring that your documents obey these rules is the only way you can guarantee that they will be properly displayed on the many different browsers your clients may use. All too often, writers prepare documents that look wonderful on one browser but end up looking horrible, or even unviewable, on others.

Although some general rules for constructing valid HTML are included in Chapters 1 and 2, Chapter 4 and the references therein should be used as detailed guides to correct HTML. In particular, Chapter 4 presents a detailed exposition of the HTML language and of the allowed nesting of the different HTML markup instructions. Chapter 5 continues along this line, but looks at the experimental HTML features that are not yet formally part of the "standard" HTML language—you should use Chapter 4 as a guide for writing universally viewable HTML documents, while Chapter 5 can be viewed as a "preview" of coming events.

Of course HTML is only a beginning. To truly take advantage of the system you need to understand the interaction between WWW client browsers and HTTP servers, and to be able to write server-side gateway programs that take advantage of this interaction. These topics are covered in Chapters 6 through 9. Chapter 6 describes the URL syntax in detail, while Chapter 7 delves into the specifics of the HTTP protocol used to communicate with HTTP servers. Chapter 8 then describes the details of the Common Gateway Interface (CGI) specification for writing server-side programs that interface with the HTTP server. Chapter 9 then gives several concrete and clearly explained examples of real-world CGI programs, to show how the issues from Chapters 6 through 8 affect gateway program design. This chapter also contains a detailed reference list of resources useful in developing CGI applications—many resources useful in writing good Web applications are already on the Web, just waiting for you to go and get them.

Chapters 4 through 9 are the technical core of this book and will be useful reference material when writing HTML documents or server CGI programs.

Chapter 10 looks at auxiliary tools useful in developing and organizing HTML documents. For example, you will no doubt need tools for preparing image files, or for preparing active imagemap files, and these tools are described here. At the same time, there are tools for converting collections of e-mail letters into HyperText archives, or for creating a HyperText table of contents for large collections of related HTML files. Almost all of these tools are available over the Internet, either from anonymous FTP sites or from HTTP servers. URLs are used to indicate the locations of these programs and of additional documentation, when available.

Preparing HTML documents can be tedious, since HTML markup tags are complicated text strings that must be included in your text document. HTML codes are not only time consuming to type but also a common source of error: it is easy to make a mistake typing all those tags! You will not be the first to notice this fact, and many individuals, groups, and companies are actively developing HTML editing software to help in the document creation process. Chapter 11 summarizes and briefly describes many of the HTML editors available on PC, Macintosh, and UNIX platforms. If you are going to do a lot of document development, you will certainly want to get one of these useful tools.

In some cases you may not want an editor, but would rather be able to convert documents from another format, for example Microsoft's Rich Text Format, FrameMaker's MIF format, or LaTeX, into HTML. Chapter 11 includes descriptions of several of these packages, including instructions on how they can be obtained. There are also a number of useful tools for "validating" the HTML document for conformity with the language specification and for checking the validity of HyperText links within a document. These tools are listed at the end of Chapter 11.

Chapter 11 also discusses some the issues involved in setting up an HTTP server. Again there are many URL references to additional documentation and to locations where server software can be obtained.

Chapter 12, the final chapter in the book, gives some examples of WWW sites containing interesting and well designed presentations. These sites range from business and entertainment to those devoted to scientific research and education. For the first edition, I asked the creators of these sites to themselves describe the creation process so that you could get a feel for what was involved. For this second edition, these individuals have added material that provides wonderful insights into the changes that have occurred over the past year. I encourage you to visit these sites and see how they work. I can guarantee you will be impressed.

Finally you should just go out and browse! Reading a book in which I spout off my ideas of good and bad design is all well and good, but you as a writer of HTML documents will only appreciate how things look and feel by going out there and looking and feeling. The content of this book is merely a framework for appreciating what tens of thousands of creative individuals are already doing. So, go and see for yourself!

NOTE FOR THE SECOND EDITION— BOOK ARCHIVE SITE

For those of you familiar with the first edition, this second edition has been both brought up-to-date and significantly expanded. There are now 12 chapters, as opposed to 9, and the book now looks at Web design issues (Chapter 3), new and future HTML extensions (Chapter 4 and Chapter 5), and the details of CGI programming, with extensive examples (Chapters 8 and 9). In addition, regular updates to the material in the book will be available online at the URL:

```
http://www.wiley.com/compbooks/
```

This site also archives all the example documents and source codes from the book—after all, if you have the Web, who needs a CD-ROM?

ACKNOWLEDGMENTS

Like the first edition, this book would not have been possible without the encouragement and support of my friends and coworkers. I would like to thank Norman Wilson (author of **listen.c** and **backtalk.c**) and Rudy Ziegler, for their help with various technical issues and their general willingness to talk over book-related questions, probably at the expense of more profitable activities and also John Bradley and Sian Meikle for reviewing Chapter 3 and for providing useful feedback and commentary. I would also like to thank my coworkers at the Information Commons and the High Performance and Research Computing group at the University of Toronto, for their kindness and understanding in the face of someone who was—on occasion—a trifle tired and grumpy. Additionally, I would like to thank my research assistants, Michael Lee and Chris Oliver. Their hard work researching Chapters 11 and 12 was invaluable, and gratefully received.

More than anyone, I would like to thank my wife, Ann Dean, for her patience and support during the long months of late nights and lonely weekends, as well as for her reassuring faxes, phone calls, and—the occasional chocolate.

DEDICATION

To my parents.

INTRODUCTION TO THE HYPERTEXT MARKUP LANGUAGE

What is a text markup language? A markup language is a way of describing, using instructions embedded within a document, what the document text means, or what it is supposed to look like. For example, suppose I wanted to indicate that the word "albatross" should be displayed in boldface. A markup language might express this desire with commands of the form

```
[beg_bold] albatross [end_bold]
```

meaning: "turn on boldface, write the word 'albatross', and then turn off boldface." In this example, the text strings `[beg_bold]` and `[end_bold]` are part of the markup language, which here turns boldface on and off. In general, a markup language has many such codes, to allow for a rich description of the document content and desired rendering.

Every electronic tool for processing text uses some kind of markup language. As a simple example, you may recall the "reveal codes" command in WordPerfect. This allows you to see the actual markup commands, which in these cases were sequences of unprintable characters (unlike the printable commands used in the above example). Nevertheless, the idea is the same: A markup language is just a collection of codes, embedded in the document, that explain the meaning or desired formatting for the marked text.

There are two basic approaches for creating markup languages. The first type is *physical markup*. With this technique, the markup tags explicitly say how the document should look, and contain commands such as: "*indent 0.5 inches, print the words 'Frozen Albatross' using an 18-point Arial font, . . .*" and so on. This is great for actually printing the text, but bad if printing is not the primary goal. Suppose, for example, you want to look at the document on a computer display that is not capable of the requested formatting. In this case the formatting information is useless, and the computer has no easy way of determining a good alternative presentation of the text content.

The second approach can be thought of as *logical* or *semantic markup*. With semantic markup, the markup language defines the *structural meaning* of the text, and not how it looks. Thus, in the above case, the semantic markup might look like

```
[beg_heading] Frozen Albatross [end_heading]
```

which simply means "*the text 'Frozen Albatross' is a heading.*" The advantage of this approach is that you have encoded the true structural meaning of the text, and not its physical representation. It is then easy to translate this heading into the commands: "*indent 0.5 inches, print the words 'Frozen Albatross' using an 18-point Arial font, . . .*" should you be printing the document to paper, or into other commands should you be presenting the document in some other medium, such as a computer display or a Braille reader. Thus, although semantic formatting is more difficult (you have to think about what each part of the document means when you add the markup instructions), it is a much more powerful and flexible way of describing text, and has become the technique of choice for modern document processing systems. This includes modern word processors such as Word or WordPerfect, which now incorporate many semantic markup features into their markup model.

What is the *HyperText Markup Language*, or HTML? Despite all the hype, HTML is simply just another markup language. However, unlike the others, HTML is designed specifically for marking up electronic documents for delivery over the Internet, and for presentation on a variety of different possible displays. As a result, HTML is very much a semantic markup language, designed to specify the *logical* organization of a text document; there are almost no physical formatting commands in HTML. In addition, HTML has important extensions that allow for *hypertext links* from one document to another, as well as other extensions that allow for user input and user interaction.

It is important to stress these design principles, because they explain the large differences between HTML and traditional word processors. Because it was designed for electronic documents, HTML was *not* designed to be the language of a "What You See Is What You Get" (WYSIWYG) word processor such as Word or WordPerfect. Instead, HTML is more a "What You Get Is What You Meant" (WYGIWYM) language that forces an author to construct documents with sections of text (and/or images) marked as *logical* entities, such as titles, paragraphs, lists, quotations, and so on. The interpretation of these marked elements is then largely left up to the browser displaying the document. This approach builds enormous flexibility into the system, and allows the same document to be displayed in different ways by browsers of very different capabilities. Consequently, there are browsers for machines ranging from fancy UNIX graphics computers to plain-text terminals such as VT-100s and to old 8086-based DOS computers. As an example, in presenting the same document, a graphical browser such as Mosaic or Netscape may display major headings with a large, perhaps slanted and boldfaced font (since elegant typesetting is possible with graphics displays), whereas a VT-100 browser may just center the title, using the single available font, while a Braille browser will present the same information in a completely different manner. However, all these representations will reproduce the logical organization and meaning of the original document, since this information was built in using the HTML language.

HTML is also designed to be an *extensible* language. "Extensible" simply means that new features, commands, and functionality can be added to the language, without "breaking" older documents that don't use these new features. In fact, HTML is a rapidly evolving language, with new features being added on a regular basis. This book summarizes most of the current and forthcoming commands, and provides references to other sources that will allow you to keep up with the changes.

Since HTML is constantly evolving, it is important to have a way of indicating which version of the language you are talking about. This is done through the *version number* of the HTML specification. The very first definition of HTML was Version 1, often called HTML 1.0. The current "definitive" version of HTML is Version 2, or HTML 2.0. *All browsers* support this HTML

2.0 standard. Much work is underway to extend the language (you've probably heard the name "HTML 3" used to describe this holy grail), and as each new piece of markup is standardized and adopted, the "definitive" HTML will be revised to a new version number, for example to HTML Version 2.1, Version 2.2, and so on. These upcoming pieces include tables, superscripts and subscripts, margin notes and footnotes, and mathematical equations. This book discusses most of these new developments, but separately from the definitive HTML 2.0 specifications. In particular, Chapter 4 presents a definitive description of HTML 2.0 and of some of the currently implemented HTML 3, Netscape Navigator (up to Version 2.0), and Microsoft Internet Explorer extensions, while Chapter 5 describes the more extensive changes proposed by HTML 3. If you are interested in designing documents that everyone can view and understand, you should focus on Chapter 4. All HTML authors should be aware that if they use advanced features, there will be a significant number of people who will not be able to properly read the document content.

OVERVIEW OF THE HYPERTEXT MARKUP LANGUAGE

So what does an HTML document look like? A simple example is shown in Figure 1.1. As you can see, this looks just like a plain text document. In fact, that is exactly what it is—an HTML document contains only the printable characters that you ordinarily type. Consequently, you can prepare an HTML document using a simple text editor, such as the NotePad editor on a Windows PC, TeachText on the Macintosh, or vi on a UNIX workstation. You don't need a special word processor or fancy HTML editor to create HTML documents.

MARKUP ELEMENTS AND TAGS

The things that make an HTML document special are the HTML markup *tags*. These are sections of text enclosed by the less than and greater than signs (<...>), and are the markup instructions that explain what each part of the document means. For example, the tag <H1> indicates the *start* of a level 1 heading, while the </H1> tag marks the *end* of a heading of level 1. Thus, the text string

```
<H1>This is a Heading</H1>
```

marks the string "This is a Heading" as a level 1 heading (there are six possible heading levels, from **H1** to **H6**). Note how a forward slash inside the tag indicates an end tag. The names inside the tags are *case-insensitive*, so that `<h1>` is equivalent to `<H1>`, and `<STRONG>` is equivalent to `<StROng>`. Capitalization is recommended to make the tags stand out from the regular text.

An HTML document is described as being composed of *elements*. The string

```
<h1>This is a Heading</H1>
```

is then an **H1** element, consisting of an **H1** start tag, the enclosed text, and an **H1** end tag. You will also often see an **H1** element referred to as the *container* of a heading.

Some elements are *empty*, which simply means they do not affect a block of text and do not require an end tag. An example is the **BR** element in Figure 1.1 in the line:

```
some kind of <STRONG> exciting <BR> fact</STRONG>...
```

The tag `<BR>` forces a line break at the location of the tag, just after the word "exciting" (see Figures 1.2 and 1.3). The **BR** element does not affect any enclosed text, since a line break does not "contain" anything, so an end tag is not required.

ELEMENT ATTRIBUTES

Sometimes, an element takes *attributes,* which are used to define properties or special information about the element. They are much like variables, and are often assigned *values* that define these special characteristics. For example, the element

```
<H1 ALIGN="center">This is a Heading</H1>
```

contains an **ALIGN** attribute, which states that, where possible, the author wants the heading to be centered on the display. Note that attributes always appear in the start tag of the element.

The **IMG** element, which is used to include an image inline within an HTML document, appears via the tag

```
<IMG SRC="filename.gif">
```

Here **SRC** is an attribute of the **IMG** element, and specifies the name of the image file to be included in the document (actually a Uniform Resource Locator [URL] "pointing" to the image file—URLs are discussed in Chapter 2 and, in detail, Chapter 6). The attribute name, like the element name itself, is case-insensitive. Thus the above line could equally well be written as `<iMg src="filename.gif">` or `<iMg SrC="filename.gif">`. However, the value *assigned* to the attribute **SRC** is *case-sensitive*; case-sensitivity can be preserved by enclosing the string in quotation marks. As you may have noticed, the **IMG** element is empty (as was the **BR** element), since it merely inserts an image and does not affect a block of text.

HTML AS A STRUCTURED LANGUAGE

HTML is a *structured* language, which means that there are rules for where element tags can and cannot go. These rules are there to enforce an overall *logical structure* upon the document. A heading element such as `<H1>` . . . `</H1>` can contain text, text marked for emphasis, and line breaks (`<BR>`), as well as inline images, and hypertext anchors (as will be discussed in Example 2)—but it cannot contain most other elements. For example, constructions like

```
<H1><H2>...text ... </H2></H1>
```

are invalid. Obviously, it does not make sense for a heading to "contain" a list or another heading, and the HTML language rules reflect this reality. In addition, elements cannot overlap—this means that statements such as

```
<EM> <H2>  EM and H2 overlap – this is illegal </EM> </H2>
```

are illegal. There are many such structural rules; they are given in detail in Chapters 4 and 5. This chapter and Chapter 2 illustrate the most obvious cases.

SUMMARY

1. HTML documents are divided into *elements*. Elements are usually marked by *start* and *end tags*, and take the form `<NAME>.. some text ..</NAME>`, where the enclosed text is the content of the element. Some elements do not affect a block of text, and are hence called "empty" elements. Empty elements do not require end tags.

2. Some elements can take *attributes*, which appear within the start tag and which define properties of the element. For example, heading elements can take the **ALIGN** attribute to specify how the heading should be aligned on the display. For example, `<H1 ALIGN="center">`.

3. Element names and attributes are case-insensitive. Thus, `<NAME ATTRIBUTE="string">`, `<NamE ATtRiButE="string">`, and `<name attribute="string">` are equivalent. However, the attribute value (here the string "string") may be case-sensitive. If you know it is case-sensitive, you should enclose the value in double quotation marks ("...").

4. The placement of elements in a document must obey the HTML nesting rules, which specify where elements can and cannot appear. For example, a heading element, such as **H1**, cannot contain a list or another heading, but can contain a hypertext anchor. In addition, elements *cannot overlap*. Details of the nesting rules for HTML elements are provided in Chapters 4 and 5.

EXAMPLE 1: A SIMPLE HTML DOCUMENT

We could go on explaining HTML, but it is easier to get a feel for the language, and for HTML documents, by looking at some examples; the details of the language are found in Chapter 4 if you are in a rush. Figure 1.1 shows a simple but complete HTML document, illustrating the overall document structure and some of the simpler markup elements. This document was created using the UNIX vi editor and was saved in a file named *ex1.html*. The *.html* filename extension is important, as WWW browsers and HTTP servers understand files with this suffix to be HTML documents, as opposed to "plain" text documents, such as e-mail letters or program listings. On PCs, this extension is *.htm*, since four-letter extensions are not possible. More will be said later about extension names and what they mean.

The rendering of Figure 1.1 by two different browsers is shown in Figures 1.2 and 1.3. All browsers allow you to load and view files created on your own computer, even if you are not connected to the Internet, simply by giving the browser the name of the local file. To view the example using the lynx browser, you type

```
lynx ex1.html
```

■■■■■■■ **Figure 1.1** Contents of the example HTML document *ex1.html*. The rendering of this document by different browsers is shown in Figures 1.2 and 1.3.

```
<HTML>

<HEAD>

<TITLE> This is the Title of the Document </TITLE>

</HEAD>

<BODY>

<H1> This is a Heading</H1>


<P>      Hello.  This is not a very exciting document.
I
    bet you were expecting <EM> poetry</EM>, or


some kind of <STRONG> exciting <BR> fact</STRONG> about the Internet and
the World Wide Web.


<P> Sorry.  No such luck.        This document
does
contain examples of HTML markup, for example, here is an "unordered
list":
<UL>
    <LI> One item of the list,
    <LI> A second list item  <LI> A third list item that goes on and on and
    on to indicate that the lists can wrap right around the page and still
    be nicely formatted by the browsers.
    <LI> The final item.
</UL>
<p> Lists are exciting. You can also have ordered lists (the items are num-
bered)
and description lists.
```

```
<HR>

<p> And you can draw horizontal lines, which are useful for dividing

sections.

</BODY>

</HTML>
```

at the DOS or UNIX command prompt. With the Macintosh MacWeb browser, you just start the program and select the Open... menu from the File pull-down menu at the top of the window, and then select the file you wish to open. Similar procedures are possible with all graphical browsers, such as Netscape, InternetWorks, or Mosaic.

Figures 1.2 and 1.3 show this document as rendered by two different WWW browsers. Figure 1.2 shows what the document looks like using the graphical

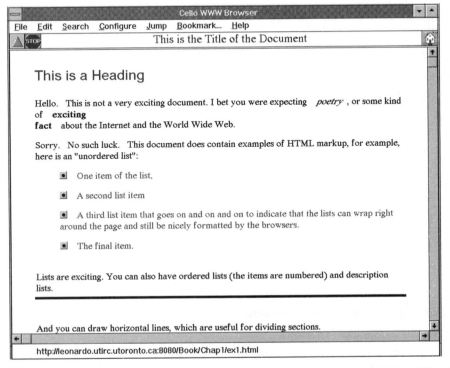

Figure 1.2 Cello rendering of the HTML document *ex1.html* (the HTML document is listed in Figure 1.1).

Cello 1.0 (for Windows 3.1) browser, while Figure 1.3 shows what you get from the character-based browser lynx.

THE HTML ELEMENT

What do the markup tags and elements mean? Since HTML is a hierarchical language, the tags and elements are best analyzed by starting from the outside and working in. The outermost element, which encompasses the entire document, is named HTML. This element indicates that the enclosed text is an HTML document. This may seem unnecessary, but it is useful in some contexts where the content of a file cannot be determined from the filename. Surprisingly enough (or perhaps not), there are several other markup languages that look superficially like HTML. The HTML tag is then a way to distinguish between these different types of documents.

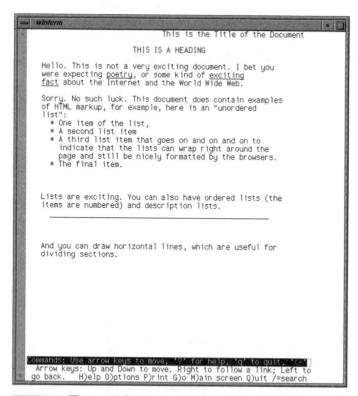

Figure 1.3 Lynx rendering of the HTML document *ex1.html* (the HTML document is listed in Figure 1.1).

THE DOCUMENT HEAD

The next element below the **HTML** element is named **HEAD**. The **HEAD** element is a container for information *about* the document, such as the **TITLE** element. **HEAD** information, if it is displayed, is not presented as part of the document. Looking at Figures 1.2 and 1.3, you will see that the content of the **TITLE** element is displayed apart from the text. With Cello, the title is displayed in the frame of the window, while with lynx, the name is displayed at the top of the screen and to the right.

The **HEAD** must always be the first document element, and must come right after the starting `<HTML>` tag.

THE DOCUMENT TITLE

Because the **TITLE** is displayed separately from the text, and usually in a restricted space such as a window title bar, a small fixed-size text box, or as a single line at the top of a text screen, you want the **TITLE** to be short. If a **TITLE** is too long, it will simply not fit. The **TITLE** should also be descriptive of the document, as it is often used as a reference to visited sites. When users store a visited link as a browser's bookmark or in a hotlist, they are actually recording the location, along with the **TITLE**. You should, therefore, be able to guess the content of a document from the **TITLE** alone.

THE DOCUMENT BODY

After the **HEAD** lies the **BODY**. This element contains *all* the text and other material that is to be displayed. Notice in Figure 1.1 that all the displayed material lies between the `<BODY>` and `</BODY>` tags.

WHY A HEAD AND BODY?

Why bother with this **HEAD/BODY** separation? Recall that HTML is designed to organize your document in a logical way. It then makes sense to separate the document itself (the **BODY**) from information *about* the document (the **HEAD**). There are several other **HEAD** elements (discussed in Chapter 4) that describe the relationships between a document and other documents (the **LINK** element), or that can provide indexing or other meta-information about the document (the **META** element). These can be extremely useful for indexing, cataloging, and organizational purposes.

HEADINGS ELEMENTS

The first element in the **BODY** is an **H1** element. H1 stands for a level 1 *heading* element; in HTML, headings come in six levels, **H1** through **H6**, with **H1** being the highest heading level, and **H6** the lowest. The **H1** element means that the enclosed text is a top-level heading and should be rendered to reflect this fact. The Cello browser (Figure 1.2) shows the heading

```
<H1> This is a Heading</H1>
```

as a large, boldfaced string of characters, left-justified and separated by a wide vertical space from the following text. Lynx, on the other hand (Figure 1.3), shows this as a capitalized text string centered on the page. This example was designed to remind you of the point made at the beginning of this section: that different browsers may render the same elements in very different ways. HTML markup instructions are designed to specify the logical structure of the document far more than the physical layout. Thus, the browser is free to find the best way to display items, such as headings, consistent with its own limitations.

INTERPRETATION OF SPACES, TABS, AND NEW LINES

Referring back to Figure 1.1, review the next few lines of text:

```
<P>    Hello.  This is not a very exciting document.
I

    bet you were expecting <EM> poetry</EM>, or


some kind of <STRONG> exciting <BR> fact</STRONG> about the Internet and

the World Wide Web.
```

You will see in Figures 1.2 and 1.3 that these lines have been rendered as a continuous paragraph of text, ignoring the blank lines, extra spaces, and tabs that are present in the original file. The rendering of an HTML document *ignores* extra spaces, tabs, and blank lines, and effectively treats any combination of these characters as a single word space. This means that you can use spaces, line breaks, and indentations for your own purposes, to organize the logical layout of an HTML document, and to make it easier to see the placement of the tags relative to the text. This is done in the bottom half of Figure 1.1, and in many of the other examples in this book. This concept will be familiar if you have written computer programs or have used typesetting languages such as TeX or Scribe, and is equivalent to using spaces and tabs to make a computer program easier to read.

CHARACTER HIGHLIGHTING

The first sentence in Figure 1.1 contains two additional elements: **EM** for *emphasis* and **STRONG** for *strong* emphasis. Note that these are *logical* descriptions of the enclosed text, and do not directly specify physical formatting styles. The recommendation in the HTML specification is that text marked with **EM** be italicized if possible, while text marked with **STRONG** should be rendered as bold. This is exactly what is done by Cello, as shown in Figure 1.2. Lynx, on the other hand, renders both **EM** and **STRONG** as underlined text (Figure 1.3). Character-based programs such as lynx can really do only four things to text: underline it, boldface it, force it to capital letters, or display it in reverse video. Given these limitations, lynx cannot render as distinct all the different elements in HTML. It therefore renders **EM** and **STRONG** in the same way. On the other hand, a text-to-speech converter would have no problem distinguishing **EM** and **BOLD**, and could simply modify the spoken intonation to account for the specified emphasis. Unfortunately, it is hard to include a text-to-speech example in a book!

Highlighting elements, such as **EM** and **STRONG**, can be placed almost anywhere you find regular text, the only exception being the **TITLE** element in the **HEAD**. The text inside a **TITLE** element can only be text; there can be no HTML elements inside a **TITLE**. Recall that the text inside a **TITLE** is not part of the document, but simply a text string providing information about the document.

HTML has several other logical highlighting elements, such as **CODE** for computer code, **KBD** for keyboard input, **VAR** for a variable, **DFN** for the defining instance of a term, **CITE** for a short citation, and so on. HTML also has *physical* highlighting elements, such as **B** for boldfaced, **I** for italics, **TT** for typewriter font (fixed-width characters), and **U** for an underlined font. It is recommended that rather than specific physical styles, you specify logical meaning for text strings, since this assigns true meaning to the associated text, and also gives the browser more flexibility in determining the best presentation.

The physical highlighting tags are useful when translating from a word processor format that already contains tags for boldface, italics, or other physical styles, since these styles can be directly converted to their HTML equivalents. They are also useful if you want to specify physical formatting for decorative purposes, but do not want to associate any special meaning to the formatted text.

PARAGRAPHS

Look at the next line, beginning with the string `<P> Sorry`:

```
<P> Sorry.  No such luck.      This document

does
```

```
contain examples of HTML markup, for example, here is an "unordered

list":

<UL>
```

The <P> tag marks the beginning of a paragraph and can best be thought of as marking the start of a paragraph *container*. Most browsers interpret the <P> that starts a paragraph by skipping a line, as shown in Figures 1.2 and 1.3. Note also that a paragraph mark can be anywhere in a line. For example, the lines:

```
the World Wide Web.


 <P> Sorry.  No such luck.      This document
```

could equally well be written as:

```
 the World Wide Web.  <P> Sorry.  No such luck.  This document
```

Recall that the rendering of an HTML document depends only on where the markup tags are located relative to the text they are marking. Of course, putting <P> at the beginning of a line makes it easier to read the "raw" HTML, and is strongly recommended.

You will notice that in Figure 1.1 there are no ending tags </P> to mark the ends of the paragraphs. In HTML, the ending paragraph tag is optional. The rule is that a paragraph is ended by the next <P> tag starting another paragraph, or by any other tag that starts another block of text, such as a heading tag (<Hn>), a quotation tag (<BLOCKQUOTE>), or list tags (<UL>, <OL>, <DIR>, <MENU>, <DL>). Thus, the paragraph ending with the words unordered list is actually ended by the following <UL> tag that marks the beginning of an *unordered list* element.

The HTML specification recommends that if two or more adjacent elements describing the logical structure of the document require some special vertical spacing, only one of the spacing values (the largest) should be used, and the other should be ignored. This implies that silly constructions such as:

```
 <p><p><p><p>  This is a paragraph
```

should yield at most a single paragraph break. More importantly, you should avoid doing such things, since, by definition, paragraphs cannot be empty. If you do try constructions like this, you will find that the document is rendered unpredictably by different Web browsers: some will leave extra space, some will not, and others will complain that the document is illegal.

If you really want extra vertical space, try using consecutive line break elements:

```
<BR> <BR> <BR>
```

This is valid HTML, and in most cases will give you the extra spacing you want.

Lists

Having clearly beaten paragraphs into the ground, we now move on to the next part of this example, namely the list of items seen in Figures 1.2 and 1.3. HTML supports several types of lists; the example here is an unordered list. An unordered list element begins with the tag <UL>, and ends with a </UL>:

```
<UL>

    <LI> One item of the list,

    <LI> A second list item  <LI> A third list item that goes on and on and

    on to indicate that the lists can wrap right around the page and still

    be nicely formatted by the browsers.

    <LI> The final item.

</UL>

<p> Lists are exciting. You can also have ordered lists (the items are numbered)
```

Lists are never not empty, and every list must be terminated with an end tag, here </UL>. Other list elements include the *ordered* list element **OL**, and the *description* or glossary list element **DL**. **DL** is discussed in Chapter 4, and is illustrated in Figures 4.12 and 4.13.

A **UL** or **OL** list can contain only **LI** (list item) elements. A *list item element* has the start tag <LI> and cannot be empty, as every list item must consist of some text. Nevertheless, an ending </LI> tag is not required, as the ending of a list item element is implied by the next <LI> or by the </UL> tag that finally terminates the list.

Unordered lists are lists of items without numbers or letters to indicate order; each item marked by an indentation of some type and a star or bullet. It is up to the browser to format them nicely. As you can see, lynx and Cello do very similar things. However, you will also note that lynx and Cello do different things to the spacing that surrounds the list; such browser-to-browser variations are common.

As mentioned, the only thing that can go directly inside a **UL** element is an **LI** element. Thus, you cannot write such things as:

```
<UL>

    here is some non-list text inside a list

    <LI>Here is list item 1.

</UL>
```

A list item (**LI**) element, however, can contain lots of things. For example, an **LI** element can contain text, the **IMG** element (for inline images), text emphasis (such as the **STRONG** element), another list, paragraphs, and even a fill-in HTML form. However, it cannot contain a heading element. Heading elements can only be directly inside the **BODY**, or inside a **FORM** (for fill-in forms) or a **BLOCKQUOTE** (for quoted text) element. **FORM**s and **BLOCKQUOTE**s are discussed in Examples 6 and 7 in Chapter 2.

LEADING SPACES INSIDE ELEMENTS

You should not leave spaces between the `<LI>` tag and the content of the list item. This is because the space will be treated as a whitespace, which may in turn change the indentation for the particular list item. Thus, the items

```
<LI> Item 1

<LI>Item 2
```

will be indented differently due to the extra whitespace in front of "Item 1." This is a subtle point, but will come up often when you are trying to format your text. It is always safest to omit spaces between the HTML tags and the enclosed text you wish to mark up.

You can also include lists within lists. For example, the markup

```
<OL>

    <LI>ordered list Item 1

    <LI>ordered list Item 2

    <UL>

        <LI>unordered item under ordered list item 2

        <LI>unordered item under ordered list item 2

    </UL>

    <LI>ordered list Item 3

</OL>
```

indicates an ordered list containing an unordered list within the second ordered list item.

HORIZONTAL RULES

The final element in Figure 1.1 is the **HR** or horizontal rule element. This element simply draws a horizontal dividing line across the page, and is useful for dividing sections. It is an empty element, since it does not act on a body of text.

LESSONS FROM EXAMPLE 1

1. Titles should be short and descriptive of the document content.

2. HTML is a hierarchical set of markup instructions. The outer layer of this organization, showing the basic document outline, is:

```
<HTML>
<HEAD>
.. document head ..
</HEAD>
<BODY>
.. document body ..
</BODY>
</HTML>
```

   The **TITLE** goes inside the **HEAD,** while the text to be displayed goes inside the **BODY.**

3. Whitespaces, tabs, and blank lines are irrelevant in the formatting of a document; the only thing that affects the display of the document by the browser is the placement of the HTML markup *tags*. You should, however, avoid whitespace between tags and the text being marked up by the tags.

4. Heading elements (**H1** through **H6**) can go only inside the **BODY, FORM,** or **BLOCKQUOTE** elements.

5. UL and OL lists can contain only **LI** (list item) elements. The **LI** elements can contain text, images, and other lists, but cannot contain headings.

EXAMPLE 2: IMAGES
AND HYPERTEXT LINKS

Figure 1.1 served to illustrate how HTML can be used to mark up the logical organization of a single document. This second example illustrates the hypertext capabilities of HTML. The example consists of two documents, *ex2a.html* and *ex2b.html*, with a hypertext link from one to the other. The documents are shown in Figures 1.4 and 1.5. *Ex2a.html* also includes inline images, to illustrate a few of the things to think about when using images in your documents. Notice how space characters are used to make the HTML documents easier to read by eye.

Figure 1.4 Contents of the example HTML document *ex2a.html*. The rendering of this document by the Mosaic for X-Windows, MacWeb, and lynx browsers is shown in Figures 1.6–1.8.

```
<HTML>

<HEAD>

<TITLE> Example 2A, Showing IMG and Hypertext Links </TITLE>

</HEAD>

<BODY>


<H1> Example 2A: Image Inclusion and Hypertext Links </H1>


<P> Greetings from the exciting world of HTML Example documents. OK, so text
    is not so exciting.  But how about some pictures!


<P> There are many ways to fit in the image.  For example,
    you could fit it in this way:
    <IMG SRC="home.gif" ALIGN="top">, this way
    <IMG SRC="home.gif" ALIGN="middle"> or this way
    <IMG SRC="home.gif" ALIGN="bottom">.


<P> Another important thing: you can make
```

```
            <a href="ex2b.html">hypertext links</a> to other files.

        You can even make hypertext links using images,  for example

            <a href="ex2b.html"><IMG SRC="sright.xbm" ALIGN="middle"></a>.


<P> Lastly, here is a row of images:

        <IMG src="home.gif" alt="[Home Icon]">

        <IMG src="home.gif" alt="[Home Icon]">

        <IMG src="home.gif" alt="[Home Icon]">

        <IMG src="home.gif" alt="[Home Icon]">

        <IMG src="home.gif" alt="[Home Icon]">

        <IMG src="home.gif" alt="[Home Icon]">

        <IMG src="home.gif" alt="[Home Icon]">

        <IMG src="home.gif" alt="[Home Icon]">



</body>

</html>
```

▬▬▬

▬▬▬ **Figure 1.5** Contents of the example HTML document *ex2b.html*. This document is the target of a hypertext link from the file *ex2a.html* shown in Figure 1.4.

```
<HTML>

<HEAD>

<TITLE> Example 2B: Target of example Hypertext Link</TITLE>

</HEAD>

<BODY>


<h2> Target of Hypertext Link </h2>

<p> OK, so now that you are here, how do you get back?  This document

    doesn't have any hypertext links, so you have to use a "back" button (or the
```

```
    'u' key if using lynx) to move back to the previously viewed document.


</BODY>

</HTML>
```

THE EXAMPLE DOCUMENT

Figure 1.4 and the contents of the file *ex2a.html* will be examined first. The first paragraph is a simple text paragraph. The second paragraph is similar, except that it contains three images, included using the **IMG** element `<IMG SRC="home.gif">`. *Home.gif* is a GIF format image file; I know this by the *.gif* filename extension (and, of course, because I created it). GIF files are one of the common image formats that can be included within HTML documents.

EXAMPLE DOCUMENT RENDERED

The rendering of the document *ex2a.html* (listed in Figure 1.4) is shown in Figures 1.6 through 1.8. Figure 1.6 shows the document as presented by the Mosaic for X-Windows browser (Version 2.4). Figure 1.7 shows the same document viewed using the Macintosh MacWeb browser, and Figure 1.8 shows the document as seen by the lynx browser. Many of the differences between them are simply due to the different window sizes and fonts. Still, there are differences that warrant mention.

INLINE IMAGES

Note the appearance of the images in Figures 1.6 and 1.7. In HTML 2.0, images are included as if they were large letters or words in line with the surrounding text and deforming the line spacing to ensure that no text overlaps any image. By default, the included image is inserted so that the bottom of the image is aligned with the bottom of the line of text leading up to the image. Note that there is no special wrapping or flowing of the text around the image and, since you have no way of guaranteeing how the document will be formatted and displayed, no guarantee that an image embedded in the middle of a sentence will appear in a particular place on the screen. In this case, the only way you can guarantee image placement is to make the image the first item following a paragraph (or other) break; then, it will always be the first item on a line. More advanced image placement control is discussed later in this example, in Example 8 in Chapter 2, and in Chapter 4.

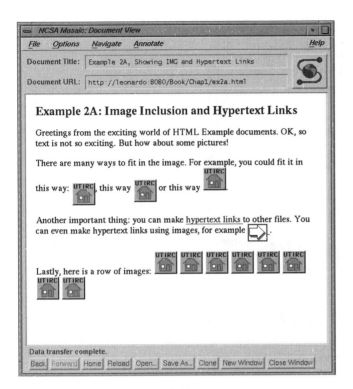

Figure 1.6 Mosaic for X-Windows rendering of the HTML document *ex2a.html* (the HTML document source is shown in Figure 1.4).

ALIGNING IMAGES WITH TEXT

In HTML 2.0, there are three alignment options for the image. These are specified by the **ALIGN** attribute, which can take three possible values: ALIGN=top, ALIGN=bottom, and ALIGN=middle (the argument is case-insensitive). ALIGN=bottom is the default. The three options are illustrated with the three "Home" icons (I am afraid I am not a great graphic artist). The first, ALIGN=top, aligns the top of the image with the top of the text, while the ALIGN=middle value aligns the middle of the image with the bottom of the text, and ALIGN=bottom aligns the bottom of the image with the bottom of the text.

IMAGES AND NONGRAPHICAL BROWSERS: THE ALT ATTRIBUTE

Figure 1.8 shows the lynx interpretation. Lynx is a text-only browser and cannot display images. Lynx simply replaces each occurrence of an image with the text string [IMAGE]. This is not very descriptive, but it at least tells

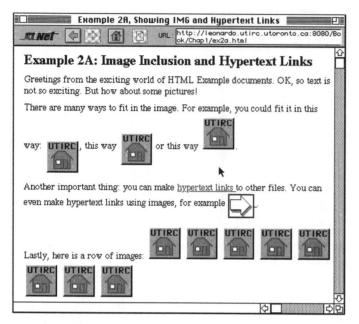

Figure 1.7 MacWeb browser rendering of the HTML document *ex2a.html* (the HTML document source is listed in Figure 1.4).

users what they are missing. If the string [IMAGE] is insufficient, you can replace it with something more useful by using the ALT="string" attribute in the **IMG** element. The **ALT** attribute specifies a text alternative for an image, which is critical to a browser that cannot display images. The usage is simply:

```
<IMG SRC="image.file" ALT="[A text alternative to the Image]">
```

The string specified for **ALT** is case-sensitive, and it is common (but not necessary) to surround the string with square brackets as is done at the bottom of *ex2a.html*, where the attribute alt="[Home Icon]" is used with all the inline images. The resulting text rendering is shown in Figure 1.8.

If you have a purely decorative image with no associated underlying meaning, you should use the **ALT** attribute to assign an empty description, that is:

```
<IMG SRC="decoration.gif" ALT="">
```

This means that a user of a nongraphical browser will see nothing. This is far better than seeing "[IMAGE]", which always make a reader wonder whether the document author forgot to provide a description of an important part of the document.

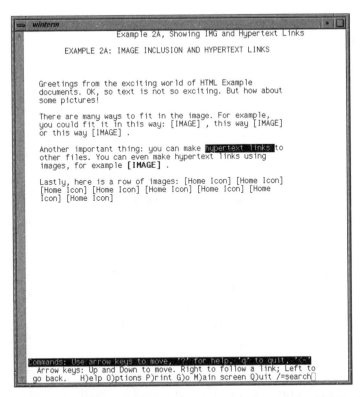

Figure 1.8 Lynx browser rendering of the HTML document *ex2a.html* (the HTML document source is listed in Figure 1.4).

IMAGE FORMATS

There are many digital formats for storing images, with various advantages and disadvantages. Unfortunately, Web browsers are able to display only a small subset of these, so that images you want to include must be converted into one of the commonly understood formats. The most useful ones are discussed in the next paragraph.

On the World Wide Web, the most universally accepted image format is the GIF or Graphics Interchange Format (filename extension *.gif*). This was the format used in Figure 1.4. In fact, GIF is the only format that can be displayed inline by all Web browsers. Another common format is JPEG (filename extension *.jpeg* or *.jpg*), which is particularly good for storing photographic images. Many (but not all) browsers support inline JPEG. Both GIF and JPEG store images in a *compressed* format, which means that images can be stored in relatively small files. This is important when downloading images as images, even when compressed, tend to require big files, which can be very slow to access over the Internet.

The third common format is X-Pixelmap, or its black-and-white equivalent, X-Bitmap (filename extensions *.xpm* and *.xbm* respectively). These store images in noncompressed format, and are a very inefficient way of storing images. In addition, some browsers (notably, early versions of Netscape Navigator) cannot display these formats. The different image formats, and ways of converting images between these formats, are discussed in more detail in Chapter 10.

NETSCAPE AND HTML 3.0 IMAGE FEATURES

The **ALIGN** attribute values just described only allow for rudimentary control over the placement of images within a document. HTML 3.0 supports additional **IMG** attributes and attribute values (e.g., `ALIGN="left"` and `ALIGN="right"`) to allow images to float on the page, which provide better control of image placement and allow the surrounding text to flow around the images. Several browsers support these newer attributes, and the Netscape Navigator supports these along with some Netscape-specific extensions. These image features are described in detail in Chapter 4.

LOADING IMAGES

How does the browser actually obtain the images and complete the document? The browser first obtains the HTML document and then looks for **IMG** elements. If it finds **IMG** elements, the browser makes additional connections to the server indicated by the **SRC** attribute to obtain the required image files. Thus, a single document containing ten images will require 11 distinct connections to load. Needless to say, this can be slow, particularly if the browser has a slow network connection to the server. Most graphical browsers, such as Mosaic or MacWeb, have a Delay Image Loading button or pull-down menu selection that disables the automatic loading of inline images. This can save time when viewing a document, but is useful only if the author has written the document to be understandable without the pictures. In addition, some browsers will display the document text and then fill in the images once the image files have arrived. This can be problematic if the browser does not know the size of the arriving image. Recent enhancements to HTML provide new **IMG** element attributes that contain image size information, which allows the browser to reserve space for images prior to loading. These features of the **IMG** element are discussed in Chapter 4.

HYPERTEXT LINKS

The third paragraph in *ex2a.html* shows a hypertext link. The form is straightforward:

```
<A HREF="ex2b.html">hypertext links</A>
```

The element marking a hypertext link is called an **A** or *anchor* element, and the marked text is referred to as a *hypertext anchor*. The area between the beginning <A> and ending </A> tags becomes a "hot" part of the text. With Mosaic, MacWeb, Netscape, or other graphical browsers, hot text is often displayed with an underline, and usually in a different color (often blue), while with lynx, this region of text is displayed in bold characters. Placing the mouse over this region and clicking the mouse button, or, with lynx, using the tab key to move the reverse-video region to lie over the hot part and pressing Enter, causes the browser to access the indicated document or other Internet resource.

You can also use images as hypertext anchors. At the end of the second paragraph in *ex2a.html* (Figure 1.4), I have marked the image *sright.xbm* as the anchor (recall that the *.xbm* means this is an X-Bitmap image). The relevant piece of HTML is:

```
<a href="ex2b.html"><IMG SRC="sright.xbm" ALIGN="middle"></a>
```

Graphical browsers indicate this by *boxing* the image with a colored or highlighted box, while lynx simply bolds the [Image] text string it puts in place of the image. With this mechanism you can use small images as *button* icons, as is commonly done in multimedia applications. This doesn't do much good with lynx, of course, so if you do use images as *navigation icons*, you had better add an ALT attribute to let lynx (or Braille browser) users know what is going on.

TEXT SPACES IN ANCHOR ELEMENTS

You will note that I did not leave spaces between the anchor tags and the surrounded **IMG** element. This was intentional, and ensures that there are no space characters inside the anchored string. If you have spaces at either end of the enclosed anchor string, the browser will assume that these spaces are part of the anchor, and will render them accordingly. This is not always pleasing, and can leave an anchored image with small lines sticking out from the bottom of the image, or anchored text with underlines hanging out beyond the beginning or end of the text. The lesson once again is: Use tags around the text you want to mark, and don't include extra spaces unless specifically intended.

UNIFORM RESOURCE LOCATORS

The *target* of the hypertext link is indicated by the anchor attribute **HREF**, which takes as its value the *Uniform Resource Locator (URL)* of the target document or resource. As mentioned in the Preface, a URL is a text string that indicates the server protocol (HTTP, FTP, WAIS, etc.) to use in accessing the resource, the Internet domain name of the server, and the name and location of the resource on that particular server. Obviously, the **HREF** attributes in Figure 1.4 do not contain all this information! These URLs are examples of *partial* URLs, which are a shorthand way of referring to files or other resources *relative* to the URL of the document currently being viewed. For Figure 1.4, this means: Use the same protocol, same Internet domain name, and same directory path of the present document (*ex2a.html*), and retrieve the indicated file *ex2b.html* from the same directory.

If you click the mouse button over the hypertext anchor, the browser downloads and displays the linked document, as shown in Figure 1.9. To return to the previously viewed document, press the Back button on the browser control panel (with lynx, press the letter "u" for *up*), which takes you back to the previously displayed document, namely *ex2a.html*. Figure 1.10 shows what

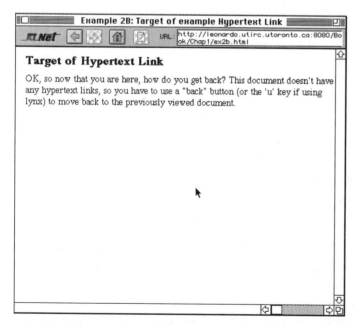

Figure 1.9 MacWeb browser rendering of the HTML document *ex2b.html* (the HTML document source is listed in Figure 1.5).

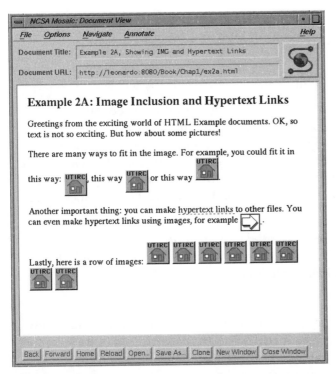

Figure 1.10 Mosaic for X-Windows browser rendering of the HTML document *ex2a.html* after returning from a hypertext jump to the document *ex2b.html*. Note how the line under the anchor is now dashed instead of solid.

this document looks like the second time around using Mosaic for X-Windows. The document is now subtly different: the portion of text that served as the launching point for the hypertext link, previously underlined by a solid line, is now underlined by a dashed line. On a color display, you also see the anchored text rendered with a changed text color. Programs such as Mosaic, MacWeb, Netscape, and InternetWorks use this change in highlighting to let you know that you have already visited this link. This helps to keep you oriented, by letting you know where you have already been. Unfortunately, this is not possible with lynx, as there are an insufficient number of highlighting modes to allow for this level of subtlety. With lynx, you have to pay a bit more attention to what you have been doing.

RELATIVE UNIFORM RESOURCE LOCATORS: LINKING DOCUMENTS TOGETHER

As mentioned, the anchor

```
<A HREF="ex2b.html">hypertext links</A>
```

uses a partial URL, which is a location relative to the URL of the displayed document itself. This partial URL idea is great news, because it means that you need not specify entire URLs for simple links between files on the same computer. Instead, you need only specify their position on the file system relative to each other, as was done in Figure 1.4.

Partial URLs can also point to directories other than the one containing the current document. Specification of these relative directories is done using a UNIX-like path structure. Suppose that the example documents *ex2a.html* and *ex2b.html* lay in the directory structure shown in Figure 1.11. That is, the files *ex2a.html* and *ex2b.html* are in the directory *Project1/Examples*, while the file *e2c.html* is in *Project1/Examples/SubDir,* and *ex2d.html* is located in *Project1/Other*.

How do you reference the files *ex2c.html* and *ex2d.html* from the file *ex2a.html*? To reference *ex2c.html*, you simply create a hypertext link that accesses the partial URL *SubDir/ex2c.html*:

```
<A HREF="SubDir/ex2c.html">hypertext links</A>
```

Notice the UNIX-like directory pathnames in which the forward slash character indicates a new directory. The specification of the URL syntax uses the forward slash to denote directories or any other hierarchical relationship (formally, URLs can reference not just files, but also programs and other resources). You *cannot* use backslashes (\) as you do with DOS and Windows, or colons (:) as you do on Macintoshes.

If you want to create a link from *ex2a.html* to *ex2d.html* in *Project/Other,* you write the URL as:

```
<A HREF="../Other/ex2d.html">hypertext links</A>
```

since the file is one directory level up (the symbol ".." meaning one directory up), and one level down into the directory *Other*. (A single dot [.] implies the current directory, so `HREF="./Subdir/ex2c.html"` and `HREF="Subdir/ex2c.html"` are equivalent.)

SPECIAL CHARACTERS IN A URL

Of course, this is going to be a problem if you actually use the slash character as part of a filename, since the URL convention will try to interpret it as a directory change. You therefore should avoid directory or filenames containing this character if at all possible. The URL specification does have a way of allowing this and other special characters within a URL, without having them interpreted specially. This *encoding* mechanism is discussed in Chapters 6 and 8.

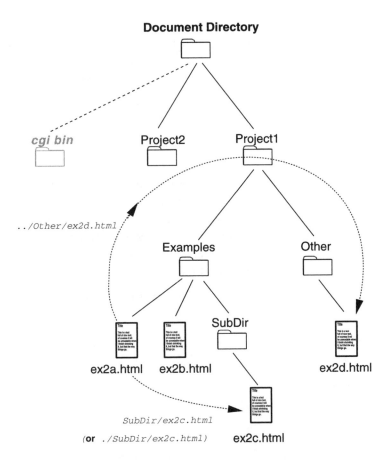

Figure 1.11 Accessing neighboring files using partial URLs. The folders and files show the organization of files lying in the *Document Directory*—the directory that contains resources available to clients accessing an HTTP server. The dotted lines and the corresponding text strings show partial URLs relating the file *ex2a.html* to the files *ex2c.html* and *ex2d.html*. The grayed directory, *cgi-bin*, is a special directory used to store programs that can be executed by the HTTP server. This directory is kept physically distinct from the true document directories, since programs present a security risk to the server and must be guarded more carefully than documents (see Chapter 11 for more details).

There are a lot of other partial URL forms and, of course, the format for full URLs has yet to be discussed. More examples of URLs appear later in this chapter and in Chapter 2, while a detailed description of the URL syntax is given in Chapter 6.

Finally we refer to the last line of *ex2a.html* (Figure 1.4), which is simply a row of inline images. Note that these wrap to best fit the width of the screen, just as if they were a sequence of words (Figures 1.6 and 1.7). Consequently, if the user changes the size of the browser window, these icons will be repositioned. This once again points out the wide variation possible between different renderings of the same document.

WRITING FOR HYPERTEXT: THE GOOD, BAD, AND UGLY

As you can see, hypertext links are easy and can be very useful—in fact, it is probably fair to say that they are the most important feature of HTML documents. However, it is easy to get carried away with hypertext links, and they can quickly become a source of irritation to someone reading a document. The following are a few suggestions for ways to include links in an HTML document without detracting from the presentation and readability of the text.

In general, it is best to create hypertext links that flow naturally from the text. Thus, it is better to write:

```
<p> The issue of hormone-controlled ostrich-feather

growth has recently been a topic of

intense <A HREF="ostrich-paper.html">interest</A>
```

than:

```
<p> For information about current hormone-controlled

ostrich-feather

growth press <A HREF="ostrich-paper.html">here</A>
```

(These examples are illustrated in Figures 1.12–1.13.)

Figure 1.12 Listing for the document *badlinks.html*. This document illustrates good and bad examples of hypertext links. A Mosaic for X-Windows rendering is shown in Figure 1.13.

```
<HTML>

<HEAD>

<TITLE> Examples of Bad Hypertext Links </TITLE>

</HEAD>

<BODY>
```

```
<H1> Examples of Good/Bad Hypertext Link Design</H1>


<p> <B> 1) Don't distort the Written Text  </B>

<P> <B> Good: </B>

<BR>The issue of hormone-controlled ostrich-feather growth has recently
    been a topic of intense <A HREF="ostrich-paper.html">interest</A>.


<P> <B> Not So Good: </B>

<BR> For information about current hormone-controlled ostrich-feather
     growth press  <A HREF="ostrich-paper.html">here</A>.

<p> <B> 2) Keep the linked text section short. </B>

<p> <B> Good: </B>

<br> The life cycle of the  <A HREF="animal.html">atlantic polar-bear
     ocelot</A> is a complex and .......


<p> <B> Not So Good: </B>

<br> <A HREF="animal.html">The life cycle of the atlantic polar-bear
     ocelot is a complex</A> and .......


<p> <B> 3) Link Icon and Text Together </B>

<p> <B> Good: </B>

<br> <A HREF="file.html"><IMG SRC="home.gif"> The latest</A> home
     security systems breakdown show......

<p> <B> Not so Good: </B>

<br> <A HREF="file.html"><IMG SRC="home.gif"></A> The latest home
     security systems breakdown show......


</BODY>

</HTML>
```

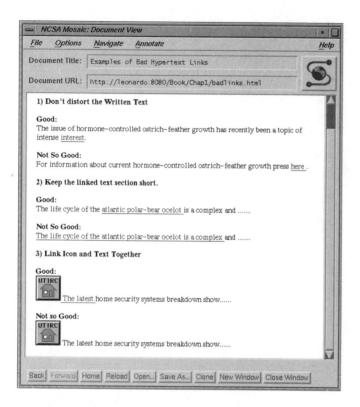

■■■■■■ **Figure 1.13** Mosaic for X-Windows rendering of the file ***badlinks.html*** (shown in Figure 1.12).

You also don't want the link to be gratuitously long. It is much more effective to link from a single word or phrase than from a whole sentence. Thus the links:

```
<p> <A HREF="animal.html">The life cycle of the atlantic polar-bear ocelot</A>

is a complex and interesting example of . . .
```

is better written as:

```
<p> The life cycle of the  <A HREF="animal.html">atlantic polar-bear ocelot</A>

is a complex and interesting example of . . .
```

These (and other) examples of good and bad hypertext links are included in the HTML document shown in Figure 1.12 and displayed in Figure 1.13. There is no hard and fast rule for creating bad and good link presentations. In general, if you are adding links within a text document that is intended to be easy to read, it is best to make the links as unobtrusive as possible.

USING THE URL AS THE LINKED TEXT

It is sometimes useful to include the URL of a document you are referencing as part of the text—you don't always have to hide the URL in the HTML markup. This is particularly useful if your document is likely to be printed, since the HTML markup tags are lost on paper. For example the WWW FAQ (Frequently Asked Questions) document, a wonderful repository of useful information about the World Wide Web, contains such lines as:

```
<p> ....The original home of the WWW FAQ is

<A HREF=" http://sunsite.unc.edu/boutell/faq/www_faq.html">

http://sunsite.unc.edu/boutell/faq/www_faq.html</A>.
```

If you are reading the HTML document containing this markup, just click on the anchored text to view the referenced document. If you are reading the printed version, you still have all the information you need to access the site when you next have access to the Internet.

LISTS, PARAGRAPHS, OR MENUS OF LINKS?

If you are putting together a collection of links, you want to think carefully about their organization. Should they be placed within a paragraph? Probably not. More likely, they should go in a list or as a menu bar (a horizontal list of text or graphical buttons linked to the desired objects). You will also want to organize them in a logical and organized manner, particularly if you have a lot of hypertext links to present—a page full of random links is exceedingly frustrating to use. Link-mania pages containing seemingly random collections of links can occur quite innocently, often when you have been slowly assembling lists of interesting URLs. The collection may be fine for you, but can be confusing to someone else.

Figure 2.2 (Chapter 2) shows a *home page* constructed using some of these features of "bad" anchor design (the source for this document is in Figure 2.1), while Figure 2.4 shows an improved and better organized home page using the suggestions given here (the source is in Figure 2.3). We will talk more about home pages in Chapter 2, but, by simple comparison, you will see that Figure 2.4 is much easier to understand than Figure 2.2, even though Figure 2.4 contains less textual information.

Finally and most important of all: Make sure all your hypertext links work and go to the right place! There is nothing worse than clicking on a hypertext link only to get "ERROR. Requested document not available" in response. Actually, that's not quite true. It is even worse to click on an anchor that indicates a particular destination, only to find that you have actually accessed something completely different and obviously incorrect. Errors like these tell readers that the document developer did not bother with even the simplest checks of his or her work, and immediately bring into question the accuracy of the documents themselves. It is easy to check your links: Just do it.

LESSONS FROM EXAMPLE 2

1. Images are included via the IMG element:

```
<IMG src="prism-small.gif" ALT="[Text stuff]">
```

SRC specifies the URL of the image file to be included. The **ALT** attribute gives a text string to be displayed by browsers that cannot display images. Images are usually treated as if they were big text letters. Some new HTML 3 attributes allow the text to flow around the images. These attributes are discussed in Chapter 4.

2. Hypertext links to another document are included using the **A** (anchor) element:

```
<A HREF="SubDir/example1.2B.html">hypertext links</A>
```

where HREF is used to specify the URL of the target of the link. The examples here are of partial URLs: partial URLs assume the same Internet site and protocol as for the document currently being viewed, and look for the file (or resource) relative to it. In this regard the slash (/) and double dot (..) characters are special, representing relative positions in the directory (or other) hierarchy.

Images can also be hypertext anchors via constructs such as:

```
<A HREF="someplace.html"><IMG SRC="image.gif"></A>
```

3. Don't use hypertext links gratuitously. If they are embedded in the text, try to make them flow with the text. If a paragraph has many links, try thinking of another way to present the material: maybe it should be a list or a menu, or perhaps the hypertext anchors could be combined

into a less intrusive form. Above all, make sure the links work; links going nowhere or to the wrong place are cardinal sins of HTML authoring.

REFERENCES

There is lots of documentation on HTML available on the Web itself, while USENET newsgroups specifically devoted to World Wide Web and HTML issues are a good place to see announcements of new products or services, or to ask questions. The newsgroups are also the best place for up-to-the-minute information on WWW happenings, and are a good place to start when trying to find out about the latest features. However, the best place to start is the World Wide Web FAQ.

WORLD WIDE WEB FAQ LIST

Thanks to Thomas Boutell, the Frequently Asked Questions (FAQ) list is one of the most useful collections of information on the Web. Sections of this list are posted regularly on the relevant newsgroups. In addition, the entire FAQ is available, in hypertext form, at:

```
http://sunsite.unc.edu/boutell/faq/www_faq.html
```

WEB USENET NEWSGROUPS

The following is a list of all the active World Wide Web newsgroups, and their associated subjects. Please, post messages only to the appropriate groups, and *cross-post* when sending the same message to more than one group!

comp.infosystems.www.announce	Announcements of new sites or services (moderated)
comp.infosystems.www.servers.mac	Macintosh HTTP servers
comp.infosystems.www.servers.ms-windows	MS-Windows/Windows NT HTTP servers
comp.infosystems.www.advocacy	Political and other advocacy issues
comp.infosystems.www.authoring.cgi	CGI programming

comp.infosystems.www.authoring.images	Images in Web documents including image formats, format conversions, and image maps
comp.infosystems.www.browsers.misc	Miscellaneous browser issues
comp.infosystems.www.browsers. ms-windows	MS-Windows Web browsers
comp.infosystems.www.authoring.misc	Miscellaneous Web authoring issues
comp.infosystems.www.browsers.mac	Macintosh browsers
comp.infosystems.www.servers.misc	Miscellaneous server issues
comp.infosystems.www.servers.unix	UNIX HTTP servers
comp.infosystems.www.browsers.x	X-Windows Web browsers
comp.infosystems.www.authoring.html	HTML authoring issues
comp.os.os2.networking.www	Web issues related to IBM OS/2
bionet.software.www	WWW applications in the biological sciences

The following groups are older, and have largely been replaced in importance (and traffic) by the preceding list of more specialized groups.

comp.infosystems.www.providers	Issues related to publishing material on the Web, such as the HTML language, and the development of server gateway programs
comp.infosystems.www.users	User-related issues, such as configuring browsers, finding browsers, or discussing browsers
comp.infosystems.www.misc	Miscellaneous topics

USER SURVEYS OF WWW RESOURCES

http://www.cc.gatech.edu/gvu/user_surveys/

GENERAL WEB REFERENCES

General references to HTML are given at the ends of Chapters 4 and 5. The following sites contain documentation that may be of interest, but at a more introductory level:

```
http://oneworld.wa.com/htmldev/devpage/dev-page.html

http://cbl.leeds.ac.uk/nikos/doc/repository.html

http://coney.gsfc.nasa.gov/www/sswg/candy_style.html

http://www.hprc.utoronto.ca/HTMLdocs/NewHTML/intro.html
```

This Yahoo! page is a useful compendium of many HTML-related Web sites:

```
http://www.yahoo.com/yahoo/Computers/World_Wide_Web/HTML/
```

HTML AND

DOCUMENT DESIGN

Chapter 1 introduced the philosophy and design behind the HTML language. It also used two example documents to illustrate some of the basic elements of an HTML document: headings, lists, character highlighting, images, horizontal rule dividers, and, most importantly, hypertext anchors. In this chapter, we look again at these elements, focusing on advanced features and document design issues. Here also, you will find an introduction to some of the other important HTML elements—namely, the **ADDRESS, BLOCKQUOTE, OL** (ordered list), **FORM,** and **TABLE** elements that significantly enrich the vocabulary of HTML document authors.

The examples in this chapter are designed to illustrate the proper use of these elements, and to point out some common mistakes. Since browsers do not check for incorrect HTML, it is easy to write badly formed HTML documents that look fine on one browser, but awful on another. Furthermore, these examples reflect design issues involved in creating a page. For example, what are good and bad ways to include hypertext anchors, or good and bad ways to include image files? Although there are no perfect answers to these questions, the examples are designed to show the characteristics and limitations of the Web, thereby illustrating why some design choices are generally better than others.

EXAMPLE 3: HEADING, ADDRESS, AND ANCHOR ELEMENTS

This example, illustrated in Figures 2.1–2.5, looks again at the **A** (anchor) and heading elements, and introduces the **ADDRESS** element (for providing address information), all in the context of a practical document design problem, namely the construction of a document collection *home page*. A home page is designed to be the first document seen by visitors to a site, and serves as your welcoming introduction to guests, both old and new. It is often used to direct people to your other interesting resources, and perhaps to other related resources elsewhere on the Internet. This particular example is based on a page constructed for the Instructional and Research Computing Group at the University of Toronto— Figures 2.1 and 2.2 illustrate bad design features, while Figures 2.3–2.5 illustrate good design. Although it comes from an academic institution, the organizational model will be similar for business, entertainment, or other developers. Chapter 12 gives some examples from a number of diverse environments.

Figure 2.1 HTML document listing for the file ***home_bad.html***, which contains a poorly designed home page. Figure 2.2 shows the rendering of this document on a PC browser (Air Mosaic).

```
<HTML> <HEAD>

<TITLE> Instructional and Research Computing </TITLE>

</HEAD> <BODY>

<hr>


<h1> Instructional and Research Computing </H1>


This is the home page of the Instructional and Research Computing

Group <STRONG>(IRC)</STRONG>, one of seven departments of the Division

of Computing and Communications.

The IRC group provides support for

<A HREF="MulVis/intro.html"> multimedia and visualization techniques</A>,

access to and support for

<A HREF="HPC/intro.html"> high performance computing</A>,

and support for <A HREF="AdTech/intro.html"> adaptive technology

</A>.  (aids for the physically challenged)  We also have some interesting
```

```
links to <A HREF="Lists/Lists.html"> WWW Starting Points </A>,

a big list of <A HREF="Lists/Lists.html"> WWW Search Tools</A>,

another list of hypertext pointers to

<A HREF="Lists/Libraries.html"> Libraries </A> resources, and a

link to the  <A HREF="http://www.utoronto.ca/uoft.html"> Main University

Home Page </A>.


<p>

If you become lost in our documents use the navigation icons.

The <EM> home </EM> icon brings you back here, while the <EM> up </EM>

icon takes up one level in the document hierarchy.  <EM> Info </EM>

and <EM> help </EM> are also useful, while the <EM> letter</EM> icon let

you send us a message, and the <EM> search </EM> icon allows you to do

a textual search of our pages.

<hr>

  <A HREF="home.html"><IMG SRC="home.gif"    ALIGN=TOP ALT="[Home]"  ></A>

  <A HREF="help.html"><IMG SRC="ic_help.gif" ALIGN=TOP ALT="[Help]"  ></A>

  <A HREF="info.html"><IMG SRC="ic_info.gif" ALIGN=TOP ALT="[Info]"  ></A>

  <A HREF="/cgi-bin/mail.pl"> <IMG SRC="ic_mail.gif" ALIGN=TOP ALT="[Mail]"
></A>

  <A HREF="home.html"><IMG SRC="ic_up.gif"   ALIGN=TOP ALT="[Up]"    ></A>..

  <A HREF="cgi-bin/doc-search.pl"> <IMG SRC="ic_find.gif" ALIGN=TOP
ALT="[Search]"></A>

<hr>

<ADDRESS>

<A HREF="Staff/web_admin.html"> webmaster@site.address.edu </A>

</ADDRESS>


</BODY>

</HTML>
```

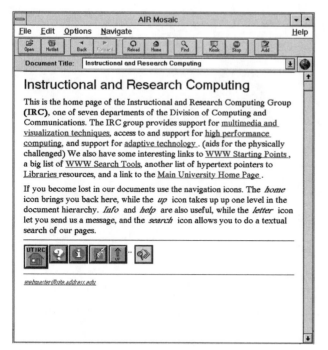

■■■■■■ **Figure 2.2** Air Mosaic rendering of the HTML document **_home_bad.html._**

Figure 2.3 shows the example "good" home page document, while Figures 2.4 and 2.5 show how this page looks using the Windows Air Mosaic and UNIX lynx browsers.

■■■■■■ **Figure 2.3** Listing of the example home page document **_home.html._**

```
<HTML> <HEAD>

<TITLE> Instructional and Research Computing </TITLE>

</HEAD> <BODY>

[<A HREF="home.html">          Home   </A>]

[<A HREF="help.html">          Help   </A>]

[<A HREF="info.html">          Info   </A>]

[<A HREF="/cgi-bin/mail.pl">   Mail   </A>]

[<A HREF="home.html">          Up     </A>]

[<A HREF="cgi-bin/doc-search.pl">Search</A>]

<hr>
```

```
<h1> Instructional and Research Computing </H1>

This is the home page of the Instructional and Research Computing

Group <STRONG>(IRC)</STRONG>, one of seven departments of the Division

of Computing and Communications.  We provide:

<UL>

<LI> support for <A HREF="MulVis/intro.html"> multimedia and visualization

     techniques</A>

<LI> access to and support for <A HREF="HPC/intro.html"> high performance

     computing</A>

<LI> support for <A HREF="AdTech/intro.html"> adaptive technology </A>

     (aids for the physically challenged).

</UL>

Some other useful University resources are:

<p>

 <A HREF="Lists/Lists.html"> WWW Starting Points </A> |

 <A HREF="Lists/Lists.html"> WWW Search Tools</A> |

 <A HREF="Lists/Libraries.html"> Libraries </A> |

 <A HREF="http://www.utoronto.ca/uoft.html"> Main University Home Page </A>

<p>

If you become lost in our documents use the navigation icons.

The <EM> home </EM> icon brings you back here, while the <EM> up </EM>

icon takes up one level in the document hierarchy.  <EM> Info </EM>

and <EM> help </EM> are also useful, while the <EM> letter</EM> icon let

you send us a message, and the <EM> search </EM> icon allows you to do

a textual search of our pages.

<hr>

  <A HREF="home.html"><IMG SRC="home.gif"    ALIGN=TOP ALT="[Home]"  ></A>

  <A HREF="help.html"><IMG SRC="ic_help.gif" ALIGN=TOP ALT="[Help]"  ></A>

  <A HREF="info.html"><IMG SRC="ic_info.gif" ALIGN=TOP ALT="[Info]"  ></A>
```

```
<A HREF="/cgi-bin/mail.pl">

    <IMG SRC="ic_mail.gif" ALIGN=TOP ALT="[Mail]"  ></A>

  <A HREF="home.html">

    <IMG SRC="ic_up.gif"   ALIGN=TOP ALT="[Up]"      ></A>..

  <A HREF="cgi-bin/doc-search.pl">

    <IMG SRC="ic_find.gif" ALIGN=TOP ALT="[Search]">

  </A>

<hr>

<ADDRESS>

<A HREF="Staff/web_admin.html"> webmaster@site.address.edu </A>

</ADDRESS>


</BODY>

</HTML>
```

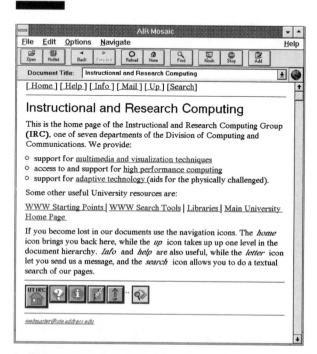

Figure 2.4 Air Mosaic rendering of the HTML document **home.html** (the HTML document is shown in Figure 2.3).

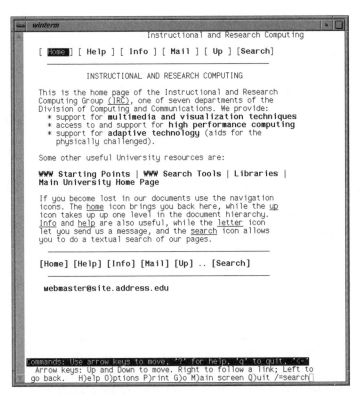

Figure 2.5 Lynx rendering of the HTML document *home.html* (the HTML document is shown in Figure 2.3).

APPROPRIATE USE OF HEADING ELEMENTS

Figure 2.3 begins with a **TITLE** and an **H1** heading.[1] These are both clearly descriptive of the content and origin of this document or document collection. As mentioned in Chapter 1, the **TITLE** should always be clearly descriptive of a page, since it will be used as a bookmark by visitors to your collection. You have much more flexibility with headings, but, in general, the main heading of a home page should also clearly reflect the contents of the collection, as this quickly lets your visitors know that they have reached the right place.

As mentioned earlier, headings can range from **H1** through **H6**, in decreasing order of importance. In designing a collection of documents, you should use heading elements that retain this sense of relative importance, as it helps to build organizational structure within and between documents. There are useful programs that can build a table of contents for large collections of HTML doc-

---

[1] The text buttons at the top of the page are text-only duplicates of the graphical buttons at the bottom of the display—the use of these buttons is discussed later in this section.

uments based on the contents and relative *levels* of the heading elements. This, of course, will work only if the headings elements were used correctly (i.e., **H1** for major sections, **H2** for subsections, **H3** for subsubsections, and so on).

SIGN YOUR DOCUMENTS WITH ADDRESS

It is always a good idea to sign your HTML documents, particularly the home pages or other major pages. This provides information allowing visitors to send feedback or commentary on what they have found at your site. The HTML **ADDRESS** element is specifically designed for address information, and is used for this purpose in Figure 2.3. In this example, the **ADDRESS** element contains an e-mail address suitable for feedback and/or commentary about the IRC collection. Also, this e-mail address is placed within the anchor element, and is a hypertext link connected to a page (*web_admin.html*) containing additional information—for example, about the server and server administrator. For more personal projects, this might be an HTML document containing a brief biography of the document author.

FULL UNIFORM RESOURCE LOCATORS

Looking at Figure 2.3, you will see that most of the URL references are relative references. There is one, however, that is not. This is the URL pointing to the *Main University Home Page*. This is a complete URL that specifies the complete information needed to access the main University HTTP server:

```
http://www.utoronto.ca/uoft.html
```

A complete HTTP URL has three main parts, as in this example:

1. `http:` The protocol specifier. The string `http:` means that the HTTP protocol is to be used. This and other schemes are discussed in Chapter 6.

2. `//www.utoronto.ca` The Internet domain name of the server. This gives the Internet name the client should contact. Sometimes, you will see this with a number after the name, for example: `www.somewhere.edu:8080`. The trailing number is a *port number* and specifies the port the server is actually talking on. Most HTTP servers "talk" at Port 80. You can leave this out if the server should be contacted at the default value.

3. `/uoft.html` The path and filename of the desired file (or other resource). Here, the URL is to the file *uoft.html* that lies right at the top of the server's *document directory*, the directory under which the HTTP server keeps the documents; thus the path consists simply of a forward slash. If the files were under a subdirectory, that would be specified, so that paths such as */Project1/Examples/ex2a.html* are possible (as in Figure 1.11).

The URL scheme allows for all sorts of protocols: `ftp:` for the FTP protocol; `gopher:` for the Gopher protocol; `wais:` for the WAIS protocol, and so on. Consequently, using URLs, you can create hypertext links to anonymous FTP servers, Gopher sites, WAIS databases, and many other Internet resources. Web browsers are designed to understand these protocols. When they encounter a hypertext reference in an HTML element such as `HREF="url"`, where `"url"` points to an anonymous FTP or Gopher site, a browser is able to contact the site, using the appropriate protocol, and access the indicated resource.

HOME PAGE DESIGN ISSUES

There are several issues to consider when designing a home page. In general:

1. **A home page should be small.** A home page should be a small HTML document with a minimum of extraneous graphics or text. Large images (meaning large image files) and the detailed resources of your site should be elsewhere.

2. **A home page should be concise.** A home page is like an introductory map to a site or to a collection of documents, explaining what the site is and where to find the local resources. Thus, it should briefly outline the resources on your server and provide hypertext links to those resources. It should also briefly outline the organization of your site, such as the meanings of icons or menus, so that visitors will know how to navigate their way around.

3. **A home page should not be dependent on graphics.** You can include graphics in this page, but they should be small. Many people have slow Internet connections and don't want to spend many minutes waiting for thousands of kilobytes of gratuitous imagery. Icons or images on a home page should therefore be small image files, totaling less than ten kilobytes (this will take approximately eight seconds to download for someone using a 14.4 kbaud modem). Also, you must ensure that a user can navigate from your home page without a graphical browser, since many users will be accessing your site with text-only browsers. Thus, if you use icons for navigation buttons, you should also provide a text-only option.

4. **A home page should include contact information.** Someone will want to contact you at some point, perhaps to point out a problem, or to compliment you on your work. The home page should include contact information for the administrator of the resources. A common, generic e-mail address for the site administrator is ***webmaster@www.domain.name***,

where *www.domain.name* is the domain name of your server. This information should be included on the home page, most commonly at the page bottom.

CLARITY OF TEXT CONTENT

To make a home page small and compact, you must make sure that the text component is both clear and concise. The text portion of the example home page document (Figure 2.3) fulfills these criteria, providing a clear and concise description of the site and the material it contains, with a minimum of extraneous detail. This can be written in whatever style you prefer: polite and well mannered, or eclectic and off the wall. In the example in Figure 2.3, the first paragraph explains what the site is and provides links to the major areas of interest. Each of these areas may, in turn, have its own home page, specific to the subject at hand. This hierarchical structure lets people quickly find what they are looking for, and also makes it easy for you to organize your documents. For example, you could have independent subdirectories for each distinct project, with your main home page having hypertext links to introductory home pages located in each of these subdirectories. Other hypertext links can then provide alternative relationships between documents, within this overall hierarchical arrangement.

The home page in Figure 2.3 also contains a second, less detailed list that provides a brief selection of alternative services. These items link to documents or services that are perhaps peripheral to the main purpose of your site, but that may be useful in directing the visitor to his or her destination. Here, this is a collection of hypertext pointers to other resources that our group commonly uses.

Referring to Figures 2.4 and 2.5, you can see how clean the organization appears. Since the document is written in correct HTML, both browsers display it clearly, subject to their own limitations. A comparison of Figure 2.5 with the less-well-thought-out version in Figure 2.2 illustrates the importance of good organizational design. A little thought about how the hypertext links should be organized makes an enormous difference in the clarity and readability of the final presentation.

It is useful to think how this home page model might apply to other applications, for example, to an electronic magazine or *e-zine*. E-zine home pages often have a magazine title bar (a graphic), followed by the magazine title (an **H1** heading), and a brief introduction to the e-zine. This is usually followed by a collection of pointers to "this month's articles," followed by a hypertext link to a reference document that, in turn, contains a list of links to the home pages of previous e-zine issues. This is very similar to the model presented in Figures 2.3–2.5. Some examples of different successful home page designs are shown in Chapter 12.

Alternatively, you might consider an all-graphical home page. Some sites, such as the Silicon Graphics Inc. site, use an imagemap as their home page. You can find this home page at the URL:

```
http://www.sgi.com/
```

(While I am reluctant to include it here, as they keep changing the graphic, it is well worth a look!) The image on this home page contains image-mapped buttons that are linked to the various resources on their Web site, much like the textual buttons and links in Figure 2.4. You will note, however, that SGI does provide a menu of text buttons for users who do not have graphical browsers (or who have disabled image loading because of slow Internet connections).

IMAGES: ACCEPTABLE SIZES AND COLOR DEPTHS

Although not included in Example 3, a decorative image containing the company or organizational logo is often placed at the top of the home page document. This can be a very attractive addition, adding appealing graphical impact to your introductory page. You must be careful, however, to ensure the image is not so large that it frustrates your users by taking a long time to download—as mentioned before, the sizes of all the images on a page should ideally sum to less than 10 kbytes. Be aware that, even if the page is attractive, the impact of this elegance will be lost on a user who has had to wait minutes for the image to arrive.

In addition, you should process the image so that it does not contain too many distinct colors. Many graphics boards on current computers are capable of displaying only 256 colors (8-bit color) simultaneously, while some World Wide Web browsers limit each image in the browser window to fewer colors than this, so that the browser can display more than one image at the same time (e.g., if the browser allows each image to have 50 distinct colors, the browser can display up to five images before reaching the 256-color limit). Therefore, attempting to display an image containing 256 colors can present problems—in fact, the image can look downright ridiculous. Most graphics editing programs allow you to process images and reduce the number of colors they contain, often with little loss of image quality (at least as displayed by the browser). This has the added bonus of making the image files smaller.

NAVIGATION ICONS

Look back to the bottom of the HTML document listed in Figure 2.3 and displayed in Figures 2.4 and 2.5. The feature to look at is the collection of small *icons*. These icons are attached, by hypertext anchors, to a collection of important reference documents of the collection; the paragraph preceding these icons explains what the icons mean. The intent is to place these icons on every HTML document, to provide a universal cue for navigating through the local document collection. For example, the *home* icon always links back to this main home page, while the *up* icon links up to the top of whatever set of documents you are looking at. Thus, if you had chosen to visit the High Performance Computing section, the *up* icon would bring you back to the High Performance Computing home page. In turn, the *Info* icon refers to a page giving a brief description of IRC and its mandate, while the *Help* icon connects to a page that briefly describes the meanings of all the icons. Finally, the *Mail* icon links to a gateway program on the HTTP server that allows the user to send mail to the server administrator, while the *Search* icon links to a different gateway program that allows the user to do keyword searches on the collection of HTML documents. Note that all these icons are equipped with an `ALT="string"` text alternative. If you are going to navigate with icons, be sure that people using a text-only browser, like lynx, know what the icons mean!

Having navigation icons is extremely important, particularly when you have a very large number of related hypertext documents. It is very easy to get lost when you are browsing through such large collections. Hypertext is not like a *linear* book, where you can always tell where you are by the page number or the thickness of the remaining pages. Navigation icons replace these tactile methods of navigation with symbols that link you to reference points within the collection. In addition, icons can direct users to general services that may be useful wherever they are in a collection, such as a search tool for searching a database or a mail tool for sending an electronic message to the site administrator.

The very top of this home page shows a text-only variant of the navigation icons (see Figures 2.3 to 2.5). This was added for contrast with the iconic approach. Text or icons, both add the same functionality, and choosing one or the other is largely a matter of taste. Text-based navigation aids can take up less space on a page and do not require that the client software access the server to obtain the icon images. If you do use image icons, the latter problem is mitigated by using the same icons in all your pages. Most web clients *cache* (retain local) copies of images once they have been accessed, and don't bother to retrieve them from the server when they are required on subsequent occasions.

Image downloading problems can also be alleviated by using small icons and a reduced number of colors per image. Most of the icons included in the document shown in Figure 2.3 and displayed in Figure 2.4 are only 36 pixels square and contain only 16 colors each (4 bits/pixel). As a result, each GIF-format icon takes only around 280 bytes, and downloading them to the browser is fast, even over a dial-up connection, and does not place large demands on the network.

LESSONS FROM EXAMPLE 3

1. A home page should be small and should not contain many large images.

2. A home page should clearly and concisely describe the contents of the World Wide Web site and should contain hypertext links to the site's resources.

3. A home page can explain and introduce navigation icons if they are used.

4. A home page should contain information for contacting the administrator of the documents managed at the site.

EXAMPLE 4: THE PRE ELEMENT AND LINEAR HYPERTEXT DOCUMENTS

This example, shown in Figures 2.6 through 2.11, looks at a hypertext collection of text-based documents. One common use of HTML is to prepare online documentation or online collections of reference materials. These can be very large collections of documents, often with some overall hierarchical structure (such as sections and subsections), but also with many hypertext links cross-linking these documents and linking them to other resources on the Internet. Often, the root structure of these documents is linear, reflecting their origins as a printed manual, or their logical presentation as a readable, linear collection. This is not necessarily a bad thing—after all, books are a rather successful communications medium. While hypertext allows for nonlinear representations of information, this does not mean that a nonlinear model is always better, or more appropriate!

THE PRE ELEMENT

Figures 2.6 and 2.7 introduce the HTML **PRE** element. This element is used to enclose preformatted text for presentation as is, preserving the space characters and carriage returns typed into the HTML document, and displaying the characters using a fixed-width typewriter font. Thus you should use the **PRE** element to display computer codes, text examples, or verbatim text sequences. This is also one way you can create tables for display in an HTML document, since this element preserves the horizontal spacing needed to align columns.

You can include character emphasis within a **PRE** element, so that you can use the **STRONG** and **EM** elements to emphasize certain text strings. You can also include hypertext anchors. Tags do not add width to the text, so you can use them to add highlighting or hypertext anchors to vertically aligned text. The usefulness of the **PRE** element is illustrated in Figure 4.19 (Chapter 4), where it is used to display both program code and a small table. Anchors and text highlighting elements are the only HTML elements allowed within a **PRE**; other elements, such as heading elements, paragraph elements, list elements, **BLOCKQUOTE** (for quotations), or **ADDRESS** elements, are prohibited.

DOCUMENT COLLECTIONS: SOME DESIGN ISSUES

The design of document collections is discussed in more detail in the next chapter. However, some major points are apparent in this example, so it makes sense to discuss them here.

1. Each document should be small, usually no more than two or three screens full of data. The advantage of the hypertext model lies in the linking of various components of the documentation package. This advantage is often lost if you are viewing a single, huge document containing hundreds or thousands of lines of displayed text. Although you can build hypertext links within a document to other points inside the same document, this is generally more difficult to navigate than a collection of smaller files.

2. Each document should have navigation tools in the form of hypertext links that connect the document to other documents in the hierarchy and to general navigation points within the collection. Thus, each page should have links to *next* and *previous* documents (if there is an obvious order to the pages) and to a table of contents or the section heading. If the document is big, say more than two or three screens full of

text, then it might be a good idea to place the navigation icons at both the top and bottom of the document, to make them easier to find.

3. Documents should show a consistent presentation style, with the same heading structure, the same navigation icons, and similar content outlines. This makes it easy to get the *feel* for the collection, and also makes it possible to index or catalog the collection using programs that take advantage of this structure.

Artistic license is, of course, allowed! But these are general guidelines, based on experience, that will help to make your work more pleasing and easier to use.

Figure 2.7 (the HTML listing is in Figure 2.6) shows an example HTML document from a large collection of related files. This particular example is one of approximately 70 documents that discuss various aspects of the HTML language. This collection of documents can be accessed at the URL:

```
http://www.hprc.utoronto.ca/HTMLdocs/NewHTML/htmlindex.html
```

▬▬▬▬ **Figure 2.6** HTML listing for the document **hrule.html**, a typical text-only HTML document.

```
<html>

<head>

<title> HR element in HTML </title>

</head>

<body>

[<a href="htmlindex.html">Index</a>]

[<a href="body.html">Up</a>]

[<a href="lists_reg.html">Back</a>]

[<a href="entities.html">Next</a>]


<H1> 4.7 Horizontal Ruled Line </H1>


The HR element is used to draw a horizontal dividing

line completely across the screen. This can be
```

to logically separate blocks of text, or to separate
icon lists from the body of the text.

<p> The HR element is empty (you don't need a <code></HR></code>).

<h2> Example </h2>
The following shows an example of the use of <HR>
and the resulting rendering (on your browser).
<blockquote>
<pre>
The following document is scanned from the back of
a cereal box. To see the scanned image, press the
icon at the bottom of the text ....
<HR>
<H1> MIGHTY CHOKEE-OS! </H1>
The cereal of chocolate deprived kiddies everywhere!
<p> Aren't you lucky your parents love you enough
to buy you CHOCKEE-OS!
<p> Remember to ask Mom and Dad for NEW SUPER
CHOCKEE-OS, now with Nicotine!!
</pre>
</blockquote>
<p> <b> This is rendered as:</b>
<p> The following document is scanned from the back of a
cereal box. To see the scanned image, press the icon at
the bottom of the text ....
<HR>
<H1> MIGHTY CHOKEE-OS! </H1>
The cereal of chocolate deprived kiddies everywhere!

```
<p> Aren't you lucky your parents love you enough

to buy you CHOCKEE-OS!

<p> Remember to ask Mom and Dad for NEW SUPER CHOCKEE-OS,

now with Nicotine!!!

<hr>

<p> [<a href="htmlindex.html">Index</a>]

[<a href="body.html">Up</a>]

[<a href="lists_reg.html">Back</a>]

[<a href="entities.html">Next</a>]

</body>

</html>
```

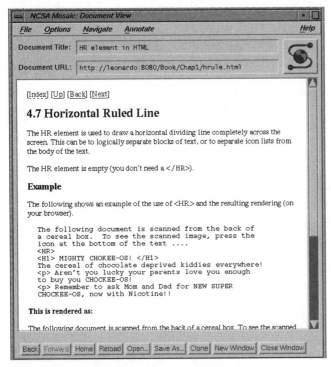

Figure 2.7 Mosaic for X-Windows display of a typical text-only document (**hrule.html**).

FLAT OR SERIAL DOCUMENT COLLECTIONS

The documents in Figures 2.6–2.11 are part of a *flat* collection of documents, in that all the files are linked together in a serial fashion. However, there are also many hypertext links relating the documents in nonserial ways (for example, one document discussing the **IMG** element has a sentence mentioning URLs, which, in turn, contains a hypertext link to a document giving a more detailed discussion of URLs). The documents are also ordered hierarchically. Thus, the document discussing the **BR** element is *under* the **BODY** document, which is, in turn, *under* the Table of Contents (see Figure 2.9). The Table of Contents page contains hypertext links to all the documents in this collection and is an easy tool for quickly finding and accessing a particular section.

NAVIGATION BUTTONS

Note the navigation text icons at the top of the page in Figure 2.7. There are four navigation buttons: *Index*, *Up*, *Back*, and *Next*. The *Index* button takes you directly to a Table of Contents page, while the *Up* button takes you one level up in the hierarchy—in this case, to the **BODY** page. The *Back* button takes you backward to the preceding document in the hierarchy, while the *Next* button takes you forward to the next document. The *Back* and *Next* buttons are the ones to use if you want to read the document straight through.

Figure 2.8 HTML source document for the Table of Contents page *htmlindex.html*. Some of this document has been omitted to save space. The rendering of the document is shown in Figure 2.9.

```
<html>

<head>

<title> HTML Documentation Table of Contents</title>

</head>


<body>


<h1> HTML Documentation Table of Contents </h1>


<dl>
```

```
<dt> <a href="htmlindex.html"> Table of Contents (this page)</a>

<dt> <a href="about_the_author.html"> About the Author</a>

</dl>

<ol>

<li> <a href="intro.html"> Introduction to this Document</a>

<li> <a href="html_intro.html"> Introduction to HTML </a>

<ol>

     <li> <a href="elements.html"> HTML Elements </a>

     <li> <a href="doc_struct.html"> HTML Document Structure</a>

     <li> <a href="naming.html"> HTML Document Naming Scheme </a>

</ol>

<li> <a href="head.html">HEAD</a> of an HTML Document

     <ol>

     <li> <a href="title.html"> TITLE</a>

     <li> <a href="isindex.html"> ISINDEX</a>

     <li> <a href="nextid.html"> NEXTID</a>

     <li> <a href="link.html"> LINK</a>

     <li> <a href="base.html"> BASE</a>

     </ol>

<li> <a href="body.html"> BODY</a> of an HTML Document

     <ol>

     <li>  <a href="headings.html"> Headings</a> (Hn)

     <li>  <a href="paragraph.html"> Paragraphs</a> (P)

     <li>  <a href="line_break.html"> Line Breaks</a> (BR)

     <li>  <a href="image.html"> Inlined Images</a> (IMG)

     <ol>

     <li>   <a href="image-examples.html"> Examples </a> of Images

     </ol>

     <li>  <a href="anchors.html"> Hypertext Anchors</a> (A)
```

```
     <ol>

          <li>  <a href="A_href.html">Link to</A> an object (HREF)

          <li>  <a href="A_name.html">Link from </A>an object (NAME)

          <li>  <a href="A_rel.html">Relationship</A> between objects (REL)

          <li>  <a href="A_rev.html"> Relationship</A> between objects (REV)

          <li>  <a href="A_urn.html"> URN </A>

          <li>  <a href="A_title.html">TITLE </A>

          <li>  <a href="A_methods.html">How</A> to link   (METHODS)

     </ol>

          .

          .

          .

     </ol>

<li> Stepping up to <a

href="http://info.cern.ch/hypertext/WWW/MarkUp/HTMLPlus/htmlplus-1.html">HT ML+</a>

<li> <a href="bibliography.html">Bibliography</a>

</ol>

</body>

</html>
```

TABLE OF CONTENTS PAGE

Figure 2.9 shows the HTML Table of Contents document for this collection (the listing is in Figure 2.8), although only part of it appears within the displayed window. Notice how this gives a complete overview of the document tree, including the relative placement of the sections in the hierarchy and the hypertext links to each section. This Table of Contents was constructed by hand—a tedious process, to say the least. Fortunately, there are programs that can automatically generate a hypertext table of contents directly from the HTML document collection, using the headings embedded in the documents to create both section names and the hierarchical organization. This is another good reason to use appropriate heading elements. Information about these indexing tools is provided in Chapter 9.

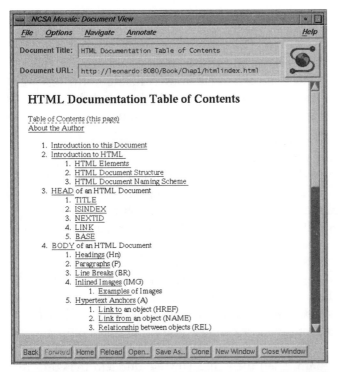

Figure 2.9 Table of Contents page (***htmlindex.html***, listed in Figure 2.8) for the HTML document collection containing the file ***hrule.html*** (shown in Figure 2.6). This collection of documents can be accessed at:

```
http://www.hprc.utoronto.ca/HTMLdocs/NewHTML/htmlindex.html
```

These documents are updated on a regular basis.

GENERAL DESIGN ISSUES:
OFFERING ALTERNATIVE FORMATS

There are several other organizational features that you may also want to include. Often, a printed version of a document collection is useful. If this is desired, you can combine the documents and present them as a single, large file that clients can download and read as HTML or print (from their browsers) as a single text file. However, you should let them know what to expect. For example, you can add text in the table of contents or some other page that provides information like the following:

```
<p> This entire archive of documents is also available as a

    single <A HREF="alldocs.html">concatenated HTML document</A>
```

```
(198 Kbytes), suitable for printing.  Note, however, that

the hypertext links in this document have been removed.</P>
```

This guides the user to a document that can be both viewed and printed, but also warns that the file is big, and that certain facilities available in the discrete files are not present. He or she can then choose whether to click on the phrase "concatenated HTML document" and access this resource.

In some cases, you might want to make the entire document collection available as an archive. Then, users who are making extensive use of the documents can copy down the entire HTML collection and install it on their own machines, reducing the load on your server and increasing the speed with which they can access the material. If you are using a PC, you might make such an archive using the PKZIP package. This allows you to archive files and directories into a single compressed file, usually with the filename extension *.zip*. Thus, you could pkzip all the files in the document collection into a file called *alldocs.zip*. StuffIt is a common archiving program on a Macintosh: the resulting archive would be named *alldocs.sit*. UNIX users will use a program called tar (for *tape archiver*), which would result in the archive file *alldocs.tar*. UNIX also has two programs for compressing programs: compress, which places a .Z at the end of the compressed filename, and gzip, which places a .z at the end of the compressed filename. This would yield the compressed archive files *alldocs.tar.Z* (using compress) or *alldocs.tar.z* (using gzip). If you were generous in preparing archives for multiple platforms, you might provide an HTML document pointing to these files. An example of such a document is shown in Figures 2.10 and 2.11.

Most HTTP server programs allow you to control access to certain files or directories on the server, and to restrict access to files to authorized users. You might, for example, choose to control access to archives should there be copyright problems associated with the archive contents.

NESTING OF LIST ELEMENTS

As a final HTML aside, note that Figure 2.11 illustrates how different lists can be nested. Here, an unordered list (**UL**) is nested inside an unordered list item element (**LI**):

```
<UL>

    <LI> <A HREF="alldocs.zip">...

    .

    .
```

```
          .

       <UL>

          <LI> (This is a concatenation of the ...

       </UL>

    </UL>
```

Figure 2.10 Example HTML document *src_link.html* that contains links to alternative formats of a document collection. Clicking on the items retrieves the archives to the client's machine.

```
<HTML>

<HEAD>

<TITLE> Archives of this Documentation </TITLE>

</HEAD>

<BODY>


<H2> Document Archives </H2>


<p> Archives of the document collection are available in the following

formats:


<UL>

<LI> <A HREF="alldocs.zip">  alldocs.zip</A>    (138 Kbytes) -- <EM> DOS PKZIP
</EM>

<LI> <A HREF="alldocs.sit">  alldocs.sit</A>    (532 Kbytes) -- <EM> Macintosh
Stuffit</EM>

<LI> <A HREF="alldocs.tar">  alldocs.tar</A>    (527 Kbytes) -- <EM> UNIX tar
</EM>

<LI> <A HREF="alldocs.tar.Z">alldocs.tar.Z</A> (133 Kbytes) -- <EM> UNIX tar
(compressed)</EM>

<LI> <A HREF="alldocs.tar.z">alldocs.tar.z</A> (104 Kbytes) -- <EM> UNIX tar
(gnuzipped) </EM>

<LI> <A HREF="alldocs.html"> alldocs.html </A> (523 Kbytes) -- <EM>
Concatenated HTML documents </EM>
```

```
<UL>

<LI> (This is a concatenation of the HTML documents, suitable for

printing from a browser. The Hypertext links have been removed).

</UL>

</UL>

</BODY>

</HTML>
```

■■■■

The browser does exactly what you would expect, and simply nests one list
inside the other. In HTML, any type of list can be nested within another list.
Recall, however, that you cannot put lists inside headings, or headings inside
lists.

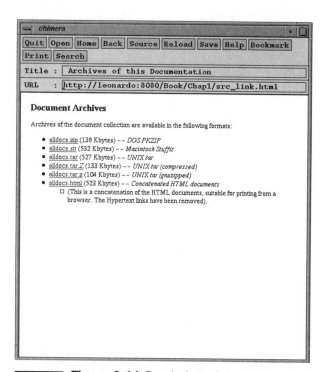

■■■■■ **Figure 2.11** Rendering of the HTML document ***src_link.html*** (shown in Figure
2.10) by the UNIX chimera browser.

LESSONS FROM EXAMPLE 4

1. Collections of documents should have a consistent design to make them easy to navigate. You should also try to create a hypertext table of contents. There are programs available that can help you do this, some of which are discussed in Chapter 9.

2. You can use navigation icons (or text) as hypertext links to help the user navigate through the document collection. Make sure that you provide a text-only navigation option for users who are using a non-graphical browser.

3. Single HTML documents should be small and self-contained. Larger documents should be broken up into smaller documents to best take advantage of the hypertext facilities.

4. Sometimes a *flat*, printable text document is also desirable. You can concatenate your HTML files together to make such a document, and then create a hypertext link from your collection to this document, but be sure to include information about the size of this file (if it is large) so that the user knows what to expect.

EXAMPLE 5: IMAGES, MOVIES, AND SOUND FILES

As mentioned earlier, WWW browsers can display only certain image formats, and often restrict GIF images to fewer than 50 or so displayed colors per image. It was also pointed out that small images are advantageous, since large images can take a long time to download and are often irritating for that reason alone.

However, sometimes these restrictions are unreasonable. Suppose you need to display a page containing a large image that is an important part of your presentation. For example, it may be an image of a campus map that can be *clicked* on to access information about various campus buildings, in which case, a tiny image is not appropriate. Alternatively, you may have truly high-quality GIF images containing 256 colors, or perhaps non-GIF format images, and want to make them available for viewing. Perhaps you even have movie or sound files. How can these be included in a document and presented to your clients?

LINKING TO LARGE IMAGES

Large GIF images can always be added to an HTML document. The key to good document design is simply to warn users, at the hypertext anchors pointing to an HTML document containing a large image, that this is what they can expect. This is a useful way of directing users to large active images (see the section on creating active images in Chapter 10) and gives them the option of disabling image loading when accessing the document, or not accessing the document altogether.

THUMBNAIL SKETCHES

A *thumbnail sketch* is a particularly useful way of linking to a large image. A *thumbnail* is simply a reduced-size icon of the actual image or of some characteristic portion of the image. Thumbnails are easy to make with almost any commercial or public-domain image editing program. You can then include the thumbnail in your document, and make a hypertext link from the thumbnail to the document containing the large image, or to the image itself. This is what was done in Figures 2.12 and 2.13, where the small images are links to larger images or movie files. In this example, the thumbnail of the larger GIF image is only 1,500 bytes, one-tenth the size of the original file. Note that sizes of the linked documents are also given (these are big files!). It is always good practice to give this information when files are large.

You should also indicate the data type of the file; in Figure 2.13, for example, the text indicates that the linked image file is in GIF format and that the linked movie is in MPEG format. There are many different movie and image formats, and most clients are capable of displaying only a subset of them. It is always a good idea to indicate the format of large data files so that users can avoid wasting time downloading files they cannot use.

HELPER APPLICATIONS

So far our hypertext links have been to HTML documents or to HTML documents containing images via the **IMG** element. What happens if the links connect to other media, such as image files, movie files, or sound files? Most World Wide Web browsers are not capable of displaying these data formats. So, what do they do?

The answer lies in so-called *helper* or *viewer* applications, which are programs on the user's computer that can be used to display images, movies, or sounds that cannot be displayed by the browser itself. Thus, in Figure 2.13, the large-screen image was produced by clicking on the upper image icon in the browser window, causing the browser to retrieve the data accessed by this

▬▬▬▬ **Figure 2.12** The HTML document *vortex.html*, showing links from image icons to full-size images and video sequences. Figure 2.13 shows the rendering of this document by the Mosaic for X-Windows browser.

```
<HTML>

<HEAD>

<TITLE>Simulated Vortex Dynamics in a Porous-Body Wake</TITLE>

</HEAD>


<BODY>

<H1>Simulated Vortex Dynamics in a Porous-Body Wake</H1>


This video presents the result of a numerical simulation on the wake
generated by a porous body.  The wake flow is simulated by inserting
small-scale discrete vortices into a uniform stream,  and  the colors
in the video represent the magnitude of vorticity.   The initial flow
field is subjected to a small perturbation based on experimental data.
The evolution of the wake flow is  manifested  by the merging  and
interactions of the small-scale vortices.<P>


The objective of this investigation is to study the merging and
inter-action processes of vortices and the formation of large eddies in
the flow.  Such an investigation is of importance to many flow-related
industrial and environmental problems, such as mixing, cooling,
combustion and dispersion of air-borne or water-borne contaminants.<P>
<HR>
<B> <A HREF="legend.gif"><IMG SRC="legicon.gif"
ALIGN=Bottom> Initial flow</A> and color legend for vorticity.</B>
(14.5 KB gif image)<p>
<HR>
<B> <A HREF="flow.mpeg"><IMG SRC="vortex.gif" ALT="[movie icon]"
```

```
ALIGN=Bottom> Visualization</A> of the evolution of the wake flow.</B>

(0.38 MB mpeg-1 movie)<p>

</BODY>

</HTML>
```

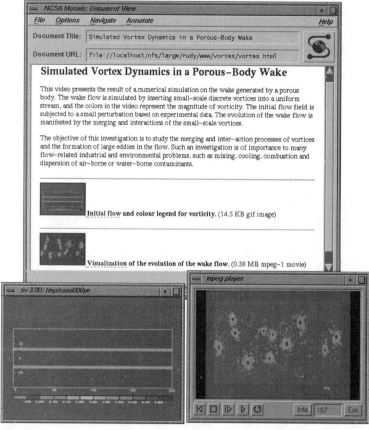

Figure 2.13 The Mosaic for X-Windows rendering of the document listed in Figure 2.12, showing thumbnail image icons linked to full-size image files and movie files. The picture overlaid on the browser resulted from clicking on the image icon at the top of the screen, while the movie-playing window was launched by pressing on the icon at the bottom of the screen. This page and the associated images and movies are courtesy of Rudy Ziegler of the University of Toronto High Performance Research Computing Group, while the data yielding the displayed image and movie frame were provided by Z. Huang, J. G. Kawall, and J. F. Keffer of the Department of Mechanical Engineering at the University of Toronto.

link, acknowledge the data to be an image file, and launch the appropriate helper application to display the image (in this case, the UNIX image viewing program xv). In the case of the movie file, the browser knew that the data was an MPEG movie, so it started up the program mpeg_play to display the video information.

How does the browser know what a file contains and what to do with it? If the data comes from an HTTP server, then the server, as part of the HTTP protocol, explicitly tells the browser the type of data it is sending. It does this with a special header message that is sent to the client just before the actual data. This message is actually a *MIME content-type* header, which, for a GIF image file, looks like:

```
Content-Type: image/gif
```

and, for an MPEG movie, is:

```
Content-Type: video/mpeg
```

When the browser receives this message, it looks in its own database of *helper* applications to find the program that matches this *MIME type*. If it finds a program to help, it passes the data to the program and lets it do its job.

If the data comes from an FTP server, or if the browser is accessing the file from the local machine and not from a server, then the browser must usually *guess* at the data content. It does this from the filename extension. Each browser has a database that matches filename extensions to the appropriate MIME type, and uses this database to determine the MIME types of file accessed locally or via FTP. In general, this database will map the *.gif* suffix to the image/gif MIME type, the suffixes *.jpeg* or *.jpg* to the image/jpeg MIME type, and the suffixes *.mpeg*, *.mpg*, or *.mpe* to the video/mpeg MIME type. These lists must be updated if you add a new filename extension. With Macintosh and some Windows browsers, the lists can be edited from a pull-down menu.

There are literally dozens of MIME types for data ranging from images, audio, and video to compressed archives and executable programs. A detailed list of MIME types is given in Appendix B, while the usage of MIME types is discussed in more detail in Chapter 7.

LESSONS FROM EXAMPLE 5

1. Warn users when you present a link to a large image document or file.

2. List the data format for large image, audio, or movie files so that users can tell if the file is in a format they can actually use.

3. You can use icons to link to larger image or movie files. This lets users know what to expect and is often a good graphical addition to your document.

EXAMPLE 6: FILL-IN FORMS

This example looks at the HTML **FORM** element, which allows you to solicit user input by constructing HTML documents containing fill-in forms. Using this element, a designer can build a document containing checkboxes, radio boxes, pull-down lists, text windows, and menus, and can configure this **FORM** to send the data gathered by these buttons and boxes to a program on an HTTP server. For example, **FORM**s can be used to collect data for a database search; solicit data for an online questionnaire; accept electronic text for submission to a database; or solicit electronic messages for forwarding to a particular user.

The example document in Figure 2.14 shows this latter case: namely, a **FORM** that allows the user to type in a text message for forwarding to a recipient selected from a list. Figure 2.15 shows how this form is rendered by Mosaic for X-Windows while Figure 2.16 shows the rendering by lynx. Finally, Figure 2.17 shows what MacMosaic Version 1.0.3 does with this HTML document; this older version of MacMosaic does not understand the **FORM** element.

THE FORM ELEMENT

Let's first look at Figure 2.14 and the <FORM..> tag beginning with the line:

```
<FORM  ACTION_"http://side.edu/cgi-bin/send-note">
```

This line starts the **FORM** element and ties the data of the form to a particular program (*send_note*) on the indicated HTTP server. All a **FORM** element does is collect data: it doesn't do any processing of the data, so the only way you can get a form to do anything useful is to send the data gathered by it to a program on the server. The <FORM...> tag in this illustration indicates that the data gathered by the form are to be sent to the program *send_note*. Data are sent to this server-side program when the user presses the *Send Message* button at the bottom of the page. The **FORM** and the program *send_note* must be designed together for the program to understand the message sent by the form.

The program *send_note* takes the data sent by the client and processes them to complete the task. In this example, the program might take the data sent by

Figure 2.14 The HTML source code for the document *form.html*.

```
<HTML><HEAD>

  <TITLE> Example of an HTML FORM  </TITLE>

</HEAD>

<BODY>

<H1> Example of an HTML FORM  </H1>

<FORM ACTION="no_action">

Data entered into a FORM is sent to a program on the server

for processing.  If you see a button at the end of this sentence

then your browser supports the HTML FORMs element.

--[<INPUT TYPE="checkbox" NAME="button" VALUE="on">]-

If you do not see a button between the square brackets go to the

<A HREF="text-only.html"> text-only interface </A>. </FORM>

<hr>

<FORM  ACTION="http://side.edu/cgi-bin/send_note">

  <p> <STRONG> 1) Send this note to: </STRONG>

  <SELECT NAME="mailto-name" >

    <OPTION SELECTED> Martin Grant

    <OPTION> Jack Smith

    <OPTION> Bruce Lee

    <OPTION> Anna Mcgarrigle

    <OPTION> Kate Bush

    <OPTION> Spike Lee

    <OPTION> Diane Koziol

    <OPTION> Ross Thomson

    <OPTION> Ann Dean

  </SELECT>
```

```
<p> 2) <STRONG>Give your e-mail address: </STRONG>

    This indicates who sent the letter

<p> <INPUT TYPE="text"  NAME="signature"

       VALUE="name@internet.address" SIZE=60>



<p> <STRONG> 3) Message Body: </STRONG>

<p>

<TEXTAREA COLS=60 ROWS=8 NAME="message_body">

 Delete this message and type your message into this

 textbox.  Press the "Send Message" button to send it

 off. You can press the "Reset" button to reset the

 form to the original values.

</TEXTAREA>

<P>

<INPUT TYPE="submit" VALUE="Send Message"> <INPUT TYPE="reset"> (reset form)

</FORM>

</BODY>

</HTML>
```

the form and compose an electronic mail message to be sent to the intended person. We will look at gateway programs and how data is actually sent from the form to the gateway program in Chapters 7 and 8.

FORM INPUT ELEMENTS

By comparing the HTML document in Figure 2.14 and its rendering in Figure 2.15, you can see some of the several input items that can go inside a form. This example shows a **SELECT** element pull-down menu (where the user selects the name of the person to whom he or she wishes to send the message—the possible names being given by the **OPTION** element); a single-line

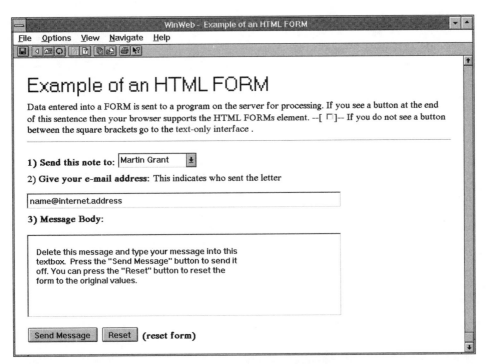

▨▨▨▨▨▨ **Figure 2.15** WinWeb rendering of the *form.html* document (the document source is displayed in Figure 2.14). The **FORM** fill-in elements are clearly evident.

text **INPUT** element (here, where the user types in his or her e-mail address); and a **TEXTAREA** element (where the user would type the body of the message). Several other input elements are available and are described in Chapter 4. The elements **SELECT, INPUT, OPTION,** and **TEXTAREA** can appear only inside a **FORM.**

Every **FORM** input element takes one key attribute. This is the **NAME** attribute, which associates a *variable name* to the data associated with the input element, for example NAME="mailto-name" or NAME="button". These names are used to differentiate between the data associated with the different input elements. Some elements, such as the **INPUT** element, can also assign a default initial *value* to the named variable using the **VALUE** attribute. An example is the element:

```
<INPUT TYPE="checkbox" NAME="button" VALUE="on">
```

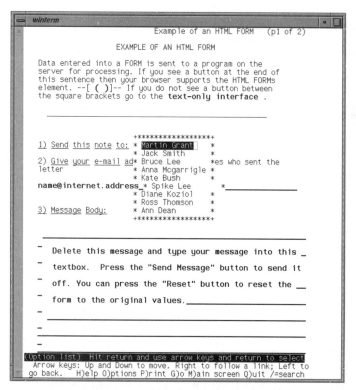

```
winterm
                        Example of an HTML FORM   (p1 of 2)

                        EXAMPLE OF AN HTML FORM

         Data entered into a FORM is sent to a program on the
         server for processing. If you see a button at the end of
         this sentence then your browser supports the HTML FORMs
         element. --[ ( )]-- If you do not see a button between
         the square brackets go to the text-only interface .



                       +*****************+
         1) Send this note to: * Martin Grant  *
                               * Jack Smith    *
         2) Give your e-mail ad* Bruce Lee     *es who sent the
         letter                * Anna Mcgarrigle *
                               * Kate Bush     *
         name@internet.address_* Spike Lee     *_____
                               * Diane Koziol  *
                               * Ross Thomson  *
         3) Message Body:      * Ann Dean      *
                               +*****************+


        ‾ Delete this message and type your message into this _

        ‾ textbox.  Press the "Send Message" button to send it

        ‾ off. You can press the "Reset" button to reset the __

        ‾ form to the original values._____

        -  _____

        -  _____

        -
        (Option list)  Hit return and use arrow keys and return to select
         Arrow keys: Up and Down to move. Right to follow a link; Left to
         go back.  H)elp O)ptions P)rint G)o M)ain screen Q)uit /=search
```

Figure 2.16 The lynx browser rendering of the *form.html* document (the document source is displayed in Figure 2.14). The **FORM** fill-in elements are clearly evident. In general, lynx gives written instructions at the bottom of the screen to help the user properly manipulate the form.

which assigns the value "on" to the name "button". These values can subsequently be changed by user input, by selecting a different entry from a pull-down menu, typing text into a box, or clicking on checkboxes or buttons.

When the user presses the special *Send Message* button (a special **INPUT** element with the attribute TYPE="submit"), the data in the form are sent to the server as a collection of strings of the form *name=value*, where *name* is the value assigned to the **NAME** attribute of an element, and *value* is the value assigned by the user's input. For example, the checkbox input element in this illustration would send the string *button=on*. The detailed algorithm for the construction of this string is discussed in Chapter 6, and also in Chapter 8.

The server program sorts out what the data mean by matching the *names* in the message to names the program is designed to recognize. Consequently, a form and the associated server-side gateway program must be designed together.

Like all HTML elements, the **FORM** element has restrictions on where it can be placed. A **FORM** cannot be inside a heading, inside another **FORM,** or inside character emphasis markup, such as a **STRONG** or **EM** element. However, a **FORM** can contain headings, character markup elements, and even lists. Again, the details of the nesting rules are given in Chapter 4.

Figure 2.16 shows the same **FORM** as displayed by lynx. The lynx browser can display all the major FORM elements and provides instructions at the bottom of the screen to explain how to fill in the different parts.

Notice the little button enclosed in square brackets near the top of Figures 2.15 and 2.16. This button does not actually do anything (note that there is no associated <INPUT TYPE="submit"> button), and is simply there to test the capabilities of the browser. There are still a few older browsers that are unable to process the **FORM** element (for example, Cello Version 1.0 and MacMosaic Version 1.0.3). It is therefore still a good idea to test the form capabilities of the browser, and let the user know if he or she will be

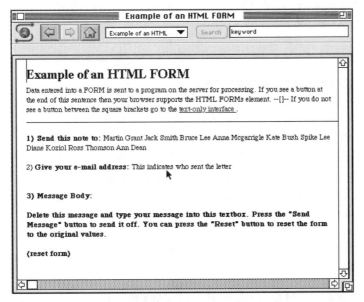

Figure 2.17 MacMosaic Version 1.0.3 rendering of the *form.html* document (the document source is displayed in Figure 2.14). This browser cannot display **FORM** elements.

unable to properly view a document. Figure 2.17 displays the same HTML document as Figure 2.15 but using the MacMosaic 1.0.3 browser. You can see that the button in the first paragraph is missing (as are all the other **FORM** boxes—in general, browsers simply ignore tags that they do not understand). The first paragraph explains why the rest of the page looks so odd, and can direct users to alternate documents designed for a FORMs-incapable browser, should such pages be available.

LESSONS FROM EXAMPLE 6

1. The document developer can use the HTML **FORM** element to solicit user input. However, each FORM document must send the data it gathers to a server-side gateway program designed to analyze the form data. This gateway program is specified by the **ACTION** attribute of the **FORM** element. The program and form must be designed together.

2. An HTML **FORM** can contain several input elements, namely, **INPUT**, **SELECT**, **OPTION**, and **TEXTAREA**. These elements can appear only inside a **FORM**.

3. A **FORM** cannot be inside a heading element or inside another **FORM**—**FORM**s cannot be nested. However, heading, list, and character markup elements can be inside a **FORM**.

EXAMPLE 7: LINKS WITHIN DOCUMENTS

Up until now, we have looked at hypertext links that connect one document to another. When such a link is accessed, the browser retrieves the linked object and displays it, starting from the beginning of the object.

This is not always what is desired. Sometimes, the document is actually a single, large document and you want to link to a particular place in the document, not just to the beginning. Alternatively, you may want to link between different places in the same document—for example, from a list of sections in the document to each of the section headings. This is simply not possible with the linking model discussed so far.

ANCHOR ELEMENT: THE NAME ATTRIBUTE

Links between locations in the same document are made possible through the **NAME** attribute of the **A** (anchor) element. The **NAME** attribute lets you assign a unique name, called a *fragment identifier*, to a particular place in a document. You can then link to this particular named location using a special form of URL that contains this special name. You can do this from within the same document, or from any other document.

Figure 2.18 shows a document containing several named locations, and illustrates one of the common uses of named locations—to create a simple index of the contents of the page. The top of the page contains links that access the different sections of the document, while each section contains links that allow you to return to the top of the page, and back to the contents listing. This page was originally developed by the author and Sian Meikle of the University of Toronto Library, and is part of a template document collection we distribute to university departments interested in developing their own document collections. The entire template is located at:

```
http://www.hprc.utoronto.ca/Template/readme.html
```

NAME ATTRIBUTE AND FRAGMENT IDENTIFIERS

There are four named anchors in Figure 2.18, but for this discussion, we will focus on the one for the history section. The relevant hypertext anchor is:

```
<A NAME="history">History of the Department</A>
```

This anchor associates a *fragment identifier*, history, with this location in the document. Looking at Figure 2.19, you will see that this section of text is not rendered in any special way. In general, a named anchor is not specially displayed. From elsewhere in this document, the location can be referenced using a URL of the form

```
<A HREF="#history">Department History</A>
```

as seen in Figure 2.18. Note how the fragment identifier is indicated by prepending the hash character (#) in front of it, to distinguish this from a regular URL. If the user clicks on the anchored text Department History, the browser will then access the named fragment identifier and scroll the page down to that location, as shown in Figure 2.20.

NAME AND HREF COMBINED

A hypertext reference can contain both **HREF** and **NAME** attributes. An example is shown in the very first anchor in Figure 2.18, namely:

```
<A HREF="depthome.html" NAME="top"><IMG SRC="home.gif" ALT="[home]"></A>
```

Clicking on this anchor links the user to the document *depthome.html* (you will note that in Figure 2.19 this image is highlighted as a linked hypertext anchor). At the same time, clicking on the internal page link:

Figure 2.18 A Typical HTML document, ***deptinfo.html***, that contains the named anchor element. Portions of the document have been omitted to save space. Comments are in italics, while markers indicating the named anchors are in boldface italics.

```
<HTML> <HEAD>

  <TITLE> Biology Department: General Information  </TITLE> </HEAD>

<BODY>

<A HREF="depthome.html" NAME="top"><IMG SRC="home.gif" ALT="[home]"></A>

<HR>

<IMG SRC="french2.gif" ALT="[Picture of our Building]">

<H1>Biology at the University of Toronto</H1>

<ADDRESS>

  University of Toronto          <BR>

  150 St George Street, Room 213 <BR>

  Toronto Ontario M5S 1A1 CANADA <BR>

  <B>Tel:</B>     (416)-978-7000  <BR>

  <B>Fax:</B>     (416)-978-9000  <BR>

  <B>E-mail:</B> <a href="mailto:infobiol@biology.utoronto.ca">
infobiol@biology.utoronto.ca</a>

</ADDRESS>


<HR>

<B>On this page:</B>

[<A HREF="#general">General Information</A>]

[<A HREF="#facilities">Research Facilities</A>]

[<A HREF="#history">Department History</A>]  [<-- References Named Anchor]

<HR>


<H2><A NAME="general">General</A></H2>

<BLOCKQUOTE>
```

```
<P>
  <EM> This is an example document only. There is no need, for example, to
  have all this information on a single page. There is one advantage,
  however, to keeping this material together -- it allows the user to
  print the entire document for reading away from the computer.</EM>
</BLOCKQUOTE>


<P> The University of Toronto is the largest university in Canada
  with 2500 graduate faculty and more than 9000 full and part-time graduate
  students. Metropolitan Toronto has a population of 3,000,000 people
  who provide a rich multicultural mix and create an interesting and
  stimulating environment outside the University.</P>


        [text1 deleted ...]
<H2><A NAME="facilities">Research Facilities</a></H2>


<P> The Department provides many facilities to aid astronomical research,
    and students and staff use national and international observatories
    all over the world and in space. The Department has a special fund for
    students to pay for travel to such observatories as the UTSO in Chile,
    CFHT in Hawaii, the VLA in New Mexico, and the IUE satellite
    groundstation in Maryland.</P>


    [text deleted]
<a HREF="#top">... to top of page</A>
<H2><A NAME="history">History of the Department</A> </H2> [<--NAMED ANCHOR]


<P> Biology became a major department in 1905.  The first chair of
    the Department, Dr. Roland Fishburn, introduced several teaching
```

```
    programs in aid of the Faculty of Medicine, and went on to

    develop major programs in Bological Research. This led to the

    construction of the Biology Building in 1911, constructed on

.......[more text deleted]

<a HREF="#top">... to top of page</A>

<HR>

<a HREF="depthome.html"><IMG SRC="icons/home.gif" ALT="[home]"></A>

</BODY> </HTML>
```

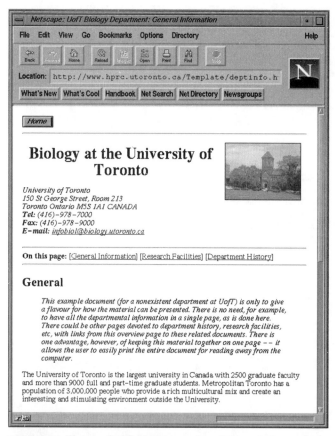

Figure 2.19 Netscape Navigator 1.1 rendering of the document *deptinfo.html* shown in Figure 2.18.

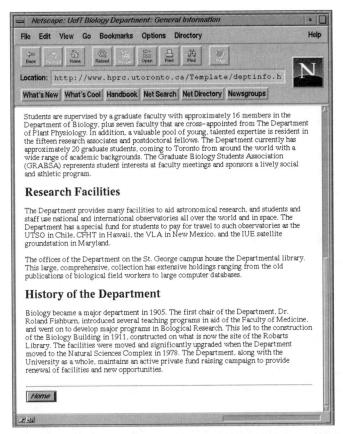

Figure 2.20 Netscape Navigator 1.1 rendering of the document **deptinfo.html** shown in Figure 2.18 after accessing the internal link referenced by the text string "Department History," shown at the top of Figure 2.19.

```
<a HREF="#top">... to top of page</A>
```

returns the user to the top of the page and to this same linked image. Thus, anchors can be both the start and destination of a hypertext link.

FRAGMENT IDENTIFIERS AND FULL URLS

You can also access named locations from outside the document. This is done by *appending* the fragment identifier to the document's locator string. For example, if the full URL for the document **deptinfo.html** were:

```
http://www.hprc.utoronto.ca/Template/deptinfo.html
```

then the URL that explicitly references the history section is just:

```
http://www.hprc.utoronto.ca/Template/deptinfo.html#history
```

Fragment identifiers and full URLs are discussed in detail in Chapter 6.

THE BLOCKQUOTE ELEMENT

Figures 2.18 and 2.19 illustrate another new element, namely **BLOCK-QUOTE**. This element is used to mark block quotations, such as an extract from a book or speech. Blockquoted text is often indented, and so HTML writers often use this element simply to highlight blocks of text (as done in this example). This is not the true intention of the **BLOCKQUOTE** element, and HTML 3 elements such as **NOTE** (which is, unfortunately, not understood by most current browsers, exceptions being emacs-w3 and Arena) are more appropriate for marking off special notes or cautions. HTML 3 elements such as **NOTE** are discussed in Chapter 5.

LESSONS FROM EXAMPLE 7

1. The **NAME** attribute assigns a name, called a *fragment identifier*, to an **A** (anchor) element. This allows an anchor to be the *destination* of a hypertext link, and allows for hypertext **HREF** anchors that target specific locations within a given document.

2. You can reference a **NAME**d location from within the same document, using an anchor element of the form `<A HREF="#frag_id">anchor text</A>`, where `frag_id` is the fragment identifier you wish to reference. The hash character is mandatory, and indicates the start of a fragment identifier.

3. You can reference a **NAME**d location from any other document by appending the fragment identifier to the URL of the document, for example:

`<A HREF="http://bla.bla.edu/Projects/doc2.html#frag-id">anchor text</A>`.

4. You can combine **HREF** and **NAME** anchors in the same anchor element:

`<A HREF="URL-string" NAME="frag-id">anchor text</A>`.

This means that the anchor is both the start and the possible destination of a hypertext link.

5. **BLOCKQUOTE** is for block quotations, and usually displays the enclosed text with indented margins. This is often used as a trick to introduce text indentation.

EXAMPLE 8: ADVANCED FEATURES: IMAGES AND PARAGRAPHS

As discussed in Example 2, HTML 2.0 allows for rudimentary control over the placement and alignment of images or text on the page. Recent extensions to HTML allow for significant improvement in control over this aspect of document presentation. These extensions occur through the addition of **ALIGN** (alignment) attributes to the **Hn** (heading) and **P** (paragraph) elements, as well as the addition of new **ALIGN** attribute values for the **IMG** element. These new attributes, and their effect, are shown in Figures 2.21 and 2.22.

HEADING AND PARAGRAPH ALIGNMENT

In HTML 2.0, the **H1** through **H6** and **P** elements do not take attributes. HTML 3 proposes several attributes for these elements, among which is **ALIGN**. **ALIGN** defines the desired alignment for the element on the page, and can take the values "left" (the default), "center," "right," and "justify." Currently, only "left" (left-align the text on the page) and "center" (center the text on the page) alignment are widely implemented. Figure 2.22 shows the effect of these different alignment options on the heading and paragraph elements, while Figure 2.23 shows the presentation by a browser that does not understand this attribute: the browser ignores the **ALIGN** attribute and uses the browser's alignment default (left-aligned). Note in Figure 2.22 how the Netscape 1.1. browser does not understand the ALIGN=right attribute value—this omission is corrected with the Version 2.0 browser.

The **ALIGN** attribute to heading and paragraph elements is understood by many browsers, including the Netscape, Arena, emacs-w3, and newer versions of Mosaic browsers.

IMAGE ALIGNMENT

Image alignment is more problematic than text alignment, since the desire is to let the image "float" to some preferred location, and then let the text flow around the image. HTML 3 proposes using **ALIGN** values of *left* and *right* for this purpose, where *left* causes the image to float to the left of the page, and *right* causes the image to float to the right-hand margin. Any text following the image, or included in the paragraph containing the image, is flowed around the image. Figure 2.22 show the effect of the left alignment value. Here the image has floated to the left margin, with the text flowing to the right around it. Figure 2.23 shows the rendering by a browser that does not

■■■■■ **Figure 2.21** HTML code for the document **_align.html_**. This document illustrates some of the newer alignment features possible with the heading, paragraph and image elements.

```
<HTML><HEAD><TITLE>

    Heading, Paragraph and Image Alignment Options

</TITLE> </HEAD>

<BODY>

<H1 ALIGN=center> Alignment Options <BR> Headings, Paragraphs and Images</H1>

<P>

<IMG ALIGN="left" HEIGHT=140 WIDTH=140 ALT="[Example Image]" SRC="image.gif">

Here is some text that flows around the image. The <CODE>ALIGN=right</CODE>

attribute value causes the image to float to the right hand margin, and
allows the text to flow around the image.  This results in much nicer
image-text placement, a better use of the page, and graphically more attrac-
tive documents.

<BR CLEAR=left>

<HR>

<H3 ALIGN=right>Here is a right aligned Heading </h3>

<P ALIGN=center> <EM> You should note that these alignment tags are not
understood

by all browsers. Well-behaved browsers will simply ignore the attributes
they do not understand, and display the document to the best of their abil-
ity </EM>

<h3 align=left>Left Aligned (the default) Heading </h3>

<p align=right> This paragraph is supposed to be right-aligned. This can
look

rather odd, but it can be useful in some contexts.

</BODY></HTML>
```

■■■■■

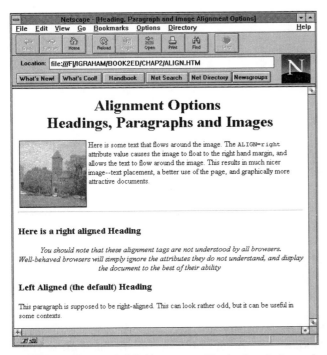

Figure 2.22 Netscape Navigator 1.1 rendering of the document *align.html*. The HTML listing for this document is shown in Figure 2.21.

understand this attribute; here, the image is simply placed inline with the text. If you want the image to appear separate from the text, you must be sure to precede and follow the image by either a paragraph or a line break element.

IMAGE WIDTH AND HEIGHT

To format the page, the browser must obviously know the size of the image to be inserted. In general, the browser does not know this until the image is actually loaded, which means that it can't begin to format the page until after the image has arrived. Because this can significantly delay the construction of the page, HTML 3 proposes the **HEIGHT** and **WIDTH** attributes, which are used to specify the desired size of the image (by default, in pixels). This allows the browser to format the document, leaving an empty box in the document ready for the image being downloaded. Also, if the image is not of

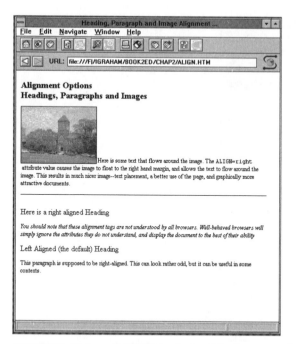

Figure 2.23 Mosaic for Windows rendering of the document *align.html*. The HTML listing for this document is shown in Figure 2.21.

the specified size, the browser will resize the image to fit the defined box. This feature is supported by several browsers, including Netscape Navigator and Arena.

CLEARING MARGINS FOR TEXT

Sometimes, you will want the text that follows an image to continue after the bottom of the figure, and not beside it. To do this, you must "clear" the text so that subsequent text moves down unconditionally below the image. Since the image can be to the left or right, you must be able to specify that the text should start only when the left margin is clear, when the right margin is clear, or when both margins are clear.

In HTML 3, you accomplish this using the **CLEAR** attribute, which is currently only available on the **BR** element. Thus, `<BR CLEAR=left>` ensures that the text following the **BR** is cleared to the left margin, while `<BR CLEAR=right>` ensures that the following text is cleared to the right margin, and `<BR CLEAR=all>` ensures that the following text is cleared to both margins. Figure 2.22 shows the effect of `CLEAR=left`—in the absence of

CLEAR=left, the subsequent horizontal rule and heading would be placed next to the image, and not below it. This attribute is currently understood by any browser that allows left- and right-aligned images.

LESSONS FROM EXAMPLE 8

1. The **ALIGN** attribute on headings and paragraphs can be used to modify the default alignment of the text content. Possible values are "left" (the default), "right," "center," and "justify."

2. On some browsers, the **ALIGN** attribute on **IMG** elements can float an image to the left (**ALIGN**="left") or right (**ALIGN**="right") of the display, and allow text to flow around the image. In these cases the attributes **WIDTH** and **HEIGHT** can be used to indicate the desired size of the image, while the element **BR**, with an appropriate **CLEAR** attribute value, can be used to clear subsequent text to start below the image.

EXAMPLE 9: ADVANCED FEATURES: TABLES AND BACKGROUNDS

This last example looks at HTML tags for modifying the background of the display window and for defining tables of items. The absence of tables was one of the major weaknesses of HTML 2.0. This has been largely solved by the HTML 3 proposals for a simple, yet effective collection of table elements. The system is discussed in detail in Chapters 4 and 5.

TABLES AND CAPTIONS

Tables are defined using the **TABLE** element, while the content of the table is laid out as a sequence of table rows (**TR**), which in turn contain table headers (**TH**) and table data (**TD**). A table can also have a caption, defined by the **CAPTION** element. The caption can contain all forms of character formatting markup, including hypertext anchors. An example is shown in Figures 2.24 and 2.25. Tables can have borders and dividing lines, or can be borderless. The start tag <TABLE BORDER> ensures that the table is drawn with borders and dividers.

TABLE ROWS AND COLUMNS

Tables are defined as a collection of rows, defined by the **TR** element. Each of these rows contains a collection of *cells*, defined by the **TH** or **TD** elements. **TH** (table header) elements are used for column or row headings, while **TD**

■■■■■■ **Figure 2.24** HTML code for the document *tables.html*. This document illustrates the **TABLE** element, as well as the **BACKGROUND** attribute to the **BODY**
element.

```
<HTML><HEAD><TITLE> Table and Background Example</TITLE>

</HEAD>

<BODY BACKGROUND="backgnd.gif">

<H1> A Simple Table Example </H1>

<TABLE BORDER>

<CAPTION> First Example <A HREF="tables.html">Table</A></CAPTION>

  <TR>

      <TH ROWSPAN=2> Segment </TH>  <TH COLSPAN=2> Total Memory </TH>

  </TR> <TR>

                                        <TH>Bytes</TH> <TH> Kbytes </TH>

  </TR> <TR>

     <TD> 005B5 </TD> <TD ALIGN=right> 78 </TD> <TD> (0K) </TD>

  </TR> <TR>

     <TD> 00780 </TD> <TD ALIGN=right > 175 </TD> <TD> 0K </TD>

  </TR> <TR>

     <TD> 020B </TD> <TD ALIGN=right > 88348 </TD> <TD> 510K </TD>

  </TR> <TR>

     <TD COLSPAN=2 ALIGN=left><A HREF="memory.html">Total Free</A></TD>

     <TD> 510K </TD>

  </TR>

</TABLE>

</TR></BODY></HTML>
```

■■■■■■

(regular tabular entry) elements are used for everything else. These are nonempty elements, but the end tags are optional. These elements can take several attributes to define the alignment of the element content (**ALIGN** and

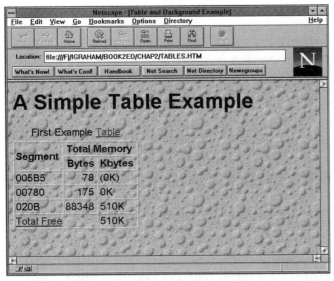

Figure 2.25 Netscape Navigator 1.1 rendering of the document *tables.html*. The HTML listing for this document is shown in Figure 2.24.

VALIGN), or the number of rows or columns (**ROWSPAN** and **COLSPAN** respectively) occupied by the element.

JUSTIFICATION OF TABLE ROWS AND COLUMNS

When you design a table, you must ensure that the number of rows and columns sums to the correct number for your table. For example, compare the markup in Figure 2.24 with the table rendering in Figure 2.25. The table is defined with three columns and six rows. Note how the number of columns in each TR element always sums to three (a cell with ROWSPAN=2, such as the first cell here, contributes an extra column to the following row, since this cell "spans" the same column in two rows). Keeping track of the rows and columns tends to be a bit tricky the first time you create a table, but you will quickly get the hang of it. If you are doing tables by hand, it is useful to lay them out in your HTML document as done in Figure 2.24, as this allows you to see the underlying tabular structure. Of course, it is easier if you can find a program that will create HTML tables for you. Some packages that can already do this are listed in Chapter 9, while several HTML editors now boast of integrated TABLE editing tools.

ALIGNMENT WITHIN TABLE CELLS

Items within elements, or along entire rows, can be aligned using the alignment attributes. **ALIGN**, which can take the values "left", "center", or

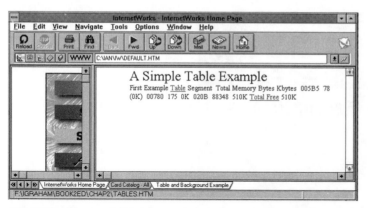

Figure 2.26 InternetWorks rendering of the document *tables.html*. The HTML listing for this document is shown in Figure 2.24.

"right", aligns the cell contents horizontally within the cell. The attribute **VALIGN** is used to vertically align the content, and can take the values "top", "middle", or "bottom". The effect of some of these alignment options is illustrated in Figure 2.25.

BACKGROUND CONTROL

HTML 3 proposes the use of the **BACKGROUND** attribute to the **BODY** element, to indicate an image file that the browser can use to tile the background of the browser display window. The general form is:

```
<BODY BACKGROUND="url_to_image_file">
```

The value of the **BACKGROUND** attribute is the URL of an image file. If capable, the browser will load this image file and use it to *tile* the background of the document being displayed. Figure 2.25 shows an example of a loaded background. This can be an attractive change to the document, but should be used with care—remember that not everyone has a good graphics monitor, and that every color you use for the background is one color less for any images you might want to display on top of the background.

Backgrounds can cause problems if the background color is similar to the default color used for the text. The Netscape Navigator browser supports several other **BODY** attributes for setting the desired default color for the text. These are discussed at the conclusion of Chapter 4.

RENDERING BY TABLE-
OR BACKGROUND-INCAPABLE BROWSERS

Tables and background tiling are supported by a limited number of browsers. What happens if a browser that does not support these features attempts to display tables or backgrounds? There is no problem with backgrounds (provided the background does not contain important information content), since the document content will be displayed regardless of whether the browser is capable of tiling the background with an image. The situation with tables is more problematic. Figure 2.26 shows what happens when a browser that does not understand table elements is presented with a **TABLE**. The table tags are ignored, and the text is jumbled together in a haphazard and unreadable fashion. Clearly, table elements are useless unless the browser understands them.

Several commonly used browsers, and all browsers released prior to the spring of 1995, do not understand the table elements. Because of this, it is wise to offer tabular data in alternative formats—for example, inside a **PRE** element, using the fixed-width font dictated by **PRE** to align the text content. Alternatively, you can present the table as an included image file. You can then provide links connecting to these two different representations, and give your users the choice of accessing the document format acceptable to their browser.

LESSONS FROM EXAMPLE 9

1. The **TABLE** element permits formally defined tables in HTML documents. However, several browsers do not support this element, so you should offer a non-**TABLE** alternative to these users, wherever possible.

2. The **BACKGROUND** attribute to the **BODY** specifies an image file to be used as a background to the displayed text. This can be very attractive, but care should be taken in case the background dominates or otherwise obscures the document content. Additional Netscape-specific **BODY** attributes that permit additional control of the text colors are described in Chapter 4.

THE DESIGN
OF HTML DOCUMENT
COLLECTIONS

Chapters 1 and 2 provided a gentle (I hope!) introduction to HTML, and to good design habits for creating HTML documents. This chapter takes a broader approach, and looks at the issues involved in designing *collections* of HTML documents and associated resources. By analogy to the printed world, this is the difference between designing a single page of text, and designing a magazine or book. "Collections" such as books and magazines require design elements that are neither necessary, nor apparent from the perspective of a single page. The same is true of hypertext collections, although here the required design elements are quite different from those required in printed books.

Why are the requirements different? The reasons lie in the different nature of the presentation media: books are spatial, physical, and static collections, with a fixed *linear* structure, while hypertext is nonspatial and nonphysical, possibly dynamic, and often *nonlinear*. Good hypertext design must reflect these differences, while preserving the easy navigability of printed books. This chapter looks at some ways of accomplishing this goal.

PAPER AND BOOKS

The easiest way to start is with the familiar example of a book. This allows us to introduce, using a familiar model, the ideas behind the construction of a document collection. The issues that arise in hypertext design can then be analyzed with respect to this more familiar paradigm.

A book, of course, is simply a collection of pages. Obviously, however, there is more to it than that! A large collection of unbound and unnumbered pages is awkward and confusing (rather like the floor of this author's office, as he sits writing this chapter), since a reader cannot tell the sequence of the pages without checking for continuity from page to page, and cannot easily tell if a page belongs with a given group of pages, should multiple collections be present. Book design solves these organizational problems by giving the pages a uniform design (top and bottom page banners, typeface, and so on), so that the pages of a given book have a distinctive look; by numbering the pages to give *linear* order to the collection; and by binding them together to enforce the correct order. If there are many pages, a book is often given a table of contents listing the page numbers of important starting pages, and perhaps an index providing page references to other important locations. By convention, these are placed at the beginning and end of the book (the exact location varies with different linguistic and national conventions), to make them easy to find. Additional cross-referencing is possible through internal page references, footnotes, bibliographies, and so on. In fact, the organizational technology of printed books is very sophisticated, covering everything from simple pamphlets to multivolume encyclopedias. This is not surprising, given that the technology of printed books has been refined over 500 years of practical experience.

LINEAR DOCUMENTS

Books and other printed media can all be described as *linear*. Here, linear means having an obvious beginning and end, and a single fixed sequence of pages in between. Indexes, tables of contents, or cross-references exist superimposed on this linear framework—they provide added value, and are often critically important, but they do not change the underlying structure. In fact they depend on the underlying structure (page numbers) to provide internal references within the book.

The reasons for the near-universality of this linear model are both physical, and psychological. Physically, the only reliable way to organize printed pages is as a bound, linear entity—it is hard to create a book as a random collection of nonlinearly accessible documents! Psychologically, a linear, well-defined structure is comfortable, familiar, and convenient, since the result is easy to read, easy to reference, and easy to communicate to others. The goal of all publishing is *communication*, and a book is a robust collection that can be reliably communicated to others (through duplicate copies), and reliably referenced and compared (through page number references), since everyone with the same book has the same information, at the same location within the book.

It is also important to note that the physical nature of the book allows a reader to know both the exact size of the book, and where he or she is in the book. This makes it easy for a reader to browse a book, for example by jumping from the table of contents to some selected location, or by simply selecting pages at random, all the while retaining a sense of location with respect to the beginning, end, table of contents, or index.

Other traditional media, such as music, video, and film, are also linear in this sense, being predetermined sequential presentations of sounds or images created by a musician or director. This, in part, reflects the temporal nature of these media—music and film move dynamically (and usually forward) in time in a sequential way. This also reflects the technical limitations of the media, as it is almost impossible to make nonlinear presentations with traditional film, video, or audio technology, just as is the case with printed text.

Figure 3.1 illustrates the structure of a book. Note how the table of contents and index merely provide referencing on top of the underlying linear structure.

NONLINEAR MEDIA

The advent in recent years of inexpensive, yet extremely powerful, computers and graphical displays has made it possible to step beyond this linear barrier, and has opened up enormous—and still largely unexplored—possibilities in the organization and presentation of information. This is because a computer has no preferred organization for stored data, and can easily store, index, relate, and access the data in a number of different ways, subject to the design of the database storing the data and the abilities of the software. In addition,

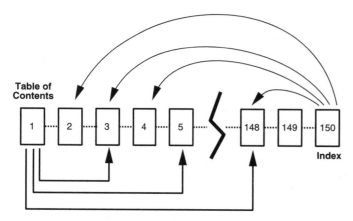

Figure 3.1 The structure of a linear document collection, in this case a book. The ordering is implicit in the page numbering. Tables of contents and indexes simply provide referencing on top of this underlying structure.

a computer can create a representation of the underlying data quickly, efficiently, and *inexpensively*, according to instructions provided by software and user input. In a sense, you can think of the stored data as a collection of book pages, which can be shuffled and rearranged almost instantaneously by the computer, at practically no cost. This is in stark contrast to the difficulty and high cost of modifying the order of printed material, or material on tape or film.[1]

At the same time, modern computer interfaces can directly, and again at low cost, present these data to a user—a Web browser is just one instance of this process. This also is a new phenomenon, since high-resolution computer display systems capable of rapidly displaying finely formatted text and graphics have only recently become affordable. Thus, not only can a computer rapidly organize data, it can also instantly present the data to a user, in almost any format (text, graphics, audio and video, etc.). A computer can consequently act like an infinitely customizable printing press, capable of customizing and presenting data in decidedly nonlinear ways, limited only by the interests of a user and the capabilities of the underlying software.

This has led, in the past 15 or so years, to the birth of several new media. The first, and possibly still most popular, was video games. Games are inherently

---

[1] This flexibility and speed also applies to audio and video, which in large part explains why text, audio, and video editing are now commonly performed on computers.

nonlinear in the sense described above, since they evolve in an unpredictable way following the input (i.e., "play") of the user. Video games preserve this model through an environment that incorporates both the game scenario and rules—the user "plays" in this environment, and can explore nearly endless game variants, the number of possible variations depending, of course, on the sophistication of the game. The first games were very simple, with primitive graphics and limited scenarios, but today's games, such as Myst and Doom, provide enormously rich environments, and enormous flexibility in the way a player can explore the game's virtual world. Anyone with an interest in the possible directions of these new media should spend time playing with modern computer games—even if sometimes it is hard to argue that this is really "work"!

HYPERTEXT AND MULTIMEDIA

At the same time, it was apparent from the earliest days of computers that this new technology could realize the long-dreamed notions of hypertext [2] and multimedia.[3] Inexpensive computers, and easy-to-use programs such as HyperCard or Macromedia Director, opened up exciting new ways of presenting combinations of otherwise weakly connected media. Very quickly, hypertext and multimedia became the hottest new topics in media design, with products ranging from multimedia wine guides and hypertext encyclopedias to multimedia/hypertext training packages. Indeed, today many corporations commission multimedia promotional kits instead of the more traditional videos or films.

Designing linear multimedia is relatively straightforward—it is the design of *hyper*text or *hyper*media collections that introduces enormous design complexities. This is because each hypertext presentation must incorporate, *within* the structure of the presentation, the tools allowing a user to successfully and comfortably explore the collected material. Since in hypertext the components can be related in decidedly nonlinear ways, there are no simple organizational schemes, such as page numbering, that can serve as ubiquitous and commonly understood paradigms of navigation and location. And, unlike a game, you want the rules to be nonintrusive and easy to follow, since it is the *content*

---

[2] *Hypertext*: a collection of text and graphics that can be explored, by the reader, in a nonlinear way.
[3] *Multimedia*: the mixture of text, graphics, sound, and video in a single presentation. Note that a multimedia presentation is often *linear*. The combination of multimedia in a nonlinear hypertext format is often called *hypermedia*. In this book, the terms hypertext can be taken as synonymous with hypermedia.

you want to communicate, and not the navigational mechanisms. Designers and researchers are still exploring ways of designing easy-to-use hypertext and hypermedia, and it is not a surprise that good design is something of an art, rather than a science.

WEB COLLECTIONS AS HYPERTEXT

Most of these design problems are apparent in large collections, or webs, of HTML documents. Web collections are a form of hypermedia, limited of course by the technologies of the Web and the Internet (a web collection is clearly not as dynamic or multimedia-oriented as a Macromedia Director presentation), but at the same time enriched by the ability to connect with resources around the world. Most importantly, the Web is inherently nonlinear, since there can be (often frustratingly) a nearly endless number of ways of getting from one page to another. Figure 3.2 shows a simple figure of a possible Web document collection—as in Figure 3.1, the solid lines indicate the links (in this case, hypertext links) between the pages, with the arrows indicating the directions of the links.

Do you see the inherent problem in Figure 3.2? Suppose you are at document *A*, and want to proceed to a topic discussed in document *B*. How do you get there? The answer is that you have absolutely no idea. If this collection were to have no structure other than the indicated links, you would be forced to move randomly through the collection until you happened, largely by chance, upon the desired page. In the absence of additional information, you do not know where to find the Table of Contents (or even if there is one), the Index, or even the beginning of a section. Even if the links were sequential (the documents connected one after the other, like a book), you would not be able to find places such as these since, with the Web, there is no way to step back, "see" the entire book, and just turn to the "front" for the Table of Contents. Indeed, you have absolutely no idea of the size of the collection. A book gives you both a local and global feel for its size and for your location: the page number tells you where you are, and where the next and previous pages are, while the feel of the book tells you approximately where you are with respect to the entire book (e.g., halfway through) and also tell you exactly where to find the Table of Contents (at the front) or the Index (at the back). The ability to see the whole picture, plus conventions for the location of contents pages and indexes, are part of the technology of books that makes them so easy to use. It is your goal, in designing a web, to include similar navigational tools, and allow visitors to your web to easily explore and find what they are looking for, without becoming lost or frustrated.

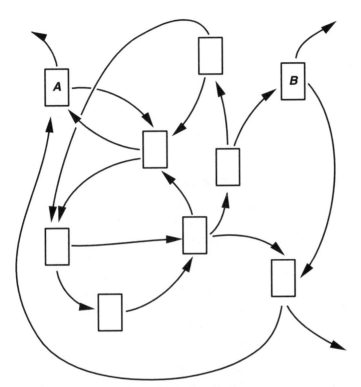

▬▬▬ **Figure 3.2** A figurative example of a web of documents—the links between the documents are indicated by the arrows. The collection is nonlinear, in that there are a number of different routes by which the collection could be visited. It is, however, very easy to get lost in such a web.

THE DESIGN OF WEB COLLECTIONS

It is time to look at some concrete examples of web collection design. The first examples will be based on a linear model—just because the Web is non-linear, doesn't mean you have to give up linearity completely! A linear approach is perfectly appropriate when converting a printed document to hypertext, for online documentation, or when you have a particular sequence that you want followed by your readers, such as a slide show.

This will be followed by a look at some nonlinear collections—in particular, at the possible organization of collections of documents at a Web site. This section will include some design pointers for these larger collections, as well as some suggestions for managing large collections developed collaboratively by several people.

Last, the chapter will look at how to make a Web site that is attractive to visitors, and that also keeps visitors coming back. This is an issue of both hypertext design and public relations. You must always remember that a Web site is a dynamic place that *encourages* interaction with its visitors, and take advantage of this characteristic, if you are going to develop a Web site that attracts and retains loyal visitors.

LINEAR DOCUMENT COLLECTIONS

Figure 3.3 shows the schematic layout for a linear document collection—the solid lines with the arrows show the locations and directions of the critical navigational links. Figures 3.4 and 3.5 show a possible design for a page in this collection. The structure in Figure 3.3 very much follows the book layout shown in Figure 3.1, except that now there are additional links to places such as the Index and Table of Contents. Recall that in a book, the reader could easily find these components because of their physical placement in the book. This is not possible with hypertext, so the web collection must have explicit links connecting each page to these important navigational tools.

It is easiest to start by looking at the structure of a single page, an example of which is given in Figures 3.4 and 3.5. The important navigational features are in the banners at the top and bottom of the pages. The first navigational feature is the title graphic. This quickly identifies the page as part of a particular collection (the "Information Commons" collection), so that users immediately know, from page to page, which collection they are "in." (The text "Information Commons" and "Help With E-Mail" is part of the graphic itself.) Every collection should carry an identifying title graphic such as this, or alternatively, an identifying string of text. It is also possible to use slight variations on a particular graphic to indicate which section is being examined. Thus the graphic shown in Figure 3.5 could be slightly varied from section to section—each section would still show the logo and the name "Information Commons," but might also show a smaller-font string with section names or headings. Some examples of this are shown later in this chapter.

The second navigational feature is the collection of text buttons that link to the important related documents. These buttons replace the navigational cues available in a printed book, and allow readers to quickly find their place in the document. Using the "Prev" and "Next" buttons, the document can be read sequentially, or it can be accessed nonsequentially through the "Table of

(A)

Table of Contents

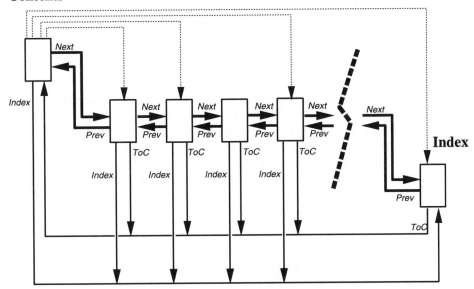

███████ **Figure 3.3** A linear collection of hypertext documents. The thick solid lines show the main navigational links, while the thin lines illustrate secondary links superimposed on this linear structure. Part (A) shows the underlying linear structure—the links from each page to the *Next* ("Next") and *Previous* ("Prev") pages, as well as to the *Table of Contents* ("ToC") and *Index* ("Index"), with the link names marked in italics. To make the figure easy to follow, the links from the Index to the individual documents have been omitted.

(B)

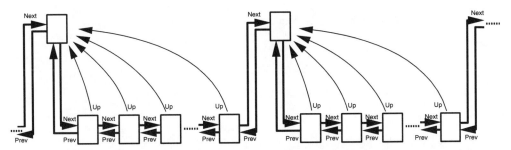

Part (B) shows the possible linking structure when there are section headings within the linear structure. Here the "Up" link connects each page to the top page of this section. For clarity, the "ToC" and "Index" links have been omitted.

Contents" or "Index." The "Up" button is linked to the top page of the local section—for example, if this were a page from Section 2 of the collection, the "Up" button might link to the first page of Section 2. Part (B) of Figure 3.3 shows how this could be organized. For convenience, this top-of-section page might contain a brief section introduction, and perhaps a contents listing for the section. This allows the user to move "Up" for an overview of the section, without having to return all the way to the full table of contents.

■■■■■■■ **Figure 3.4** Template HTML document for a linear collection (here, part of a collection of documentation on HTML), illustrating how navigational links can be included within the page design. Each page in a collection will have an identical banner design and labeling graphic that uniquely identifies the collection and allows the user to quickly get used to the look and feel of the pages. Figure 3.5 shows this document as displayed by the Netscape Navigator browser. Note that the text adjacent to the logo ("Information Commons" and "Help With E-Mail") is part of the header graphic.

```
<HTML><HEAD>

<TITLE> REL and REV Attributes for Hypertext Links</TITLE>

</HEAD><BODY>

<P ALIGN="center"><IMG ALIGN="bottom" SRC="iclogo.gif"
        ALT="{Information Commons -- HTML Documentation]"><BR>

[<A HREF="page2_1.html" REL="previous">Prev</A>]

[<A HREF="page2_3.html" REL="next">Next</A>]

[<A HREF="page2_0.html" REL="parent">Up</A>]

. . .


[<A HREF="contents.html"       REL="contents"><B>ToC</B></A>]

[<A HREF="/cgi-bin/index.pl" REL="index"><B>Index</B></A>]

. . .

[<A HREF="info.html"><EM>Info</EM></A>]

[<A HREF="/cgi-bin/feedback.pl"><EM>Feedback</EM></A>]

<HR>

<H2> REL and REV Attributes </H2>

<P> REL and REV attribute are used, with LINK and A (anchor)
```

```
elements, to describe the relationship between the document

containing the element, and the document referenced by the

hypertext link .....

<P> And yet more babble about REL and REV...

<HR>

<CENTER> <EM><A HREF="mailto:ic_html_doc@ic.utor.ca >IC

HTML Documentation</A> . . . . . .</EM>

<EM>Last Update:</EM> 12 September 1995 </CENTER>

</BODY>

</HTML>
```

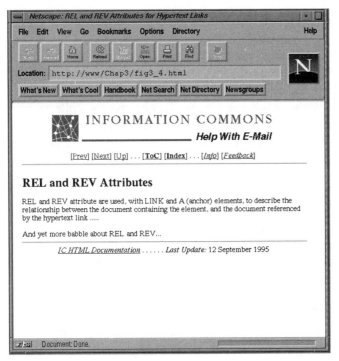

Figure 3.5 Display, by the Netscape Navigator browser, of the document listed in Figure 3.4.

Note how the anchor elements include the **REL** attributes, with values corresponding to the meanings of the links. Although **REL** and the converse, **REV**, do not currently affect the behavior of browsers, they are exceedingly useful in identifying the intent of a link, both to someone editing documents and to someone trying to understand, perhaps through automated web-mapping programs, the overall layout of a collection. Thus, you are advised to include these attributes if you know the relationship(s) defined by the hypertext link. **REL** and **REV** attribute values and their meanings are discussed in Chapter 4, and in Appendix F.

Some informational hypertext links are also provided in this linear collection—these connect to resources that are not really part of the collection, but that provide information useful to the user. For example, the "Feedback" link might connect to a gateway program (or simply a **mailto** URL) that lets the visitor send feedback to the document author(s), while the "Info" link could provide information explaining what all the navigation buttons mean, and how they work. Both features are useful, and should be present in a complete collection.

The last thing to stress is the importance of clean design of the text layout, and the use of the same design layout for all pages in the collection. Thus, if you decide to use centered **H2** headings for main sections, and left-justified **H3** headings for subsections, you should do this for all pages. This reinforces the familiar pattern implied by the graphic and banner design and makes it easy for a reader to navigate within each page, as well as across the collection. Note in Figure 3.5 that the page is dated, and also contains a hypertext link to the author or maintainer of the page. Although these items are not necessary on every page, dating the pages lets visitors know when the material was last modified, while the feedback mechanism lets you hear what your readers think. You should use a dating scheme that will not be misinterpreted internationally—thus the form 8/9/95 is not ideal, since some countries use the order day/month/year, while others use month/day/year. If you don't want feedback, you can omit the feedback link—but my experience is that feedback is overwhelmingly positive and constructive, and that feedback helps enormously when building and maintaining large document collections.

STRUCTURED (TREELIKE) COLLECTIONS

The next hypertext model is that of a tree, or hierarchical document collection. An example is shown in Figure 3.6, which shows a single, extended tree. A real-world example is the Yahoo collection (`http://www.yahoo.com`), which is a list of Web-accessible resources. The Yahoo documents are organized hierarchically. For example, the Yahoo! page on aids for people with disabilities, shown in Figure 3.7B, lies under the category "Companies" listed in Figure 3.7A. This page in turn lies under the category "Disabilities," which in turn lies under the category "Health." If you have information that organizes itself in a hierarchical manner, this is your obvious approach. Of course, the hierarchy need not be as large or as extensive as the Yahoo collection for this approach to be valuable. Another more modest example is presented later in this chapter.

The navigation tools required within a hierarchy are different from those needed in a linear collection. For example, the linear concepts of *next*, *previous*, and *Table of Contents* are no longer meaningful, while links to "Up" are usually equivalent to the browser's "back" button, and are often not necessary. Instead, you want links back to the root of the tree (the link to "Yahoo" in Figure 3.7), perhaps to a "Search" or "Index" tool (essentially a searchable

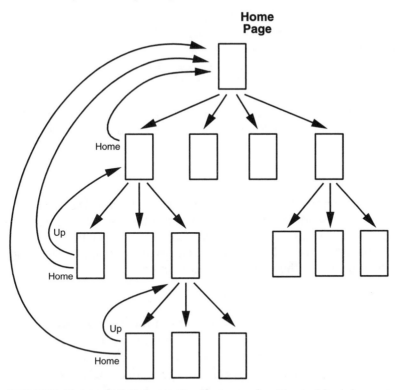

▬▬▬▬ **Figure 3.6** Schematic diagram of a *hierarchical* document web. The documents are organized in a treelike structure, descending from a single home document.

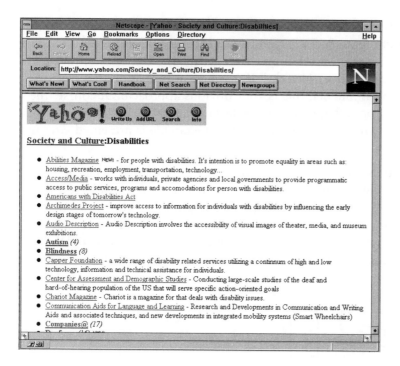

■■■■■ **Figure 3.7A** Example pages from the Yahoo hierarchical catalog of Web sites. (A) is an example of an index page for this collection—you can find this page by accessing the site:

```
http://www.yahoo.com/
```

and selecting the category "Health," followed by the category "Disabilities." Note the boldface items, indicating a further layer in the hierarchical tree. The "@" indicates that the link is to a "leaf" that is attached to multiple "branches" of the Yahoo tree. (B) shows the document returned by selecting the "Companies(@)" link in the document shown in part (A).

index), and also to important informational pages. As in the linear collection discussed previously, the document in Figure 3.7 also has links to a feedback utility ("Write Us") and to general information—here, about the Yahoo hierarchical resource list ("Info"). Finally, the special-purpose link "Add URL" lets a visitor register new URLs for inclusion in the collection. Obviously, each collection will have its own special-purpose utilities, depending on the site's function and purpose.

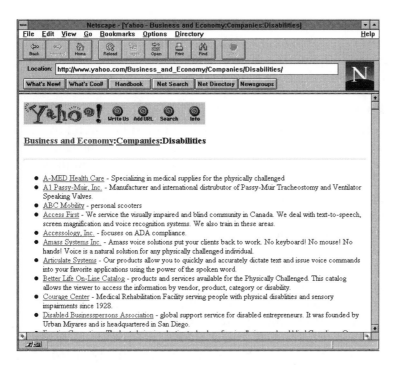

Figure 3.7B

At Yahoo, the page *layout* also contains important information. In all the Yahoo index pages (e.g., Figure 3.7A), links to additional subcategories are indicated by boldface hypertext anchors, while the bracketed number after each such anchor indicates the number of items cataloged in that subcategory. A trailing "at" (@) character means that the subcategory is actually located in more than one place in the hierarchy, implying that the node has *multiple parents* in the hierarchy—the tree is not a simple tree, but contains cross-linked branches. In this case, the top of the page lists the different possible parent nodes; in Figure 3.7 these are "Business and Economy," "Companies," and "Disabilities." This feature can be confusing, and an inexperienced Yahoo user, unfamiliar with this nonlinear structure and the meaning of the character "@", can quickly get lost by selecting one of these alternative parents. Fortunately, if you access nodes with only a single parent, this possibly confusing line is absent.

The Yahoo design is undergoing constant evolution, as better page layout models are developed, and as the collection of references grows—the Yahoo tree(s) keep growing new document "branches" and "leaves" to account for the ever-increasing size of the database. Overall, the design has evolved comfortably (at least as far as a user is concerned!) within the original structure, which is a good indication of the robust nature of the hierarchical approach.

DESIGNING A GOOD HIERARCHY

The hierarchical model can be extremely useful, but you must be careful to make an easily navigable hierarchy. In particular, you do not want the hierarchy to be too deep, or too shallow. If the hierarchy is too shallow, then there will be too many categories at each level and it will be difficult for visitors to find what they are looking for. At the same time, if there are too many levels in the hierarchy, it will again be hard for visitors to find what they want, as after four or five selections they will lose confidence that they are on the right track. You should strive to keep the tree depth as shallow as possible, without making each level too unwieldy. A depth of 3 to 5 is ideal, while anything greater than 6 is likely a bad choice. Your design must also reflect the material you wish to present, and the way you wish to present it—there is no one hierarchical structure that is universally appropriate. Thus the Yahoo layout, which works well for Yahoo, is not where you should start—you should start by looking at *your* data, and determining how you want *it* to be organized and accessed.

A WEB DOCUMENT HIERARCHY

Another example of a well-organized hierarchy is found at the URL:

```
http://www.hprc.utoronto.ca/HTMLdocs/tools_home.html
```

which is the top node for a document collection describing the various Web browsers, HTML editors, and support tools available on Mac, UNIX, and PC platforms. This collection is organized hierarchically, first by platform (Windows, Macintosh, OS/2, UNIX, Miscellaneous tools) and second by subcategories based on tool type (TCP/IP Software, WWW Browsers, Browser Helper Applications, HTML Editors, and HTML Translators/Filters). Figure 3.8 shows a typical page from this collection, in this case the top-level page of the hierarchy. Note how this page has navigational links to the documents one level down in the hierarchy, namely "Widows Tools," "Macintosh Tools," "OS/2 Tools," "UNIX Tools," and "Miscellaneous Tools." This organization makes it extremely easy to navigate through the hierarchy and find the desired information. Although not apparent from this page, the hierarchy is only three levels deep, so that it is easy to quickly reach the desired information.

Note also that there is a link from this page all the way back to the home page for this Web site ("HPRC Home"), which is essentially the top node for the entire local collection. The overall design and organization of a Web site is discussed later in this chapter.

HIERARCHIES AND LINEAR COMPONENTS TOGETHER

Obviously, it is easy to include linear collections, described at the beginning of this section, within this hierarchical model. Individual nodes within the hierarchy simply become the starting pages for the linear collection, so that a node in the hierarchy essentially points to an entire, large, linear collection. The hierarchy then gives an overall, and easily navigable, structure to the entire collection, rather like shelf labels in a library or bookstore.

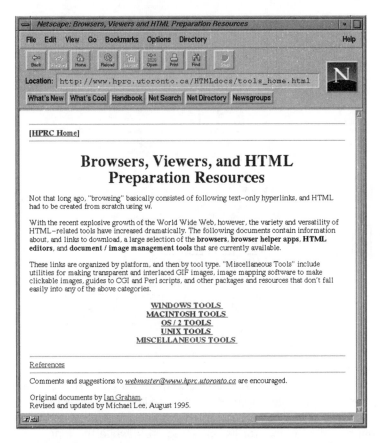

■■■■■■ **Figure 3.8** A page from a hierarchical list of Web programming resources, showing the important design features in a hierarchical collection. This page is available over the Web at

`http://www.hprc.utoronto.ca/HTMLdocs/tools_home.html`

This page was designed by Michael Lee of the University of Toronto's Information Commons.

DESIGNING A COMPLETE WEB

Figure 3.9 illustrates a possible organization of a large site's web collection. In general a web has a single top node, or *home page*, which is the publicly advertised location for the document collection. The home page then has links to other pages that lead down to the remaining resources in the collection. In this example, the home page has links to small introductory documents that explain the origins of the site and provide some useful site information; in addition, links to the top-level nodes of the various hierarchical collections beneath the home page are also provided. Figures 3.10 and 3.11 show two example home pages—despite their superficial dissimilarity, both pages follow precisely this model.

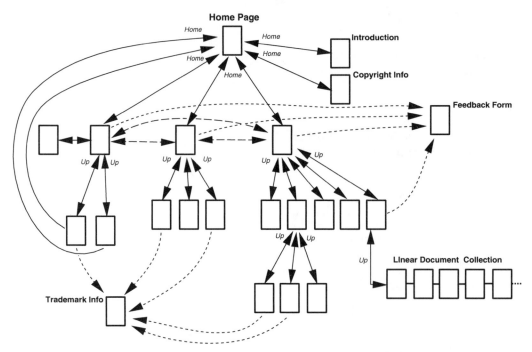

■■■■■■ **Figure 3.9** Schematic layout of a large web collection, showing the HTML-coded hypertext relationships between the home page, the top-level organizational nodes, and other elements of the collection. The solid lines indicate main links between items within the hierarchical (or linear) structures, while the long-dashed lines indicate links between "siblings" at the same level in a hierarchy. The arrows indicate the possible directions of the links, as coded into the HTML anchor elements in the documents. The short-dashed links indicate links to general-purpose pages—note that these hypertext anchors are unidirectional, since it is unreasonable to code in all the possible return paths. Typical home pages for such large collections are shown in Figures 3.10 and 3.11.

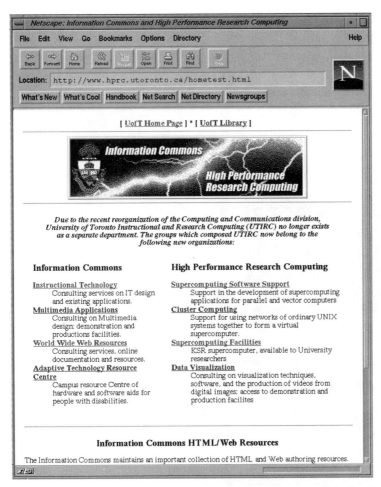

Figure 3.10 Prototype home page for the High Performance Research Computing Group at the University of Toronto. The page has links to single documents describing the mandate of the organization and the organization of the local Web site, in addition to links to the main organizational areas. These latter links are to top-level nodes of subsequent hierarchical trees.

Almost all sites on the Web follow this home page design model. As an exercise, you should spend some time exploring Web sites and the associated home pages, comparing the home page design and site layout with the model presented here. You will quickly begin to see the overall design similarities.

DISTINGUISHING BRANCHES IN A LARGE WEB

Often, a Web site will have many different main sections rooted in the home page, as seen in both the *Silicon Surf* home page (Figure 3.11) and the

Figure 3.11 Home page of *Silicon Surf*, the electronic publication of Silicon Graphics Inc. This is a graphically oriented home page, with links to the main information categories at the *Silicon Surf* Web site. Despite the very different look, the organization of this page is very similar to that in Figure 3.10. You should note that the *Silicon Surf* home page can also be sensibly viewed by nongraphical browsers, as all the image buttons are equipped with appropriate **ALT** attribute text descriptions explaining the destination of the link. (Be aware that image-mapped active images are *never* functional with a nongraphical browser, so if you use an image-mapped image as a navigational tool, you should also offer a text-only menu.) Image used by permission of Silicon Graphics (`http://www.sgi.com`) and copyright 1995 Silicon Graphics Inc. All rights reserved.

academically oriented High Performance Research Computing page (Figure 3.10). In general, the Web manager will want to use similar document layouts and design models in the different branches, since this makes it easier for users to navigate through the collection. At the same time, the designer will want to distinguish between these different sections, so that users will know where they are.

As with the linear collections discussed previously, the obvious way to do this is by modifying the banner text graphic at the top of the page to reflect the identity of the site and the specific features of the local tree. For example, the banner graphic shown in Figure 3.5, which contains the Information Commons logo and name, could be modified for each section at the Information Commons Web site, retaining the logo and name but adding a subtitle appropriate to each section. The logo immediately communicates that the page belongs within the Information Commons collection, while the subtitle quickly indicates the particular subsection or topic. In addition, different-sized logos can be used for sections and subsections, to give a graphical feel for the hierarchical location of the document in the overall collection. Finally, the **BACKGROUND** attribute to the **BODY** element can be used to tile the background with a "watermark" reflecting this same information. (This is not sufficient on its own, however, as the information provided by the background graphic is entirely lost with a nongraphical browser.)

Figure 3.12 shows some possible banner designs for the Information Commons, based on the ideas just presented. Note how each of them preserves the Information Commons look and feel, while quickly communicating the function of the page and its location within the overall hierarchy.

Use the ALT Attribute!

If you use graphical banners to distinguish your pages, you must also use the **ALT** attribute of the **IMG** element to assign appropriate alternative text strings to the images. Then, the important organizational information contained within the image is available to a visitor who is not able to view graphics. As an example, an Information Commons banner within a document describing e-mail services should have an **ALT** attribute value such as `"INFORMATION COMMONS — Help With E-Mail."`

Multiple Entry Points/Views

Ideally, you want to design all your pages, including your home page, so that they can be understood on any Web browser. However, sometimes this is not

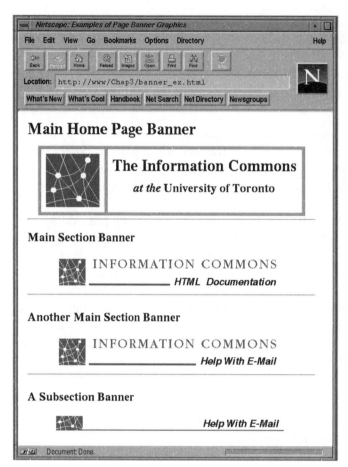

Figure 3.12 Possible page banners for different Web pages at the Information Commons. Note how the banner graphics preserve the identity of the site, while at the same time communicating the subcategories of each page. In addition, major section banners are bigger than minor page banners, allowing for easy determination of place in the hierarchy.

possible, or is inconvenient—for example, you may be presenting information both to users who have learning disabilities and prefer graphics over text, and to users who are blind and can *only* use text. To deal with this type of conflict, some Web sites offer *multiple* home pages.[4] A good example of this is

---

[4] This is also useful for sites that insist on using active imagemaps on their home pages—active image maps do not work for visitors using lynx, or who have disabled image loading, so these visitors need an alternative, graphics-free home page.

found at the University of Toronto's Adaptive Technology Resource Centre site home page, shown in Figure 3.13. This page is graphically rich, but offers *two* alternative home pages—one designed for users with screen readers, and the other for users who can use graphics, but who prefer a less graphically intense presentation.

You may also want to offer alternative home, and other, navigational pages that structure the contents of the site from different points of view. For example, a collection of material on Adaptive Technology (aids for persons with disabilities) can be organized as a tree presenting important issues and

Figure 3.13 Home page for the Adaptive Technology Resource Centre at the University of Toronto. Note how this page offers two alternative home pages, optimized for different audiences. This page is available at the URL :

```
http://www.hprc.utoronto.ca/AdTech/ATRCmain.html
```

technologies, as in Figure 3.13, but could also be presented as a problem-solving tree, where the various branches represent options in a decision-tree for obtaining technology solutions for particular user disabilities. A schematic illustrating this type of structure is given in Figure 3.14, which shows two organizational trees linked to the same document content.

You must be careful with this type of design, since the documents at the bottom of the tree (the actual data in your collection) have no way of knowing whether they were accessed from tree *A* or tree *B*. The navigational icons on each document must therefore point to both trees, and to the appropriate places on each tree. This presents difficulties similar to those at the Yahoo site, where several list categories appeared below multiple nodes in the tree. At Yahoo, the referenced page lists all the possible parent nodes. Unfortunately, accessing these alternative parents can be quite disorienting for an inexperienced user, unless their nature as optional routes is well explained—note all

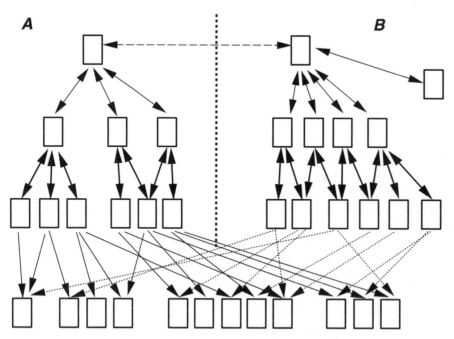

■■■■■■ **Figure 3.14** Possible structure of a Web site having two home pages and two parallel organizational structures, labeled *A* and *B*. Both trees access the same underlying collection of documents, shown at the bottom of the figure.

the efforts the Yahoo administrators have made to make this as easy to navigate as possible. You should visit Yahoo, and try this out for yourself.

GATEWAY FILTERING OF DOCUMENTS

Although the Web is a dynamic medium, HTML documents by themselves are static and unintelligent—as just noted, a retrieved page contains no information about the history of your interaction, and cannot know, for example, which home (or other) page you used to access it. This means that if you use multiple home pages, then all your documents must have multiple "Go to HOME" buttons for each of these possible home pages—or you have to leave out these links entirely—to avoid disorienting your visitors.

You can in part deal with this issue by using a *gateway* program[5] to dynamically modify *every* document returned from the server. For example, suppose there are two alternative structures for a document collection, labeled *pathA* and *pathB*, each path starting from a different home page. You can implement this collection such that the home pages do not access the remaining documents directly, but instead access them *through* a gateway program. This program processes the documents so that they include the navigational icons and other information that reflects the path being explored. Suppose the first page to be explored from home page *A* is the document ***monsters.html***. In this example, the page is accessed via the URL:

```
http:/www.we.edu/cgi-bin/docfilter/dir1/dir2/monsters.html?path-a
```

where the gateway filtering program is `docfilter`, the path to the desired document is `/dir1/dir2/monsters.html`, and the query string `path-a` indicates which path is being explored. The `docfilter` program retrieves the indicated document, and modifies all URL strings in that document so that they also use `docfilter` to access documents from the local collection, and so that they reflect which path is being explored. In addition, `docfilter` modifies the document banner, inserting the navigational icons and linkages appropriate to this particular path.

This is not a trivial exercise, since the filtering process is complicated and must take into account the structure of the entire document collection. Thus, to date, use of this approach has been limited. However, a wonderful (and far more sophisticated) example of the power of this approach can be found at the Electronic Books Technology site:

```
http://www.ebt.com/
```

---

[5] Gateway programs are discussed in Chapters 8 and 9.

Here, the document collection is entirely served from an underlying database of non-HTML documents—filtering programs dynamically convert the database entries (coded in another SGML language) into HTML, and automatically configure the presentation depending, for example, on the path being explored.

MULTIPLE WEB DESIGNERS

Large HTML document collections are usually designed by more than one person. As a site becomes large, maintenance and development become major issues, so it is useful to have a model for collection management that allows for scalability with size, and for a well-defined delineation of responsibilities.

MAIN HOME PAGE AND ORGANIZATIONAL PAGES

A Web site should have an overall Web manager who organizes the home page and the main navigational pages. This manager is responsible for ensuring valid links to the top pages of the underlying collections, but cannot be responsible for the internal consistency of those underlying collections. This makes for a reasonable division of responsibilities and obligations, giving the individual project development groups full control over their own document collections, while leaving the overall management of the site in the hands of a site manager.

A site manager should prepare a template of HTML documents for use by the groups developing their own resources. This template might contain a generic graphical logo for the site, some document templates that reflect a generic page design, and finally, a list of URLs that link to the main navigational pages maintained by the site manager. Each project group can then integrate these links into their own project pages, and create links back to the site main home page. They can also use the logos and page templates to preserve, if they wish (or are mandated) to do so, the site's look and feel.

PROJECT DIRECTORIES

Each major document subcollection should be placed in its own document directory, distinct from the directory housing the Web site home page and main organizational pages. Users responsible for maintaining each collection can then be given permission to create and modify files in their particular directory, but nowhere else. This isolates the projects from each other, and ensures that no one can accidentally modify another group's pages.

TEST AND PRODUCTION DIRECTORIES

In some cases, it may be convenient to give each group two directories—one for the finished and publicly available material, the other as a development or test area. In this way, the development team can develop and modify documents in the test directory, without worrying about affecting the documents being seen by visitors to the site. Once the new material has been fully developed and tested, in can be collectively copied into the public directory, making it available to the general public.

There are several Web development packages—for example, the Silicon Graphics **WebMagic** HTML editor—that support this type of development and "publication," while several HTTP servers, such as **NaviServer** and **BASIS Webserver**, integrate database management of the document collection with the server. You can expect more tools such as these to become available in the near future.

REVISION CONTROL

In many cases, a single collection will be designed collaboratively by many different users. In this case, it is often convenient to use revision control or document management software to manage the collaborative development process. Such software can archive the changes made to a collection, and can also ensure that only a single person can modify a particular document at a time. The servers mentioned in the previous section support this type of facility. There are many revision and document management packages available on every platform (most were originally designed for software development projects, for which similar issues are important). Some, such as **rcs** (Revision Control System) and **sccs** (Source Code Control System), often come bundled with UNIX systems, and were designed to manage large software development projects. If you are developing a large project involving many document developers, you should definitely consider one of these tools. Sites such as Yahoo have links to information about several such packages. If you are interested in this option, you should search Yahoo (or other) sites, using search strings such as "revision control" or "document management."

In the absence (or even in the presence) of document management software, you will want to take the following points into account when designing and maintaining a large document collection:

- Keep your documents well organized on disk, using subdirectories to appropriately organize the material by topic or workgroup.

- Use HTML comments (`<!-- comment -->`), or some other mechanism, to record modifications to the documents. Document management systems often maintain a secondary database for these data. HTML comments are described in Chapter 4.
- Use partial URLs to reference documents on the same server. This makes the collection transportable, as the relative references will be correct regardless of the absolute location of the collection.
- Preserve the original high-resolution image files you used to create your page graphics, logos, and buttons, so that at a later date you can easily create new document graphics from these original data.

STORYBOARD YOUR WEB DESIGN

You have probably noticed the usefulness of schematic drawings in picturing the interrelationships and linkages between Web documents. In fact, such drawings are extremely useful in *designing* web collections—it is always a good idea to sketch out the web layout on paper (or on a computer, if you have a suitable drafting program) and work out the desired relationships *before* you actually begin preparing the documents. Design and navigation problems quickly become apparent when you lay out the overall organization of the pages, as do the choices for the navigational links that must be built into each page. Storyboarding is easy to do, and will save you time and effort in the long run.

OTHER DESIGN ISSUES

This section summarizes some general design ideas that were not mentioned elsewhere, but that are applicable in all cases. Although these may seem only common sense, they are often difficult to implement unless thought about in the early design phase of a large project.

PLAN YOUR DOCUMENT COLLECTION

This may seem obvious, but it is not—or, at least, many people seem to ignore this aspect of design. A well-designed collection will both age and grow well. Aging well means that pages can be redesigned, with new graphics and better layout, without affecting the underlying hypertext structure. The same is true for growth. A well-designed collection will have room for new nodes, new trees, and new branches, without requiring the pruning or dismemberment or outright destruction of the original structure. You must plan ahead, because any good Web site will grow quickly, at which point it is exceedingly difficult to go back and fix your original mistakes. I know this from experience!

MAKE THE COLLECTION EASY TO NAVIGATE

This may seem mindless repetition, but it is essential that you use good design consistently. All your pages should have links back to some master navigational page, such as the local linear collection's table of contents, or the home page of the local document tree. Also, all your pages must have obvious exit points—you don't want users guessing at what to do next. And, last, make sure your links work! All the navigation buttons in the world won't help if you made a mistake in the underlying URLs. Chapters 10 and 11 list some utilities that are useful for testing hypertext links in a collection of documents.

NEVER MOVE THE MAIN NAVIGATIONAL PAGES

Once you have built a popular site, your visitors will bookmark your important navigational pages so that they can return directly to these locations. Therefore, once these pages are put in place, you should *never, ever,* move them. Doing so will break all your visitors' stored hotlist or bookmark entries, and will cause no end of grief. If you must move pages, make sure to provide server redirection for the main pages, or to provide temporary pages that point to the new location.

When expanding a collection, you should also never eliminate pages—only add new ones. This avoids the problem just mentioned, and ensures that hotlist entries are not broken. This reiterates the importance of properly thinking out the organization of your collection before you start. A well-organized collection has room for easy expansion, whereas an ill-thought-out jumble of pages will not grow easily, and will lead to problems when you find you must re-organize the pages due to fundamental flaws in the initial structure.

You should also assign a special domain name to your HTTP server—a name of the form www.site.edu is quite common, with the string www quickly identifying this as a WWW server site. This special domain name can then easily be moved from one machine to another, without disturbing your site visitors. For example, you might initially have www.site.edu on a shared machine or some other temporary location. Later on, the server and the domain name can be moved to a machine dedicated to HTTP services, without affecting the URL used to access your resources.

MAKE IT EASY TO FIND RESOURCES

Your collection is there to be read, so don't make it hard for users to find what they are looking for. A visitor should be able to get to your main resources after only a couple of clicks—most visitors will give up if the resource they are interested in is too far away. You can monitor the use of your documents by analyzing the server log files. If you find that a particular resource is very popular you can always add direct links from your home page to this resource, and make it more easily accessible to your visitors.

INDICATE CHANGES AS THEY OCCUR

Indicate on your Web pages when you make changes or additions. This makes it easy for frequent visitors to find things that are new, and lets new visitors know that the collection is being continuously improved—visitors will keep coming back if they know you are constantly adding new and interesting material.

KEEP YOUR VISITORS FROM LEAVING

No doubt you want people to spend some time at your site once they arrive at your home page—and, of course, if you have followed all my design ideas, they are bound to do so! However, one easy way to unwittingly send visitors away is to explicitly give them, just after they have arrived at your site, links to places outside your local web. It is generally a bad idea to include, on your home (or other high-level) pages, links to "KooL SiTEs" or "Important Resources" elsewhere on the Web, as your visitors are likely to head right there and never come back. Instead, put this information further down in your collection, thereby forcing users to step through and see some of your own work before arriving at these external links.

PAY ATTENTION TO USER FEEDBACK

If users bother to write with commentary about your collection, you should pay attention to what they say—almost universally, such letters either point out problems with your collection (perhaps a broken link), contain suggestions for improvements or changes, or contain requests for additional information. You should also respond to these notes—after all, if they have bothered to send you a comment, the least you can do is send a note of thanks. This is not only good manners, it is also good public relations.

MONITOR SITE USAGE

There are many tools that allow you to monitor the usage log files of your Web site, and these can be constructively used to find out which parts of the collection are popular (and which are not), and can also be used to find out how people are exploring your collection. If you find that one component is popular but difficult to access, you can then rebuild the links to make access easier.

PRESERVE THE PRIVACY OF YOUR VISITORS

At the same time, you must guard your visitor's privacy. No user would be happy knowing that you were directly monitoring his or her access to information, just as you would be unhappy if your librarian were to monitor the list of books you checked out. If you do access the log files, you should do so in a way that preserves user anonymity, for example by hiding the domain names of the clients, or by looking at aggregate information averaged over many users.

CREATING AN *ATTRACTIVE* WEB SITE

This is clearly an open-ended section, as the design of a popular and attractive Web site depends enormously on both the material being presented and the intended audience. This section summarizes those features that, in the author's opinion, apply in almost all cases.

PROVIDE USEFUL, TIMELY, AND INTERESTING INFORMATION

If your site does not provide something newer or better than another Web site, no one will bother to come back. Before you design a site, think about how your material will be different, or better, than already existing resources. If you can't, then you should try thinking of something else to do. And, if you are presenting something new and different, be sure to explain to your visitors why it is better, and why it is different.

MAKE YOUR SITE DYNAMIC

The Web is dynamic, and encourages communication. Your site should recognize and embrace these facts by encouraging user feedback and user interaction, and by providing information that is updated on a regular (that is, daily or weekly) basis. Some of the more attractive Web resources, such as daily cartoons (Dilbert or NetBoy), Web contests, the amazing Fishcam, browsable archives of mailing lists, and so on, do exactly this—you can find most of these examples by searching the Yahoo index. You should strive to implement similar dynamic and interactive features at your site.

MAKE SURE YOUR SITE IS *FAST*

You must make sure that your visitors can access your information as fast as possible. Thus, you want your site to have a high-speed connection to the Internet, so that any delays in getting your material to your visitors are not due to your own low-speed link—this is particularly important if your site contains a lot of images, which are notoriously big files and correspondingly slow to download. At a minimum, you should have an ISDN-speed connection (64–128 kbps), and ideally you should have something much faster. You don't always need to buy this for yourself—if you are buying space on a commercial HTTP server, just make sure that the service provider has a fast Internet connection. You should also check this by accessing the site from some other network. This will quickly tell you if visitors to your collection are going to have speed or other access problems.

KEEP YOUR EYES PEELED FOR NEW IDEAS

There are thousands of people creating new and exciting Web collections, every day of the week. Certainly, much of what I have learned has been the result of surfing around the Web and seeing what others are doing. You must do the same! The design possibilities are growing quickly, as a result of novel design by talented individuals, and as a result of new Web technologies that permit new design elements (backgrounds, tables, animation, and so on). You must explore the Web, and see how these tools are implemented elsewhere, before you can intelligently implement them yourself.

REFERENCES

An excellent online discussion of hypertext design issues and their relevance to the Web is found at:

```
http://info.med.yale.edu/caim/StyleManual_Top.HTML
```

This resource has a large and very useful annotated bibliography. The author of the collection is Patrick J. Lynch, codirector of the Center for Advanced Instructional Media at the Yale University School of Medicine, and a lecturer in graphic design at the Yale University School of Art.

Jakob Nielsen's book *Multimedia and Hypertext: The Internet and Beyond* (Cambridge, MA: Academic Press, 1995) is an expansive overview of multimedia and hypertext, with important discussions of usability and design issues. With its almost 70 pages of references, you will never again be at a loss for what to read!

The World Wide Web Unleashed, by John December and Neil Randall (Sams Publishing, 1994), is an enormous book (1,040 pages in the first edition) covering almost every aspect of the Web, with several chapters covering document and Web site design. This is not as complete as Nielsen's, but is more focused on Web-related issues, and easier at an introductory level.

4

HTML IN DETAIL

This chapter gives a detailed exposition of the *HyperText Markup Language,* or *HTML.* It is written from a document developer's point of view, and is designed to help authors create valid HTML documents. The chapter presents a detailed description of every HTML element and of allowed hierarchical relationships among these elements. It also assumes a basic understanding of HTML at the level outlined in Chapters 1 and 2 of this book.

The presentation focuses on the current definitive version of HTML, known as HTML 2.0. However, several extensions to this version that are already in common use are also presented here—in these cases we point out that these are newer features, and may not function on some browsers. This is important to consider if you want your document to be accessible to the largest possible audience.

INTRODUCTION TO HTML

As mentioned in Chapter 1, the HyperText Markup Language is designed to specify the *logical* organization and formatting of text documents, with extensions to include inline images, fill-in forms, and hypertext links to other documents and Internet resources. The result of this approach is a markup language that:

- is not bound to a particular hardware or software environment

- represents the logical structure of a document, and not its presentation

This emphasis reflects the fact that in a distributed environment, individuals viewing a document can use many different "browser" programs of very different physical capabilities. For example, it is pointless specifying that a particular piece of text must be presented with a 14-point Times Roman font, if the person viewing the document is sitting in front of a VT-100 terminal. For this reason, HTML does not specify details of the document typesetting, and instead marks logical elements of document structure, such as headings, lists, or paragraphs. The details of the presentation of these elements are left to the browser, which can use the logical description of the document, built in using HTML, to present the material in the best possible way. Thus, the same document can be clearly presented on graphical or nongraphical browsers, and also by nonvisual browsers, such as text-to-speech browsers or Braille readers.

HTML is defined in terms of the International Standards Organization (ISO) Standard Generalized Markup Language (SGML). SGML is a sophisticated system for defining types of structured documents, and for defining markup languages for use in documents of these types. HTML is just one instance of this process. The details of SGML are complex, and fortunately not critical to an HTML document developer. One component that is particularly useful, however, is the SGML *definition* of the HTML syntax, which is contained in a special SGML document called a *Document Type Definition,* or *DTD.* This is a simple text file, often having an imaginative name like *html.dtd.* This file can be used, in combination with SGML parsing programs such as **sgmls**, to validate the syntax of any HTML document. The "References" section at the end of this chapter suggests places where you can obtain the official DTD file for HTML, while Chapter 11 discusses using **sgmls** to validate HTML documents.

HTML is an evolving language, and has undergone substantial change over the past year. The current *standard* version of HTML is referred to as HTML Version 2.0, or HTML 2.0. This chapter focuses on writing HTML documents using the HTML 2.0 specification. However, it also presents many of the features proposed as part of the HTML 3 development process, and which are already available on several browsers. The use of these elements is encouraged, but with caution: you should always be aware that these features will be unavailable to some users attempting to access your documents. In addition, browser developers such as Netscape Communications and Microsoft have introduced special HTML elements outside of the standards process. These elements are presented in this chapter, but you are cautioned that many of them are unlikely to become part of the *official* HTML language, and thus they are unlikely to be recognized by other browsers.

This book is a guide to authoring HTML documents, and although it provides a quite complete description of HTML, it should not be considered the definitive reference for the language. For comprehensive details, you are referred to the Internet Engineering Task Force (IETF) documents listed in the "References" section at the end of this chapter.

ALLOWED CHARACTERS IN HTML DOCUMENTS

As illustrated in Chapter 1, an HTML document is just a text document that can be created and edited with any text editor. An HTML 2.0 document can contain any of the valid *printable* (i.e., excluding control or undefined) characters from the 8-bit ISO Latin-1 character set (also known as ISO 8859-1— see Appendix A for more information about ISO Latin-1 characters and character sets in general). The 256 characters of the ISO Latin-1 character set consists of the 128 characters of the 7-bit US-ASCII character set (ISO 646) plus 128 additional characters that use the eighth bit. These extra 128 contain many of the accented and other characters commonly used in western European languages. Many keyboards and editors make it difficult to type these non-ASCII characters. Partly for this reason, the HTML language has mechanisms for representing such characters using sequences of 7-bit ASCII characters. These are called *character references* and *entity references*. For example, the character reference for the character é is `&#233;` (the semicolon is necessary and terminates the special reference), while the entity reference for this same character is `&eacute;`. These mechanisms are also useful for sending HTML documents by electronic mail, since many electronic mail programs mishandle 8-bit characters. However, transferring HTML documents containing 8-bit characters is not a problem with hypertext servers, since the HTTP access protocol always allows 8-bit transfers and the browsers all understand that the character set is ISO Latin-1.

In addition, some computers such as Macintoshes and PCs running DOS do not use the ISO Latin-1 character set for their internal representation of characters (Microsoft Windows does use the ISO Latin-1 set), and instead use a proprietary mapping between the binary codes and the characters they represent. Fortunately this only affects the 128 non-ASCII characters, so that restricting yourself to ASCII characters ensures a valid HTML document, while the character and entity reference mechanisms allow you to include characters from the full ISO Latin-1 character set.

Character sets are discussed in more detail in Appendix A. Figure A.1 shows the use of HTML entity references in an HTML document—this document, as displayed by a browser, is shown in Figure A.2.

The ISO Latin-1 character set restriction is clearly a problem for non–Western European languages. Some of the efforts to generalize the character-set options for HTML documents are discussed in Chapter 5 and in Appendix A.

SPECIAL CHARACTERS

Certain ASCII characters codes are treated as special in an HTML document. For example, the ampersand character (&) is used to indicate an entity or character reference, the left and right angle brackets (< and >) are used to denote the markup tags, and the double quotation mark (") is used to mark strings within the markup tags. Since an HTML parser interprets these characters in a special manner, they cannot be used as normal characters—the parser always interprets them as special. If you want one of these characters to be displayed in your text instead of being interpreted as a command, you must include it as a character or entity reference. The character and entity references for these four special characters are given in Table 4.1.

When a browser interprets an HTML document, it looks for the special character strings and interprets them accordingly. Thus, when it encounters the string

```
<H1> Heading string </H1>
```

it interprets the strings inside each pair of angle brackets (<>) as markup tags, and renders the string that is enclosed by a pair of *tags* as a heading. However, when the parser encounters a string such as

```
&lt;H1&gt; Heading string &lt;/H1&gt;
```

it interprets the < and > as entity references, and displays, as a string of regular text, the characters

```
<H1> Heading string </H1>
```

■■■■■■ **Table 4.1** Special Characters in HTML

Character	Character Reference	Entity Reference
Left angle bracket (<)	&#60;	&lt;
Right angle bracket (>)	&#62;	&gt;
Ampersand sign (&)	&#38;	&amp;
Double quotation sign (")	&#34;	&quot;

COMMENTS IN HTML DOCUMENTS

In most HTML documents you will see comments denoted by the special character strings `<!--` and `-->`. Here, the first string (`<!--`) is considered the start of a comment, while the second (`-->`) ends it, and anything between the two is a comment. Comments are not displayed by the browser, even if they occur in the **BODY** of a document. There can be spaces between the `--` and the `>` that ends a comment, but the string `<!--` that starts a comment declaration must be present without any spaces between the characters. The following is an example of a simple comment:

```
<!-- This is a comment -->
```

Comments can span more than one line, but cannot nest or overlap. However, some browsers mishandle comments that span more than one line, so for safety you should include comment strings around every line you wish to comment out. You should also not use this mechanism to comment out HTML code that would otherwise be displayed, because some browsers mistakenly use the greater than sign (`>`) in regular HTML markup tags to prematurely terminate the comment.

■■■■■■ **TIP**

More formally, a comment consists of a comment declaration (consisting of the starting string `<!` and ended by a `>`) which can, in turn, contain any number of comments; each comment is defined as a text string surrounded by the character strings `--` and `--` (two adjacent dashes); for example, `-- this is a comment --` is a single comment. There must be no white space between the starting string of the comment (`<!`) and the start of the first comment, so that all comments must begin with the string `<!--`. (Pathologically, you can have empty comments of the form `<! >`). However, white space is allowed *after* every comment, so that the `--` marking the end of the final comment can be separated by white space from the `>` character marking the end of the comment declaration.

■■■■■■

Here are some examples of comments:

```
<!-- This is a comment --
   -- This is a second comment within the same comment declaration -- >
<!-- This is also a comment

     This comment spans more than one line. Note that some browsers improperly
```

```
interpret comments that span multiple lines, so this usage should be
avoided.

-- >
```

You should note that many browsers mishandle these more sophisticated comments, so you are best advised to use the simpler comment structure.

HTML AS A MIME TYPE

HTML is proposed as a MIME content-type. MIME, for Multipart Independent Mail Extensions, is a scheme originally designed for sending mixed media mail messages (containing pictures, text, and other formats) using the standard electronic mail protocol. The MIME scheme uses MIME *content-type* headers to define the content of each different type of data being sent in the mail message. On the World Wide Web, MIME types are used by the HTTP protocol to communicate the *type* of a document being served. When an HTTP server sends a file to a client, it includes, as part of the header that precedes the data, a MIME content-type header indicating the type of data being sent. For example, a JPEG format image file being sent from an HTTP server to a client would have the message string

```
Content-Type: image/jpeg
```

as part of the HTTP header that precedes the actual data.

HTTP servers treat HTML documents as just another MIME type. When an HTML document is served, it is preceded by the header

```
Content-Type: text/html
```

which tells the browser that the document is HTML and not just plain text. HTTP and MIME types are discussed in more detail in Chapter 7 and Appendix B.

HTML PUBLIC TEXT IDENTIFIER

As mentioned several times, HTML is an evolving language. You can formally specify the version of the language supported by a document by including, as the first line in the text, a string known as a *public text identifier*. The standard declaration for HTML 2.0 is simply (or perhaps not so simply):

```
<!DOCTYPE HTML PUBLIC "-//IETF//DTD HTML 2.0//EN">
```

The HTML 2.0 DTD supports several other document type specifications, depending on the facilities supported or the strictness of the specification. For example, the declaration

```
<!DOCTYPE HTML PUBLIC "-//IETF//DTD HTML 2.0 Strict Level 2//EN">
```

indicates that the document conforms to Level 2 of the HTML 2.0 specification (Level 1 is just HTML 2.0, but without **FORM** elements) and that the syntax is to be interpreted strictly (obsolete tags are forbidden, etc.).

DOCTYPE specifications should always be added to a document by any HTML editor (such as SoftQuad's **HoTMetaL**) that rigorously enforces correct HTML markup as defined by the language DTD.

HTML ELEMENTS AND MARKUP TAGS

The overall structure of the HTML language was covered in Chapter 1. The following is a review of the basic concepts, using the HTML document in Figure 4.1 as an example. Figure 4.2 shows this document as displayed by a browser.

An HTML document is simply a text file in which certain strings of characters, called *tags*, mark regions of the document and assign special meanings to them. In the jargon of SGML, these regions and the enclosing tags are called *elements*. The tags are strings of characters surrounded by the less than (<) and greater than (>) characters. For example:

```
<H1>
```

is the *start tag* for an **H1** (level 1 heading) element, while

```
</H1>
```

is the *end tag* for that element. The entire **H1** *element* is then the string:

```
<H1> Environmental Change Project </H1>
```

Most elements are similar to this example, and mark regions of the document into blocks of text, which in turn may contain other elements containing other blocks of text, and so on. You can think of a document as a hierarchy of these elements, with the complete hierarchy defining the entire document. Elements that mark blocks of text are often called *containers*. Some elements do not have any content and are called *empty* elements. The **IMG** element (which inserts an *inline* image into a document) and the **HR** element (which draws a horizontal dividing line across the screen), are examples of empty elements that do not affect a block of text.

Each element has a name, which appears inside the tags, and which is related to what the element means. For example, the **H1** element is used to mark a level 1 heading. An element may also have *attributes*, which are quantities that specify properties for that particular element. For example, the **A** (hypertext anchor) element can take the **HREF** attribute, which specifies the target of a hypertext link. Most attributes are assigned *values*. For example, **HREF** is assigned the URL of the target document for a hypertext link, as in:

■■■■ **Figure 4.1** An example of a simple HTML document.

```
<HTML>

<HEAD>

<TITLE> Environmental Change Project </TITLE>

</HEAD>

<BODY>

<h1> Environmental Change Project </h1>

<p> Welcome to the home page of the Environmental Change Project.

This project is different from other projects with similar names. In our case we

actually wish to change the climate. For example, we would like hot beaches in

Northern Quebec, and deserts near Chicago.

<p> So how will we do this. Well we do the following

<ul>

<li> <A HREF="burn.html">Burn </A> more forests.

<li> Destroy the <A HREF="http://who.zoo.do/ozone.html">Ozone</A> layer.

<li> Breed more <A HREF="ftp://foo.do.do/cows.gif">cows</a> (for extra

    greenhouse gas).

</ul>


</BODY>

</HTML>
```

■■■■

```
<A HREF="http://who.zoo.do/Ozone.html"> Ozone </A> layer
```

Attributes always appear as part of the start tag, and never the end tag.
Attributes are often optional.

In some cases the end tag is optional. This is the case when the end of an element can be unambiguously determined from the surrounding elements. As an example, look at the LI element in Figure 4.1. This element defines a single list item inside the UL unordered list element and does not require a </LI> end tag even though the element is not empty. This is because the end of a given list item is implied by the next <LI> start tag, or by the </UL> end tag ending the list.

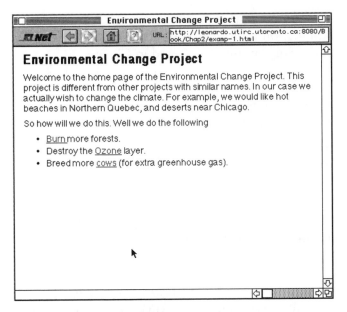

Figure 4.2 Display, using the MacWeb browser, of the document listed in Figure 4.1.

EMPTY ELEMENTS

Some elements (such as the **IMG, HR,** and **BR** [line break] elements) are *empty* and do not require end tags. Formally, you can include end tags to match the start tags, provided you do not place any text between the two tags. In practice, however, several browsers do not function properly when you include end tags for empty elements, so this usage is discouraged.

ELEMENT NESTING

Elements are always *nested*, with this nesting reflecting the structure of the document (for example, emphasized text inside a paragraph, inside a form, inside the **BODY**). However, elements can *never* overlap. Thus the structure:

```
<A HREF=....> <EM> Burn </EM> </A> more forests
```

is valid HTML markup, while:

```
<A HREF=....> <EM> Burn  </A> </EM> more forests
```

is not. In addition, all elements have restrictions as to what can be nested inside them and where they, themselves, can be nested. Details of allowed nestings will be presented later in this chapter as each element is discussed.

Some browsers will let you get away with nesting errors, so that such errors are often hard to spot. If you are lucky (or unlucky), you will get mail from someone who is questioning why he or she cannot properly view your document. A better choice is to use a validation tool, such as sgmls, to check your documents for invalid constructions. This option is discussed in Chapter 11.

CASE SENSITIVITY

The element and attribute names inside the markup tags are case-insensitive. Thus, the strings `<H1>` and `<h1>` are equivalent, as are

```
<a HreF="Dir1/foo.html"> <EM> Burn </eM> </a> more forests
```

and

```
<A href="Dir1/foo.html"> <em> Burn </eM> </A> more forests
```

Element and attribute names are nevertheless often written in uppercase to make the HTML document easier for the developer to read.

ATTRIBUTE VALUES

While element and attribute names are case-insensitive, the *values* assigned to attributes are often case-sensitive. An obvious example is the URL string assigned to the **HREF** attribute. A URL can contain both directory and filename information. Many computers allow both upper- and lowercase characters in file and directory names, so it is crucial that case be preserved. For a document author, this is ensured by enclosing the attribute argument in double quotes, as done in Figure 4.1. If quotes are omitted, the value may be promoted to uppercase.

LITERAL STRINGS

Formally, HTML has two main mechanisms for handling values assigned to attributes: *literal strings* and *name tokens*. A literal string is just that—a string of characters to be accepted literally as typed by the author, including the preservation of case. Note that you must, as a document author, surround a literal string with double quotation marks, since otherwise the string may be prematurely ended at a space or other character. Literal strings can contain any sequence of printable characters, including HTML character and entity references. Particularly, you must use character or entity references to include the double quotation mark (`&quot;`), since this character otherwise marks the beginning and end of a literal string.

Most attributes that can be assigned arbitrary author-defined strings, such as **HREF** and **SRC** (uniform resource locators), **ALT** (**IMG** elements), and **NAME** (fragment identifiers for anchor elements), are handled as literal strings.

NAME TOKENS

Name tokens are strings of characters that need not be surrounded by quotation marks, for example, the string "text" in the assignment TYPE=text. Name tokens can only contain certain characters, namely the letters a–z and A–Z, the numbers 0–9, periods (.), and hyphens (-). They must also begin with a letter. In addition, name tokens are *not* case-sensitive, so that the token abba is equivalent to ABbA. You cannot use name tokens to represent URLs or text strings that contain spaces.

Name tokens are often used for values defined as part of HTML, such as the value "text" in the element <INPUT TYPE=text...>, used to select a text input box inside a form. This example demonstrates that you can leave out the quotation marks, if only a single string is assigned to an attribute taking a name token. However, it is never an error to include quotation marks, so it is safest to leave them in. Furthermore, quotation marks are necessary if you want to assign *multiple* name tokens to the same attribute. In this case, you need to use an expression of the form ATTRIBUTE="token1 token2 token3".

The HTML DTD specifies whether or not the value assigned to an attribute should be a literal string or a name token. In this book, attribute values are, in general, placed inside quotation marks, since name tokens are always valid inside quotation marks, and the added quotation marks help to make them stand out from the regular text.

BROWSER HANDLING OF HTML ERRORS, UNKNOWN ELEMENTS, AND UNKNOWN ATTRIBUTES

On the World Wide Web, browsers are supposed to be generous in their interpretation and presentation of HTML documents. Thus, even if a document is badly constructed, for example with missing or misplaced tags, a browser will do the best it can to present the document content. Sometimes the document will look very odd due to the resulting formatting decisions, but from the user's point of view this is infinitely better than displaying nothing. This of course reiterates the importance, on the author's side, of ensuring a valid HTML document that can be properly viewed by any browser.

At the same time, HTML is an evolving language, and new elements and attributes are constantly being added, either as part of the formal language development process (HTML 2.0, HTML 2.1, etc.), or as customized extensions introduced by browser designers (such as the Netscape HTML extensions). For such an evolution to work, there must be some mechanism for a browser to handle HTML elements, or element attributes, that it does not understand.

In general, a browser is supposed to *ignore* elements, or element attributes, that it does not understand. For example, the **BLINK** or **FONT** elements are Netscape-specific: on other browsers, the `<BLINK>` . . . `</BLINK>` and `<FONT>` . . . `</FONT>` tags are ignored, and the enclosed text is rendered as regular text (given whatever other elements the string is inside). Similarly, in HTML 3, paragraphs can be centered using the new attribute **ALIGN**, that is, `<P ALIGN=center>`. If a browser does not understand this attribute, or the value assigned to the attribute, it simply ignores the attribute and uses its own default paragraph alignment.

Most of the HTML extensions introduced by Netscape Communications Inc. were added to improve document formatting control, so that they do not affect the logical structure of a document. Consequently, in most cases, browsers that do not understand the Netscape extensions will still be able to present these documents in a readable and relatively well-formatted manner, albeit missing the extra features introduced by those elements. The main exceptions to this rule are the Netscape extensions to the **IMG** element that allow for floating images. If you are not careful in the design of your document, you will find that documents containing floating images look very poor on browsers that do not support this feature.

Finally, many of the newer HTML 3 extensions will not produce readable documents if the browser does not understand the relevant tags. Particular examples are the **TABLE** element discussed in this chapter, and the **FIG** element discussed in Chapter 5. In general, you can assume that any new element that implies both logical and physical structure will be poorly displayed by a browser that does not understand the element.

OVERALL DOCUMENT STRUCTURE

Every HTML document can be divided into two main parts: the *body*, which contains the part of the document to be displayed by a browser, and the *head*, which contains information about the document, but which is not displayed. These parts are defined by the **BODY** and **HEAD** elements respectively. The resulting overall structure of an HTML document should then be:

```
<HTML>

    <HEAD>

        .... elements valid in the document HEAD

    </HEAD>

    <BODY>

        .... elements valid in the document BODY
```

```
    </BODY>

  </HTML>
```

Note how Figure 4.1 follows this outline. The outer **HTML** element declares the enclosed text to be an HTML document. Directly inside this lie the **HEAD** and the **BODY**. The **BODY** contains the text and associated HTML markup instructions of the material you want displayed. The **HEAD**, which must appear before the **BODY**, contains elements that define information *about* the document, such as its title or its logical relationships with other documents. Certain elements can only appear in the **HEAD**, while others can only appear in the **BODY**. These elements, and the overall structure of the **BODY** and **HEAD**, are the focus of the remainder of this chapter.

HYPERTEXT MARKUP LANGUAGE SPECIFICATION

This section lists each HTML element, a description of the purpose of the element, a list of where the element can be used, and examples of its use. Most of the elements in this list are from the HTML 2.0 specification. Much work is underway to extend and revise the HTML language—these efforts fall under the rubric HTML 3. The HTML 3 effort has defined elements for tabular data, sub- and superscripts, and so on, that add important functionality to the HTML language. Indeed, several (but not all) browsers already implement some of these HTML 3 features. This section mentions these more popular HTML 3 elements and attributes, but marks them as HTML 3 contributions to denote their experimental nature. Chapter 5 discusses some of the larger-scale changes that will come about from the HTML 3 effort.

In addition, the current chapter describes those HTML extensions introduced by Netscape, which are currently supported only by the Netscape Navigator browser. These elements are in widespread use, but are unlikely, in the long term, to become part of "official" HTML. In most cases, HTML 3 provides better mechanisms for accomplishing the same goals.

In general, if you want your documents to be viewable by a wide audience, you must beware of all these new (HTML 3) and browser-specific (Netscape) elements, since some browsers may not be able to display them. If you really want to use some of these features, it is a good idea to provide alternate HTML 2.0 documents for those people who are unable to view your more sophisticated creations.

KEY TO THIS SECTION

Because HTML is a hierarchical language, is it important to know not only how to use an element, but also where it can be used. This information is given in the four lines at the beginning of the description of each element. The general format looks like the following:

Usage:	`<NAME> . . . </NAME>`
Can Contain:	**element list**
Can Be Inside:	**element list**
Attributes:	**attribute list**

Here is an example, using the **LI** list item element:

LI ELEMENT: LIST ITEM

Usage:	`<LI> . . . (</LI>)`
Can Contain:	**characters, character highlighting, A, BR, IMG, DIR, DL, MENU, OL, UL, BLOCKQUOTE, FORM, P, PRE, [ISINDEX]**
Can Be Inside:	**DIR, MENU, UL, OL**
Attributes:	(**SRC**: proposed HTML 3)

These four fields define the rules for using the different elements. The meanings of the four fields are shown in Table 4.2.

SHORT-FORM DEFINITIONS

The following short forms are used in the "Can Contain" and "Can Be Inside" fields:

Hn:	The six heading elements **H1, H2, H3, H4, H5,** and **H6**
characters:	Any valid ISO Latin-1 character, character reference, or entity reference
character highlighting:	**CITE, CODE, EM, KBD, SAMP, STRONG, VAR, B, I, TT,** and *U* (proposed HTML 3). These are the physical (italics, boldface, etc.) and logical highlighting elements that are used to mark text for formatting purposes.

▮▮▮▮▮▮▮ **Table 4.2** Meanings of Fields in Element Definitions

Usage:	Shows how the element is used. An end tag indicates that an element is a container (the *Can Contain* field lists what can go inside the element). If the end tag is enclosed by parentheses, then it is optional. If no end tag is given, then the element is empty.
Can Contain:	This field indicates what elements can go inside this element. The string **"characters"** indicates elements that can contain text. If the element is empty, the word "empty" appears here. In several places, the **ISINDEX** name appears enclosed by square brackets. This indicates that the element is allowed, but that it should more appropriately appear in the **HEAD**. Elements that are proposed as part of HTML 3 are shown in bold italics while Netscape- or Microsoft-specific elements are shown in bold with underlines.
Can Be Inside:	Indicates the elements inside which this element can be placed. The above example indicates that the **LI** element can be inside a **DIR, MENU, OL,** or **UL** element, but nowhere else. Elements that are proposed as part of HTML 3 are shown in bold italics.
Attributes:	This lists the names of the attributes that can be taken by the element. The word "none" means that the element takes no attributes. Attributes that are proposed as part of HTML 3 are shown in boldface italics, while Netscape- or Microsoft-specific attributes are shown in bold with underlines.

ATTRIBUTE VALUES

Attribute values can be arbitrary strings selected by the user, such as URLs as hypertext anchors, form input element variable names and values, and so on (usually literal strings); or they can be particular values (generally name tokens) that are defined as part of HTML (e.g., the **TYPE** of an **INPUT** element, or the **METHOD** of a **FORM** element). To distinguish between these two types, user-definable values are presented in quoted italics (*"value"*), while values that are defined as part of HTML are presented as quoted regular text ("value").

ORGANIZATION

The following sections present a hierarchically organized look at the HTML elements. Thus, the first section describes the **HTML** element that contains the entire document. The next section describes the **HEAD** element, and is followed by descriptions of the elements that can lie inside the **HEAD**. This is followed by a description of the **BODY** element, which, in turn, is followed by sections describing the elements that go inside the **BODY**. Generically, the **BODY** elements can be divided into the following six categories:

Heading elements	**H1** through **H6**
Block elements	**ADDRESS, BLOCKQUOTE, HR, P, PRE, FORM,** list elements, *TABLE* (proposed HTML 3)
List elements	**DIR, DL, MENU, UL, OL**
Text/phrase markup	**CITE, CODE, EM, KBD, SAMP, STRONG, VAR, B, I, TT,** *U*
Hypertext anchors	**A**
Character-like elements	**BR, IMG**

Figure 4.3 summarizes all the HTML elements in this chapter, within this overall organization, and provides page references to the relevant sections. The description of elements in this chapter closely follows this organization.

HTML ELEMENT: AN HTML DOCUMENT

Usage:	`<HTML> . . . </HTML>`
Can Contain:	**HEAD, BODY**
Can Be Inside:	nothing
Attributes:	none

The **HTML** element declares the enclosed text to be an HTML document. It may directly contain only two elements: **HEAD** and **BODY**. Although formally optional, you should always include an **HTML** element in new documents.

Example of **HTML**:

```
<HTML>
    <HEAD>
    ... head content....
    </HEAD>
    <BODY>
    ... body content....
    </BODY>
</HTML>
```

Element	*Description*	*Page*
HTML	*An HTML document*	*140*
HEAD	*Document Meta Information*	*142*
BASE	*Base URL of the document*	*143*
ISINDEX	*Searchable document*	*144*
LINK	*Relationships to other documents*	*146*
META	*Meta information*	*147*
NEXTID	*Counter for automated editors*	*149*
TITLE	*Document title*	*150*
BODY	*Text Body*	*151*
ADDRESS	*Address information*	*153*
BLOCKQUOTE	*Block quotations*	*153*
DIV	*Divisions of a document (HTML 3)*	*222*
FORM	*User input form*	*158*
INPUT	*Input fields*	*159*
SELECT	*Selectable fields*	*165*
OPTION	*Option in a selectable field*	*167*
TEXTAREA	*Text input region*	*169*
H1 H6	*Headings (Levels 1 6)*	*170*
HR	*Horizontal rule*	*171*
DL	*Description/Glossary list*	*172*
DT	*Term*	*174*
DD	*Description*	*175*
OL	*Ordered list*	*176*
LI	*List item*	*182*
UL	*Unordered list*	*177*
LI	*List item*	*182*
DIR	*DIrectory list*	*179*
LI	*List item*	*182*
MENU	*Menu list*	*180*
LI	*List item*	*182*
P	*Paragraphs*	*184*
PRE	*Preformatted text*	*185*
TABLE	*Tables (HTML 3)*	*210*
CAPTION	*Table caption (HTML 3)*	*217*
TR	*Table row (HTML 3)*	*218*
TD	*Table data cell (HTML 3)*	*221*
TH	*Table header cell (HTML 3)*	*219*

text level markup {

Physical Phrase Markup

B	**Bold**	*209*
I	*Italics*	*209*
TT	`Fixed width font`	*209*
BIG	enlarged *text (HTML 3)*	*225*
SMALL	reduced size *text (HTML3)*	*225*
SUB	subscript *(HTML3)*	*224*
SUP	superscript *(HTML 3)*..	*224*
U	<u>Underline</u> *(HTML 3)*	*210*

Semantic Phrase Markup

CITE	*Citation*	*205*
CODE	*Typed computer code*	*206*
EM	*Emphasized text*	*206*
KBD	*Keyboard input*	*206*
SAMP	*Sample text*	*207*
STRONG	*Strongly emphasized*	*207*
VAR	*A Variable*	*208*

Character Level and Special Elements

BR	*Line break*	*201*
IMG	*Inline Image*	*192*
A	*Hypertext Anchor*	*186*

████ **Figure 4.3** Summary of HTML elements described in this chapter, showing their relative locations in the element hierarchy. HTML 3 elements are shown in italics, while Netscape-specific elements are shown with underlines.

Element	*Description*	*Page*

Figure 4.3 Continued.

HEAD ELEMENT:
DOCUMENT META-INFORMATION

Usage:	`<HEAD> . . . </HEAD>`
Can Contain:	**TITLE, ISINDEX, BASE, NEXTID, LINK, META**
Can Be Inside:	**HTML**
Attributes:	none

HEAD contains general information about the document. The information found in the head is not displayed as part of the document text; consequently, only certain elements are appropriate within the **HEAD**. All the head elements, except **TITLE**, are empty, and they can appear in the **HEAD** in any order. The only mandatory **HEAD** element is **TITLE**; all others are optional. The possible **HEAD** elements are, in decreasing order of importance (in terms of current usage):

TITLE	The title of the document
ISINDEX	Indicates the document is searchable
BASE	A record of the original URL of the document
LINK	Defines a relationship between the document and another document

META   Used for embedding, within the **HEAD**, information about the document that cannot be expressed in the preceding elements

NEXTID   Used by automated HTML editors to create unique document identifiers

You are most likely to see and use the **TITLE, ISINDEX,** and **BASE** elements. The **LINK** element is not widely supported, nor is **META**. The **NEXTID** element was designed for use by special HTML editing tools, and is largely unused—it is likely to be dropped in future versions of HTML.

The division between the **HEAD** and the **BODY** is important, as there are ways for programs to retrieve just the information in the document **HEAD**. Since the **HEAD** is always much smaller than the body, this is faster than accessing an entire document, and can be extremely useful for generating catalogs or indexes based on the **HEAD** content.

BASE Element: Base URL

Usage:	`<BASE>`
Can Contain:	empty
Can Be Inside:	**HEAD**
Attributes	**HREF** (<u>**TARGET**</u>: Netscape Navigator 2.0)

BASE is an empty element, and is optional. If present, **BASE** has a single mandatory attribute, **HREF**, which is assigned the *base URL* of the document.

The base URL is the URL indicating where a document was originally located. If a document is moved away from its original URL and related documents, relative URLs that referenced neighboring documents are no longer valid. However, if the original URL address is specified in the **BASE** element, then relative URLs from this document are evaluated relative to this "base" URL and are correctly located.

If the **BASE** element is absent, the browser determines relative URLs with respect to the URL used to access the document.

You should be aware that some older browsers do not support the **BASE** element. In addition, browsers differ in their interpretation of **BASE** when it comes to "bookmarking" a document—some browsers bookmark the **BASE** URL, while others bookmark the actual URL used to retrieve the displayed document.

Example of appropriate use of **BASE**: if a document was originally found at the URL `http://somewhere.org/Dir/Subdir/file.html`, the appropriate **BASE** element to be included in this document is then:

```
<HEAD>

    <TITLE> some sort of title.... </TITLE>

    <BASE HREF="http://somewhere.org/Dir/Subdir/file.html">

</HEAD>
```

Version 2.0 of the Netscape Navigator 2.0 browser supports *targeted* links—this lets a document author direct the data returned, upon selecting a hypertext link, to a particular *named* browser window—recall that Netscape can produce multiple copies of itself, each copy capable of displaying a different document. With Netscape Navigator, named windows are targeted using a **TARGET** attribute to the **A** (anchor) clement, as discussed later in this chapter.

In support of this feature, Netscape also implements a **TARGET** attribute with the **BASE** element. Analogous to the value of the **HREF** attribute, the **TARGET** value defines the default name of the target window for all the hypertext links within the document. For example, the element

```
<BASE TARGET="window3">
```

would mean that all accessed hypertext links will be displayed in the window named "window3". If a window named "window3" does not already exist, then it will be created the first time a link is accessed.

The base target can always be overridden by an explicit **TARGET** within an anchor, such as

```
<A HREF="/path/file.html" TARGET="window2">anchor text</A>
```

The document returned upon accessing this anchor will be directed to the window named "window2," overriding any target implied by the base target value.

The default target is always the window containing the document currently being displayed.

ISINDEX ELEMENT: SEARCHABLE DOCUMENT

Usage: `<ISINDEX>`

Can Contain: empty

Can Be Inside:	HEAD [BODY, BLOCKQUOTE, FORM, LI, DD]
Attributes:	(*HREF, PROMPT*: proposed HTML 3)

ISINDEX is an empty element and is optional. Because there are many older documents that have the **ISINDEX** declaration in the **BODY**, the HTML definition still allows this form. New documents should always place **ISINDEX** inside the **HEAD**. This element informs the browser program that the document can be examined using a keyword search, and that the browser should query the user for a search or query string.

ISINDEX does *not* mean a search of the text you are reading. Documents containing **ISINDEX** elements are usually sent to the client from server-side gateway programs designed for database searches. You can think of such a document as a front end to a gateway program, and the document you search as the database *represented* by the document you see.

When you submit the search, the keywords are sent from the client to the server by appending them to the document's URL. The mechanism for appending these data is discussed in the HTTP URL section of Chapter 6, and also in Chapter 8.

Example of **ISINDEX**:

```
<HEAD>

  <ISINDEX>

  <TITLE> title text </TITLE>

  ...

</HEAD>

<BODY>

  ... body of document

</BODY>
```

HTML 3 proposes two new attributes for the **ISINDEX** element. The attribute **PROMPT** allows the document author to define a character string for use by the browser as a query prompt. The attribute **HREF** allows the author to define a URL to which the query should be directed that is *different* from the URL of the accessed document. An example of their usage is:

```
<ISINDEX PROMPT="Name/Phone Number:"  HREF="/cgi-bin/staff-srch">
```

The **PROMPT** attribute is implemented by a few browsers, notably Netscape and Arena. **HREF** is still largely unimplemented, and is ignored by almost all browsers.

LINK ELEMENT: RELATIONSHIP TO OTHER DOCUMENTS

Usage:	`<LINK>`
Can Contain:	empty
Can Be Inside:	**HEAD**
Attributes:	Same as **A** (Anchor) element, namely **HREF, METHODS, NAME, REL, REV, TITLE, URN**

The **LINK** element describes a *relationship* between the document and other documents or objects. For example, you might use **LINK** to indicate a related index, a glossary, or perhaps different versions of the same document. Alternatively, you could use it to point to likely *next* or *previous* documents. This could be used by a browser, among other things, to predict and preload documents it is likely to need, or to configure customized navigational buttons or menus. A document may have any number of **LINK** elements to represent these various relationships to other documents.

LINK is an empty element, and is optional.

Link takes the same attributes as the Anchor (**A**) element. These are discussed in detail in the anchor element section.

Examples of **LINK**:

```
<HEAD>

  <LINK HREF="file1.html" REL="next"

        TITLE="Title of Related Document" >

  <LINK HREF="/cgi-bin/indexer" REL="index">

</HEAD>
```

The first **LINK** indicates that the indicated document is the next document to visit in some sequential series of documents, and gives the title of the document. The second **LINK** indicates that the linked document is an index of the current document.

LINK elements, with **REL** (or **REV**) attributes, are only useful given well-understood meanings for the values assigned to them. The process of defining a set of values is currently underway: some of the commonly understood relationships are given in the examples below. In the absence of well-defined meanings, the **LINK** element is largely nonfunctional, and is little used. Chapter 5 and Appendix F discuss current efforts at establishing well-defined **REL/REV** relationships.

Examples of **LINK**:

`<LINK REV="made" HREF="mailto:igraham@hprc.utoronto.ca">` The **HREF** points to information about the creator of the document containing the **LINK**.

`<LINK REL="next" HREF="another_url">` The **HREF** points to the *next* document in some logical document sequence.

`<LINK REL="previous" HREF="another_url">` The **HREF** points to the *previous* document in some logical document sequence.

`<LINK REL="index" HREF="another_url">` The **HREF** points to an *index* related to the collection containing the document containing the **LINK**.

`<LINK REL="contents" HREF="another_url">` The **HREF** points to a *Table of Contents* related to the document containing the **LINK**.

`<LINK REL="navigate" HREF="another_url">` The **HREF** points to a *navigational aid*, perhaps a Table of Contents extract, relevant to the document containing the **LINK**.

META ELEMENT:
DOCUMENT META-INFORMATION

Usage:	`<META>`
Can Contain:	empty
Can Be Inside:	**HEAD**
Attributes:	**HTTP-EQUIV, NAME, CONTENT**

The **META** element provides a place to put meta-information that is not defined by the other **HEAD** elements. This allows an author to more richly describe the document content for indexing and cataloging purposes, as illustrated in the following discussion of **META** attributes. You should not, however, use **META** as a substitute for the other **HEAD** elements.

The **META** element is optional. If present, it must take the **CONTENT** attribute and one of the **NAME** or **HTTP-EQUIV** attributes (but not both). The meanings of the attributes are:

NAME="*name*" (one of **NAME** or **HTTP-EQUIV** must be present) This specifies the meta-information name. The client (browser or other program) must understand what this name means. HTML does not currently define any values for **NAME**. **META** must contain one of **NAME** or **HTTP-EQUIV**, but not both.

HTTP-EQUIV="*string*" This can be used instead of the **NAME** attribute. **META** elements with **HTTP-EQUIV** attributes should be parsed by the HTTP server, with the values of the **HTTP-EQUIV** and **CONTENT** attributes being converted into the appropriate HTTP *response headers*. HTTP response headers are discussed in Chapter 7. **META** must contain one of **NAME** or **HTTP-EQUIV**, but not both.

CONTENT="*string*" (mandatory) This assigns the content associated with the **NAME** or **HTTP-EQUIV** value of the **META** element.

An example using the **NAME** attribute is:

```
<META NAME="keywords" CONTENT="pets dogs cats rocks lizards">
```

This might tell the client that the words "pets," "dogs," "cats," "rocks," and "lizards" are keywords useful for indexing the current document. The client or indexing program that is accessing the **HEAD** of this document must consequently understand the meanings behind the names.

The attribute **HTTP-EQUIV** allows the document to pass information to the server delivering the document. An example is:

```
<META HTTP-EQUIV="Creation-Date" CONTENT="23-Sep-94 18:28:33 GMT">
```

This element requests that the server take the **CONTENT** (the string 23-Sep-94 18:28:33 GMT) and include this information as part of an HTTP header field, named Creation-Date. If the server actually parses the document head, then it will create an HTTP header field

```
Creation-Date: 23-Sep-94 18:28:33 GMT
```

and include this with the HTTP *response header* that precedes the document during an HTTP transaction. (The HTTP protocol and HTTP response headers are discussed in Chapter 7.) HTTP response headers contain information about the document and server, such as the type of data being sent from the server, the date it is being sent, the type of server being used, and so on. The response headers can also contain more descriptive information about the document, comparable to the information found in the document **HEAD**.

NOTE

You should not use <META HTTP-EQUIV...> to override a server response header field that is normally returned by the server.

Most browsers and servers do not parse a document for **META** elements. Chapter 9 demonstrates an exception to this, in the context of the Netscape *client pull* browser animation mechanism.

NEXTID ELEMENT:
COUNTER FOR AUTOMATED EDITORS

Usage:	<NEXTID>
Can Contain:	empty
Can Be Inside:	**HEAD**
Attributes:	**N**

NEXTID is an empty element and is optional. It is used by HTML editing programs to uniquely identify documents created in the editing process—it is not designed for use by mere humans, by WWW browsers, or by hypertext servers.

NEXTID has a single mandatory attribute **N**, which specifies a numeric identifier for the document. Since the numbers should uniquely identify documents, an HTML editor should never reuse old identity numbers.

Example of **NEXTID**:

```
<HEAD>
<NEXTID N=132>
  .

  .
</HEAD>
```

NEXTID is rarely used, and is likely to be dropped from the HTML specification. Its use is therefore discouraged.

TITLE ELEMENT: DOCUMENT TITLE

Usage:	`<TITLE> . . . </TITLE>`
Can Contain:	**characters**
Can Be Inside:	**HEAD**
Attributes:	none

The title of a document is specified by the **TITLE** element. Every document must have a **TITLE**, and can have only one. The text inside a **TITLE** should indicate the document content in a concise and general way. It serves several purposes:

- To label the display window or text screen

- To serve as a record in a history or bookmark list marking documents a user has viewed

- To allow quick indexing of a document, in place of indexing the entire text

The **TITLE** is not part of the document text, and cannot contain hypertext links or any other markup commands—it can only contain text, including entity or character references.

The **TITLE** should be short so that it can easily label a window or fit in a history or bookmark list: preferably less than 60 or so characters. Users should also be able to determine the content of the document from the **TITLE** itself. Otherwise, a person reviewing his or her browser history will see the **TITLE** but not know to what it refers. Here are some examples of good **TITLE**s:

```
<TITLE>Paper on Rings by Baggins and Gandalf, 1989</TITLE>
```

```
<TITLE>Introduction to MIME types </TITLE>
```

and bad **TITLE**s:

```
<TITLE>Introduction</TITLE>
```

```
<TITLE>A Summary of the Ring-Ring Interaction Cross-Section
Measurement of B. Baggins, et al. in both Low-Temperature and
High-Temperature Studies, including Water Immersion and
Non-Destructive Testing: A Brief Review plus Commentary on
the "Missing Ring" Problem.</TITLE>
```

BODY ELEMENT: THE DISPLAYED TEXT BODY

Usage:	<BODY> . . . </BODY>
Can Contain:	**Hn, P, HR,**
	DIR, DL, MENU, OL, UL,
	ADDRESS, BLOCKQUOTE, FORM, PRE, [ISINDEX]
Can Be Inside:	**HTML**
Attributes:	*(BACKGROUND:* proposed HTML 3),
	(<u>BGCOLOR</u>, <u>TEXT</u>, <u>LINK</u>, <u>VLINK</u>: Netscape only)
	(<u>BGPROPERTIES</u>: Internet Explorer only)

The **BODY** contains the document proper, as opposed to the information about the document found in the **HEAD**. Formally, the **BODY** cannot directly contain text. Instead, it must contain elements that themselves contain the text, because the **BODY** element states only "this is the body of the document" and supplies no additional meaning to its contents. It is the job of the other elements nested within the **BODY** to organize the text and assign it meaning. This is accomplished by the elements that define headings, lists, addresses, paragraphs, and so on.

The contents of the **HEAD** and **BODY** are exclusive—elements that belong inside the **HEAD** cannot go inside the **BODY**, and vice versa.

HTML 3 proposes the **BACKGROUND** attribute to the **BODY** element. **BACKGROUND** is used to specify an image file to be used as a window background. The referenced image is used to tile the background, rather like a wallpaper, and the text and any included images are displayed superimposed on this wallpaper. The usage is:

```
<BODY BACKGROUND=".....image.gif">
```

where the argument of **BACKGROUND** is a URL pointing to the desired background image.

BACKGROUND is currently supported by the Netscape and Arena browsers, with others expected shortly. With Netscape, the background can be a GIF or JPEG image.

The Netscape browser supports four additional attributes: **BGCOLOR**, **TEXT**, **LINK**, and **VLINK**, while the Microsoft Internet Explorer also supports the attribute **BGPROPERTIES**. Note that these are *not* part of the HTML 3 specification. Nevertheless, several other browsers will soon support these attributes. The better long-term solution for elegant page formatting (which is what backgrounds really are) is the *stylesheet* mechanism, discussed in the next chapter.

The Netscape attributes are used to specify the desired color for the background, text, hypertext linked text, and visited hypertext linked text. The color is specified as an RGB code: an RGB code (**Red-Green-Blue**) specifies a color as a composite of red, green, and blue components. Each color can be in the range 0–255 (eight bits), and each color is referenced, in the RGB value, by its hexadecimal code. Thus the color red, which is full red, zero blue, and zero green, is coded `"#ff0000"`, while white (all colors on full) is `"#ffffff"`. The default colors are specified by the browser configuration. Note that when using a background, a developer may need to change the text color, using the attributes discussed below, to make the text distinguishable from the background.

The Internet Explorer **BGPROPERTIES** attribute allows for nonscrolling background images, as opposed to the default scrolling backgrounds.

BGCOLOR=*"rrggbb"* (optional) **BGCOLOR** specifies the background color for the display window. If a **BACKGROUND** image is also specified, the background will first be tiled with this color, and then with the image. If the **BACKGROUND** image is transparent, the color behind the background is given by **BGCOLOR**.

TEXT=*"#rrggbb"* (optional) **TEXT** specifies the color for the text in the document (the default is black).

LINK=*"#rrggbb"* (optional) **LINK** specifies the color for text within unvisited hypertext links (the default is blue).

VLINK=*"#rrggbb"* (optional) **VLINK** specifies the color for text within visited hypertext links.

BGPROPERTIES=*"fixed"* (optional) The **BGPROPERTIES** allows for nonscrolling background images, as opposed to the default scrolling backgrounds. **BGPROPERTIES** can take the single value "Fixed," which indicates a fixed (nonscrolling) background. This attribute is supported only by the Microsoft Internet Explorer.

ADDRESS Element: Address Information

Usage:	`<ADDRESS> . . . </ADDRESS>`
Can Contain:	**characters, character highlighting, A, BR, IMG**
Can Be Inside:	**BLOCKQUOTE, BODY, FORM**
Attributes:	none

The **ADDRESS** element is used to denote information such as addresses, electronic signatures, lists of authors, and so on. Typically, a document author will use the **ADDRESS** to sign his or her documents. In this case, the **ADDRESS** is often placed at the bottom of the HTML document to keep it separate from the main text. In a family of documents, the **ADDRESS** may contain just the author's initials, connected by a hypertext link to a biographical page. Alternatively, a collection of documents may have an introductory document that has **ADDRESS** elements containing detailed contact information for the author or authors, with the remaining documents having **ADDRESS** elements containing hypertext links back to this page.

As with all elements, the rendering of the contents of **ADDRESS** is left up to the browser. For example, Mosaic usually renders an **ADDRESS** in italics, while Cello indents it.

Figures 4.4 and 4.6 show some typical applications of the **ADDRESS** element. Browser renderings of these documents are shown in Figures 4.5 and 4.7 respectively.

BLOCKQUOTE Element: Block Quotations

Usage:	`<BLOCKQUOTE> . . . </BLOCKQUOTE>`
Can Contain:	**Hn, P, HR,**
	DIR, DL, MENU, OL, UL,
	ADDRESS, BLOCKQUOTE, FORM, PRE, [ISINDEX]
Can Be Inside:	**BLOCKQUOTE, BODY, DD, FORM, LI**
Attributes:	none

■■■■■■ **Figure 4.4** HTML example document illustrating headings, **BLOCKQUOTE,** and **ADDRESS** elements. Figure 4.5 shows this document viewed by Cello.

```
<html>

<head>

<title> Examples of ADDRESS and BLOCKQUOTE elements</title>

</head>


<body>


<h1> Example 2: The Meaning of Life </h1>


<p> How many times have you sat down and asked yourself <quote>

What is the meaning of life? </quote>  I certainly have.  I've

even read many of the good books, from C.S. Lewis, to Kant, to

Sartre to Zoltan the Magnificent.  But I think the most profound

statement about life was made by Jack Handley, who said:


<BLOCKQUOTE>

<P>I can still recall old Mister Barnslow getting out every morning and

nailing a fresh load of tadpoles to that old board of his.  Then he'd

spin it around and around, like a wheel of fortune, and no matter where

it stopped he'd yell out, "Tadpoles!  Tadpoles is a winner!"

We all thought he was crazy.  But then, we had some growing up to do.

</BLOCKQUOTE>


That pretty well sums it up.


<HR>

<ADDRESS>  <A HREF="about_the_author.html"> C.S.O </A> </ADDRESS>


</body>

</html>
```

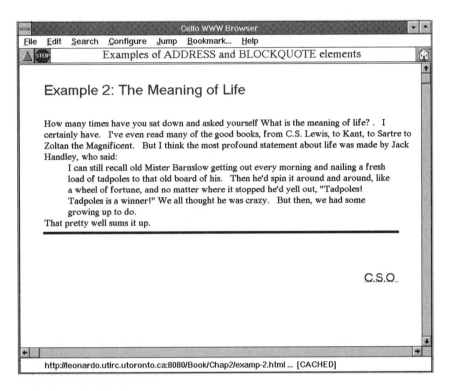

▬▬▬▬ **Figure 4.5** Display, by the Cello browser, of the document shown in Figure 4.4.

▬▬▬▬ **Figure 4.6** HTML example document illustrating **TITLE,** heading, and **ADDRESS** elements. Figure 4.7 shows this document viewed by Netscape Navigator 1.1. Note how the Netscape browser understands heading elements with **ALIGN**="center", but not the attribute **ALIGN**="right".

```
<html>

<head>

<title> Some examples of ADDRESS and heading elements </title>

</head>


<body>


<h1 align="center"> Example 3:<br> The Truth About Santa </h1>
```

```
<p> Breaking the news to a small child that Santa Claus is

merely a tool of the modern capitalist is one of

the saddest moments in raising children.   Nevertheless, such

truths must be brought to life, for fear that your child

become another Pangloss lost in the idealism so prevalent

amongst our youth. Here are some different methods to

introduce this topic.


<h2 align="right"> Santa's Exploitation of the Working Class </h2>

<p>  Begin by talking about Santa's enslaved workforce.   How

can those poor gnomes make all those gifts?   Clearly

by driven overwork.....


<h3> Elves and the Union Movement </h3>

<p> and so on.......


<h4> Elf Exploitation </h3>

<p> And still more text.


<hr>

<ADDRESS>

Santa Claus<br>

Christmas Holiday Specialist <br>

North Pole, CANADA H0H 0H0<br>

Tel (555) 555 POLE

</ADDRESS>


</body>

</html>
```

■■■■■

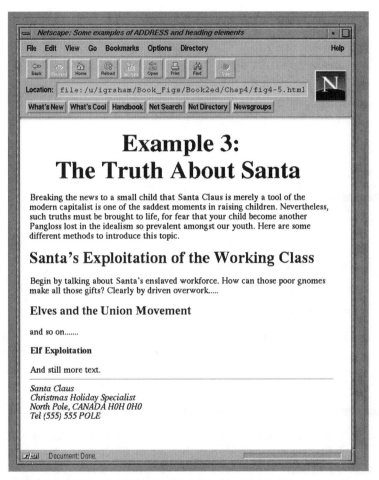

Example content from browser window:

Example 3:
The Truth About Santa

Breaking the news to a small child that Santa Claus is merely a tool of the modern capitalist is one of the saddest moments in raising children. Nevertheless, such truths must be brought to life, for fear that your child become another Pangloss lost in the idealism so prevalent amongst our youth. Here are some different methods to introduce this topic.

Santa's Exploitation of the Working Class

Begin by talking about Santa's enslaved workforce. How can those poor gnomes make all those gifts? Clearly by driven overwork.....

Elves and the Union Movement

and so on.......

Elf Exploitation

And still more text.

Santa Claus
Christmas Holiday Specialist
North Pole, CANADA H0H 0H0
Tel (555) 555 POLE

▬▬▬▬ **Figure 4.7** Display, by the Netscape Navigator 1.1 browser, of the document shown in Figure 4.6.

The **BLOCKQUOTE** element is used to mark a block of text as a quotation. Browsers can render this in various ways; for example, by indenting the **BLOCKQUOTE** contents, and by offsetting it from the preceding and following text. A **BLOCKQUOTE** also causes a paragraph break, and terminates preceding paragraphs.

Note that the definition does not allow text directly inside a **BLOCKQUOTE**; instead, text should lie inside other elements (such as paragraphs and lists) lying inside the **BLOCKQUOTE**. Thus, the form:

```
<BLOCKQUOTE>

<P> This is the quotation. ...
```

```
  ..

</BLOCKQUOTE>
```

is correct, while the form:

```
 <BLOCKQUOTE>

 This is the quotation. ...

  ..

</BLOCKQUOTE>
```

is not. A typical **BLOCKQUOTE** is shown in Figures 4.4 and 4.5.

FORM ELEMENT: FILL-IN FORMS

Usage:	`<FORM> . . . </FORM>`
Can Contain:	**INPUT, SELECT, TEXTAREA,**
	Hn, P, HR,
	DIR, DL, MENU, OL, UL,
	ADDRESS, BLOCKQUOTE, PRE, [ISINDEX]
Can Be Inside:	**BLOCKQUOTE, BODY, DD, LI**
Attributes:	**ACTION, ENCTYPE, METHOD**

The **FORM** element encompasses the content of an HTML *fill-in form*. This is the element you use to create fill-in forms with checkboxes, radio boxes, text input windows, and buttons. Data from a **FORM** *must* be sent to server-side gateway programs for processing; recall that **FORM** collects data, but does not process it. In general, a **FORM** and the server-side program handling the **FORM** output must be designed together so that the program understands the data being sent from the **FORM**. Some simple examples showing the variety of possible **FORM**s are shown in Figures 4.8 through 4.11.

The **FORM** element takes three attributes. These determine where the **FORM** input data is to be sent; what HTTP protocol to use when sending the data; and the data type of the content (as a MIME content-type). Note that **FORM**s do not nest—you *cannot* have a **FORM** within a **FORM**.

The attributes are:

ACTION="*URL*" (mandatory) The **ACTION** specifies the URL to which the **FORM** content is to be sent. Usually this is a URL pointing to a program on an HTTP server, since only HTTP servers allow significant interaction between the client and the server. However, the **ACTION** can specify other URLs. For example, in the case of a **mailto** URL, the **FORM** content would be mailed to the indicated address. Most browsers, however, do not support **mailto** URLs in the context of a **FORM**.

METHOD= "GET" or "POST" (optional) When the **ACTION** indicates an **http** URL, the **METHOD** gives the HTTP *method* for sending information to the server. HTTP methods are discussed in Chapter 7. The default value for **METHOD** is GET. With GET, the content of the form is appended to the URL in a manner identical to query data from an **ISINDEX** search (as discussed in Chapter 8). With the POST method, the form content is sent to the server as a message body, and not as part of the URL.

ENCTYPE= "MIME_type" (optional) ENCTYPE specifies the MIME type of data sent, using the POST method. The default value is `application/x-www-form-urlencoded`. At present, this is the only generally supported value. The Netscape Navigator 2.0 browser also supports the type `multipart/form-data`. The MIME type is briefly discussed in Appendix B.

User input into a form is solicited by the three elements **INPUT**, **SELECT**, and **TEXTAREA**. These elements can appear only inside a form.

INPUT ELEMENT: TEXT BOXES, CHECKBOXES, AND RADIO BUTTONS

Usage:	`<INPUT>`
Can Contain:	empty
Can Be Inside:	**FORM,** any nonempty element allowed inside a **FORM,** except **TEXTAREA** and **SELECT**
Attributes:	**ALIGN, CHECKED, MAXLENGTH, NAME, SIZE, SRC, TYPE, VALUE**

The **INPUT** element specifies a variety of *editable fields* inside a form. It takes several attributes that define the type of input mechanism (text field, buttons, checkboxes, etc.), the *variable name* associated with the input data, and the alignment and size of the input element when displayed. Although the **INPUT** element can appear only inside a **FORM** element, **BLOCKQUOTE, P, PRE,** and list elements (and, in principle, **TABLE**) can also be inside a **FORM,** and can be used to organize the **INPUT** elements into lists or paragraphs. Some examples of the **INPUT** element, and the organization allowed by these other elements, are shown in Figures 4.8 through 4.11.

Figure 4.8 HTML example document illustrating several FORMs **INPUT** elements and the **SELECT** element. Figure 4.9 shows this document as displayed by the Mosaic for X-Windows browser.

```html
<html>

<head>

<title> Examples of HTML FORMS </title>

</head>


<body>


<h1> Example 4:  Examples of FORMS</h1>

<p> sends search information to a script.


<FORM  ACTION="http://side.edu/cgi-bin/script">


    <p> Search string: <INPUT TYPE="text" NAME="search_string" SIZE=24>

    <p> Search Type:

          <SELECT NAME="search_type">

               <OPTION> Insensitive Substring

               <OPTION SELECTED> Exact Match

               <OPTION> Sensitive Substring

               <OPTION> Regular Expression

          </SELECT>

    <p> Search databases in:

        [<INPUT TYPE="checkbox" NAME="servers" VALUE="Canada" CHECKED>Canada]

        [<INPUT TYPE="checkbox" NAME="servers" VALUE="Russia">Russia]

        [<INPUT TYPE="checkbox" NAME="servers" VALUE="Sweden">Sweden]

        [<INPUT TYPE="checkbox" NAME="servers" VALUE="U.S.A.">U.S.A.]

        <em>(multiple items can be selected.)</em>

    <p> Niceness:

        <menu>

          <li> <INPUT TYPE="radio" NAME="niceness" VALUE="nicest" CHECKED > Nicest

          <li> <INPUT TYPE="radio" NAME="niceness" VALUE="nice" >    Nice
```

```
        <li> <INPUT TYPE="radio" NAME="niceness" VALUE="not nice"> Not Nice

        <li> <INPUT TYPE="radio" NAME="niceness" VALUE="nasty" >  Nasty

     </menu>

  <P> <INPUT TYPE="submit"> <INPUT TYPE=reset>.



</FORM>



<HR>

<ADDRESS>  Form by <A HREF="about_the_author.html"> I.S.G</A> </ADDRESS>



</body>

</html>
```

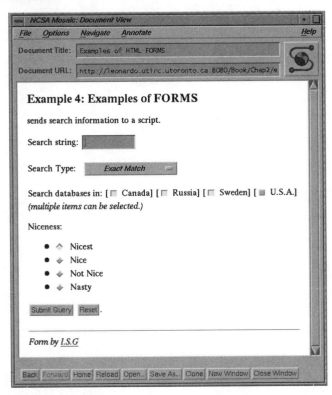

Figure 4.9 Display of the document shown in Figure 4.8 by the Mosaic for X-Windows browser.

■■■■■■■ **Figure 4.10** HTML example document illustrating FORM **INPUT, SELECT,** and **TEXT AREA** input elements. Figure 4.11 shows this document as displayed by the Mosaic for X-Windows browser.

```
<html>

<head>

<title> Examples of HTML FORMS </title>

</head>


<body>


<h1>Example 5: More Forms Examples</h1>

<p> This might send an abstract for registration to a selection

of databases.


<FORM  ACTION="http://side.edu/cgi-bin/submit_abstract">

   <h2> Please give name and password: </h2>

   <p> Name:       <INPUT TYPE="text"  NAME="userid" VALUE="guest" SIZE=20>

       Password: <INPUT TYPE="password" NAME="password" VALUE="bozo..." SIZE=8>

   <hr>

   <h2> Select Databases: </h2>

   <p> Physics: <SELECT NAME="physics_database" MULTIPLE SIZE=3>

                    <OPTION SELECTED> Condensed-Matter

                    <OPTION> High Energy

                    <OPTION> Solid-State

                    <OPTION> Quantum Cosmology

                    <OPTION> Astrophysics

                    </SELECT>

   Chemistry: <SELECT NAME="chemistry_database" MULTIPLE SIZE=3>

                    <OPTION> Surface Dynamics

                    <OPTION> Quantum Chemistry

                    <OPTION SELECTED> Polymer Dynamics
```

```
                    <OPTION> Biochemistry

                    <OPTION> Nuclear Chemistry

                    </SELECT>

    <h2> Enter Abstract: </h2>

    <p> <TEXTAREA COLS=60 ROWS=4> If you are submitting an abstract, select

the desired databases from the above list, delete this text,

type (or paste) the abstract into this box and press the

"Deposit Abstract" button.

        </TEXTAREA>

    <P> <STRONG> Press </STRONG> <INPUT TYPE="submit" VALUE="Deposit Abstract">

        to deposit, or <INPUT TYPE=reset> to reset form.


</FORM>


<HR>

<ADDRESS>  Form by <A HREF="about_the_author.html"> I.S.G</A> </ADDRESS>


</body>

</html>
```

The most important attribute to the **INPUT** element is **NAME,** which assigns a *variable name* to the *value* entered into the element. The data entered into a **FORM** are sent to the server as a collection of strings of the form *name=value,* where *name* is the variable name and *value* is the value that is input or selected by the user (the *name* and *value* strings are encoded prior to being sent to the server, as discussed in Chapters 6 and 8). The program parsing the **FORM** data uses the variable *name* to interpret the contents of the corresponding *value* and must therefore understand the different *names.* For this reason, a **FORM** and the gateway program that handles the **FORM** data must be designed together.

The other main attribute is **TYPE,** which selects the type of the **INPUT** element. There are several other attributes, but their usage and relevance depends on the **TYPE.**

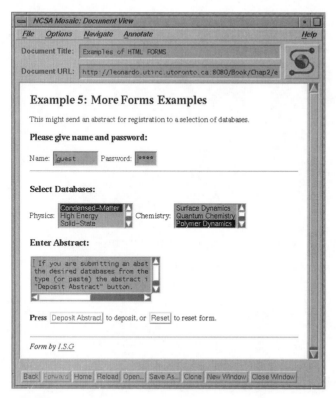

Figure 4.11 Display of the document shown in Figure 4.10 by the Mosaic for X-Windows browser.

The attributes are:

NAME= "*name*" (mandatory) This assigns the variable name "*name*" to the data contents of this **INPUT** element. Values for this attribute are selected by the user, and should best be strings that logically relate to their purpose or content.

TYPE="checkbox", "hidden", "image", "password", "radio", "reset", "submit", "text," and "file" (mandatory) **TYPE** determines the type of input element, from among a list of nine possible types. The meaning and function of these different types is given below.

TYPE="checkbox" "Checkbox" **INPUT** elements are Boolean (on/off) quantities; the default value is *off* (this can be modified with the **CHECKED** attribute). The **VALUE** attribute sets the *value* assigned to an *on* checkbox. When you submit a **FORM**, the *name=value* pair is sent only if the checkbox is *on*.

Different checkboxes may associate different *values* with the same variable *name*. This is convenient, for example, if you have six different databases to search and want to allow the user to select one, two, or all of them. When the **FORM** is submitted, the browser sends all the *values* from the *on* checkboxes, yielding several *name=value* pairs with the same *name*. An example is shown in Figure 4.8.

TYPE="hidden" This **INPUT** element is not displayed to the user. The content of a "hidden" element, set with the **VALUE** attribute, is always sent to the server when the **FORM** is submitted. This is useful for passing information back and forth between the client and server, and is typically used to record the *state* of the client/server interaction. Recall that the HTTP protocol is stateless, so that without such passed information, the gateway program handling the **FORM** data has no record of any past interaction. Typically, a "hidden" **INPUT** element is placed in a **FORM** by a server-side gateway program that assembles the **FORM**. This point is discussed in more detail in Chapter 9.

TYPE="image" The **INPUT** element is an active *inline* image (analogous to the **ISMAP** attribute of the **IMG** element). The **SRC** attribute specifies the URL of the image.

Clicking on the image immediately submits the **FORM** data, including the coordinates of the mouse pointer (measured in pixels from the upper left-hand corner of the image). The coordinates are sent in two *name=value* pairs. The "name" is created by taking the **NAME** attribute and appending the strings ".x" and ".y" to indicate the x or y coordinate. Thus, if the **NAME** was set to "*king*", the coordinates are sent in the *name=value* pairs *king.x=x_coord* and *king.y=y_coord*.

TYPE="password" The **INPUT** element is a single-line text field, but the text typed into the field is obscured by asterisks or by some other method. This is used for password entry. An example password field is shown in Figures 4.10 and 4.11.

TYPE="radio" The **INPUT** element is a radio button. Radio buttons are linked together by assigning them the same **NAME**. By definition, only one radio button can be "on" at a given instant; therefore, when a user turns *on* one radio button, all other buttons associated with the same **NAME** are automatically turned *off*. Each radio button must have a value so that every **INPUT** element of **TYPE**="radio" must have a **VALUE** attribute.

TYPE="reset" The **INPUT** element is a reset button. When pressed, all the fields in the **FORM** are reset to the values given by their **VALUE** attributes, thereby erasing all user input.

TYPE="submit" The **INPUT** element is a Submit button. Pressing the Submit button sends the **FORM** data to the specified URL. A form can have more than one such button, each with different **NAME** and **VALUE** attributes; the **FORM** sends only the *name=value* pair associated with the pressed Submit button. The *value* is not editable by the client and is displayed as the button label.

■■■■■ **NOTE**

Some older browsers do not support multiple Submit buttons with different *name=value* pairs.

■■■■■

TYPE="text" The **INPUT** element is a single-line text entry field. The physically displayed size of the input field is set by the **SIZE** attribute.

TYPE="file" (HTML 3; currently only supported by Netscape Navigator 2.0) The **INPUT** element is a file-selection tool or widget, with which the user can select an arbitrary file to be sent with the **FORM**. For this to work, the **ENCTYPE** of the **FORM** must be set to `multipart/form-data`. This MIME type is briefly discussed in Appendix B.

ALIGN="top", "middle", "bottom" (optional) **ALIGN** specifies the alignment of the image with respect to the surrounding text. The usage is equivalent to the **ALIGN** attribute to the **IMG** element (described later in this section). This is a valid attribute only with **TYPE**="image".

CHECKED (optional) The **CHECKED** attribute indicates that a checkbox or radio button is selected (turned "on"). This attribute is valid only with **TYPE**="checkbox" or **TYPE**="radio." If **TYPE**="radio," then only one of a collection of linked radio buttons can be **CHECKED**.

MAXLENGTH="n" (optional) **MAXLENGTH** specifies the length of the character buffer for a text box, where "n" is the buffer length. This is a valid attribute only with **TYPE**="text" or **TYPE**="password". **MAXLENGTH** can be larger than the displayed text box, in which case, the arrow keys may be used to scroll the text. The default length is unlimited. This attribute can be used to restrict the maximum size of the string input by the user.

SIZE="*n*" (optional) **SIZE** specifies the actual size of the displayed field. When **TYPE**="text", or **TYPE**="password", **SIZE** specifies the width, in characters, of the input text box.

SRC="*URL*" (mandatory with **TYPE**="image") **SRC** specifies the URL of the image to be included *inline* and is valid only with **TYPE**="image".

VALUE="*value*" (mandatory with **TYPE**="radio") **VALUE** specifies the initial value of the input element.

Figures 4.8 through 4.11 give typical examples of **INPUT** element usage. **FORM**s are also discussed in Chapters 2 and 8.

SELECT Element: Select from Among Multiple Options

Usage:	`<SELECT> . . . </SELECT>`
Can Contain:	**OPTION**
Can Be Inside:	**FORM,** any nonempty element inside a **FORM,** except **TEXTAREA** or **SELECT**
Attributes:	**MULTIPLE, NAME, SIZE**

The **SELECT** element allows the user to select from among a set of values presented as a selectable list of text strings; the possible *values* are specified by the **OPTION** element. The attribute **MULTIPLE** allows multiple values to be selected; otherwise, only one value can be chosen. As with the **INPUT** elements, the selected data is sent to the server as one or more *name=value* pairs.

The attributes are:

MULTIPLE (optional) If **MULTIPLE** is present, the user is able to select multiple items from a single **SELECT** element. If **MULTIPLE** is not present, the user can select only a single item from the **SELECT** list.

NAME="*name*" (mandatory) **NAME** specifies the variable name associated with the **SELECT** element.

SIZE="*n*" (optional) **SIZE** specifies the number of displayed text lines. The default value is 1 and, consequently, the list is often presented as a pull-down menu. For other values, the list is usually presented as a scrollbox. If **MULTIPLE** is set, browsers choose a minimum **SIZE** greater than 1 and will not let you use **SIZE** to select a smaller value.

Figures 4.10 and 4.11 show typical examples of **SELECT** (and **OPTION**) elements.

OPTION ELEMENT: LIST OF OPTIONS FOR SELECT

Usage:	`<OPTION> . . . (</OPTION>)`
Can Contain:	**characters**
Can Be Inside:	**SELECT**
Attributes:	**VALUE, SELECTED** *(DISABLED*: proposed HTML 3)

The **OPTION** element sets the different character-string options for a **SELECT** element. This element is not empty but the terminating `</OPTION>` is optional, as the element is by default terminated by the next `<OPTION>` tag or by the `</SELECT>` tag ending the list. **OPTION** can contain characters, character references, or entity references only; it cannot contain markup. The content of **OPTION** is used as the *value* unless a **VALUE** attribute is explicitly set.

The attributes are:

DISABLED (optional) (proposed HTML 3) **DISABLED** marks a particular **OPTION** as disabled—if displayed, it may be shown as grayed or faded. The user is unable to select or deselect this option. This attribute is supported by only a few current browsers.

SELECTED (optional) This marks the **OPTION** as selected. If the **SELECT** element has the **MULTIPLE** attribute, more than one **OPTION** can be marked as **SELECTED**. Figures 4.10 and 4.11 show examples. **SELECTED** items can be deselected by the user; thus, **SELECTED** can be used to set default selection values.

VALUE="*value*" (optional) Specifies the *value* assigned to the **OPTION**. If absent, the content of **OPTION** is sent as the *value*.

TEXTAREA ELEMENT

Usage:	`<TEXTAREA> . . . </TEXTAREA>`
Can Contain:	**characters**
Can Be Inside:	**FORM**
Attributes:	**COLS, NAME, ROWS** (<u>**WRAP**</u>: Netscape 2.0 only)

TEXTAREA allows the user to enter a block of text. The input block of text can grow to almost unlimited size, and is not limited by the size of the area displayed on the screen. Scrollbars are often present, if the text entered into a **TEXTAREA** grows to be (or initially is) bigger than the displayed region.

A **TEXTAREA** window displays characters in fixed-width fonts so that the attributes **COLS** and **ROWS** specify text area window sizes in character widths and heights. **TEXTAREA** can contain any printable characters. HTML markup is not interpreted here: the **TEXTAREA** data are simply characters to be sent elsewhere. Thus a person typing text into a **TEXTAREA** can in principle send an entire HTML document to a server using this element.

By default, the text in a **TEXTAREA** does not wrap—lines can be as long as desired, the only line wrapping that exists is due to carriage return/line feeds explicitly entered by the user. In some cases, it is more convenient if the **TEXTAREA** element itself automatically wraps the text, either virtually (the lines are displayed with wrapping, but the software-imposed new-line characters are not sent as part of the **TEXTAREA** data) or physically (the new-line characters introduced by the **TEXTAREA** formatting are sent as part of the **TEXTAREA** data). Netscape Navigator 2.0 supports the attribute **WRAP** with the **TEXTAREA** element, which can take the three values "off", "virtual," and "physical" to support these three options.

The attributes are:

COLS="*n*" (mandatory) **COLS** specifies the displayed width of the **TEXTAREA**, in columns.

NAME="*name*" (mandatory) **NAME** specifies the variable name associated with the **TEXTAREA** contents.

ROWS="*n*" (mandatory) **ROWS** specifies the displayed height of the **TEXTAREA** in rows.

WRAP="off", "virtual", "physical" (optional; Netscape Navigator 2.0 only) **WRAP** specifies the handling of word-wrapping within the **TEXTAREA**

element. **WRAP**="off" disables word-wrapping completely—the only new line characters are those explicitly included with the input data. **WRAP**="virtual" causes virtual word-wrapping—new line characters are introduced to ensure that the text fits within the specified area, but these characters are not included with the data when the **FORM** is submitted. **WRAP**="physical" causes word-wrapping equivalent to **WRAP**="virtual", but in this case the extra new line characters are included with the data when the **FORM** is submitted. The default behavior is **WRAP**="off", which reproduces the behavior of most current browsers.

Text placed within a **TEXTAREA** is displayed as an initial value. Note that HTML markup tags are not valid here. A browser provides some way to edit the displayed text.

Figures 4.10 and 4.11 show a typical example of a **TEXTAREA** element.

Hn Elements: Headings

Usage:	`<Hn> . . . </Hn>`
Can Contain:	**characters, character highlighting, A, BR, IMG**
Can Be Inside:	**BLOCKQUOTE, BODY, FORM**
Attributes:	(*ALIGN:* proposed HTML 3)

HTML allows six levels of headings, from **H1** through **H6**. There is no forced hierarchy in these headings, but for consistency you should use the top level (**H1**) for main headings, and lower levels for progressively less important ones. You should also avoid skipping a heading level within a given document, as this breaks the logical structure of the document and may cause problems when converting the document into another form, or automatically generating HTML table of contents documents.

Hn elements have no attributes under HTML 2.0.

Current renderings of headings are very much browser-dependent. For example, Mosaic and Netscape Navigator render **H1** headings with a large font and left-justified, while lynx renders **H1** headings as capitalized strings centered on the page. Some typical renderings are shown in Figures 4.2 through 4.25.

As a general rule, hypertext documents should be broken up, such that each page does not occupy more than one or two browser screen areas. You can then use the **H1** heading to mark the main heading for the collection of documents, and the others to mark subheadings.

HTML 3 proposes an **ALIGN** attribute for heading elements. **ALIGN** provides a hint to the browser as to the desired page alignment of the heading. The allowed values for **ALIGN** are **ALIGN**="left", "center", "right", and "justify". The value "left" left-justifies the title flush with the left margin (this is the default), while the value "right" flushes the title to the right window margin. The value "center" causes the heading to be centered on the display window, while the value"justify" justifies the title between the left and right margins, falling back to left alignment when the heading is too short. Some examples of aligned headings are shown in Figures 4.6 and 4.7, 4.18 and 4.19, and 4.28 through 4.29.

The **ALIGN** attribute is supported to some degree (not all alignment values are supported) by several browsers, including emacs-w3, Arena, Netscape, and WebExplorer.

HR ELEMENT: HORIZONTAL RULE

Usage:	`<HR>`
Can Contain:	empty
Can Be Inside:	**BODY, BLOCKQUOTE, FORM**
Attributes	(**SIZE**, **WIDTH**, **ALIGN**, **NOSHADE**: Netscape only)

The **HR** element draws a horizontal line completely across the screen. An `<HR>` terminates any preceding paragraph, so a new paragraph mark should follow an `<HR>` if there is subsequent text. An `<HR>` is commonly used to divide sections within a single document. One common example is to use an `<HR>` at the bottom of a document, followed by an **ADDRESS** element. This is illustrated in Figures 4.5 through 4.11.

The **HR** element is empty.

The Netscape browser supports several attributes that are not part of the proposed HTML 3 specifications. You should be aware that these features *will not work* on other browsers. These Netscape-only attributes are:

SIZE="*n*" (optional) (Netscape only) **SIZE** specifies, in pixels, the vertical thickness of the horizontal rule.

WIDTH="*n*", or WIDTH="*n*%" (optional) (Netscape only) **WIDTH** specifies the horizontal width of the **HR** element. The form **WIDTH**="*n*" specifies the width in pixels (note how the result depends on the screen resolution of the display), while the form **WIDTH**="n%" specifies the width as a percentage of the document width (e.g., **WIDTH**="80%").

ALIGN="left", "right", "center" (optional) (Netscape only) If an **HR** does not span the page, then it can, like a heading, be aligned on the page. The alignment is controlled by the **ALIGN** attribute, which can take the values "left", "right", or "center" (center is the default).

NOSHADE (optional) (Netscape only) By default, Netscape renders an HR as a shaded bar, which gives the impression of a chiseled bar in the page. The attribute **NOSHADE** (which takes no value) tells Netscape to render the element as a solid black bar, with no shading.

LIST ELEMENTS

HTML has several elements for defining different types of lists. They can be divided into two types: glossary lists (the element **DL**) and regular lists (the elements **DIR, MENU, OL,** and **UL**). Lists of the same or of different types can be nested. Thus, you can have a regular list within a regular list, a regular list within a glossary list, and so on. Some examples are shown in the following section.

DL ELEMENT: GLOSSARY LIST

Usage:	`<DL> . . . </DL>`
Can Contain:	**DT, DD**
Can Be Inside:	**BLOCKQUOTE, BODY, DD, FORM, LI**
Attributes:	**COMPACT**

This list type, also known as a definition list, presents a list of items, each with a descriptive paragraph. This can be used, for example, for traditional glossaries.

DL takes a single optional attribute, **COMPACT**, to signify that the list should be rendered in a physically compact way. You could use this to compact a list of small items, or to compact a large list that would be easier to read if rendered in a compact manner.

A **DL** list can contain two elements:

DT	The term being defined
DD	The definition of the term

DT and **DD** elements should appear in pairs. The specification also allows for successive **DT** elements, followed by a single **DD**, corresponding to multiple terms having the same definition. The current specification does not permit multiple, consecutive **DD** elements.

Figures 4.12 and 4.13 show an example of a **DL** list.

■■■■■■ **Figure 4.12** HTML example document illustrating the **DL** glossary list elements, and a **UL** unordered list nested inside a glossary list. Figure 4.13 shows this document as displayed by the Cello browser.

```
<html>


<head>
<title> Example of Glossary List elements </title>
</head>


<body>


<h1> Example 6: Example of Glossary Lists </h1>


<p> Here is an example of a glossary list. The third item in the list

has a regular unordered list nested within it. Note that the first

term (marked by the DT element) does not have a matching description

(marked by the DD element).  This is perfectly legal.  The converse:

a DD without a matching DT, is illegal.


<dl>
<dt> Things to do:
<dt> Things to avoid:
    <dd> You should not use elements that define paragraph

    formatting within the PRE element. This means you should

    not use <code> &lt;P>, &lt;ADDRESS>, &lt;Hn> </code> and so on.

    You should avoid the use of tab characters -- use single blank
```

```
        characters to space text apart.
<dt> Things That are OK:
    <dd>You <em> can </em> use the anchor element A.  A typed carriage
    return will cause a new line in the presented text.
    People you should never let format lists include:
    <ul
        <li> Bozo the Clown
        <li> Uncle Fester
        <li> Knights who go nii
    </ul>
    as they generally do a poor job.


</dl>


</body>
</html>
```

DT Element: Term in a Glossary List

Usage:	`<DT>` . . . `(</DT>)`
Can Contain:	**characters, character highlighting, A, BR, IMG**
Can Be Inside:	**DL**
Attributes:	none

The **DT** element contains the term part of a glossary or description list entry. The contents of a **DT** element should be short—typically, a few words, and certainly shorter than a line. The element can contain standard character markup, images, line breaks, and hypertext anchors.

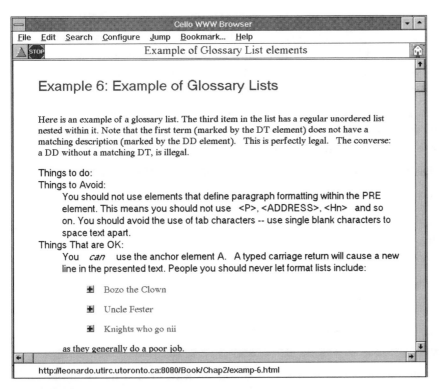

Figure 4.13 Display, by the Cello browser, of the document shown in Figure 4.12.

The **DT** element is not empty, but the terminating `</DT>` is optional, as it is implied either by the start of another `<DT>` or `<DD>` element, or by the `</DL>` ending the list.

DD ELEMENT: DESCRIPTION IN A GLOSSARY LIST

Usage:	`<DD>` . . . `(</DD>)`
Can Contain:	**characters, character highlighting,**
	A, BR, IMG,
	DIR, DL, MENU, OL, UL,
	BLOCKQUOTE, FORM, P, PRE, [ISINDEX]
Can Be Inside:	**DL**
Attributes:	**none**

The **DD** element gives the description corresponding to the previous **DT** element or elements. It can be a long description, broken into paragraphs and containing other lists, **FORMs**, quotations, and so on. A **DD** element must always follow a **DT** element—and should not occur alone. You should also not have subsequent **DD** elements in a **DL** list.

The **DD** element is not empty, but the terminating `</DD>` is optional, since the end of a **DD** element is implied either by the `<DT>` tag starting another **DT** element, or by the `</DL>` tag terminating the list.

OL ELEMENT: ORDERED LIST

Usage:	`<OL> . . . </OL>`
Can Contain:	**LI**
Can Be Inside:	**BLOCKQUOTE, BODY, DD, FORM, LI**
Attributes:	**COMPACT** (*CONTINUE, SEQNUM:* proposed HTML 3) (<u>**START**</u>, <u>**TYPE**</u>: Netscape only)

The **OL** element defines an ordered list. A browser indicates ordering by numbering the items, or by assigning them ascending letters, and so on. The **OL** element has one attribute under the HTML 2.0 specifications, namely the optional attribute **COMPACT**. **COMPACT** does not take a value, and simply requests that the browser compact the list—for example, reducing whitespaces between list entries. This attribute is not understood by most current browsers.

Each item in an **OL** list is contained within an **LI** (list item) element; the **LI** element is the *only* thing that can appear inside an **OL** list. Items can be paragraphs of text, but should be kept reasonably short; as otherwise, the idea of a list is lost. If the list items are big, perhaps it is not really a list: try paragraphs with appropriate section headings. A typical ordered list is shown in Figures 4.14 and 4.15.

HTML 3 proposes two new attributes for the **OL** element. Although currently unimplemented by most browsers (including Netscape), they are mentioned here to contrast them with the two Netscape-only attributes.

CONTINUE (optional) (HTML 3) **CONTINUE** directs the browser to continue the sequence numbering of the list elements from where the last ordered list item ended. This is not understood by current browsers.

SEQNUM="*n*" (optional) (HTML 3) **SEQNUM** sets the starting number for the first item in the list, where *n* is an integer specifying the starting number. This is not understood by current browsers.

Netscape supports two alternative attributes for defining the style of the item numbering and the starting number for the items.

START="*n*" (optional) (Netscape only) **START** specifies the starting number for the first item in the list, where *n* is an integer specifying the starting number.

TYPE="A", "a", "I", "i", "1" **TYPE** specifies the type of the marker by which the items should be numbered. Thus, **TYPE=**"A" and **TYPE=**"a" imply ordering with capital or lowercase letters respectively, while **TYPE=**"I" and **TYPE=**"i" imply ordering with uppercase or lowercase roman numerals respectively. **TYPE=**"1" invokes standard numerical ordering.

These **TYPE** attribute values violate important SGML syntax rules, so they cannot become part of standard HTML.

UL ELEMENT: UNORDERED LIST

Usage:	`<UL>` . . . `</UL>`
Can Contain:	**LI**
Can Be Inside:	**BLOCKQUOTE, BODY, DD, FORM, LI**
Attributes:	**COMPACT, (TYPE Netscape only)**

The **UL** element defines an unordered list of items, where each list item is indicated by a special symbol, such as a bullet or an asterisk. The **OL** element has one attribute under the HTML 2.0 specifications, namely the optional attribute **COMPACT. COMPACT** does not take a value, and simply requests that the browser compact the list by, for example, reducing whitespaces between list entries. This attribute is not understood by most current browsers.

Each item in a **UL** list is contained within an **LI** (list item) element; the **LI** element is the *only* thing that can appear inside a **UL** list. Items can be paragraphs of text, but should be kept reasonably short; otherwise, the idea of a list is lost. If the list items are big, perhaps it is not really a list: try paragraphs with appropriate section headings.

Netscape supports the additional attribute **TYPE**, which is used to specify the type of bullet you wish to use for the list items. The allowed values are **TYPE=**"disc" (for a small circular disc), **TYPE=**"circle" (for a small, open circle), or **TYPE=**"square" (for a small square).

Figures 4.14 to 4.17 show examples of HTML 2.0 unordered lists.

Figure 4.14 HTML example document illustrating **UL** and **OL** lists, and the nesting of list elements. Figure 4.15 shows this document as displayed by the WinWeb browser.

```
<html>


<head>
<title> Example of Regular List elements </title>
</head>


<body>


<h1> Example 7: Examples of Regular Lists </h1>


<h2> Ordered Lists </h2>
<p> This shows an ordered list, with another ordered list nested
within it.
<OL>
    <LI> First item.  Note that there can be lots of stuff in a list
    item, including images, paragraph breaks, BLOCKQUOTEs, and even
    other lists.
    <LI> A Second item in the list.
    <LI> And a third item.  This item breaks down into some
    subcategories:
        <OL>
        <LI> The first sub-item
        <LI> The second sub-item, and so on.....
        </OL>
</OL>
<hr>
<h2> Unordered Lists </h2>
<p> This also contains an ordered sublist.
```

```
<UL>

    <LI> A list item.

    <LI> Another list item; again these can containing IMG elements,

        Paragraphs, and so on.

    <LI> And sub-lists like this:

    <UL>

        <LI> An item in the list.

        <LI> Something else that is important, and so on.

    </UL>

</UL>



</body>

</html>
```

DIR ELEMENT: DIRECTORY LIST

Usage:	`<DIR> . . . </DIR>`
Can Contain:	**LI**
Can Be Inside:	**BLOCKQUOTE, BODY, DD, FORM, LI**
Attributes:	**COMPACT**

The **DIR** element defines a directory list: a list of short items, each no more than about 20 characters. If capable, a browser can display such items in columns across the screen, as opposed to one above the other.

In HTML 2.0, the **DIR** element can take the single optional attribute, **COMPACT**. This attribute does not require a value, and simply directs the browser to render the list in a compact manner. This attribute is not understood by most current browsers.

Each item in a **DIR** list is contained within an **LI** (list item) element; the **LI** element is the *only* thing that can appear inside a **DIR** list.

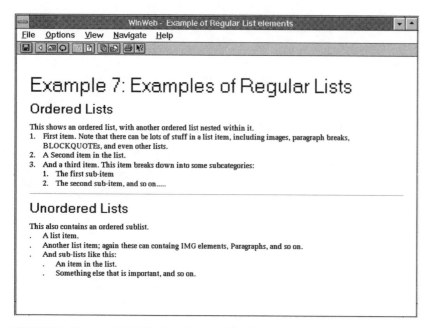

■■■■■■ **Figure 4.15** Display, by the WinWeb browser, of the document shown in Figure 4.14.

Although **DIR** is supported by current browsers, most treat it identically with **UL** lists. **DIR** lists are recommended for elimination in HTML 3, so their use in new documents is discouraged.

An example of a directory list is shown in Figures 4.16 and 4.17.

MENU ELEMENT: MENU LIST

Usage:	<MENU> . . . </MENU>
Can Contain:	**LI**
Can Be Inside:	**BLOCKQUOTE, BODY, DD, FORM, LI**
Attributes:	none

The **MENU** element defines a list of short menu items, each preferably less than a sentence long. The **MENU** list is designed to work like the **UL** but to be formatted in a more compact manner similar to a <UL COMPACT> list, except that formatting may be optimized to favor short list items.

In HTML 2.0, the **MENU** element can take the single optional attribute **COMPACT**. This attribute does not require a value, and simply directs the browser to render the list in a compact manner. This attribute is not understood by most current browsers.

MENU can contain only **LI** elements. It is an error to place text directly inside a **MENU**.

Although **MENU** is supported by current browsers, most treat it identically with **UL** lists. **MENU** lists are recommended for elimination in HTML 3, so their use in new documents is discouraged.

Figures 4.16 and 4.17 give an example of a **MENU** list.

Figure 4.16 HTML example document illustrating the **MENU** and **DIR** lists. Figure 4.17 shows this document as displayed by the MidasWWW browser.

```
<html>


<head>
<title> Example of Regular List elements </title>
</head>


<body>


<h1> Example 8: Still More Lists </h1>


<h2> Unordered Lists </h2>
<p> This also contains an ordered sublist.
<UL>

   <LI> A list item.

   <LI> Another list item,

   <LI> and still more items.

</UL>

<hr>

<h2> Directory Lists </h2>

<DIR>
```

```
    <LI> Abraham - Carbon

    <LI> Cardshark - Elegant

    <LI> Elegiac - Food

    <LI> Foot - Hogs

</DIR>

<hr>

<h2> Menu Lists </h2>

<MENU>

    <LI> First item

    <LI> Second item

    <LI> Third item

    <LI> Fourth item

</MENU>



</body>

</html>
```

LI ELEMENT: LIST ITEM

Usage:	`<LI> . . . (</LI>)`
Can Contain:	**characters, character highlighting,**
	A, BR, IMG,
	DIR, DL, MENU, OL, UL,
	BLOCKQUOTE, FORM, P, PRE, [ISINDEX]
Can Be Inside:	**DIR, MENU, UL, OL**
Attributes:	(**TYPE**, **VALUE**: Netscape only)

The **LI** element marks an item within a list. The item can contain text, character markup, and hypertext anchors, as well as subsidiary lists and text blocks. In HTML 2.0, the **LI** element has no attributes.

██████████ **Figure 4.17** Display of the document shown in Figure 4.16 by the MidasWWW browser. This is one of the few browsers to render **UL, MENU,** and **DIR** in distinct ways.

The Netscape browser supports two attributes, for defining the type of the bullets in the list, and for controlling numbering in ordered lists. These are:

TYPE="disc", "circle", "square" (within **UL** unordered lists), or

"I", "i", "A", "a," "1" (within **OL** ordered lists) **TYPE** determines the manner in which list items are marked. In unordered lists, the values "disc", "circle", and "square" produce solid circles, open circles, and squares respectively. In ordered lists, "I" and "i" produced uppercase and lowercase roman numerals respectively; "A" and "a" produce upper- and lowercase alphabetized lists, and "1" produces numbered lists.

VALUE="n" **VALUE** sets the numeric counter for the current list item, where n is an integer. Thus **VALUE**=5 sets the current list item to item number 5. Subsequent numbered items are incremented from this value.

HTML 3 proposes several new attributes to the LI element that allow for customized marking of list items. These are discussed in the next chapter.

P Element: Paragraphs

Usage:	`<P> . . . (</P>)`
Can Contain:	**characters, character highlighting, A, BR, IMG**
Can Be Inside:	**BODY, BLOCKQUOTE, FORM, DD, LI**
Attributes	(*ALIGN*: proposed HTML 3)

The **P** element marks the beginning of a paragraph and implies a paragraph break. This is different from the **BR** element that represents a simple line break. Paragraphs should be thought of as logical blocks of text, similar to a **BLOCKQUOTE, ADDRESS,** or heading **Hn**, while a **BR** is simply a "character" that causes a line break. In HTML 2.0, the **P** element has no attributes.

Typically, a paragraph is rendered with extra space separating it from the previous and following blocks of text. Sometimes the first line is also indented.

For historical reasons, an end tag `</P>` is not required. Instead, the end of a paragraph is implied by the beginning of another paragraph or by another element marking a block of text. However, an end tag `</P>` can be used to mark the end of a paragraph, and this is the recommended form.

Examples of paragraph elements are given in Figures 4.1 through 4.29.

You should not use paragraphs to add spacing, for example, by writing:

```
....text
<P>
<P>
<P>
<H2> And another thing of Interest </H2>
```

Formally, a paragraph cannot be empty, so this is illegal. Most browsers will tolerate it, but their interpretations will vary: some leave extra spaces, and some ignore the extra `<P>` tags completely.

HTML 3 proposes several additional attributes. The only one currently implemented is:

ALIGN="center", "left", "right", "justify" (optional) (proposed HTML 3)
Changes the paragraph alignment (the default is left) or paragraph justifica-

tion. This option is implemented on several browsers, notably emacs-w3, Arena, and Netscape (although not all alignment options are supported). **ALIGN** is a formatting hint that can be ignored by the browser.

Some examples of aligned paragraphs are shown in Figures 4.18 and 4.19.

PRE ELEMENT: PREFORMATTED TEXT

Usage:	`<PRE>` . . . `</PRE>`
Can Contain:	**characters, character highlighting, A**
Can Be Inside:	**BODY, BLOCKQUOTE FORM, DD, LI**
Attributes:	**WIDTH**

The **PRE** element marks text to be displayed with a fixed-width typewriter font. In particular, the **PRE** environment preserves the line breaks and space characters in the original text. This is the only element in HTML that does so. **PRE** is therefore useful for presenting text that has been formatted for a fixed-width character display, such as a plain text terminal.

Within strict HTML 2.0, the **PRE** element is the only mechanism for displaying tabular data or any other information that requires well-defined columns or relative positions of the text. All the other elements format text with variable-width fonts and adjust the horizontal and vertical white spaces between words and blocks of text.

PRE takes the single optional attribute **WIDTH**. This specifies the maximum number of characters that can be displayed on a single line, and tells a browser that it can wrap the line at this point. Graphical browsers often ignore the **WIDTH** attribute completely and let the lines in a **PRE** element be as long as they wish. You can then use a scrollbar to see text that runs off the display. The **WIDTH** attribute is largely unused, and HTML 3 suggests deprecating (dropping) it from the official language specification.

Things to Avoid

You cannot use elements that define paragraph formatting within the **PRE** element. This means you cannot use `<P>`, `<ADDRESS>`, `<Hn>`, and so on (you also cannot use `<BR>`). You should also avoid tab characters, since different browsers interpret the size of a tab differently. Instead use space characters to control horizontal spacing and to vertically align text.

> **Useful Features**
>
> You can use the **A** (anchor) element to create hypertext anchors inside **PRE.** You can also use all the character highlighting elements (**STRONG, EM,** and so on), although these highlighting elements may be ignored by the browser if appropriate rendering is not possible.

An example of the **PRE** element is shown in Figures 4.18 and 4.19. Note the use of character highlighting. Character highlighting elements inside a **PRE** contribute zero character width.

A ELEMENT: HYPERTEXT ANCHORS

Usage:	<A> . . . </A>
Can Contain:	**characters, character highlighting, BR, IMG**
Can Be Inside:	**ADDRESS, Hn, P, PRE, DT, DD, LI, character highlighting**
Attributes:	**HREF, METHODS, NAME, REL, REV, TITLE, URN (<u>TARGET</u>:** Netscape Navigator 2.0 only)

The **A,** or *anchor*, element marks a block of the document as a hypertext link. This block can be highlighted text or an image. More complex elements, such as headings, cannot be inside an anchor. In particular, note that an anchor element *cannot* contain another anchor element.

A can take several attributes. At least one of these *must* be either **HREF** or **NAME;** these specify the destination of the hypertext link or indicate that the marked text can be the target of a hypertext link. Both can be present, indicating that the anchor is both the start and destination of a link.

Anchors containing **HREFs** are rendered differently than plain text or images. Often, the anchored text or image is underlined, boldfaced, or rendered with a different color. Some browsers change this rendering once a link has been accessed, to inform the user that the link has been *explored*. Anchors with only a **NAME** attribute are usually not rendered in a special way.

▬▬▬▬ **Figure 4.18** HTML example document illustrating the use of the **PRE** element. Figure 4.19 shows this document as displayed by the Netscape Navigator 1.1 browser.

```
<html>

<head>

<title> Example of the PRE elements </title>

</head>


<body>


<h1 align="center"> Example 9: The Use of PRE </h1>

<p align="center"> The PRE element is often used to include blocks

of plain text.  For example you can use it to include

examples of typed code, such as the following C program:

<hr>

<PRE>

/* main program for fitting program */


extern int *sharv;

static char boggle[100];


main (int argc, char *argv)

double x_transpose, y_transpose, f_ack=2.3;

{

    .

</PRE>

<hr>

<p> PRE is also used for <em> tables</em>:  HTML2.0 does not have

elements for defining tables:

<PRE>
```

```
    Item            Price     Tax     Total         Category


    fileserver      10000     300     10300         <a href="cat_a.html">A</a>

    disk drive       900       30      930          <a href="cat_b.html">B</a>

    <strong>transmission</strong>     4400    110     4510              C

    <em>fertilizer</em>        5500    100     5600          F
</PRE>
<p>The markup codes take up no space: if you delete everything between the
angle brackets (in the raw HTML) all the columns align perfectly.




</body>
</html>
```

Several examples of **A** elements are given in Figures 4.2, 4.19, and 4.20.

The element attributes are:

HREF="*URL*" (mandatory if **NAME** is absent) **HREF** gives the target of a hypertext link. URL is the Uniform Resource Locator referencing the target object.

NAME="*string*" (mandatory if **HREF** is absent) **NAME** is used to mark a place in an HTML document as a specific destination of a hypertext link. The value "*string*" identifies this destination. For example, the anchor element:

```
<A NAME="poison"> Deadly Toadstools </A>
```

marks "Deadly Toadstools" as a possible hypertext target, referenced by the string poison. This string is called a *fragment identifier*. Within the same document, the location can be referenced by the hypertext reference:

```
<A HREF="#poison"> Poisonous nonmushrooms </A>
```

Clicking on the phrase "Poisonous nonmushrooms" will then link you back to the place in the current document marked by the <A NAME="poi-son">...</A> anchor.

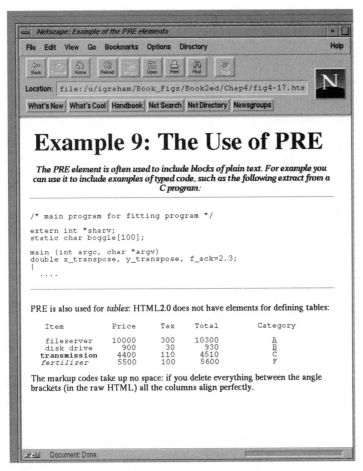

Figure 4.19 Display, by the Netscape Navigator 1.1 browser, of the document shown in Figure 4.18.

From another document, you would write:

```
<A HREF="http://www.site.edu/slimy/toads.html#poison">Poisonous </A>
```

where

```
http://www.site.edu/slimy/toads.html
```

is the URL for this document. Clicking on the word "Poisonous" will then link you to the document *toads.html* and to the particular location indicated by the `<A NAME="poison">...</A>` anchor.

REL="*string*" (optional) The **REL** attribute gives the relationship(s) described by the hypertext link; consequently, **REL** cannot be used unless an **HREF** is present. The relationship is defined between the two entire documents and is not just related to the particular link. As an example, **REL** could indicate that the linked document is an index for the current one, or is an annotation to the current one (which a browser might want to display as a pop-up). It is a pity that the **REL** (and **REV,** which is the converse of **REL**) attribute is so little used, as it can impart significant meaning and organization to large sets of related documents.

The value for **REL** is a space-separated list of case-insensitive relationship values (our old friend, the name token). An example is:

```
<A HREF="http://foo.edu/fe.html" REL="next">sdfsddf</a>
```

This would mean that the document *fe.html,* at the given URL, is the next document in some author-defined document sequence. Values for the relationships and their semantics are currently being defined: the current status is summarized in Appendix F. Some other examples are:

```
<A HREF="http://foo.edu/note1.html" REL="annotation">related notes </a>
```

The information in the document *note1.html* is additional and subsidiary to the current document. A browser might display this as margin notes.

```
<A HREF="http://foo.edu/vers2.html" REL="supersedes">previously </a>
```

The document *vers2.html* is an earlier version of the document.

At present, the **REL** and **REV** attributes are rarely used, and most browsers do not understand them. They will be of growing importance as HTML documents and document development environments become more sophisticated. For additional information on **REL** and **REV,** please see Appendix F.

REV="*string*" (optional) **REV** is like **REL** but with the relationship reversed. For example,

```
<A HREF="http://foo.edu/vers2.html" REV="supersedes"> later </a>
```

means that the document *vers2.html* is a later version of the document containing this link. Most browsers do not understand **REV** or **REL**.

URN="*URN*" (optional) **URN** is intended to specify *Universal Resource Name* for the linked document. URNs are designed to be universal document references that do not depend on server specification, as do URLs. Unfortunately, the specification for URNs is still under discussion, so this attribute is not functional.

TITLE="string" (optional) The **TITLE** attribute gives the **TITLE** of the linked document, and can be used by the browser to *preview* the title before contacting the server for the actual document. Note that you cannot guarantee that the **TITLE** is correct until you actually access the linked document. Alternatively, **TITLE** can be used to give a title to a document that would otherwise not have a title, such as a plain text file, an image file, a directory accessed via FTP, or a Gopher menu. Most browsers do not understand the **TITLE** attribute.

METHODS="*method***"** (optional) The **METHODS** attribute specifies a space-separated list of HTTP *methods* supported by the target of the hypertext link. HTTP methods specify the way a resource is accessed, and are discussed in Chapter 7.

The **METHODS** attribute is only a hint to the browser, as the actual methods that can be used can only be determined after communicating with the HTTP server. The intent is to give the browser a hint of what the link will do so that it can, for example, render the link anchor differently (perhaps using a different font, or applying a special icon) to represent the different methods.

Most browsers do not understand the **METHODS** attribute.

TARGET="*window-name***"** (optional, Netscape Navigator 2.0 only) Version 2.0 of the Netscape Navigator 2.0 browser supports targeted links—which let a document author direct data returned, upon selecting a hypertext link, to a particular *named* browser window. Recall that Netscape Navigator, like other browsers, can produce multiple copies of itself, each copy capable of displaying a different document. With Netscape Navigator, *named* copies of Netscape can be produced using the **TARGET** attribute to the **A** (anchor) element. For example:

```
<A HREF="/path/file.html" TARGET="window2">anchor text</A>
```

indicates that the document returned, upon accessing this anchor, should be directed to the window named "window2." If a window (or window frame—see below) with this name does not yet exist, the browser will clone a new copy of the browser, assign the name "window2" to this new window, and will direct the returned data to it.

In the absence of a specified target, the document is retrieved to the window from which the link was accessed, as per standard practice.

TARGETs are most often *named frames* or panes within a given browser window: Netscape Navigator 2.0 supports the new **FRAMESET** and **FRAME** elements, which permit multiple, independent document viewing panes within the same browser window. If a frame is declared via <FRAME SRC="url" NAME="frame1">, then an anchor of the form:

```
<A HREF="/Path/file.html" TARGET="frame1"anchor text</A>
```

will direct the returned document to the designated **FRAME. FRAME**s are discussed a bit later, in the section on Netscape-specific HTML extensions.

Several target names are predefined by the Netscape Navigator 2.0 browser, and are reserved for special use. These names (all beginning with the underscore character) and the associated meanings are:

TARGET="_blank"	Load the referenced data into a new, unnamed window.
TARGET="_self"	Load the referenced data in place of the current document (load on top of yourself).
TARGET="_parent"	Load the referenced data into the window containing (or, that contained) the *parent* of the current document (the document from which the current document was accessed). If there is no parent document, default to **TARGET="_self"**.
TARGET="_top"	Load the referenced data into the window containing (or, that contained) the "top" document (the document obtained by iteratively searching through successive parent documents until arriving at the initial, starting document). If there is no top document, default to **TARGET="_self"**.

All other names beginning with an underscore (_) will be ignored by the browser.

CHARACTER-RELATED ELEMENTS

The following elements are empty, and are treated much like characters. These elements lie at the bottom of the HTML element hierarchy.

IMG ELEMENT: INLINE IMAGES

Usage:	<IMG>
Can Contain:	empty
Can Be Inside:	**character highlighting,****A, Hn, P,****ADDRESS, DD, DT, LI**

Attributes: **ALIGN, ALT, ISMAP, SRC**
(*HEIGHT, UNITS, WIDTH*: proposed HTML 3)

(<u>**BORDER**</u>, <u>**VSPACE**</u>, <u>**HSPACE**</u>, <u>**LOWSRC**</u>: Netscape only)

(<u>**USEMAP**</u>: Netscape Navigator 2.0 and above only),

(<u>**CONTROLS**</u>, <u>**DYNSRC**</u>, <u>**LOOP**</u>, <u>**LOOPDELAY**</u>, <u>**START**</u>: Internet Explorer 2.0 only)

The **IMG** element includes an image file *inline* with the document text, the image being specified by the **SRC** attribute.

There are currently four common image formats used for *inline* images. These are: GIF format (with the filename suffix *.gif*); X-Bitmaps (with the filename suffix *.xbm*); X-Pixelmaps (with the filename suffix *.xpm*), and JPEG format (filename suffix *.jpeg* or *.jpg*). Unfortunately, not all browsers understand all formats. The only format universally understood by all browsers is GIF; there-fore, if you want to make your documents universally usable you should con-vert your *inline* images to the GIF format.

To a large extent, images within a document are treated like words or characters. You can place an image almost anywhere you have regular text, except within the **PRE** (preformatted text) element, which should not contain **IMG** elements.

In HTML 3, images can "float" on the page, allowing text to flow around the images. This is facilitated with special **ALIGN** attribute options, discussed below.

The **IMG** element can take four main attributes. **SRC** is mandatory and speci-fies the URL of the image file to be included. **ALIGN** specifies the alignment of the image with the surrounding text, while **ALT** gives an alternative text string for browsers that cannot display images. Finally, **ISMAP** indicates that the image is an *active image* (imagemap). Some other Netscape-specific and HTML 3 attributes are also currently implemented on several browsers, and these are also discussed below.

The Netscape Navigator and Microsoft Internet Explorer browsers support several extra attributes to control image alignment (**VSPACE** and **HSPACE**), the use of client-side imagemaps (**USEMAP**), and to allow the insertion of inline Microsoft AVI-format video files or VRML scenes (**CONTROLS, DYN-SRC, LOOP, LOOPDELAY,** and **START**). These attributes are discussed at the end of this section.

The HTML 2.0 attributes for **IMG** are:

SRC="*URL*" (mandatory) **SRC** gives the URL of the image file to be included inline.

ALT="*text alternative*" (optional) **ALT** gives a text alternative to the image for use by text-only browsers. This should always be included, to let users with text-only browsers know what they are missing, or to let graphical browsers preview the image using this text description. If the image is purely decorative and warrants no description, you can always enter a null string using the form **ALT=**"".

ISMAP (optional) This attribute marks the image as an *active* image; when the user clicks the mouse over the image, the coordinates of the mouse pointer are sent back to the server. The **ISMAP**-activated **IMG** element must, consequently, be enclosed within an anchor element, specifying the URL to which the data should be sent. Typical markup for an active image is:

```
<A HREF="http://www.utirc.ca/cgi-bin/imagemap/map_bozo">

    <IMG SRC="bozo.gif" ISMAP>

</A>
```

where *imagemap* is a server-side gateway program that can interpret the map coordinates. When the user clicks on the image, the browser uses the HTTP GET method to access the URL, indicated by the anchor element, and appends the coordinates of the mouse click (relative to the upper left-hand corner of the image) to the accessed URL. The details of this procedure are discussed in Chapter 10.

ALIGN="bottom", "middle", "top" (optional)

("left", "right": proposed HTML 3)

("texttop", "absmiddle", "baseline", "absbottom": Netscape only) **ALIGN** specifies the alignment of the image with the neighboring text. "Bottom" aligns the bottom of the image with the baseline of the surrounding text—this is the default. "Middle" aligns the middle of the image with the baseline of the text, and "top" aligns the top of the image with the top of the largest item in a line (including other images). Note that, in general, text does not wrap around an image aligned using the "top", "middle", or "bottom" attribute values, so that images within a sentence can create big gaps between adjacent lines.

HTML 3 allows for text flow around images. This is implemented using two additional values to control image placement with respect to the text. **ALIGN=**"left" floats the image over to the left margin, and allows subsequent text to wrap around the right side of the image. **ALIGN=**"right" floats the image to the right side of the window, and allows subsequent text to wrap around the left side of the image. These attribute values are understood by emacs-w3, Arena, and Netscape browsers. Browsers that do not understand these values assume the **ALIGN**="bottom" default. Figures 4.20 and 4.21 illustrate the use of the standard HTML 2.0 values, as well as **ALIGN**="left".

The Netscape browser supports additional align values. These are ignored by other browsers, which assume the **ALIGN**="bottom" default. **ALIGN**="texttop" aligns the top of the image with the top of the surrounding text. **ALIGN**="absmiddle" aligns the middle of the image with the middle of the line of text, while **ALIGN**="baseline" aligns the bottom of the image with the baseline of the line of text (this is the same as **ALIGN**="bottom"). **ALIGN**="absbottom" aligns the bottom of the image with the bottom of the line (which may include other images, and not just text).

HEIGHT="*n*" (optional) (HTML 3) **HEIGHT** specifies the actual height, *n*, of the image to be displayed, in integer units. The units are specified by the **UNITS** attribute, the default being pixels. The **HEIGHT** and **WIDTH** attributes allow the browser to format the text before actually loading the image. Browsers will scale the image to fit this box if the image is actually a different size. **HEIGHT** and **WIDTH** are understood by the Netscape, emacs-w3, and Arena browsers.

UNITS="*pixels*", "*en*" (optional) (HTML 3) **UNITS** specifies the units for the **WIDTH** and **HEIGHT** attributes. The default is **UNITS**="*pixels.*" The only other allowed value is **UNITS**="*en*" (one-half the point size of the text). The Netscape browser does not understand the **UNITS** attribute, and assumes that all **HEIGHT** and **WIDTH** specifications are in pixels.

WIDTH="*n*" (optional) (HTML 3) **WIDTH** specifies the actual height, *n*, of the image to be displayed, in integer units. The units are specified by the **UNITS** attribute, the default being pixels. The **HEIGHT** and **WIDTH** attributes allow the browser to format the text before actually loading the image. Browsers will scale the image to fit this box if the image is actually a different size. **HEIGHT** and **WIDTH** are understood by the Netscape, emacs-w3, and Arena browsers.

The Netscape browser supports five additional attributes that are not part of the HTML 3 specification. These are:

BORDER="*n*" (optional) (Netscape only) **BORDER** specifies the border width, in pixels, around images that are marked as hypertext anchors (recall that images are generally surrounded by a colored border, if they are inside an anchor). Setting **BORDER**=0 implies no border around the image.

BORDER=0 allows you to create clickable imagemaps that do not have a surrounding border.

HSPACE="*n*" (optional) (Netscape only) **HSPACE** is used by floating images, and specifies, in pixels, the horizontal space to be left between the image and the surrounding text.

VSPACE="*n*" (optional) (Netscape only) **VSPACE** is used by floating images, and specifies, in pixels, the vertical space to be left between the image and the surrounding text (above or below).

LOWSRC="*URL*" (optional) (Netscape only) This is used to specify a small low-resolution file of the inline image. Netscape will preload this small image and then replace it with the high-resolution copy (specified by **SRC**).

USEMAP="URL" (optional) (Navigator 2.0 and Internet Explorer 2.0 only) The Netscape Navigator Version 2.0 and Internet Explorer Version 2.0 browsers support client-side imagemaps, whereby a document can contain, within the new **MAP** element (discussed a bit later), imagemap coordinate data. This lets a browser itself determine which link to access when a user clicks the mouse over an active image, as opposed to the traditional (**ISMAP**) method of sending the click coordinates to a server gateway program for subsequent processing. An **IMG** element can reference a particular **MAP** element via the **USEMAP** attribute, which takes, as its value, either a fragment identifier (the **MAP** is in the same file as the **IMG** element) or a full URL plus a fragment identifier (the **MAP** is in a separate document). Each **MAP** element must consequently be identified by an appropriate **NAME** attribute value.

A developer can specify both **USEMAP** and **ISMAP** in the same **IMG** element, with **USEMAP** having precedence. Thus, if a browser understands **USEMAP**, it will use the local **MAP**; if the browser does not understand **USEMAP**, it will access the standard server-side imagemap program referenced by the surrounding hypertext anchor. For example:

```
<A HREF="/cgi-bin/imagmep/mapfile1"><IMG SRC="image.gif"

     USEMAP="#MAP1" ISMAP></A>

<MAP NAME="map1">

<AREA SHAPE="rect" COORD="10,20,50,50" HREF="stuff.html">

<AREA SHAPE="rect" COORD="30,40,60,60" HREF="otherstuff.html">

. . .

</MAP>
```

If the browser interpreting this document understands **USEMAP**, it will use the local map `<MAP NAME="map">` when the user clicks on the active image. If the browser does not understand **USEMAP**, it will revert to **ISMAP**, and will send the click coordinates to the referenced server-side program, as per standard practice.

The Microsoft Internet Explorer supports the following additional attributes:

DYNSRC="*URL*" (optional) (Internet Explorer 2.0 only) **DYNSRC** specifies the URL of an AVI-format video clip, or a VRML world description file to be included inline with the document. The attributes **CONTROLS, LOOP, LOOPDELAY,** and **START** are used to control the behavior of the video clip or VRML scene. Both **DYNSRC** and **SRC** can be specified in the same IMG clement, so that **DYNSRC**-incapable browsers can display a regular image file.

CONTROLS (optional) (Internet Explorer 2.0 only) The **CONTROLS** attribute (which takes no value) indicates that a set of video or VRML controls should be displayed along with the inline viewer. If **CONTROLS** is absent, then the controls are not displayed.

START="fileopen", "mouseover" (optional) (Internet Explorer 2.0 only) **START** indicates when a video clip should begin playing: **START=**"fileopen" implies as soon as the video file is downloaded, while **START=**"mouseover" implies that the movie should start playing as soon as the mouse button is moved over the inline viewer. Both can be specified, separated by commas—for example, **START=**"fileopen,mouseover" will invoke both behaviors.

LOOP="*n*", "infinite" (optional) (Internet Explorer 2.0 only) **LOOP** specifies how many times the video clip should be looped before stopping. **LOOP=**"–1 " or **LOOP=**"infinite" means that the loop will play indefinitely. The default value is 1.

LOOPDELAY="*n*" (optional) (Internet Explorer 2.0 only) **LOOPDELAY** specifies the delay, in milliseconds, between subsequent replays of the video clip. The default value is 0.

MAP ELEMENT: CLIENT-SIDE IMAGEMAP DATABASE

Usage:	`<MAP> . . . </MAP>`
Can Contain:	**AREA**
Can Be Inside:	Undefined; probably any block-text element within the **BODY**.
Attributes:	**NAME** (mandatory)

A **MAP** element contains client-side imagemap mapping data. Each **MAP** must be uniquely identified using a **NAME** attribute: for example, `<MAP NAME="map1">`. Such a map is referenced from an **IMG** element using the **USEMAP** attribute, for example:

```
<IMG SRC="image.gif" . . . . USEMAP="#map1">
```

A single document can contain any number of **MAP** elements, each uniquely identified by a **NAME**. A **MAP** need not be in the same document as the **IMG** from which it is referenced, so that the previous reference might also be written:

```
<IMG SRC="image.gif" . . . . USEMAP="http://some.where.edu/maps/maps.html#map1">
```

where the file *maps.html* contains **MAP** elements used in several different documents.

A **MAP** element must contain **AREA** elements—these are the only elements allowed within a **MAP**. **AREA** elements mark out the regions of an image and the URLs to which these regions are linked. For example:

```
<MAP NAME="map1">

.<AREA SHAPE="rect" COORD="10,20,50,50" HREF="stuff.html">

<AREA SHAPE="rect" COORD="30,40,60,60" HREF="otherstuff.html">

. . . .

</MAP>
```

SHAPE and coordinate specifications are discussed in the next section.

AREA ELEMENT:
CLIENT-SIDE IMAGEMAP MAPPING AREAS

Usage:	`<AREA>`
Can Contain:	empty
Can Be Inside:	**MAP**
Attributes:	**COORDS, HREF, NOHREF, SHAPE**

The **AREA** element specifies shaped regions in a mapped image and the URLs associated with the shape. The meanings and uses of the four attributes are:

SHAPE="rect" **SHAPE** indicates the type of shape being specified in the **AREA** element—the only currently supported shape is "rect", for rectangle. If **SHAPE** is not specified, a browser assumes the default SHAPE="rect".

COORDS="*xl,yl,x2,y2.......*" (mandatory) **COORDS** specifies the comma-separated coordinates of the defined **SHAPE**, as a sequence of (*x,y*) pairs—the required number of pairs depends on the specified **SHAPE**. Coordinates are specified in pixels measured from the upper left-hand corner of the image. With SHAPE="rect" the specified coordinates are the upper left-hand corner (*x1,y1*) followed by the lower right-hand corner (*x2,y2*).

It is possible for different **AREA**s to overlap—in this case, the browser searches sequentially through the **AREA** elements of the given **MAP**, and selects the first acceptable entry.

NOHREF If present, **NOHREF** indicates that the browser should take no action if the user clicks inside the specified region, and should continue to display the current document. This is the default behavior for regions of the image that are not mapped by any **AREA** element.

HREF="*URL*" **HREF** specifies the URL to which the region is linked. Note that partial URLs are evaluated relative to the URL of the **MAP** file—recall that the **MAP** need not be in the same document as the **IMG** element referencing the **MAP**. Similarly, if the document containing the **MAP** element

Figure 4.20 HTML example document illustrating the **IMG** inline image element. Figure 4.21 shows this document as displayed by the Netscape Navigator 1.1 browser.

```
<html>


<head>

<title> Example of IMG Element </title>

</head>


<body>


<h1> Example 10: Examples of IMG Elements</h1>
```

```
<P> <IMG SRC="icon-help.gif" ALT="[Test image]" ALIGN=TOP>
Here is some text related to the test image.   The text is aligned with
the top of the image. Note that the text does not flow around the image.


<P> <IMG SRC="icon-help.gif" ALT="[Test image]" ALIGN=MIDDLE>
Here is some text related to the test image.   The text is aligned with
the middle of the image. Note that the text does not flow around the image.


<P> <A HREF="http://www.bozo.edu/test.html">
<IMG SRC="icon-help.gif" ALT="[Test image]"
ALIGN=BOTTOM> Here is some text </A>  related
to the test image.   The text is aligned with the bottom of
the image, and is also part of the <em> hypertext link.</em>


<P>  Here is an HTML 3
<IMG SRC="icon-help.gif" ALT="" ALIGN="left">
left-aligned image. Note how the text flows around this image, unlike the
top, middle and bottom aligned images shown above. The element
<CODE>&lt;BR CLEAR="left"></CODE> (here's one...)
<BR CLEAR="left">
(....there it was) creates a line break that clears the text to
follow the left-flushed image.
</body>
</html>
```

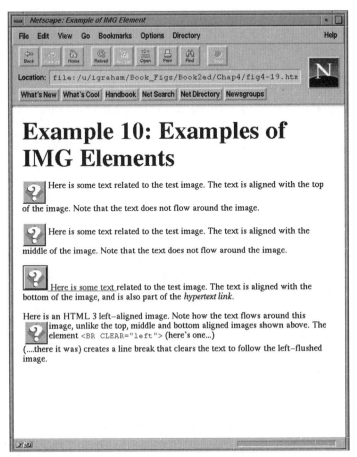

Figure 4.21 Display, by the Netscape Navigator 1.1 browser, of the document shown in Figure 4.20.

also contains a **BASE** element, relative URLs specified by the **HREF** will be evaluated relative to the base URL.

BR ELEMENT: LINE BREAK

Usage:	
Can Contain:	empty
Can Be Inside:	**A, character highlighting, ADDRESS, Hn, P, DD, DT, LI**
Attributes:	(*CLEAR*: proposed HTML 3)

BR indicates a line break. This is fundamentally different from a paragraph mark. A `<BR>` is treated as a character (like a *hard* carriage return), whereas **P** defines a block of text as a paragraph element. `<BR>` is commonly used in the **ADDRESS** element; an example of this usage is shown in Figure 4.7. **BR** can also break lines in a poem, with **P** elements marking the different verses.

HTML 3 proposes the attribute **CLEAR** to the **BR** element. **CLEAR** is useful when text is flowed around an image or figure. In this case, it is not clear if **BR** should break the line and return to the next text line that runs alongside the image, or the next line that flushes with the left or right margin. The **CLEAR** attribute allows the author to make this specification. The possible values are:

CLEAR="left", "right", "all" (optional) (proposed HTML 3) `<BR CLEAR= left>` breaks the line and moves the text, after the **BR**, down until the text can be flushed with the left margin. `<BR CLEAR=right>` breaks the line and moves the text, after the **BR**, down until the right margin is clear. `<BR CLEAR=all>` breaks the line and moves the text, after the **BR**, down until both margins are clear.

The **CLEAR** attribute is understood by the Netscape, Arena, and emacs-w3 browsers. An example is given in Figures 4.20 and 4.21.

CHARACTER HIGHLIGHTING/ PHRASE MARKUP ELEMENTS

HTML has elements that allow you to associate special logical meanings, or physical formatting styles, with a phrase or a string of characters. These elements do not cause page breaks, or in any way affect the structural layout of the document. Their purpose is to assign special meanings to the enclosed text, or to request special physical formatting, such as boldface or italics.

These two methods can be described as logical highlighting (also called information-type formatting or idiomatic phrase markup), and physical highlighting (also called character or typographic formatting). Logical highlighting is more in keeping with the markup language model. That is, you can use logical highlighting to mark a block of text as a piece of typed computer code, a variable, or something to be emphasized. The rendering details are then left to the browser, although hints as to appropriate renderings are part of the HTML specifications. You are strongly encouraged to use logical highlighting elements as opposed to physical ones.

Physical highlighting requests a specific physical format, such as boldface or italics. This, of course, gives no clue to the underlying meaning behind the marked-up phrase. Thus, if a browser is unable to implement the indicated markup (e.g., a dumb terminal cannot do italics), it cannot easily determine an alternative logical highlighting style.

Logical styles may not be distinct (i.e., different logical styles may be rendered in the same way). Also, some browsers do not support all physical styles. For example, lynx does not support italics, and renders it as underlined.

LOGICAL CHARACTER HIGHLIGHTING/FORMATTING

Here are the different logical highlighting elements, and typical renderings:

CITE	A citation (usually italics)
CODE	Example of typed code (usually fixed-width font)
EM	Emphasis (usually italics)
KBD	Keyboard input (for example, in a manual)
SAMP	A sequence of literal characters
STRONG	Strong emphasis (usually boldface)
VAR	A variable name

HTML 3 proposes several additional text highlighting elements. These are discussed in the next chapter.

You can nest highlighting modes inside one another. However, this is often not sensible, given the rather specific meanings assigned to the elements. Also, different browsers interpret these nestings in different ways, so that the presentation can be unpredictable.

Examples of the different highlighting elements are shown in Figures 4.22 and 4.23.

■■■■■■ **Figure 4.22** HTML example document illustrating the different text highlighting elements. Figure 4.23 shows this document as displayed by the Netscape Navigator 1.1 browser.

```
<html>



<head>

<title> Example of Highlighting Markup elements </title>

</head>
```

```
<body>


<h1> Example 11 - Highlighting Elements </h1>
<h2> Examples of Logical Highlighting </h2>


<ul>
<li> CITE - This is <CITE> citation </CITE>text
<li> CODE - This is <CODE> typed computer code </CODE>text.
<li> DFN - This is <DFN> a defining instance </DFN>text. (Proposed HTML 3)
<li> EM - This is <EM> emphasized </EM>text.
<li> KBD - This is <KBD> keyboard input </KBD>text.
<li> SAMP - This is <SAMP> literal character </SAMP>text.
<li> STRIKE - This is <STRIKE> strike-out</STRIKE> text. (Proposed HTML 3)
<li> STRONG - This is <STRONG> strongly emphasized </STRONG>text.
<li> VAR - This is <VAR> a variable </VAR>text.
</ul>


<h2> Examples of Character Highlighting </h2>


<ul>
<li> B - This is <B> boldfaced </B>text.
<li> I - This is <I> italicized </I>text.
<li> TT - This is <TT> fixed-width typewriter font </TT>text.
<li> U - This is <U> underlined </U>text. (Proposed HTML 3)
</ul>


</body>
</html>
```

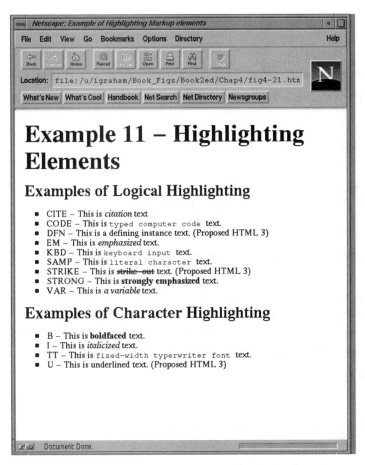

Figure 4.23 Display, by the Netscape Navigator 1.1 browser, of the document shown in Figure 4.22.

CITE ELEMENT: CITATION

Usage:	`<CITE> . . . </CITE>`
Can Contain:	**characters, character highlighting, A, BR, IMG**
Can Be Inside:	**A, character highlighting, ADDRESS, Hn, P, PRE, DD, DT, LI**
Attributes:	none

The **CITE** element marks a small citation—for example, a book or other document reference. Typically, this block of text will be rendered in italics, subject to the capabilities of the browser.

CODE ELEMENT: TYPED CODE

Usage:	`<CODE> . . . </CODE>`
Can Contain:	**characters, character highlighting, A, BR, IMG**
Can Be Inside:	**A, character highlighting, ADDRESS, Hn, P, PRE, DD, DT, LI**
Attributes:	none

The **CODE** element marks a selection of typed computer code—for example, a single line of code from a program. Large selections of code should be displayed using a **PRE** element, which properly reproduces space characters and line breaks. **CODE** element contents should be rendered in a fixed-width typewriter font.

EM ELEMENT: EMPHASIS

Usage:	`<EM> . . . </EM>`
Can Contain:	**characters, character highlighting, A, BR, IMG**
Can Be Inside:	**A, character highlighting, ADDRESS, Hn, P, PRE, DD, DT, LI**
Attributes:	none

The **EM** element marks a block of text for emphasis. Typically, the marked block of text is rendered in italics, subject to the capabilities of the browser. For example, lynx represents **EM** emphasized text by an underline.

KBD ELEMENT: KEYBOARD INPUT

Usage:	`<KBD> . . . </KBD>`
Can Contain:	**characters, character highlighting, A, BR, IMG**

Can Be Inside:	**A, character highlighting, ADDRESS, Hn, P, PRE, DD, DT, LI**
Attributes:	none

The **KBD** element marks a block of text as keyboard input. Typically, this is displayed with a fixed-width typewriter font.

SAMP ELEMENT: LITERAL CHARACTERS

Usage:	<SAMP> . . . </SAMP>
Can Contain:	**characters, character highlighting, A, BR, IMG**
Can Be Inside:	**A, character highlighting, ADDRESS, Hn, P, PRE, DD, DT, LI**
Attributes:	none

The **SAMP** element marks a block of text as a sequence of literal or *sample* characters. Typically, this is rendered in a fixed-width typewriter font.

STRONG ELEMENT: STRONG EMPHASIS

Usage:	<STRONG> . . . </STRONG>
Can Contain:	**characters, character highlighting, A, BR, IMG**
Can Be Inside:	**A, character highlighting, ADDRESS, Hn, P, PRE, DD, DT, LI**
Attributes:	none

The **STRONG** element marks a block of text for strong emphasis. Typically, this is rendered in boldface, although text-only browsers, such as lynx, use an underline (with lynx, **EM** and **STRONG** emphasis are displayed in the same way).

VAR Element: A Variable

Usage:	`<VAR>` . . . `</VAR>`
Can Contain:	**characters, character highlighting, A, BR, IMG**
Can Be Inside:	**A, character highlighting, ADDRESS, Hn, P, PRE, DD, DT, LI**
Attributes:	none

The **VAR** element marks a variable name. This is typically rendered in italics or bold italics.

PHYSICAL CHARACTER HIGHLIGHTING/FORMATTING

Physical highlighting elements request physically desired renderings. Physical styles are often useful when translating from another document to HTML, where the only information available may be physical markup instructions. Use logical highlighting in new documents whenever possible.

Physical highlighting elements can be nested, and these nestings often make sense (as they do not with most logical highlighting elements). Therefore, requesting that a block of text be rendered in underlined-boldface-italics is entirely reasonable. However, be aware that some browsers presently mishandle these nestings, and render them in unexpected ways—for example, rendering `<B><I>text</I></B>` in boldface, and not bold-italics.

The physical style elements, and their renderings, are:

B	Boldface (where possible)
I	Italics (may be rendered as slanted in some cases)
TT	Fixed-width typewriter font
U	Underlined (proposed: HTML 3)

Examples of the renderings of these styles are shown in Figure 4.23.

HTML 3 proposes several additional physical highlighting elements, some of which are discussed later in this chapter.

B Element: Boldface

Usage:	`<B>` . . . `</B>`

Can Contain:	**characters, character highlighting, A, BR, IMG**
Can Be Inside:	**A, character highlighting, ADDRESS, Hn, P, PRE, DD, DT, LI**
Attributes:	none

The **B** element marks a text block to be rendered in boldface. If this is impossible, the browser can render this in some other way (lynx uses an underline).

I ELEMENT: ITALICS

Usage:	`<I> . . . </I>`
Can Contain:	**characters, character highlighting, A, BR, IMG**
Can Be Inside:	**A, character highlighting, ADDRESS, Hn, P, PRE, DD, DT, LI**
Attributes:	none

The **I** element marks a text block to be rendered in italics. If this is impossible, the browser can render it in some other way (lynx uses an underline).

TT ELEMENT: FIXED-WIDTH TYPEWRITER FONT

Usage:	`<TT> . . . </TT>`
Can Contain:	**characters, character highlighting, A, BR, IMG**
Can Be Inside:	**A, character highlighting, ADDRESS, Hn, P, PRE, DD, DT, LI**
Attributes:	none

The **TT** element marks a text block to be rendered with a fixed-width typewriter font.

U ELEMENT: UNDERLINE (PROPOSED: HTML 3)

Usage:	`<U> . . . </U>`
Can Contain:	**characters, character highlighting, A, BR, IMG**

Can Be Inside:	**A, character highlighting,** **ADDRESS, Hn, P, PRE, DD, DT, LI**
Attributes:	none

The U element marks a text block to be rendered with an underline. This element is understood by some, but not all, browsers.

CURRENTLY SUPPORTED HTML 3 ELEMENTS

Three HTML 3 elements are currently finding widespread support by browser developers. The most widely implemented is the **TABLE** element, used for tables and tabular data. Also implemented are four new character highlighting elements: **SUB** and **SUP**, respectively, for text subscripts and superscripts; and **BIG** and **SMALL**, respectively, for bigger and smaller text fonts relative to the surrounding text. **SUB** and **SUP** are currently implemented by Mosaic and by the Netscape Navigator 2.0 browser, while **BIG** and **SMALL** are only implemented by the latter program. Finally, the Netscape Navigator 2.0 browser supports the **DIV** element, used for marking off blocks of a document.

TABLE ELEMENT: TABLE (AN HTML 3 ELEMENT)

Usage:	<TABLE> . . . </TABLE>
Can Contain:	*CAPTION, TR*
Can Be Inside:	Not finalized, probably:
	BLOCKQUOTE, BODY, FORM, DD, LI, *TD, TH*
Attributes:	*BORDER* (<u>CELLPADDING</u>, <u>CELLSPACING</u>, <u>WIDTH</u>: Netscape only)

Elements for defining tables were developed as part of the HTML 3 proposals, and are still undergoing refinement. Because tables are currently implemented in several browsers, they are discussed here, as well as in the next chapter. Several of the finer points of the table specification may change before the specification is finalized. Table elements, based on the following descriptions, are implemented on the Netscape, Arena, emacs-w3, and certain versions of Mosaic. Future specifications of the **TABLE** element should be backwards-compatible with this current implementation.

The **TABLE** element contains tabular data; the structure and content of the table are defined by additional elements that can appear only inside the **TABLE**. The **TABLE** element has several optional attributes. These are:

BORDER (optional) The **BORDER** attribute tells the browser to draw a box around each cell in the table, if possible. This attribute is understood by all browsers now capable of rendering tables. The default behavior is to draw a borderless table.

The Netscape browser allows the **BORDER** attribute to take an integer value specifying the thickness of the borders (the default value is 1). Thus **BORDER=4** specifies a table with a large outside border. This extension is only supported by Netscape.

CELLPADDING="*n*" (optional) (Netscape only) The **CELLPADDING** attribute specifies the space, in pixels, left between the borders of the cell and the cell contents (image or text). The default value is 1. Note that, for presentation purposes, cells containing text are generally rendered with extra whitespace above and below the text, so that a **CELLPADDING** of 0 does not collapse the border to touch both the sides and top of the text.

CELLSPACING="*n*" (optional) (Netscape only) The **CELLSPACING** attribute specifies the horizontal and vertical space, in pixels, left between individual cells in a table (the "thickness" of the dividing lines). The default value is 1.

WIDTH="*n*", or "*n*%" (optional) (Netscape only) **WIDTH** prescribes the desired width of the table, either as a percentage of the width of the display window (0% to 100%) or as an absolute width, *n*, in pixels. Note that fixing a table size may introduce formatting difficulties, should the table not fit easily within the specified size.

A **TABLE** element can contain only two elements. These are:

CAPTION: Gives the caption or title of the table

TR: Table row: Defines a row in a table. The row can contain two different elements, **TH** (table header) and **TD** (table data).

The design of HTML **TABLE**s will be familiar to those who have used the tabular environment in LaTeX. Tables are defined as a collection of *cells*, where a cell is an item (a box) within the table. The content of each cell is specified using the **TD** (table data) and **TH** (table header) elements. Cells are further organized into rows, defined by the element **TR** (table row), where a table row can contain any number of **TD** and **TH** elements. However, the content of the *first* table row defines the number of allowed columns for every other row in the table. Thus, a row containing two **TD** and two **TH** elements means that the table, and every row in the table, must have four columns.

The following is a small table containing four rows of three columns each. This table is shown in Figures 4.24 and 4.25.

```
<TABLE BORDER>
    <TR>  <th> Heading 1 </th>  <th> Heading 2 </th>  <th> Heading 3 </th> </TR>
    <TR>  <td> item 1    </td>  <td> item 2    </td>  <td> item 3   </td> </TR>
    <TR>  <td> item 4    </td>  <td> item 5    </td>  <td> item 6   </td> </TR>
    <TR>  <td> item 7    </td>  <td> item 8    </td>  <td> item 9   </td> </TR>
</TABLE>
```

Note how each row contains three cells, defined either by **TH** header or **TD** data cells. In this example the first row contains the three headings, while subsequent rows contain the data.

Tables are made somewhat more interesting by letting **TH** and **TD** cells occupy more than one row or column. This is accomplished through two special attributes. The **ROWSPAN** attribute specifies how many rows are occupied by the cell, counted to the right of the cell, while the **COLSPAN** attribute specifies how many columns are occupied by the cell, counting downwards. A multicolumn or multirow cell means that the **TR** row definitions for some rows will contain fewer **TD** or **TH** items in the row than you would expect, since some of the cells are occupied by the cell "hanging down" from the row above, or pushing over from the cell to the left. It is the author's responsibility to make sure that all the items in a row sum to the correct number of total columns.

The use of **ROWSPAN** and **COLSPAN** is illustrated in the following example, which is also shown in Figures 4.24 and 4.25.

```
<TABLE BORDER>
<CAPTION>Here is the caption to this exciting table</CAPTION>
<TR>  <th colspan=2> Heading 1                      </th>  <th> Heading 3</th> </TR>
 <TR>  <td rowspan=2> item 1</td>  <td> item 2  </td>  <td> item 3  </td>  </TR>
 <TR>                             <td> item 4  </td>  <td  item 5  </td>  </TR>
 <TR>  <td> item 6              </td>  <td> item 7  </td>  <td> item 8  </td>  </TR>
```

```
<TR>   <td> item 9          </td>  <td rowspan=2 colspan=2>  item 10  </td>   </TR>

<TR>   <td> item 1          </td>                                              </TR>

<TR>   <td colspan=3> a big wide item 11   </td>                               </TR>

</TABLE>
```

The first row indicates that this table has three columns, although the first **TH** cell spans two of these columns, so that there are only two **TH** elements in this row. The second row contains the required three cells, but the **ROWSPAN**=2 attribute, in the first cell, indicates that this cell spans two rows. Consequently, there are only two cells declared in the third row, since the first column is occupied by the cell that started in the preceding row.

The fourth row is a regular row with three single-column and single-row cells. The fifth row, however, contains only two cells; the second of these occupies two rows and two columns. Consequently, the sixth row contains only one cell, as the remaining columns are occupied by the two-column-wide cell hanging down from row 5. Finally, the last row contains a single cell that spans the entire table.

The contents of cells can also be aligned within **TD** and **TH** cells, using the **ALIGN** (horizontal alignment) and **VALIGN** (vertical alignment) attributes. These are discussed in detail later in this section.

Figure 4.24 HTML example document illustrating the **TABLE** elements. Figure 4.25 shows this document as displayed by the Netscape Navigator browser.

```
<html><head>

<title> HTML 3 TABLEs </title>

</head><body>


<h1> Example 12 HTML 3 Tables</h1>

<P> The following two simple examples look at basic HTML 3 tables.

<h2> First Example -- A Simple Table </h2>

<TABLE BORDER>
```

```
<TR>   <th> Heading 1 </th>   <th> Heading 2 </th>   <th> Heading 3 </th>  </TR>

<TR>   <td> item 1    </td>   <td> item 2    </td>   <td> item 3    </td> </TR>

<TR>   <td> item 4    </td>   <td> item 5    </td>   <td> item 6    </td> </TR>

<TR>   <td> item 7    </td>   <td> item 8    </td>   <td> item 9    </td> </TR>

</TABLE>



<h2>Second Example with COLSPAN and ROWSPAN </h2>

<TABLE BORDER>

<CAPTION>Here is the caption to this exciting table</CAPTION>

<TR>   <th colspan=2> Heading 1                     </th>   <th> Heading 3</th> </TR>

<TR>   <td rowspan=2> item 1</td>   <td> item 2   </td>   <td> item 3   </td> </TR>

<TR>                               <td> item 4   </td>   <td> item 5   </td> </TR>

<TR>   <td> item 6      </td>   <td> item 7   </td>   <td> item 8   </td> </TR>

<TR>   <td> item 9      </td>   <td rowspan=2 colspan=2> item 10   </td> </TR>

<TR>   <td> item 1      </td>                                          </TR>

<TR>   <td colspan=3> a big wide item 11   </td>                      </TR>

</TABLE>



</body></html>
```

The last examples are shown in Figures 4.26 and 4.27. These show some convenient uses of tables, such as for boxing images and text, and creating dou-
ble-column text. Although the latter looks quite nice here, just imagine how it
would look with a larger font size or a smaller display window!

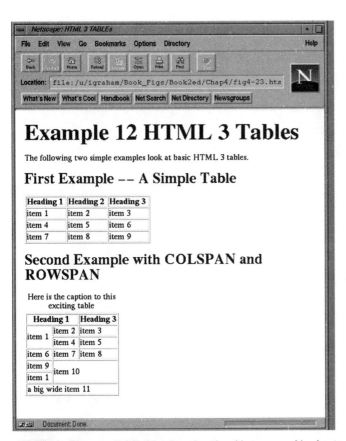

Figure 4.25 Display, by the Netscape Navigator 1.1 browser, of the document shown in Figure 4.24.

Figure 4.26 A second HTML example document illustrating the **TABLE** elements. Figure 4.27 shows this document as displayed by the Netscape Navigator browser.

```
<html><head>
<title> HTML 3 TABLEs (part 2)</title>
</head><body>


<h1> Example 13 HTML 3 Tables</h1>
<P> These examples illustrate some other uses of tables: to organize text,
    or to organize images.
<h2> First Example -- Images in Tables</h2>
<table border=5 cellspacing=5 cellpadding=10>
<tr> <td>
```

```
<IMG SRC="./logo.gif" ALT="[Information Commons Logo]" ><br>
<td>
<H2 align="center">The Information Commons <br><em>at the</em>
<br>University of Toronto </H2>
</tr>
</table>
<h2>Second Example: Text in two columns.</h2>
<table>
<tr>
<td>
<p> Here is the first column of text. This could go on, and on, and on
and on, and on, and on, which is to say that I have completely lost any
any sense of what to type for these examples. Oh, I know --
how about throwing in a list:
<UL>
<li> here's a nice item
<li>and here's another
</UL>
<P> But that's enough, now for the second column.
<td>
<P> Here we go with the second column. This column sits nicely next to
the other one, and is separated by the invisible cell border. Cells can
contain all sorts of markup elements, so you can create very sophisticated
things inside these cells, such as:
<h3>Heading</h3>
<P> If a browser does not understand tables, then this will be presented as
a single page of single-column text: this is one example where things will
still be readable, even if the browser does not understand tables.
</tr>
</table>
</body>
</html>
```

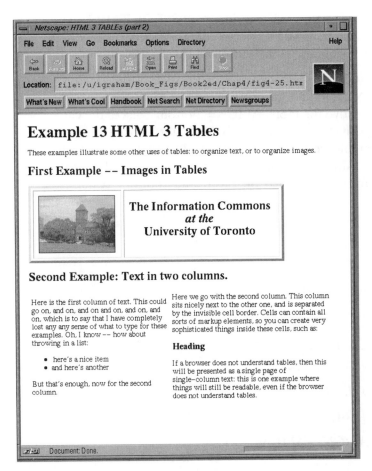

Figure 4.27 Display, by the Netscape Navigator 1.1 browser, of the document shown in Figure 4.26.

CAPTION ELEMENT: TABLE CAPTION

Usage:	`<CAPTION> . . . </CAPTION>`
Can Contain:	**characters, character highlighting, A, BR, IMG, (WBR, NOBR, FONT:** Netscape only)
Can Be Inside:	*TABLE*
Attributes:	*ALIGN* (proposed HTML 3)

The **CAPTION** element specifies the table caption or title. Each **TABLE** can have at most one **CAPTION**. The **CAPTION** can contain text, character high-lighting elements, and **IMG** elements, along with hypertext anchors.

The optional HTML 3 **ALIGN** attribute specifies the location of the caption relative to the table. **ALIGN** can take four possible values: **ALIGN**="top" (the default) places the caption above the table, **ALIGN**="bottom" places the cap-tion below the table, and **ALIGN**="left" and **ALIGN**="right" place the caption to the left and right of the table, respectively. Figures 4.24 and 4.25 show an example of a table caption. **ALIGN** is supported by the Netscape and Arena browsers, although Netscape only supports the "top" and "bottom" values.

Example of **CAPTION**:

```
<TABLE BORDER>

<CAPTION> Profits In each Year: 1983-1993 </CAPTION>

<TR> ......

</TABLE>
```

TR ELEMENT: TABLE ROW

Usage:	`<TR>. . .</TR>`
Can Contain:	*TH, TD*
Can Be Inside:	*TABLE*
Attributes:	*ALIGN, VALIGN*

The **TR** element denotes a row of a table. Thus, a row in a table might be coded:

```
<TR>

    <TH> Heading <TD> data 1 <TD> data2 <TD> data3 <TD> data4

</TR>
```

which indicates a row containing five columns, the first column being a table heading, and the rest containing table data. Every row must be terminated by a </TR>, except for the final row, where the final </TR> can be inferred from the </TABLE> tag ending the table.

The **TR** element can take two optional attributes, **ALIGN** and **VALIGN**. These attributes define the horizontal (**ALIGN**) and vertical (**VALIGN**) align-ment of the contents of the cells within the row. These settings can be overridden by alignment attributes specific to a cell. The specific meaning of the attributes are:

ALIGN="left", "right", "center" (optional) **ALIGN** specifies the alignment of the table cell content within every cell in the row. **ALIGN**="left" aligns the content flush left within the cell, **ALIGN**="right" aligns the content flush right within the cell, while **ALIGN**="center" centers the content within the cell.

VALIGN="top", "middle", "bottom", "baseline" (optional) **VALIGN** specifies the vertical alignment of the content within the cell. The values "top", "middle", and "bottom" vertically align the cell content at the top, middle, or bottom of the cell, respectively, while **VALIGN**="baseline" specifies that the baseline of the cell content should be vertically aligned with the baseline of the text in adjacent cells of the same row.

TH ELEMENT: TABLE HEADING

Usage:	`<TH> . . . (</TH>)`
Can Contain:	Not formalized, but probably: **characters, character highlighting, A, IMG, BR,** **ADDRESS, BLOCKQUOTE, FORM, P, PRE, Hn,** *TABLE,* **DIR, MENU, OL, UL**
Can Be Inside:	*TR*
Attributes:	**ALIGN, VALIGN, COLSPAN, ROWSPAN, NOWRAP** (<u>BGCOLOR</u>: Internet Explorer only)

The **TH** element specifies a Table Header cell—the cell that defines the heading of a row or column. The **TH** element is not empty, but the end tag `</TH>` is optional as its existence is implied by the next `<TH>`, `<TR>`, or `<TD>` tag. The **TH** element can be empty, which means that the cell is blank. **TABLE**s can have more than one **TH** for a given row or column. It is up to the table designer to ensure that table headings are placed appropriately. The **TH** element has five optional attributes that define the alignment of the cell contents within the cell (**ALIGN, VALIGN**), how many columns or rows of the entire table are to be spanned by the cell (**COLSPAN, ROWSPAN**), and whether word wrapping is allowed within the cell (**NOWRAP**).

The **TH** element attributes are:

ALIGN="left", "right", "center" (optional) **ALIGN** specifies the alignment of the table cell content within the cell. **ALIGN**="left" aligns the content flush left within the cell, **ALIGN**="right" aligns the content flush right within the cell, while **ALIGN**="center" centers the content within the cell. The **ALIGN** attribute of a **TH** element overrides any **ALIGN** attribute value set in the surrounding **TR** element.

VALIGN="top", "middle", "bottom", "baseline" (optional) **VALIGN** specifies the vertical alignment of the content within the cell. The values "top", "middle", and "bottom" vertically align the cell content at the top, middle, or bottom of the cell respectively, while **VALIGN**="baseline" specifies that the baseline of the cell content should be vertically aligned with the baseline of the text in adjacent cells of the same row. The **VALIGN** attribute of a **TH** element overrides any **VALIGN** attribute value set in the surrounding **TR** element.

ROWSPAN = "*n*" (optional) **ROWSPAN** specifies how many table rows are spanned by the cell—the default value is 1. Counting of rows is downward from the top of the table. It is the author's responsibility to ensure that the cells in each column sum to the correct number of rows.

COLSPAN = "*n*" (optional) **COLSPAN** specifies how many table columns are spanned by the cell—the default value is 1. Counting of columns starts from the left side of the table. It is the author's responsibility to ensure that the cells in each row sum to the correct number of columns.

NOWRAP (optional) **NOWRAP** indicates that text within a cell may not wrap; the browser may not use soft line breaks. You can use **BR** elements to force hard line breaks, where desired. **NOWRAP** should be used with caution, as it can lead to extremely wide cells.

BGCOLOR="*#rrggbb*","color_name" (optional) The Internet Explorer browser supports the **BGCOLOR** attribute, which permits for cell-specific background colors. Colors are specified as hexadecimal-coded RGB triplets, or by using a short list of supported color names. The supported color names are "Black", "Olive", "Teal", "Red", "Blue", "Maroon", "Navy", "Gray", "Lime", "Fuchsia", "White", "Green", "Purple", "Silver", "Yellow", and "Aqua".

Example of **TH** element:

```
<TH ALIGN=LEFT> Housing Prices: </TH>
```

This example specifies a table heading cell that spans one row and one column, and that contains the heading "*Housing Prices:*". **TH** cells need not contain simple text strings. They can also contain other **TABLE**s, lists, images, hypertext anchors, and so on.

TD ELEMENT: TABLE DATA

Usage:	`<TD> . . . (</TD>)`
Can Contain:	Not formalized, probably: **characters, character highlighting, A, IMG, BR, ADDRESS, BLOCKQUOTE, FORM, P, PRE, Hn, *TABLE*, DIR, MENU, OL, UL**
Can Be Inside:	*TR*
Attributes:	*ALIGN, VALIGN, COLSPAN, ROWSPAN, NOWRAP* (**BGCOLOR**: Internet Explorer only)

The **TD** element specifies a table data cell, which is a cell that contains the tabular data. The **TD** element is not empty, but the end tag `</TD>` is optional, as the end of a **TD** element is implied by the next `<TH>`, `<TR>`, or `<TD>` tag. The **TD** element can have empty content, which simply means that the cell is blank. The **TD** element has five optional attributes that define the centering of the contents of the cell (**ALIGN, VALIGN**), how many columns or rows of the entire table are to be spanned by the cell (**ROWSPAN, COLSPAN**), and whether wordwrapping is allowed within the cell (**NOWRAP**). These have the same meanings as defined in the description of the **TH** element.

The **TD** element attributes are:

ALIGN="left", "right", "center" (optional) **ALIGN** specifies the alignment of the table cell content within the cell. **ALIGN**="left" aligns the content flush left within the cell, **ALIGN**="right" aligns the content flush right within the cell, while **ALIGN**="center" centers the content within the cell. The **ALIGN** attribute of a **TD** element overrides any **ALIGN** attribute value set in the surrounding **TR** element.

VALIGN="top", "middle", "bottom", "baseline" (optional) **VALIGN** specifies the vertical alignment of the content within the cell. The values "top", "middle", and "bottom" vertically align the cell content at the top, middle, or bottom of the cell, respectively, while **VALIGN**="baseline" specifies that the baseline of the cell content should be vertically aligned with the baseline of the text in adjacent cells of the same row. The **VALIGN** attribute of a **TD** element overrides any **VALIGN** attribute value set in the surrounding **TR** element.

ROWSPAN="*n*" (optional) **ROWSPAN** specifies how many table rows are spanned by the cell—the default value is 1. Counting of rows is downward from the top of the table. It is the author's responsibility to ensure that the cells in each column sum to the correct number of rows.

COLSPAN="*n*" (optional) **COLSPAN** specifies how many table columns are spanned by the cell—the default value is 1. Counting of columns starts from the left side of the table. It is the author's responsibility to ensure that the cells in each row sum to the correct number of columns.

NOWRAP (optional) **NOWRAP** indicates that text within a cell may not wrap; the browser may not insert line breaks. An author can use **BR** elements to force hard line breaks, where desired. **NOWRAP** should be used with caution, as it can lead to extremely wide cells.

BGCOLOR="*#rrggbb*", "color_name" (optional) The Internet Explorer browser supports the **BGCOLOR** attribute, which permits cell-specific background colors. Colors are specified as hexadecimal-coded RGB triplets, or by using a short list of supported color names. The supported color names are "Black", "Olive", "Teal", "Red", "Blue", "Maroon", "Navy", "Gray", "Lime", "Fuchsia", "White", "Green", "Purple", "Silver", "Yellow", and "Aqua".

Example of **TD** element:

```
<TD center colspan=1 rowspan=2> 23.22 </TD>
```

This example specifies a table data cell that spans one column and two rows, and that contains the data value 23.22. **TD** cells need not contain numbers, or even simple text strings—they can also contain other **TABLE**s, lists, images, hypertext anchors, and so on.

DIV ELEMENT: A BLOCK DIVISION OF THE BODY

Usage:	`<DIV> . . . </DIV>`
Can Contain:	**Hn, P, HR,**
	DL, OL, UL, DIR, MENU,
	ADDRESS, BLOCKQUOTE, *DIV*, FORM, PRE, *TABLE*, [ISINDEX]
Can Be Inside:	**BODY, BLOCKQUOTE, *DIV*, FORM *TD*, TH**
Attributes:	**ALIGN**

DIV marks a block of the document as a logical group or *division*, and is used to specify generic properties for the entire block. For example, `<DIV ALIGN="right">` implies that all the text within the **DIV** element should be right-aligned, unless this alignment specification is overridden by an element within the **DIV**. In principle, **DIV** allows for a formal description of the document content, as discussed in Chapter 5.

DIV implies the end of any preceding paragraph. Other than this, DIV does not affect the formatting or presentation of a document, and is simply used to more formally organize the document content.

DIV can be used within properly written HTML 2.0 documents, since it can be safely ignored. However, be careful that you do not use **DIV** tags to end otherwise unterminated block elements, such as paragraphs.

Example of **DIV**:

```
<BODY>
<DIV ALIGN="left">
<H1>A Left-Aligned Heading</H1>
<P>A left-aligned paragraph. . . .
. . . more paragraph text .  ..
</P>
<DIV ALIGN="right">
   <H2>A right-aligned heading</H2>
   <BLOCKQUOTE>
   <P>A paragraph inside a block quotation--the entire
      quotation is right-aligned.</P>
   </BLOCKQUOTE>
</DIV>
<P>Another left-aligned paragraph. . . .
. . .
   </P>
</DIV>
```

SUB ELEMENT: SUBSCRIPTS

Usage: `<SUB>  .  .  .  </SUB>`

Can Contain:	**characters, character highlighting** (including *SUP, SUB, BIG, SMALL*),
	A, BR, IMG
Can Be Inside:	**A, character highlighting** (including *SUP, SUB, BIG, SMALL*),
	ADDRESS, Hn, P, PRE, DD, DT, LI
Attributes:	none

SUB marks text that should be rendered as a subscript relative to the preceding text. The content of a **SUB** may also be rendered in a smaller font, if possible. This is an unsafe element for browsers that only support HTML 2.0, since subscripted text will be incorrectly presented by a browser that does not understand SUB. Some browsers (e.g., recent versions of Mosaic and Netscape Navigator 2.0) support this element. An example is

```
caCO<SUB>3</SUB>
```

SUP ELEMENT: SUPERSCRIPTS

Usage:	`<SUP> . . . </SUP>`
Can Contain:	**characters, character highlighting** (including *SUP, SUB, BIG, SMALL*),
	A, BR, IMG
Can Be Inside:	**A, character highlighting** (including *SUP, SUB, BIG, SMALL*),
	ADDRESS, Hn, P, PRE, DD, DT, LI
Attributes:	none

SUP marks text that should be rendered as a superscript relative to the preceding text. The content of a **SUP** may also be rendered in a smaller font, if possible. This is an unsafe element for browsers that only support HTML 2.0, since superscripted text will be incorrectly presented by a browser that does not understand **SUP**. Some browsers (e.g., recent versions of Mosaic and Netscape Navigator 2.0) support this element. An example is:

```
X<SUP>2</SUP>
```

BIG ELEMENT: TEXT WITH ENLARGED FONT

Usage:	`<BIG> . . . </BIG>`
Can Contain:	**characters, character highlighting** (including *SUP, SUB, BIG, SMALL*),
	A, BR, IMG
Can Be Inside:	**A, character highlighting** (including *SUP, SUB, BIG, SMALL*),
	ADDRESS, Hn, P, PRE, DD, DT, LI
Attributes:	none

BIG marks text that should be rendered, when possible, with a font slightly larger than the font of the surrounding text. Enclosed images are not affected. **BIG** will be ignored if a larger font is not available. **BIG** is currently only supported by the Netscape Navigator 2.0 browser, where it is essentially equivalent to using the **FONT** element With `<FONT SIZE="+1">`.

SMALL ELEMENT: SUPERSCRIPTS

Usage:	`<SMALL> . . . </SMALL>`
Can Contain:	**characters, character highlighting** (including *SUP, SUB, BIG, SMALL*),
	A, BR, IMG
Can Be Inside:	**A, character highlighting** (including *SUP, SUB, BIG, SMALL*),
	ADDRESS, Hn, P, PRE, DD, DT, LI
Attributes:	none

SMALL marks text that should be rendered, when possible, with a font slightly smaller than the font of the surrounding text. Enclosed images are not affected. **SMALL** will be ignored if a smaller font is not available. **SMALL** is currently only supported by the Netscape Navigator 2.0 browser, where it is essentially equivalent to using the **FONT** element with `<FONT SIZE="-1">`.

NETSCAPE-SPECIFIC HTML EXTENSIONS

In addition to the aforementioned HTML 3 elements, and enhancements to already existing HTML elements, Netscape has implemented several completely new elements. These are currently only recognized by the Netscape Navigator browser, and are unlikely (in most cases) to be integrated into upcoming revisions of "official" HTML. These Netscape extensions are largely designed to give an author greater control over document layout. Thus, browsers that do not understand these elements will often (but not always!) be able to present the document with minor loss of information content.

The new **FRAMESET**, **APPLET**, and **SCRIPT** elements introduced with Netscape Navigator 2.0 are exceptions to this rule. The **FRAMESET** element lets a document designer partition the browser display window into a collection of independent framed panes, each pane containing a distinct HTML document. The **SCRIPT** element lets an author include a script program, written in *LiveScript* (a.k.a. *JavaScript*), within an HTML document, while the **APPLET** element allows inlining of external programs, called applets, into the document. These are exciting features—but unfortunately the markup introduced by these elements is often incompatible with HTML 2.0 and with standard Web browsers. Consequently, if you want your documents to be understood when displayed by other browsers, you must be very careful in the use of these elements.

As a reminder in the usage summaries, the Netscape-only elements are indicated by an underline, while the HTML 3 elements are placed in italics. The Netscape elements **FONT**, **NOBR**, and **BLINK** can be thought of as new-character highlighting elements, while the **WBR** (word break) element can be thought of as a variant of **BR**.

CENTER Element:

Center the Enclosed Text (Netscape Only)

Usage:	`<CENTER> . . . </CENTER>`
Can Contain:	Unspecified, probably: **ADDRESS, BLOCKQUOTE, CENTER, Hn, HR, [ISINDEX], PRE,** *TABLE,* **DL, OL, MENU, DIR, FORM, A, BR, IMG**

Can Be Inside:	BLOCKQUOTE, BODY, *CENTER*, DD, FORM, LI, *TD*, *TH*
Attributes:	none

The **CENTER** element centers any enclosed blocks of text, with the exception of `<IMG ALIGN=left . . . .>` or `<IMG ALIGN=right . . .>` elements, for which the alignment is specified by the image alignment attribute. In particular, the **CENTER** element can be used to center a **TABLE** on the page (which is otherwise not possible). Both the start and stop tags (`<CENTER>` and `</CENTER>`) introduce a line break in the text flow.

Formally **CENTER** should be thought of as a block element, meaning that it can only contain other block elements (**P, PRE**, etc.) and not raw text. However, the Netscape browser is very lenient in this regard, and does allow for raw text inside **CENTER**. This has the advantage of reducing the vertical spacing between the centered text and the blocks of text above and below, which is often a convenient way of improving text formatting. However, you should not assume that **CENTER** will provide a break, since a browser that ignores the tag will neither introduce a break nor center the text.

One useful trick is to use **CENTER** to center-align text placed between two **HR** elements:

```
<hr width=80%>

<center>

   These simple notes form a useful, single document

   explaining the rationale and organization of the Web Document

   template collection. Please print this out for off-line

   reference.

</center>

<hr width=80%>
```

If the browser does not support **CENTER**, the text within **CENTER** will still be broken from any preceding or following text because of the `<HR>` tags.

Figures 4.28 and 4.29 show how this differs from the following example code (which includes a **P** element inside the **CENTER**ed text):

Note how the `<P>` tag introduces extra vertical space between the first HR and the subsequent text. HTML markup, such as in the first example, is useful for marking special notes or cautions. In HTML 3, this is better done using the **NOTE** element, as discussed in the next chapter.

The **CENTER** element will not become part of the official HTML specification. In "official" HTML, formatting issues, such as text alignment, are handled through element attributes (for example, `<P ALIGN=center>`) or through stylesheets, as discussed in the next chapter.

NOBR ELEMENT: NO LINE BREAK (NETSCAPE ONLY)

Usage:	`<NOBR>. . .</NOBR>`
Can Contain:	Unspecified, probably: **characters, character highlighting,** <u>**BASEFONT**</u>, <u>**BLINK**</u>, <u>**FONT**</u>, <u>**NOBR**</u>, <u>**WBR**</u>, A, BR, IMG
Can Be Inside:	Unspecified, probably: **A, character highlighting,** <u>**BLINK**</u>, <u>**FONT**</u>, <u>**NOBR**</u>, ADDRESS, *CAPTION*, Hn, P, PRE, DD, DT, LI
Attributes:	none

The **NOBR** element marks a block of text that cannot contain line breaks. Thus, a block of text enclosed by a **NOBR** will be presented as a single line of text, even if it scrolls off theword spaces, regardless of the page layout.

It is possible that an element such as **NOBR** will be integrated into a future revision of the "official" HTML.

WBR ELEMENT: WORD BREAK (NETSCAPE ONLY)

Usage:	`<WBR>`
Can Contain:	empty
Can Be Inside:	Unspecified, probably: **A, character highlighting,** <u>**BLINK**</u>, <u>**FONT**</u>, <u>**NOBR**</u>, ADDRESS, *CAPTION*, Hn, P, PRE, DD, DT, LI
Attributes:	none

Figure 4.28 Demonstration HTML document showing the use of the Netscape-specific **CENTER** and **FONT** elements, as well as the **WIDTH** attribute to the **HR** element. These elements and features do not work on other browsers.

```
<html><head>

<title> Netscape HTML Extensions </title>

</head><body>


<h2> Example 14: FONT and CENTER, and BR</h2>


<p> You can use <b>FONT</b> to control font size.

For example,

<font size=2>t<font size=3>h<font size=4>i<font size=5>s

<font size=6>i</font>s </font>o</font>d</font>d </font>

looking, as I adjusted the font.

You can use this for large capital letters in

headings:

<p><font size=+1>I</font>AN <font size=+1>G</font>RAHAM'S

    <font size=+1>H</font>OME

    <font size=+1>P</font>AGE -- (with size change on

    leading letters)


<hr size=4>


<h2>2. Centering Things </h2>

<p> It is always better to use ALIGN="center" for this, but sometimes

CENTER does have its nice points. For example, look at the following:

text, centered between two HR elements:

<br><br>

<hr width=80%>

<center>

These simple notes form a useful, single document
```

```
explaining the rationale and organization of the Web Document

template collection. Please print this out for off-line reference.

</center>

<hr width=80%>

<br>


<P>But look here, where I put the enclosed text inside a paragraph:

the extra spacing above the text and before the first HR is not

really desired:

<br><br>


<hr width=80%>

<center>

<P> These simple notes form a useful, single document

explaining the rationale and organization of the Web Document

template collection. Please print this out for off-line

reference.

</center>

<hr width=80%>


</body>

</html>
```

The **WBR** element is used to mark a word space, within a **NOBR** element, at which word breaks are actually allowed. **WBR** does not force a break, but simply tells the browser where a word break is allowed, should one be needed. Consequently, **WBR** is only meaningful within a **NOBR** element.

It is likely that an element such as **WBR** will be integrated into a future revision of the "official" HTML.

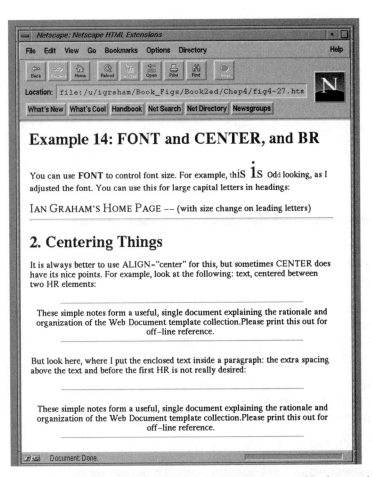

Figure 4.29 Rendering, using Netscape Navigator 1.1, of the HTML document shown in Figure 4.28.

BASEFONT ELEMENT:
SET THE DEFAULT FONT (NETSCAPE ONLY)

Usage:	<BASEFONT>
Can Contain:	empty
Can Be Inside:	Unspecified; **BASEFONT** can apparently appear inside any element.
Attributes:	**SIZE**

BASEFONT is used to specify the default font size for the document, using the **SIZE** attribute, which can take any value from 1 to 7 (the default is 3).

BASEFONT should appear prior to any displayed text in the **BODY** of the document. Localized changes to the font size should be implemented using the **FONT** element.

BASEFONT will not be implemented as part of standard HTML (see the **FONT** element following).

Example of **BASEFONT**:

```
<BASEFONT SIZE=4>
```

FONT ELEMENT:
SELECT TEXT FONT SIZE (NETSCAPE ONLY)

Usage:	`<FONT> . . . </FONT>`
Can Contain:	Unspecified, probably: **characters, character highlighting,** **BASEFONT, BLINK, FONT, NOBR, WBR, A, BR, IMG**
Can Be Inside:	Unspecified, probably: **A, character highlighting,** **BLINK, FONT, NOBR,** **ADDRESS,** *CAPTION,* **Hn, P, PRE, DD, DT, LI**
Attributes:	**SIZE, COLOR** (**FACE:** Microsoft Browser only)

The **FONT** element changes the font size of the enclosed text. **FONT** has no effect on enclosed **IMG** elements. **FONT** takes the single attribute **SIZE**, which specifies the font size. Font sizes can range from `<FONT SIZE=1>` to `<FONT SIZE=7>` (the default is 3). The assigned attribute value can also be preceded by a plus (+) or minus (–) sign to indicate a change in font size relative to the default basefont of the document (the default basefont size is 3). Thus, `<FONT SIZE=-1>` indicates a font one size reduced from the basefont. The default basefont can be changed using the **BASEFONT** element.

With the Netscape Navigator 2.0 browser, Netscape has added support for a **COLOR** attribute, which lets the author specify the desired text color as an

RGB triplet—for example, `<FONT COLOR="#FF0000">` . . . `</FONT>` for pure red text. This attribute is also understood by the Microsoft Internet Explorer browser.

Microsoft has further added the attribute value **FACE** to this element, which allows you to specify the typeface (**FACE**="Arial", "Times", etc.) to be used for the displayed text. The names, however, are specifically tied to the Microsoft Windows font names, so that this is not generalizable to other platforms (Mac or UNIX) or other PC operating systems (OS/2), and in fact may not work on all Windows systems, if the specified font is unavailable.

The **FONT** element is unlikely to be integrated into future revisions of HTML, as it goes against the logical document design paradigm of the language. The designers of HTML 3 have proposed the nonempty character highlighting elements **BIG** and **SMALL** to indicate changes in the font size of the tagged text; however, these are unimplemented by most current browsers, with the exception of Arena, emacs-w3, and some versions of Mosaic.

Examples showing the use of **FONT** are shown in Figures 4.28 and 4.29.

BLINK ELEMENT:
BLINKING TEXT (NETSCAPE ONLY)

Usage:	`<BLINK>` . . . `</BLINK>`
Can Contain:	Unspecified, probably: **characters, character highlighting,** **BASEFONT, BLINK, FONT, NOBR, WBR,** **A, BR, IMG**
Can Be Inside:	Unspecified, probably: **A, character highlighting,** **BLINK, FONT, NOBR,** **ADDRESS,** *CAPTION,* **Hn, P, PRE, DD, DT, LI**
Attributes:	none

The **BLINK** element marks the enclosed text as blinking text: Netscape Navigator flashes the text on and off. **BLINK** affects any enclosed text, but has no effect on enclosed images, **FORM** input elements (although regular text inside a **FORM** is rendered as blinking), or list item markers (bullets, numbers, etc.).

In principle, you should explicitly mark each block of text (paragraph, list item, etc.) for blinking, as opposed to marking large blocks (several paragraphs and lists) of the document. In practice, you can use a single <BLINK> tag to mark an entire document as blinking, and thereby drive all viewers toward madness.

The slightest mention of the **BLINK** element causes formal HTML language designers to pull out crosses, garlic, and/or wooden stakes and begin chanting, in rising voices, "evil, evil, horrible evil!!" It is, therefore, unlikely that **BLINK** will be integrated into the official HTML specification.

APPLET ELEMENT: INCLUDE AN EMBEDDED APPLET (NETSCAPE NAVIGATOR 2.0 ONLY)

Usage:	<APPLET> . . . </APPLET>
Can Contain:	**PARAM**
Can Be Inside:	undefined; probably **BODY**
Attributes:	**CODE, WIDTH, HEIGHT**

APPLET is used to include an inline applet—at present, Java applets are the only supported applications. The attribute **CODE** specifies the URL at which the applet is located (analogous to the **SRC** attribute of the **IMG** element), while the attributes **WIDTH** and **HEIGHT** specify the height and width required by the applet, in pixels. Parameter values required by the applet are obtained from **PARAM** elements contained within the **APPLET** element. The use of applets is discussed in a bit more detail in Chapter 5.

Example of **APPLET**:

```
<APPLET CODE="HuntingMammoths.class" WIDTH="300" HEIGHT="300">

    <PARAM NAME="x_offset" VALUE="0.224">

    <PARAM NAME="image" VALUE="images/hairy_mammoth.gif">
```

```
<PARAM NAME="weapon" VALUE="rubber biscuit">

</APPLET>
```

■■■■■ **NOTE**

The **APPLET** tag is under active development. In particular, the Netscape developers hope to integrate the **APPLET, FIG** (see Chapter 5), and the proposed **EMBED** elements to create a generalized element for embedding complex objects such as video sequences, figures, VRML scenes, or embedded applications within an HTML.

PARAM Element:
Define a Parameter for an APPLET
(Netscape Navigator 2.0 Only)

Usage:	`<PARAM>`
Can Contain:	empty
Can Be Inside:	**APPLET**
Attributes:	**NAME, VALUE**

PARAM is used to assign a value to any required applet-dependent variable name. The variable name is specified via the **NAME** attribute, while the value of this variable is specified with **VALUE**. **NAME**s and **VALUE**s are, of course, entirely specific to the applet being invoked.

FRAMESET Element:
Declare a FRAME Document
(Netscape Navigator 2.0 Only)

Usage:	`<FRAMESET> . . . </FRAMESET>`
Can Contain:	<u>**FRAME**</u>, <u>**FRAMESET**</u>, <u>**NOFRAMES**</u>
Can Be Inside:	**HTML**
Attributes:	**COLS, ROWS**

The Netscape Navigator 2.0 browser supports a new type of HTML document called a *frame* document. In a frame document, the **BODY** element is replaced by a **FRAMESET** element—this element defines the layout of window *frames* within the browser window. Each frame is a distinct viewing region that can contain its own, unique HTML document. The *content* of a frame is defined by the **FRAME** or **FRAMESET** elements located inside the **FRAMESET**—**FRAME** elements define the content and properties of a particular frame, while additional **FRAMESET** elements simply divide the corresponding frame into additional subframes.

The only other element allowed inside a **FRAMESET** is **NOFRAMES**. This element contains standard **BODY**-content HTML markup for use by browsers that do not understand the **FRAMESET** elements. Browsers that understand **FRAMESET** ignore the content of **NOFRAMES**.

An HTML document containing a **FRAMESET** cannot contain **BODY** content, other than that allowed within a **FRAMESET**. If you include regular **BODY** element tags prior to the first **FRAMESET**, the Netscape Navigator browser will entirely ignore the **FRAMESET**.

The layout and size of the frames defined by a **FRAMESET** are specified by the **COLS** or **ROWS** attribute. **COLS** indicates that the frames are laid out in columns, with the value assigned to **COLS** specifying the number and sizes of the columns. **ROWS** indicates that the frames are laid out in rows, with the value assigned to **ROWS** specifying the number and sizes of the rows. A **FRAMESET** must take one of **ROWS** or **COLS**, but cannot take both.

ROWS and **COLS** values are specified as a column-separated list of values. The number of comma-separated items is equal to the number of frames contained within the **FRAMESET**, while the values of the items determine the frame sizes. The values can take three possible forms:

Type	Format	Description
Fixed Pixel	n	Specifies the absolute frame size, in pixels, where n is the integer number of pixels.
Percentage	$n\%$	Specifies the frame size as a percentage of the total available height (or width), where n is the percentage. If the total of all specified frames is greater than 100%, then all frames are rescaled until the total is 100%. If the total is less than 100%, and there are no relative frames (see

below), then all frames are rescaled until the total is 100%. If the total is less than 100% and there are relative-sized frames, the space is assigned to the relative frames.

Relative Size	n^*	Specifies the size as a free-floating, relative value—all space remaining after allocating fixed pixel or percentage frames is divided among all relative-sized frames. An optional integer preceding the asterisk weights the space contribution: thus the string "2*,3*,*" would allocate 2/6 of the remaining space to the first frame, 3/6 to the second frame, and 1/6 to the third frame.

Here are some examples:

```
<FRAMESET ROWS="80, 3*, *, 100">
```

declares four row-oriented frames: the first (top) frame is 80 pixels high, while the fourth (bottom) frame is 100 pixels high. The second frame will occupy three-quarters of the remaining height, while the third frame will occupy the final one-quarter of the remaining height.

```
<FRAMESET COLS="20%, 80%">
```

declares two column-oriented frames. The first frame occupies 20 percent of the available width, and the second occupies the remaining 80 percent.

Additional examples, illustrating nested **FRAMESET**s, are given below. The Netscape frame elements are still under development, so it is possible that the specifications presented here will change. Please consult online information resources for up-to-date information.

FRAME ELEMENT:
A FRAME WITHIN A FRAMESET
(NETSCAPE NAVIGATOR 2.0 ONLY)

Usage:	<FRAME>
Can Contain:	empty
Can Be Inside:	**FRAMESET**
Attributes:	**MARGINWIDTH, MARGINHEIGHT, NAME, NORESIZE, SCROLLING, SRC**

The **FRAME** element defines the properties of each of the frames declared by the **FRAMESET** element. The attributes **MARGINWIDTH**, **MARGIN-HEIGHT**, **NORESIZE**, and **SCROLLING** define the physical properties of the frame. The **NAME** attribute is used to assign a specific name to the **FRAME**, which allows the frame to be targeted using the **TARGET** attribute to the anchor clement. The **SRC** attribute references the HTML document to be inserted within the **FRAME**. All attributes are optional, including **SRC**: if **SRC** is absent, the frame is simply left empty. **FRAME** is an empty element, as the content of the frame is defined via the **SRC** attribute.

The **ROWS** or **COLS** attribute specifies the number of frames that must be inside the **FRAMESET**—it is an error if a **FRAMESET** does not actually contain this number of **FRAME** and/or **FRAMESET** elements.

Here is an example of correctly defined **FRAME**s (comments in italics):

```
<FRAMESET ROWS="10%, 80%, 10%>                           3 rows, narrow top and bottom

    <FRAME SCROLLING="no" SRC="logo+buttonbar.html">     1st frame

    <FRAMESET COLS="20%, 80%">                           2d frame is a FRAMESET
                                                         containing 2 frames
        <FRAME NAME="navigation" SRC="navigate.html">

        <FRAME NAME="main" SRC="main/start.html">

    </FRAMESET>

    <FRAME SCROLLING="no" SRC="credits.html">            3d frame

</FRAMESET>

. . . .
```

In the above example, the display is first divided into three rows: the top and bottom rows are narrow (10 percent of the available height) and contain noscrolling documents. The middle row is further divided into two columns: the first takes up 20 percent of the window width; the second takes up the remaining 80 percent. Both these frames are scrollable, and are named using **NAME** attributes.

Here is an example of incorrectly defined **FRAME**s (comments in italics):

```
<FRAMESET ROWS="10%, 80%, 10%>                           3 rows, narrow top and bottom

    <FRAME SCROLLING="no" SRC="logo+buttonbar.html">     1st frame

    <FRAMESET COLS="20%, 80%">                           2d frame is a FRAMESET
                                                         containing 2 frames
        <FRAME NAME="navigation" SRC="navigate.html">
```

```
      <FRAME NAME="main" SRC="main/start.html">

  </FRAMESET>

  <FRAME SCROLLING="no" SRC="credits.html">          3d frame

  <FRAME SRC="oops.htm">                             ERROR--FRAMESET declares
                                                     3 rows, but this is the
                                                     fourth frame!!

  </FRAMESET>
```

The following are the definitions of the **FRAME** attributes:

MARGINWIDTH="*n*" (optional) **MARGINWIDTH** specifies the width, in pixels, of the left and right margins for the frame. The **MARGINWIDTH** cannot be less than 1, to ensure that there is some blank space left between the frame content and the frame borders. If this attribute is absent, the browser will itself determine a (hopefully) appropriate margin width.

MARGINHEIGHT="*n*" (optional) **MARGINHEIGHT** specifies the height, in pixels, of the top and bottom margins for the frame. The **MARGIN-HEIGHT** cannot be less than 1, to ensure that there is some blank space left between the frame content and the frame borders. If this attribute is absent, the browser will itself determine a (hopefully) appropriate margin height.

NAME="*name_string*" (optional) **NAME** is used to assign a name string to the particular frame: the **TARGET** attribute to the **A** or **BASE** elements can then be used to direct retrieved documents or data to this named frame. If **NAME** is absent, the frame name is undefined. Values for names must be name tokens, as defined previously in this chapter.

NORESIZE (optional) **NORESIZE** informs the browser that the frame size is fixed and cannot be modified by the user—this will clearly also inhibit the resizing of adjacent frames in the same window. If this attribute is absent, the frame can be resized, usually by using the mouse to drag a border of the frame.

SCROLLING="yes", "no", "auto" (optional) **SCROLLING** specifies the status of scrollbars for the frame. A value of "yes" means that the frame must always have scrollbars, while "no" means that the frame should never have scrollbars—if you use this latter value, you must be sure that the frame is large enough to contain the desired document. The value "auto" lets the browser include scrollbars when necessary. The default value is "auto."

SRC="URL" (optional) **SRC** specifies the URL of the HTML document to be displayed within the frame. **SRC** can be absent, in which case the frame is initially blank.

NOFRAMES ELEMENT:
HTML MARKUP FOR FRAME-INCAPABLE BROWSERS
(NETSCAPE NAVIGATOR 2.0 ONLY)

Usage:	<NOFRAMES> . . . <NOFRAMES>
Can Contain:	**BODY**
Can Be Inside:	**FRAMESET**
Attributes:	none

The **NOFRAMES** element contains HTML markup to be displayed by browsers that do not understand the **FRAMESET** or **FRAME** elements. A **FRAME**-capable browser will ignore the content of the **NOFRAMES** element and will instead display the indicated **FRAME**s. On the other hand, a **FRAME**-incapable browser will ignore the **FRAMESET, FRAME,** and **NOFRAMES** tags and will display the **NOFRAMES** content as the **BODY** of a regular HTML document.

NOFRAMES should contain a **BODY** element and regular **BODY** content. The following is an example of the use of **NOFRAMES**:

```
<HTML>

<HEAD>

<TITLE>Test of the NOFRAMES Element</TITLE>

</HEAD>

<FRAMESET ROWS="50%, 50%">

    <NOFRAMES>

    <BODY BACKGROUND="graywhale.gif">

    <H1 ALIGN="center"> Warning! </H1>

    <P ALIGN="center"><EM>If you are reading this text, you are viewing
    this document with a FRAMEs-incapable browser--this document was
    designed to be viewed by a FRAMEs-capable browser, such as Netscape
    Navigator 2.0. If you do not have such a browser, please access the
    alternative
```

```
<A HREF="noframes.html">noframes</A> collection.

</BODY>

</NOFRAMES>


<FRAME  SRC="top_part.html" NAME="wind1">

<FRAME  SRC="bot_part.html" NAME="wind2">


</FRAMESET>

</HTML>
```

SCRIPT ELEMENT: INCLUDE A PROGRAM SCRIPT (NETSCAPE NAVIGATOR 2.0 ONLY)

Usage:	`<SCRIPT>` . . . `<SCRIPT>`
Can Contain:	script program code (*LiveScript*—a.k.a. *JavaScript*)
Can Be Inside:	**HEAD**
Attributes:	**LANGUAGE, SRC**

The **SCRIPT** element is used to include program scripts within an HTML document. Scripts can be included in two ways: as the content of the **SCRIPT** element, or externally via an **SRC** attribute that references the URL of the script. If the script is embedded within the **SCRIPT**, then the end tag `</SCRIPT>` is mandatory. However, if the script is included via the **SRC** attribute, then the `</SCRIPT>` tag must be absent.

The mandatory **LANGUAGE** attribute specifies the language of the script: the only currently supported value is "LiveScript" (*JavaScript*), which refers to a scripting language explicitly designed by Netscape and integrated into the Netscape Navigator 2.0 browser.

Embedding a script within an HTML document can cause problems, as the string "`</x`", where `x` is any ASCII letter, will prematurely terminate the element. In this case, a LiveScript script author must be careful to escape such sequences and hide them from the HTML parser.

The **SCRIPT** tag and the LiveScript language are still under development, and may change before being definitively implemented. For up-to-date information, please consult the references at the end of this chapter.

MICROSOFT INTERNET EXPLORER–SPECIFIC HTML EXTENSIONS

The Microsoft Internet Explorer supports two additional elements: **MARQUEE**, for scrollable text marquees, and **BGSOUND**, for inline audio. These elements are currently not supported by other browsers.

MARQUEE ELEMENT: A SCROLLING TEXT MARQUEE (INTERNET EXPLORER 2.0 ONLY)

Usage:	`<MARQUEE> . . . </MARQUEE>`
Can Contain:	not specified; probably **text, text highlighting**
Can Be Inside:	not specified; probably **BODY, BLOCKQUOTE, FORM, DD, LI, TD, TH**
Attributes:	**ALIGN, BEHAVIOR, BGCOLOR, DIRECTION, HEIGHT, HSPACE, LOOP, SCROLLAMOUNT, SCROLLDELAY, VSPACE**

MARQUEE denotes a text string to be scrolled horizontally on the display: the content of the element is the text to be scrolled. **MARQUEE** takes a number of attributes to control the size and placement of the marquee on the page (**ALIGN, HEIGHT, HSPACE,** and **VSPACE**), and to control the behavior of the scrolled text (**BEHAVIOR, DIRECTION, LOOP, SCROLLAMOUNT, SCROLLDELAY**). The **BGCOLOR** attribute can be used to specify a background color specific to the marquee text.

Example of **MARQUEE**:

```
<MARQUEE ALIGN="middle" HSPACE="10" LOOP="-1"

    SCROLLAMOUNT="1"

    SCROLLDELAY="4">Here is the marquee text</MARQUEE>
```

The attributes and their specific meanings are as follows:

ALIGN="top", "middle", "bottom" (optional) **ALIGN** specifies the alignment of the surrounding text with the marquee. **ALIGN**="top" means that the top of the **MARQUEE** should be aligned with the top of the surrounding text. **ALIGN**="middle" means that the middle of the **MARQUEE** should be aligned with the middle of the surrounding text. **ALIGN**="bottom" means that the bottom of the **MARQUEE** should be aligned with the bottom of the surrounding text. The default alignment is "bottom."

BEHAVIOR="scroll", "slide", "alternate" (optional) **BEHAVIOR** specifies the behavior of the marquee text. **BEHAVIOR**="scroll" means that the text should start from beyond one margin (left or right), scroll completely across to the other margin, and disappear completely. **BEHAVIOR**="slide" means that the text will start from beyond one margin (left or right) and will scroll onto the screen until it touches the other margin, whereupon it should cease scrolling. **BEHAVIOR**="alternate" means that the text should bounce back and forth between the left- and right-hand margins of the **MARQUEE**. The default is **BEHAVIOR**="scroll".

BGCOLOR="#*rrggbb*", "color_name" (optional) **BGCOLOR** specifies the background color for the marquee. Colors are specified as hexadecimal-coded RGB triplets, or by using a short list of supported color names. The supported color names are "Black", "Olive", "Teal", "Red", "Blue", "Maroon", "Navy", "Gray", "Lime", "Fuchsia", "White", "Green", "Purple", "Silver", "Yellow", and "Aqua." The default is the display window color.

DIRECTION="left", "right" (optional) **DIRECTION** specifies the scrolling direction for the text. **DIRECTION**="left" means that the text will scroll from left to right, while **DIRECTION**="right" means that the text will scroll from right to left. The default is **DIRECTION**="left."

HEIGHT="*n*", "*n*%" (optional) **HEIGHT** specifies the height of the marquee. This height can either be specified in pixels (**HEIGHT**="*n*") or as a percentage of the display window height (**HEIGHT**="*n*%"). You should be careful not to make the **MARQUEE** too thin, as this will obscure the marquee text. The default will be just tall enough to contain the text in the given font.

HSPACE="*n*" (optional) **HSPACE** specifies the margin, in pixels, to leave to the left and right of the **MARQUEE**. The default value is 0.

LOOP="*n*", "infinite" (optional) **LOOP** specifies the number of times the marquee will loop before stopping. The values **LOOP**="−1" or **LOOP**="infinite" cause the marquee to loop forever. The default value is "−1".

SCROLLAMOUNT="*n*" (optional) **SCROLLAMOUNT** specifies the number of pixels between subsequent redraws of the marquee text—a large value yields a marquee that jumps rapidly across the screen, while a small value yields smoothly scrolled text.

SCROLLDELAY="*n*" (optional) **SCROLLDELAY** specifies the time delay, in milliseconds, between subsequent redraws of the marquee text—a small value implies a rapidly scrolling marquee.

VSPACE="*n*" (optional) **VSPACE** specifies the margin, in pixels, to leave above and below the **MARQUEE**. The default value is 0.

WIDTH="*n*", "*n*%" (optional) **WIDTH** specifies the width of the marquee. This width can either be specified in pixels (**WIDTH=**"*n*") or as a percentage of the display window width (**WIDTH=**"*n*%"). You should be careful not to make the **MARQUEE** too narrow, as this may make it difficult to read the marquee text.

BGSOUND ELEMENT: INLINE AUDIO SNIPPETS (INTERNET EXPLORER 2.0 ONLY)

Usage:	<BGSOUND>
Can Contain:	empty
Can Be Inside:	not defined; probably allowed inside any nonempty **BODY** element.
Attributes:	**SRC, LOOP**

BGSOUND inserts an inline audio snippet—the location of the audio file is specified by the **SRC** attribute to the **BGSOUND** element. By default, the sound is loaded and played once. The LOOP attribute can be used to change the number of times the sound is played. Thus **LOOP=**"10" instructs the browser to play the sound file ten times, and then stop. The values **LOOP=**"–1" or **LOOP=**"infinite" instruct the browser to continuously play the sound file until the user selects another document. Here is an example of **BGSOUND**:

```
<BGSOUND HREF="/project1/sounds/bubbles.wav" LOOP="-1">
```

MATHEMATICS
AND OTHER MISSING FEATURES

HTML 2.0 is missing a number of important hypertext document description features, such as page banners (sections of text that do not scroll with the document, but stay at the top or bottom of the window), tabbing control, properly defined figures, quotations (complete with citations and captions), and a method for expressing mathematical equations. The absence of a mathematics mode is quite surprising, given the origin of HTML in the scientific community. In HTML 2.0, mathematical equations can be included only by using a separate application to create a GIF format image of the equation, which is then included as a GIF image within the HTML document.

The LaTeX typesetting and document formatting language is ubiquitous in the scientific community for writing mathematically oriented documents. For this community, Nikos Drakos of the University of Leeds has produced a sophisticated program that can convert a LaTeX document into an HTML document, including conversion of mathematical expressions into inline GIF images. This remarkably efficient and useful program is called **latex2html**, and is described briefly in Chapter 11.

HTML 3 largely overcomes the limitations of HTML 2.0 by including new elements that allow for banners, tabbing control, figures, mathematics, and so on. The changes that will result from HTML 3 are discussed in the next chapter.

REFERENCES

A gentle introduction to SGML—Quite readable, and understandable for the beginner:

```
http://etext.virginia.edu/bin/tei-tocs?div=DIV1&id=SG
```

```
http://www.lib.virginia.edu/etext/tagging-intro.html
```

For further online reading, see Robin Cover's collection of SGML resources and references:

```
http://www.sil.org/sgml/sgml.html
```

The gruesome, detailed details of SGML—Definitely not easily read, but it contains all the details of SGML—only for the truly serious:

The SGML Handbook
Charles F. Goldfarb
Oxford University Press, 1990

The HTML 2.0 draft specification—The current best reference for HTML 2.0 information, and of particular use to editor and browser developers:

http://www.w3.org/hypertext/WWW/MarkUp/html-spec/html-spec_toc.html

HTML 2.0 Document Type Definitions—Needed if you are to validate syntax of HTML documents using programs such as **SGMLs.**

SGML Declaration for HTML—The declaration of SGML properties implemented in the DTD; this must be read by any SGML parser, such as **SGMLs,** before it can parse the DTD:

http://www.w3.org/hypertext/WWW/MarkUp/html-spec/html.decl

HTML 2.0 DTD—The official SGML description of the HTML 2.0 language:

http://www.w3.org/hypertext/WWW/MarkUp/html-spec/html.dtd

HTML 2.0 DTD—Strict Interpretation of Syntax—A header file for the DTD listed above:

http://www.w3.org/hypertext/WWW/MarkUp/html-spec/html-s.dtd

World Wide Web Organization HTML Reference Materials page—An extremely useful collection of pointers for HTML 2.0, HTML 3, and other information of interest to HTML authors and Web software designers:

http://www.w3.org/hypertext/WWW/MarkUp/

Catalog of online HTML references—This site contains many pointers concerning information resources about HTML; however, these resources are of widely varying levels of utility and accuracy:

http://www.yahoo.com/Computers/World_Wide_Web/HTML/

Netscape **SCRIPT** and **FRAMESET** element documentation:

http://www.netscape.com/comprod/products/navigator/version_2.0/script/script_info/

http://www.netscape.com/assist/net_sites/frames.html

# Chapter 5

THE NEXT GENERATION— HTML 3, STYLESHEETS, AND APPLETS

The name "HTML 3" represents an ambitious project aimed at significantly revamping HTML, to provide important new features and functionality. The result of this process is HTML Version 3—a "developmental" version of the language that demonstrates and tests many proposed enhancements. Thus, despite all the hype, it is important to view HTML 3 as a testbed, and not as a widely implemented "production" language. Indeed, many of the elements and attributes proposed in HTML 3 may change significantly before they are integrated into a formal HTML specification. You should definitely not use the material in this chapter as a guide to designing universally viewable Web pages!

That being said, it is true that several HTML 3 features, such as the **ALIGN** attribute to paragraphs and headings, and the **TABLE** element, have been implemented by current browsers and are seeing wide popularity, while other HTML 3 elements are likely to soon see widespread use. Thus, the content of this chapter serves as an important indication of upcoming developments.

At present, very few browsers support HTML 3 features other than those features mentioned above and in Chapter 4. If you want to experiment with more advanced aspects of HTML 3, you should obtain the Arena browser. Arena is a testbed platform for HTML 3, and implements many of the elements described here. However, Arena is only available for a limited number of UNIX platforms, and does not have the speed or broad functionality found in commercial browsers. As an alternative you can consider the emacs-w3 browser, which also implements many HTML 3 features.

CHAPTER OUTLINE

The first and largest section of this chapter consists of an introduction to the ideas behind HTML 3, and the important changes with respect to HTML 2.0. It includes a detailed description of the new elements, and their proposed implementation. Important incompatibilities with HTML 2.0 and HTML 2.0–compliant browsers are pointed out, to help you integrate HTML 3 features into new documents.

This is followed by a section on *stylesheets*. Stylesheets allow HTML authors to specify, using a separate stylesheet document, the desired formatting of their HTML documents. Two stylesheet *languages* are currently under development. This section looks briefly at one of these languages, and uses some simple examples to show how it works.

The final section looks briefly at embedded applications within HTML documents, and particularly at the Java language. The applets made possible by languages like Java allow for much richer multimedia behavior in HTML documents, and promise to significantly enrich the multimedia character of the World Wide Web.

INTRODUCTION TO HTML 3

As mentioned previously, HTML 3 is an ambitious effort to revamp HTML 2.0, taking into account many of the lessons learned over recent years. The results of this process fit into three broad categories:

1. Addition of new attributes to *all* existing HTML 2.0 **BODY** content elements, to allow for definition of *country-* or *language-specific features* (e.g., what symbol to use for quotation marks), for *labeling* of any element as a possible named hypertext target, and for *classifying* elements according to their logical intent (e.g., this paragraph is a stanza in a poem).

2. Addition of *new elements* allowing additional description of logical document content. Examples are elements for figures, footnotes, block divisions, and mathematical terms.

3. Addition of *stylesheet* support. As already mentioned (probably more often that you'd like), HTML describes logical document organization,

and not document formatting. Stylesheets allow you to associate physical formatting suggestions (as a separate data file, or as a special collection of data within an HTML document) with an HTML document. Browsers that understand stylesheets can access the HTML document along with the designated stylesheet (if a separate file), and can use the instructions in the stylesheet to determine formatting details.

It is likely that many HTML 3 features will be added incrementally to HTML 2.0, yielding HTML 2.1, HTML 2.2, and so on. In the following, I try to note those features that are relatively stable and that are likely (but not guaranteed!) to be soon implemented by browser developers.

COMPATIBILITY OF HTML 3 WITH HTML 2.0 BROWSERS

Many of the elements introduced in HTML 3 are not compatible with HTML 2.0 browsers, in that the rendering of the contents of these elements is not understandable to the user. Particular examples are the **FIG** (figure) and **MATH** (mathematics) elements, which produce gibberish when displayed by an HTML 2.0-compliant browser. It is therefore recommended that HTML 3.0 documents be assigned the MIME content-type

```
Content-type: text/html; version=3.0
```

namely, the text/html content type, but with a *version* number parameter. Most current (i.e., HTML 2.0-compatible) browsers do not understand the "version" extension field, and interpret this as an undefined type. The browser then either gives the user the option of saving the file to disk, or presents the document as uninterpreted plain text.

Servers must then be able to distinguish HTML 3 documents from HTML 2.0. An easy way is to use the filename extension *.html3* (or *.ht3* for MS-DOS/Windows machines), and configure the server to serve such documents as the required MIME type. Some servers have problems with content-type headers having extra parameters, so be sure to check that your server can do this before implementing this special content type.

Some HTML 3 elements are largely "safe" when viewed by an HTML 2.0 browser. If you only use these elements or attributes, you can serve the document without the version number—and hope for the best!

RELATIONSHIP OF THIS CHAPTER TO CHAPTER 4

To avoid duplication, this chapter does not discuss elements and attributes that are unchanged from HTML 2.0—the grayed-out entries in Figure 5.1

Element	*Description*	*Page*
HTML	*An HTML document*	253
HEAD	*Document Meta Information*	142
BASE	*Base URL of the document*	143
ISINDEX	*Searchable document*	144
LINK	*Relationships to other documents*	146
META	*Meta information*	147
NEXTID	*Counter for automated editors*	149
RANGE	Mark a range in a document	254
STYLE	Stylesheet information	255
TITLE	*Document title*	150
BODY	*Text Body*	151
ADDRESS	*Address information*	153
BANNER	A document banner	263
BLOCKQUOTE (*BQ*)	Block quotations	263
CREDIT	FIG or BLOCKQUOTE credit	263
DIV	Block division of the BODY	264
FIG	Figures	266
OVERLAY	Image overlay on a FIG	272
CAPTION	Caption to a FIG or TABLE	273
FN	Footnotes	274
FORM	User input form	276
INPUT	Input fields	279
SELECT	Selectable fields	282
OPTION	Option in a selectable field	283
TEXTAREA	Text input region	281
H1 H6	Headings (Levels 1 6)	284
HR	Horizontal rule	285
NOTE	Notes or Admonishments	286
DL	*Description/Glossary list*	172
LH	List Heading	287
DT	*Term*	174
DD	*Description*	175
OL	Ordered list	288
LH	List Heading	287
LI	List item	289
UL	Unordered list	288
LH	List Heading	287
LI	List item	289
DIR	*Directory list*	179
LI	*List item*	182
MENU	*Menu list*	180
LI	*List item*	182
P	*Paragraphs*	184
PRE	*Preformatted text*	185
TABLE	Tables	293
CAPTION	*Table caption*	217
COL	Column Widths and Properties	295
COLGROUP	Group Columns	296
THEAD	Table Header	297
TBODY	Table Body	298
TFOOT	Table Footer	298
TR	Table row	299
TD	Table data cell	299
TH	Table header cell	300

■■■■ **Figure 5.1** Hierarchical breakdown of HTML 3 elements. Elements that were present in HTML 2.0 are shown in a bold font, while elements that are new to HTML 3 are shown in boldface-italics. Elements that are essentially unmodified from HTML 2.0, and that are only discussed in Chapter 4, are grayed out. You are referred to Chapter 4 for information about these elements.

Element	*Description*	*Page*

Physical Phrase Markup

B	Bold	209
BIG	Increased Font Size	310
I	Italics	209
S	Strike through	310
SMALL	Reduced size Font	310
SUB	Subscript	310
SUP	Superscript	311
TT	Fixed width	209
U	Underline	311

Semantic Phrase Markup

ACRONYM	Acronyms	308
ABBREV	Abbreviations	308
AU	Author	308
CITE	Citation	205
CODE	Typed computer code	206
DEL	Deleted text	309
DFN	Defining instance of a term	309
EM	Emphasized text	206
INS	Inserted text	309
KBD	Keyboard input	206
LANG	Language context	309
PERSON	Names of people	309
Q	Short in line quotation	310
SAMP	Sample text	207
STRONG	Strongly emphasized	207
VAR	A Variable	208

Character Level and Special Elements

BR	Line break	201
IMG	Inline Image	192
A	Hypertext Anchor	300
SPOT	Mark a location in a document	302
TAB	Tabbing Control	302
MATH	Mathematical Expressions	311

text level markup

Netscape and Microsoft Extensions

HEAD Elements

| SCRIPT | Inline scripting program (Netscape only) | 241 |

BODY Elements

APPLET	Include an inline Java applet (Netscape only)	234
PARAM	Define a variable required by the applet (Netscape only)	235
BASEFONT	Set the base font	232
BGSOUND	Include an inline sound file (Microsoft only)	244
CENTER	Center contents horizontally	226
FRAMESET	Declare a FRAME document (Netscape only)	235
FRAME	Content for a particular FRAME (Netscape only)	237
NOFRAMES	Markup for non FRAME browsers (Netscape only)	240
MAP	A client side imagemap	197
AREA	Region in a client side imagemap	190
MARQUEE	Define a scrolling text marquee (Microsoft only)	242

Physical Phrase Markup

FONT	Change the font size	232
BLINK	Blinking text	233
NOBR	No Line Break	231
WBR	Word Break	231

▰▰▰▰ **Figure 5.1** Continued.

indicate such elements. As you may recall, the previous chapter covered certain widely implemented HTML 3 *attributes* (e.g., the **ALIGN** attribute for paragraphs and headings), as well as an early but widely implemented version of the HTML 3 **TABLE** element. This information is also not reproduced here. Figure 5.1 summarizes the HTML 3 elements. Elements new to HTML 3 are shown in boldface-italics. Elements that are essentially unmodified from HTML 2.0, and that are only discussed in Chapter 4, are grayed out.

KEY TO THIS CHAPTER

As in Chapter 4, information about where and how an element can be used is given in the four lines at the beginning of the element description. The general form is:

Usage:	`<NAME> . . . </NAME>`
Can Contain:	**element list**
Can Be Inside:	**element list**
Attributes:	**attribute list**

Here is an example, using the HTML 3 **LH** list header element:

Usage:	`<LH> . . . (</LH>)`
Can Contain:	**characters, character highlighting, A, BR, IMG,** *MATH, TAB*
Can Be Inside:	**DL, OL, UL**
Attributes:	*CLASS, ID, LANG*

The four fields define the rules for using the different elements—their meanings were discussed in Chapter 4, and are summarized in Figure 4.3. The difference for this chapter lies in the presence of the new HTML 3 elements and attributes—elements and attributes new to HTML 3 are in italics.

HTML 3 SHORT-FORM DEFINITIONS

The following short forms are used in the "Can Contain" and "Can Be Inside" fields. Again, elements new with HTML 3 are in italics.

Hn	The six heading elements **H1, H2, H3, H4, H5,** and **H6**
characters	Any valid ISO Latin-1 character, character reference, or entity reference
character highlighting	*ABBREV, ACRONYM, AU,* CITE, CODE, *DEL, DFN,* EM, *INS,* KBD, *LANG, PERSON, Q,* SAMP, STRONG, VAR, B, *BIG,* I, *S, SMALL, SUB, SUP,* TT, and *U*
	These are the logical (**CITE, CODE, STRONG,** etc.) and physical (**B, *BIG,*** etc.) formatting elements.
math entities	Mathematical entity references, as tentatively defined in Tables 5.1 through 5.6
math elements	*ABOVE, BELOW, B, T, BT, BAR, BOX, DDOT, DOT, HAT, ROOT, SQRT, TILDE, VEC*
	These elements can only appear inside *MATH.*

The **Hn, characters,** and **character highlighting** definitions are largely unchanged from HTML 2.0, while **math entities** and **math elements** are entirely new to HTML 3.

ATTRIBUTE VALUES

As in Chapter 4, attribute values are in all cases enclosed by double quotation marks. The *value* is placed in italics when it is an arbitrary, user-defined string, and in a regular font when it is a parameter value fixed by the HTML specification.

HTML ELEMENT: AN HTML DOCUMENT

Usage:	`<HTML> . . . </HTML>`
Can Contain:	**HEAD, BODY**
Can be Inside:	nothing
Attributes:	*CLASS, URN, VERSION*

The **HTML** element declares the enclosed text to be an HTML document. HTML 3 recommends that this element take three optional attributes:

CLASS=*"string"* (optional) **CLASS** specifies the *class* for the entire document. The meaning of class is discussed in the "Changes in Body Content" section, later in this chapter.

URN=*"urn"* (optional) **URN** specifies the *Universal Resource Name* for the document, and serves as locator to back-reference moved documents. The syntax and design of URNs is still under discussion, so this attribute is not presently implemented.

VERSION=*"version_definition"* (optional) **VERSION** specifies the HTML version, as defined by the DOCTYPE definition in the DTD (see Chapter 4). For HTML 3 this is:

```
<HTML VERSION="-//W3O//DTD W# HTML 3.0//EN">
```

Since HTML 2.0 now recommends that a DOCTYPE definition be included with every HTML document (see Chapter 4), this attribute is likely unnecessary.

DOCUMENT HEAD— CHANGES IN HEAD CONTENT

The HTML 2.0 **HEAD** element and the head-level elements discussed in Chapter 4 are unchanged in HTML 3. HTML 3 introduces two new **HEAD** elements, designed to provide information about marked regions in a document (**RANGE**) and a mechanism for including *stylesheet* information within a document head (**STYLE**).

RANGE ELEMENT: MARK A RANGE IN THE DOCUMENT

Usage:	<RANGE>
Can Contain:	empty
Can Be Inside:	**HEAD**
Attributes:	*CLASS, FROM, ID, TO*

RANGE is an empty element, and indicates a particular *range* in the document body, denoted by the values of the attributes **FROM** and **TO**. This allows the document creator (perhaps an automated program) to mark blocks for special logical or rendering purposes—for example, a section highlighted to indicate that it was picked out by a database search program. The form of a **RANGE** is:

```
<RANGE FROM="location-1"  TO="location-2">
```

where `location-1` and `location-2` are locations in the document marked by **ID** attributes. In HTML 3, the **ID** attribute denotes named locations within a document, replacing the **NAME** attribute to the **A** element in HTML 2.0. HTML 3 also supports the new **BODY** element **SPOT**, an empty element that permits insertion of location **IDs** anywhere in a document using the tag `<SPOT ID="location">`.

The attributes of **RANGE** are:

ID=*"string"* (optional) **ID** contains a fragment identifier that labels the particular range elements. This allows multiple ranges to be defined within the same document, each referenced through its specific **ID**.

CLASS=*"string"* (optional) **CLASS** contains a character string used to classify the element. This allows you to define the nature of the **RANGE**. For example, **CLASS**=*"search.target"* might mean that the defined **RANGE** was the portion of the document correlated with the search that returned the current document.

FROM=*"location-id"* (mandatory) **FROM** marks the start of a marked range in the document. The location must be defined in the document, or else the **RANGE** is invalid.

TO=*"location-id"* (mandatory) **TO** marks the end of a marked range in the document. The location must be defined in the document, or else the **RANGE** is invalid.

RANGE is a harmless element to an HTML 2.0 browser, since it is empty, and is ignored. There are currently no browsers that process **RANGE** elements.

STYLE Element: Stylesheet or Rendering Information

Usage:	`<STYLE> . . . </STYLE>`
Can Contain:	**characters**
Can Be Inside:	**HEAD**
Attributes:	none

The **STYLE** element contains stylesheet rendering instructions, to be applied to the document when displayed by the browser. **STYLE** allows the rendering information to be present within the document, and not as a second file referenced through a **LINK** element. The latter may be accomplished using **LINK** elements of the form:

```
<LINK REL="stylesheet" HREF="http:some.where.dom/path/stylesheet">
```

It is possible that future versions of HTML will employ a distinct element, separate from **LINK**, to indicate external stylesheets.

The **STYLE** element allows for browsers that do not support linked stylesheets. In this instance, **STYLE** is best thought of as an interim mechanism for including stylesheet information, as it has several disadvantages compared with linked stylesheets:

- **STYLE** is incompatible with HTML 2.0: HTML 2.0 browsers ignore the **STYLE** tags, and interpret the element content as **BODY** text, displaying it to the user.
- A linked stylesheet can be shared among many documents, while the **STYLE** element forces every document to contain the stylesheet. This is both wasteful (every document must contain the stylesheet) and difficult to update.

Here is an example **STYLE** element:

```
<HEAD>

   <STYLE>

   h1         : font.color = #900000

   h1         : margin.top = 10

   h1.center : align = center


   ul         : indent = 20

   ul         : margin.left = 20


   b, strong : font.color = #598

   em         : font.color = #009000

   a          : font.color = #0050C0

   ...

   </STYLE>

   ....
```

```
</HEAD>

<BODY>
```

CHANGES IN BODY CONTENT

Most new HTML 3 features are found in the **BODY**. There are several new elements, most notably **BANNER** for page banners, **DIV** for blocks of the document, **FIG** for figures, and **MATH** for mathematical expressions. HTML 3 also recommends dropping the **DIR** and **MENU** list types: in HTML 3, the layout specified by these list types can be produced using UL elements with appropriate attribute values.

NEW UNIVERSAL ATTRIBUTES: CLASS, ID, AND LANG

HTML 3 adds several new attributes to the HTML language attribute repertoire. In particular, the three attributes **CLASS**, **ID**, and **LANG** are allowed with almost *every* element inside the document **BODY** (the exception being the mathematics elements). These attributes are likely to soon become part of "official" HTML. The meanings are:

CLASS="*class.subclass*" (optional) **CLASS** is used to *subclass* an element. In practice, this means that **CLASS** provides information about the unique semantic characteristics of a particular element or *class* of elements. For example, the tag `<P CLASS="song.verse">` would mean that the paragraph is a verse of a song, while `<P CLASS="song.refrain">` would mean that the paragraph is a song's refrain. This is very useful in providing additional information about the structure of a document. **CLASS** is also important for document formatting, as the *stylesheet* mechanism is linked to **CLASS** definitions of an element. For example, a stylesheet might contain information that states:

- Regular paragraphs are not indented, and are in 12-point TimesRoman font.
- Paragraphs that are song verses should be indented, in 12-point Arial font.
- Paragraphs that are song refrains should be indented further than song verses, and in 12-point Arial bold font.

Class names are *name tokens* (see Chapter 4)—case-insensitive strings that must begin with a letter and that can contain only ASCII letters (a–z, A–Z), numbers (0–9), periods (.), and hyphens (-). With class names, the convention is that a period is used to denote a change in class level, with the most general class being to the left of the period and less general ones to the right, hence the examples song.verse and song.refrain.

The specification allows multiple class names within the same **CLASS** attribute value, by leaving a space between the class names and enclosing the entire string in double quotes. For example:

```
<P CLASS="song.refrain clapton.layla">
```

assigns class names song.refrain and clapton.layla to this paragraph element.

At present the Arena and, to some degree, the emacs-w3 browsers recognize the **CLASS** attribute for stylesheet purposes, but other browsers do not. This is a safe attribute for HTML 2.0 browsers, as it can be ignored without affecting the presentation of the document.

ID="*location*" The **ID** attribute assigns an identifier to a particular element—the location can then be referenced using a hypertext anchor element. For example, the location

```
<P ID="location">
```

can be referenced using the anchor element:

```
<A HREF="#location">...</a>
```

For consistency, HTML 3 replaces the **NAME** attribute of the **A** (anchor) element by **ID**. Thus the forms:

```
<A NAME="flopsy">marked text</a>
```

and

```
<A ID="flopsy">marked text</a>
```

are equivalent in HTML 3, with the latter being the recommended form.

NOTE

Most browsers do not recognize the **ID** attribute. The **ID** attribute can be included in an HTML 2.0 document, but is nonfunctional: you can't use the **ID** attribute to mark locations that are to be the targets of a hypertext link.

LANG="*aa-ccode*" (optional) **LANG** is used to indicate the language of the document, and the national variant of that language. This is done using a collection of special codes for languages, along with a second collection of codes for individual countries—for example, `fr-ca` for Canadian French. These codes are summarized in Appendix E. The country code is optional, so that you can use just a language code.

This attribute allows the browser to choose appropriate language and national formatting for things such as monetary symbols, decimal point characters, hyphenation rules, and punctuation for quoted text.

At present no browsers use the **LANG** value to modify document formatting.

OTHER COMMON ATTRIBUTES: CLEAR, MD, ALIGN, AND NOWRAP

The optional elements **ALIGN, CLEAR, NOWRAP,** and **MD** are allowed with many **BODY**-content elements. **ALIGN** is allowed with elements that define blocks of text, and specifies how paragraphs within the block should be aligned. **CLEAR** can be present with elements used to define blocks of text or flow of text, and controls how text flows around embedded objects (figures, images, or tables). **NOWRAP** can also be present with elements used to define blocks of text, and disables word wrapping inside these elements. Finally, **MD** is allowed whenever there is a hypertext link to an external object, either through an **A** (anchor) element or through a **SRC** attribute referencing an object. **MD** contains an encoded checksum, called a *message digest*, that lets the browser authenticate the linked object as indeed being the one intended by the document author.

The following describes, in detail, these four attributes, and where they can be used.

ALIGN="left", "center", "right", "justify" (optional) All elements that define blocks of text can take the optional **ALIGN** attribute. **ALIGN** specifies how paragraphs within the block are to be aligned, and takes four possible values:

ALIGN="left"   paragraphs are left-aligned (flush with the left margin)

ALIGN="center"   paragraphs are centered

ALIGN="right"   paragraphs are right-aligned (flush with the right margin)

ALIGN="justify"   paragraph text is left- and right-justified, where possible, with the left margin being equivalent to the left margin associated with **ALIGN**="left".

Note that the alignment setting of an outer element is overridden by an **ALIGN** on an enclosed element. For example, consider the following block of HTML:

```
<DIV ALIGN="right">

    <P> bla bla bla impster ipsut flubb milfium bdilfim nossic asdf blob globum

    <P ALIGN="left">more goofy text—it's hard to think of intelligent things

        to say while making up these examples....

</DIV>
```

This indicates that the first paragraph inside the **DIV** should be right-aligned, while the second should be left-aligned. The default alignment is **ALIGN**="left".

The **ALIGN** attribute is a hint as to text formatting, and can be ignored without affecting the meaning of a document. It is therefore safe for HTML 2.0 browsers.

NOTES

NOTE 1: ALIGN, as described above, can be used in the following HTML 3 elements:

     DIV, Hn (headings), **P**

NOTE 2: The **ALIGN** attribute is used, but with a different meaning, by the elements **IMG**, **FIG**, **TABLE**, various elements within **TABLE**, and **CAPTION**. Please see the descriptions of these elements for the meanings of **ALIGN** in these contexts.

CLEAR="left", "right", "all", "n en", "n pixels" (optional) **CLEAR** specifies, for elements that control text blocks, how the text should flow around embedded objects such as **IMG**, **FIG**, and **TABLE** elements. This is equivalent to the **CLEAR** attribute of the **BR** element as implemented by the Netscape browser, as discussed in Chapter 4. The possible values are:

CLEAR="left" An element with this **CLEAR** attribute should be moved down until the left margin is clear.

CLEAR="right" An element with this **CLEAR** attribute should be moved down until the right margin is clear.

CLEAR="all" An element with this **CLEAR** attribute should be moved down until both margins are clear.

CLEAR="*n* en" An element with this **CLEAR** attribute should be moved down until there is a region into which text can be entered that has a *width* greater than or equal to "*n*" en units, where "*n*" is an integer. An en unit is one-half the width of current point size.

CLEAR="*n* pixels" An element containing this **CLEAR** attribute should be moved down until there is a region into which text can be entered that has a width greater than or equal to "*n*" pixels, where "*n*" is an integer.

CLEAR is a harmless attribute for HTML 2.0 browsers, and is simply ignored.

■■■■■■ **NOTE**

CLEAR can be used in the following elements:

ADDRESS, BLOCKQUOTE, HR, Hn (headings), P, PRE, OL, UL, DL, LI, DT, DD, and BR

■■■■■

NOWRAP (optional) **NOWRAP** indicates that the text within the element should *not* be word-wrapped. Consequently, **NOWRAP** can be used by elements that define blocks of text. When **NOWRAP** is specified, word wrapping occurs only at explicit <BR> tags. **NOWRAP** affects all enclosed elements, so that:

```
<DIV NOWRAP>

    <P> paragraph 1

    <P> paragraph 2

</DIV>
```

disables word wrapping in both paragraphs. At present, there is no HTML 3 attribute or element to reverse the effect of **NOWRAP** to allow optional word wrapping. It is likely that an element analogous to Netscape's **WBR** (word break) will be required. Currently, there are no browsers that implement **NOWRAP**.

MD=*"digest_string"* (optional) MD specifies a *message digest* for an object specified by a hypertext link, and can be present inside an **A** (anchor) element, or wherever an external image is referenced using a **SRC** attribute. A message digest is essentially a digital signature for a data file, created by a program employing a special cryptographic checksum algorithm: the program reads in a data file and produces the message digest as output. Because of the way the algorithm works, it is virtually impossible for a person to intentionally create a second, substitute file that yields the same digital signature. Thus the message digest becomes an independent check on the validity of the referenced data.

When an author creates a hypertext link to a file, he or she can use the **MD** attribute to include the message digest string within the element linked to the file. When a client uses the link to access the object, the browser accesses the file and can use the checksum algorithm to calculate the message digest. If the message digest calculated by the browser is the same as that included in the **MD** attribute, then the linked object is the one expected by the document author. If the two message digests are not the same, then the linked file was altered in some way, and is untrustworthy.

Here are two examples, in both cases assuming the MD5 message digest algorithm. The algorithm is indicated by the md5: prefix to the encoded checksum:

```
<A HREF="../accounts.html" MD="md5:jVadfxmasdfSAdfa">

<IMG SRC="pie_chart.gif" MD="md5:132dsf/;.aF">
```

At present, there are no browsers that actually validate linked files using message digests. **MD** is ignored by HTML 2.0 browsers.

BANNER ELEMENT: A DOCUMENT BANNER

Usage:	<BANNER> . . . </BANNER>
Can Contain:	**Hn, P, HR,**
	DL, OL, UL,
	ADDRESS, BLOCKQUOTE, *DIV, FIG, FN,* **FORM,** *NOTE,* **PRE,** *TABLE,* **[ISINDEX]**
Can Be Inside:	**BODY**
Attributes:	*CLASS, ID, LANG*

BANNER defines a block of the document as a *page banner*. The marked block should appear at the top or bottom of the display window, and should not scroll with the rest of the document. Thus a **BANNER** is an ideal place for things such as corporate or organizational logos, or collections of graphical/text "buttons" used for navigational purposes within a large document collection.

A **BANNER** should be the first element in a document **BODY**; this way, if the browser does not support **BANNER**, the element content will still appear at the top of the display window. This allows you to include **BANNER** elements in HTML 2.0 documents. You must make sure, however, that the **BANNER** content is a self-contained block—for example, by putting it inside a closed paragraph (use that </P> tag!).

In the future, you will likely be able to specify a document banner using a **LINK** element of the form <LINK REL="banner" HREF="banner_url">.

There are no browsers that currently support **BANNER**.

BLOCKQUOTE (BQ) ELEMENT: BLOCK QUOTATION

Usage:	<BLOCKQUOTE> . . . </BLOCKQUOTE>
Can Contain:	*CREDIT,* **Hn, P, HR,**
	DL, OL, UL,
	ADDRESS, BLOCKQUOTE, *DIV, FIG, FN,* **FORM,** *NOTE,* **PRE,** *TABLE,* **[ISINDEX]**

Can Be Inside: *BANNER*, BODY, BLOCKQUOTE, *DIV*, *FIG*, *FN*, FORM, *NOTE*,

DD, LI, *TD*, *TH*

Attributes: *CLASS*, *CLEAR*, *ID*, *LANG*, *NOWRAP*

BLOCKQUOTE is unchanged from HTML 2.0; HTML 3 recommends dropping the name **BLOCKQUOTE** in favor of the shorter name, **BQ**. HTML 3 also adds **CREDIT** to the allowed content of **BLOCKQUOTE**, for including a credit for the quotation. At present, there are no browsers that support **CREDIT**.

CREDIT ELEMENT: CREDIT TO A FIG OR ELEMENT

Usage: `<CREDIT> . . . </CREDIT>`

Can Contain: **characters, character highlighting, A, BR, IMG, MATH, TAB**

Can Be Inside: *BLOCKQUOTE, FIG*

Attributes: *CLASS, ID, LANG*

CREDIT contains a credit or acknowledgment associated with a **BLOCKQUOTE** or **FIG** element. Consequently, the content of **CREDIT** should be short and concise. Figures 5.2–5.4 show a credited **FIG**. **CREDIT** is not supported by HTML 2.0 browsers. However, a **CREDIT** *may* be rendered reasonably if it appears at the end of a **BLOCKQUOTE**, and if all preceding block elements were properly closed with end tags.

DIV ELEMENT: A BLOCK DIVISION OF THE BODY

Usage: `<DIV> . . . </DIV>`

Can Contain: **Hn, P, HR,**

DL, OL, UL,

ADDRESS, BLOCKQUOTE, *DIV*, *FIG*, *FN*, FORM, *NOTE*, PRE, *TABLE*, [ISINDEX]

Can Be Inside:	*BANNER*, BODY, BLOCKQUOTE, *DIV, FIG, FN,* FORM, *NOTE, TD, TH*
Attributes:	*ALIGN, CLASS, CLEAR, ID, LANG, NOWRAP*

DIV marks a block of the document as a logical group or *division*: the **CLASS** attribute can be used to indicate the type of block (e.g., **CLASS**="subsection"). In principle, every document should be prepared as a nested collection of divisions, although this is not formally required. **DIV** allows for a formal description of the document content, and can be used, for example, to restrict indexing or searching software to particular components of a document. In addition, stylesheets can be used to associate desired formatting with different divisions, according to the value of their **CLASS** attributes.

DIV implies the end of any preceding paragraph. Other than for this, **DIV** does not affect the formatting or presentation of a document, and is simply used to more formally organize the document content.

DIV can be used within properly written HTML 2.0 documents, since it can be safely ignored. However, be careful that you do not expect **DIV** tags to end otherwise unterminated block elements, such as paragraphs.

Example of **DIV**:

```
<BODY>

<DIV CLASS="article">

    <DIV CLASS="abstract">

    ...

    </DIV>

    <DIV CLASS="section">

      ...

        <DIV CLASS="subsection">

        ...

        </DIV>

    </DIV>

</DIV>

</BODY>
```

FIG ELEMENT: FIGURES

Usage:	`<FIG> . . . </FIG>`
Can Contain:	*CAPTION, CREDIT, OVERLAY*, Hn, P, HR, DL, OL, UL, ADDRESS, BLOCKQUOTE, *DIV, FN,* FORM, *NOTE*, PRE, *TABLE,* [ISINDEX]
Can Be Inside:	*BANNER*, BODY, BLOCKQUOTE, *DIV, FIG, FN,* FORM, *NOTE, DD*, LI, *TD, TH*
Attributes:	*ALIGN, CLASS, CLEAR, HEIGHT, ID, IMAGEMAP, LANG, MD, NOFLOW, SRC, UNITS, WIDTH*

FIG is used to include a formal figure in a document—in HTML 3, **IMG** should be used only for inserting decorative graphics. **FIG** can contain elements for captions (**CAPTION**) and credits (**CREDIT**), and has sophisticated mechanisms for image overlays (**OVERLAY**), client-side imagemaps, and a mechanism for including text-only descriptions of the figure and related imagemap.

Figures are designed as "floating" objects, and can be positioned on the display using the **ALIGN** attribute. Text then flows around the figure, or not: the optional **NOFLOW** attribute stops text flow around the figure, and ensures it is kept clear of surrounding text.

A simple **FIG** is as follows:

```
<FIG SRC="albatross.gif">

  <CAPTION> Get Your Frozen Albatross!</CAPTION>

  <P>A movie theater ice-cream seller, carrying a

     frozen albatross, on a stick.

   <CREDIT><A HREF="monty.html">Monty Python</A>, The

          Illustrated History

   </CREDIT>

</FIG>
```

This example contains the image *albatross.gif*, a caption, and a figure credit. The content of the **FIG**, in this case the paragraph of text `<P>A movie the-ater . . .` , is not displayed by a graphical browser capable of displaying the image. However, if an HTML 3-aware browser is incapable of displaying the figure, or if image display is disabled, it will present this text content in place of the image. This is similar to the **ALT** attribute value of the **IMG** element, except that the text is now document body content, and can contain a large assortment of HTML elements. Thus you can use this portion of the **FIG** element to create a very complete textual description of the image, and make your documents much more usable to those using nongraphical tools.

Active images can be included in two ways. The first is similar to the use of **ISMAP** with an **IMG** element, although the coding is much easier. Here is an example, with the extra text required for the active imagemap shown in bold-face:

```
<FIG SRC="albatross.gif" IMAGEMAP="http://bla.ca/cgi-bin/imagemap">

  <CAPTION> Get Your Frozen Albatross!</CAPTION>

  <P>A movie theater ice-cream seller, carrying a

     frozen albatross, on a stick.

   <P>Select on the following options:

  <UL>

     <LI><A HREF="albatross.html">Albatross Information</A>

     <LI><A HREF="cleese.html">About John Cleese</A>

     <LI><A HREF="albatross.html">Ice Cream?</A>

   </UL>

</CREDIT>

</FIG>
```

The **IMAGEMAP** attribute tells the browser that this is an active image, and also provides the URL to which the click coordinates should be sent—you no longer need a surrounding anchor element, as was required with `<IMG ... ISMAP>`. Note also that the **FIG** example was designed so that if the browser is incapable of displaying images, the user is presented with a list of selectable options instead of a clickable map.

The second alternative allows you to include information linking regions within the image to desired hypertext links *within* the **FIG** element. This allows the browser itself to both measure the click coordinates and determine which anchor to access. As a result, the browser no longer needs to access an imagemap program on a server. Here is an HTML fragment showing how this is done, based on the preceding example—again, the extra markup needed to implement this *client-side imagemap* approach is shown in boldface:

```
<FIG SRC="albatross.gif">

 <CAPTION> Get Your Frozen Albatross!</CAPTION>

 <P>A movie theater ice-cream seller, carrying a

    frozen albatross, on a stick.

 <P>Select on the following options:

 <UL>

   <LI><A HREF="albatross.html" SHAPE="default">Albatross Information</A>

   <LI><A HREF="cleese.html" SHAPE="circle 100,100,20">About John
Cleese</A>

   <LI><A HREF="albatross.html" SHAPE="rect 100,200,150,220">Ice
Cream?</A>

 </UL>

</CREDIT>

</FIG>
```

The difference lies in two places: first, in the absence of the **IMAGEMAP** attribute, and second, in the **SHAPE** attributes of the anchor elements. This method requires that hypertext anchors to the desired resources be included within the **FIG**. The **SHAPE** attributes specify both the type and location of the region in the image that is associated with each hypertext link. These coordinates can be specified in pixels (integer numbers, measured downward and to the right from the upper left-hand corner) or as decimal quantities from (0.0, 0.0) (upper left-hand corner) to (1.0, 1.0) (bottom right-hand corner). The **FIG** element recognizes the **SHAPE** attribute as tying the enclosed hypertext links to the image. Once again, if the browser is unable to display the image, it will display the enclosed text, including the list of hypertext links.

The construction of **SHAPE** attribute values is described in the **A** (anchor) element section, later in this chapter.

Finally, a **FIG** can include *overlay* images. For example, the following **FIG** consists of a city map of Toronto, with an overlay containing directions to the Toronto Islands Park:

```
<FIG SRC="downtown.gif">

<OVERLAY SRC="to_islands.gif">

  <P> Directions to Toronto Island Park.

        Take the subway south to Union Station, followed by

        the streetcar south one station. Then follow the

        signs to the Ferry Docks.

</FIG>
```

OVERLAYs can themselves be active imagemaps, either through an **IMAGEMAP** attribute or through the **SHAPE** attribute to the anchor element, as discussed above.

The **FIG** element is largely incompatible with HTML 2.0, since the image file is not presented, and **CAPTION**s and **CREDIT**s are incorrectly displayed. However, the text content of a **FIG** may provide some guide to the missing image, if care is taken to design a **FIG** that allows for HTML 2.0 limitations. Figures 5.2–5.4 show an example of the **FIG** element and its rendering on HTML 3 and HTML 2.0 browsers.

As mentioned in Chapter 4, there are efforts underway to combine the features of the current **FIG**, **APPLET**, and **EMBED** elements to develop a generic element appropriate for embedding complex objects within an HTML document. It is thus likely that **FIG**, as described here, will not be widely implemented as part of standard HTML.

███████ **Figure 5.2** An example HTML 3 document illustrating the use of the **FIG** element. Figure 5.3 shows this document rendered by the Arena browser, while Figure 5.4 shows the rendering by Netscape Navigator.

```
<HTML>

<HEAD>

  <TITLE>Example of FIG Element</TITLE>
```

```
    <LINK REV="made" HREF="mailto:igraham@hprc.utoronto.ca">
</HEAD>


<BODY>
  <DIV>

    <H2 ALIGN=center> Example of a FIG Element</H2>
    <P> Here is a paragraph, leading up to the figure. The Figure. will

    appear following this paragraph.</P>
    <FIG SRC="french.gif" ALIGN="left">

        <CAPTION><B>Department of French</B></CAPTION>
        <P>Photo of the building housing the Department of French.

        This paragraph of text is only displayed by browsers that cannot

        display the image included by the FIG.</P>

    </FIG>

    <P>This is some text that follows the figure—not how it flows

        around the figure, as is desired with properly laid-out documents.

        The Figure also has a CAPTION (at the bottom) .</P>

    <P>Browsers that do not understand FIG will not display the image.

        They will also have a rough time displaying the FIG element content,

        unless you were very careful to block all text into well-defined

        paragraphs or lists! </P>

  </DIV>

  <DIV CLASS="contact-info">

    <HR>

    <ADDRESS><A HREF="maintenance.html">I.S.G</A></ADDRESS>

  </DIV>

</BODY>

</HTML>
```

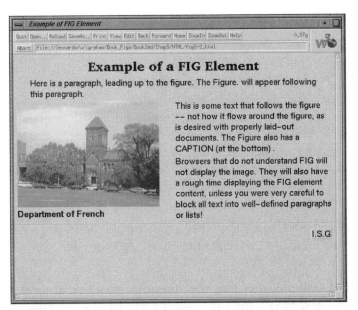

Figure 5.3 Rendering of the HTML document listed in Figure 5.2 by the Arena 0.97 browser. The **FIG** element is clearly illustrated.

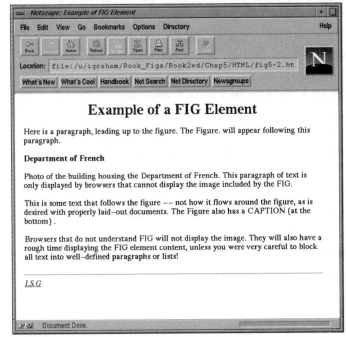

Figure 5.4 Rendering of the HTML document listed in Figure 5.2 by the Netscape Navigator 1.1 browser. This browser does not understand the HTML 3 **FIG** element, and so cannot display the image.

The following are the important attributes specific to **FIG**:

ALIGN="bleedleft", "left", "center", "right", "bleedright", "justify" (optional) **ALIGN** specifies the horizontal alignment of the figure. **ALIGN**="left" and **ALIGN**="right" align the figure flush left and flush right with the text margin, respectively. **ALIGN**="bleedleft" and **ALIGN**="bleedright", on the other hand, align the figure flush with the left and right window borders. **ALIGN**="center" (the default) aligns the figure with the center of the window, and disables text flow around the figure. **ALIGN**="justify" causes the browser to attempt to rescale the figure so that it completely fills the region between the left and right text margins, and consequently disables text flow around the figure.

SRC="*url_string*" (mandatory) **SRC** gives the URL of the image file to be included as the figure. The file can be validated using the **MD** attribute, as discussed earlier in this chapter.

NOFLOW (optional) **NOFLOW** indicates that the author does not want text to flow around the image, and forces any subsequent text, **TABLE**, or **FIG** to start below the figure.

HEIGHT="*n*" (optional) **HEIGHT** specifies the desired integer height of the image, in units specified by the **UNITS** attribute; the default units are pixels. A browser should rescale the image to fit this height.

WIDTH="*n*" (optional) **WIDTH** specifies the desired integer width of the image, in units specified by the **UNITS** attribute; the default units are pixels. A browser should rescale the image to fit this width.

UNITS="pixels", "en" (optional) **UNITS** specifies the units by which the desired **HEIGHT** and **WIDTH** of the image are specified. The possible values are "pixels" (the default) and "en". One en unit is one-half the point size of the current font.

IMAGEMAP="*url_string*" (optional) **IMAGEMAP** specifies a URL to which click coordinates should be sent, and indicates that the figure is an active image.

OVERLAY ELEMENT: IMAGE OVERLAY IN A FIG

Usage:	<OVERLAY>
Can Contain:	empty
Can Be Inside:	*FIG*

Attributes:	*HEIGHT, IMAGEMAP, MD, SRC, UNITS, WIDTH, X, Y*

OVERLAY is used to load an image overlay on top of a **FIG** image; if present, it must be the first element inside a **FIG**. The **SRC** attribute is mandatory for an **OVERLAY**, and gives the URL of the overlay image. The optional **MD** attribute can be used to validate the linked overlay image. **OVERLAY** takes several other optional attributes, which have the following uses:

X="*x*" (optional) **X** specifies the desired *x* (horizontal) offset, relative to the left edge of the image, of the overlay relative to the figure image—the units are specified by the **UNITS** attribute (the default units are pixels).

Y="*y*" (optional) **Y** specifies the desired *y* (vertical) offset, relative to the top edge and measured downward, of the overlay relative to the figure image—the units are specified by the **UNITS** attribute (the default units are pixels).

IMAGEMAP="*url*" (optional) **IMAGEMAP** specifies a URL to which click coordinates should be sent, and implies that the overlay is an active image. An overlay imagemap overrides any **IMAGEMAP** referenced in the original **FIG**.

UNITS="pixels", "en" (optional) **UNITS** specifies the units by which the desired **HEIGHT** and **WIDTH**, and the **X** and **Y** offsets, are specified. The possible values are "pixels" (the default) and "en". One en unit is one-half the point size of the current font.

OVERLAYs are not supported by any existing browsers.

CAPTION ELEMENT: CAPTION TO A FIG OR TABLE

Usage:	<CAPTION> . . . </CAPTION>
Can Contain:	**characters, character highlighting, A, BR, IMG, MATH, TAB**
Can Be Inside:	*FIG, TABLE*
Attributes:	*ALIGN, CLASS, ID, LANG*

CAPTION contains a caption to a **FIG** or **TABLE** element, and can be placed anywhere inside a **FIG** or **TABLE** element. The browser will render the caption in an appropriate way, with the optional attribute **ALIGN** specifying a preferred location for the caption. The possible options are **ALIGN**="top", "bottom", "left", and "right", with the obvious associated meanings. The default setting is **ALIGN**="top".

For best compatibility with HTML 2.0, **CAPTION**s should be placed at the beginning or end of the **FIG** content.

Figures 5.2–5.4 illustrate a figure **CAPTION**.

FN ELEMENT: FOOTNOTES

Usage:	`<FN> . . . </FN>`
Can Contain:	**Hn, P, HR,**
	DL, OL, UL,
	ADDRESS, BLOCKQUOTE, *DIV, FIG, FN,* **FORM,** *NOTE,* **PRE,** *TABLE,* [ISINDEX]
Can Be Inside:	*BANNER,* **BODY, BLOCKQUOTE,** *DIV, FIG, FN,* **FORM,** *NOTE,*
	DD, LI, *TD, TH*
Attributes:	*CLASS, ID, LANG*

FN denotes a footnote. Footnotes are referenced using the **ID** attribute, so that **ID** is a mandatory attribute of **FN**. A browser should hide footnotes, and present them to the user only when requested. For example, when an anchor linked to a footnote is selected, the footnote might then be presented in a pop-up window.

FN is an *unsafe* element in HTML 2.0, since the enclosed text is not hidden, and will appear out-of-context in the document. You can preserve separation of footnotes from the document by collecting **FN** elements together and placing them at the bottom of the document. An HTML 2.0 browser will then display the footnotes as text at the bottom of the page. Of course, the hypertext links to the footnotes will not function on an HTML 2.0 browser.

Example of **FN**:

```
<P>Photon-inflated boogons are an important new concept in

elementary boogon <A HREF="boog1">theory</A>.
```

```
.... more text .....

<FN ID="boog1">

  <P>Boogon theory was first introduced by Bak in 1995,

    as discussed in his seminal <A HREF="http://www.x.ca/boog/pap.ps">paper</a>.

  <P>Inflationary aspects were first introduced by Thomson, in a

    succesful attempt at solving the dangling-boogon

    <a href="http://www.boog.ca/booger/paradox.html">paradox</a>

</FN>
```

Figures 5.5–5.7 illustrate the use of **FN**. There are currently no browsers that support **FN**.

▬▬▬ **Figure 5.5** An example HTML 3 document illustrating the use of the **FN** and **NOTE** elements. Figure 5.6 shows this document rendered by the Arena browser, while Figure 5.7 shows the rendering by Netscape Navigator.

```
<HTML>

<HEAD>

  <TITLE>Example of FN and NOTE Elements</TITLE>

  <LINK REV=made HREF="mailto:igraham@hprc.utoronto.ca">

</HEAD>

<BODY>

  <DIV>

    <H2>Example of FN and NOTE Elements</H2>

    <P>This text contains <A HREF="#fn1">footnotes</A>.  Each of the

      hypertext references leads to a footnote found in the body of

      the <A HREF="#fn2">document</A>.  A bowser should hide the

      footnotes until they are accessed.  </P>

    <HR>

    <NOTE ROLE="caution">

        <P> FNs and NOTEs may look absurd on HTML 2 browsers.  To
```

```
                help make things better, collect your footnotes together, and

                place them at the bottom of the document. Notes should be \

                written with appropriate text and block elements. </P>

        </NOTE>

        <HR>

        <P>And here is more exciting text, not part of the NOTE. Well, what

            did you expect at these prices—art?</P>

    </DIV>

    <DIV CLASS="footnotes">

        <HR>

        <FN ID="fn1"><P>This is <B>footnote 1</B>. A FN-aware browser should

            hide this text until the FN is accessed!.</P> </FN>

        <FN ID="fn2"><P>Here is the <B>second footnote</B>. These have been

            placed at the bottom of the page, to help them display better on

            an HTML 2.0 browser. Note that links to the footnotes don't work.

        </P> </FN>

    </DIV>

</BODY>

</HTML>
```

FORM ELEMENT: FILL-IN FORMS

Usage:	`<FORM>` . . . `</FORM>`
Can Contain:	**INPUT, SELECT, TEXTAREA, Hn, P, HR,**
	DL, OL, UL,
	ADDRESS, BLOCKQUOTE, *DIV, FIG, FN, NOTE,* **PRE,** *TABLE,* **[ISINDEX]**

Can Be Inside:	*BANNER*, BODY, BLOCKQUOTE, *DIV*, *FIG*, *FN*, *NOTE*,
	DD, LI, *TD*, *TH*
Attributes:	ACTION, ENCTYPE, METHOD, *SCRIPT*

HTML 3 adds new functionality to a form, through additional user input elements plus a **SCRIPT** attribute. **SCRIPT** specifies the URL of an *executable script* that can be accessed by the client, and used to process the **FORM** fields and user input. As an example, the script might auto-calculate certain fields based on the content of other fields, might change the keyboard focus by following the mouse pointer, or might process mouse clicks on a graphical input field. There is currently no specification for such a scripting language, and this feature is not implemented on current browsers.

As discussed in Chapter 4, Netscape Navigator 2.0 implements the new **HEAD** element **SCRIPT**, which is used to include a scripting program that

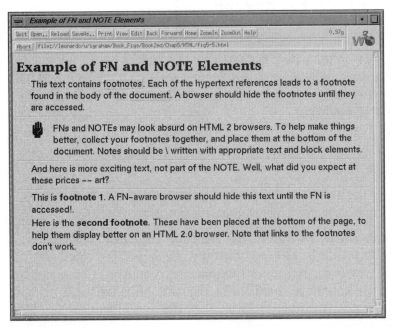

Figure 5.6 Rendering of the HTML document listed in Figure 5.5 by the Arena 0.97 browser.

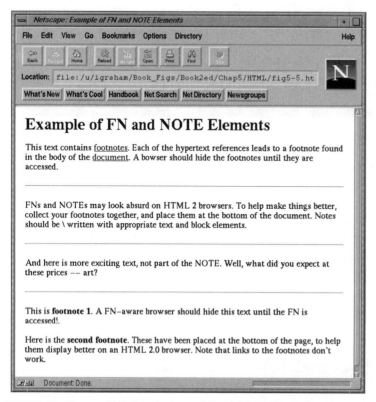

■■■■■ **Figure 5.7** Rendering of the HTML document listed in Figure 5.5 by the Netscape Navigator 1.1 browser. This browser does not understand the HTML 3 elements. However, careful placement of the **FN** and **TIP** elements helps to make the document readable.

can interact with the HTML document, including **FORM**s. In fact, the Netscape *LiveScript* scripting language contains explicit functions for interacting with **FORM** input elements.

HTML 3 also allows the new optional attributes **DISABLED** and **ERROR** on every **FORM** user input element. The meanings of these attributes are:

DISABLED (optional; any **FORM** user input element) **DISABLED** marks an input element as disabled: the element content is displayed, but should be rendered in some way (e.g., grayed out) to indicate its status. The content of a disabled element cannot be modified by the user. An HTML 2.0 browser will ignore this attribute, and will allow the user to edit the field.

ERROR=*"error_message"* (optional; any **FORM** user input element) **ERROR** indicates that the content of a field is in error, while the value of the **ERROR** attribute explains the reason(s) for this error. A browser should display this information in some way to the user. An HTML 2.0 browser will ignore this attribute.

INPUT ELEMENT: FORM INPUT ELEMENTS

Usage:	<INPUT>
Can Contain:	empty
Can Be Inside:	**FORM,** any nonempty element allowed inside a **FORM**
Attributes:	*ACCEPT,* **ALIGN, CHECKED,** *CLASS, DISABLED, ERROR, FILE, ID, LANG, MAX,* **MAXLENGTH,** *MD, MIN,* **NAME, SIZE, SRC, TYPE, VALUE**

As in HTML 2.0, the **INPUT** element specifies a variety of *editable fields*; you are referred to Chapter 4 for an introduction to **INPUT** elements. HTML 3 adds several new attributes to all input elements: **DISABLED** for disabled input fields; **ERROR** for errors associated with a field; and **MD** for use whenever a **SRC** attribute is specified. There are also two new input mechanisms: **TYPE**="range", for an input slider, with the ranges of the slider specified by the **MIN** and **MAX** attributes, and **TYPE**="scribble" for user input (using a mouse or other pointing device) onto a graphical scratchpad. These new attributes and input types are described below; new attribute values associated with attributes already present in HTML 2.0 are underlined.

TYPE= "text", "checkbox", "radio", "password", "range", "scribble", "file", "hidden", "submit", "image", "reset" (mandatory)

The differences from HTML 2.0 types are summarized below. At present there are no browsers supporting these new input types.

TYPE="range" This allows a user to select a numeric value in a specified range: the range is specified by the attributes **MIN** and **MAX**, which are mandatory for this **TYPE**. The default value is (**MAX+MIN**)/2. A browser might display this as a slider or any other appropriate input device. The following is a simple example of this input type:

```
<INPUT TYPE="range" MIN="2.0"  MAX="5.0" NAME="gain" VALUE="2.6">
```

It is an error if the **VALUE** or user input lies outside the specified range.

TYPE="scribble" This specifies pointing device input: the browser should display an image (specified with the **SRC** attribute, mandatory for **TYPE="scribble"**), onto which the user can "scribble" using an input device such as a mouse. If the browser is unable to display images or create an appropriate graphic input device, this input type should be treated as **TYPE="text"**—in this case, the **VALUE** attribute can be used as an initial value. The **VALUE** attribute is ignored if the browser is capable of properly handling the "scribble" type. Here is an example:

```
<INPUT TYPE="scribble" NAME="diagram_notes"

      SRC="diagram.gif"

      VALUE="diag_unable-to-scribble">
```

This type is unimplemented, as there is no defined mechanism for transmitting scribble input data to a server.

TYPE="file" This specifies file input, and allows the user to attach a local file to the data being sent to the server. The optional **ACCEPT** attribute specifies the types of files that can be sent, as a list of comma-separated MIME content-types. For example:

```
<INPUT  TYPE="file" NAME="image_data"

ACCEPT="image/gif, image/jpeg, image/tiff">
```

This input type is largely unimplemented, as until recently there was no defined mechanism for transmitting file data content to a server. There is currently a draft specification for a new mechanism that would allow **FORM**-based file uploads to a server from a client using a `multipart/form-data` MIME content-type. References to this new MIME type are given at the end of this chapter. The "file" input type is implemented by the Netscape Navigator 2.0 browser.

TYPE="submit" In HTML 3, the **SRC** attribute is allowed in a **TYPE="submit"** input element. This allows an image in place of a simple Submit button. When the user clicks on the image, the form is submitted, along with the coordinates of the pointing device relative to the upper left-hand image corner. For example, the following element:

```
<INPUT TYPE="submit" NAME="option"  VALUE="Option 2" SRC="opt2.gif">
```

would send the data `option.x=x_coord` and `option.y=y_coord` to the server, along with the other **FORM** data, as soon as the user clicked on top of the image. This is not compatible with HTML 2.0 unless the click coordinates are not required—in this case you need merely ensure an appropriate **VALUE**. This extension is not supported on current browsers.

TYPE="reset" In HTML 3, the **SRC** attribute is allowed a **TYPE**="reset" input element. This allows an image to be used in place of a Reset button. The following is an example:

```
<INPUT TYPE="RESET" VALUE="Initialize" SRC="opt2.gif">
```

This is backward-compatible with HTML 2.0, since **RESET** merely resets the **FORM** to its initial values.

ACCEPT="*type1/subtype1, type2/subtype2*" (optional; **TYPE**="file" only) **ACCEPT** specifies, as a comma-separated list of MIME types, the allowed data formats that can be accepted by a **TYPE**="file" input element.

ALIGN="top", "middle", "bottom", "left", "right" (optional; only with **TYPE**="scribble" "image", "submit", or "reset") **ALIGN** is valid for input elements containing images: namely, **TYPE**="scribble" and "image", as well as "submit" and "reset" when an image file is inserted via a **SRC** attribute. The values "top", "middle", and "bottom" align the top, middle, or bottom of the image with the baseline of the surrounding text, while the values "left" and "right" allow the image to float to the left and right margins, as with the **IMG** element. Text can flow around these floated images. HTML 2.0 only allows "top", "middle", and "bottom" alignment of **TYPE**="image" **INPUT** elements.

MIN="*x*" (mandatory with **TYPE**="range") **MIN** specifies the lower limit of a range field, as either an integer or real number.

MAX="*x*" (mandatory with **TYPE**="range") **MAX** specifies the upper limit of a range field, as either an integer or real number.

TEXTAREA Element: FORM Text Input

Usage: `<TEXTAREA> . . . </TEXTAREA>`

Can Contain: **characters**

Can Be Inside:	FORM
Attributes:	*ALIGN, CLASS,* COLS, *DISABLED, ERROR, ID, LANG,* NAME, ROWS

The use of **TEXTAREA** is unchanged from HTML 2.0. In addition to **DISABLED** and **ERROR**, discussed previously, HTML 3 adds the following attribute:

ALIGN= "top", "middle", "bottom", "left", "right" (optional) HTML 3 treats a **TEXTAREA** element like an embedded image; the **ALIGN** attribute allows control of the alignment of the region on the display. The values "top", "middle", and "bottom" align the top, middle, or bottom of the image with the baseline of the surrounding text, while the values "left" and "right" allow the image to float to the left and right margins.

SELECT Element: FORM Multiple-choice Input

Usage:	<SELECT> . . . </SELECT>
Can Contain:	OPTION
Can Be Inside:	FORM, any nonempty element allowed inside a FORM *except* TEXTAREA or SELECT
Attributes:	*ALIGN, CLASS, DISABLED, ERROR, HEIGHT, ID, LANG, MD,* MULTIPLE, NAME, *SRC, UNITS, WIDTH*

The **SELECT** element allows for selectable lists of items. In HTML 2.0 this was a list of text items. HTML 3 allows the selectable list to be presented as a graphical image (included using the **SRC** attribute). The included image is sized and placed on the page in the same manner as an **IMG** element—consequently, if the **SELECT** element has the **SRC** attribute, it can also take the attributes **ALIGN, HEIGHT, WIDTH, UNITS,** and **MD**. The meanings of these attributes are exactly as described in the **IMG** element section, and are not reproduced here.

If the **SELECT** element takes an image, then the active regions of the image are indicated using **OPTION** elements taking a **SHAPE** attribute; this attribute specifies the region of the image associated with each option, just as with anchor elements inside a **FIG** element. If the browser is unable to display the image, this simply reduces to a list of selectable text items, and **SHAPE** attributes are ignored. Here is an example of a **SELECT** element using images:

```
<SELECT NAME="python_character" IMG="monty_p.gif" ALIGN="left">

    <OPTION SHAPE="circle 50, 50, 8" VALUE="cleese">John Cleese

    <OPTION SHAPE="circle 50, 70, 8" VALUE="gilliam">Terry Gilliam

    <OPTION SHAPE="circle 50, 100, 8" VALUE="idle">Eric Idle

    . . .

    <OPTION SHAPE="default" VALUE="nobody">Nobody

</SELECT>
```

The use of the **SHAPE** attributes is exactly the same as with anchor elements inside a **FIG**. At present, there are no browsers that implement the <SELECT SRC=...> form of the **SELECT** element. This new **SELECT** format is compatible with HTML 2.0 browsers, since they will present the text list instead of the selectable image.

The use of the **SRC** attribute in a **SELECT**:

SRC="*url_string*" (optional) **SRC** gives the URL associated with the image to be included as a graphical menu. If **SRC** is specified, the **SELECT** element can also take the **ALIGN**, **HEIGHT**, **WIDTH**, **UNITS**, and **MD** attributes. The meanings of these attributes are not reproduced here; see the **IMG** element section for a description of their use. An HTML 2.0 browser will ignore this attribute.

OPTION Element: Option Within a SELECT

Usage:	<OPTION> . . . (</OPTION>)
Can Contain:	**characters**
Can Be Inside:	**SELECT**
Attributes:	*CLASS, DISABLED, ERROR, ID, LANG,* **SELECTED**, *SHAPE,* VALUE

As in HTML 2.0, **OPTION** indicates the possible choices in a **SELECT** element—please see Chapter 4 for a summary of the use of **OPTION**. HTML 3 extends the HTML 2.0 text-only mode **SELECT** by allowing **OPTION** to link regions, within a **SELECT** image, to different selectable items. This is accomplished via the **SHAPE** attribute, which specifies a geometric region within the image. The use of a **SHAPE** attribute within an **OPTION** element is identical with the use of the **SHAPE** attribute within an **A** (anchor) element—please see the **A** and **FIG** element sections for details. Briefly, the use of **SHAPE** is as follows:

SHAPE=“*shape coord1, coord2, . . .* ” **SHAPE** specifies the region of the image linked to the specified option. In the above notation “*shape*” is a keyword indicating the type of shape, possible values being “square”, “circle”, “polygon”, and “default” (to be used if no other region is selected). “*coord1, coord2, . . .* ” is a comma-separated list of numbers that give coordinate and other information (radius, height, etc.) relevant to the indicated shape. The use of a **SHAPE** attribute within an **OPTION** element is identical with the use of the **SHAPE** attribute in an **A** (anchor) element— please see the **A** element section for details.

Hn Elements: Headings

Usage:	`<Hn> . . . </Hn>`
Can Contain:	**characters, character highlighting, A, BR, IMG,** *MATH, TAB*
Can Be Inside:	*BANNER,* BLOCKQUOTE, *DIV, FIG, FN,* FORM, *NOTE,* *TD, TH*
Attributes:	*ALIGN, CLEAR, DINGBAT, ID, LANG, MD, NOWRAP, SEQNUM, SKIP, SRC*

The meaning of heading elements is unchanged from Chapter 4. In HTML 3, you should use headings in combination with **DIV** elements to organize the text, since heading elements are just headings, and do not impose organization. For example, a **DIV** defining a subsection might contain the subsection heading (**H2**), followed by the section content.

In HTML 3, headings can take attributes that allow numbered headings (**SEQNUM, SKIP**), or that assign “bullets” to a heading, as an inlined image (**SRC**) or a special symbol (**DINGBAT**). The use of these attributes is discussed below.

SEQNUM="*n*" (optional) **SEQNUM** sets a *sequence number* for the heading element, and for subsequent heading elements of the same order; the browser can then number the heading appropriately, if instructed to do so in a stylesheet. The **SEQNUM** value is optional, the default being 1. The sequence counter is reset to 1 upon encountering a heading element of a higher level. This is illustrated in the following example:

Heading Elements	Counter Value	Comments
`<H1 SEQNUM=3>...</H1>`	3	
`<H2>...</H2>`	3.1	
`<H2>...</H2>`	3.2	
`<H1>...</H1>`	4	
`<H2>...</H2>`	4.1	(Level 2 counter reset to 1 because of intervening Level 1 heading)
`<H2 SKIP=2>...</H2>`	4.4	(Skipped two intervening steps)

HTML 2.0 browsers simply ignore **SEQNUM** and **SKIP**, and present unnumbered headings.

SKIP="*n*" (optional) **SKIP** skips sequence numbers, incrementing the sequence number before generating the heading. The default increment (in the absence of a specified increment) is 1.

DINGBAT="*entity_name*" (optional) **DINGBAT** gives the entity name of a symbol to be placed in front of the heading. **DINGBAT** names are yet to be specified. You cannot specify both **SRC** and **DINGBAT** in the same heading. An example is:

```
<H1 DINBGAT="disk.drive">
```

SRC="*url_string*" (optional) **SRC** give the URL of an image file to be included as a symbol in front of the heading. You cannot specify both **SRC** and **DINGBAT** in the same heading element.

HR ELEMENT: HORIZONTAL RULE

Usage:	`<HR>`
Can Contain:	empty

Can Be Inside:	*BANNER*, BODY, BLOCKQUOTE, *DIV*, *FIG*, *FN*, FORM, *NOTE,*
	TD, *TH*
Attributes	*CLASS*, *CLEAR*, *ID*, *MD*, *SRC*

The **HR** element is largely unchanged from HTML 2.0. HTML 3 proposes that **HR** take an optional **SRC** attribute, which specifies the **URL** of an image file to be used as the dividing symbol. There are currently no browsers that support this **SRC** attribute. HTML 2.0 browsers simply ignore these attributes, and draw the default dividing line.

NOTE ELEMENT: NOTES OR ADMONISHMENTS

Usage:	<NOTE> . . . </NOTE>
Can Contain:	**Hn, P, HR,**
	DL, OL, UL,
	ADDRESS, BLOCKQUOTE, *DIV*, *FIG*, *FN*, **FORM,** *NOTE*, **PRE,** *TABLE*, [ISINDEX]
Can Be Inside:	*BANNER*, BODY, BLOCKQUOTE, *DIV*, *FIG*, FN, FORM, *NOTE,*
	DD, LI, TD, TH
Attributes:	*CLASS*, *CLEAR*, *ID*, *LANG*, *MD*, *SRC*

NOTE is designed for including comments within a document, such as cautions or warnings. The type or role of a **NOTE** is defined by the **CLASS** attribute. HTML 3 recommends three class names for use with **NOTE**—CLASS="note", **CLASS**="caution", and **CLASS**="warning"—although others are possible. A browser should render the content of a **NOTE** with a sidebar graphic or icon appropriate to the **CLASS** value. Alternatively, the **SRC** attribute can specify a graphic.

HTML 2.0 browsers will ignore the **NOTE** tags, which leads to incorrectly formatted text if previous paragraphs were not closed. You should therefore make sure that all **NOTE** elements contain block elements, and not just raw text, and that the nature of the note is clear from the text content alone.

Figures 5.5–5.7 illustrate the **NOTE** element.

LIST ELEMENTS

HTML 3 recommends dropping **MENU** and **DIR** lists, since they are rarely used. In their place, you can use the unordered list elements <UL PLAIN> and <UL PLAIN WRAP="VERT">.

HTML 3 also adds several attributes to the list elements, to provide list rendering hints, and to allow for more flexible control of list numbering, bulleting, and organization. It also adds a new list header element, **LH**, which serves as a short heading for the list content. An **LH** must appear as the first element inside a list. **LH** will cause problems for HTML 2.0 browsers, as discussed below.

▬▬▬ **NOTE**

There is substantial ongoing discussion of list elements, with the intent of adding support for features such as cascading or "accordion" lists. This may lead to a substantial redesign of list elements, compared with the material presented here.

▬▬▬

LH ELEMENT: LIST HEADING FOR A **DL**, **UL**, OR **OL** LIST

Usage:	<LH> . . . (</LH>)
Can Contain:	**characters, character highlighting, A, BR, IMG, MATH, TAB**
Can Be Inside:	**DL, OL, UL**
Attributes:	*CLASS, ID, LANG*

The **LH** element contains a heading for a list. **LH** can be inside any of the HTML 3 heading elements, and must be the *first* element following the list start tag. **LH** can contain standard character markup, images, line breaks, and hypertext anchors.

HTML 2.0 browsers will not understand the **LH** element and will treat the **LH** element content as plain text. As a result, HTML 2.0 browsers may have trouble rendering its content —recall that in HTML 2.0, a list could only contain **DT** and **DD** tags, or **LI** tags (depending on the list type), and not plain text. Fortunately most HTML 2.0 browsers are lenient, and will present the heading text, although not marked up in any special way.

OL ELEMENT: ORDERED LIST

Usage:	`<OL> . . . </OL>`
Can Contain:	*LH*, LI
Can Be Inside:	*BANNER*, BODY, BLOCKQUOTE, *DIV*, *FIG*, FN, FORM, *NOTE*,
	DD, LI, TD, TH
Attributes:	*CLASS*, *CLEAR*, COMPACT, *CONTINUE*, *ID*, *LANG*, *SEQNUM*

The **OL** element is largely unchanged from HTML 2.0. In HTML 3, **OL** can take the attributes **CONTINUE** and **SEQNUM**, discussed below, which control numbering of list items. These are incompatible with HTML 2.0, so that if **CONTINUE** and **SEQNUM** are used, the numbering on an HTML 2.0 browser will be incorrect.

HTML 3 supports an **LH** element as the first element inside a list—this contains a list heading, as described previously. **LH** is incompatible with HTML 2.0.

CONTINUE (optional) **CONTINUE** directs a browser to continue the numbering of list items from where the previous ordered list left off. This is ignored by HTML 2.0 browsers.

SEQNUM="n" (optional) **SEQNUM** sets the starting number for the first item in the list to n (an integer). This is ignored by HTML 2.0 browsers.

UL ELEMENT: UNORDERED LIST

Usage:	`<UL> . . . </UL>`
Can Contain:	*LH*, LI
Can Be Inside:	*BANNER*, BODY, BLOCKQUOTE, *DIV*, *FIG*, FN, FORM, *NOTE*,
	DD, LI, TD, TH
Attributes:	*CLASS*, *CLEAR*, COMPACT, *DINGBAT*, *ID*, *LANG*, *MD*, *PLAIN*, *SRC*, *WRAP*

The **UL** (unordered list) is largely unchanged from HTML 2.0. HTML 3 proposes new attributes for selecting list item bullets (**DINGBAT, SRC**) or for control of list item arrangement (**PLAIN, WRAP**). The meanings are:

DINGBAT="*entity_name*" (optional) **DINGBAT** specifies an icon to be used as the bullet in an unordered list. This is specified as a special "dingbat" entity name—such entity names are as yet undefined. **DINGBAT** is currently unimplemented.

PLAIN (optional) Leave the list items unmarked (i.e., leave out the bullets).

SRC= "*URL*" (optional) **SRC** specifies the URL of an image to be used as the list item bullet.

WRAP= "horiz", "vert" (optional) Implies multicolumn lists, and declares how the items should be wrapped on the screen.

These attributes are not understood by current browsers. Note that HTML 3 recommends dropping the **MENU** and **DIR** elements. In their place you can use the unordered list elements <UL PLAIN> and <UL PLAIN WRAP=VERT>, respectively.

LI Element: List Item

Usage:	<LI> . . . (</LI>)
Can Contain:	P, PRE, DL, OL, UL,
	BLOCKQUOTE, *FIG, FN, FORM, NOTE,* [ISINDEX]
Can Be Inside:	UL, OL
Attributes:	*DINGBAT, MD, SKIP, SRC*

The **LI** element marks an item within a list. In HTML 3, LI can only contain block elements; this is unlike HTML 2.0, which allows list items to directly contain text and character highlighting elements. New attributes with HTML 3 are:

DINGBAT="*entity_name*" (optional) **DINGBAT** specifies an icon to be used as the bullet in the unordered list. This is sensible only for **LI** elements inside **UL** lists. **DINGBAT** entity names are yet to be specified.

SKIP="*n*" (optional) In an ordered list, **SKIP** advances the sequence number before rendering the item. For example, if the previous item was item 4, **SKIP**=2 would cause the current item to be labeled as number 6, skipping two numbers in the sequence. **SKIP** is sensible only inside **OL** lists.

SRC="*URL*" (optional) **SRC** specifies the URL of an image to use as the list item bullet. If present, the **MD** attribute can validate the linked image. This is sensible only inside **UL** lists.

These attributes are not understood by HTML 2.0 browsers, which can lead to errors in item numbering, or to unexpected layout of unordered lists.

HTML 3 TABLES

The HTML table elements were discussed in Chapter 4, as several implementations of tables are already in current use. The HTML development process, however, has now produced a richer table environment, with several new attributes and elements. These new features are discussed in the following section. However, you should read the **TABLE** element section from Chapter 4 to understand the organizational ideas behind a **TABLE**. The specification presented below is backwards-compatible with the **TABLE** implementation described in Chapter 4, and includes the additional attributes introduced by Netscape Inc.

LENGTH MEASURING UNITS

The **TABLE** elements support several units for measuring lengths. The units are indicated by adding an appropriate two-letter suffix to the numerical value—you *cannot* leave any space between the number and this suffix. The two-letter suffixes and their meanings are:

Suffix	Units
cm	centimeters
em	em units (height of the default font)
in	inches
mm	millimeters
pi	picas (there are 12 points per pica)
pt	points (there are 72.27 points/inch)
px	pixels (the default units)

For example, a length of 5 millimeters can be specified as "5mm" or "0.5cm." Pixel units are assumed if the suffix is left out. Decimal fractions are possible (e.g., 0.5cm) but exponential notation (e.g., 1.5e2) is not.

In some cases, lengths can also be expressed as integral percentages. This is indicated by placing a percentage symbol after the number. For example, the start tag `<TABLE WIDTH="80%">` specifies a table that spans 80 percent of the screen width. Lengths can also, in some cases, be expressed relative to other lengths—this is indicated by appending the asterisk symbol "*" after the number. This is useful when defining relative widths of columns, where you do not know the absolute width of the table. For example, the element `<COL WIDTH="3*">` (**COL** is defined later in this section) indicates a column with a width three times bigger than a column specified by `<COL WIDTH="1*">` (or `<COL WIDTH="*">`), and six times bigger than a column specified by `<COL WIDTH="0.5*">`.

Generic TABLE Attributes

In addition to **ID**, **CLASS**, and **LANG**, many of the **TABLE** elements take the following attributes. These are described here to avoid duplication throughout this section.

DIR="ltr", "rtl" (optional) **DIR** specifies the *direction* in which the characters should be written, and overrides any direction implied by the **LANG** attribute value. Possible values are "ltr" (left to right), or "rtl" (right to left). When applied to the **TABLE** element, DIR affects the layout direction of the text and table cells. Thus, `<TABLE DIR="rtl">` means that the table columns should be laid out from right to left, and also that the text within table cells should run from right to left.

STYLE="*stylesheet_info*" (optional) **STYLE** attribute content is interpreted as stylesheet-language instructions, to be used in formatting the element content (the stylesheet language being used must be specified by a **STYLE** element in the document **HEAD**). Stylesheets are not currently implemented, so there is no specification for constructing **STYLE** strings.

ALIGN="center", "char", "justify", "left", "right" (optional) **ALIGN** specifies the horizontal alignment of the content of the table cells enclosed by the element. The alignments "center", "left", "right", and "justify" have their obvious meanings ("justify" reverts to left-aligned, should justification not be possible), while "char" indicates alignment upon a particular character. The default alignment is "left". The default character for character alignment is the decimal point character implied by the **LANG** value (a period). Alternate alignment characters are specified by the **CHAR** attribute. The **CHAROFF** attribute specifies the horizontal offset of the alignment character.

CHAR=*"c"* (optional) **CHAR** specifies the character upon which the cell should be aligned. This overrides the default value, which is the decimal point character implied by the current language (set by the **LANG** attribute or by the default). This is only meaningful with **ALIGN**="char".

CHAROFF=*"length"* (optional) **CHAROFF** specifies the offset of the alignment character: if a text line does not contain the alignment character, then the *end* of the text line should be aligned with this position. The offset is measured from the left or right side of the cell, depending on **DIR**. The length can be specified in the standard physical units, or as a percentage offset: the latter is calculated as a percentage of the cell width. This is only meaningful with **ALIGN**="char".

VALIGN="baseline", "bottom", "middle", "top" (optional) **VALIGN** specifies the vertical alignment of the contents of the cells contained within the clement. The values "bottom", "middle", and "top" align the content within the cell, as per the obvious meanings. **VALIGN**="baseline" can be applied only to a collection of cells in a given row, in which case the first line of text in the cells is aligned at the text baseline. The default is **ALIGN**="middle".

GENERAL TABLE FEATURES

In the table model described in Chapter 4, a **TABLE** contained **TR** (table rows) elements and, optionally, a **CAPTION**. In the newer table model, a **TABLE** does not directly contain table rows, but instead should contain the **THEAD**, **TFOOT**, and **TBODY** elements, which in turn group table rows into a header (**THEAD**), footer (**TFOOT**), and a table body (**TBODY**). In addition, the **TABLE** clement can contain two new elements, **COL** and **COLGROUP**, which define properties such as cell alignment and/or width for particular columns or groups of columns. **COL** and **COLGROUP** elements must precede all table rows, since the program rendering the table must know this alignment or width information before it can begin formatting the table.

Here is a simple example of a table illustrating the use of some new components:

```
<TABLE WIDTH=80%>

    <COL WIDTH="1*">

    <COL WIDTH="2*">

    <COL WIDTH="1*">

    <THEAD>

        <TR>    <TH> Rodent    <TH> Description    <TH> Cost </TR>
```

```
</THEAD>

<TBODY>

    <TR>     <TD> Mouse  <TD> Small and cuddly     <TD> $1.99 </TR>

    <TR>     <TD> Gerbil <TD> Small and stinky     <TD> $2.99 </TR>

    <TR>     <TD> Rat    <TD> Absolutely disgusting <TD> $5.99 </TR>

</TBODY>

</TABLE>
```

In this example, the **COL** elements specify the relative widths of the three columns in the table (1|2|1). The table then consists of a table head (the row containing the table headings) plus a table body.

████████ **NOTE**

The **TABLE** element is still under development, and although the above appears close to being standardized, it is still subject to change.

████████

TABLE Element: Tables and Tabular Structures

Usage:	<TABLE> ... </TABLE>
Can Contain:	*CAPTION, COL, COLGROUP, THEAD, TBODY, TFOOT*
Can Be Inside:	*BANNER,* BODY, BLOCKQUOTE, *DIV, FIG,* FORM, *NOTE,* DD, LI, *TD, TH*
Attributes:	*ALIGN, BORDER, CLASS, CELLPADDING, CELLSPACING,*
	COLS, DIR, FRAME, ID, LANG, RULES, STYLE, WIDTH

The **TABLE** element defines a table. In the earlier table specification (see Chapter 4), the **TABLE** element directly contained **TR** elements. In the newer specification, a **TABLE** should only contain **THEAD**, **TBODY**, and **TFOOT** elements, which in turn contain the **TR**s. However, the start and stop tags of **TBODY** are optional, so that the **TABLE** can, in fact, contain **TR** elements.

Thus, the current specification is backwards-compatible with that given in Chapter 4. As discussed above, **TABLE** can also contain a **CAPTION**, as well as **COL** and **COLGROUP** elements that contain column-specific formatting and layout information.

The revised **TABLE** element can take a number of new attributes. These are:

ALIGN="center", "left", "right" (optional) **ALIGN** specifies the horizontal position of the table with respect to the text margins. Text can flow around left- or right-aligned tables, but not around centered tables.

BORDER=*"length"* (optional) **BORDER** specifies the width of the border framing the table. This can be specified in any of the physical units described previously. The default units are pixels. For backwards compatibility, the attribute can be specified without a value. The value **BORDER**="0" implies a table without borders, and is equivalent to specifying **FRAME**="void" (see below). Any other value (or an unspecified value) for **BORDER** implies **FRAME**="border".

CELLSPACING=*"length"* (optional) **CELLSPACING** specifies the horizontal and vertical spacing between cells in the table. The length can be specified in any of the standard physical units, the default being pixels.

CELLPADDING=*"length"* (optional) **CELLPADDING** specifies the horizontal and vertical spacing between the content of a cell and the cell borders. The length can be specified in any of the standard physical units, the default being pixels.

COLS=*"n"* (optional) **COLS** specifies the actual number of columns in the table. This allows the browser to begin formatting the table as the table data arrive.

FRAME="void", "above", "below", "hsides", "lhs", "rhs", "vsides", "box", "border" (optional) **FRAME** specifies which sides of the framing border should be rendered. The possible values, and their meanings, are:

"void"—render no sides of the table (a table without drawn borders)

"above"—render only the top side of the table frame

"below"—render only the bottom side of the table frame

"box" or "border"—render all four sides of the table frame

"hsides"—render only the top and bottom sides of the table frame "lhs"—render only the left-hand side of the table frame

"rhs"—render only the right-hand side of the table frame

"vsides"—render only the left- and right-hand sides of the table frame

RULES="none", "basic", "rows", "cols", "all" (optional) RULES specifies which dividing lines should be drawn within the table. The meanings of the five possible values are:

"none"—do not draw any interior dividing lines

"basic"—draw horizontal dividing lines between the **THEAD, TFOOT,** and **TBODY** content

"rows"—draw horizontal dividing lines between all table rows. A browser may use heavier lines between **THEAD, TFOOT,** and **TBODY** than between regular cells.

"cols"—draw vertical dividing lines between groups of columns (groups are defined by the **COLGROUP** and **COL** elements), and also draw horizontal dividing lines between the different row groupings (as in **RULES**="basic").

"all"—draw dividing lines between all rows and all columns. A browser may use heavier lines between groups of columns, or between **THEAD, TFOOT,** and **TBODY.** This is the default.

WIDTH="*length*" (optional) **WIDTH** specifies the desired width of the table. This can be specified in any of the physical units described previously in this section. The width can also be given as a percentage, determined relative to the width of the display—this can be ignored if the resulting table would be too small. The default is the full width of the display.

COL ELEMENT: SPECIFY PROPERTIES OF A COLUMN

Usage:	<COL>
Can Contain:	empty
Can Be Inside:	*COLGROUP, TABLE*
Attributes:	*ALIGN, CHAR, CHAROFF, CLASS, DIR, ID, LANG, SPAN, STYLE, WIDTH, VALIGN*

COL is an optional element, and is used to specify default properties for a column or a group of columns. A table will generally have several **COL** elements, to specify the properties of the different columns. For example,

```
<COL WIDTH="1*">

<COL WIDTH="2*">

<COL WIDTH="1*">
```

indicates that the second column is twice as wide as the first column, and that the third column is the same width as the first. The number of columns affected by a **COL** element is set by the **SPAN** attribute. Thus, **SPAN**=3 means that the properties specified by the **COL** element apply to three adjacent columns. For example,

```
<COL WIDTH="1*" ALIGN="left">

<COL SPAN=3 WIDTH="2*" ALIGN="center">

<COL WIDTH="1*" ALIGN="right">
```

indicates that the second, third, and fourth columns are each twice as wide as the first column, and that the fifth column is the same width as the first. The value **SPAN**="0" is special, and indicates that the properties should be applied to all columns from the current column up to the last column in the table.

Column properties can be specified using the **STYLE, LANG, DIR**, and various alignment attributes described at the beginning of this section. In addition, **WIDTH**s can be specified in absolute units, percentage width units (relative to the width of the table), or in the relative width units demonstrated in the above example.

COLGROUP ELEMENT: HORIZONTAL ALIGNMENT PROPERTIES OF A COLLECTION OF CELLS

Usage:	<COLGROUP> . . . (</COLGROUP>)
Can Contain:	*COL*
Can Be Inside:	*TABLE*
Attributes:	*ALIGN, CHAR, CHAROFF, CLASS, DIR, ID, LANG, STYLE, VALIGN*

It is often useful to *group* columns together. For example, you might want to group the leftmost two columns as a vertical collection of subject headings, or the two rightmost columns as spreadsheet totals. Such groupings are possible using the **COLGROUP** element. This element allows you to group columns, and also assign the group default alignment settings. An example is:

```
<COLGROUP ALIGN="char"  CHAR="." CHAROFF="40%" VALIGN="baseline">

    <COL  WIDTH="1*">

    <COL   WIDTH="2*">

<COLGROUP ALIGN="center">

    <COL WIDTH="1*">

    <COL WIDTH="1.5*">

<THEAD> ....
```

which defines two column groups: the first with character alignment, the second with centered cell contents. Note how the **COLGROUP** properties apply to all the columns specified within the **COLGROUP**.

A browser may render the boundaries between grouped columns with a heavier dividing line than the boundaries between ungrouped columns. This is a reminder that the **COLGROUPS** should be used to group cells that logically belong together.

THEAD Element: Table Header

Usage:	`<THEAD> . . . (</THEAD>)`
Can Contain:	*TR*
Can Be Inside:	*TABLE*
Attributes:	*ALIGN, CHAR, CHAROFF, CLASS, DIR, ID, LANG, STYLE, VALIGN*

THEAD defines the table header. A table header consists of table rows that make up the header of the table (for example, a **THEAD** might contain one or more rows of **TH** table header cells). **THEAD** content is designed to act, where appropriate, like a banner, so that if the table is longer than the display, the **THEAD** cells stay at the top of the displayed table as the user scrolls through the table body.

THEAD must precede the **TBODY**, which in turn must precede the **TFOOT**. If a browser does not understand the **THEAD**, **TFOOT**, or **TBODY** elements it will then display the table appropriately, but without floating headers and footers.

TBODY Element: Table Body

Usage:	(<TBODY>) . . . (</TBODY>)
Can Contain:	*TR*
Can Be Inside:	*TABLE*
Attributes:	*ALIGN, CHAR, CHAROFF, CLASS, DIR, ID, LANG, STYLE, VALIGN*

TBODY defines the body of the table. Formally you do not need the start and stop tags in the absence of **THEAD** or **TFOOT** elements, but it is safest to put them in.

TFOOT Element: Table Footer

Usage:	<TFOOT> . . . (</TFOOT>)
Can Contain:	*TR*
Can Be Inside:	*TABLE*
Attributes:	*ALIGN, CHAR, CHAROFF, CLASS, DIR, ID, LANG, STYLE, VALIGN*

TFOOT defines the table footer. A table footer consists of table rows that make up the footer of the table. **TFOOT** content is designed to act, where appropriate, like a **BANNER**, so that if the table is longer than the display, the **TFOOT** cells stay at the bottom of the displayed table as the user browses through the table body.

TFOOT must be the final element in a table, just after **TBODY**. If a browser does not understand the **THEAD**, **TFOOT**, and **TBODY** elements, it will then display the table appropriately but without floating headers and footers.

TR ELEMENT: TABLE ROW

Usage:	<TR> . . . (</TR>)
Can Contain:	*TD, TH*
Can Be Inside:	*THEAD, TFOOT, TBODY*
Attributes:	*ALIGN, CHAR, CHAROFF, CLASS, DIR, ID, LANG, STYLE, VALIGN*

TR defines a table row. Its usage is unchanged from that described in Chapter 4, other than for the different attributes possible under the new specification.

TD ELEMENT: TABLE DATA

Usage:	<TD> . . . (</TD>)
Can Contain:	Hn, P, HR,
	DL, OL, UL,
	ADDRESS, BLOCKQUOTE, *DIV, FIG, FN,* FORM, *NOTE,* PRE, *TABLE,* [ISINDEX]
Can Be Inside:	*TR*
Attributes:	*AXES, AXIS, ALIGN, CHAR, CHAROFF, CLASS, COLSPAN, DIR, ID, LANG, NOWRAP, ROWSPAN, STYLE, VALIGN*

TD denotes a cell containing table data. TD can contain almost any form of body content, but formally cannot contain plain text—you must place the text within at least a paragraph, and then place the paragraph in the cell.

As in the previous table specification, the attributes **ROWSPAN** and **COLSPAN** define the number of rows and columns spanned by the cell—their use is discussed in Chapter 4. Note that the special values **ROWSPAN="0"** indicates that the cell spans all rows from the current row to the end of the table, while **COLSPAN="0"** indicates that the cell spans all columns from the current column to the end of the table. TD cells can also take the attributes **ALIGN, CHAR, CHAROFF,** and **VALIGN** to specify the alignment of the cell content. These values override any alignment settings specified in surrounding elements. Attributes specific to the individual cells are:

AXIS=*"string"* (optional) **AXIS** specifies an abbreviated name for a header cell, for use by software that renders a table into speech. In the absence of this element, the browser will use the cell content as a spoken label.

AXES=*"string"* (optional) **AXES** specifies a comma-separated collection of **AXIS** names, which then specify the row and column headers appropriate to the cell. A header cell may have both an **AXIS** and **AXES**, which indicates that the cell is actually a subheading.

TH ELEMENT: TABLE HEADER

Usage:	`<TH> . . . (</TH>)`
Can Contain:	**Hn, P, HR,**
	DL, OL, UL,
	ADDRESS, BLOCKQUOTE, *DIV, FIG, FN,* FORM, *NOTE,*
	PRE, *TABLE,* [ISINDEX]
Can Be Inside:	*TR*
Attributes:	*AXES, AXIS, ALIGN, CHAR, CHAROFF, CLASS, COLSPAN, DIR, ID, LANG, NOWRAP, ROWSPAN, STYLE, VALIGN*

TH denotes a cell containing a table header. **TH** can contain almost any form of body content, but formally cannot contain plain text. Minimally, you must place the text within a paragraph, and then place the paragraph in the cell.

TH cells can take the same attributes as **TD** elements, discussed in the previous section; you are therefore referred to the **TD** section for a discussion of the attributes.

A ELEMENT: HYPERTEXT ANCHORS

Usage:	`<A> . . . </A>`
Can Contain:	**characters, character highlighting, BR, IMG, *MATH, TAB***
Can Be Inside:	**character highlighting, ADDRESS, Hn, P, PRE,**

<table>
<tr><td></td><td>*CAPTION, CREDIT,* DT, *LH*</td></tr>
<tr><td>Attributes:</td><td>*CLASS,* HREF, *ID, LANG, MD,* METHODS, NAME, REL, REV, *SHAPE,* TITLE, URN</td></tr>
</table>

As in HTML 2.0, **A** marks a text or image block as the beginning and/or end (target) of a hypertext link. Within a **FIG** element, **A** supports the **SHAPE** attribute, which is used to relate the anchor hypertext reference to regions within the figure image. The details of this mechanism are discussed in the **FIG** element section, elsewhere in this chapter. The following is a brief discussion of the **SHAPE** attribute:

SHAPE= *"shape coordinates"* (optional: used inside a **FIG** only) **SHAPE** is valid only for anchor elements within **FIG** elements, as discussed in the **FIG** element section, earlier in this chapter. **SHAPE** defines active regions of the figure image, and attaches them to the indicated hypertext links. In the above notation, *"shape"* is a keyword indicating the type of shape, possible values being "square", "circle", "polygon", and "default" (to be used to define actions taken if the user's cursor is not inside a defined square, circle, or polygon. *"Coordinates"* is a comma-separated list of numbers that gives coordinate and other information (radius, height, etc.) appropriate to the indicated shape. Coordinates can either be integer quantities, in which case they are measurements in pixels from the upper left-hand corner, or real numbers in the range (0.0,0.0) (the upper left-hand corner) to (1.0,1.0) (lower right-hand corner).

The following examples show the appropriate form of the **SHAPE** attribute values. Here x, y, r, w, h, xn, and yn represent coordinates in either of the above units schemes. Note that all quantities in a given **SHAPE** value should be in the same units. Here are the different shapes, and the meanings of the associated coordinates:

"circle x, y, r"	Indicates a circle centered at (x,y) and of radius r.
"rect x, y, w, h"	A rectangle: (x,y) is the upper left-hand corner of the rectangle, while w is the width (to the right) and h is the height.
"polygon $x1$, $y1$, . . . xn, yn"	A polygon: the coordinates $(x1,y1)$ . . . (xn,yn) are the vertices of the polygon (minimum of three vertices). The polygon is joined by connecting the point $(x1,y1)$ to (xn, yn).

If a user selects a point lying within more than one region, the browser will calculate the distance between the point and the center of gravity of the different regions. The chosen link will be the one whose center of gravity is closest to the selected point.

In HTML 3, **A** can also take the generic attributes **CLASS**, **ID**, and **LANG**, as well as the **MD** attribute used to validate linked resources. These are harmless to an HTML 2.0 browser, with the exception of **ID**. HTML 3 recommends replacing the attribute **NAME** by the attribute **ID**. However, **ID** is not recognized by an HTML 2.0 browser. You should therefore stick to the **NAME** attribute (or use both **NAME** and **ID**), if you want your fragment identifiers to work!

SPOT ELEMENT: MARK A LOCATION WITHIN A DOCUMENT

Usage:	<SPOT>
Can Contain:	empty
Can Be Inside:	**any element**
Attributes:	*ID*

SPOT is used to mark a location within a document, and can occur *anywhere* in the body of a document. **SPOT** takes a single mandatory attribute, **ID**, which must be assigned a label referencing the location. The **RANGE** element (in the document **HEAD**) can use the range specified by two **SPOT** elements to mark a section of the document for special treatment, such as highlighting. This is entirely browser-dependent.

When surrounded by text, **SPOT** is considered a null character, and does not imply a word space. **SPOT** is ignored by HTML 2.0 browsers, which clearly cannot detect the **SPOT**-labeled location.

TAB ELEMENT: TABBING CONTROL

Usage:	<TAB>
Can Contain:	empty
Can Be Inside:	**A, character highlighting, ADDRESS, Hn, P, PRE,**

	CAPTION, CREDIT, DT, *LH*
Attributes:	*ALIGN, CHAR, ID, INDENT, TO*

▮▮▮ **NOTE**

There are currently no browsers that support the **TAB** element. The **TAB** element is currently undergoing substantial discussion, so that the specification is likely to change from that discussed below.

▮▮▮

TAB provides control of horizontal tabbing. Tab stops can be set in two ways: by using a **TAB** to mark a location in a document, or by using the **INDENT** attribute of a **TAB** to specify a physically desired indent. In both cases, the location of each tab is indicated using the **ID** attribute. Then, each of these labeled tabs can be accessed using the **TO** attribute, which references the **ID**-labeled tab. Here are two examples, showing the two methods of setting tabs:

EXAMPLE 1: INTERNALLY SET TAB POSITIONS

```
<P>I want the next line to start <TAB ID="tab-1">here, so I set the

    tab mark, and then <br>

                          <TAB TO="tab-1"> tab "to" this marked indent.
```

EXAMPLE 2: PRESET TAB POSITIONS

```
<TAB INDENT=10 ID="indent-1">

<TAB INDENT=30 ID="indent-2">

<P CLASS="poem.verse">Alas, I implore<BR>

            <TAB TO="indent-1"> --against sacrificial greed,<BR>

That life's truth, and beauty<BR>

                      <TAB TO="indent-2">should comfort me<BR>

.......
```

Once you have assigned a tab stop, the tab **ID** is valid anywhere in the remainder of the document.

Ordinarily, a tab aligns the leading character of the text that follows the **TAB**. In some cases, however, you want to align on some other character, such as a decimal point. This allows you to align a column of numbers, such that the decimals are tabbed into alignment. This option is accomplished using the attribute **ALIGN**="char", which specifies alignment on a special character (the default is the decimal point, or whatever character is appropriate given the current **LANG** context). You can use **CHAR**="c" to set an alternative alignment character, where c is the character you wish to align on. For example, the following:

```
<TAB INDENT=20 ID="tab1">

<TAB TO="tab1" ALIGN="char"> 12.2212<BR>

<TAB TO="tab1" ALIGN="char"> 1213.4<BR>

<TAB TO="tab1" ALIGN="char"> 43.12<BR>
```

would, on a graphical display capable of tabbing, produce the formatted output:

12.2212

1213.4

43.12

where all the numbers are tab indented, but aligned on the decimal point.

The **ALIGN** attribute has several other uses. For example, <TAB ALIGN="right"> will cause the text following the tab to be flushed to the right-hand margin, while <TAB ALIGN="right" TO="tabstop"> flushes the text to the right, using the designated tab stop as the right margin. Other options are possible, and are summarized in the following attribute descriptions.

ALIGN= "left", "center", "right", "char" (optional) **ALIGN** specifies the alignment within the tabbed fields. The meanings are:

ALIGN="left" (the default) The text following the **TAB** starts immediately after the designated tab stop.

ALIGN="center" The text following the **TAB** and up to the next tab or line break is centered on the designated tab stop. If there is no designated tab stop (i.e., there is no **TO** attribute to the **TAB** element), then the text is centered between the left and right margins.

ALIGN="right" The text following the **TAB** and up to the next tab or line break is flushed right with the designated tab stop. If there is no designated tab stop (i.e., there is no **TO** attribute to the **TAB** element), then the text is flushed to the right margin.

ALIGN="char" The text following the **TAB** is decimal aligned—the first occurrence of the decimal point character in the text following the **TAB** is aligned with the designated tab stop. If there is no designated tab stop (i.e., there is no **TO** attribute to the **TAB** element), the **TAB** is treated as a single-space character.

ID="*string*" (mandatory if specifying a tab position) **ID** is an identifier used to reference the tab stop, and must always be present if a tab is being defined. Once set, a tab stop is defined for the remainder of the document.

INDENT="*n*" (optional) **INDENT** specifies a physical indent for a tab stop. Indents are specified in en units, where one en is equal to one-half the point size of the current font. **INDENT** is only valid when combined with **ID** to define a tab stop.

TO="*string*" (mandatory if aligning to a tab stop) **TO** references a tab stop; the text following the tab is then indented to the tab stop indicated by the named **TAB**. **TO** cannot be used if **ID** is present, since **ID** is used to define the tab stop.

LOGICAL CHARACTER HIGHLIGHTING/FORMATTING

HTML 3 proposes several new logical text highlighting elements that provide some purely semantic, as well as semantic/structural, information about the text. All these elements share the same content model, so to avoid reproducing it repeatedly, it is presented just once (`element` represents the generic element name):

Usage:	`<element> . . . </element>`
Can Contain:	**characters, character highlighting, A, BR, IMG,** *MATH, TAB*
Can Be Inside:	**A, character highlighting, ADDRESS, Hn, P, PRE,** *CAPTION, CREDIT,* **DT,** *LH*
Attributes:	*CLASS, ID, LANG*

The new highlighting elements are demonstrated in Figures 5.8, 5.9, and 5.10.

■■■■■■ **Figure 5.8** An example HTML 3 document illustrating the use of the new HTML character highlighting elements.. Figure 5.9 shows this document rendered by the Arena browser, while Figure 5.10 shows the rendering by the HTML 2.0 browser Mosaic for X-Windows Version 2.7b1.

```
<HEAD>

  <TITLE>HTML 3 Character Emphasis Elements</TITLE>

  <LINK REV=made HREF="mailto:igraham@hprc.utoronto.ca">

</HEAD>

<BODY>


<DIV>

  <h2 align=center>HTML 3 Character Emphasis Elements</h1>

  <h3>Logical Highlighting</h2>


  <ul>

    <li> ACRONYM- This is an <ACRONYM>acronym</ACRONYM>.

    <li> ABBREV - This is an <ABBREV> abbrev. </ABBREV> (abbreviation).

    <li> AU - <AU>Ian Graham</AU> is an author.

    <li> DEL - This is <DEL> deleted text. </DEL>

    <li> DFN - This is a <DFN> term's </DFN> defining instance.

    <li> INS - This is <INS> inserted text. </INS>

    <li> LANG - This is a modified <LANG>language context</LANG>.

    <li> PERSON - <PERSON>Frank Jones</PERSON> is a person.

    <li> Q - This is short <Q>quotation</Q>.

  </ul>


  <h2> Physical Highlighting </h2>


  <ul>
```

```
        <li> BIG - This is <BIG> enlarged size (BIG) </BIG> text.

        <li> S - This is <S> struck-out </S>text.

        <li> SMALL - This is <SMALL> reduced size (small) </SMALL> text.

        <li> SUB - This is text with a<SUB>subscript</SUB>.

        <li> SUP - This is text with a<SUP>superscript</SUP>.

        <li> U - This is <U>underlined</U> text.

    </ul>

</DIV>


</BODY>

</HTML>
```

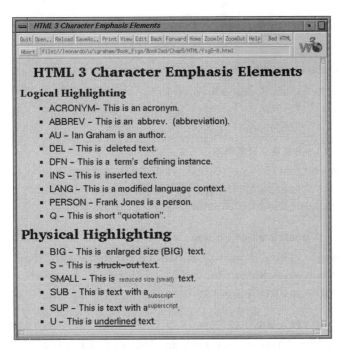

Figure 5.9 Rendering of the HTML document listed in Figure 5.8 by the Arena 0.97 browser.

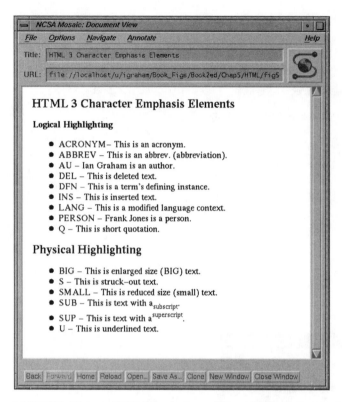

■■■■■■ **Figure 5.10** Rendering of the HTML document listed in Figure 5.8 by the Mosaic for X-Windows 2.7b1 browser.

ACRONYM ELEMENT: ACRONYMS

ACRONYM marks an acronym. There is no recommended formatting for the content of this element. This is a safe element for HTML 2.0, since a browser will simply render the text without modified formatting.

ABBREV ELEMENT: ABBREVIATIONS

ABBREV marks an abbreviation. There is no recommended formatting for the content of this element. This is a safe element for HTML 2.0, since a browser will simply render the text without modified formatting.

AU ELEMENT: AUTHOR NAME

AU marks the name of an author. There is no recommended formatting for the content of this element. This is a safe element for HTML 2.0, since a browser will simply render the text without modified formatting.

DEL ELEMENT: DELETED TEXT

DEL marks deleted text. The intent here is to mark deleted text that has a logical purpose for deletion, such as text deleted from a legal document. There is no recommended formatting for the content of this element, although struck-out text may in some instances be appropriate. A browser might also, for example, allow the user to toggle the deleted text in and out from the displayed document. This is an *unsafe* element for HTML 2.0, since a browser will simply display the enclosed text, unmodified. In most cases this will produce a very confusing document!

DFN ELEMENT: DEFINING INSTANCE

DFN marks the defining instance of a term. A browser will typically render this in italics or bold italics. This is a safe element for HTML 2.0, since a browser will simply render the text without modified formatting.

INS ELEMENT: INSERTED TEXT

INS marks text that has been inserted in a document. The intent here is to mark inserted text that has a logical purpose for insertion, such as a text addition to a legal document. There is no recommended formatting for the content of this element, although highlighting or italics may be appropriate in some instances. A browser might also, for example, allow the user to toggle the deleted text in and out from the displayed document. This is an *unsafe* element for HTML 2.0, since a browser will simply display the enclosed text, unmodified. In most cases this will produce a very confusing document!

LANG ELEMENT: LANGUAGE CONTEXT

LANG marks the language context for a block of text, and should be used where this cannot be appropriately accomplished using other elements. The LANG attribute is mandatory for the LANG element. This element introduces no change in text formatting, other than those changes caused by a change in language context—typically LANG would modify punctuation symbols. This is a safe element for HTML 2.0, since a browser will simply render the text without modified formatting.

PERSON ELEMENT: NAMES OF PEOPLE

The **PERSON** element marks the name of a person. There is no recommended formatting for the content of this element. This is a safe element for HTML 2.0, since a browser will simply render the text without modified formatting.

Q ELEMENT: SHORT QUOTATION

The **Q** element marks a short quotation, as opposed to a **BQ** (or **BLOCK-QUOTE** in HTML 2.0) element that is used to mark large quotations. This will typically be rendered in quotation marks appropriate to the language context (as set by the **LANG** attribute). In an English-language context, the text would be surrounded by single or double quotation marks. This is a *partially* safe element for HTML 2.0, since a browser will render the text without modified formatting, but the quoted nature of the text may no longer be obvious.

PHYSICAL CHARACTER HIGHLIGHTING/FORMATTING ELEMENTS

HTML 3 proposes six new physical text highlighting modes. These all follow the same content model as the logical highlighting elements discussed in the previous section. The new physical elements are illustrated in Figures 5.8 and 5.9.

BIG ELEMENT: INCREASE FONT SIZE

BIG marks text to be rendered, if possible, in a larger font. An HTML 2.0 browser will simply render the text without modified formatting. This element is understood by the Netscape Navigator 2.0 browser.

S ELEMENT: STRIKE-THROUGH

S marks text to be rendered as struck-out text, that is, with a horizontal line drawn through the enclosed text. This may be similar in presentation to **DEL** (deleted) text, but does not have the logical sense of deletion that is associated with the **DEL** element. This is *unsafe* in HTML 2.0, as the text content will be rendered without modified formatting.

SMALL ELEMENT: DECREASE FONT SIZE

SMALL marks text to be rendered, if possible, in a smaller font. An HTML 2.0 browser will simply render the text without modified formatting. This element is understood by the Netscape Navigator 2.0 browser.

SUB ELEMENT: SUBSCRIPT

SUB marks text that should be rendered as a subscript relative to the preceding text. The content of a **SUB** may also be rendered in a smaller font, if possible. This is an *unsafe* element for HTML 2.0, since subscripted text will be incorrectly presented by a browser that does not understand **SUB**. Some browsers (e.g., Mosaic and Netscape Navigator 2.0) support this element.

SUP ELEMENT: SUPERSCRIPT

SUP marks text that should be rendered as a superscript relative to the preceding text. The content of a SUP may also be rendered in a smaller font, if possible. This is an *unsafe* element for HTML 2.0, since superscripted text will be incorrectly presented by a browser that does not understand SUP. Some browsers (e.g., Mosaic and Netscape Navigator 2.0) support this element.

U ELEMENT: UNDERLINE

U renders the enclosed text with an underline, where possible. This element was proposed, and then dropped, from the HTML 2.0 specification, and is currently part of HTML 3. Some browsers support the U element.

MATH ELEMENT: MATHEMATICAL EXPRESSIONS

Usage:	`<MATH> . . . </MATH>`
Can Contain:	**characters, math entity references** (see below), *ABOVE, BELOW, BOX, SUB, SUP, VEC, BAR, DOT, DDOT, HAT, TILDE, SQRT, ROOT, ARRAY, B, T, BT*
Can Be Inside:	**A, character highlighting, ADDRESS, Hn, P, PRE,** *CAPTION, CREDIT,* **DT,** *LH*
Attributes:	*BOX, CLASS, ID*

The **MATH** element is used to include mathematical expressions in an HTML document. The formatting of mathematical elements is significantly more complex that the formatting of regular text, so that the **MATH** element can (and usually must) contain a number of math-specific elements (**ABOVE, BELOW, BAR,** etc.) that describe the construction of mathematical expressions. In addition, the **MATH** element can contain many special entity references that represent mathematical symbols such as Greek letters, product and integration signs, as well as special spacing characters for fine-tuning the space left between symbols. These special mathematics entities are summarized in Tables 5.1 through 5.7.

Those familiar with LaTeX will find the experimental HTML **MATH** element both familiar and frustrating—familiar in that things look a lot like LaTeX, frustrating in that there are several major differences.

MATH can take the optional attributes **ID** and **CLASS**, but *not* the **LANG** attribute. Mathematical formatting does not depend on language, but rather on the type of expression: for example, a chemistry formula, a genetic code sequence, or an old-fashioned equation (the default). In **MATH**, the **CLASS** attribute specifies this expression type, which can modify the rendering of the element content. For example, if the expression is a regular equation, a well-equipped graphical browser will render text letters using special italics designed for representing mathematical variables. If, however, the author specifies **CLASS**="chem", the text font should be nonitalicized, while with **CLASS**="gene" the text font should be one appropriate for expressing genetic code sequences. At present, only **CLASS**="chem" is understood as a defined style.

MATH can also take the optional element **BOX**, which requests that the browser draw a box around the expression.

NOTE

> The **MATH** element is experimental, and subject to change. In particular, entity names are defined for only a limited number of the required mathematical symbols (logical and, or, arrows, etc.). The specification is likely to change greatly over the next year.

The **MATH** element is not widely supported: currently only the Arena browser supports HTML mathematics, and even then only partially. Figures 5.11 through 5.16 contain some examples of HTML mathematical expressions.

MATHEMATICAL ENTITY REFERENCES

Mathematics is a world of non-ISO Latin-1 characters, so that the HTML **MATH** element supports a large collection of new entity references. These entities are only valid within a **MATH**. Currently defined entities are listed in Tables 5.1 through 5.7; these lists are at present incomplete.

GREEK LETTERS

Table 5.1 lists all the lowercase Greek letters and their corresponding entity references. In some cases there are common variations of the same character. These variations are denoted by preceding the character name with the word

■■■■ **Table 5.1** Entity References for Lowercase Greek Letters, Including Standard Variations Commonly Used in Mathematical Typesetting

Letter	Entity	Letter	Entity	Letter	Entity
alpha (α)	&alpha;	beta (β)	&beta;	gamma (γ)	&gamma;
delta (δ)	&delta;	epsilon (∈)	&epsilon;	var epsilon (ε)	&vepsilon;
zeta (ζ)	&zeta;	eta (η)	&eta;	theta (θ)	&theta;
var theta (ϑ)	&vtheta;	iota (ι)	&iota;	kappa (κ)	&kappa;
lambda (λ)	&lambda;	mu (μ)	&mu;	nu (υ)	&nu;
xi (ξ)	&xi;	omicron (o)	&omicron;	pi (π)	&pi;
var pi (ϖ)	&varpi;	rho (ρ)	&rho;	var rho (ϱ)	&varrho;
sigma (σ)	&sigma;	var sigma (ς)	&vsigma;	tau (τ)	&tau;
upsilon (υ)	&upsilon;	phi (φ)	&phi;	var phi (φ)	&varphi;
chi (χ)	&chi;	psi (ψ)	&psi;	omega (ω)	&omega;

"var", as in "var theta". Table 5.2 lists uppercase Greek letters (some are not shown, as they are the same as Latin letters).

MATHEMATICAL SYMBOLS

Mathematical expressions require many special symbols to express things such as integration, summation, logical relationships, and so on. Some symbols, such as less than (<) and greater than (>), are standard ASCII. Most, however, are not, so that special entity references are required. Currently defined entities are shown in Table 5.3.

For simplicity, HTML 3 interprets certain regular character strings as special characters. Thus the string "int" is interpreted as an integral sign, while "sum" indicates a summation symbol. Several such shortcuts are available, and are listed in Table 5.4.

■■■■ **Table 5.2** Entity References for Uppercase Greek Letters

Letter	Entity	Letter	Entity	Letter	Entity
Gamma (Γ)	&Gamma;	Delta (Δ)	&Delta;	Theta (Θ)	&Theta;
Lambda (Λ)	&Lambda;	Xi (Ξ)	&Xi;	Pi (Π)	&Pi;
Sigma (Σ)	&Sigma;	Upsilon (ϒ)	&Upsilon;	Phi (Φ)	&Phi;
Chi (X)	&Chi;	Psi (Ψ)	&Psi;	Omega (Ω)	&Omega;

■■■■■ **Table 5.3** Mathematical and Special Symbol Entity References Valid within a **MATH** Element

Character	Entity	Character	Entity	Character	Entity
⊥	⊥	±	±	∨	∨
∧	∧	≤	≤	≥	≥
≡	≡	≈	≈	≠	≠
⊂	⊂	⊆	⊆	⊃	⊃
⊇	⊇	∈	∈	←	←
→	→	↑	↑	↓	↓
↔	↔	⇐	⇐	⇒	⇒
⇑	⇑	⇓	⇓	⇔	⇔
∀	∀	∃	∃	∞	&inf;
∇	∇	⟨	⟨	∝	∝
⟩	⟩	⇔	⇔	∅	∅

SPACE CHARACTERS

Inside a **MATH** element, whitespace characters are generally removed during the typesetting process. Thus an expression such as

```
<MATH>&alpha;       &beta;        &gamma;</MATH>
```

is rendered as

αβγ

with no space between the characters. In some well-understood cases, spacing will be added (e.g., next to an integral sign). However, very often clear typesetting requires that the author add space between symbols. Table 5.5 lists four entities that introduce fixed-width spaces between characters. These are analogous to the nonbreaking space ( ) character of the ISO Latin-1 character set, but with finer control of the width.

■■■■■ **Table 5.4** Regular Character Strings Interpreted within **MATH** Elements as Special Symbols

Symbol	String	Symbol	String	Symbol	String
Summation (Σ)	sum	Integral ($\int$)	int	Product (Π)	prod

■■■■ **Table 5.5** Space Character Entity References Valid within a **MATH** Element

Description	Entity Reference	Description	Entity Reference
thin space (1/4 em)		medium space (1/2 em)	&sp;
thick space (1 em)		huge space (4 em's)	&quadsp;

CONTINUATION SYMBOLS/ELLIPSES

Mathematical expressions often require several different types of ellipsis symbols, such as the three dots on a baseline (...) commonly used in regular text, but aligned vertically or diagonally rather than horizontally. Also, they may require horizontal ellipses aligned at the level of the characters (for example, aligned with a minus sign). The entity references in Table 5.6 allow these ellipsis forms inside a **MATH** element.

SPECIAL CHARACTERS

Certain ASCII characters are special inside a **MATH** element, as they are used as short form representations for **MATH**-content element tags:

caret (^)	represents the start or end **SUP** (superscript) tag, depending on context
underscore (_)	represents the start or end **SUB** (subscript) tag, depending on context
left curly bracket ({)	represents the \<BOX> (start box) tag
right curly bracket (})	represents the \</BOX> (end box) tag

■■■■ **Table 5.6** Continuation Dots (Ellipsis) Entity References Valid within a
MATH Element

Description	Entity Reference
Three dots aligned with the text baseline (...)	&ldots;
Three dots mid-aligned with the text (⋯)	&cdots;
Three vertical dots (⋮)	&vdots;
Three diagonal dots (upper left to lower right) (⋱)	&ddots;
Valid within an **ARRAY** element only: fills the entire column of an **ARRAY** with vertical dots, or an entire row with horizontal dots.	&dotfill;

Table 5.7 Character and Entity References for Special Characters Inside a **MATH** Element (Some Are Not Yet Specified)

Description	Character Reference	Entity Reference
Caret (^)	&#94;	-- unknown --
Underscore (_)	&#95;	-- unknown --
Left curly bracket ({)	&#123;	&lcub;
Right curly bracket (})	&#125;	&rcub;

Examples of these are given in later sections. If you want these *characters* to appear within a **MATH** element, you must use their character or entity references. The relevant character and entity references are shown in Table 5.7.

SUPERSCRIPTS (SUP) AND SUBSCRIPTS (SUB)

Mathematical superscripts and subscripts are obtained using the **SUP** and **SUB** elements. These elements are also available outside of the **MATH** element, but their implementation is different inside **MATH**, as noted below.

Here are shown the letter "A" with a Greek alpha superscript, and "B" with a Greek beta subscript, which can be found in Figures 5.11 and 5.12:

```
<MATH> A<SUP> &alpha; </SUP> </MATH> <BR>

<MATH> B<SUB> &beta; </SUB> </MATH>
```

Because sub- and superscripts are common in mathematics, HTML 3 contains a shorthand notation for writing these expressions. The notation replaces both the start and end **SUP** tags by the caret character (^), and the start and end **SUB** tabs by the underscore character (_). Thus the above super- and subscript expressions can be equally written as:

```
<MATH> A^&alpha;^</MATH> <BR>

<MATH> B_&beta;_</MATH>
```

This is easier to type, and the caret (^) and underscore (_) suggest the idea of superscript and subscript. Note that in either case the <SUP> or <SUB> tag is placed right next to the term taking the super- or subscript. This is important, as it indicates to which expression the super- or subscript should be applied.

Superscripts and Subscripts on the Same Character

You can assign a superscript and subscript to the same character simply by following the character by both a subscript and superscript element. For example, the following gives the letter "*A*" the subscript "*01*" and the superscript "*Greek-alpha plus 1*":

```
<MATH> A_01_^ &alpha; + 1^ </MATH>
```

as shown in Figures 5.11 and 5.12 The rule to remember is: once a superscript (or subscript) element is ended, the next superscript or subscript element applies to the original baseline element.

Super- and Subscripts Preceding a Character

Super- and subscripts can be in front of, as well as after, a character—for example, the expression _a_X^b^ indicates the letter "*X*" with a leading subscript "*a*" and a trailing superscript "*b*". In general, a super- or subscript is applied to the term adjacent the expression: consequently, you must leave spaces to separate the subscript or superscript from the term you do *not* want them attached to. For example, the expression

```
<MATH> A^&alpha;^  _&beta;_B<MATH>
```

indicates an "*A*" with a superscript Greek alpha followed by a "*B*" with a leading subscript Greek beta, while the expression:

```
<MATH> A^&alpha;^_&beta;_B<MATH>
```

is unclear: should the subscript Greek beta be applied to the letter "*A*" or the letter "*B*"? By convention, the **MATH** interpreter parses from left to right, and will apply superscripts and subscripts to the first legitimate character, placing the subscript Greek beta on the letter "*A*".

Unfortunately, the current version of Arena cannot format leading sub- or superscripts. In principle, you can also use **ALIGN**="left" or "right" attributes to a **SUP/SUB** element, to specify super- or subscript placement. This is also not currently implemented.

▮▮▮▮ **Figure 5.11** Example HTML 3 document *fig5-11.html*, which illustrates mathematical superscripts and subscripts. The rendering of this document by the Arena browser is shown in Figure 5.12.

```
<HTML>

<HEAD>

<TITLE> Example Math Document #1 </TITLE>

</HEAD>



<BODY>
```

```
<H1 align=center> Example Math Document #1 </h1>

<HR>

<HR>


<h2>Simple Superscripts and Subscripts </h2>

<table border>

<tr> <td> <tt>&lt;MATH>A&lt;SUP>&amp;alpha;&lt;/SUP>&lt;/MATH></tt>

     <td> <MATH> A <SUP> &alpha; </SUP> </MATH>

<tr> <td> <tt>&lt;MATH>B&lt;SUB>&amp;beta;&lt;/SUB> &lt;/MATH> </tt>

     <td> <MATH> B <SUB> &beta; </SUB> </MATH>

<tr> <td align=left colspec=2> <b><i>Alternate Notation:</i></b>

<tr> <td> <tt>&lt;MATH>A^&amp;alpha;^&lt;/MATH> </tt>

     <td> <MATH> A^&alpha;^ </MATH>

<tr> <td> <tt> &lt;MATH> B_&amp;beta;_ &lt;/MATH>  </tt>

     <td> <MATH> B_&beta;_ </MATH>

</table>


<hr>

<h2> Combined Superscripts and Subscripts </h2>

<table border>

  <tr> <td> <tt> &lt;MATH>A_01_^&amp;alpha;+1^&lt;/MATH> </tt>

       <td> <MATH> A_01_^ &alpha; + 1^ </MATH>

</table>


<hr>

<h2> Superscripts on Superscripts </h2>

<P>

<table border>

<tr> <th> Correct </th>

     <td> <TT> &lt;MATH>A&lt;SUP>b&lt;SUP>&amp;alpha;&lt;/SUP>
```

```
            &lt;SUB>&amp;beta;&lt;/SUB>&lt;/SUP>&lt;/MATH></TT>

        </td>

        <td> <MATH> A <SUP> b <SUP>&alpha;</SUP><SUB>&beta;</SUB></SUP>

         </MATH>

        </td>

<tr> <th> Incorrect </th>

        <td> <TT>&lt;MATH> A^b^&alpha;^_&amp;beta;_^ &lt;/MATH> </TT>

        </td>

        <td> <MATH> A^b^&alpha;^_&beta;_^ </MATH> </td>

</table>


</BODY>

</HTML>
```

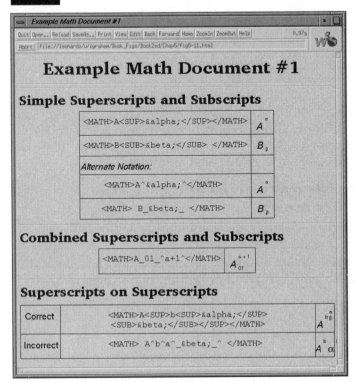

Figure 5.12 Rendering, by the Arena browser, of the document shown in Figure 5.12.

Superscripts on Superscripts

Sub- or superscripts can be placed on sub- or superscripts by appropriate nestings of **SUP** and/or **SUB** elements. For example, suppose you want the letter "*A*" to have a superscript "*b*", where the "*b*" has a subscript Greek beta and a superscript Greek alpha. The appropriate markup is (see Figures 5.11 and 5.12):

```
<MATH>
      A <SUP> b <SUP> &alpha;</SUP> <SUB> &beta;</SUB> </SUP>
</MATH>
```

Note that you *cannot* use the short forms (_) or (^). This is because with complex expressions such as this, the parser has no way of determining if you want an underscore to be a start or stop **SUB** tag. For example, if the **SUP** and **SUB** tags are replaced by the short forms, the expression is:

```
<MATH>
      A^ b ^ &alpha;^ _ &beta;_ ^
</MATH>
```

which is interpreted as meaning:

```
<MATH>
      A <SUP> b </SUP> &alpha;<SUP> <SUB> &beta;</SUB> </SUP>
</MATH>
```

which is wrong (see the bottom of Figure 5.12—the expression is slightly truncated due to a formatting error by the browser). If you want complex superscript and subscript notations, avoid the shorthand notations.

Superscripts on Superscripts:
Using the BOX Element

You can also create complex superscripts and subscripts using the **BOX** element. For example, let's reconsider the example above: an "*A*" with a superscript "*b*", with the "*b*" itself having a superscript Greek alpha and subscript Greek beta. Using the **BOX** element, this can be written as (see Figures 5.13 and 5.14):

```
A^ <BOX> b^ &alpha;^_&beta;_ </BOX> ^
```

or

```
A^ { b^ &alpha;^_&beta;_ } ^
```

The **BOX** element groups together the "*A*" superscript, with the box content having its own super- and subscripts. Note that the curly bracket shorthand for the **BOX** start and end tags does not have the problem of the underscore and caret.

SUB and SUP: Putting Expressions over Mathematical Operators

The **SUP** and **SUB** elements can be used to place super- or subscripts on most characters. However, when applied to mathematical *operators* represented by ordinary character strings, such as summation (sum), integration (int), or product (prod), **SUP** and **SUB** place the expression directly above or below the symbol. This is how you create limits to summations or integral expressions, or labeling of relational operators. Figure 5.13 shows three examples, using the integration, summation, and product symbols.

Grouping Equation Components: Putting Things Over Things

As seen previously, **BOX** is used to group parts of an equation for treatment as a group. It can also be used to box together components that should be treated separately from the rest of the expression. Suppose you want to put one expression over another, so as to imply division. This is done by boxing the top and bottom expressions together, and using the <OVER> tag to indicate what is over what. For example, the expression "q(m,n) = n! divided by m!(n-m)!" can be written in one of the two following ways:

    q(m,n) &sp; = <BOX> n! <OVER> m! (n-m!) <BOX>

    q(m,n) &sp; = { n! <OVER> m! (n-m!) }

as shown in Figures 5.13 and 5.14. Note how the space entity &sp; is used to add extra space between the leading term and the equals sign.

Figure 5.13 Example HTML 3 document *fig5-13.html*, which illustrates **BOX** and **OVER** elements. The rendering of this document by the Arena browser is shown in Figure 5.14.

```
<HTML>

<HEAD>

<TITLE> Example Math Document #2 </TITLE>

</HEAD>


<BODY>
```

```
<H1 align=center> Example Math Document #2 </h1>

<HR>

<HR>

<h2> Superscripts on Superscripts with BOX</h2>


<table border>

<tr>

   <td> <TT>&lt;MATH>A^{b^&amp;alpha;^_&amp;beta;_}^&lt;/MATH> </TT>

   <td> <MATH> A^ { b^&alpha;^_&beta;_} ^ </MATH>

</table>


<H2> Limits on Math Operators </H2>

<P>

<TABLE>

<tr> <td> <MATH> int_0_^&inf;^ </MATH>

     <td> <MATH> sum_m=0_^m=n-1^ </MATH>

     <td> <MATH> prod_m=0_^m=n-1^ </MATH>

</TABLE>


<HR>

<H2> Putting Things over Things</H2>

<table border>

<tr> <th align=left>Division<br>(<B>OVER</B>)</th>

     <td> <TT> q(m,n)&amp;sp;={n! &lt;OVER> m!(n-m)!}

         </TT>

     <td> <MATH>q(m,n)&sp; = {n! <OVER> m! (n-m)! } </MATH>

</table>


<HR>

<H2> Putting symbols ABOVE and BELOW </H2>
```

```
<table border>

<tr> <td><TT> &lt;ABOVE> &lt; f(x)+1 &gt;&lt;/ABOVE>

        </TT>

    <td><MATH> <ABOVE> &lt;f(x)+1&gt; </ABOVE> </MATH>


<tr> <td><TT> &lt;BELOW> &lt;f(x)+1&gt; &lt;/BELOW>

        </TT>

    <td> <MATH> <BELOW> &lt; f(x) + 1 &gt; </BELOW> </MATH> <br>

</TABLE>

</BODY>

</HTML>
```

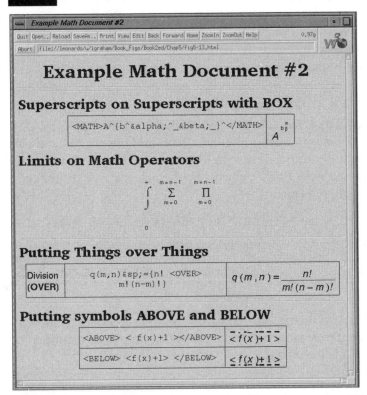

Figure 5.14 Rendering, by the Arena browser, of the document shown in Figure 5.13.

ATOP AND CHOOSE: OTHER WAYS OF PUTTING THINGS OVER THINGS

The **OVER** element implies mathematical division, and puts a dividing line between the top and bottom components. **ATOP** similarly places one item atop another, but without a dividing line, while **CHOOSE** also places one item above another, but in the context of the combinatorial notation *a choose b*. Neither of these are currently implemented.

PLACING A SYMBOL ABOVE OR BELOW ANOTHER SYMBOL: ABOVE AND BELOW

Finally, it is often necessary to modify the notation of an expression by placing a bar or other symbol above or below the expression. This is accomplished with the **ABOVE** or **BELOW** elements. The usage is:

```
<above> &lt; f(x) + 1 &gt; </above>

<below> &lt; f(x) + 1 &gt; </below>
```

as shown in Figures 5.13 and 5.14, which would, respectively, render a horizontal bar above or below the enclosed expression. The **SYM** attribute to **ABOVE** and **BELOW** is used to change the symbol lying above or below the expression: **SYM** takes as its value the entity name of the desired character. This is not currently implemented.

LEFT AND RIGHT DELIMITERS

Often when building large mathematical expressions you need to employ enlarged grouping delimiters, such as brackets, summations, or integral signs, that are dimensioned appropriately for the expression. The **LEFT** and **RIGHT** elements, combined with the **BOX** element, mark such scalable delimiters. The form for these empty elements is:

LEFT Delimiter: character followed by <LEFT> tag

     Example: x<LEFT>

RIGHT Delimiter: <RIGHT> tag followed by character

     Example: <RIGHT>y

Delimited characters size themselves to encompass the surrounding **BOX**ed expression—they therefore must lie inside the **BOX**. Here is an example (shown in Figures 5.15 and 5.16):

```
{int<LEFT> x^3^ {[<LEFT> f(x) <OVER> g(x) <RIGHT>] } dx }
```

You need not balance a left delimiter with a right delimiter, nor use the same character for the left and right sides, should both be present. Any character can be used as the delimiter, but the most common ones are angle brackets (< and &rt;), round brackets [(and)], curly brackets ({ and }), square brackets ([and]), vertical bar (|), integral sign (int), and summation symbol (sum).

Figure 5.15 Example HTML 3 document *fig5-15.html*, which illustrates **LEFT, RIGHT**, and formatting elements. The rendering of this document by the Arena browser is shown in Figure 5.16.

```
<HTML>

<HEAD>

<TITLE> Example Math Document #3 </TITLE>

</HEAD>


<BODY>

<H1 align=center> Example Math Document #3 </h1>

<HR>

<HR>


<H2> Left and Right Delimiters</H2>

<table border>

<tr> <td align=left> <TT>

     {int&lt;LEFT> x^3^ {[&lt;LEFT> f(x)&lt;OVER>g(x) &lt;RIGHT>] } dx }

     </TT>

   <td> <MATH> {int<left> x^3^ {[<left> f(x)<OVER>g(x) <right>]} dx }

     </MATH>

</table>
```

```
<hr>
<H2> Special Functions and Accenting Elements

<table>
<tr> <td> <MATH> <SQRT> a + b </SQRT> </MATH>
    <td> <MATH> <ROOT> 3 <OF>   a + b</ROOT> </MATH> <BR><BR>
<tr> <th> <B>VEC:</B>
    <td> <MATH> <VEC> &alpha; </VEC> </MATH>
<tr> <th> <B>DOT:</B>
    <td> <MATH> <DOT> &alpha; </DOT> </MATH>
<tr> <th> <B>DDOT:</B>
    <td> <MATH> <DDOT> &alpha; </DDOT> </MATH>
<tr> <th> <B>BAR:</B>
    <td> <MATH> <BAR> &alpha; </BAR> </MATH>
<tr> <th> <B>TILDE:</B>
    <td> <MATH> <TILDE> &alpha; </TILDE> </MATH>
<tr> <th> <B>HAT:</B>
    <td> <MATH> <HAT> &alpha; </HAT> </MATH>
<tr> <th> <B>B</B>
    <td> <MATH> regular and B-<B>MODIFIED</B> </MATH>
<tr> <th> <B>BT:</B>
    <td> <MATH> regular and BT-<BT>MODIFIED</BT> </MATH>
<tr> <th> <B>T:</B>
    <td> <MATH> regular and T-<T>MODIFIED</T> </MATH>
</table>
</BODY>
</HTML>
```

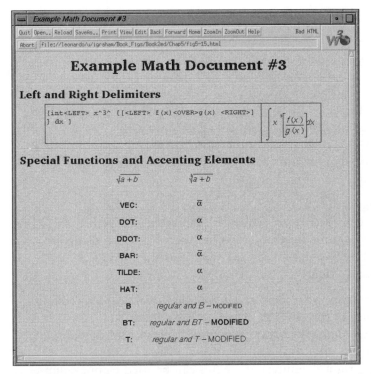

▬▬▬ **Figure 5.16** Rendering, by the Arena browser, of the document shown in Figure 5.15.

SIZEᴅ BOXᴇs

If the **BOX** is simply not big enough, you can use the **SIZE** attribute to the **BOX** element to force a large box. **SIZE** can take the values "normal", "medium", "large", and "huge", the default being "normal".

ARRAY: Mᴀᴛʜᴇᴍᴀᴛɪᴄᴀʟ Aʀʀᴀʏs

In mathematics, you often want to organize terms into arrays. **ARRAY** allows you to construct these structures. In an **ARRAY**, an array of terms is broken into **ROWS**, while each row is in turn broken into **ITEMS** (analogous to cells in a **TABLE**). As with tables, it is up to the person creating the **ARRAY** to ensure that there are the correct number of items in each row. As in a **TABLE**, the **ITEM** elements can take a **COLSPAN** attribute, allowing a single item to span multiple columns. Here is a simple array:

```
<ARRAY>

   <ROW> <ITEM> a <ITEM> b <ITEM> c <ITEM> w
```

```
<ROW> <ITEM> e <ITEM> f <ITEM> g <ITEM> x

<ROW> <ITEM> h <ITEM> i <ITEM> j <ITEM> y

<ROW> <ITEM> k <ITEM> l <ITEM> m <ITEM> z

</ARRAY>
```

The **COLDEF** attribute to the **ARRAY** element controls array formatting. For example, `<ARRAY COLDEF="CCCC">` indicates a four-column array, while `<ARRAY COLDEF="C+C-C=C">` indicates a four-column array, but with the array items separated by a plus sign (columns 1 and 2), a minus sign (columns 2 and 3), and an equals sign (columns 3 and 4).

You can control the alignment of column items using the **COLDEF** attribute: the letter "C" indicates centered items, while "L" indicates left-aligned and "R", right-aligned. These can be overridden within each **ITEM** by using an **ALIGN** attribute (e.g., `<ITEM ALIGN="left">`), with possible **VALUES** "left", "center" (the default), and "right".

You can align the entire array with the surrounding mathematical expression using an **ALIGN** attribute of the **ARRAY** element. The default is **ALIGN**="middle", which aligns the array with the baseline of the surrounding text. Other possible options are "top" and "bottom". The **LDELIM** (left delimiter) and **RDELIM** (right delimiter) attributes can be used to put delimiters around the array—for example, **LDELIM**="(" for a round bracket left delimiter, or **RDELIM**="|" for a vertical bar right delimiter.

Finally, you can use a **LABELS** attribute to **ARRAY** to indicate that the first row and column of the array are labels for the array. This causes the first row and column to be displayed slightly displaced from the bulk of the array, and also hides from display the item in the first row and column. Note, however, that you must still have this first **ITEM** there, to maintain a consistent count of the number of items in a row.

Unfortunately, the **ARRAY** element is currently unimplemented.

SPECIAL MATHEMATICAL FUNCTIONS

Certain mathematical functions are integrated into the math mode. Currently there are only two of these: **SQRT**, which renders the element content within a square root symbol; and **ROOT**, which renders the content as an arbitrary root—the order of the root is specified with the **OF** element. For example (see Figures 5.15 and 5.16):

```
<SQRT> a + b </SQRT>   </MATH>

<MATH> <ROOT>3<OF> a + b </ROOT>
```

ACCENTING SYMBOLS (HATS, TILDES, ETC.) AND SPECIAL FONTS

Accenting of mathematical symbols is accomplished using special accenting elements. The currently defined elements are **VEC** (vector), **BAR** (overbar), **DOT** (dot centered and above), **DDOT** (two horizontal dots centered and above), **HAT** (hat/circumflex above), and **TILDE** (tilde above). An example is `<DDOT>x</DDOT>`. The elements **B, T,** and **BT** allow modification of the style of the mathematical symbols; by default they are rendered in a mathematical italics font. **B** element content is in bold, while **T** element content is upright, and not italics. **BT** element content is upright-bold, and is equivalent to a combination of **B** and **T**. The different accenting elements are shown in Figures 5.15 and 5.16. Most are currently unimplemented.

HTML 3 MATH ELEMENTS

The following is a list of all the currently defined HTML 3 math elements. These short forms are used in the definitions:

math entity references	the entity references given in Tables 5.1 through 5.7
math elements	*ABOVE, BELOW, B, T, BT, BAR, BOX, DDOT, DOT, HAT, ROOT, SQRT, TILDE, VEC*

B ELEMENT: BOLD FONT

Usage:	`<B> . . . </B>`
Can Contain:	**characters, math entity references, math elements,** *ARRAY, SUB, SUP*
Can Be Inside:	*MATH, ITEM, OF,* **math elements**
Attributes:	**CLASS**

B marks a term to be rendered in bold font. The optional attribute **CLASS** can be used to define the term as being of a special class (e.g., tensor or vector); a browser can use this information to modify the font and rendering. At present there are no browsers that understand this attribute in this context.

BT ELEMENT: BOLD UPRIGHT FONT

Usage: `<BT> . . . </BT>`

BT marks a term to be rendered in a bold-upright font, and takes the same content model and attributes as **B** (see above). The optional attribute **CLASS** can be used to define the term as being of a special class (e.g., tensor or vector); a browser can use this information to modify the font and rendering.

T ELEMENT: UPRIGHT FONT

Usage: `<T> . . . </T>`

T marks a term to be rendered in an upright font, and takes the same content and attributes as **B** (see above). The optional attribute **CLASS** can be used to define the term as being of a special class (e.g., tensor or vector); a browser can use this information to modify the font and rendering.

BAR ELEMENT: DRAW AN OVERBAR OVER AN EXPRESSION

Usage:	`<BAR> . . . </BAR>`
Can Contain:	**characters, math entity references, math elements, *ARRAY*, *SUB*, *SUP***
Can Be Inside:	*MATH, ITEM, OF*, **math elements**
Attributes:	none

BAR places a horizontal bar across the enclosed mathematical expression.

DDOT ELEMENT: DRAW A DOUBLE-DOT OVER AN EXPRESSION

Usage: `<DDOT> . . . </DDOT>`

DDOT places a double-dot symbol above the enclosed mathematical expression. **DDOT** takes the same content model as **BAR** (see above).

DOT ELEMENT: DRAW A DOT OVER AN EXPRESSION

Usage: `<DOT> . . . </DOT>`

DOT places a single dot atop the enclosed mathematical expression. DOT takes the same content model as **BAR** (see above).

HAT ELEMENT: DRAW A HAT OVER AN EXPRESSION

Usage: `<HAT> . . . </HAT>`

HAT places a hat character (caret) atop the enclosed mathematical expression. HAT takes the same content model as **BAR** (see above).

TILDE ELEMENT: DRAW A TILDE OVER AN EXPRESSION

Usage: `<TILDE> . . . </TILDE>`

TILDE places a tilde character atop the enclosed mathematical expression. TILDE takes the same content model as **BAR** (see above).

VEC ELEMENT: DRAW A VECTOR SYMBOL OVER AN EXPRESSION

Usage: `<VEC> . . . </VEC>`

VEC places a vector symbol (typically an arrow) atop the enclosed mathematical expression, and takes the same content as **BAR**.

ABOVE ELEMENT: DRAW A STRETCHED SYMBOL ABOVE A TERM

Usage: `<ABOVE> . . . </ABOVE>`

Can Contain:	**characters, math entity references, math elements,** *ARRAY, SUB, SUP*
Can Be Inside:	*MATH, ITEM, OF,* **math elements**
Attributes:	**SYM**

ABOVE places a character symbol, specified using the optional **SYM** attribute, above the enclosed term. The default, in the absence of **SYM**, is a horizontal line.

BELOW ELEMENT: DRAW A STRETCHED SYMBOL BELOW A TERM

Usage:	`<BELOW> . . . </BELOW>`

BELOW places a character symbol, specified using the optional **SYM** attribute, below the enclosed term. The default, in the absence of **SYM**, is a horizontal line. **BELOW** takes the same content model as **ABOVE** (see previous).

BOX ELEMENT: GROUP A COLLECTION OF TERMS

Usage:	`<BOX> . . . </BOX>`
Can Contain:	**characters, math entity references, math elements,** *ARRAY, SUB, SUP, ATOP, CHOOSE, LEFT, OVER, RIGHT*
Can Be Inside:	*MATH, ITEM, OF,* **math elements**
Attributes:	**SIZE**

BOX groups together a collection of terms to be treated as a unit. This can be used to group denominators and numerators together, with additional elements (**OVER, ATOP,** and **CHOOSE**) being used to separate top from bottom. In addition, **BOX** can be used to control the size of delimiting symbols, such as brackets (specified with the **LEFT** and **RIGHT** elements), which scale to the size of the **BOX**. Finally, **BOX** can be used to force automatic scaling of integral, product, and summation symbols that should scale to be larger than their arguments.

The symbols { and } are shorthand representations of <BOX> and </BOX>, respectively.

BOX takes the single optional attribute **SIZE**. **SIZE** is used to specify a box size larger than that implied by the actual content of the box. This is used to force the size of delimiting characters to be larger than expected. Possible values for **SIZE** are **SIZE**="normal" (default normal size), "medium", "large", and "huge".

OVER Element: Place Denominator over Numerator

Usage:	<OVER>
Can Contain:	empty
Can Be Inside:	**BOX**
Attributes:	none

OVER implies mathematical division, and arranges the content of a box into a denominator (the part before the <OVER> tag) and a numerator (the part after the tag). When rendered, the denominator and numerator are separated by a division line.

OVER is an empty element, and can only appear inside a **BOX**.

ATOP Element: Place Term atop a Second Term

Usage:	<ATOP>

ATOP is an empty element. It is similar to **OVER** but does not imply division; instead, **ATOP** places the first part of a **BOX** element content (the part before the <ATOP> tag) above the second part (the part after the tag), with no symbol separating top from bottom.

ATOP has the same content model as **OVER** (see above).

CHOOSE Element: Combinatorial Choose

Usage:	<CHOOSE>

CHOOSE is an empty element, and implies a combinatorial choose function; it arranges the content of a box into a first term (the part before the `<CHOOSE>` tag) and a second term (the part after the tag). When rendered, the first term is placed above the second term (with no separating character), and both terms are jointly enclosed by left and right round brackets.

CHOOSE has the same content model as **OVER** (see above).

LEFT Element: Define a Left Delimiter

Usage: `<LEFT>`

LEFT is an empty element that defines a left delimiter inside a **BOX** element: the character or character expression preceding the `<LEFT>` tag is the delimiter character or expression. In rendering, the delimiter is scaled in size to encompass the entire **BOX**. In general, delimiters should only be appropriate mathematical delimiters, such as brackets, vertical bars, integrals, and summation or product symbols. A delimiter can in fact be combinations of terms, such as a combination of multiple integral symbols, complete with super- and subscripts (the integral limits). For example, `&int;^2^_1_<LEFT>` indicates that the integral sign, with the indicated limits, is a left delimiter.

LEFT has the same content model as **OVER** (see above).

RIGHT Element: Define a Right Delimiter

Usage: `<RIGHT>`

RIGHT is an empty element that defines a right delimiter inside a **BOX** element: the character or character expression following the `<RIGHT>` tag is the delimiter character or expression. In rendering, the delimiter is scaled in size to encompass the entire **BOX**. In general, delimiters should only be appropriate mathematical delimiters, such as brackets, vertical bars, integrals, summation, or product symbols. A delimiter can in fact be combinations of terms, such as a combination of brackets, complete with super- and subscripts (e.g., exponents). For example, `<RIGHT>]^2^` indicates that the right square bracket, with the indicated superscript, is a right delimiter.

RIGHT has the same content model as **OVER** (see above).

ARRAY Element: An Array of Mathematical Terms

Usage:	`<ARRAY> . . . </ARRAY>`
Can Contain:	*ROW*
Can Be Inside:	*MATH, ITEM, OF,* math elements
Attributes:	*ALIGN, COLDEF, LABELS, LDELIM, RDELIM*

ARRAY denotes an array of mathematical terms. An array consists of one or more **ROWS** of terms, each row containing one or more **ITEMs**. The construction of arrays is similar to the construction of tables.

ARRAY can take five optional attributes. These are:

ALIGN="top", "middle", "bottom" (optional) **ALIGN** controls the vertical alignment of the array with respect to the surrounding text. The default is "middle", which aligns the middle of the array with the baseline of the surrounding text. The values "top" and "bottom", respectively, align the top and bottom rows of the array with the baseline of the surrounding text.

COLDEF="*string*" (optional) **COLDEF** can be used to define the number of columns, the default alignment of the terms in a column, and the character to use in separating the columns. Alignment is determined by the uppercase letters C (centered), L (left-aligned), and R (right-aligned). A four-column array can then be defined using **COLDEF**="CLRL", so that the first column is centered, the third is right-aligned, and the second and fourth are left-aligned. By default, there is no separator character between columns. The separators "+", "-", and "=" can be introduced by placing them between the columns you wish separated by the symbol. Thus **COLDEF**="C+L+R=L" indicates that columns 1 and 2 and columns 2 and 3 are separated by plus signs, while columns 3 and 4 are separated by equals signs.

LABELS (optional) **LABELS** defines the array as a labeled array, so that the first row and column of the array are treated as row and column labels, separate from the array content.

LDELIM="*c*" (optional) **LDELIM** defines the character to use as the left delimiter of the array; the default is no character. Here "*c*" is any character or entity name. Commonly used characters are "[", "(", and "|" (vertical bar).

RDELIM="*c*" (optional) **RDELIM** defines the character to use as the right delimiter of the array; the default is no character. Here "*c*" is any character or entity name. Commonly used characters are "]", ")", and "|" (vertical bar).

ROW ELEMENT: A ROW IN AN ARRAY

Usage:	`<ROW> . . . (</ROW>)`
Can Contain:	*ITEM*
Can Be Inside:	*ARRAY*
Attributes:	none

The **ROW** element delimits a row within an **ARRAY**. The end tag is optional, since it can be inferred from the next `<ROW>` tag or from the `</ARRAY>` tag ending the array.

ITEM ELEMENT: ITEM IN A MATH ARRAY

Usage:	`<ITEM> . . . (</ITEM>)`
Can Contain:	**characters, math entity references, math elements,** *ARRAY, SUB, SUP*
Can Be Inside:	*ROW*
Attributes:	*ALIGN, COLSPAN, ROWSPAN*

ITEM marks an item within a mathematical array, and must appear inside an array **ROW**. It is a nonempty element, but the end tag is optional, as its presence can be inferred from the next `<ITEM>` or from the `<ROW>` tag starting the next row. **ITEM** can contain any mathematical expression, including other arrays. **ITEM** can take three attributes:

ALIGN="left", "center", "right" (optional) **ALIGN** aligns the content of an **ITEM** within the column. The default is centered, but left and right alignment is also possible.

COLSPAN="*n*" A single **ITEM** can span more than one columns. **COLSPAN** specifies the number of columns occupied by the item, as a positive integer (the default is one column). The author must ensure the number of columns sum appropriately.

ROWSPAN="*n*" A single **ITEM** can span more than one row. **ROWSPAN** specifies the number of rows occupied by the item, as a positive integer (the default is one row). The author must ensure the number of rows sums appropriately.

SQRT ELEMENT: A SQUARE ROOT

Usage:	`<SQRT> . . . </SQRT>`
Can Contain:	**characters, math entity references, math elements, *ARRAY, SUB, SUP***
Can Be Inside:	*MATH, ITEM, OF*, **math elements**
Attributes:	none

The **SQRT** element renders the element content inside a square root symbol.

ROOT ELEMENT: A ROOT OF ARBITRARY ORDER

Usage:	`<ROOT> . . . </ROOT>`
Can Contain:	**characters, math entity references, math elements, *ARRAY, SUB, SUP, OF***
Can Be Inside:	*MATH, ITEM, OF*, **math elements**
Attributes:	none

The **ROOT** element renders the element content as a root of arbitrary order. The order of the root is specified by the first mathematical expression inside the **ROOT** element: the order of the root is separated from the body of the root by the empty element **OF**. Thus the "n+1 root of x" is written as: `<ROOT>n+1<OF>x</ROOT>`.

OF ELEMENT: ORDER OF A ROOT

Usage:	`<OF>`

Can Contain:	**characters, math entity references, math elements,** *ARRAY, SUB, SUP*
Can Be Inside:	*ROOT*
Attributes:	none

The empty **OF** element is used inside a **ROOT** element to mark the order of a root.

SUP ELEMENT: SUPERSCRIPT

Usage:	`<SUP> . . . </SUP>`
Can Contain:	**characters, math entity references, math elements,** *ARRAY, SUB, SUP*
Can Be Inside:	*MATH, ITEM, OF,* **math elements**
Attributes:	*ALIGN*

SUP marks a superscript to an associated character or mathematical term, or an expression to be placed above a mathematical operator such as an integral sign. Inside a **MATH** element, **SUP** can take the single optional attribute **ALIGN**, which specifies whether the superscript should be placed to the left (**ALIGN**="left") or right (**ALIGN**="right") of the associated character or term.

SUB ELEMENT: SUBSCRIPT

Usage:	`<SUB> . . . </SUB>`
Can Contain:	**characters, math entity references, math elements,** *ARRAY, SUB, SUP*
Can Be Inside:	*MATH, ITEM, OF,* **math elements**
Attributes:	**ALIGN**

SUB marks a subscript to an associated character or mathematical term, or an expression to be placed below a mathematical operator such as an integral sign. Inside a **MATH** element, **SUB** can take the single optional attribute

ALIGN, which specifies whether the subscript should be placed to the left (**ALIGN**="left") or right (**ALIGN**="right") of the associated character or term.

STYLESHEETS

As has been mentioned many times, HTML is a semantic markup language that describes the *meaning* of the parts of a document, and not the physical representation. And, as noted repeatedly, there are many advantages to this technique. First, semantic markup *adds* information to the text, by explaining what the text is for (e.g., headings, figures, or paragraphs) or what the text means (e.g., block quotations, address, or emphasis). In addition, the elements of HTML are constructed such that information appropriate for nonvisual display can be contained within the elements, examples being the **ALT** attribute content of **IMG** elements or the text contained within a **FIG**. As a result, an HTML document can be transcribed into a number of different representations, such as graphical displays, text-only displays on nongraphical workstations, Braille readers, or spoken words via a text-to-speech converter, with no loss of information content.

At the same time, an author does not want to be limited to a semantic description alone. Authors and readers alike care what a document looks like, be it a printed page, a computer display, or any other format. Each author (or reader) will have his or her preferred way of representing things such as headings, quotations, or emphasis. These issues fall under the general category of *style*—how the author wants the different parts of the document to look or feel. Thus to be a fully functional markup language, HTML should support a mechanism whereby authors (or readers) can specify the styles they want applied to the written words.

Up until now, HTML has largely ignored this issue. Browser software often provided limited user-modifiable control of document presentation (font sizes and types, colors, etc.), while limited author-derived control was possible through a few element attributes, such as **ALIGN**. However, using attributes to specify formatting details is not a good long-term solution, since there is no "universal" collection of appropriate formatting attributes—instructions relevant to a Braille reader, a graphical display, or a laser printer are simply not the same. What is required, then, is a *second* mechanism, independent but related to HTML, for specifying the desired formatting of a document. Then the style information and document can be maintained separately, with the display device (graphic display, printer, text-to-speech, etc.) selecting and applying the style information appropriate for its display format.

This mechanism, currently under development, is known as a *stylesheet*. A stylesheet is simply a collection of instructions that define the desired formatting properties for each of the HTML elements. A stylesheet is designed to be *applied* to the HTML document during the formatting process. As an example, a stylesheet might contain instructions such as:

```
H1: font_size=24 point; font_type=arial; align=page_centered

H2: font_size=18 point; font_type=times; align=page_left

EM: font_type=italics
```

which could mean:

"Center **H1** headings on the page, and display them using a 24-point Arial font"

"Left-align **H2** headings, and display them using an 18-point Times Roman font"

"Format text inside **EM** using an italics version of the current font"

and so on. When a browser reads an HTML document, it can also access this stylesheet information (mechanisms for finding this information are discussed later) and apply these instructions as it formats the document for display. This gives an author the ability, through an author-designed stylesheet, to suggest formatting prescriptions for his or her documents. I use the word "suggest" because the browser, or the user, will always have the option of ignoring the style information, should it be inappropriate for some reason. Final control of presentation must always rest with readers, since they are the ones who are actually using the text.

There are additional benefits to the stylesheet model. As an author, you can develop a single stylesheet, and apply it to all documents in a given collection. Thus the work of developing a style for a single document can be shared with a number of other documents, making life easier for the author, and also giving the collection a common look and feel. Finally, separating the style information from the HTML document means that the HTML document stays compact and easy to understand—it does not become cluttered with lots of device-specific formatting instructions. It would be far harder to write an HTML document if the author, each time, had to add in all sorts of physical formatting hints. Using stylesheets, the author has only to create a stylesheet once, and can then forget about this part of the problem and get back to creating real content.

STYLESHEET LANGUAGES

So why don't we already have stylesheets? The answer is that the Web will soon support stylesheets, but that two things must be done for this to happen. The first thing that is required is a formal *stylesheet language* that allows an author to write down explicit instructions as to how the elements of a document should be rendered. The second is browser support of this language, since the language is useless if it is not understood by a browser. There are currently two stylesheet languages in development. The first, known as *cascading stylesheets*, or *CSS*, is designed to be particularly simple to use and understand, so that most HTML authors will not have much difficulty constructing useful stylesheets. CSS is being developed in conjunction with the Arena browser, and Arena provides a testbed for CSS stylesheets. The second language under development is called *DSSSL-Lite*. This is being designed as a "lite" version of *Document Style Semantics and Specification Language* (*DSSSL*), an extremely advanced (and complicated!) stylesheet language. DSSSL-Lite is significantly more complicated than CSS, but also is more powerful.

Both these languages are still being designed, and are currently undergoing rapid change. This section therefore does not attempt to describe either language in detail. Instead it uses the current version of the cascading stylesheet approach to illustrate how these languages work, and how they are related to the HTML elements and attributes. The references at the end of this chapter provide links to online stylesheet information resources—you will be able to find the latest specification for these stylesheet languages at one of the listed sites.

EXAMPLE: CASCADING STYLESHEETS

The cascading stylesheet approach is being led by Håkon Lie. The intent of CSS is to design a language that is simple and easy to understand, allowing authors to easily create CSS stylesheets by hand, without the need of fancy editing tools. It is also designed to understand HTML 3 features, and in particular the **CLASS** attribute: **CLASS** attributes can be used to give different presentation styles to elements (for example, two paragraphs) having different **CLASS** attribute values. The examples below will explain how this works.

Figure 5.17 shows a simple example stylesheet. The first two lines specify the desired size of the browser display window, in pixels. The third and fourth lines specify the margins for the document within the display window, relative to the edges of the display area. Thus the left and right document margins are indented 0.5 centimeters from the edges of the window. The fifth and sixth lines define generic properties of all the elements in the document (the star is a wildcard symbol, and represents all possible element names): in this case these lines specify that the default font for all elements is Times Roman and that, by default, the left margin for all elements should be 1 centimeter in from the document edge.

Lines 7, 8, and 9 provide formatting information specific to particular elements. Line 7 sets the font for **H1, H2,** and **H3** elements to Helvetica, while leaving the font for **H4** through **H6** unchanged. Line 8 then sets the text margin for **H2** and **H3** headings to 0 centimeters: since the default indent for text was set to 1 centimeter at line 6, this means that the headings will begin 1 centimeter to the left of any following text. Finally, line 9 says that **H1** headings should be centered between the two margins. This setting may in turn be overridden by any **ALIGN** attributes in the HTML document.

Combinations of requirements are also possible. For example, the instruction:

```
/ H1(STRONG) /  font.style = bold & italics
```

Figure 5.17 Portion of a demonstration *cascading* stylesheet (CSS). The meanings of the various lines are discussed in the text. The italicized line numbers on the left are not part of the stylesheet, and are present for reference purposes only.

```
1    width = 500px

2    height = 600px

3    margin.left = 0.5cm

4    margin.right = 0.5cm

5    *:           font.family = times

6    *:           margin.left = 1cm

7    h1, h2, h3: font.family = helvetica

8    h2, h3:      margin.left = 0cm

9    h1:          text.align = center

....
```

means that the content of a **STRONG** element, when inside an **H1** heading, should be rendered in a combination of boldface and italics. Similarly, an expression such as:

```
/ H1 P/ margin.above = 0.75cm
```

means that there should be a 0.75-centimeter vertical space between any **H1** heading and the subsequent paragraph.

RELATION TO CLASS ATTRIBUTES

Stylesheet rendering instructions can be applied to particular HTML elements by means of the **CLASS** attribute. Consider, for example, the following HTML excerpt:

```
<H2 CLASS="abstract"> Abstract </H2>

<P CLASS="abstract"> first paragraph .......

<P CLASS="abstract"> second paragraph.....

<H2> Introduction to HTML </H2>

<P> HTML is the best thing since sliced bread......
```

In rendering this document, I want the abstract titles to be centered, and the paragraphs significantly indented, but without changing the headings or paragraphs elsewhere in the document. I can do this by first *subclassing* the relevant elements—that is, I use the class attribute to specify what particular class (in this case, "abstract") each paragraph or heading belongs to. Then, I modify the stylesheet (in this example, the stylesheet in Figure 5.17) to produce the new stylesheet shown in Figure 5.18. The additions are shown in boldface.

▬▬▬ **Figure 5.18** Portion of a demonstration *cascading* stylesheet (CSS), showing how stylesheet information can be attached to particular elements through the **CLASS** attribute value. The meanings of the various lines are discussed in the text. The italicized line numbers on the left are not part of the stylesheet, and are there for reference purposes only. The lines in bold are new lines relative to Figure 5.17.

```
1    width = 500px

2    height = 600px

3    margin.left = 0.5cm
```

```
 4    margin.right = 0.5cm

 5    *:              font.family = times

 6    *:              margin.left = 1cm

 7    h1, h2, h3:     font.family = helvetica

 8    h2, h3:         margin.left = 0cm

 9    h1:             text.align = center

10    h2.abstract:    text.align = center

11    p.abstract:     margin.left = 2.5cm

12    p.abstract:     margin.right = 2.5cm

....
```

The changes are found in lines 10 through 12. Here the class attribute value has been appended to the desired element, so that one can specify formatting information relevant only to elements of that class. Thus line 10 states that **H2** headings with a **CLASS** value of "abstract" should be centered, while lines 11 and 12 say that **P** (paragraph) elements with a **CLASS** value of "abstract" should have left and right margins indented 2.5 centimeters. These do not affect **H2** or **P** elements with any other **CLASS** attribute value, or without a **CLASS** attribute in the first place.

Again, I stress that stylesheets are still under development, and that the above is just an example of how they work. You are referred to the references at the end of this chapter for up-to-date information about the current state of CSS (and DSSSL-Lite) stylesheets.

STYLESHEETS AND HTML

How are stylesheets indicated in an HTML document? Currently there are two proposed mechanisms. In HTML 3 stylesheet information can be contained in a **STYLE** element in the document **HEAD**. For example:

```
<HEAD>

    <TITLE> Test Stylesheet Document </TITLE>

    <STYLE  NOTATION=css>

        h1,h2:  font.family=helvetica

        h1:     font.size=24pt

        h2:     font.size=18pt
```

```
        margin.left = 1cm

    *:          margin.left = 1.5cm

</STYLE>

</HEAD>
```

Alternatively, the author can use a **LINK** element to link to an appropriate stylesheet. For example:

```
<HEAD>

  <TITLE> Test Stylesheet Document </TITLE>

  <LINK REL=stylesheet HREF="./mystyle.css">

</STYLE>

</HEAD>
```

As with all data types, stylesheets will need a MIME content-type header so that the browser will know what type of stylesheet is being delivered. The above assumes that the filename extension *.css* will be used to indicate CSS stylesheets: the corresponding MIME content type *might* then be `application/x-stylesheet-css`. These MIME types are not yet formally specified.

What happens if a document contains both a **LINK**ed stylesheet and internal **STYLE** stylesheet information?

```
<HEAD>

  <TITLE> Test Stylesheet Document </TITLE>

  <STYLE   NOTATION=dss>

      h1,h2:  font.family=helvetica

      h1:     font.size=24pt

      h2:     font.size=18pt

      margin.left = 1cm

    *:          margin.left = 1.5cm

  </STYLE>

  <LINK REL=stylesheet HREF="./my_style.css">

</HEAD>
```

This is where the cascading idea comes into play. With cascading stylesheets, the browser will first access the **LINK**ed stylesheet, and will then *overlay* (cascade) any stylesheet information contained in a **STYLE** element *on top* of the instructions of the linked stylesheet. Thus if the **LINK**ed stylesheet said:

```
h1,h2:  font.family=times
```

and the **STYLE** element contained the instruction

```
h1:  font.family=helvetica
```

the cascading of the two would format **H1** headings with a Helvetica font, and **H2** headings with Times Roman.

Finally, the user should be able, through the browser, to configure his or her own style preferences, which in turn would override those set by **LINK**ed or **STYLE**-defined instructions. To facilitate this cascading, CSS supports a collection of directives that allow the stylesheet author to declare how important the formatting selections are. Thus a document author might write, in a linked stylesheet:

```
h1: font.size=18pt ! important
```

```
h1: font.family=helvetica ! normal
```

which gives the importance of the different instructions. As a result, an "important" instruction in a linked stylesheet might not be replaced by a "normal" instruction in a **STYLE** element, and so on. The rules for how this mechanism would work are still under discussion.

EMBEDDED APPLICATIONS: JAVA

If you haven't heard the name Java by now, then you must have been on holiday, far from electronic civilization. Java is being hyped as the most exciting development since the birth of the World Wide Web, and as the tool that is going to revolutionize the Internet—didn't we hear that once before? Behind all this hype, there is a kernel of truth—Java is exciting, and does open up some remarkable possibilities for Web applications. For example, Java programs, embedded within HTML documents, can produce dynamic graphics and animations, and can allow sophisticated interaction between the Java *applet* and the user. In a very real sense, Java can "bring to life" otherwise static HTML pages.

Java is being developed by Sun Microsystems, and is currently integrated into the Sun HotJava Web browser, which runs on SparcStations running Solaris

2.4 or on Windows NT/Windows 95—this is currently the only browser that includes Java capabilities. However, Netscape has signed a licensing agreement with Sun, and plans to include Java functionality in the next release of the Netscape Navigator browser.

To make sense of it, this section briefly explains what Java actually is, and how it is being integrated into the Web.

Java is, to put it baldly, just another computer language. It is an object-oriented language, patterned after C++ but designed to be both easier and safer to use—easier in that it is a simpler language, safer in that various features, such as variable typing and memory allocation and management, are strictly enforced and automatically performed.

More importantly, Java is designed for writing applications, or *applets*, that can roam the Internet, and that can run on any computer processor architecture. The Java system comes with special features that allow this both to work and to be safe for the machine running the applet.

This system works because of the three components of the Java system. The first part, of course, is the Java language. The second component is the Java compiler—compiling a Java program produces a specially formatted Java object file, written in a processor-independent *byte-code*. The compiler also builds a cryptographic checksum into this object file, so that the program, once created, cannot be tampered with. The third component is the Java runtime system (essentially a Java interpreter), which is what actually runs the Java program. The runtime system, which must be present on any machine that runs a Java program, contains various checks to make sure the object file was not tampered with, and also ensures that the Java program cannot affect restricted resources on the client system. The combination of a Java compiler, the platform-independent, cryptographically secure Java object file, and a secure Java interpreter, means that Java programs can be sent to, and run safely on, any computer.

The Java runtime system includes modules for user interaction and graphics, which permit Java programs to generate dynamic graphics and interact with the user.

As discussed in Chapter 4, the Netscape Navigator 2.0 browser now supports embedded Java applets through the **APPLET** element, as does the Sun HotJava browser. However, there is currently much effort underway to integrate the features of the **APPLET** and **FIG** tags into a new composite element having the best of both worlds. It is thus likely that the **APPLET** tag will change substantially in the near future.

It is hard to put into words the types of things that can be done with Java applets. I have seen simple clickable images turned into festively animated pages, and have seen applets containing images of molecules—but where the molecules are actually three-dimensional objects that can be rotated by the user. The power of this technique is profound, and truly does represent an exciting new addition to HTML documents, and to the Web in general.

REFERENCES

HTML 3—General starting place

http://www.w3.org/hypertext/WWW/MarkUp/MarkUp.html

HTML 3 Specifications3

http://www.w3.org/hypertext/WWW/MarkUp/html3/CoverPage.html

http://www.w3.org/hypertext/WWW/MarkUp/html3-tables/tables.txt (text version)

Internationalization and character set issues (see also Appendix A)

http://www.w3.org/hypertext/WWW/International/Overview.html

http://www.w3.org/hypertext/WWW/MarkUp/html-spec/charset-harmful.html

http://www.alis.com:8085/ietf/html/

   (files with names like "draft-ietf-html-i18n...")

MD2 and MD5 message digest algorithms

ftp://ds.internic.net/rfc/rfc1319.txt (MD2)

ftp://ds.internic.net/rfc/rfc1321.txt (MD5)

FORM-based file uploads

http://www.ics.uci.edu/pub/ietf/html/draft-ietf-html-fileupload-03.txt (or larger number)

Stylesheets: General overview

http://www.w3.org/hypertext/WWW/Style/

Cascading stylesheets draft

```
http://www.w3.org/hypertext/WWW/Style/css/draft.html
```

DSSSL-Lite stylesheet proposal

```
http://www.falch.no/~pepper/DSSSL-Lite/
```

```
http://www.jclark.com/dsssl/lite.html
```

The Java language: Overview and details

```
http://java.sun.com/
```

Embedding Applets in HTML documents

The following may be out of date—you should be able to find up-to-date references from the preceding URL.

```
http://java.sun.com/1.0alpha3/doc/appguide/AppTag.html
```

```
http://java.sun.com/1.0alpha3/doc/appguide/AddingApplet.html
```

Java and other types of mobile code

```
http://www.w3.org/hypertext/WWW/MobileCode/
```

6

UNIFORM RESOURCE

LOCATORS (URLS)

CONSTRUCTION AND SYNTAX OF URLS

Uniform Resource Locators, or *URLs*, are a scheme for specifying Internet resources using a single line of printable ASCII characters. This scheme encompasses all major Internet protocols including FTP, Gopher, HTTP, and WAIS. URLs are one of the foundation tools of the World Wide Web and are used within HTML documents to reference the targets of a hypertext link. However, URLs are not restricted to the World Wide Web, and can be used to communicate information about Internet resources in e-mail letters, handwritten notes, or even books.

A URL contains the following information:

- The *protocol* to use when accessing the server (e.g., HTTP, Gopher, WAIS).

- The Internet *domain name* of the site on which the server is running, along with any required username and password information.

- The *port number* of the server. If this is omitted, the browser assumes a commonly understood default value of the indicated protocol.

- The *location* of the resource in the hierarchical (often directory, or directory-like) structure of the server.

Here is a typical example, in this case for the HTTP protocol:

```
http://www.cern.ch/hypertext/WWW/RDBgate/Implementation.html
```

This references the file ***Implementation.html*** in the directory ***/hypertext/WWW/RDBgate*** accessible at the server ***www.cern.ch*** using the HTTP protocol.

ALLOWED CHARACTERS IN URLS

Every URL must be written using *printable* ASCII characters (the bottom half of the ISO Latin-1 character set, as discussed in Appendix A, and excluding control characters), and *cannot* be written using the full ISO Latin-1 character set. This restriction ensures that URLs can be sent by electronic mail; many electronic mail programs mishandle characters from the upper half of the ISO Latin-1 character set. In a URL, non-ASCII characters can be represented using a *character encoding* scheme. This is analogous to the character entities used with HTML. However, the schemes are distinctly different, and you should never use HTML character or entity references in a URL.

For ISO Latin-1 characters, the encoding is simple: any ISO Latin-1 character can be represented by the encoding:

```
%xx
```

where the percent sign is a special character indicating the start of the encoding, and *xx* is the *hexadecimal code* for the desired ISO Latin-1 character (the *x* represents a hexadecimal digit in the range [0-9,A-F]). Table A.1 (Appendix A) lists all the ISO Latin-1 characters alongside their hexadecimal codes. As an example, the encoding for the character *é* (the letter *e* with an acute accent) is %E9.

DISALLOWED CHARACTERS

Several ASCII characters are disallowed in URLs, and can be present only in encoded form, because these characters often have special meanings in a non-URL context, and their presence can lead to misinterpretation of the URL. For example, HTML documents use the double quotation mark (") to delimit a URL in a hypertext anchor, so that a quotation mark inside the URL would end the URL prematurely. Therefore, the double quote is disallowed. The space character is also disallowed, since many programs will consider the space as a break between two separate strings. Space characters often appear

▬▬▬▬ **Table 6.1** Disallowed ASCII Characters in URLs

Character	Hex	Character	Hex
TAB	09	SPACE	20
"	22	<	3C
>	3E	[	5B
\	5C	]	5D
^	5E	`	60
{	7B	|	7C
}	7D	~	7E

in Macintosh file or folder names. For example, the filename "Network Info" (where there is a single space between the words "Network" and "Info") must be encoded in a URL as:

```
Network%20Info
```

Finally, all 33 control characters (hex codes 00 to 1F, and 7F) are disallowed. Table 6.1 summarizes the disallowed printable characters, including TAB (although TAB is formally a control character). You will sometimes see unencoded disallowed characters in a URL that still seem to work; but to avoid possible problems you are advised to encode all these characters.

SPECIAL CHARACTERS

In a URL, several ASCII characters have special meanings, such as the percent character (%), which denotes character encodings. The forward slash character (/) is also special, and denotes a change in hierarchy, such as a directory change. These special characters must be encoded if you want them to appear as regular, uninterpreted characters. Thus, to include the string:

```
ian%euler
```

in a URL you must encode it as:

```
ian%25euler
```

where %25 is the encoding for the percent character. If you do not do this, a program parsing the URL will try to interpret %eu as a character encoding. Conversely, you must not encode a special character if you require its special meaning. For example, the string:

```
dir/subdir
```

indicates that `subdir` is a subdirectory of `dir`, while:

`dir%2Fsubdir`

is just the character string `dir/subdir` (`%2F` is the encoding for the slash).

The general rule is: Encode any character that might be special if you do not want to use its special meaning.

The most common special characters are:

- The percent sign (`%`). This is the escape character for character encodings, and is special in all URLs.
- The hash (`#`). This separates the URL of a resource from the *fragment identifier* for that resource. A fragment identifier references a particular location within a resource. This character is special in all URLs.
- The slash (`/`). This is used to indicate hierarchical structures such as directories.
- The question mark (`?`). This indicates a *query string*; everything after the question mark is query information to be passed to the server. Special in Gopher, WAIS, and HTTP URLs only.

Other characters that are special in certain URL schemes are the colon (`:`), semicolon (`;`), at (`@`), equals (`=`), and ampersand (`&`). These special cases will be noted as they arise.

EXAMPLE OF A UNIFORM RESOURCE LOCATOR

Figure 6.1 illustrates a typical URL (in this case, for the HTTP protocol) showing the different parts and the associated meanings.

1. **Protocol** The first string in the URL specifies the Internet *protocol* to use in accessing the resource; this example requests the HTTP protocol. The protocol is indicated by the name appearing before the first colon in the URL. The string specifying the protocol (here `http`) can contain only lowercase letters (`a-z`). URL schemes are defined for most Internet protocols, including FTP, Gopher, HTTP, telnet, and WAIS. The details of the different schemes are presented later on.

2. **Domain Name and Port Number (Address)** The second part of this URL is the Internet address of the server; this information lies between the double forward slash (//) and a terminating forward slash (/). This example gives

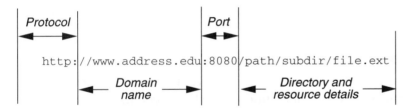

■■■■■■ **Figure 6.1** Example of a URL (here an **http** URL), showing the main components. Not all URLs follow this model, as discussed in the text.

the *domain name* of the server and the *port number* to contact. Omitting the port number implies the default value for the given protocol. Numeric IP addresses can be used instead of domain names, for example:

```
//132.206.9.22:1234/
```

You can often (depending on protocol) include username and password information if this is needed to access a resource. The format is:

```
//username:password@www.address.edu:1234/
```

Note that the password can be read by anyone who reads the URL, so this is not a secure way to allow access to a resource.

3. **Resource Location** The forward slash after the host and port number field indicates the beginning of the *path* information required to locate the resource on the server. This field varies considerably, depending on the service being accessed. Often, it resembles a directory path leading down to a file, as in Figure 6.1. In this context, the forward slash character (/) is used in place of *all* system-dependent symbols defining directories, such as the backslash (\) on DOS or Windows computers, the colon (:) on Macintoshes, and the [dir.subdir.subsubdir] expressions used by VAX/VMS systems.

PASSING SEARCH STRINGS

The URL syntax allows you to pass query strings to the designated resource, in situations (typically Gopher, HTTP, or WAIS) that support such service. This is accomplished by appending the query strings to the URL, separated from the URL by a question mark. Two examples are:

```
gopher://gopher.somewhere.edu/77/searches.phone?bob+steve
```

```
http://www.somewhere.edu/cgi-bin/srch-data?archie+database
```

Thus, question marks must be encoded if you do *not* want to indicate a query string.

ENCODING OF QUERY STRINGS

Of course query strings, since they are part of a URL, must also be encoded. However, query string data takes an additional level of encoding, over and above the regular character encodings discussed to this point. By way of illustration, space characters within query strings are encoded as plus (+) signs and not via hex character encodings, as illustrated in the above examples. Query string encoding can be specific to the protocol being used, and also to the mechanism being used to gather data from the user (**ISINDEX**, **FORM**, or **ISMAP** active image). These mechanisms are discussed later on, in the section on **http** URLs.

SPECIAL CASES

In some cases, Internet domain names are not part of a URL. This is the case for protocols that are not dependent on a particular server, such as those for sending electronic mail or accessing USENET newsgroup articles.

SOME SIMPLE URL EXAMPLES

`http://info.cern.ch/hypertext/WWW/Addressing/URL/Overview.html`
This references the file *Overview.html* in the directory */hypertext/WWW/Addressing/URL/* from the server *info.cern.ch* using the HTTP protocol and the default port number (80 for HTTP).

`gopher://gumby.brain.headache.edu:151/7fonebook.txt` This references the searchable index *fonebook.txt* from the Gopher server at *gumby.brain.headache.edu* running on port number 151.

`news:alt.rec.motorcycle` This references the newsgroup *alt.rec.motorcycle*.

`mailto:ross@physics.mcg.ca` This sends an electronic mail message to the indicated e-mail address.

PARTIAL URLS WITHIN HTML DOCUMENTS

Within a given HTML document, you do not always need to specify the entire URL of a second document. This is because being *in* the document already implies information about the current URL, which allows you to reference neighboring documents or resources using a *partial* URL, giving the location *relative* to the current document.

For example, suppose you access the document *file.html* using the full URL

```
http://www.stuff.edu/main/docs/file.html
```

Within this document there is a hypertext reference containing the *partial* URL

```
<A HREF="stuff.html"> anchor text </A>
```

Where is this file? From inside *file.html*, any information not present in a URL reference is considered the *same* as that used to access the current document. Thus, the partial URL `stuff.html` is transformed into a full URL by appropriating the required URL components from the URL used to access *file.html*. The completed URL is then:

```
http://www.stuff.edu/main/docs/stuff.html
```

which indicates, as expected, that *stuff.html* is on the same server and in the same directory as *file.html*. Other equivalent partial URLs are:

```
/main/docs/stuff.html
```

```
//www.stuff.edu/main/docs/stuff.html
```

The former appropriates `http://www.stuff.edu` from the current URL to complete the reference, while the latter appropriates only the `http:` part from the *base* URL of the current document.

You can also use partial URLs to reference files in other directories; for example, from the example *file.html* the relative URL:

```
../../main.html
```

indicates the file *main.html* in the root HTTP directory, namely:

```
http://www.stuff.edu/main.html
```

Partial URLs are very useful when constructing large collections of documents that will be kept together. Of course, relative URLs become invalid if a document is moved to a new directory or a new Internet site. This problem can be mitigated by using the **BASE** element of the HTML language, which is used to record a *BASE* URL for a document. If the document is moved, all relative URLs are determined relative to the URL recorded by **BASE**.

FRAGMENT IDENTIFIERS

In some cases, you will see locator strings of the form:

```
http://some.where.edu/Stuff/Path/plonk.html#location-1
```

The portion of the URL following the hash (#) character is called a *fragment identifier*, which references a particular location within the designated URL. In an HTML document, a location is indicated using an anchor element of the form:

```
<A NAME="location-1">text marker</A>
```

where the string `location-1` is an arbitrary string (a name taken) marking the location indicated by the text enclosed within the element.

When a browser is instructed to access a resource specified by a URL, it first strips off *all* characters following and including an unencoded hash (#), and uses the remaining string as the resource URL. Consequently, for the stripped URL to be valid, the fragment identifier must be the very last substring on a URL. The browser preserves the fragment identifier as local browser-specific information and, after retrieving the indicated resource, looks for the indicated location. The browser will present the document to the user, such that the location is prominently displayed, either by placing the location at the top of the screen, or by highlighting it in some way.

Formally, fragment identifiers are not part of the URL specification, but they appear so often in the context of a URL that they bear mention here. Fragment identifiers are discussed in more detail in the **http** URL section.

URL SPECIFICATIONS

We now look at the details of the different URL forms. The protocols most commonly referenced by URLs are:

```
ftp:

gopher:

http:

mailto:

news:

telnet: (rlogin:, tn3270:)

wais:

file: (local file access)
```

FTP URLS

Ftp URLs designate files and directories accessible using the FTP protocol. In the absence of any username and password information, anonymous FTP access is assumed. This connects you to the designated server as user *anonymous*, and uses your Internet mail address as the password. Here is a typical example, referencing the file *splunge.txt* located in the directory *path* at the Internet site *internet.address.edu*:

```
ftp://internet.address.edu/path/splunge.txt
```

You can specify an FTP access of a directory using a URL such as:

```
ftp://internet.address.edu/path/
```

In this case, FTP servers provide a list of directory contents. WWW browsers display this information as a menu, allowing the user to navigate through the filesystem or select particular files for downloading.

SPECIAL CHARACTERS IN FTP URLs

The forward slash (/) and semicolon (;) characters are special in an ftp URL. The forward slash indicates directory or other hierarchical structures, while the semicolon is used to indicate the start of a *typecode* string, which must be the last string of the URL. Typecode strings are discussed below.

NONANONYMOUS FTP ACCESS

You can reference nonanonymous FTP resources by specifying, within the URL, the username and password of the account you wish to access. For example:

```
ftp://joe_bozo:bl123@internet.address.edu/dir1/Dir2/file.gz
```

allows a user to access files on machine *internet.address.edu* belonging to user joe_bozo with password bl123. This is, however, not a secure way of giving access to this file, since anyone who reads the URL knows joe_bozo's password. If you have information you want to make available via FTP, set up a proper anonymous FTP service.

FTP DIRECTORY PATHS

Directory paths in FTP accesses are defined relative to a particular home directory. This home directory is different, depending on how the user accomplishes the FTP connection. A user who connects to a machine via anonymous FTP is placed in the anonymous FTP home directory, and has restricted access to the server filesystem. This is a security feature that allows you to make certain files publicly available without exposing the rest of your system to unauthorized users. On the other hand, if a visiting user connects to the same machine as a registered user, the home directory will be that of the registered user, entirely different from that attained via anonymous FTP.

All of this means that the path you use to access a file as a regular user can be quite different from the path used to access a file by anonymous FTP. You must keep this in mind when archiving data into anonymous FTP archives, and when creating URLs that point to these data.

MODES FOR FILE TRANSFERS

The FTP protocol allows several modes for transferring files. The most important is *image* or *binary* mode, which makes a byte-by-byte copy of the file. This is the mode to use when transferring programs, compressed data, or image files. Also common is *ASCII* mode, which should be used to transfer plain, printable text files. This mode is useful because it "corrects" for the fact that PCs, Macintoshes, and UNIX computers use different characters to mark the end of a line of text. In particular, Macintoshes use the carriage-return character CR; UNIX computers use the line-feed character LF; and DOS/Windows computers use both CR and LF (often written CRLF). In ASCII mode, FTP automatically converts between these three end-of-line markers to ensure that the received file has the new line codes appropriate to the local system. You cannot use this mode to transfer programs, however, since programs and data files will contain bytes with the same codes as CR or LF characters, and under ASCII mode, these codes will be converted into the new line codes appropriate to the local system, which destroys the data content of binary data files.

The FTP protocol has no knowledge of the data content of a file and must be told what mode to use in a file transfer. Thus your WWW browser must have some way of determining the data type of a file being accessed via an **ftp** URL. In general the browser "guesses" the type from the suffix of the filename. All WWW clients maintain a local database that maps filename extensions onto data types. For example, Mosaic for X-Windows maintains this database in a file called *mime.types*, while other browsers allow you to define this information using configuration menus or pop-up windows. WWW browsers use this information to guess the content of a file and to select the appropriate transfer mode.

TYPECODE STRINGS

Typecode strings allow you to explicitly set the transfer mode for an FTP access. For example, the following URL

```
ftp://internet.address.edu/path/splunge.txt;type=a
```

indicates that the designated resource (the file *splunge.txt*) should be accessed using ASCII mode. The semicolon is used to separate the end of the resource locator string from the type indicator. Other possible type indicators are `type=i` for image (binary) transfers, and `type=d` for accessing a directory listing. Typecode strings are optional, in which case the transfers will be in image (binary) mode. Fragment strings, if used, are appended after the typecode string; for example:

```
ftp://internet.address.edu/path/goof.html;type=a#location
```

NOTE

Several browsers do not support typecode strings, and erroneously assume that the string is part of the filename. It is probably best to avoid using typecode strings until support for them is more widespread.

TIP

TROUBLESHOOTING FTP URLs

At times, an **ftp** URL request may fail, either because the network is down or because the machine you are trying to access is overloaded with FTP accesses and refuses your request. Alternatively, the server may be configured to restrict access to only certain Internet sites. WWW browsers are notoriously terse in handling FTP connections, and say very little if a connection has failed. You can check for the cause of the problem by using an FTP connection outside of your WWW application. A stand-alone FTP session can provide much more commentary on the state of your connection and will often give you a message explaining why the connection cannot be made.

GOPHER URLS

Gopher servers can be accessed via URLs in a manner that looks superficially similar to that of FTP or HTTP servers, but is, in fact, quite different. This is because Gopher resources are referenced using a combination of *resource identifier* codes and *selector strings*, so that a **gopher** URL is quite different from an **ftp** or **http** URL. Resource identifiers are single-digit codes that specify the *type* of the Gopher resource—for example, that it is a text file, a directory, or a searchable index. The Gopher selector string is just a name associated with this resource. This can be a directory or filename, but can also be a redirection to a database search procedure, or to a telnet session. Sometimes the selector string has, as its first character, a duplicate of the single-character resource type identifier. This can lead to hair-pulling confusion, with resource identifiers appearing alone, or in pairs, seemingly at random. Table 6.2 summarizes the Gopher resource identifier codes.

GENERAL FORM OF A GOPHER URL

The general form for a basic Gopher URL is:

```
gopher://domain.name.edu/Tselector_string
```

where T is the Gopher typecode and `selector_string` is the Gopher selector string. The root information of a Gopher server can be obtained by leaving out all type and selector string information. Thus, the root information of the above Gopher server is available at the URL:

Table 6.2 Gopher Resource Identifier Codes

Code	File/Resource Type
0	Text file
1	Directory
2	CSO name/phone book server
3	error
4	Macintosh binhexed (*.hqx) file
5	DOS binary file of some type
6	UNIX unencoded file
7	Full-text index search
8	Telnet session
9	Binary file

```
gopher://domain.name.edu/
```

Hierarchical relationships are possible. For example:

```
gopher://domain.name.edu/1stuff
```

indicates that `stuff` is a directory, and will retrieve the Gopher contents of `stuff`, while the URL

```
gopher://domain.name.edu/7stuff/index
```

indicates access to the *index* search in the directory *stuff*. Accessing this URL would cause the browser to ask the user for query string information to be used in the search.

PASSING SEARCH INFORMATION

Search information is sent to the Gopher server by appending the search strings to the URL, separated from the URL by a question mark. Thus to pass the strings `bob`, `carol`, and `ted` to the Gopher search index noted above, the URL is:

```
gopher://domain.name.edu/7stuff/index?bob+carol+ted
```

Note that the URL syntax for Gopher queries uses a plus (+) sign to separate different search strings. Therefore, if you want to include a literal plus sign with a string, it must be encoded. (The encoding for a plus sign is `%2B`.)

CLIENT CONSTRUCTION OF QUERY STRINGS

Inserting plus sign separators and converting plus signs in query strings into encoded values is done by the WWW or Gopher client. When a user accesses a Gopher search from a WWW browser, he or she is prompted for search strings. These are generally entered in a text box, using space characters or tabs to separate the different strings. When the search information is submitted, the search strings are appended, with appropriate encodings, to the URL. The client software is responsible for replacing space characters by plus signs and for encoding characters in your search string that might be incorrectly interpreted.

The following are some simple examples of Gopher URLs.

GOPHER URL EXAMPLES

`gopher://gopher.utirc.utoronto.ca/` Retrieve the home menu from the Gopher server running on the machine *gopher.utirc.utoronto.ca* at the default port number (70).

`gopher://gopher.utirc.utoronto.ca/11adaptive.technology`
Retrieve the `adaptive technology` menu from the indicated Gopher server running on the default port number. The selector string for this directory is `1adaptive.technology`.

`gopher://gumby.brain.headache.edu:151/7fonebook.txt?bob+` `carol+ted+alice` Access the searchable index `fonebook.txt` from the named Gopher server, running on port number 151, and pass to it the four indicated search strings. The Gopher selector string is `fonebook.txt`.

The Gopher protocol is currently being enhanced, and more sophisticated URLs will be needed to access the newer Gopher features. Please see the references at the end of this chapter for additional information.

HTTP URLS

Http URLs designate files, directories, or server-side programs accessible using the HTTP protocol. **Http** URLs follow the general form indicated in Figure 6.1. Here are some examples:

`http://www.site.edu:3232/cgi-bin/srch-example?query-string`
References the resource ***srch-example*** at the site ***www.site.edu***, accessible through the HTTP server running on port 3232, and passes to this resource the string `query-string`.

`http://www.utirc.utoronto.ca/` Access the root directory of the indicated HTTP server. The server can be configured to deliver a standard HTML document, a listing of the directory contents, or an error message.

An **http** URL must always point to a file (text or program) or a directory. A directory is indicated by terminating the directory name with a forward slash, such as:

`http://www.site.utoronto.ca/HTMLdocs/`

The following reference to this directory is an error and implies that you are referring to a file, and not a directory:

`http://www.site.utoronto.ca/HTMLdocs`

However, you can leave out the trailing slash if you are referencing the root of a Web site, and not specifying any path information. Thus, the following two URLs are formally equivalent and correct:

`http://www.hprc.utoronto.ca/`

`http://www.hprc.utoronto.ca`

SPECIAL CHARACTERS IN HTTP URLs

The forward slash (/), semicolon (;), and question mark (?) are special characters in the path and query string portions of an **http** URL. The slash denotes a change in hierarchy (such as a directory), while the question mark ends the resource location path and indicates the start of a query string. The semicolon is reserved for future use, and should therefore be encoded in all cases where you intend a literal semicolon character.

PASSING QUERY STRINGS TO A SERVER

Http URLs can contain query string data to be passed to the server. These strings are appended to the URL, separated by a question mark, as with Gopher query strings. Two common examples are:

`http://some.site.edu/cgi-bin/foo?arg1+arg2+arg3` This is equivalent to the Gopher mechanism discussed in the previous section. Once again, the plus signs are the special query string encoding for space characters.

`http://some.site.edu/cgi-bin/imagemap?ix,iy` This mechanism is used by active images. For example, URLs of this form are produced by the following HTML anchor element markup:

```
<A HREF=http://some.site.edu/cgi-bin/imagemap>

        <IMG SRC="image.gif" ISMAP>

</A>
```

The **ISMAP** directive declares this image to be an active imagemap, while the surrounding hypertext anchor indicates the URL to which image coordinates should be sent. When the user clicks the mouse over the image, the coordinates of the mouse pointer relative to the upper left-hand corner of the image are sent to the server by appending them to the indicated URL. The *imagemap* program must know how to parse this information. This is discussed in more detail in Chapters 8 and 10.

In these examples, the information is passed to a resource in the */cgi-bin* directory. In general, HTTP servers do not directly handle query data directly and instead pass it on to other "gateway" programs for further processing. The directory name */cgi-bin* is a configurable symbolic name, commonly used to reference a directory containing gateway programs.

ENCODING OF QUERY STRINGS

In addition to the character encodings required within URLs, query strings undergo additional levels of encoding to preserve information within the query string data. This is necessary because certain characters in a query string are assigned special encoded meanings—for example, the plus character (+) used to encode spaces, as noted previously.

Document authors do not usually have to worry about the encoding phase; browsers take **ISINDEX** or **FORM** input data and do the encoding automatically. However, a gateway program author must explicitly decode these data; thus he or she must understand the encoding, in order to reverse it. The following is a brief review of the encoding steps; you are referred to Chapters 4 (discussion of **FORM** elements) and 8 for more details.

1. Percent characters (%) are converted into their URL encodings (%2f).
2. Plus signs (+) are converted into their URL encodings (%2b).
3. Ampersands (&) are converted into their URL encodings (%26).
4. Equals signs (=) are converted into their URL encodings (%3d).
5. The possibly special characters, namely # ; / ? : $! , ' ( ), are converted into their URL encodings.
6. Space characters are encoded as plus signs (+)
7. All non-ASCII characters (hex codes greater than 7f), all ASCII control characters (hex 00–31, and 7f), and the unsafe ASCII characters listed in Table 6.1, are converted into their URL encodings (note that spaces have already been converted into plus signs).

At this point, every ASCII punctuation character has been encoded, except for the characters

    _ - . * @

If the data are from an **ISINDEX** query, the encoding is complete. If they are from a **FORM**, there are several more stages. To encode **FORM** data, one needs to ensure that:

8. The name and value strings from each **FORM** input element are encoded as just described.
9. The name and value strings are combined into composite strings of the form name=value. Note that the first encoding phase (Step 8) encoded all equals signs in the name and value strings, so that the only *un*encoded equals signs in the string are those used to separate a name from its associated values.

10. The `name=value` strings from all the **FORM** elements are combined into a single string, separated by ampersand (`&`) characters. For example:

    `name1=value1&name2=value2`

    Note that the first encoding phase (Step 8) encoded all ampersands in the `name` and `value` strings, so that the only unencoded ampersands are those used to separate name/value pairs.

Query string data encoded by these mechanisms are said to be *URL-encoded.* In fact, this encoding mechanism is assigned its own MIME type, namely

`Content-type: application/x-www-form-urlencoded`

Note that you can easily tell if the data are from a **FORM** or **ISINDEX** query just by checking for an unencoded equals sign.

ENCODING OF **ISMAP** ACTIVE IMAGE QUERIES

A typical active image is written, in an HTML document, as:

`<A HREF="http://some.where.edu/prg-bin/program"><IMG`

`    SRC="funny_image.gif" ISMAP></A>`

The **ISMAP** attribute makes the **IMG** element active, while the surrounding anchor element gives the URL to which the image coordinates should be sent. **ISMAP** active image queries are composed by taking the integer x and y coordinates of the mouse click, in pixels with respect to the upper left-hand corner of the active image, and appending them to the URL of the enclosing anchor element, using the format:

`http://some.where.edu/prg-bin/program?x,y`

In this case, the only valid characters in the query strings are the integer numbers (x and y) and a comma. All other characters are invalid.

FRAGMENT IDENTIFIERS

A single HTML document can use the **NAME** attribute of the anchor element to specify distinct targets of hypertext references. For example:

`<A NAME="raw">hypertext link target</A>`

marks the string as a possible target of a hypertext link. These named locations are called *fragment identifiers*, and can be referenced, in a URL, by appending the fragment identifier to the document URL, separated from it by the hash (#) sign. For example, suppose the above-named anchor is found in the document:

```
http://site.world.edu/dir/data.html
```

The string `hypertext link target` is then explicitly referenced by the URL:

```
http://site.world.edu/dir/data.html#raw
```

You can also use fragment identifiers from within a single document, by using a partial URL that references *just* the fragment identifier, prepended by the hash character. Thus, within the document *data.html*, the string `hypertext link target` is referenced with the URL `#raw`. For example:

```
<A HREF="#raw">raw data</A>
```

■■■■■■ **NOTE**

As mentioned previously, fragment identifiers are not formally part of a URL. Fragment identifiers are name tokens, and should be written using letters, numbers, and dashes, and should have a letter as their first character. Thus the string `fig-2` is a good choice for a fragment identifier, while `23-x` is incorrect.

■■■■■

SERVER ISSUES: SPECIAL PROGRAM DIRECTORIES

URL resource specification strings beginning with the strings `/cgi-bin` or `/htbin` are often special, and refer to directories containing programs and scripts (this is an HTTP server feature and these names can be changed in the server configuration files). When a server is contacted via a URL referencing a *gateway* program, the server launches the program and passes data from the client (if any) to this program for further processing. This is discussed in more detail in Chapter 8. However, here are two simple examples, with brief explanations:

`http://some.site.edu/cgi-bin/srch-example` The server executes the program *srch-example* found in the *cgi-bin* directory. Any output from *srch-example* is sent back to the client.

`http://www.site.edu/cgi-bin/srch-example/path/other?srch_string` The server again executes the program *srch-example* found in the *cgi-bin* directory. The extra *path information* path/other is passed as a parameter to *srch-example*, as is the query information srch_string.

SERVER ISSUES: PERSONAL HTML DIRECTORIES

Users who have accounts on a machine running the NCSA HTTP, Apache, or Netscape Netsite servers (and probably others) can have world-accessible HTML documents in their own home directories, distinct from those files in the server document hierarchy. These "personal" HTTP document directories are indicated in a URL by a tilde (~) character prepended in front of the path information (the first item in the path hierarchy following the tilde must be the account name of the user). The tilde tells the server that this is not a regular directory, but a *redirection* to a personal document archive of the user with the indicated account. For example, if the user iang has a personal document directory, this could be accessed using the URL:

```
http://site.world.edu/%7Eiang/
```

where %7E is the encoding for the tilde character. You will often see a real tilde in such URLs, since the tilde is safe in most situations. However, to be perfectly correct you should encode the tilde—this will always work.

HTTPS (HTTP-SECURE) URLS

The Netscape Netsite Commerce HTTP server supports a special variant of the **http** URL, known as **https.** **Https** URLs are composed in exactly the same manner as **http** URLs, except that the connection between client and server is encrypted using an encryption technology called Secure Sockets Layer (SSL), so that data can pass securely between client and server. Currently, only the Netscape Navigator supports this SSL technology and **https** URLs. SSL is discussed in more detail in Chapter 7.

MAILTO URLS

The **mailto** URL sends mail to the designated electronic mail address. The format for **mailto** is:

```
mailto:mail_address
```

where mail_address is the Internet mail address (as specified in RFC 822, the document that defines the Internet mail protocol) to which the message should be sent. Typically, this is of the form name@host, where name is the user name of the person and host is the name of the machine. A browser will allow the user to type in the mail message.

Some mail addresses contain the percent character. This character must be encoded, since it is a special character (marking the beginning of a character encoding string). As an example, the e-mail address:

```
jello%ian@irc.utoronto.ca
```

must be converted into the **mailto** URL:

```
mailto:jello%25ian@irc.utoronto.ca
```

Several browsers, such as MacWeb and some older versions of Mosaic, do not support **mailto** URLs.

A **mailto** URL does not indicate how the mail should be sent. In general, a client mail program must contact a *mailserver*, a program that validates the mail and forwards it on to its destination. **Mailto** URLs do not specify a mailserver, so this information must be separately configured into a browser. In general, a Web browser provides a configuration utility allowing users to provide this information.

NEWS URLS

News URLs reference USENET newsgroups or individual USENET news articles. Newsgroups are specified via URLs of the form

```
news:news.group.name
```

where `news.group.name` is the name of a particular newsgroup. The special form

```
news:*
```

is used to reference *all* available newsgroups. Note that this does not specify an NNTP server from which news can be accessed—this must be specified elsewhere, in a browser-specific manner. For example, MacWeb users can configure this with a pull-down menu, while UNIX Mosaic for X-Windows users must set the *NNTPSERVER* environment variable to the name of the desired server.

An alternative format is used to request particular news articles. The general form is:

```
news:message_id@domain.name.edu
```

where `message_id` is the unique ID associated with a particular article originating from the machine `domain.name.edu` (this is all discussed in gruesome detail in RFC 1036, referenced at the end of the chapter). The at (@) character is special in a **news** URL, and indicates this alternative form of reference. This format is not generally useful, since most news servers delete articles after a few days or weeks, so that any referenced article is soon unavailable.

NNTP URLS

The **nntp** URL scheme provides a way of explicitly referencing a news article from a particular NNTP news server. A typical **nntp** URL might be:

```
nntp://alchem.chem.tor.ca/alt.rubber-chickens/12311121.121
```

which references *article number* `12311121.121`, in the newsgroup `alt.rubber-chickens`, from the NNTP server running on the machine `alchem.chem.tor.ca` (at the default port number 119). The NNTP protocol is described in RFC 977, should you want additional details.

Unfortunately, most news servers are configured to restrict access to local users, so that this mechanism does not truly designate a world-accessible resource. Furthermore, most Web browsers do not support **nntp** URLs. **News** URLs are generally more useful.

TELNET URLS

You can use a **telnet** URL to reference a telnet link to a remote machine. An example is:

```
telnet://flober.rodent.edu
```

More generally, you can use a URL of the form:

```
telnet://username:password@flober.rodent.edu/
```

to indicate the username and password that the user should employ. The colon (:) and at (@) characters are special in a **telnet** URL, since they designate the different fields in this form. In general, this username and password information will not be used by the client to make and complete the connection. Rather, this information may be presented to users as a hint as to what they should do once the connection is made. Obviously you do not want to use this more general form if you want to keep your passwords a secret!

Some browsers support a variant of a **telnet** URL, called a **tn3270** URL. This indicates a connection that requires IBM 3270 terminal emulation on the part of the client. In general, this is only useful if the client computer supports a tn3270 client program (tn3270 clients are rarely built into a Web browser), and provided the WWW client is configured to know about this program. If not, most browsers default to a regular telnet connection.

Rlogin connections are often possible using an **rlogin** URL. The specification is:

```
rlogin://username@flober.rodent.edu
```

where `username` is the account name for the rlogin. You will be prompted for a password in the resulting window unless one is not required. Many browsers emulate **rlogin** URLs using a telnet connection.

WAIS URLS

WAIS servers can be accessed via URLs in a manner similar to HTTP servers. The major difference is in the file specification: here, we must pass the correct search instructions to the WAIS server, in addition to information about what is to be searched.

The standard form for accessing a WAIS server is:

```
wais://wais.server.edu/database?search
```

where `wais.server.edu` is the Internet domain name of the host running the WAIS server (including a port number, if required; the default is 210); `database` is the name of the WAIS database to be searched; and `search` is a list of search instructions to pass to the database. Another form is

```
wais://wais.server.edu/database
```

which designates a particular searchable database. A browser will understand that this URL references a searchable database and will prompt for query string input.

Finally, **wais** URLs can be used to reference individual resources on the WAIS database. The form for this URL is

```
wais://wais.server.edu/database/wais_type/resource_path
```

where `wais_type` is a type indicator, which gives the type of the object being accessed, and `resource_path` is the document ID, used internally by the WAIS database. In general these strings are generated by the WAIS server itself, and it is rare that a user will actually compose the `wais_type` and `resource_path` fields. However, if you are burning to do it yourself, you should read the WAIS documentation listed at the end of this chapter.

FILE URLS

File URLs are specific to a local system and should not be used in documents to be publicly accessed over the Internet. A **file** URL represents access of files from computers on a network, particularly from the local computer, but does not specify a protocol for accessing these files. The general form for a **file** URL is

```
file://hostname/path/file
```

where `hostname` is the domain name for the system and `path/file` is the locator of the file. The **file** URL is most commonly used to represent local file access. All browsers allow local file access, often with a pull-down menu, and represent the location using a **file** URL. The domain name for local file access can be either the special string `localhost`, or an empty field (`file:///...`). For example, if you are accessing the local file */big/web/docs.html*, the **file** URL could be either of the following:

```
file://localhost/big/web/docs.html
```

```
file:///big/web/docs.html
```

The file could be on a local disc, or on a file system mounted from elsewhere.

PROSPERO URLS

This scheme is used to access resources accessible using the Prospero Directory Service, which acts rather like a sophisticated caching and proxying service. However, since very few Web browsers (i.e., practically none) support **prospero** URLs, this form is not discussed here. Further information is found in the references.

COMING ATTRACTIONS

Several new URL schemes are under development. These include **afs** (global file access using the Andrew File System), **mid** (message identifiers for electronic mail), **cid** (content identifiers for MIME message parts), **mailserver** (access to data from mailservers), and **z39.50** (access to ANSI standard Z39.50 database and searching services). These are still in the developmental stages, and have not been widely implemented.

URLS, URIS, URNS, URCS—NAMING THINGS ON THE WEB

The URL scheme is the most common naming scheme used on the Web, but it is not the only one. This brief section summarizes the names and general features of the different proposed schemes.

UNIFORM RESOURCE NAMES: URN

Uniform Resource Names, or URNs, are designed to be a location-independent way of referencing an object. Thus, a URN would not specify the specific location of the desired resource, but would specify a generic name. The software processing the name would then locate the named object at the closest or most accessible location, using a name lookup service. The specification of URNs is incomplete, and they are not in current use.

UNIFORM RESOURCE LOCATOR: URL

Uniform Resource Locators, or URLs, are protocol- and location-specific schemes for referencing resources on the Internet. This is currently the only implemented mechanism for referencing resources on the Internet.

UNIFORM RESOURCE IDENTIFIER: URI

Uniform Resource Identifiers, or URIs, generically represent any naming schemes used to reference resources on the Internet. Thus, both URLs and URNs fall under the category of URIs. The names URI and URL are often used synonymously, but this is only accurate in the absence of a defined naming scheme for URNs.

UNIFORM RESOURCE CITATION: URC

Uniform Resource Citations, or URCs, are designed to be collections of attribute/value pairs that describe a particular object (referenced using a URI). Some of the values in these pairs may also be URIs. A URC can act in many ways, for example as a cross-indexing resource for a large resource collection, or simply as a collection of references to related data. The specification for URCs is not complete, so they are not in current use.

REFERENCES

These specifications originate from the various Internet working groups currently developing Internet and Web standards. In most cases, the Internet protocols or standards are formalized in documents known as Requests for Comments, or RFCs. Once approved by the appropriate Internet Engineering Task Force (IETF), these documents are officially numbered, giving rise to the referenced RFC numbers quoted here.

General overview of addressing issues on the Web

```
http://www.w3.org/hypertext/WWW/Addressing/Addressing.html
```

URI Specification, in HTML format

```
http://www.w3.org/hypertext/WWW/Addressing/URL/URI_Overview.html
```

URI Specification (RFC 1630)

```
ftp://ds.internic.net/rfc/1630.txt
```

URL Specification (RFC 1738)

```
http://www.w3.org/hypertext/WWW/Addressing/rfc1738.txt
```

```
ftp://ds.internic.net/rfc/rfc1738.txt
```

Relative URL Specification (RFC 1808)

```
http://www.w3.org/hypertext/WWW/Addressing/rfc1808.txt
```

```
ftp://ds.internic.net/rfc/rfc1808.txt
```

URNs: The PATH Specification

```
http://union.ncsa.uiuc.edu/~liberte/www/path.html
```

URCs: Uniform Resource Characteristics

```
http://union.ncsa.uiuc.edu/HyperNews/get/www/URCs.html
```

```
http://www.acl.lanl.gov/URI/ExtRep/urc0.html
```

Electronic Mail/ARPA Internet Text Messages Specification (RFC 822)

```
ftp://ds.internic.net/rfc/rfc822.txt
```

Standard for Interchange of USENET Messages (RFC 1036)

```
ftp://ds.internic.net/rfc/rfc1036.txt
```

Network News Transfer Protocol Specification (RFC 977)

```
ftp://ds.internic.net/rfc/rfc977.txt
```

THE HTTP PROTOCOL

To develop interactive HTML documents, a Web designer needs to understand the interaction between WWW clients and an HTTP server. This interaction involves two distinct but closely related issues. The first is the HTTP protocol used for communication with HTTP servers. This protocol has several specific communication *methods* (for example, *GET, POST,* or *HEAD*) that allow clients to request data from the server, and send information to the server. It also contains mechanisms for communicating additional critical information, such as the general status of a transaction (successful or not, and if unsuccessful, why not) the capabilities of the client (what data types, character sets, or languages are acceptable), and user authentication information (when required).

The second issue is the way HTTP servers handle a client's request. If the request is for a file, the server locates the appropriate file and sends it back to the client, or sends the relevant error message if the file is unavailable. Of particular interest is the situation when the client wants to send information to the server for more complicated processing. In most cases, servers do not do this processing themselves, and instead "hand off" the work to other programs, called *gateway programs*. The *Common Gateway Interface (CGI)* specification, described in the next chapter, defines the mechanisms by which HTTP servers communicate with gateway programs. You need to understand both the HTTP protocol and the CGI specification to write server-side gateway programs and HTML documents that access these programs.

Gateway programs, like files, are referenced using URLs. When a client accesses a URL pointing to a gateway program, the server activates the program and uses the CGI mechanisms to pass to the program data sent by the client (if any). The gateway program acts on the data and returns its response back to the server, again using the CGI mechanisms. The server then forwards the data to the client that initiated the request using the HTTP protocol, completing the transaction. Again, the details of CGI are discussed in the next chapter.

This chapter first outlines the general principles of the HTTP protocol, and then illustrates its operation using six example cases. The chapter concludes with a detailed list of the control messages that can be sent from client to server, and vice versa, along with a summary of references for further inquiry.

THE HTTP PROTOCOL

HTTP is an Internet client/server protocol designed for the rapid and efficient delivery of hypertext materials. HTTP is a stateless protocol, which means that once a server has delivered the requested data to a client, the server breaks the connection, and retains no memory of the event that just took place. Statelessness is in part what makes an HTTP server fast.

All HTTP communication transmits data as a stream of 8-bit characters, or *octets*. This ensures the safe transmission of all forms of data, including images, executable programs, or HTML documents containing 8-bit ISO Latin-1 characters.

An HTTP connection has four stages:

1. **Open the connection.** The client contacts the server at the Internet address and port number specified in the URL (the default port is 80).

2. **Make the request.** The client sends a message to the server, requesting service. The request consists of HTTP *request headers* that define the *method* requested for the transaction and provide information about the capabilities

of the client, followed by the data being sent to the server (if any). Typical HTTP methods are *GET*, for getting an object from a server, or *POST*, for posting data to an object (e.g., a gateway program) on the server.

3. **Send the response.** The server sends a response to the client. This consists of *response headers* describing the state of the transaction (for example, the status of the response [successful or not] and also the type of data being sent), followed by the actual data.

4. **Close the connection.** The connection is closed; the server does not retain any knowledge of the transaction just completed.

This procedure means that each connection processes a single transaction, and can therefore only download a single data file to the client, while the stateless nature of the transaction means that each connection knows nothing about previous connections. The implications of these features are illustrated in the following example transactions.

SINGLE TRANSACTION PER CONNECTION

As an example, assume that HTTP is used to access an HTML document containing ten inline images via the **IMG** element. Composing the entire document requires 11 distinct connections to the HTTP server: one to retrieve the HTML document itself and ten others to retrieve the ten image files.

STATELESSNESS OF THE CONNECTION

Suppose a user retrieves a fill-in HTML **FORM** from a server. The **FORM** has a field into which the user types a name, which in turn allows the user to access some name-specific information in a personnel database. When the user submits the **FORM**, the username (and any other information gathered by the **FORM**) is sent to a gateway program residing on the server for subsequent processing of the request (the URL of the gateway program is specified as an attribute to the **FORM** element, as discussed in Chapter 4).

This gateway program processes the data and returns, as a second HTML document, the results to the user. This document contains a second **FORM** allowing further requests of the database. But, in this case, the second **FORM** does not contain a place for a name. Since the server is stateless and thus has no memory of the first connection, how does it know the name of the person the second time around?

The answer: the server does not know. Instead, the gateway program must explicitly keep track of this information for each client, for example by placing the name information *inside* the HTML document returned to the user. This can be accomplished by including, in the **FORM** returned to the user, an `<INPUT TYPE="hidden" ...>` element. *Hidden* elements are used to record the *state* of the client/server transaction, and in this case to record the name. For example, the element might be:

```
<INPUT TYPE="hidden" NAME="name_of_person" VALUE="Robert Johnston">
```

When the client submits the **FORM** for the second time, the content of the hidden element is sent along with any user-input data, thereby returning the name information to the server. Using hidden elements, information can be passed back and forth between the client and server, preserving knowledge of the name for each subsequent transaction.

EXAMPLE HTTP CLIENT/SERVER SESSIONS

The easiest way to understand the HTTP protocol is through simple examples. The following sections document six examples covering the most common HTTP methods. Each presentation shows both the data sent from the client to HTTP server and the data returned from the server to client. First, a few words about how this "eavesdropping" was accomplished.

MONITORING CLIENT/SERVER INTERACTION

It is easy to monitor the interaction between HTTP servers and World Wide Web clients, since the communication is entirely in character data sent to a particular port. Consequently, all you need do is *listen* at a port, or *talk* to a port. You can listen at a port using the program **listen**, given in Appendix D, while you can talk to a port using the standard Internet program, **telnet**.

You use **listen** to find out what a Web client sends to a server. To obtain this information, you run the **listen** program on a computer: as an example, let's suppose you run **listen** on the computer with domain name *leonardo.subnet.ca*. When started, **listen** prints out the port number it is listening at, for example:

```
listening at port 1743
```

and then falls silent, waiting to print any data that arrive at that port. You now configure a WWW client to send HTTP requests to this port. You do this by *pointing* the browser to port 1743 on *leonardo.subnet.ca,* using a URL such as

```
http://leonardo.subnet.ca:1743/Tests/file.html
```

(the port number is marked in boldface). The client dutifully sends the HTTP request headers to port number 1743 on *leonardo.subnet.ca,* whereupon **listen** receives the data and prints them to the screen.

Determining what the server sends in response to the client takes a bit more work. In this case, you can use the telnet program to connect to the server, and must then enter by hand the HTTP request headers that were sent by the client (and which you intercepted using the **listen** program). Suppose, for example, that the server is running at port 80 on *leonardo.subnet.ca.* To connect to this server, simply make a telnet connection to this port. On a UNIX system, you would type:

```
telnet leonardo.subnet.ca 80

Trying 128.100.121.33...

Connected to leonardo.subnet.ca

Escape character is '^]'.
```

The string you type is in boldface. (PC and Macintosh versions of **telnet** are somewhat different, but all allow you to do the same thing.) **Telnet** gives three lines of information to let you know what it is doing and then falls silent. Whatever you type is sent to the server running on *leonardo.subnet.ca,* so you now type in the required request headers. Whatever the server sends in response is sent to the telnet program and printed on the screen.

A third alternative is the utility program **backtalk,** listed in Appendix D. **Backtalk** is a derivative of **listen** that allows you both to monitor data arriving at a port, and to send data to the remote program talking to that port. When launched, **backtalk** allocates a port and, just like **listen,** prints out the port number, for example:

```
listening at port 1743
```

Thereafter, anything the remote program sends to port 1743 is printed to the display by **backtalk,** while anything the user types into the console is sent out through port 1743 and back to the remote program. This allows you to mimic the response headers of a server, albeit by hand. This is useful for examining client response to special server response headers, such as a request for user authentication.

These tools were used, in the following six examples, to determine the information passed between the client and server in typical HTTP transactions. These six examples look at:

1. a GET method request for a file

2. a GET method request to a gateway program, with a query string appended to the URL

3. an HTML **FORM** accessing a server gateway program using the GET method

4. an HTML **FORM** accessing a server gateway program using the POST method

5. an HTTP HEAD method request of a file

6. a request for a file that requires user authentication

These examples build on an understanding of URLs and of the way data are gathered by an HTML form and composed as a message for the server. These topics were covered in Chapters 4 (**FORMs**) and 6 (construction of query strings).

EXAMPLE 1:
A SIMPLE GET METHOD REQUEST

This request accesses a server and requests that a document be sent to the client. The request could be initiated by the user clicking on a hypertext anchor pointing to the file, for example:

```
<A HREF="http://some.server.edu/Tests/file.html">

    anchor text

</A>
```

The transaction can be broken into two parts: the passing of the request to the server, and the response information sent by the server back to the client.

THE CLIENT REQUEST

Figure 7.1 shows the actual data sent by a Netscape Navigator 1.1 client to the server. Other clients send qualitatively the same information (we will look at some others later on). The dots indicate `Accept` header fields that were omitted to save space.

Figure 7.1 Data sent from a client to an HTTP server during a simple GET request. *Comments are in italics.*

```
GET /Tests/file.html HTTP/1.0

Accept: text/plain

.

.


Accept: */*

If-Modified-Since: Wed, 02 Aug 1995 17:23:31 GMT

Referer: http://www.hprc.utoronto.ca/HTMLdocs/NewHTML/intro.html

User-Agent: Mozilla/1.1
           [a blank line, containing only CRLF ]
```

This request message consists of a *request header* containing several *request header fields*. Each field is a simple line of text, terminated by a carriage-return linefeed character pair (CRLF). The blank line (containing only a CRLF pair) at the end of the collection of header fields indicates the end of the headers and the beginning of any *data* being sent from the client to the server. This example transaction does not send data to the server, so the blank line is the end of the request.

The request message contains two parts. The first part, namely the first line of the request, is the *method* field, which specifies both the HTTP method to be used and the location of the desired resource on the server. This is followed by several HTTP *request* fields, which provide information to the server about the capabilities of the client, and about the nature of the data (if any) being sent by the client to the server.

CLIENT REQUEST: THE METHOD FIELD

The method field contains three text fields, separated by whitespace (whitespace is any combination of space and/or tab characters). In this example, the method header is:

```
GET /Tests/file.html HTTP/1.0
```

while the general form of this field is:

```
HTTP_method   identifier   HTTP_version
```

These three strings contain:

`HTTP_method:`	The HTTP method specification—GET in this example. The method specifies what is to be done to the object specified by the URL. Some other common methods are HEAD, which requests header information about an object, and POST, which is used to send information to the object.
`identifier:`	The identifier of the resource. In this example the identifier is the URL stripped of the protocol and Internet domain name strings. If this were a message to a *proxy server*, it would be the entire URL. Proxy servers are discussed later in this chapter.
`HTTP_version:`	The HTTP protocol version used by the client, currently `HTTP/1.0`.

CLIENT REQUEST: THE ACCEPT FIELD

The example shows several additional request headers. The `Accept` fields pass to the server a list of data types acceptable to the client. These are given as MIME content-types, and simply tell the server what types of data the client can handle. MIME types are discussed in more detail in Appendix B, and later in this chapter. The meanings for simple requests are relatively straightforward. For example, the line `Accept: text/plain` means that the client can accept plain-text files, while the line `Accept: audio/*` means that the client can accept any form of audio data.

This field should only be used to indicate that the client only wants a certain type of data, and no other. Currently, most clients send the header:

```
Accept: */*
```

which indicates that they will accept anything.

A client can send additional information in the `accept` header fields stating the relative desirability of particular types of data. This is expressed through two quantities: the q or quality factor (a number in the range 0.0 to 1.0, where 0.0 is equivalent to not accepting a type, and 1.0 is equivalent to always accepting a type), and mxb, which stands for the maximum size in bytes. If the resource is bigger than the mxb value, then it is not acceptable to the client. The default values are q=1.0 and mxb=undefined (that is, any size is acceptable).

For example, the following:

```
Accept: image/*

Accept: image/jpeg; q=0.7; mxb=50000

Accept: image/gif; q=0.5
```

mean that the client prefers image/jpeg files, provided they are smaller than 50 kbytes. If there is a JPEG file, but it is too big, then the client would prefer a GIF. If there are no GIF files, then the client will take any available image file.

Accept types can be combined in a single field, by separating them using commas. For example, the above three fields can be also written:

```
Accept: image/*, image/jpeg; q=0.7; mxb=50000, image/gif; q=0.5
```

CLIENT REQUEST: OTHER COMMON FIELDS

There are several other possible request header fields. The User-agent header

```
User-Agent: mozilla/1.1
```

provides information about the client making the request.

Another common field is Referer. Referer contains the URL of the document from which the request originated. Thus, if a user first obtained the document

```
http://www.hprc.utoronto.ca/HTMLdocs/NewHTML/intro.html
```

and from there accessed another document, the header field

```
Referer: http://www.hprc.utoronto.ca/HTMLdocs/NewHTML/intro.html
```

would be one of the request header fields sent to the server when requesting the second document.

A third common header is If-Modified-Since. This contains a time and date, in Greenwich Mean Time, and is used to retrieve a document (or data) only if it has changed since the specified time and date. This is usually sent by a client that retains a local copy of the document, and is used to check whether or not the client needs to update its local copy. In Figure 7.1, the client sent the header:

```
If-Modified-Since: Wed, 02 Aug 1995 17:23:31 GMT
```

If the requested resource */path/file.html* has been modified since this time and date, then the server should send the client a new copy. However, if the resource has not been modified since this time and date, the server should not send a new copy, but instead a special message indicating that the resource has not changed, and that the client should use its existing copy. These messages are discussed in the upcoming section on server response.

REQUEST HEADERS AND GATEWAY PROGRAMS

In this example, the request headers are used by the server to determine whether or not a data file should be sent to the server, and, if so, what type of data to send. (Servers can use the `Accept:` fields to decide from among a variety of different possible return types. At present this feature, known as *content* or *format negotiation*, is implemented on the CERN and Apache HTTP servers.) If the request is to a gateway program, and not for a file, then the server cannot make this decision. Instead, the server passes *all* the request header information to the gateway program, as a collection of environment variables, and lets the gateway program decide what to do. Thus, a gateway program author must understand the meanings of these header fields, since he or she will have to write gateway programs that interpret them. A complete list of the possible request headers is given at the end of this chapter.

THE SERVER RESPONSE

When the server receives the request, it tries to apply the designated method to the specified object (file or program), and passes the results of this effort back to the client. The returned data are preceded by a response header, consisting of *response header fields*, which communicates information about the state of the transaction back to the client. As with the request header fields sent from the client to the server, these are single lines of text terminated by a CRLF, while the end of the response header is indicated by a single blank line containing only a CRLF. The data of the response follow the blank line.

Figure 7.2 shows the data returned by the server to the client in response to the request of Figure 7.1.

The first seven lines are the response header. The end of the response header is indicated by the single blank line. The data response of the request (in this case, the requested HTML document) follows this blank line.

SERVER RESPONSE: THE STATUS LINE

The first line in the response header is a status line, which lets the client know what protocol the server uses, and whether or not the request was successfully completed. The general format for this line is

```
http_version  status_code  explanation
```

■■■■■■ **Figure 7.2** Data returned from the server to the client subsequent to the GET request of Figure 7.1. *Comments are in italics.*

```
HTTP/1.0 200 OK

Date: Thu, 03 Aug 1995 16:04:09 GMT

Server: NCSA/1.4.2

MIME-version: 1.0

Content-type: text/html

Last-modified: Thu, 03 Aug 1995 16:03:27 GMT

Content-length: 145

     [a blank line, containing only CRLF ]

<html>

<head>

<title> Test HTML file </title>

</head>


<body>


<h1> This is a test file</h1>

<p> So what did you expect, art?


</body>

</html>
```

■■■■■

which in our example was

```
HTTP/1.0 200 OK
```

The HTTP_version field gives the protocol version used by the server, currently HTTP/1.0. The status_code is a number between 200 and 599 that gives the status of the connection, while the explanation field is a text string that provides descriptive information about the status. Explanation strings may vary from server to server, whereas status codes are explicitly defined by the HTTP specification. Status codes between 200 and 299 indicate successful transactions, while numbers 300–399 indicate *redirection*, which means that the object specified by the URL has moved, and that the server is also sending the client the new URL of the object (the server sends the new URL in a Location response header field). Numbers 400–599 are error messages. When you encounter an error, the server usually sends a small HTML document explaining the error, to help the user understand what happened and why. The different status codes and their meanings are summarized in Table 7.2, at the end of this chapter. In this example, the code 200 means that everything went fine, and that the server is returning the requested data.

SERVER RESPONSE: RESPONSE HEADERS

The remaining response header fields contain information about the server and about the response being sent. The example in Figure 7.2 returns six lines of response header information. The first three, the Date, Server, and MIME-Version fields, describe the server and the details of the transaction, while the Content-type, Last-modified, and Content-length fields pass information specific to the document or data being returned. The formats and meanings of these header fields are:

Date: date_time Contains the time and date when the current object was assembled for transmission, in the format Thu, 03 Aug 1995 16:04:09 GMT. Note that the time *must* be Greenwich Mean Time (GMT) to ensure that all servers share a common time zone. Other possible time formats are discussed at the end of this chapter.

MIME-version: version_number Gives the MIME protocol version used by the server. The current version is 1.0.

Server: name/version This gives the name and version of the server, with a slash character separating the server name from the version number, such as NCSA/1.4 or CERN/3.0.

Content-length: length Gives the length, in bytes, of the data portion of the message (in this example, 145). In some transactions, the length is unknown (for example, if it is output from a gateway program), in which case this field is absent, and the client will continue to read data until the server breaks the connection.

Content-type: type/subtype Gives the MIME Content-type of the data being sent. This tells the client what type of data is being sent by the server. In this example, the MIME type is `text/html`, which informs the browser that the data is an HTML document. MIME types are discussed in detail in Appendix B.

`Last-modified: date_time` Gives the date and time that the document was last modified, here in the format `Thu, 03 Aug 1995 16:02:27 GMT`. As with the `Date` field, the date must be given in Greenwich Mean Time.

How is this header generated? If the request is for a file, the HTTP server constructs the header itself. If the request is to a CGI gateway program, then the gateway program must provide header information that specifies details about the returned data, such as the `Content-type`, that cannot be otherwise determined by the server. The server parses this information, and adds some of its own, to construct a complete server response header. Alternatively, the gateway program can return the entire response header and bypass the server. This *nonparsed header* option is described in Chapter 8.

SERVER RESPONSE: FILE NOT MODIFIED

How would the server respond if the requested file was not modified subsequent to the time specified in the `If-modified-since` field sent with the request header? In this case, the server would respond with the short message:

```
HTTP/1.0 304 Not Modified

Date: Thu, 03 Aug 1995 16:04:09 GMT

Server: NCSA/1.3

MIME-version: 1.0

[Blank line, containing CRLF]
```

Thus, the server returns just a header containing the status code 304. This tells the client that the file was unchanged, and that the client should use its cached copy of the data.

LESSONS FROM EXAMPLE 1

1. When a client contacts an HTTP server, it sends the server a request header consisting of *request header* fields. These header fields include the *method field*, which specifies the HTTP method being requested by the client and the *location* on the server of the resource being requested, followed by other request header fields that pass information about the capabilities of the client. The collection of request headers is terminated by a single blank line.

2. The server responds with a message consisting of a *response header* followed by the requested data. The response header fields communicate information about the state of the transaction, including a MIME *content-type* header that explicitly tells the client the type of data being sent. The response header is terminated by a single blank line. The data being sent to the client follows after the blank line.

EXAMPLE 2: A GET METHOD REQUEST WITH SEARCH STRINGS

The second example is a GET method, but with query information appended to the URL. As discussed in Chapter 2, query information is appended to the URL, separated by a question mark. This is done automatically by World Wide Web browsers when you submit **ISINDEX** queries or HTML **FORM**s data. A typical URL might be

```
http://www.stuff.ca/cgi-bin/srch-example?item1+item2+item3+item4
```

which passes four items from an **ISINDEX** query to the program *srch-example*.

Figure 7.3 shows the request headers sent by the MacWeb browser when it accesses this URL. Again, some `accept` header fields are omitted to save space.

This request header is essentially the same as that in Figure 7.1, the only difference being the query string appended to the locator string. The server's interpretation of this string is described in the next chapter.

LESSONS FROM EXAMPLE 2

Query data appended to a URL during a GET request to a server is passed as part of the locator string in the HTTP *method field* of the request headers. All other request headers are the same as those for a standard GET request, as described in Example 1.

EXAMPLE 3: SUBMITTING A FORM USING THE GET METHOD

This example examines how an HTML **FORM** submits the form data content to a server, using the HTTP GET method. The example HTML **FORM** is shown in Figure 7.4. The actual rendering of this form by a WWW browser is shown in Figure 7.5.

The **FORM** element is discussed in detail in Chapter 4. This **FORM** defines the three variable names *srch*, *srch_type*, and *srvr*. These have been assigned,

Figure 7.3 Data sent from a MacWeb client to an HTTP server during a GET request with query strings appended to the URL. *Comments are in italics.*

```
GET /cgi-bin/srch-example?item1+item2+item3+item4 HTTP/1.0

Accept: video/quicktime

Accept: video/mpeg

Accept: image/x-xbitmap

Accept: image/pict

Accept: image/jpeg

  .

  .

  .

Accept: text/plain

Accept: text/html

User-Agent: MacWeb/1.00ALPHA2 libwww/2.13

    [a blank line, containing only CRLF ]
```

by user input, the values *srch=dogfish*, *srch_type=Exact Match*, *srvr=Canada*, and srvr=Sweden. The example uses the Mosaic for X-Windows Version 2.4 browser, and Figure 7.6 shows the data sent by this **FORM** to the server. The dots again indicate `accept` header fields that were deleted to save space.

As discussed in Chapters 4 and 6, submitting a **FORM** sends the data to the server as a collection of *name/value* pairs. In practice, this is accomplished by sending the data as a collection of strings of the form `name=value`, linked by ampersand characters (`&`) (e.g., `name1=value1&name2=value2...`). In addition, blank characters are encoded into plus signs. With the GET method, this string is appended to the URL, separated from it by a question mark. When the HTTP server receives these data, it forwards the entire *query string* to the gateway program *form1*. These details are discussed in Chapter 8.

Figure 7.4 Example HTML **FORM** that uses the GET method to submit data to a server.

```
<FORM ACTION="http://leonardo.utirc.utoronto.ca:8080/cgi-bin/form1" METHOD=GET>

<p> Search string: <INPUT TYPE="text" NAME="srch" VALUE="dogfish">

<p> Search Type:

  <SELECT NAME="srch_type">

    <OPTION> Insensitive Substring

    <OPTION SELECTED> Exact Match

    <OPTION> Sensitive Substring

    <OPTION> Regular Expression

  </SELECT>

<p> Search databases in:

  <INPUT TYPE="checkbox" NAME="srvr" VALUE="Canada" CHECKED> Canada

  <INPUT TYPE="checkbox" NAME="srvr" VALUE="Russia"  > Russia

  <INPUT TYPE="checkbox" NAME="srvr" VALUE="Sweden" CHECKED> Sweden

  <INPUT TYPE="checkbox" NAME="srvr" VALUE="U.S.A."  > U.S.A.

  <em>(multiple items can be selected.)</em>

<P> <INPUT TYPE="submit"> <INPUT TYPE=reset>.

</FORM>
```

LESSONS FROM EXAMPLE 3

When an HTML **FORM** submits data to an HTTP server using the GET method, the **FORM** data are appended to the URL as a query string. Consequently, the **FORM** data are sent to the server in the query string part of the locator string, in the request header method field. The **FORM** data are encoded according to the **FORM**-URL encoding scheme discussed in Chapters 4 and 6.

EXAMPLE 4: SUBMITTING A FORM USING THE POST METHOD

This example uses the **FORM** shown in Figure 7.5 but with one subtle change: It uses the HTTP POST method instead of GET. Consequently, the same data are sent to the server, but in a different way.

As in Example 3, this form has variable names *srch, srch_type*, and *srvr*. These have been assigned values *srch=dogfish, srch_type=Exact Match, srvr=Canada*, and *srvr=Sweden*. Figure 7.7 shows the data sent to the server, again from the Mosaic for X-Windows browser.

The POST method sends data in a message body, and not in the URL. The difference is indicated in three places. The first is in the method header field, which now specifies the POST method and which has no data appended to the URL. The second is in the two new request header fields: `Content-type` and `Content-length`. The third is in the line of data following the header. This line is the actual data being sent to the server.

The two new header fields tell the server that there will be data following the request header. The `content-length` field gives the length in bytes of the message, while the `content-type` field specifies the MIME type of the message being sent to the server. There is currently only one widely implemented content-type for **FORM** data being sent to a server, namely:

```
Content-type: application/x-www-form-urlencoded
```

This header indicates that the data is from a **FORM** and that it is encoded in the same manner as when appended to a URL. You can compare the message

```
GET /cgi-bin/form1?srch=dogfish&srch_type=Exact+Match&srvr=Canada&srvr=Sweden HTTP/1.0
Accept: text/plain
Accept: application/x-html
Accept: application/html
Accept: text/x-html
Accept: text/html
Accept: audio/*
   .
   .
   .
Accept: text/x-setext
Accept: */*
User-Agent: NCSA Mosaic for the X Window System/2.4 libwww/2.12 modified
   [a blank line, containing only CRLF ]
```

body at the bottom of Figure 7.7 with the data appended to the URL in Figure 7.6 to verify this equivalence. The details of how the data are passed from the server to the CGI program are described in Chapter 8.

LESSONS FROM EXAMPLE 4

When an HTML **FORM** submits data to an HTTP server using the POST method, the **FORM** data are sent to the server as a *message body* that follows the request header. This message body is generally encoded in the same manner as when appended to the URL. Additional request header fields tell the server the content-type of the arriving message (application/x-www-form-urlencoded) and the length of the message. No data are appended to the URL.

Figure 7.7 Data sent from a client to an HTTP server during a **FORM**s-based POST request.

```
POST /cgi-bin/form1 HTTP/1.0

Accept: text/plain

Accept: application/x-html

Accept: application/html

Accept: text/x-html

Accept: text/html

Accept: audio/*

    .

    .

    .

Accept: text/x-setext

Accept: */*

User-Agent: NCSA Mosaic for the X Window System/2.4 libwww/2.12 modified

Content-type: application/x-www-form-urlencoded

Content-length: 58

    [a blank line, containing only CRLF]

srch=dogfish&srch_type=Exact+Match&srvr=Canada&srvr=Sweden
```

EXAMPLE 5: ACCESSING A DOCUMENT WITH THE HEAD METHOD

The HEAD method is often used by programs that automatically search for documents on WWW servers. This method requests that the server send the response headers relevant to the requested URL, but not the full content of the referenced object. This is a quick way of seeing if a document or gateway program is actually present, and of obtaining some general information about it, such as its MIME content-type or the date it was last modified, without downloading an entire resource.

Suppose you access the document in Example 1 using the HEAD method. This request is written:

```
HEAD /Tests/file.html HTTP/1.0

User-Agent: HEAD Test Agent

From: name@domain.name.edu
```

You do not need all the accept header fields, since you are not requesting a complete document. The `From` field gives the server the electronic mail address of the person making the HEAD request. The response to this request (in this case, from the NCSA Version 1.3 HTTP server) is:

```
HTTP/1.0 200 OK

Date: Saturday, 24-Sep-94 23:10:55 GMT

Server: NCSA/1.3

MIME-version: 1.0

Content-type: text/html

Last-modified: Sunday, 18-Sep-94 19:44:28 GMT

Content-length: 0
```

This indicates that the document is there (the status code 200 indicates a valid URL), and includes information about the document type and the date it was last modified. In principle, the HTML **META** element, discussed in Chapter 4, allows the server to parse the document and include additional information about the document in these header fields, but few servers currently implement this feature.

LESSONS FROM EXAMPLE 5

A HEAD request retrieves only the response header for the indicated URL— the document itself is not retrieved. If the HEAD request is for an HTML document, some servers parse the *document* **HEAD** for information to include in the response header, but this server feature is not widely implemented.

The preceding discussion and examples provided an overview of the HTTP protocol. The next section looks briefly at more complex features of the HTTP protocol, such as user authentication, format negotiation, and other less-used methods, and gives a summary of commonly used request headers, response headers, and HTTP methods.

USER AUTHENTICATION, DATA ENCRYPTION, AND ACCESS CONTROL

So far, we have not discussed controlling access to an HTTP server, or the encryption of data for transmission between client and server. There are several mechanisms available for doing these things, but as yet no well-established standard. This section briefly discusses some options open to a server administrator, and refers the interested reader to more advanced documentation on this topic.

For low-level security, most servers can be configured to allow access only to machines in an authorized Internet domain or subdomain. For example, servers can be configured such that only machine domain names ending in .domain.site.edu (actually, the corresponding IP addresses) are permitted access. In general, this restriction can be applied on a per directory basis. This is not very secure, however, since a clever cracker can *spoof* a domain name and access the data. It is also not very specific, since anyone can access the restricted material provided they can access one of the allowed machines.

Somewhat finer control is possible using the *Basic* authentication scheme. Basic authentication is part of the HTTP protocol, and allows a server to request that the client send a username and password, which the server uses to determine the authenticity of the user, and evaluate whether he or she is authorized to access the requested resource. However, in the Basic authentication scheme, the username and password are sent in unencrypted format, so that it is relatively easy for anyone sniffing the network traffic to extract the username and password information. Thus, the Basic scheme is not secure, unless the underlying data are encrypted in some way.

Truly secure communication and user authentication requires encryption of the data being sent from client to server and from server to client. *Negotiated encryption* means that the server and client must exchange information, usually encryption keys, allowing each of them to send encrypted information that can be decoded only by the other. This requires that both client and server contain encryption/decryption software, and that they both understand the same encryption schemes. There are several such schemes currently in use, but as yet no common standard. In addition, several of the schemes have U.S. trade or security restrictions, and cannot be exported from the United States. This is an important consideration if you wish to serve secure documents and information to an international audience. User authentication is an important feature for most commercial providers of WWW software products, as is encryption (do you really want the entire world to know your credit card number?), so, if encryption is important to you, you will want to consider commercial providers of server and browser software.

The next section reviews the Basic authentication scheme, which is available on almost all Web browsers and HTTP servers. The section that follows reviews some of the currently deployed HTTP encryption schemes.

EXAMPLE 6:
THE "BASIC" AUTHENTICATION SCHEME

The Basic authentication scheme is the only user authentication scheme universally available on the World Wide Web. This scheme is *not* secure, as username and password information are not encrypted when sent from client to server (they are encoded, however, which at least hides them from nonexperts). You should, consequently, not think of this as a secure authentication scheme, unless combined with an encryption mechanism such as the Netscape SSL technology (more about this later).

The Basic scheme involves the exchange of special HTTP request and response header messages. In the following example, we follow a request for a resource that requires authentication, and illustrate how these headers negotiate the request for this information.

STEP 1: CLIENT REQUESTS THE RESOURCE

The client first makes a regular request for the resource (here, an HTML document). A typical request header is shown in Figure 7.8.

■■■■■ **Figure 7.8** Typical GET request from the Netscape Navigator browser.

```
GET /SecDir1/foo.html HTTP/1.0

User-Agent: Mozilla/1.1N (X11; I; IRIX 5.3 IP22)

Accept: */*

Accept: image/gif

Accept: image/x-xbitmap

Accept: image/jpeg
```

■■■■■

STEP **2:**

SERVER **R**ESPONSE—**A**UTHENTICATION **R**EQUIRED

The response message is shown in Figure 7.9. The server status message

```
HTTP/1.0 401 Unauthorized
```

tells the client that the resource was not returned because the resource requires user authentication. In addition, the server sends the new header field

```
WWW-Authenticate: Basic realm="SecRealm1"
```

The WWW-Authenticate tells the client which authentication scheme is being used (Basic is currently the only type), and also what *realm* is involved, here realm="PasswdDoc" (realms are discussed a bit later on). The response message also includes a short HTML document that is presented by the browser if it does not understand WWW-Authenticate headers, or if the user was unable to provide valid authentication information.

Figure 7.9 HTTP server response upon a request for a resource protected by the Basic authentication scheme.

```
HTTP/1.0 401 Unauthorized

Date: Thursday, 03-Aug-95 14:38:57 GMT

Server: NCSA/1.3

MIME-version: 1.0

Content-type: text/html

WWW-Authenticate: Basic realm="SecRealm1"


<HEAD><TITLE>Authorization Required</TITLE></HEAD>

<BODY><H1>Authorization Required</H1>

Browser not authentication-capable or

authentication failed.

</BODY>
```

STEP 3: CLIENT REQUESTS RESOURCE

The client, upon receipt of the 401 HTTP response header, prompts the user for his or her username and password. The client takes the username and password and forms the concatenated string

```
username:password
```

This is then *uuencoded* into a pseudo-encrypted string (I say pseudo-encrypted, because it is trivial to decode). The client then tries, once again, to access the resource, this time passing the encoded username and password information within an `Authorization` request header field, of the form:

```
Authorization: Basic aWFuOmJvb2J5
```

where the string `aWFuOmJvb2J5` is the encoded username and password string. Figure 7.10 shows a typical request header containing this authentication information.

If the authentication is accepted, the server returns the resource. If not, it again returns the response shown in Figure 7.9, to indicate that authentication failed and that the user should try again.

THE MEANING OF A REALM

A `Realm` is simply a way of grouping username and password information, so that the browser need not keep prompting the user for a new username and password if subsequent requests are for access to the same realm. For example, suppose that a server administrator creates two secure directories,

■■■■■ **Figure 7.10** Typical client request for a resource protected by the Basic authentication scheme—the `Authorization:` field indicates the authentication scheme being used (`Basic`) along with the encoded username and password.

```
GET /SecDir1/foo.html HTTP/1.0

User-Agent: Mozilla/1.1N (X11; I; IRIX 5.3 IP22)

Accept: */*

Accept: image/gif

Accept: image/x-xbitmap

Accept: image/jpeg

Authorization: Basic aWFuOmJvb2J5
```

■■■■■

SecDir1 and *SecDir2*, and controls access to them using the password files *pass1* and *pass2*, respectively. The administrator must also assign realm names to these directories, so that in communicating with a client, the server can inform the client which realm is involved, without giving away the name of the password file. In this example, we can assume the administrator assigned the name "SecRealm1" to the directory *SecDir1*, and the name "SecRealm2" to the directory *SecDir2*.

The first time a user accesses a document in *SecDir1*, he or she will be prompted for a username and password. The browser will store this name/password string under the realm name "SecRealm1." On subsequent accesses to this directory, the server sends the header indicating that this is a request for authentication relating to realm "SecRealm1." The browser then simply returns the authentication password stored in its local database, and does not prompt the user for this information.

If, on the other hand, the user tries to access a document in *SecDir2*, the server sends back the header

```
WWW-Authenticate: Basic realm="SecRealm2"
```

which tells the browser that authentication is required for this new, as yet unentered, realm. As the browser has never accessed this realm, it has no record of an appropriate username and password. The browser therefore prompts the user for this information, and stores this information under this additional realm keyword.

CLIENT/SERVER DATA ENCRYPTION

As mentioned in the previous section, any authentication scheme is insecure if the messages and data passed between client and server are unencrypted: if the username and password are not encrypted, then they can be copied and used by someone else, while if the transported data are not encrypted, then data can be intercepted regardless of any password protection. There are two main approaches to encryption currently being deployed on the Web, and these are summarized below. Additional information about these schemes is found in the references at the end of this chapter.

NETSCAPE'S SECURE SOCKETS LAYER (SSL)

The *Secure Sockets Layer* protocol is designed as an encryption layer *below* the HTTP protocol. Thus, HTTP messages are unaffected, with encryption occurring just prior to converting the messages into TCP/IP packets for transmission over the Internet. To indicate the special nature of this connection,

Netscape Communications created the new URL scheme **https** (HTTP-Secure). **Https** URLs are encoded identically to **http** URLs. The default port for **https** URLs is 443, and not 80, so that a single machine can run both secure and nonsecure servers.

In principle, SSL can be used for any Internet tool that uses the underlying TCP/IP protocol for data communications. For example, Netscape Communications Inc. has released an NNTP news server employing SSL, and intends to implement SSL more widely in the future.

SSL works at several levels. At the encryption level, the protocol employs a sophisticated security handshake protocol: when a client contacts a secure server, they exchange encryption keys, which are subsequently used to encrypt all data passed between the server and client. Encryption keys are never reused, to ensure that keys cannot be intercepted and used by an unauthorized party. The server also sends the client a cryptographic certificate that tells the client which server it is in contact with, and that is used to validate that the server is indeed who it claims to be. Finally, the client and server send, ahead of the transmitted data, a message digest calculated from the data; the receiving party uses this message digest to ensure that the data content has not been modified in some way by any intervening party.

The Netscape Navigator contains built-in support for SSL, but only for short (40-bit) encryption keys (this is the maximum size allowed for encryption products exported outside the United States). The Netscape Commerce Server supports server encryption (with 40-bit keys) and server cryptographic certificates. Netscape plans to distribute U.S.-only versions of these programs that support 128-bit keys—these will be restricted to U.S. customers. The SSL protocol can negotiate the size of the keys, so that if a browser is only capable of 40-bit keys, the encryption keys will be reduced to that level.

At present, the Netscape Navigator and Commerce Server are the only products to support SSL.

Secure HTTP Protocol (S-HTTP)

Enterprise Information Technologies (EIT), recently purchased by Veriphone Inc. (things change quickly on the Web, and it's not just technology!), has developed a complementary encryption and authentication scheme known as *Secure HTTP* or *S-HTTP*. This scheme is implemented as part of the HTTP protocol, and involves additional HTTP request and response headers that *negotiate* the type of encryption being used, the exchange of encryption keys, the passing of message digest information, and so on. This is similar to the

Basic authentication scheme, except that S-HTTP allows the client and server to exchange cryptographic certificates and encryption keys, allowing each party to authenticate the other and to encrypt data it is sending to the other.

S-HTTP and SSL are complementary schemes. SSL has the advantage of encrypting all underlying communication, but the disadvantage that the same encryption is applied to all messages: there is no way to change the encryption scheme based, for example, on the personal encryption key of a user. S-HTTP, on the other hand, can allow this form of encryption, since the keys can be passed in the HTTP headers. It is quite likely that both schemes will be widely implemented in the near future.

Open Market and Spry both offer commercial HTTP servers that support the S-HTTP extensions, while the Spry Web browser supports S-HTTP from the client side.

PROXY SERVERS AND SERVER CACHING

Proxy servers are often used by local area networks (LANs) that want to protect themselves from unauthorized entry over the Internet. Such protection can be accomplished by installing *firewall* software on the gateway machine that links the local network to the outside world. A firewall keeps TCP/IP packets from entering the local network from the outside world, and thereby protects the LAN from the dangerous world outside.

Unfortunately, a firewall means that users inside the LAN cannot access WWW resources outside, since communication is blocked at the firewall. The solution is to install a *proxy server* on the firewall, and to configure your WWW browsers to refer to this proxy server instead of the real servers outside your LAN. A proxy server has access to both the inside and outside worlds, and can safely pass information back and forth across the firewall. When your browser wants to request information from outside the firewall, it sends this request to the proxy server on the firewall. The proxy server then *proxies* the request—that is, it completes the request on your behalf, and forwards you the result.

This two-stage process can be slow. To speed up service, proxy servers can *cache* the retrieved files. Thus, the first time you request a document, the server goes to the outside world and fetches it, but it then also retains a copy on its own local disc. If you make another request for this same file, the proxy server gives you the locally cached copy of the document, and does not go refetch it. This saves time, and can also significantly reduce the load on the network connection.

This can be a problem, however, if the file is one that changes with time, as can be the case for pages containing periodically updated data, or for documents created dynamically by CGI programs. This problem can be solved using the Expires server response header field, which is used to inform a proxy server how long it can keep a cached copy of a downloaded document. When the proxy server retrieves a document from the primary server outside the firewall, the primary server can place, in the server response header, the line

    Expires: time_and_date

where time_and_date, in one of the time and date formats allowed on the Web, specifies the time and date after which the cached copy should be considered out-of-date. This tells the proxy server how long it can keep the document before it needs to obtain an updated copy from the original server.

There are several HTTP header messages designed explicitly to handle proxying issues. For example, each time a proxy server proxies a request, it should add a response header of the form:

    Forwarded: by server_URL for domain_name

which keeps track of how the data were obtained. If multiple proxy servers were involved (one proxy calling another proxy, and so on), then the returned header should have such multiple headers, one for each step in the chain.

Another important header is the request header field Pragma, which takes the form:

    Pragma: no-cache

When a client (or a proxy server) sends a request header containing this field, the targeted server must always access a new copy of the requested URL, and can never use a cached copy. This ensures that the requesting client always gets the most up-to-date version, regardless of which proxy server(s) the requests pass through.

CERN HTTP PROXY SERVER

There are two ways of implementing proxy servers. The first is to use a full HTTP server that has proxying capabilities. For example, the CERN HTTP proxy server was explicitly designed both to be an HTTP server and to support proxy access. The CERN HTTP server also implements document caching, and is an ideal choice for implementing HTTP service inside a firewall-secured environment. Chapter 11 discusses the issues involved in selecting an HTTP server platform and server software.

SOCKS PROXY SUPPORT

The second alternative is to employ a general-purpose Internet proxying package. The SOCKS package is one such package, but was not designed specifically for HTTP service; it consequently does not have caching capabilities and ignores all the HTTP header messages relevant to proxy HTTP servers. However, this is an ideal choice if you do not need an HTTP server, and is significantly easier to implement than the full CERN HTTP server. Additional information about SOCKS can be found at:

```
ftp://ftp.nec.com/pub/security/socks.cstc
```

A proxy server is useful only if your browser can be configured to use it. At present, almost all browsers support proxy servers.

FORMAT NEGOTIATION

The last item to discuss is *format negotiation*. As mentioned in the discussion of `accept` request headers, a client can send information to a server explaining the types of data it prefers, and the order of preference. The example request headers given were

```
Accept: image/*

Accept: image/jpeg; q=0.7; mxb=50000

Accept: image/gif; q=0.5
```

which indicated that the client preferred image/jpeg files, provided they were smaller than 50 kbytes; that it next preferred GIFs (if the JPEGs were too big); and, finally, that it would take any format of image if the first two were unavailable. However, the HTTP requests described in this chapter have been directed at specific files, and did not allow the option of returning another format. How can optional formats be allowed?

The mechanisms supporting optional formats are server-specific, and are implemented differently on the servers (CERN and Apache) that currently support this feature. The CERN server, for example, implements via server configuration *map* directives. This permits requests for files with particular name extensions to be mapped onto a special-purpose gateway program.[1]

---

[1] Thanks to Chris Lilley for this explanation—any errors are, of course, mine.

Suppose you want to generically refer to images using the filename extension
.image, and want to use the special gateway program **select** to determine
which image format to return to a given client. The appropriate map directives in the server configuration file would be

```
Pass     *.image /select/*.image

Exec     /select/*        /path/to/gateways/cgi-bin/select/*
```

The Pass line maps all filenames with extensions .image onto the special
gateway program **select,** while the Exec line provides the absolute path to this
gateway program (equivalent to the ScriptAlias command with the NCSA
HTTPD server).

When a URL requests a file with the extension .image, the URL data, HTTP
accept headers, and all other related data (as discussed in Chapter 8) are
passed to the gateway program **select,** which in turn must determine which
type of data to return. The remainder of the problem is a programming exercise (there is no generic **select** program, and you will have to write one yourself, or find a suitable program elsewhere). The gateway program could, for
example, directly return the correct format image data (as determined from
the accept or User-agent headers, and from knowledge of what formats
actually exist on the server), or it could return a *redirect* header that redirects
the client to the correct file.

The Apache server implements format negotiation using two non–CGI-based
mechanisms, both somewhat different from the above (the Apache documentation refers to the process as *content negotiation*). By one mechanism, the
server administrator creates a special map file that contains information about
the different data variants. The following is an example map file called
monty_python.image. This contains the following:

```
URI: monty_python; vary="type"

URI: monty_python.jpeg

Content-type: image/jpeg; qs=0.85


URI: monty_python.gif

Content-type: image/gif; qs=0.5


URI: monty_python.xpm

Content-type: image/xpm; qs=0.2
```

which indicates that there are three different image variants for this file, and which also gives the relative qualities of the images (through the parameter qs). A URL pointing to the file `monty_python.image` will then retrieve the appropriate image file from among the three possible formats, depending on the `accept` headers sent by the client.

The second method is known as *MultiViews*. This lets a user request a generic resource *minus* the filename extension, for example `http://.../path/monty_python`, whereupon the server locates all files with this filename prefix in the indicated directory, and dynamically creates a map file similar to the one above (but without qs parameters). The server then uses the `accept` headers to determine which file to return to the client.

The CERN and Apache techniques provide additional features, such as the ability to specify the content-language of a document and/or the content-encoding of the data (e.g., compressed). The references at the end of this chapter provide additional information on both the CERN and Apache content/format negotiation techniques.

HTTP METHODS AND HEADERS REFERENCE

The following four sections summarize the currently implemented HTTP methods, request headers, response headers, and status codes (including server error messages). Also discussed in a section following are the time and date formats allowed in request and response headers that provide this information. Additional details are found in the references at the end of this chapter.

HTTP METHODS

The most common methods are the GET, HEAD, and POST methods discussed previously in this chapter. Table 7.1 summarizes the commonly implemented HTTP methods.

HTTP REQUEST HEADER FIELDS

`Accept: `*`type/subtype`* This field contains a list of MIME content-types that are acceptable to the client, separated by commas. Types can also contain parameters describing their relative merit (q=0.0 to q=1.0), and the maximum allowed size for a resource (mxb=*num_bytes*). The use of these terms was discussed earlier in this chapter.

Table 7.1. The Different HTTP Methods

HTTP Method	Description
GET	Retrieve the indicated URL. Data can also be sent to the URL by including a query string with the URL. This is the situation for data sent from **ISMAP** active imagemaps, from **ISINDEX** queries, and from **FORM** elements with the **FORM** attribute **METHOD="GET"**.
HEAD	Retrieve the HTTP header information for the indicated URL.
POST	Send the data to the indicated URL, if the URL already exists. This method is used by HTML **FORM** elements with the attribute value **METHOD="POST"**.
PUT	Place the data sent by the client in the indicated URL, replacing the old contents if the URL already exists. The CERN HTTP server has an implementation of PUT.
DELETE	Delete the resource located at the indicated URL. The CERN HTTP server has an implementation of DELETE.
LINK	Links an existing object to another object. For an HTML document, this would imply editing the document and adding **LINK** information to the document **HEAD**. This method is unimplemented by current HTTP servers.
UNLINK	Remove the link information inserted, for example, by a LINK method. This method is unimplemented by current HTTP servers.

Accept-Charset: *charset-type, charset-type* ... Lists the character sets preferred by the browser, other than the default (ASCII or ISO Latin-1). Thus the server, if capable, can deliver the resource using the character set preferred by the browser. This header is unimplemented on current browsers and servers.

Accept-Encoding: *encoding_type* Lists the data encoding types acceptable to the client. For example,

Accept-Encoding: x-compress

tells the server that the client can accept compressed data in the compress format. Currently understood encoding types are x-compress and x-gzip, which may also be seen under the names compress or gzip. Other possible (but largely unimplemented) encoding types are base64 and quoted-printable. If a browser can accept multiple encodings, the header can be written

```
Accept-Encoding: type1, type2, ...
```

If a server knowingly sends a document in one of these encodings, it must include an appropriate `Content-encoding` response header.

`Accept-language: language` This field lists the languages preferred by the browser. The languages are specified using the schemes discussed in Appendix E. The field:

```
Accept-language fr-ca, fr, en
```

would mean that the browser prefers Canadian French, will accept standard French if Canadian French is not available, and, lastly, will accept English if the other two are not available. This header is unimplemented on most current browsers.

`Authorization: scheme data` This passes user authentication and encryption scheme information to the server. If authentication is not required, this field is absent.

`Content-length: length` Gives the length, in bytes, of the message being sent to the server. If no message is sent, then this field is absent.

`Content-type: type/subtype` This gives the MIME content-type of the message being sent to the server. If no message is sent, then this field is absent.

`Date: date_time` Contains the time and date when the current object was assembled for transmission, here in the format `Thu, 03 Aug 1995 16:04:09 GMT`. Note that the time must be Greenwich Mean Time (GMT) to ensure that all servers share a common time zone. Other possible time formats are discussed at the end of this chapter.

`From: mail_address` This contains the address, in Internet mail format, of the user accessing the server. In general, a browser does not send this information, out of concern for a user's privacy.

`If-Modified-Since: date_time` This request header is used with the GET method to make the GET request conditional—if the requested document has not changed since the indicated time and date, the document is not sent. The date must follow the format: `Friday, 23-Sep-95 18:28:33 GMT`, or one of the other valid formats described at the end of this chapter. If the document is not sent, the server should send the response header message 304 (not modified).

`MIME-version:` *version_number* This gives the MIME protocol version used by the server; the current version is 1.0.

`Pragma:` *directives_for_server* `Pragma` directives are designed for passing special-purpose information to servers. Currently, there is only one server directive,

`Pragma: no-cache`

which instructs a proxy server (or servers, if it takes multiple proxy servers to reach the resource) always to fetch the document from the actual server, and never use a locally cached copy.

`Referer:` *URL* This gives the URL of the document from which the request originated. This can be a partial URL, in which case it is interpreted *relative* to the URL of the document being requested. If a document contains an HTML BASE element, then the content of this content should be sent instead.

`User-Agent:` *program/version comments* Provides information about the client software making the request.

HTTP RESPONSE HEADER FIELDS

The following is a list of currently implemented HTTP response header fields. A more detailed list can be found in the References to the HTTP specification listed at the end of this chapter.

`Allow:` *methods_list* Specifies a comma-separated list of HTTP methods supported by the resource. This must be returned if the status code 405 (HTTP method not allowed) is being returned. This can contain any supported method, including nonstandard ones supported by the server.

`Content-Encoding:` *encoding_type* Specifies the encoding type mechanism used in generating the results. The only currently valid types are `compress` and `gzip`, and their synonyms `x-compress` and `x-gzip` (the latter are obsolete, and are being phased out). You can have only one content-encoding type per header. This allows compressed files to be uncompressed on-the-fly by the client.

`Content-length:` *length* Gives the length (in bytes) of the message being sent to the client.

`Content-Transfer-Encoding:` *encoding_type* This is a MIME protocol header, and gives the encoding mechanism used by the included MIME
message. The default is 8-bit character encoding (binary). Other possible
values (uncommon with HTTP) are `quoted-printable` and `base64`.

`Content-type:` *type/subtype* This gives the MIME content-type of the
message being sent to the client. The content-type can contain optional
parameter fields, separated from the type/subtype by a semicolon. For
example,

`Content-type: text/html; charset=ISO-10646-1`

indicates that the message is an HTML document, written using the ISO
10646-1 character set. Note that these parameter fields are largely ignored
by current clients.

`Date:` *date_time* Contains the time and date when the current object was
assembled for transmission, here in the format `Thu, 03 Aug 1995
16:04:09 GMT`. Note that the time must be Greenwich Mean Time
(GMT) to ensure that all servers share a common time zone. Possible time
formats are discussed at the end of this chapter.

`Derived-From:` *version_number* This indicates the version of the
resource from which the enclosed data (being sent by the client to the
server) was derived. This is used in version control of collaboratively developed resources, and is required if the method is PUT. This field is largely
unimplemented on current browsers.

`Expires:` *date_time* Gives the time and date after which the information
being sent should be considered invalid. This tells clients when to refresh
data in their local cache. Proxy servers can use this field to determine when
a cached copy of a document should be refreshed.

`Forwarded: by` *server_URL* `for` *domain_name* This field is added by
proxy servers to indicate the proxying steps taken between the client
requesting the resource, and the server from which the resource originates.
For example:

`Forwarded: by http://www.utoronto.ca:8001/ for linux.hvv.utoronto.ca`

Multiple `Forwarded` fields will be present if multiple proxy servers were
used.

Last-modified: *date_time* Gives the date and time that the document was last modified, here in the format Thu, 03 Aug 1995 16:02:27 GMT. As for the Date field, the date must be given in Greenwich Mean Time.

Link: *link_information* This is equivalent to the HTML LINK element, in that it is used to define relationships between the data being returned by the server and other resources. If derived for an HTML document, this field (or multiple fields) should contain the information from the LINK elements in the document. This allows the HTTP header to contain LINK information about a resource, and allows a client, using HEAD methods, to access information about the document that is useful for cataloging, organizational, or indexing purposes. Link is currently unimplemented.

Location: *URL* This contains the actual URL of the resource, and is returned by a server if the requested document was not found on the server, but the server does know the correct (moved) location of the resource. A Location header is included when a *redirection* header (status 301 or 302) is returned.

Location is considered obsolete, and is being phased out in place of the URI field. However, URI is largely unimplemented, so servers that do return URI headers also return location headers, for compatibility with current clients and proxy servers.

MIME-version: *version_number* Gives the MIME protocol version used by the server. The current version 1.0.

Public: *method_list* This contains a comma-separated list of nonstandard (experimental) methods supported by the server. This header is largely unimplemented on current servers.

Retry-after: *date_time* (or *seconds*) This field contains a time and date (or a time in seconds) after which a client should retry to access a resource that was temporarily unavailable. This field is appropriate when the status header 503 (service unavailable) is being returned. It might be returned by a server or gateway program that is temporarily unable to comply with a request. Typical forms are:

```
Retry-after: Thursday, 10-Aug-95 12:23:12 GMT

Retry-after: 60
```

The latter indicates that the client should retry after a 60-second wait. Most browsers (and proxy servers) do not understand the `retry-after` field.

`Server:` *`program/version`* This contains information about the server software from which the resource originated. The program and version information fields are separated by a slash.

`Title:` *`title`* The title of the document. This should be identical to the contents of the document's TITLE element.

`URI:` *`<location>`*`;vary="`*`parameters`*`"` The URI field contains the Uniform Resource Identifier (URI) of the resource, and is designed to replace the `Location` field for that purpose. In particular, the URI field allows the server to specify multiple URIs for a particular resource, or multiple versions of the same resource. Here the string, *`<location>`*, gives the resource URI (surrounded by left and right angle brackets), while the *`parameters`* specify details about the different versions available at the URI. For example, `vary="type,language"` could mean that the designated URI can return the resource in different types and languages, depending on the `accept` headers of the requesting client.

`URI:` is not widely implemented, so that gateway programs that wish to return `URI:` headers should also return `location` headers, for compatibility with older software.

`Version:` *`version_info`* This field contains version information for a server resource, and is designed, along with the `derived-from` field, for use in cooperative development of server resources. This field is largely unimplemented by current servers and browsers.

`WWW-Authenticate:` *`scheme scheme_message`* This passes information to the client stating the encryption and authorization schemes the server wants to use. This is only used for directories, files, or CGI programs that require user authentication. *`Scheme`* gives the name of the authorization scheme (e.g., Basic), while *`scheme_message`* gives related data.

HTTP STATUS CODES

Table 7.2 describes the meanings of the different HTTP status codes. In general, codes 200 through 299 indicate a successful transaction, while codes 400–599 indicates an error of some type. Codes 300–399 imply redirection:

either the resource has moved and the server is returning the URL of the new location to the client, or the resource has not changed since it was last requested by the client, in which case the server does not bother to return the document the second time around.

■■■■■■■■ **Table 7.2** HTTP Status Codes

Successful Transactions

200	The request was completed successfully.
201	The request was a POST (or PUT) method and was completed successfully. 201 indicates that data were sent to the server, and that the server created a new resource as a result of the request.
202	The request has been accepted for processing, but the results of this processing are unknown. This would be returned, for example, if the client deposited data for batch processing at a later date.
203	The GET (or HEAD) request was fulfilled, but has returned partial information.
204	The request was fulfilled, but there is no new information to send to the client. The browser should do nothing, and should continue to display the document from which the request originated.

Redirection Transactions

300	The requested resource is available from more than one location, but the client and server could not negotiate a preferred choice. The response should contain a list of the locations and their characteristics. The client should then choose the one that is most appropriate.
301	The data requested have been permanently moved to a new URL. If this status is returned, the server should also send the client the URL of the new location via the header

```
Location: URL comments
```

where URL is the new document URL. Browsers that understand the Location field will automatically connect to the new URL.

302	The data were found but actually reside at a different URL. If this status is returned, the server should also send the client the correct URL via the header

```
Location: URL comments
```

Browsers that understand the Location field will automatically connect to the new URL. Users will get a 302 redirection if a URL pointing to a directory is missing the trailing slash character.

▀▀▀▀▀▀ **Table 7.2** Continued

304   A GET request was sent that contained the `If-Modified-Since` field. However, the server found that the document had not been modified since the date specified in this field. Consequently, the server responds with this code and does not resend the document.

Error Messages

400   The request syntax was wrong.

401   The request required an `Authorization:` field, and the client did not specify one. The server also returns a list of the allowed authorization schemes using a `WWW-Authenticate` response header. This mechanism is used by a client and server to negotiate data encryption and user authentication schemes.

402   The requested operation costs money and the client did not specify a valid `Chargeto` field in the request header. This is not currently implemented.

403   The client has requested a resource that is forbidden.

404   The server cannot find the URL requested.

405   The client tried to access a resource using a method that is not allowed for that resource. The response must include a list of allowed methods, contained within an `Allow:` field.

406   The resource was found, but could not be delivered because the *type* of the resource is incompatible with the acceptable types indicated by the `accept` or `accept-encoding` headers sent to the server by the client.

410   The resource is no longer available at the server and there is no forwarding information available.

500   The server has encountered an internal error and cannot continue with the request.

501   The request made is legal, but the server does not support this method.

502   The client requested a resource from a server that, in turn, attempted to access the resource from another server or gateway. In this case, the secondary server or gateway did not return a valid response to the server.

503   The service is unavailable, because the server is too busy. The server may also send a `Retry-After` header, which tells the client how long to wait before trying again.

504   The client requested a resource from a server that, in turn, attempted to access the resource from another server or gateway. This is similar to 502, except that in this case, the transaction failed because the secondary server or gateway took too long to respond.

FORMATS FOR TIME AND DATE FIELDS

The HTTP protocol supports two formats for time and date fields. The recommended format takes the form:

```
Wed, 09 Aug 1995 07:49:37 GMT
```

where the first field is the day of the week (Mon, Tue, Wed, Thu, Fri, Sat, or Sun), the second field the date (01 to 31), the third the month (Jan, Feb, Mar, Apr, May, Jun, Jul, Aug, Sep, Oct, Nov, or Dec); the remaining hours (0 to 24), minutes, and seconds fields are obvious.

An alternative (and currently, the most common) supported format is as follows:

```
Wednesday, 09-Aug-94 07:49:37 GMT
```

where the first field is the day of the week (Monday, Tuesday, Wednesday, Thursday, Friday, Saturday, or Sunday), the third is the month (as given above), and the remaining fields are obvious. This second format is currently very common, but will clearly cause chaos at midnight, December 31, 1999. You should design your gateway programs (or any other Internet software) to use the first of these two time formats, but to understand both.

REFERENCES

The HTTP specifications are currently under development. Some useful reference documents follow.

Overview of HTTP resources (with pointers to various drafts of the protocol)

```
http://www.w3.org/hypertext/WWW/Protocols/Overview.html
```

HTTP Draft Specification

```
http://www.w3.org/hypertext/WWW/Protocols/HTTP1.0/draft-ietf-http-spec.html
```

Authentication, encryption, and the Web overview

```
http://www.w3.org/hypertext/WWW/Security/Overview.html
```

The Basic authentication scheme

```
http://www.w3.org/hypertext/WWW/AccessAuthorization/Overview.html
```

EIT's Secure HTTP (S-HTTP) proposal

```
http://www.eit.com/projects/s-http/
```

Netscape Communications Security Technology Overview

http://home.mcom.com/info/security-doc.html

Netscape Communications Secure Sockets Layer (SSL) Proposal

http://www.mcom.com/newsref/std/SSL.html

http://home.mcom.com/info/SSL.html

Spyglass Authentication Scheme—Digest Access Authentication

http://ds.internic.net/internet-drafts/draft-ietf-http-digest-aa-01.txt

CERN proxy HTTP server

http://www.w3.org/hypertext/WWW/Daemon/User/Proxies/Proxies.html

CERN Server Format Negotiation

http://www.w3.org/hypertext/WWW/Daemon/User/Config/Rules/html#Map

Apache Server Content Negotiation

http://www.apache.org/docs/content-negotiation.html

Some thoughts on the "Next Generation" of HTTP

http://www.w3.org/hypertext/WWW/Protocols/HTTP-NT/http-ng-status.html

THE COMMON
GATEWAY INTERFACE

The Common Gateway Interface (CGI) is the specified standard for communication between HTTP servers and server-side gateway programs. When you access a gateway program, the server activates the program and passes it any **ISINDEX, FORM,** or other data that was sent from the client. When the gateway program has finished processing the data, it sends the result back to the server, whereupon the server sends it back to the client. The CGI specifications define how these data are passed from the server to the gateway program, and vice versa.

Gateway programs can be compiled programs written in languages such as C, C++, or Pascal, or they can be executable scripts written in languages such as perl, tcl, and the various shell programs. In fact, most gateway programs are scripts, since these are easy to write and modify and are inherently transportable from machine to machine. In addition, execution speed is often not an important factor when writing a gateway program, since the slowest part of the process is usually the resource the gateway connects to, and not the gateway program itself.

This chapter first presents an overview of how data are communicated between a client and server (using the HTTP protocol) and of how data are communicated between the server and a gateway program (the CGI mechanisms). This is followed by five examples that explore the details of the CGI mechanisms for different types of HTTP methods (GET and POST), and different HTML tools for gathering user input (**ISINDEX** and **FORM** elements). Lastly there are brief discussions of how data passed from a client are decoded in gateway programs, and security issues to consider when writing gateway programs.

Chapter 9 follows up with a discussion of specific CGI programming examples, along with a list of useful CGI utility programs and libraries currently available over the Internet.

COMMUNICATION WITH GATEWAY PROGRAMS

The CGI mechanisms describe how (and what) data are passed from a server to a server-side gateway program, and vice versa. In general, all data that a client sends to a server (using the HTTP protocol) are made available, using three CGI mechanisms, to the referenced gateway program. The gateway program has two CGI mechanisms for returning data to the server, and from there to the client. These mechanisms are discussed in the following sections.

SENDING DATA FROM CLIENT TO SERVER (HTTP)

There are three ways data is sent from the client to the server. These are:

1. *As a URL query string.* For example:

   ```
   http://some.site.edu/cgi-bin/ex_prog?query_info
   ```

   passes the query string query_info to the server. The server, in turn, launches the gateway program *ex_prog* and passes it the query string.

2. *As* extra path *information in the URL.* *Extra path* information is placed in the URL by adding directory-like information to the URL just after the name of the gateway program. For example, in:

   ```
   http://some.site.edu/cgi-bin/ex_prog/dir/file?query_info
   ```

the string /dir/file is interpreted by the server as extra path information, while query_info is again the query string. When the server launches the gateway program *ex_prog*, it passes both the query string query_info and the extra path string /dir/file to *ex_prog*. In both cases, the CGI mechanisms pass these data to the gateway program using *environment variables*.

3. *As data sent to the server in a message body.* This is possible with the HTTP POST method, and is commonly used with HTML **FORM**s. When a server receives a POST method message from a **FORM**, it sends the POSTed data to the designated gateway program. The gateway program reads the data in from standard input.

SENDING DATA FROM SERVER TO GATEWAY PROGRAM (CGI)

The CGI specifications define the mechanisms by which data are forwarded by a server to a gateway program. There are three mechanisms:

1. *Command-line arguments* The server launches the gateway program with command-line arguments. This happens only with a GET method request arising from an **ISINDEX** query.

2. *Standard input* The gateway program reads in data from standard input. This is how data sent by a client via the POST HTTP method are passed to the gateway program.

3. *Environment variables* The server puts information in special *environment variables* before starting the gateway program. The gateway program can access these variables and obtain their contents. *Everything* sent by the client, except POST data, is passed to the gateway program within environment variables. Thus, there are environment variables containing the query string, the extra path information, and the content of *every* request header field sent by the client to the server.

The mechanisms that are relevant during a particular transaction depend on the HTTP method of the request (GET or POST), and also on the nature of the query string appended to the URL (**ISINDEX** versus non-**ISINDEX** queries). Examples to illustrate typical cases are given later in this chapter.

RETURNING DATA FROM
GATEWAY PROGRAM TO SERVER (CGI)

There are two ways in which a CGI program can send information back to the server:

1. *By writing to standard output* The gateway program passes data back to the server by writing data to standard output. This is the *only* way that gateway programs can return data to a client. In general, there are two parts to the returned data. The first part is a collection of server directives, which are parsed by the server and are used to compose the response header that precedes the returned data. The second part is the data being returned by the gateway program.

2. *By the* name *of the gateway program* Gateway programs with names beginning with the string *nph-* are called *nonparsed header* programs, and are treated specially by the server. As mentioned previously, the server usually parses the output of a gateway program, and looks for server directives to use in creating the HTTP response header sent to the client ahead of the returned data. If a gateway program name begins with *nph-*, the server sends the gateway program output directly to the client and does *not* add any header information. In this case, the gateway program author must ensure that all required HTTP response header fields are returned by the gateway program.

These methods are illustrated in the following five examples. Example 1 looks at an HTML **ISINDEX** document request. Example 2 demonstrates non-parsed header gateway programs, which send data directly back to the client, bypassing any server processing. Example 3 shows how environment variables are passed to the gateway program, and explains the contents of these variables. Examples 4 and 5 show how data from HTML **FORM**s—using the GET and POST methods, respectively—are passed to a gateway program. These examples also explain how these data are decoded by a gateway program.

EXAMPLE 1: ISINDEX SEARCHES

ISINDEX queries are the *only* query method that pass data to a gateway program as command-line arguments. It is a simple technique, and a useful starting point for understanding client/server/gateway interactions.

This example accesses the gateway program *srch-example* listed in Figure 8.1, which is a Bourne-shell script designed to search a phone-number database using the search program *grep*. The script searches for names in a phone-number database, and uses the **ISINDEX** element to prompt for the search string. In this example, the search string is just the list of names you want to search for. When the script receives this data, it searches the database for the indicated names and returns the names and phone numbers of any matches. The script is designed both to prompt for search strings and to return the results of the search.

From Chapters 2 and 4, you will recall that **ISINDEX** queries send data to the server by appending the query data onto the URL being viewed, for example:

```
http://some.where.edu/cgi-bin/srch_program?query_string
```

When this information reaches the server, and if it is an **ISINDEX** query, the server decodes the URL (converts plus [+] signs into spaces, and converts URL character encodings into the correct 8-bit characters), uses the space characters to break the query string into individual terms, and then passes these terms to the indicated gateway program as command-line arguments.

How does the server know if a query is an **ISINDEX** query? The convention is that an ISINDEX query string *does not contain* any unencoded equals signs (=). As noted in Chapter 6 (which gave the details of the URL encoding mechanism), and also in Example 3 in Chapter 7, **FORM** data are encoded as a collection of strings of the form name=value, which always contains at least one unencoded equals sign (any equals signs originally present in the name or value strings are encoded as %3d). Therefore, the presence of an unencoded equals sign indicates a query string from a **FORM**, and not from an **ISINDEX**.

STEP 1: FIRST ACCESS OF THE URL

In this example, the script *srch-example* is initially accessed via the URL

```
http://leonardo.utirc.utoronto.ca:8080/cgi-bin/srch-example
```

Figure 8.1 Bourne-shell script CGI gateway program *srch-example*.

```
01 #!/bin/sh
02 echo Content-TYPE:  text/html
03 echo
04
05 if [ $# = 0 ]            # is the number of arguments == 0 ?
06 then                     # do this part if there are NO arguments
07   echo "<HEAD>"
08   echo "<TITLE>Local Phonebook Search</TITLE>"
09   echo "<ISINDEX>"
10   echo "</HEAD>"
11   echo "<BODY>"
12   echo "<H1>Local Phonebook Search</H1>"
13   echo "Enter your search in the search field.<P>"
14   echo "This is a case-insensitive substring search: thus"
15   echo "searching for 'ian' will find 'Ian' and Adriana'."
16   echo "</BODY>"
17 else                      # this part if there ARE arguments
18   echo "<HEAD>"
19   echo "<TITLE>Result of search for \"$*\".</TITLE>"
20   echo "</HEAD>"
21   echo "<BODY>"
22   echo "<H1>Result of search for \"$*\".</H1>"
23   echo "<PRE>"
24   for i in $*
25   do
26      grep -i $i /vast/igraham/Personnel
27 done
```

```
28   echo "</PRE>"

39   echo "</BODY>"

40   fi
```

Note that there is no query information attached to the URL; this is an important factor in the initial behavior of the script.

Line 1 tells the computer to interpret this script using the **/bin/sh** program, which is the traditional location and name for the Bourne shell. The second two lines *echo* information to standard output (echo is the Bourne-shell command that prints to standard output). Standard output is sent back to the server, and from there, back to the client.

The first line returns an HTTP *server directive*, which gives the server information about the data to come. This is absolutely necessary, as the server has no other way of knowing the type of data being returned by the program. The first line prints the header

```
Content-TYPE: text/html
```

to tell the server that the data to follow is an HTML document. The next line prints a blank line. This marks the end of the headers; subsequent output is message data.

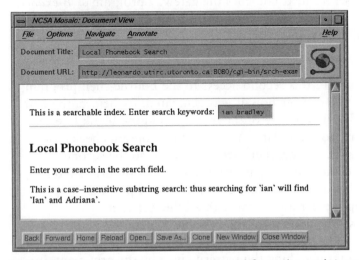

Figure 8.2 Document returned from the script *srch-example* when accessed *without* a query string appended to the URL.

Several other server directives are allowed—they are summarized in Example 2.

Line 5 tests the number of command-line arguments. In this case, there was no query string, so there are no command-line arguments and the first branch of the `if` is executed. This first branch prints, to standard output, a simple HTML document explaining the nature of the search; this is shown in Figure 8.2. The returned document also contains the **ISINDEX** element, which instructs the browser to prompt for search information; this results in the query box shown in Figure 8.2. The names *ian* and *bradley* are typed into this box, separated by a single space. These are the names to be used in the search.

STEP 2: SECOND ACCESS OF THE URL

Submitting this **ISINDEX** search information accesses the same URL, but appends the names *ian* and *bradley* to the URL as query strings. Thus, in this second phase, the accessed URL is

```
http://leonardo.utirc.utoronto.ca:8080/cgi-bin/srch-example?ian+bradley
```

where the space between *ian* and *bradley* has been encoded as a plus sign, following the URL query string encoding scheme described in Chapter 6.

When the server receives this URL, it parses the query string and finds that there are no unencoded equals signs, so it knows that this is an **ISINDEX** query. It therefore takes the query string and breaks it into individual strings, using the plus signs to mark the string separators. This yields the two strings `ian` and `bradley`. The server next launches the gateway program *srch-example*, using the names `ian` and `bradley` as command-line arguments. If you were to do this by hand, you would type:

```
srch-example ian bradley
```

Figure 8.3 shows the results of this second access to the Bourne-shell program; by following Figure 8.1, you can see how it was generated. As before, the first two lines print the MIME content-type of the message and the blank line separating the HTTP headers from the data. At line 5, the program checks for command-line arguments. This time, there are arguments, so the second branch of the script is executed starting at line 18. This section prints a different HTML document—this time, including output from the program *grep*. Lines 24 through 27 loop the variable i through all the different command-line arguments. The content of the variable i (denoted by i) is given as an argument to the program *grep*, which scans the file */vast/ igraham/Personnel* for names matching the pattern given by the argument

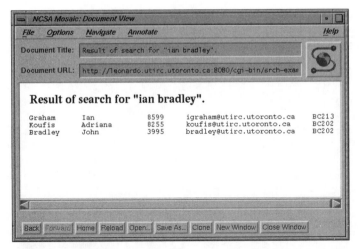

Figure 8.3 Document returned from the script *srch-example* when accessed *with* a query string appended to the URL.

i. Grep prints the matches to standard output. The result of the searches is shown in Figure 8.3. Note that there is now no query box, as the second branch of the script in Figure 8.1 did not return an **ISINDEX** element.

EXAMPLE 2: GATEWAY PROGRAM SERVER DIRECTIVES

In this example, we look at how the HTTP server composes response header information for the document returned by the gateway program. Consider first the actual data sent by the server to the client when it first accessed the *srch-example* (see Figure 8.4; these are the data that produced Figure 8.2).

Comparing Figure 8.4 with Figure 8.1, you will see that the headers are not, in fact, those returned by the script: the content-type headers are typographically different (`Content-TYPE` versus `Content-type`). In fact, the headers returned to the client were generated by the HTTP server, with help from the headers passed from the gateway program.

SERVER DIRECTIVES

The server takes the header data returned by the gateway program and parses each of the header fields. Most of these headers are passed through unaltered, and are included with headers returned to the client. Some, however, are

■■■■ **Figure 8.4** Data returned to the client upon accessing the URL `http://leonardo.utirc.utoronto.ca:8080/cgi-bin/` `srch-example`. These are the data that produce Figure 8.2.

```
HTTP/1.0 200 OK

Date: Tuesday, 27-Sep-94 16:43:48 GMT

Server: NCSA/1.3 MIME-version: 1.0

Content-type: text/html


<HEAD>

<TITLE>Local Phonebook Search</TITLE>

<ISINDEX>

</HEAD>

<BODY>

<H1>Local Phonebook Search</H1>

Enter your search in the search field.<P>

This is a case-insensitive substring search:thus

searching for 'ian' will find 'Ian' and Adriana'.

</BODY>
```

■■■■

treated as *server directives* and are used by the server to *modify* the HTTP response header fields it normally returns in the response header. The three currently valid server-directive headers are:

1. `Content-type:` *type/subtype* (`;` *parameters*) This gives the MIME type for the data being sent by the gateway program. The server replaces its default `Content-type` server response header with the type/subtype values given here. The (`;` *parameters*) string notes the optional semicolon-separated MIME type parameter fields.

2. `Location:` *URL* This tells the server that the gateway program is specifying the URL to which the client should be redirected. The server

adds this header to the server response and also changes its header status line from:

HTTP/1.0 200 OK

to:

HTTP/1.0 302 Redirection

which tells the client that there is redirection information in the response headers, and that it should use the Location field URL to access the desired resource.

3. Status: *code string* This passes an HTTP status string to the server for use in place of the standard value. For example, if the *srch-example* gateway script returned the header:

Status: 444 four-fourty-four

the response headers returned to the client would look like:

HTTP/1.0 444 four-fourty-four

Date: Tuesday, 27-Sep-94 16:43:48 GMT

Server: NCSA/1.3

MIME-version: 1.0

Content-type: text/html

...

Note that you are not limited to these server directives, and can include many response header fields among the server directives—they will simply be forwarded to the client as response header fields, following those headers generated by the server itself. For example, if your gateway program is returning data from a database that is updated on a regular basis, you could insert an Expires: header to indicate when the data will be stale, thereby allowing clients to reliably cache copies of the data until it is time for them to be renewed.

However, you *must not* use this mechanism to send duplicate copies of the headers ordinarily returned by the server. In general, most servers, after parsing a gateway program's server directives, also return the Server:, Date, and MIME-Version: header fields. You should therefore not return these fields from your gateway program, unless it is a *nonparsed header* program.

NONPARSED HEADER GATEWAY PROGRAMS

It is possible to return gateway program output directly to the client without parsing by the HTTP server. This is done by appending the string *nph-*, for *nonparsed header*, to the name of the script. When the server sees gateway program names beginning with *nph-*, it passes the gateway program output directly to the client. For example, Figure 8.5 shows the data returned from the gateway program *nph-srch-example*—this is an exact duplicate of the program *srch-example* listed in Figure 8.1, the only change being the *nph-* added before the filename.

Comparing Figure 8.5 with the program listing in Figure 8.1 shows that the response now contains just the data printed by the gateway program, with nothing added or modified by the server. The advantage of nonparsed header gateway programs is speed, since the server is not required to parse the returned data and generate appropriate headers. In exchange, the gateway program itself must produce all the required headers. Note how the returned data in Figure 8.5 are an *invalid* server response, as the response does not contain a status line, nor does it indicate the date, server type, or MIME version. Thus an *nph-* script must print, at a minimum, the following response headers (with values appropriate to the script):

Figure 8.5 Nonparsed header output returned upon accessing the URL
`http://leonardo.utirc.utoronto.ca:8080/cgi-bin/nph-srch-example.`

```
Content-TYPE: text/html

<HEAD>

 <TITLE>Local Phonebook Search</TITLE>

<ISINDEX>

</HEAD>

<BODY>

<H1>Local Phonebook Search</H1>

Enter your search in the search field.<P>

This is a case-insensitive substring search: thus

searching for 'ian' will find 'Ian' and Adriana'.

</BODY>
```

```
HTTP/1.0 200 OK

Date: Tuesday, 27-Sep-94 16:43:48 GMT

Server: NCSA/1.3

MIME-version: 1.0

Content-type: type/subtype
```

Nonparsed header programs are very useful, but are obviously more complicated to use than parsed gateway programs.

EXAMPLE 3: ENVIRONMENT VARIABLES

The preceding examples would imply that the server passes very little information to a gateway program. In fact, the server is not so ungenerous. Before launching a gateway program, the server initializes several *environment variables* that are subsequently accessible to the gateway. In particular, this mechanism is used to pass *extra path* information to a gateway program. The names and contents of common environment variables are shown in Figures 8.6 and 8.7. Figure 8.6 shows the gateway script *srch-example-2*; this is the same **ISINDEX** script shown in Figure 8.1, modified to print the contents of the environment variables. The HTML document generated upon accessing this script at the URL

```
http://leonardo.utirc.utoronto.ca:8080/cgi-bin/srch-example-2/dir/file?ian+bradley
```

is shown in Figure 8.7. Accessing this URL passes both query string (ian+bradley) and extra path information (/dir/file) to the referenced gateway program.

Most of the environment variables in Figure 8.7 are easy to understand. Some are set by default and do not depend on the nature of the request, while others are set only when particular client/server/gateway interactions are involved. The next section lists the different variables, discussed with reference to the data displayed in Figure 8.7.

GATEWAY PROGRAM ENVIRONMENT VARIABLES

The following are the environment variables generated by the server and passed to the gateway program (environment variable names are in capital-italics):

■■■■■ **Figure 8.6** Bourne-shell script ***srch-example-2***. This is a modification of the script in Figure 7.6 to explicitly print the environment variables and the command-line arguments.

```
#!/bin/sh
echo Content-TYPE:  text/html
echo

 if [ $# = 0 ]    # is the number of arguments == 0 ?
then               # do this part if there are NO arguments
     echo "<HEAD>"
     echo "<TITLE>Local Phonebook Search</TITLE>"
     echo "<ISINDEX>"
     echo "</HEAD>"
     echo "<BODY>"
     echo "<H1>Local Phonebook Search</H1>"
     echo "Enter your search in the search field.<P>"
     echo "This is a case-insensitive substring search: thus"
     echo "searching for 'ian' will find 'Ian' and Adriana'."
     echo "</BODY>"
else               # this part if there ARE arguments
     echo "<HEAD>"
     echo "<TITLE>Result of search for \"$*\".</TITLE>"
     echo "</HEAD>"
     echo "<BODY>"
     echo "<P> Number of Command-line Arguments = $#.    They are:"
     for i in $*
     do
          echo " <code> $i </code> "
     done
     echo "<h2> The Environment Variables </h2>"
```

```
    echo "<pre>"        # print the environment variables
    echo " SERVER_SOFTWARE = $SERVER_SOFTWARE"
    echo " SERVER_NAME = $SERVER_NAME"
    echo " GATEWAY_INTERFACE = $GATEWAY_INTERFACE"
    echo " SERVER_PROTOCOL = $SERVER_PROTOCOL"
    echo " SERVER_PORT = $SERVER_PORT"
    echo " REQUEST_METHOD = $REQUEST_METHOD"
    echo " HTTP_ACCEPT = $HTTP_ACCEPT"
    echo " PATH_INFO = $PATH_INFO"
    echo " PATH_TRANSLATED = $PATH_TRANSLATED"
    echo " SCRIPT_NAME = $SCRIPT_NAME"
    echo " QUERY_STRING = $QUERY_STRING"
    echo " REMOTE_HOST = $REMOTE_HOST"
    echo " REMOTE_ADDR = $REMOTE_ADDR"
    echo " REMOTE_USER = $REMOTE_USER"
    echo " AUTH_TYPE = $AUTH_TYPE"
    echo " CONTENT_TYPE = $CONTENT_TYPE"
    echo " CONTENT_LENGTH = $CONTENT_LENGTH"
    echo "</pre>"
    echo "<H2>Result of search for \"$*\".</H2>"
    echo "<PRE>"
    for i in $*
    do
        grep -i $i /vast/igraham/Personnel
done
    echo "</PRE>"
    echo "</BODY>"
fi
```

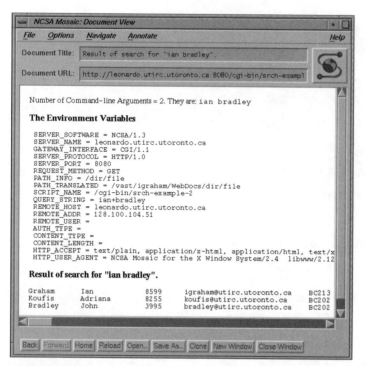

Figure 8.7 Document returned from the script in Figure 8.6 after accessing the URL `http://leonardo.utirc.utoronto.ca:8080/cgi-bin/srch-example-2/dir/file?ian+bradley`.

SERVER_SOFTWARE=server_name/version The name and version of the server software answering the request. The format is `name/version`, as in `NCSA/1.3` for this example.

SERVER_NAME=domain.name The Internet domain name of the server—here, `leonardo.utirc.utoronto.ca`. If the domain name is not available, this will be the numerical IP address.

GATEWAY_INTERFACE=CGI/version The particular version of the CGI interface specification being used by the server. The current version is 1.1, so this should be `CGI/1.1`.

SERVER_PROTOCOL=HTTP/version The protocol being used, namely HTTP, and the related version number. This allows gateway programs that support different versions of the HTTP protocol, or that support multiple protocols (for example, both Gopher and HTTP). In these cases, the program would use the contents of this variable to execute the appropriate code section. The current HTTP protocol version is 1.0, so this should be HTTP/1.0.

SERVER_PORT=number The port number called by the client: 8080 in this example.

REQUEST_METHOD=HTTP_method The method associated with the request. For HTTP server access this will be GET, HEAD, POST, PUT, and so on. This allows you to write a single gateway script or program supporting multiple methods; the script can use the contents of this variable to decide which portions of the program to execute.

PATH_INFO=extra_path This contains any extra path information found in the URL. In the current example, this contains the string /dir/file.

PATH_TRANSLATED=/transl/extra_path The *PATH_INFO* path translated into an *absolute* document path on the local system. For example, suppose the server document directory (the directory below which all documents are kept) is */vast/igraham/WebDocs*. The translated path is then:

PATH_TRANSLATED=/vast/igraham/WebDocs/dir/file

Note that this is not related to where the gateway program is physically kept. The translated path is often used to reference gateway program configuration files.

SCRIPT_NAME=/path/script_name The path and name of the script being accessed as it would be referenced in a URL. This can be used to construct URLs that refer back to this same gateway program, for insertion in script-generated HTML documents. For example, the following concatenated string

http://*$SERVER_NAME:$SERVER_PORT$SCRIPT_NAME*

generates the URL of the script from information contained in the environment variables (here $NAME refers to the *content* of the environment variable NAME).

QUERY_STRING=query_string The query string that follows the question mark in a URL—in this case, ian+bradley. It is still encoded, so that blanks are represented by plus signs, FORM name=value pairs are separated by the ampersand character, and so on. The person writing the gateway program must explicitly decode these data to extract the data sent by the client. If this string results from an **ISINDEX** search request, then

QUERY_STRING information is also passed to the program as decoded command-line arguments. However, you can access the same information from the *QUERY_STRING* variable, albeit in undecoded form.

REMOTE_HOST=client.domain.name The Internet domain name of the host making the request. If the domain name is unavailable, this field is left blank. The numerical IP address is available in the *REMOTE_ADDR* variable. In this example, I accessed the server on leonardo from leonardo itself.

REMOTE_ADDR=xxx.xxx.xxx.xxx The numeric IP address of the remote host accessing the server.

AUTH_TYPE=type The authentication method required to authenticate a user who desires access. This is only used with scripts that are protected. If authentication is not required this variable is empty. The only currently implemented value is Basic, for the Basic authentication scheme.

REMOTE_USER=name The authenticated name of the user. This is set only if authentication is required. It can be used to record the user's name and to control access depending on the user's identity. It is empty if authentication was not required.

REMOTE_IDENT=name The remote user name retrieved by the server using the **identd** identification daemon. This is largely unused.

CONTENT_TYPE=MIME_type If the client is POSTing or PUTting data to the server, this variable contains the MIME content-type of the data. If no data is being sent, this is left blank. The data itself is available to the gateway program by reading from standard input. The only widely implemented type is application/x-www-form-urlencoded.

CONTENT_LENGTH=length If the client POSTs or PUTs data to the server, this contains the length of the data message. If no data are being sent, this is left blank. The gateway program does not have to read all the data before returning data to the client, or before exiting.

In addition to these environment variables, *every* piece of information in the HTTP request headers (the headers sent from the client to the server) is passed to the gateway program in an environment variable. The environment variable names are constructed by:

- capitalizing the name in the request header field
- converting dash (–) characters into underscores (_)
- adding the prefix *HTTP_*

Thus, the `User-Agent` headers become the environment variable *HTTP_USER_AGENT*, while the `Accept` header values are concatenated (comma-separated) into the *HTTP_ACCEPT* environment variable. In this example, the browser sent only two types of fields, namely `Accept` and `User-Agent`, so there are only these two *HTTP_* environment variables:

HTTP_ACCEPT=type/subtype, type/subtype ... A comma-separated list of all the MIME types acceptable to the client, as indicated by the `Accept` headers sent from the client to the server. A gateway program can use this information to determine which type of data to return to the client.

HTTP_USER_AGENT=program/version The contents of the request header `User_Agent` field.

In general, any of the request headers listed in Chapter 7 can be passed to the server, in which case they will also be passed to the gateway program. Other commonly set environment variables are *HTTP_REFERER* and *HTTP_IF_MOD-IFIED_SINCE*.

EXAMPLE 4: HTML FORMS VIA A GET REQUEST

This example examines the data passed, by an HTML **FORM,** to the program shown in Figure 8.8. The **FORM** used is the same one employed in Example 3 in Chapter 7, which uses the GET method to send the data to the program (the **FORM** document is shown in Figure 7.4, and as rendered by a browser, in Figure 7.5). The Bourne-shell program in Figure 8.8 prints out the relevant environment variables, and also reads in data from standard input (the `read var` command, on the fourth line from the bottom) and prints the input data to standard output.

Figure 8.8 Test script *form1* accessed by the HTML **FORM** in Figure 7.4. This script returns an HTML document listing the script command-line arguments (if there are any), the contents of all the environment variables, and any data read from standard input (if any exist).

```
#!/bin/sh

echo Content-TYPE:  text/html

echo

# is a FORMs test script — it prints the environment variable

# contents generated by a FORM access to this script.
```

```
echo "<HEAD>"

echo "<TITLE>FORMs Test Page </TITLE>"

echo "</HEAD>"

echo "<P> Number of Command-line Arguments = $#. They are:" for i in $*

do

    echo " <code> $i </code> "

done

echo "<h2> The Environment Variables </h2>"

echo "<pre>"

echo "SERVER_NAME = $SERVER_NAME"

echo "SERVER_PORT = $SERVER_PORT"

echo "REQUEST_METHOD = $REQUEST_METHOD"

echo "PATH_INFO = $PATH_INFO"

echo "PATH_TRANSLATED = $PATH_TRANSLATED"

echo "SCRIPT_NAME = $SCRIPT_NAME"

echo "QUERY_STRING = $QUERY_STRING"

echo "CONTENT_TYPE = $CONTENT_TYPE"

echo "CONTENT_LENGTH = $CONTENT_LENGTH"

echo

if [ -n "$CONTENT_LENGTH" ]; then # Read/print input data (if any).

    echo "<H2>data at Standard Input is:</h2>"

    echo "<PRE>"

    read "var"  # read data from standard input into "var"

    echo "$var" # print var to standard output

    echo "</PRE>"

else

    echo "<h2> No Data at standard input </h2>"

fi

echo "</BODY>
```

Figure 7.6 shows the data actually sent to the server, and shows how the **FORM** data are encoded for transmission and appended to the URL. As a reminder, these data are reproduced here:

```
GET /cgi-bin/form1?srch=dogfish&srch_type=Exact+Match&srvr=Canada&srvr=Sweden HTTP/1.0

Accept: text/plain

Accept: application/x-html

Accept: application/html

Accept: text/x-html

Accept: text/html

Accept: audio/*

.

.
```

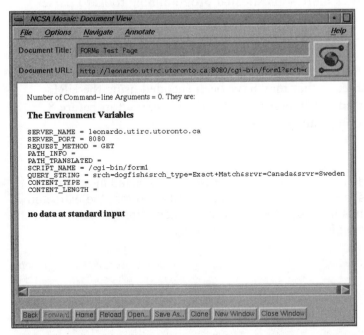

▬▬▬▬ **Figure 8.9** Data returned from the script shown in Figure 8.8, when accessed using the GET method, by the **FORM** shown in Figures 7.4 and 7.5.

```
Accept: text/x-setext

Accept: */*

User-Agent: NCSA Mosaic for the X Window System/2.4 libwww/2.12 modified
```

   [a blank line, containing only CRLF]

Figure 8.9 shows the document returned by the script in Figure 8.8. You will note that there are no command-line arguments. In parsing the URL, the server detected unencoded equal signs in the query string. This implies a non-**ISINDEX** query, so the server does not create command-line arguments. The remaining quantities are obvious. The *REQUEST_METHOD* environment variable is set to GET, and the query string is placed in the *QUERY_STRING* environment variable. The *CONTENT_TYPE* and *CONTENT_LENGTH* variables are empty, since there is no data sent in a GET method, while the *PATH_INFO* and *PATH_TRANSLATED* variables are also empty, since there was no extra path information in the query.

Further processing requires more sophisticated programming tools to parse the *QUERY_STRING* and break it into its component parts. This is not difficult, recalling that the ampersand character divided the different segments; the equals sign is used to relate FORM variable names to the assigned values; and spaces in the query strings are encoded as plus signs. Finally, you must unencode all the special characters that may have been encoded using the URL encoding scheme discussed in Chapter 6. The perl code extract in Figure 8.10 illustrates how this decoding can be done.

Figure 8.10 Perl code extract for decoding **FORM** data passed in a query string. Note that this is not a functional piece of code and that the extracted name and value strings must be placed in a permanent storage location (such as an associative array) for subsequent processing.

```
if( !defined($ENV{"QUERY_STRING"})) {     # Check for Query String environment
    &pk_error("No Query String\n");       # Variable — if absent, then error.
}

$input=$ENV{"QUERY_STRING"}               # get FORM data from query string
```

```
                                              # Check for unencoded equals sign — if
                                              # there are none, the string didn't
if( $input !~ /=/ ) {                         # come from a FORM, which is an error.

    &pk_error("Query String not from FORM\n");

}
                                              # If we get to here, all is OK. Now
@fields=split("&",$input);                    # split data into separate name=value
                                              # fields(@fields is an array)


#   Now loop over each of the entries in the @fields array and break
#   them into the name and value parts. Then decode each part to get
#   back the strings typed into the form by the user


foreach $one (@fields) {
    ($name, $value) = split("=",$one);        # split,at the equals sign,into
                                              # the name and value strings. Next,
                                              # decode the strings.
    $name  =~ s/\+/ /g;                       # convert +'s to spaces
    $name  =~ s/%(..)/pack("c",hex($1))/ge;   # convert URL hex codings to Latin-1
    $value =~ s/\+/ /g;                       # convert +'s to spaces
    $value =~ s/%(..)/pack("c",hex($1))/ge;   # convert URL hex codings to Latin-1


    #   What you do now depends on how the program works. If you know that each
    #   name is unique (your FORM does not have checkbox or SELECT items that
    #   allow multiple name=value strings with the same name) then you can place
    #   all the data in an associative array (a useful little perl feature!):


    $array{"$name"} = $value;
```

```
#      If your form does have SELECT or <INPUT TYPE=checkbox..> items,

#      then you'll have to be a bit more careful...



}
```

Some useful collections of CGI utilities are listed in Chapter 9.

EXAMPLE 5:
HTML FORMS VIA A POST REQUEST

This example again accesses the program shown in Figure 8.8 using a **FORM** equivalent to the one in Figure 7.4, but, this time, using the POST method. Figure 7.7 shows the data actually sent to the server; as a reminder, these data were:

```
POST /cgi-bin/form1 HTTP/1.0

Accept: text/plain

Accept: application/x-html

Accept: application/html

Accept: text/x-html

Accept: text/html

Accept: audio/*

    .

    .

    .

Accept: text/x-setext

Accept: */*

User-Agent: NCSA Mosaic for the X Window System/2.4 libwww/2.12 modified

Content-type: application/x-www-form-urlencoded
```

```
Content-length: 58
```

```
srch=dogfish&srch_type=Exact+Match&srvr=Canada&srvr=Sweden
```

In this case, the data is sent to the server as an encoded message following the headers. There are two extra headers: the content-length header, which tells the server the length of the following message; and the content-type header, which tells the server that this is an `application/x-www-form-urlencoded` MIME type—a special MIME type used to indicate **FORM** data that have been encoded using the URL encoding scheme.

Figure 8.11 shows the results returned by the script in Figure 8.8, and displays the data that arrived at the script. There are no command-line arguments this time, because there is no query string. Most of the environment variables are the same as with the GET request shown in Figure 8.9. Obvious differences are the *REQUEST_METHOD* variable, which is now POST instead of GET, and the null *QUERY_STRING*. In addition, the *CONTENT_TYPE* and *CONTENT_LENGTH* are not empty but contain the length of the message and the content-type, as indicated in the fields sent by the client.

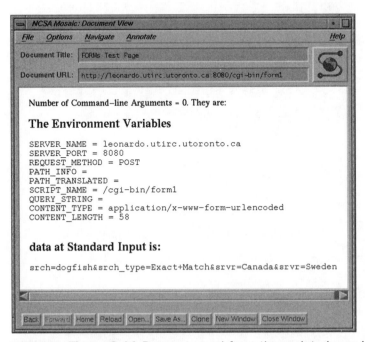

Figure 8.11 Data returned from the script shown in Figure 8.8 when accessed by the **FORM** shown in Figure 7.4 and modified to use the POST HTTP method.

Where are the **FORM** data? With the POST method, these data are sent to the gateway program as an input stream, which the program reads from standard input. The script in Figure 8.8 reads data from standard input, and prints the results back to standard output. The result is printed at the bottom of Figure 8.11, which clearly shows the query data sent by the client. These data are encoded using the same URL encoding mechanisms employed with the GET query in Figure 8.9. To further process these data, you must parse it and separate the fields. Figure 8.12 shows an extract of a perl program illustrating how this decoding can be done. This is very similar to the code in Figure 8.10—the differences occur only at the beginning of the script, and are marked in italics. Again, there are CGI libraries, mentioned in Chapter 9, that can help in the processing of these data.

■■■■■■■ **Figure 8.12** Perl code extract for decoding **FORM** data passed to the program via standard input. Differences from the extract in Figure 8.10 are shown in italics. Note that this is not a functional piece of code, and that the extracted name and value strings must be placed in a permanent storage location (such as an associative array) for subsequent processing.

```
$input=<STDIN>;                  # read FORM data from stdin
chop($input); chop($input);      # chop CR/LF trailing characters:
                                 # recall that the data sent by a client
                                 # is always terminated by a single line
                                 # containing only a CRLF pair. This
                                 # must be removed, since it is not
                                 # part of the message body.
                                 # Check for unencoded equals sign — if
                                 # there are none, the string didn't
if( $input !~ /=/ ) {            # come from a FORM, which is an error.
    &pk_error("Query String not from FORM\n");
}
                                 # If we get to here, all is OK. Now
@fields=split("&",$input);       # split data into separate name=value
```

```
                                        # fields(@fields is an array)


#   Now loop over each of the entries in the @fields array and break

#   them into the name and value parts. Then decode each part to get

#   back the strings typed into the form by the user.


foreach $one (@fields) {
    ($name, $value) = split("=",$one);        # split,at the equals sign,into
                                              # the name and value strings. Next,
                                              # decode the strings.

    $name  =~ s/\+/ /g;                        # convert +'s to spaces
    $name  =~ s/%(..)/pack("c",hex($1))/ge;   # convert URL hex codings to Latin-1
    $value =~ s/\+/ /g;                        # convert +'s to spaces
    $value =~ s/%(..)/pack("c",hex($1))/ge;   # convert URL hex codings to Latin-1


    #   What you do now depends on how the program works. If you know that each
    #   name is unique (your FORM does not have checkbox or SELECT items that
    #   allow multiple name=value strings with the same name) then you can place
    #   all the data in an associative array (a useful little perl feature!):


    $array{"$name"} = $value;


    #   If your form does have SELECT or <INPUT TYPE=checkbox..> items,
    #   then you'll have to be a bit more careful...


}
```

Example 5 may seem little different from Example 4, but it is, in fact, different in important ways. First, many computer operating systems have a finite data space for environment variables, so that large messages passed via GET URLs can be truncated. In addition, the POST method in principle allows for complicated MIME messages to be sent from client to server, something that is impractical, if not impossible, with the GET method.

RELATIVE ADVANTAGES OF GET AND POST

The GET and POST methods for handling **FORM** input have different strengths and weaknesses. POST is clearly much superior if you are sending large quantities of data to the server, and should always be used in this case. If you are sending small quantities of data, the choice is less clear. One useful criterion is to ask yourself if you want the user to be able to store ("bookmark") a URL that will return the user to this particular resource. If the answer is yes, then use the GET method, since the relevant data will be placed in the query string portion of a URL, which is stored when a URL is recorded. If, on the other hand, you do not want the user to be able to quickly return to this resource, or if you want to hide the **FORM** content as much as possible, then you should use POST.

HTML ENCODING OF TEXT WITHIN A FORM

With gateway programs, you often need to place data inside the **FORM** sent to the client—this might be initial field values assigned to the **VALUE** attributes of **INPUT** or **OPTION** elements or within the body of a **TEXTAREA** element, or it might be state information preserved within the **VALUE** attributes of **TYPE**="hidden" **INPUT** elements. However, in doing so, you must remember that the text received by the client will be *parsed*. This means that any entity or character references embedded in the **VALUE** (or even **NAME**) strings, or within the body of a **TEXTAREA** element, will be automatically converted into the correct ISO Latin-1 characters. For example, if a document sent to a client contains the hidden element

```
<INPUT TYPE="hidden" NAME="stuff" VALUE="&lt;BOO&quot;&gt;">
```

the client will *parse* the **VALUE** string and convert it into the string <BOO">. When the **FORM** containing this hidden element is submitted, the string <BOO"> will be URL-encoded and sent to the server, so that the entity encoding in the original data is lost.

This is sensible if you recall that, as far as the browser is concerned, entity references and character references *are* no different from the characters they represent. This can be a problem, however, if the data within the hidden form contains HTML markup, since here you often need to *preserve* entity references distinct from the characters they represent—for example, so that simple character strings (<tag>) do not get converted into markup tags (<tag>) by this conversion process. Thus, if you need to preserve entity references, you must do the following encodings of the string prior to assigning it to a **VALUE** or **NAME**, or prior to placing it within a **TEXTAREA** element:

- encode all ampersand characters in the text string as &amp
- encode all double quotation symbols as &quot
- encode all right angle brackets as &gt

The second and third steps are necessary, as any raw double quote characters (") will prematurely terminate a **VALUE** or **NAME** string, while some browsers mistakenly use an unencoded greater-than symbol (>) to prematurely end **INPUT** elements. The first step encodes the leading character of each entity or character reference—for example, the original string é becomes &eacute;. This is processed by the client browser back to the string é, which brings you back full circle when the data are returned to the server.

STATE PRESERVATION

In a complex gateway application, a complete transaction may require a series of interactions between the client and server. Since the HTTP protocol is stateless, the server and any gateway program retain no knowledge of any previous transaction. Thus you, as the gateway program designer, must build in mechanisms for keeping track of what happened in a previous stage of a transaction.

In general, there are two ways to do this. First, the gateway program can place all the data received from the client within <INPUT TYPE= "hidden"...> elements returned within the **FORM** used in the next stage of a transaction. Then, the subsequent access to a server-side gateway program will resend all data from the previous interaction(s). The second method is to create a temporary file on the server and store the transaction data within this file. In this case the gateway program must return an <INPUT TYPE= "hidden"...> element containing the *name* of this temporary file, so that the gateway program, on any subsequent requests, will know which file to reference. This reduces the amount of data that must be sent from client to server (and back again), but also means that the gateway programs must manage these temporary files. For example, many remote users may not complete the transaction, which will leave temporary files in place unless there are auxiliary routines for deleting "stale" temporary files.

SECURITY CONSIDERATIONS

There is always a security risk associated with running a gateway program on a server, since a rogue program can easily corrupt the data files being managed by the server. Most HTTP servers restrict executable programs to special URLs (typically those pointing to the directories */cgi-bin* or */htbin*), and do not permit executable gateway programs in the area where regular documents are kept. The server administrator can then maintain strict control over the installation of programs in these areas, and can verify that installed gateways are not dangerous to the integrity of the server.

The details of security management depend on the server that you are using. In general, most servers allow significant customization of these features.

DESIGNING SAFE GATEWAY PROGRAMS

As a gateway program designer, you must be careful to design safe gateway programs. Although it is hard to define specific rules for doing so, here are three main points you should particularly watch out for:

1. **Guard system information.** Gateway programs should never return to the client any information about the local system, such as absolute paths to files, system usernames, password information, and so on, that could compromise system security. If you must return path information, pass it as a *relative* path that gives away no information about the server's filesystem design.

2. **Never trust client data.** A gateway program should never trust data sent by a client—the data could be in error, either due to a simple typing mistake, or due to an intentional effort on the part of the client to break into your system. As a relatively benign example, you should never blindly trust the e-mail address (either the *from* or *to* address) provided by a user in a fill-in HTML FORM—you could be mailing data to the wrong user, or to a nonexistent mail address. More importantly, you should be careful to the

point of paranoia about using strings provided by a client as arguments to system calls—example system calls are the C or perl `system()` or `popen()` calls, or the perl or shell `eval` commands. Blindly passing client strings to these calls is a classic route to disaster, since commands executed by these calls can easily delete files, mail your password file to a remote user, and commit other venial sins. If you must execute strings passed by the user, be sure to check them for dangerous commands, and to *escape* special shell characters that can cause grievous problems. The possibly dangerous shell characters are:

` ~ ! # $ ^ & * ( ) = | \ { } [ ] ; : ' " < > , . ?

3. **Execute in a secure environment.** You can often run a script under a secure, or restricted, shell that takes proactive action to prevent problems. For example, if you are using perl gateway programs you should use taint-perl instead of perl. This version of perl treats all quantities that come from environment variables or external input as *tainted*, and refuses to pass these quantities, unprocessed, to system calls.

NON-CGI GATEWAYS VIA APPLICATION PROGRAMMING INTERFACES

The gateway mechanism is simple and effective. However, it is slow, since the gateway program must be started up, as a distinct running process, each time it is referenced. As mentioned earlier, this is often not a problem, particularly if the resource behind the gateway program is not speedy. Nevertheless, there are many occasions when speed is of the essence, and for which it would be useful if the gateway designer could bypass the CGI mechanisms completely, and instead build the interface routines directly into the server.

A few servers support this feature through custom-designed gateway *application programming interfaces*, or *APIs*. Notable among these are the Netscape Netsite server's NSAPI (Netscape API) and an API under development as part of the Apache server project. The Netscape home page (`http://www.netscape.com`) maintains some online documentation on the API (just search for the string `"nsapi"`), but this is badly organized and poorly written (Netscape does, however, sell an NSAPI manual, should you be so bold!). On the other hand, the Apache documentation site (`http://www.apache.org/`) maintains somewhat better online information on its own API, which is distinctly different from the Netscape variant.

Gateways built using an API are much faster than those built using the CGI interface. However, they gain this speed at the expense of portability—APIs are strongly server-specific, so if you write an API-based gateway for the Netscape Netsite server, you will be forever tied to that server, as no other vendor supports that interface specification.

REFERENCES

The following URLs provide useful documentation on the CGI specification. References to CGI utilities and libraries and to online CGI tutorials are given at the end of Chapter 9.

CGI specifications

    http://hoohoo.ncsa.uiuc.edu/cgi/overview.html

NCSA Demonstration CGI documents

    http://hoohoo.ncsa.uiuc.edu/cgi/examples.html

CGI PROGRAMS

AND TOOLS

This chapter discusses some practical examples of CGI programming, and provides a reference list of sites on the Web maintaining archives of programs or tools useful in developing gateway applications. The first issues addressed are the Netscape *client push/server pull* HTML and HTTP extensions, which are currently implemented only by the Netscape Navigator browser. These extensions allow for rudimentary animation of Web presentations. Examples are provided that illustrate how these extensions work. Next is a discussion of *server-side includes*. This is a special HTTP server feature that allows for *parsable* HTML documents, which are processed by the server prior to being delivered to a client. The third section gives a detailed presentation of three gateway programming examples, illustrating some of the important issues in gateway program design. This is in turn followed by an outline of *client-side program execution*, a technique whereby a server can distribute program resources for execution on a client. The chapter concludes with sections listing known CGI utility programs, CGI database interface programs, and, finally, archive sites containing collections of gateway programs and information related to CGI database interface routines.

NETSCAPE CGI ANIMATION TECHNIQUES

The Netscape Navigator browser supports two special mechanisms that allow for slide show–like presentations and for a rudimentary form of animation. The animation scheme, called *server push*, employs a new *multipart* MIME type that lets a server send a client a series of images or documents, which are in turn displayed by the Navigator browser as an animated sequence. To use this technique, you must write a gateway program that sends the data to the client using this special MIME type. Alternatively, the *client pull* technique uses a new HTTP response header, Refresh, which instructs the browser, after a specified delay, either to actively refresh the displayed document, or to access another document at a specified URL. Again, a gateway program is needed to produce the refresh HTTP header field. However, authors can instead include, in their HTML documents, **META** elements containing the refresh header field content (using the **HTTP-EQUIV** attribute value, as discussed in Chapter 4)—the Netscape Navigator browser parses the documents for the **META** element, and understands refresh header information. This latter method is useful for creating document slide shows.

The following sections look in detail at these two animation techniques.

CLIENT PULL

In *client pull*, the server sends the client a special HTTP Refresh response header field (Netscape Navigator is presently the only browser to understand this field). The field has the general form

```
Refresh: xx; URL=url_string
```

where *xx* is an integer giving the time, in seconds, that the browser should wait before *refreshing* the document, and *url_string* is the *full* (not relative) URL that the browser should access when it is time to do the refresh. The header

```
Refresh: 10; URL=http://www.hprc.utoronto.ca/home.html
```

tells the browser to wait 10 seconds, and to then access the indicated URL. The URL portion can be left out, in which case the browser will reaccess the same URL. Thus, a header of the form

```
Refresh: 30
```

tells a browser to refresh the currently displayed URL, after a 30-second delay. The refresh time can be set to zero, in which case the browser will refresh the display as soon as the currently requested data are fully loaded.

There are several things to note about this procedure. First, this response header field is only understood by the Netscape Navigator browser; it won't work with other browsers, which will simply display the accessed document, and then stop. Second, the `Refresh` field must be returned by a gateway program—servers themselves do not return refresh header fields. Third, each request by the client counts as a separate HTTP transaction, as the connection is broken between refresh requests.

As an alternative to using HTTP response headers, the same information can be placed within a **META** element in an HTML document. This allows you to easily place refresh capability into already existing parsed HTML documents (parsed HTML documents are discussed later in this chapter), or allows you to build slide shows into a sequence of regular HTML documents, using the URL references in the `refresh` fields to reference consecutive documents. This approach is convenient, as you do not need a CGI program (but note that it still only works with the Navigator browser). The **META** element content equivalent to the general form of the refresh response header is

```
<META HTTP-EQUIV="Refresh" CONTENT="xx; URL=url_string">
```

while **META** elements equivalent to the two examples just given are:

```
<META HTTP-EQUIV="Refresh" CONTENT="10
      URL="http://www.hprc.utoronto.ca/home.html">

<META HTTP-EQUIV="Refresh" CONTENT="30">
```

The Netscape Navigator browser understands these **META** elements and interprets their content as HTTP response header fields (this is the purpose of the **HTTP-EQUIV** attribute, as discussed in Chapter 4). This, of course, is only possible with HTML documents; if you are returning other forms of data, you will need to write a gateway program that returns an HTTP `refresh` header field.

SERVER PUSH

Server push is a second and fundamentally different way of creating dynamic documents. When a client accesses a resource delivered using server push, the client/server connection remains open, and the server sends a sequence of data objects, one after the other, over the open connection. This is done using a special Netscape-specific MIME *multipart* message format, discussed below. The advantages of this method are twofold. First, you do not need to recontact the server to get the second (or subsequent) data objects. As a result, the data are delivered more quickly, since the client does not need to renegotiate a connection for each part. The load is also lighter on the server, for the same reasons. Second, you can use server push to download a sequence of images into an `<IMG SRC="...">` element. This allows you to embed an *animation sequence* into an HTML document by referencing, from an **IMG** element, a gateway program that delivers a sequence of image files using server push. The disadvantage is that you absolutely need to write a special-purpose gateway program—unlike client pull, server push cannot be implemented using **META** elements.

To implement server push, Netscape has implemented the experimental MIME type `multipart/x-mixed-replace`. Using this MIME type, a server can deliver a sequence (in principle, an endless sequence) of data files, one after the other. This is done by defining, as part of the MIME type, a *boundary* string: a special string of ASCII characters that is used to separate each part of the multipart message from the preceding and following parts. The MIME content-type declaration takes the form:

```
Content-type: multipart/x-mixed-replace;boundary=RandomAsciiString
```

where *RandomAsciiString* is the (random) string of ASCII characters used as the separator between the different parts of the message. The general form for this MIME multipart message is shown in Figure 9.1, with comments in italics.

Figure 9.1 Structure of a `multipart/x-mixed-replace` MIME message. Here, `RandomAsciiString` is a random string of ASCII characters, which is used to mark the separator between the message parts, and `type/subtype` is the data type of the data being sent. This MIME type is only understood by Netscape Navigator.

```
Content-type:  multipart/x-mixed-replace;boundary=RandomAsciiString

                              [blank line, containing a CRLF pair ]
--RandomAsciiString           [marker denoting boundary between parts]
Content-type: type/subtype

   [blank line, containing a CRLF pair ]
.... content of first chunk ....

.... and more content ....

--RandomAsciiString
Content-type: type/subtype

   [blank line, containing a CRLF pair ]
```

```
.... content of second chunk ....

.... and more content ....

--RandomAsciiString

Content-type: type/subtype

    [blank line, containing a CRLF pair ]

.... content of third chunk ....

.... and more content ....

--RandomAsciiString

.

.

. [and so on....]

.

--RandomAsciiString--          [The end of the multipart message]
```

Note how the boundary between different parts of the multipart message is denoted by the string RandomAsciiString preceded by two dashes, that is:

    --RandomAsciiString

The end of the multipart message is denoted by the same string but with two additional trailing dashes:

    --RandomAsciiString--

In practice, you can leave out this termination string, and send an unending sequence of messages. A browser user can end this sequence by selecting the browser's "Stop" button, or by explicitly selecting an alternate URL.

Here are two gateway program examples showing how server push works.

EXAMPLE 1:
A SIMPLE "SERVER PUSH" SHELL SCRIPT

This simple shell script, listed in Figure 9.2, repeatedly returns a document listing the "top" process running on the computer.

▓▓▓▓▓▓▓ **Figure 9.2** The Bourne-shell script **nph-top-list.sh**, which returns, every 10 seconds, a list of the top 10 running processes on the computer. *Line numbers are in italics.*

```
1   #!/bin/sh
2   echo "HTTP/1.0  200 OK"                    # [ Server
3   date -u '+Date: %A, %d-%b-%y %T GMT'      #     Response
4   echo Server: $SERVER_SOFTWARE             #     Headers ]
5   echo MIME-Version: 1.0
6   echo "Content-type: multipart/x-mixed-replace;boundary=a1lpRf5fgFd1dr"
7   echo ""
8   echo "--a1lpRf5fgFd1dr"        # [initial boundary for first part]
9   while true
10    do
11        echo "Content-type: text/html"
12        echo ""
13        echo "<HTML><HEAD>"
14        echo "<TITLE> Top Running Processes </TITLE></HEAD><BODY>"
15        echo "<H1 ALIGN=center> Top Running Processes at time: <BR>"
16        date                       # [date prints the current time and date]
17        echo "</H1><HR>"
18        echo "<PRE>"
19        /usr/local/bin/top -d1  # Print out "top" running processes
20        echo "</PRE></BODY></HTML>"
21        echo echo "--a1lpRf5fgFd1dr"
22        sleep 10
23    done
```

This first thing to note is that this is a *nonparsed header* script—this is usually necessary with server push, as many servers *buffer* the data returned from a gateway program, and only forward data when the buffer is full or when the gateway program terminates. In the current example we want each part of our multipart message delivered immediately to the client. We can ensure this only by using a nonparsed header script, which bypasses the server buffering and dumps data directly down the port to the client.

As a result, lines 2 through 6 return *all* the required HTTP response headers—namely, the status header (response 200, implying success), the date (the format ensures the return of a date header in the correct format), and the server type (obtained from the environment variable) and MIME version, followed by the content-type declaration for the type `multipart/x-mixed-replace`. In this example, the multipart boundary is the string `allpRf5fgFd1dr`. Note that there are no space characters in this content-type header. Ordinarily, you can have spaces before and after the semicolons separating the type/subtype from the associated parameters, but this is incorrectly processed by some servers (in particular, some versions of the NCSA HTTP server), so it is safest to remove all unnecessary whitespace. Finally, line 7 returns a blank line, which indicates the end of server directives and the start of the data stream being returned to the client.

Line 8 prints the first boundary marker—this indicates the start of the first *part* of the message. The script then executes a loop, starting from line 10, which is executed every 10 seconds (note the `sleep 10` command at the bottom of the loop). The loop returns a content-type header (here `text/html`) followed by a blank line—this also is mandatory. This is followed by the desired HTML document which includes, inside a **PRE** element, the output from the program **top**. The last thing returned is the boundary marker`--allpRf5fgFd1dr`. This tells the client that the message has been completely delivered and that it can stop waiting for more data. It also tells the client to keep the connection to the server open, in anticipation of the next part of the message.

This program will in principle run forever, sending down top information every 10 seconds. A Netscape Navigator user can interrupt this by simply pressing the "Stop" button, or by choosing to access another URL. The server should detect the broken connection and issue a kill signal to the gateway program. Unfortunately, this is not always possible with nonparsed header programs, in which case it is up to the gateway program to detect when the connection is broken. Shell languages, such as the Bourne shell used in the example, are notoriously bad at this—they often "forget" to die—so you should write server push scripts in languages such as perl or C, which properly terminate when the connection is broken. The script in Figure 9.2, for example, does not always terminate when the client breaks the connection—

this has, on occasion, left a dozen of these scripts happily running on our server, long after the connection that started them had been broken.

EXAMPLE 2: A C PROGRAM FOR "PUSHING" IMAGES

The example C program *nph-doit-2,* shown in Figure 9.3, uses server push to send a sequence of GIF images. Assume this CGI program is located in the server's *cgi-bin* directory. Then, to insert an animated image in an HTML document, you would write the following HTML markup:

```
<IMG SRC="/cgi-bin/nph-doit-2">
```

which assumes that the HTML document and gateway program are served out of the same server. The client will then access the indicated URL to download the requested image. The Netscape Navigator understands the returned multipart message, and will play the image sequence as a simple animation. Most other browsers do not understand the multipart MIME type and display nothing, or else display a generic symbol representing a missing or broken image. We now look at the program, and follow how it functions.

Figure 9.3 Simple C program **nph-doit2.c**, for pushing a sequence of images to a client. The files are read from the indicated directory. *Commentary not originally in the program listing is in **bold italics**.*

```
/*

 * doit-2.c

 * Based on doit.c --

 *   Quick hack to play a sequence of GIF files, by Rob McCool.

 *      This code is released into the public domain. Do whatever

 *      you want with it.

 *

 * Doit-2.c Modifications by By Ian Graham, July 23 1995

 * to make it a simpler demonstration example -- or so I thought!

 */


#include <sys/types.h>
```

```c
#include <unistd.h>
#include <stdlib.h>
#include <fcntl.h>
#include <sys/stat.h>
#include <dirent.h>
#include <stdio.h>


/* Define the server directives and response headers              */


#define HEADER1  "HTTP/1.0 200 OK\r\n"      /* Nph-response header    */
#define HEADER2 \
  "Content-type: multipart/x-mixed-replace;boundary=aRd4xBloobies\r\n"


/* Define the boundary strings, the Content-type header, and the   */
/* path to the directory containing the images                     */


#define BOUNDARY     "\r\n--aRd4xBloobies\r\n"
#define END_BOUND    "\r\n--aRd4xBloobies--\r\n\r\n"
#define CONTENT      "Content-type: image/gif\r\n\r\n"
#define IMG_DIR      "/absolute/path/img-dir"     /*  where the files are */


int main(int argc, char *argv[])
{
    static char   *file;
    char          *files[1024], *tmp, buf[127];
    caddr_t       fp;
    int           fd, i, ndir=0;
    DIR           *dirp;
```

```
struct dirent *dp;
struct stat    fi;


/* Get list of all files in image directory -- we will            */
/* spit them out in alphabetical order                            */
                                            /* ** GET LIST    ** */
dirp = opendir(IMG_DIR);
while ( ((dp = readdir(dirp)) != NULL) && (ndir < 1024) ) {
    if( strncmp(dp->d_name,".", 1)) {
        files[ndir] = malloc(strlen(dp->d_name)+1+strlen(IMG_DIR));
        sprintf(files[ndir], "%s/%s", IMG_DIR, dp->d_name);
        ndir++;
    }
}
closedir(dirp);
                                            /* ** GOT LIST    ** */
/* Write out server directives, and first multipart boundary      */


                        /* ** PRINT SERVER RESPONSE HEADERS     ** */
if(write(STDOUT_FILENO, HEADER1, strlen(HEADER1)) == -1)    exit(0);
if(write(STDOUT_FILENO, HEADER2, strlen(HEADER2)) == -1)    exit(0);
if(write(STDOUT_FILENO, BOUNDARY, strlen(BOUNDARY)) == -1) exit(0);


/* Now loop over all files, and write to client                   */
for (i=0; i<ndir; i++)  {
    fprintf(stderr, "Doing output loop -- i=%i\n", i);
    sleep(1);
                        /* ** WRITE PART CONTENT-TYPE      ***/
```

```
    if(write(STDOUT_FILENO, CONTENT, strlen(CONTENT)) == -1) exit(0);
    if( ( fd=open(files[i],O_RDONLY)) == -1 ) {
        fprintf(stderr,"Unable to open file %s\n", files[i]);
        continue;
    }
    fstat(fd, &fi);                         /*  find size of file and    */
    tmp=malloc(fi.st_size*sizeof(char)); /*  allocate memory for it    */
    read(fd, tmp, fi.st_size);
                                         /* ** WRITE THE IMAGE DATA ** */
    if(write(STDOUT_FILENO, tmp, fi.st_size) == -1) exit(0);
                                /* ERROR: unable to write image        */
    free(tmp);
    close(fd);
                                         /* ** WRITE THE PART BOUNDARY ** */
    if(write(STDOUT_FILENO, BOUNDARY, strlen(BOUNDARY)) == -1) exit(0);
                                /* ERROR unable to write boundary       */
}


/* Write out the boundary marking the end of the multipart            */
/* message. Then we are done.                                         */


write(STDOUT_FILENO, END_BOUND, strlen(END_BOUND));
exit(0);

}
```

The first part of the program (between the *GET LIST* and *GOT LIST*
comments) gets a list of all the image files in the directory
/absolute/path/img_dir, and creates an array (`files[]`) of absolute path

filenames pointing to these files. The program then writes out the necessary server response headers, and the initial multipart headers and message dividers required by the multipart message (just after the **PRINT SERVER RESPONSE HEADERS** comment). The subsequent loop iterates over the different image files, sending them one after the other to the client, each file followed by the required multipart boundary marker (after the **WRITE THE PART BOUNDARY** comment). When the program is finished with the list, it exits, writes out the final boundary marking the end of the multipart message, and ends the connection.

Because this is a gateway program, you can pass variables to the program using the usual tricks. Thus you can use extra path information to pass the location of the image directory, instead of using a hard-wired location as was done in this example.

Both client pull and server push are rudimentary techniques for implementing animation, and are likely to be replaced by more sophisticated methods currently under development. For example, HTML **LINK** elements can in principle be used to represent "Next" and "Previous" documents in a linear document collection, allowing the browser to produce a slide show, if desired. Animation is also better handled through alternate mechanisms. In particular, embedded applications, such as Java or Macromedia Director applets, allow for much richer animation sequences, and also for user interaction with the animation.

SERVER-SIDE DOCUMENT INCLUDES

A recurring question by HTML authors is: "Can I include a file within my HTML document in the same way I include an image?" The answer is, in general, no, as there are no elements (yet!) within HTML that allow arbitrary document inclusions. If you want to have documents that are created dynamically (which is what is implied by inclusion), you are supposed to use a CGI program. Needless to say, this can be annoying if all you want to do is patch a small piece of text into an otherwise stable document. Some kind of *include* HTML command would be a far easier mechanism than a full-blown CGI script.

The NCSA, Netscape, Apache, and several other HTTP servers allow server-side file inclusion, using a special server interpretation of HTML comment strings that allows for *parsable* HTML. This allows you to include, in your documents, commands that can inline text files, or even execute server programs and include the program output inline with the document. This is a powerful feature but should not be abused, since every parsable file must be specially processed by the server, which can significantly slow server response. You should reserve use of parsable files for situations where it is the only realistic choice.

By default, most servers supporting server-side includes/parsable HTML documents come with this feature disabled—you have to explicitly turn it on. Your server's documentation package will explain how this is done, if it is supported. In general, you will want to configure your system so that parsable HTML documents have a different filename extension than HTML documents, for example *.shtml* instead of *.html*. This ensures that the server does not waste time parsing regular HTML documents that do not contain parsable commands.

Server-side includes are well documented in the NCSA HTTPD server online manuals, referenced at the end of this chapter. Also referenced are several sites on the Web that provide useful interactive tutorials illustrating server-side includes.

INCLUDE COMMAND FORMAT

The server-side include command is framed inside an HTML comment string:

```
<!-- include_command -->
```

When parsed by a server supporting this feature, the entire comment string is replaced by the output of `include_command`. Enclosing this command within a comment string ensures that the document will not cause problems if it is processed by a server that does not support this feature, or that has this feature disabled. Such servers will simply deliver the document, including the comment line, and the client will treat the enclosed string as a comment, and ignore it.

The general form for the include command is:

```
<!--#command arg1="value1" arg2="value2" -->
```

where `command` is the name of the command to be executed and `arg1` and `arg2` are arguments passed to the command. There must be no space between the hash sign (#) and the command name. The number and name of the argument(s) depend on the actual command; most commands take a single argument. Note that, despite its structure, this is *not* a comment statement. You *cannot* include comment descriptions inside an include command. Consequently, lines like:

```
<!--#command arg1="value1" This prints the time of day  -->
```

are invalid.

There are six possible commands: `config`, `include`, `echo`, `fsize`, `flastmod`, and `exec`. `Config` configures the way the server parses the document. `Include` includes another document (*not* a CGI program) at the indicated location, while `echo` includes the contents of one of the special environment variables set for parsed documents. `Fsize` and `flastmod` are similar to `echo`; `fsize` prints the size of a specified file, while `flastmod` prints the last modification date of a specified file. Finally, `exec` executes a single-line Bourne-shell command, or a CGI program. For security reasons, the `exec` facility can be disabled in the server configuration files while leaving the other features operational.

Here are the details of the six different commands, with examples.

INCLUDE

`Include` is used to include another document (or another parsed document) at the given location in the current document. `Include` can only include a document, and cannot include CGI program output. `Include` takes one argument that specifies the file to be included. The possible arguments and their values are:

`virtual="`*virtual/path*`"` `Virtual` specifies the *virtual* path to the document relative to the server's document directory or to a user's personal server directory. For example, user fosdick with his or her own public HTML area would access files in this area with the virtual path:

```
<!--#include virtual="~fosdick/path/file.html"-->
```

`file="`*relative_path/file*`"` `File` specifies the path to the document relative to the current document. You cannot use `file` to move up in the hierarchy, only down (e.g., you can't use `../stuff.html`). For example, to include the file *junk.html* from the same directory, you would type:

```
<!--#include file="junk.html" -->
```

The following are some examples of `include`:

```
<!--#include file="templates/template2.html" -->

<!--#include virtual="/path/subpath/templates/template2.html -->
```

ECHO

`Echo` includes in the document the contents of a named environment variable. The variable name you wish to include is indicated via the argument `var="variable_name"`. `Variable_name` can be any of the CGI environment variables listed in Chapter 8, and can also be one of the following special environment variables, valid only in parsable files:

DOCUMENT_NAME The name of the current file.

DOCUMENT_URI The virtual (relative to server document directory) path to the document, such as ~fosdick/path/file.html, or /path/subpath/templates/template2.html.

DATE_LOCAL The current date, using the local time zone. The format of this date can be controlled using the timefmt argument of the config command.

DATE_GMT Same as *DATE_LOCAL*, but in Greenwich Mean Time.

LAST_MODIFIED The last modification date of the current document. The format is specified by *timefmt*.

▬▬▬▬ **TIP**

> These variables are also available to gateway or shell programs executed using the exec command. Also, some servers, such as Apache, have an extended list of available variables. Consult your server documentation for more information on any extra local features.

▬▬▬▬

Example of echo:

```
The file is found at: <!--#echo var="DOCUMENT_URI" -->
This file was accessed at the time: <!--#echo var="DATE_LOCAL" -->
```

FSIZE

Fsize includes the size, in bytes, of a specified file. The file is specified using the file or virtual arguments, as described with the include command. Fsize is useful for presenting information about a file to be downloaded, allowing the document to tell the user the size of the file even if the file size varies often (as it might, for example, for a mail archive). Fsize can also be useful for presenting file indexes that include file size information. The output format can be controlled using the sizefmt argument of the config command.

Example of fsize:

```
The size of the file main.html is: <!--#fsize file="main.html" -->
```

FLASTMOD

`Flastmod` includes the last modification time of a specified file. The file is specified using the `file` or `virtual` arguments, as described with the `include` command. Like `fsize`, `flastmod` is useful for providing up-to-date information about files that are periodically changed. The output format can be controlled using the `timefmt` argument of the `config` command.

Example of `flastmod`:

```
This file was last changed on:

<!--#flastmod virtual="/path/dir1/dir2/main.html"  -->
```

EXEC

`Exec` executes the given Bourne-shell command or CGI program. `Exec` can have one of two possible arguments:

`cmd="cmd_string"` Causes the string `"cmd_string"` to be executed using the Bourne shell **/bin/sh.** `Cmd_string` can be a simple one-line shell program to do simple things, like listing directory contents or running a program to filter a data file for presentation.

`cgi="cgi_program"` Executes the given CGI program, where the location of the program is given by the *virtual* path to the program. Note that the script must return a valid MIME type. Unfortunately, you cannot pass query strings or path information to the script using the standard URL mechanisms. Thus expressions like:

```
<!--#exec cgi="/cgi-bin/script.cgi/path1/path2?query" -->
```

are invalid. The only way you can access the script is with the command:

```
<!--#exec cgi="/cgi-bin/script.cgi" -->
```

However, suppose the parsable script *stuff.shtml* contained the command:

```
<!--#exec cgi="/cgi-bin/script.cgi" -->
```

and you access the file *stuff.shtml* via the URL:

```
.../stuff.shtml/extra/path?query_string
```

In this case, `query_string` and `/extra/path` information *are* available to the script *script.cgi* called from *stuff.shtml*. This is illustrated in an example at the end of this section.

CONFIG

The `Config` command controls aspects of the output of the parsed commands, such as the formats of the date and size output strings, or the error message string to include if parsing fails. `Config` can take three different arguments, one argument per command. These are:

`errmsg="error_string"` Gives the error string to use if there is an error in parsing the parsable commands.

`timefmt="format"` Sets the format for printing dates. This format is specified as with the C `strftime` library call (`strftime` is commonly found on UNIX computers).

`sizefmt="bytes","abbrev"` Sets the format for the specification of file sizes. The value `bytes` prints file sizes in bytes, while `abbrev` uses kilobytes or megabytes as abbreviated forms, where applicable.

Examples of `Config`:

```
<!--#config sizefmt="abbrev"  -->

<!--#config timefmt="%m%d%y"  -->

<!--#config errmsg="Unable to parse scripts"  -->
```

EXAMPLE 3: SERVER-SIDE INCLUDES

The following example (shown in Figures 9.4 and 9.5) shows the use of server-side includes. The example consists of a main document *stuff.shtml* (the suffix *.shtml* is used to indicate parsable HTML documents) that includes a second parsable document *inc_file.shtml*, and that also executes the CGI program *test_script.cgi*. The listings for these examples are shown in Figure 9.4, while the browser rendering of the document *stuff.shtml* is shown in Figure 9.5.

In this example the document *stuff.shtml* is accessed using the URL:

```
http://leonardo:8080/stuff.shtml/extra/path/info?arg1+arg2
```

Note that this passes query strings and extra path information to *stuff.shtml*, just as if it were a gateway program (see Chapter 8 for more information about CGI programs and passed variables). The information is passed through the environment variables *QUERY_STRING* and *PATH_INFO*. All of these example documents are designed to print these environment variables. As seen in Figure 9.4, these variables are empty inside the parsable HTML documents. However, as shown at the bottom of Figure 9.5, these variables *are* present inside the

CGI program executed from within the parsable document. You can, therefore, access a parsable document and, through it, pass query information to a CGI program, just as if you were accessing the CGI program directly.

The `include` and `echo` commands are also illustrated in Figures 9.4 and 9.5. These can be used to print useful information about the current file. Remember, however, that you really want to avoid this type of include as much as possible, as every server execution slows the server response. For example, it is a waste of server resources to use the *LAST_MODIFIED* variable to display the last time you edited a simple HTML document, since you could just as easily add this information while editing it.

■■■■■■■ **Figure 9.4** Example of server-side includes. The main file is ***stuff.shtml***, which *includes* the file ***inc_file.shtml*** and also the output of the CGI program **test_script.cgi**. The listings for these three files are shown. The resulting HTML document, upon accessing the URL `http://leonardo:8080/stuff.shtml/extra/path/info?arg1+arg2`, is shown in Figure 9.5.

```
1. stuff.shtml

<html>

<head>

<title> Test of NCSA Server-side Includes </title>


<body>

<h1> Test of NCSA Server-side Includes </h1>


<pre>

Stuff.shtml was last modified:    <!--#flastmod virtual="/stuff.shtml"  -->.

Size of stuff.shtml is:           <!--#fsize file="stuff.shtml"  -->.

DOCUMENT_NAME =                    <!--#echo var="DOCUMENT_NAME" -->

DOCUMENT_URI =                     <!--#echo var="DOCUMENT_URI" -->

DATE_LOCAL =                       <!--#echo var="DATE_LOCAL" -->

QUERY_STRING =                     <!--#echo var="QUERY_STRING" -->

PATH_LOCAL =                       <!--#echo var="QUERY_STRING" -->
```

```
DATE_GMT =                         <!--#echo var="DATE_GMT" -->
LAST_MODIFIED =                    <!--#echo var="LAST_MODIFIED" -->
</pre>


<!--#config errmsg="Unable to parse scripts"  -->


<p><em>....now include inc_example.shtml....</em>


<!--#include file="inc_file.shtml" -->


<p> <em>..... now include test_script.cgi CGI program output...... </em>


<!--#exec cgi="/cgi-bin/test_script.cgi" -->
</body>
</html>
```

2. *inc_file.shtml*

```
<pre>
Inc_file.shtml last modified:     <!--#flastmod virtual="/inc_file.shtml"-->.
Size of inc_file.shtml is:        <!--#fsize file="inc_file.shtml"  -->.
DOCUMENT_NAME:                    <!--#echo var="DOCUMENT_NAME" -->
DOCUMENT_URI:                     <!--#echo var="DOCUMENT_URI" -->
DATE_LOCAL:                       <!--#echo var="DATE_LOCAL" -->
DATE_GMT                          <!--#echo var="DATE_GMT" -->
LAST_MODIFIED                     <!--#echo var="LAST_MODIFIED" -->


</pre>
```

3. *test_script.cgi* (in the `cgi-bin` directory)

```sh
#!/bin/sh


echo "Content-type: text/html"

echo

echo "<pre>"

echo "This is  CGI script output."

echo "QUERY_STRING is \"$QUERY_STRING\"."

echo "PATH_INFO =  \"$PATH_INFO\". "

echo "</pre>"
```

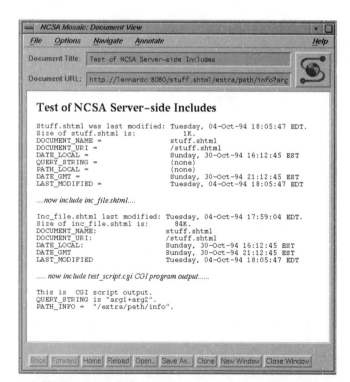

■■■■ **Figure 9.5** Browser rendering of the server-side executable document ***stuff.shtml*** when accessed using the URL `http://leonardo:8080/ stuff.shtml/extra/path/info?arg1+arg2.`

For additional information about server-side includes, and in particular for information on how to configure the NCSA HTTP server to allow server-side includes, you should consult the NCSA online documentation at:

```
http://hoohoo.ncsa.uiuc.edu/docs/tutorials/includes.html
```

SOME EXAMPLE CGI PROGRAMS

This section looks at a few example CGI programs, representing some of the common uses of this facility. The first example looks at a gateway program that returns a document containing a count of the number of times the page was accessed. The second looks at using a gateway program and the server-side include feature to insert a randomly selected HTML snippet into an HTML document. Finally, the third example looks at WebNotice, a large-scale gateway-program application, designed by the author. This package integrates 28 gateway programs, 19 HTML document templates, and 10 HTML documents, to create a Web-based system for depositing and viewing public notices.

EXAMPLE 4: PAGE ACCESS COUNTER

The following script answers the common question, "How do I include, within my page, a number indicating how many times the document has been accessed?" The following simple perl gateway program does just that. This program reads in the document to be returned to the client and edits it, replacing a dummy comment string in the document (the string `<!-- counter -->`) by the desired count. The count is obtained from a log file that counts the number of times the file has been accessed. The gateway program opens this log file, and increments the counter by 1. The program listing is found in Figure 9.6.

To use this gateway program, you must access the document via a URL of the form

```
http://some.where.edu/cgi-bin/counter.pl/path/file.html
```

where `path/file.html` is the path to the document, relative to the root of the server document directory.

The specific location of the file to be returned is given in the *PATH_TRANS-LATED* environment variable, which is assigned to the variable $path at line 5. Line 2 checks to make sure this variable actually exists—if it does not, this means that there was no extra path information in the URL, implying that the author forgot to reference a file. Lines 8 through 11 process the variable $path, to extract the path to the directory containing the document being returned ($path) as well as the name of the file being returned. The count file is then given the same name as the file, but preceded by a dot. Thus if the file

Figure 9.6 Listing of the perl gateway program **counter.pl**, which inserts an access count into a designated HTML document. The path to the designated HTML document is passed as *extra path* information in the URL used to access this program. Line numbers, in italics, are added for reference purposes only—they are not present in the original program.

```
1  #!/usr/local/bin/perl
2  if (defined($ENV{"PATH_TRANSLATED"}) ) {
3      $path = $ENV{"PATH_TRANSLATED"}   # get file from extra path info
4  }
5  else {
6      &f_error("No file specified\n");
7  }
8  $file     = $path;                    # Path to file to be processed
9  $cnt_file = $path;
10 $cnt_file =~ s/.*\///;                # Extract substring for counter filename
11 $path     =~ s/\/[\w-.;~]*$/\//;      # get path to directory
12
13 $cnt_file = $path.".".$cnt_file;      # counter filename = path/.filename
14
15 if( !(-e $cnt_file) ) {               # If count file doesn't exist, create it
16    open(CNTFILE, "> $cnt_file") ||
17            &f_error("Unable to create count file\n");
18    print CNTFILE "0";
19    close(CNTFILE);
20 }
21 $loops = 0;                           # try 4 times to lock the count file
22 while ( flock($cnt_file,2) == -1 )  {
23    $loops++;
24    if( $loops > 4) {
25        $cnt = "-1 (Unable to lock counter)\n";
```

```
26      goto PROCESS;                    # If unable to lock, skip it.
27  }
28      sleep 1;
29 }
30 open(CNTFILE, "+< $cnt_file")         # open the counter file
31          || &f_error("Unable to open counter file\n");
32 $cnt = <CNTFILE>;                      # get the current count
33 $cnt++;                                # increment count by one
34 seek(CNTFILE, 0, 0);                   # rewind to start of file
35 print CNTFILE "$cnt";                  # write out new count
36 close(CNTFILE);                        # close the count file
37 flock($cntfile, 8);                    # Unlock the count file
38
39 PROCESS:
40 open(FILE, $file)                      # Open file to process
41      || &f_error("Unable to open file for processing\n");
42 @array= <FILE>;                        # Read in the file
43 close(FILE);
44                                        # Print out the document
45 print "Content-type: text/html\n\n";
46 foreach (@array) {                     # scan for special string, and
47    s/<!-- counter -->/ $cnt /i;        # replace it by the count
48    print $_;
49 }
50 # Error Handling Subroutine
51 sub f_error {
52   print "Content-type text/plain\n\n";
53   print "<HTML><HEAD>\n<TITLE>Error In Counter Script</TITLE>";
54   print "\n</HEAD><BODY>\n<h2>Error</h2>\n<P>Error message: $_[0]";
```

```
55   print "\n<P> Please report this problem to someone.";

56   print "\n</BODY></HTML>";

57   die;

58 }
```

being returned is *home.html*, the count file will be named *.home.html*. Consequently, every file has its own distinct count file, with a matching name.

Line 15 checks to see if the count file exists—if it does not, lines 16 through 19 create it, and give it an initial value of 0.

Lines 22 through 29 attempt to *lock* the file (flock($cntfile,2)). Locking the file means that the perl program becomes the *only* program that can modify the file, and ensures that two users cannot simultaneously attempt to change the count file. The program tries four times to lock the file, waiting one second between attempts. If it fails, it sets a default value for the string containing the counter value ($cnt) and skips the part of the program that actually reads the count file. If it succeeds in locking the file, it proceeds to the next phase, beginning at line 30, where the count file is opened, the counter is read in and incremented by 1, and the count is rewritten to the file, overwriting the old value. The file is then closed and the lock is released (flock($cntfile, 8)), freeing it for use by other users.

Line 39 begins the processing of the file being returned to the client. The file is opened at line 40; at line 42 it is read, line by line, into the array @array. When this is finished, the file is closed (line 43).

Line 45 prints the required content-type header. Lines 46 through 48 print these data to standard output, and *replace* every occurrence of the string <!-- counter --> by the counter string (line 47)—this is either the counter value from line 33, or the error string from line 25.

And that is it. The count is inserted, the document is returned, and the counter has been incremented by 1.

What is missing from this program? Well, you might want to exclude accesses by your own machine or domain from the counting process, so one modification might be to restrict counting to certain domain names. Also, you may prefer to keep all the counters in a single counter database file, as opposed to having one file for each document. Finally, you should note that this example program only counts accesses that pass through the gateway program—if the document is accessed via the URL

```
http://some.where.edu/path/file.html
```

then the access is not counted. To avoid this problem you must invoke a counter from within a parsed HTML document.

These variations on page counters are available in a number of counter programs, many of which are far more sophisticated than the example. Some popular implementations are found at:

```
http://melmac.corp.harris.com/access_counts.html
```

```
http://www.best.com/~kroberts/acc_kntr.html
```

You will find many other examples by searching the Yahoo, Lycos, or other sites using the string "page counter." Yahoo, I believe, devotes an entire page to this topic.

EXAMPLE 5: INSERTING
A RANDOMLY SELECTED HTML FRAGMENT

One cute parsable HTML document trick is to use a gateway program to insert a randomly selected HTML snippet within a given HTML document. The perl program **rot-new.pl** is a simple implementation that selects a file at random from a specified directory and inserts it inline within the parsed document. Assuming that the program is located in the server's *cgi-bin/* directory, the relevant HTML parsable comment for adding this server-side include instruction is:

```
<!--#exec cgi="/cgi-bin/rot-new.pl" -->
```

When the server parses this document, it will replace this comment string by the output of the program **rot-new.pl**.

Figure 9.7 gives the listing for the program **rot-new.pl**.

This program is simple. At line 8 it prints a text/html content-type header— recall that this is required of programs returning data to a parsed HTML document. The second block, at lines 12–14, gets a directory listing for the directory /svc/www/InsTest—this is the directory that contains the insertions. Lines 15–17 convert the filenames into absolute paths, excluding non-data files (i.e., directories), and store the list of files in the array @filenames.

■■■■■■ **Figure 9.7** Listing for the program **rot-new.pl,** which randomly selects an HTML document segment for insertion within an HTML document. Line numbers (in italics) are added for illustration only, and are not present in the original program.

```
1    #!/usr/local/bin/perl

2    # rotator.pl

3    # Author:  Ian Graham

4    #          Information Commons, University of Toronto

5    #          <igraham@hprc.utoronto.ca>

6    # Version: 0.1b.    Date:    July 13 1995

7

8    print "Content-type: text/html\n\n";        # print content-type header

9

10   $include_path="/svc/www/InsTest";           # Directory containing include files

11                                               # Second Block: Get listing for

12   if( !opendir(DIR, $include_path)) { # the directory containing the inserts

13      &f_error("Unable to open notices directory\n", __LINE__, __FILE__); }

14   @tmp = readdir(DIR);                         # Read list of filenames; then check

15     foreach (@tmp) {                           # to see if they are files, and not

16                                                # directories(-T tests for "real" files

17       push(@filenames, $include_path."/".$_) if -T $include_path."/".$_; }

18   close(DIR);

19   $last_index = $#filenames;                   # Get index of last entry

20   $last_index += 1;                            # in array of filenames

21

22   if($last_index < 0) {

23     print " no files to insert ...\n"; die; # no stuff, so don't do nuthin'

24   }

25   else {                                       # If there are files to be

26                                                # inserted, select one at random
```

```
27      srand(time);                                # and print it to stdout.

28      $rand_index = int(rand($last_index));

29      open(TEMP, $filenames[$rand_index]) ||      # Open selected file --

30          &f_error("Unable to open insertion file.\n", __LINE__,__FILE__);

31      @insertion = <TEMP>; close(TEMP);

32      print @insertion;                           # Print contents to standard output

33  }

34  # -------------- FINISHED ----------- FINISHED --------------

35  # Error Handling Subroutine

36

37  sub f_error {                                   # What to do if there is an error

38    print "Content-type text/html\n\n";

39    print "Fatal error  at line $_[1] in file $_[2].\n";

40    print "Please send mail to: <BR>\n";

41    print "<A HREF=\"mailto:webmaster@comm.ut.ca\">webmaster@comm.ut.ca</A><BR>\n";

42    print "to inform us of this error. If you can please, quote the URL\n";

43    print "of the page that gave this error.\n<HR>\n";

44    die "Fatal Error: $_[0] at line $_[1] in file $_[2] \n";

45  }
```

The subsequent if statement at line 22 checks to see if there are any files in this list—the program exits if there are none. The alternate block of the if, beginning at line 25, selects a filename at random (line 28), opens the file (line 29), reads in the file content and then closes the file (line 31), and prints the content to standard output (line 32). The output is the text included within the HTML document.

EXAMPLE 6: WEBNOTICE—A WEB-BASED SYSTEM FOR DISTRIBUTING NOTICES

WebNotice is a Web-based package for posting and distributing notices on the World Wide Web. WebNotice uses the **FORM** interface to collect information from users, and uses gateway programs to process the submitted data, to archive that data in a server-side database, and to extract data from the database for return to the user. Any user can access the database to retrieve posted notices, but only authorized users can add new notices to the system—authorization is accomplished using the Basic authentication scheme, discussed in Chapter 7. The stored notices are organized into *groups*, so that notices can be posted under different group categories (in this example, the groups are different university departments). Each group has its own distinct set of authorized users, and a user can only post under groups for which he or she is authorized.

WebNotice consists of 28 gateway programs, 19 HTML document templates (read in by the gateway programs, and processed into complete HTML documents), 10 HTML documents, and a 30-page instruction manual, so it is clearly impossible to explain the whole package in this short section. The following will simply give an outline of the package, and will provide an explanation of how some of the important parts work. The intent here is not to explain the detailed functioning of any particular component, but to give an idea of how the overall design of a large gateway programming system takes place.

The WebNotice system is currently running at a number of sites. To see how it works, you can visit the original home of the package, at

```
http://www.hprc.utoronto.ca/cgi-reg/notices_main.pl
```

Figure 9.8 shows the organization of the different programs in the WebNotice system. The arrows show the flow as the user traverses the system. Everything starts with the program **notices_main.pl**. This program returns a simple HTML document that describes the various options. The program generates the document by reading in a simple HTML template and customizing it for the directory locations and filenames of the local site. An example of the resulting page is shown in Figure 9.9.

ADDING A NOTICE WITH WEBNOTICE

There are several possible options shown in Figure 9.9—as an example, we shall follow the link to "Add a notice." Selecting this link accesses the gate-

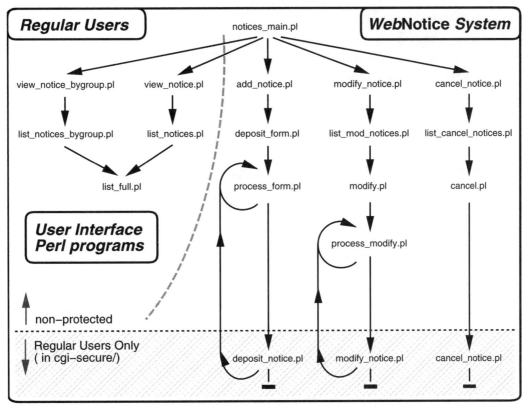

Figure 9.8 A schematic diagram showing some of the different perl programs in the WebNotice notice distribution system. The arrows show the possible hypertext links that relate the different documents. The loops following the **process_form.pl** and **process_modify.pl** programs indicate that the results returned by these programs can produce HTML **FORM**s that have **ACTION**s linked to either of the two destinations, depending on the data.

way program **add_notice.pl**. This program checks a server-side database to obtain a list of all the groups registered with the system, and returns a page containing this list, within a selectable **FORM**. This page is shown in Figure 9.10. The list of groups (here, a list of university departments) is presented as a list of selectable items (radio buttons) in a fill-in **FORM**. The user selects the group under which he or she wishes to submit a notice, and presses the **FORM** Submit button—in this example, the user has selected the *Department of Statistics*. Pressing the Submit button sends the **FORM** data to the server, and to the program **deposit_form.pl**.

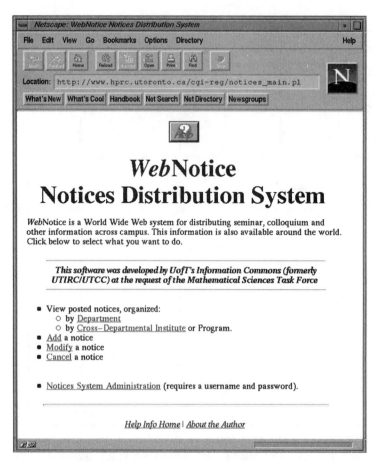

■■■■■■ **Figure 9.9** The HTML document returned by the program **notices_main.pl**. This is the home page for the WebNotice system and provides links to all the functional components of the system.

THE NOTICE FILL-IN FORM—DEPOSIT_FORM.PL

Figure 9.11 shows the document returned by the program **deposit_form.pl**. Note how this gateway program was accessed using the GET method—you can see the encoded group information appended to the URL. This allows the user to *bookmark* this page, so that he or she can return here without having to restart at the **notices_home.pl** page. This judicious choice of the GET method makes it easy for users to bookmark pages they are likely to reference often.

The document returned by **deposit_form.pl** contains an extensive fill-in FORM, into which the user enters the information required of a notice

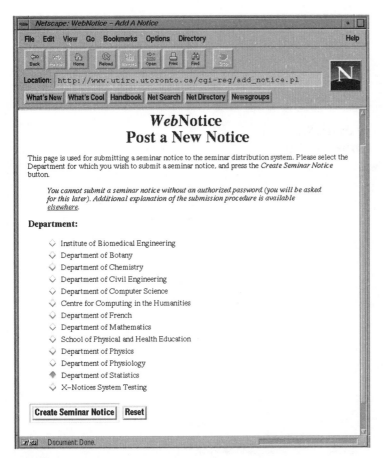

Figure 9.10 The HTML document returned by the program **add_notice.pl**. This page lists, within an HTML **FORM**, all the groups under which notices can be deposited. The program **add_notice.pl** obtains this information by reading a server database.

announcement—there are fields for the time, date, and location of the event (this system is designed for notification of events such as concerts or seminars), the name of the presenter, and so on.

Not obvious here is that the **FORM** also contains the "hidden" input element:

```
<INPUT TYPE="hidden" NAME="dept" VALUE="stats">
```

This was inserted into the **FORM** by the program **deposit_form.pl,** based on the data passed in the query string. Thus, when the data in this new **FORM** are sent the server, they will still include the name of the group under which the notice is to be recorded.

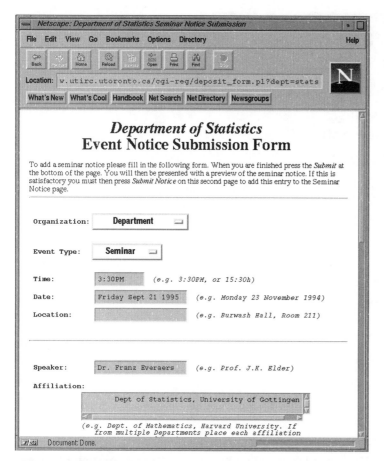

Figure 9.11 The HTML document returned by the program **deposit_form.pl**. This document contains a **FORM** into which the user enters the information required by the notices system. This program is accessed using the GET method (see the URL in the "Location" window), so that this fill-in **FORM** document can be bookmarked for future reference.

PROCESSING AND CHECKING
THE FORM DATA—PROCESS_FORM.PL

When the user completes the **FORM**, he or she presses the Submit button at the bottom of the page. This **FORM** uses the POST method to send the form data to the gateway program **process_form.pl**. **Process_form.pl** processes the incoming data and checks for obvious errors, such as missing fields, errors in the time and date, and so on. If there are no errors, the program returns a preview of the posted notice for confirmation by the user—an example preview document is shown in Figure 9.12. Notice the "Accept?" yes-or-no checkboxes, and the associated Submit button. The *entire* data content of the notice is stored, using `<INPUT TYPE="hidden" ...>` elements, within the "Yes/No" acceptance **FORM**. The **ACTION** of this **FORM** points to the program **deposit_notice.pl**, which actually adds the notice to the notices database. If the user decides the notice is acceptable, selects "Yes," and presses Submit, the data contained within the hidden elements are sent to the program **deposit_notice.pl**.

ENCODING DATA IN "HIDDEN" ELEMENTS

The **FORM** data must be processed prior to being placed within the **VALUE** strings of "hidden" elements `<INPUT NAME="..." TYPE="hidden" VALUE="...">`. In particular, double quotation marks (") must be encoded using their entity references, as otherwise they will prematurely terminate the value string. In addition, any greater than (>) character should be encoded, as some browsers mistakenly use these characters to terminate the **INPUT** element in which they are contained.

When the browser receives this string, it will parse the string, and replace any character or entity reference by the correct character, but only after it has interpreted the HTML markup. Thus if the returned HTML markup contains the hidden element

```
<INPUT TYPE="hidden" NAME="stuff" VALUE="&lt;BOO&quot;&gt;">
```

the client will parse the **VALUE** string and convert it into the string `<BOO">`. When the **FORM** containing this hidden element is submitted, the string `<BOO">` will be URL-encoded and sent to the server, so that the entity encoding in the original data is lost. Recall that, as far as the browser is concerned, entity references and character references *are* no different from the characters they represent. This can be a problem if the data within the hidden form contains HTML markup, since here you often need to *preserve* entity references— for example, so that simple character strings (`&lt;tag&gt;`) do not get converted into markup tags (`<tag>`) by this conversion process. Thus, if you need to preserve entity references, you must do the following encodings of the string [prior to placing it the **VALUE:**]

- encode all ampersand characters in the text string as `&amp;`
- encode all double quotation symbols as `&quot;`
- encode all right angle brackets as `&gt;`

The first step encodes the leading character of each entity or character reference—for example, the original string é becomes &eacute;. This is processed by the client browser back to the string é, which brings you back full circle when the data are returned to the server.

PROCESSING AN ERROR-FREE FORM

As indicated in Figure 9.8, the program **deposit_notice.pl** is located in a directory (here labeled *cgi-secure/*) different from that containing **process_form.pl**, **deposit_form.pl**, and so on—**deposit_notice.pl** is located in a directory *protected* by the Basic authentication scheme. As soon as a user accesses **deposit_notice.pl**, he or she is challenged for an authorization username and password. If the username and password information entered by the user are in error, access is immediately refused. If the username/password pair is acceptable because it is a valid pair, the program **deposit_notice.pl** then checks to make sure this user is authorized to deposit under the group being considered—the username and password may be valid, but only for *another* departmental group (e.g., for the Department of Physiology). The WebNotice system checks the username against a database that matches usernames with groups—if the user is *not* authorized to submit notices under the Department of Statistics, the program **deposit_notice.pl** returns the server directive

```
Status: 401 Not authorized
```

which is the HTTP status message indicating authorization failure. The server subsequently returns the 401 header message to the client. In general, the client will tell the user that authorization failed, and will give the user the option of trying again with another username and password.

Finally, if the username/password pair is acceptable, and the particular user is allowed to deposit notices under the given department, then the notices data are decoded and stored in the notices database. The deposited notice can then be retrieved for viewing (**list_notices.pl** and **list_notices_bygroup.pl**), modification (**modify.pl**), or deletion (**cancel.pl**). The process of modification and cancellation both pass through programs in the *cgi-secure* directory, ensuring that authentication is again required before changes are permitted.

PROCESSING A FORM CONTAINING FIELD ERRORS—PROCESS_FORM.PL

It is also possible that the data passed to **process_form.pl** contained errors in the time, date, or other fields. In this case, **process_form.pl** creates a table of the errors and returns a document containing both a list of these errors and a

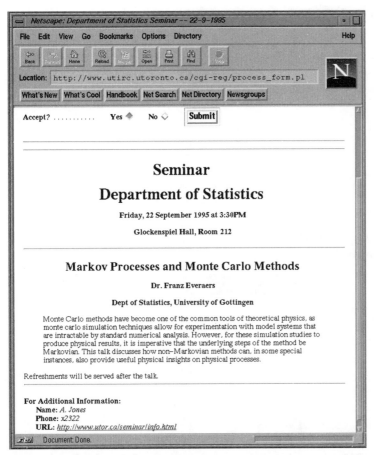

Figure 9.12 If the **FORM** in Figure 9.11 is properly completed and submitted, the user is presented with this "preview" of the notice. It contains a small **FORM**, which the user uses to accept or reject the notice. This **FORM** contains `<INPUT TYPE="hidden"...>` elements that contain the entire data content of the fill-in **FORM** shown in Figure 9.11.

duplicate fill-in **FORM** containing the data from the user's first attempt. An example of such a document is shown in Figure 9.13.

ENCODING **VALUE**s IN **INPUT** AND **OPTION** ELEMENTS

As when constructing "hidden" **INPUT** elements, the double quote (") and right angle bracket (>) placed in the **VALUE** (or **NAME**) attributes of any **INPUT** or **OPTION** element must encoded, so that the double quotation

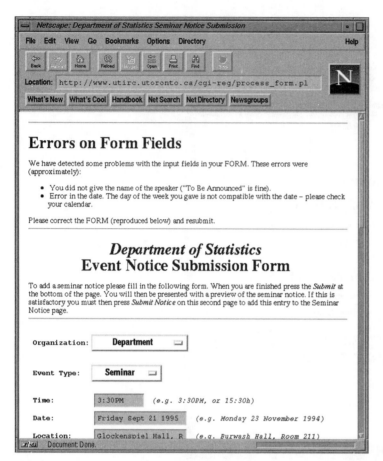

Figure 9.13 The **FORM** returned by the program **process_form.pl** if there were errors in the **FORM** input fields. This document lists the errors at the top, and then reproduces the fill-in **FORM** for correction by the user. This **FORM**, when submitted, once again accesses the program **process_form.pl**. The issues involved in assuring that the **FORM** data are safely returned in this second form, and in "hidden" elements within a **FORM**, are discussed in the text.

mark does not prematurely end the string, and so that the greater than symbol does not prematurely end the element on poorly behaved browsers. Similarly, if you wish to preserve the distinction between characters and their encodings, which is required if you wish to preserve HTML markup strings (particularly for the special characters <, >, &, and "), you must also encode all ampersand characters as &.

USE **TEXTAREA** INPUT ELEMENT
FOR USER INPUT OF **HTML** MARKUP

Many of the possible problems with parsing HTML code within **VALUE** or other strings can be solved by using **TEXTAREA** input elements whenever HTML markup input is desired. In particular, any **TEXTAREA** text content sent by the server to the client is parsed by the client (entity references are converted to the appropriate characters), but HTML *markup* is not interpreted. Therefore, when generating **TEXTAREA** content to be returned with a **FORM,** you do not have the same concerns about converting angle brackets to entity references, although you must still convert all ampersand characters into & to preserve the original entity references.

GENERAL ISSUES
IN GATEWAY PROGRAM DESIGN

There are many problems that will crop up as you write gateway programs, as is the case with any programming project. There are four particularly common errors, in this author's experience, that occur when writing gateway programs. Your list will assuredly be different, but hopefully this section will help you avoid some basic pitfalls!

Check for the correct HTTP method. The environment variable *REQUEST_METHOD* indicates the method being used to access the script. If the method is incorrect (the request used the GET method, but the program expects POST), you should return an HTML document containing an appropriate error message.

Check for input. Your gateway program should always check for the existence of input (if input is expected), either in the *QUERY_STRING* environment variable or at standard input, depending on the HTTP method. Programs often behave very badly if they attempt to read nonexistent environment variables, or an empty standard input stream. You should check for this error, and return an appropriate error message if an error occurs.

Check for errors in input fields. Check the input fields for obvious errors— and never trust the data that has been sent. Innocuous mistakes, such as an unexpected negative number where a positive one is anticipated, can create havoc if you haven't "trapped" for all possible errors.

Remember that the client parses returned text. Remember that the text you return inside a **NAME** or **VALUE** string or inside a **TEXTAREA** region will be parsed, and that all character and entity references will be converted, by the browser, into the corresponding ISO Latin-1 characters. If you do not want this to happen, you must *encode* the ampersand characters in the original data prior to placing the data in the **FORM** being sent to the client.

WANT TO OBTAIN WEBNOTICE?

The WebNotice software package is, like many World Wide Web applications, freely available over the Internet. If you want to find out more about WebNotice, and perhaps obtain your own copy of the software, just access the URL:

```
http://www.hprc.utoronto.ca/Software/webnotice.html
```

This document provides additional information about WebNotice, as well as instructions for obtaining the software.

CLIENT-SIDE EXECUTABLE PROGRAMS

The emphasis to this point has been on programs that run on the server using data passed from the client. Sometimes, however, you want to execute a program on the *client*. For example, you might want the user to be able to start up a USENET news reading program on the client by pressing a **FORMs** button or a hypertext link. Or, you might want the user to be able to start up an interactive teleconferencing session in the same manner. Both these situations require that the server send information to the client requesting the execution of a program, or actually send a program to the client for execution. For example, the newsreader could be launched by sending the client a simple start-up script, while the teleconferencing example would require a more complicated script that both launches the teleconferencing program and provides the information needed to contact the other party.

Although clearly a powerful tool, client-side executable programs incur many security risks, because the program arriving from the server is an unknown quantity—the client has no way of knowing what it will actually do. For example, a vicious server administrator could create a script that deletes files on the client computer. These very real possibilities warrant efforts on your part to protect your system.

The following discussion outlines how client-side program execution is allowed, and includes hints for ensuring the security of this procedure. It also discusses the packages vsafecsh and w3launch, which are useful tools for facilitating safe execution of client-side programs.

SENDING THE SCRIPT TO THE CLIENT

The first stage is to send the executable script or program from the server to the client. This is done from a CGI gateway program, using a special MIME content-type in the response headers (see Chapter 8) that tells the client that the data being sent by the gateway program is a program or script that the client should execute. As an example, the following header could be used:

```
Content-type:  application/x-www-local-exec
```

Note that the type *must* be application, while the subtype name must begin with x-. The x- prefix is used for all local, experimental, or otherwise unregistered MIME types. This example uses x-www-local-exec, but you can choose whatever you like.

Here is an example of a server-side CGI program that sends the above content-type header, followed by the executable script, to the client. The example is a simple UNIX Bourne-shell script:

```
#!/bin/sh

echo Content-type:  application/x-www-local-exec

echo

echo "#!/bin/sh"

#

#    Bourne shell scripts to run on the client. For example, this

#    could start up some client program, and use server environment

#    variables to control the configuration of the program

#

#    This UNIX example simply launches a local xterm window running the

#    tin Usenet newsreader program

#

echo

echo "xterm -display $DISPLAY -e  /usr/local/bin/tin"

echo
```

When a client browser accesses this CGI program, the browser receives the following message from the HTTP server:

```
HTTP/1.0 200 OK

Date: Monday, 03-Oct-94 22:19:31 GMT

Server: NCSA/1.3

MIME-version: 1.0

Content-type:  application/x-www-local-exec

Content-Length: 57


#!/bin/sh


xterm -display $DISPLAY -e  /usr/local/bin/tin
```

which includes the content-type header that was generated by the CGI program. The next step is to configure the client to know what to do with this special content-type, and with the message body.

CONFIGURING THE CLIENT

The browser must be configured to know what to do with messages of the `application/x-www-local-exec` MIME type. This is done by adding information about this content-type to the browser's configuration files. For Mosaic for X-Windows, this means editing the *mailcap* file, which is the Mosaic for X-Windows file that matches MIME types to helper programs. For this simple example, the required line is

```
application/x-www-local-exec;  /bin/sh %s
```

which tells Mosaic for X-Windows to pass any document of type `application/x-www-local-exec` to the program **/bin/sh** (the Bourne shell) for execution. The `%s` is the symbolic representation of the document sent to the client. Similar configurations are possible on Macintosh or PC browsers, in which case, the new MIME types can often be added using a pull-down menu for helper applications.

The above example of a client-side program requires a UNIX client—because of the UNIX Bourne-shell script being passed as an executable program, and because of the use of the UNIX tin newsreader as the client-side program. This illustrates how strongly client-side program execution can be tied to the client architecture. One way to resolve these differences is to have the server-side script try to guess the platform, based on the content of the

HTTP_USER_AGENT environment variable. The gateway program can then send the program or script file relevant to the client hardware and software.

SECURITY ISSUES

The preceding example program is harmless; however, scripts that contain the following lines pose greater concern to the local user running the script:

```
#!/bin/sh
```

```
xterm -display my.home.display:0      # pop Xterm somewhere else

/bin/rm -r $HOME                      # delete all your files!!
```

This script would open an xterm window on the remote machine my.home.display but connected to the local user's machine and account, thus giving the person at my.home.display access to the local user's entire directory. The second command deletes, recursively, all the local user's files. Obviously you do not want to allow scripts that can do such things! Fortunately client-side security features can be added that significantly reduce or eliminate the risk of such nightmarish events.

There are essentially two approaches to improved security. The first approach is to execute all programs on a client using a "secure" local shell. To do this, the *mailcap* (or other) file can be modified to direct execution to this safe shell, for example:

```
application/x-www-local-exec;   /usr/local/bin/secure_sh %s
```

where secure_sh is a special shell program that includes extra security features. This might run under the client system's restricted shell (often called **rsh**), which restricts a program's ability to modify variables or files, or it might contain internal tests that check for dangerous commands. (The vsafecsh program, described below, is one package that implements this type of protection, in this case for scripts that are executed using the UNIX csh shell.)

The second option is to design special client-side programs, place them on every client and in a special directory, and allow the program passed from the server to access *only* these predesigned packages. For example, specially prepared, safe client scripts for starting up the newsreader or the teleconferencing package could be placed on each client machine, with the scripts sent from the server being allowed to access only these safe client scripts. Careful design of the small client scripts can significantly enhance the security of the local systems. This, in part, is the approach taken by w3launch.

The following are brief descriptions of the vsafecsh and w3launch utilities.

Vsafecsh

Vsafecsh is a C program that acts as a protective gateway for client-side csh programs executed on UNIX platforms. Ordinarily, you would enable csh execution on a client using a *mailcap* entry such as:

```
application/x-www-localc-exec; csh -f %s
```

However, as described previously, this is not secure. Security can be improved by replacing this entry with

```
application/x-www-localc-exec; vsafecsh -f %s
```

which causes the csh script passed from the server to be initially parsed, and checked, by vsafecsh. Thus, vsafecsh acts as a safety filter for downloaded csh scripts.

Vsafecsh forks and executes *only* those executable programs that are authorized by the user. Currently, the list of allowed programs is compiled into the code of vsafecsh, so the user or workstation administrator must recompile vsafecsh for any newly allowed programs. However, this is a small price to pay in exchange for safe client-side execution.

Additional information about vsafecsh is found at:

```
http://www.eit.com/software/vsafecsh/vsafecsh.html
```

Vsafecsh was written by Vinay Kumar of Enterprise Integration Technologies.

W3launch

Much of the difficulty in setting up secure client-side execution is solved through a package called w3launch. W3launch, available for both UNIX systems and PCs running Windows, allows a client site administrator to register certain special programs as *launchable* from a server-provided script. This registration ensures that only secure programs can be executed, and allows the administrator to control access to these programs. W3launch consists of client and server software for administering these registered programs, and for creating server-side "launch" scripts that access these programs.

Additional information about w3launch is found at:

```
http://bmbwww.leeds.ac.uk/w3launch/home.htm
```

The source codes and executables are available from this document. W3launch was written by Jon Maber of the University of Leeds.

CGI TOOLS

This section lists various CGI gateway programs and utilities. Some, such as e-mail handlers, may be generally useful, while others may be too specific to be of general use. However, in general they do serve as useful models for developing custom applications.

This collection is not complete—nor could it be. You are advised to check the Yahoo (or other) Net directory for more extensive lists of gateway programming resources. Some other useful lists of CGI programming resources are at:

```
http://homepage.seas.upenn.edu/~mengwong/perlhtml.html
```

```
http://www.oac.uci.edu/indiv/ehood/perlWWW/
```

```
http://www.cyserv.com/pttong/cgi.html
```

```
http://edb518ea.edb.utexas.edu/cgix/cgix.html
```  (Macintosh CGI)

```
http://128.172.69.106:8080/cgi-bin/cgis.html
```  (Shareware CGI site)

CGI EMAIL HANDLER

This package, created by Thomas Boutell, is a simple CGI program that allows WWW clients to send e-mail messages to a restricted set of allowed recipients. To configure the package you will need to create FORMs-based HTML documents for composing the letter: you need to create a separate FORM for each of the permitted recipients. You also need to create a server-side database of allowed recipients, used by email to verify that the user is sending mail to an authorized person.

This package is quite simple, and has been used as a model for several other, more extensive, implementations. Additional information about this package, including directions to the various component parts you will need, is found at:

```
http://siva.cshl.org/email/index.html
```

CGI FEEDBACK FORM

This package of utilities, by Arjan de Vet, uses a FORMs interface to let the client send feedback information to the server administrator. It consists of a small C-language CGI program that reads the FORM data and converts the FORM information into a mail message to the site administrator.

The package is available at:

```
ftp://ftp.win.tue.nl/pub/infosystems/www/wwwutils.tar.gz
```

This archive also contains other interesting gateway utilities.

CYBERVIEW 3D DOCUMENT GENERATOR

Cyberview 3D is a CGI package, combined with an underlying 3D graphics engine, that can return rendered 3D graphics images to a client, with viewpoints and orientations determined from the user's input. This is an elegant package, and illustrates nicely some of the interesting ways that the CGI can be used to interface the Web with extremely sophisticated server-side resources.

Additional information about Cyberview 3D, including information on obtaining the package, is found at:

```
http://www.geom.umn.edu/apps/cyberview3d/about.html
```

Cyberview 3D was created by Paul Burchard.

FAKESSI.PL—CERN SERVER-SIDE INCLUDES SCRIPT

Fakessi.pl is a perl script that provides NCSA server-side include functionality to the CERN server. Fakessi.pl is a gateway program that parses appropriate HTML documents (i.e., those documents marked as "parsable") for the NCSA-style server-side include directives, and replaces these directives by the appropriate data. For this to work, the CERN server must be configured to map all files with extension *.shtml* (or whatever extension is chosen for parsable HTML) onto the fakessi.pl gateway.

Additional information about fakessi.pl, including downloading instructions, is found at

```
http://sw.cse.bris.ac.uk/WebTools/fakessi.html
```

Fakessi.pl is being developed by Steff Watkins.

MORE PAGE COUNTERS

Of course, there are many, many page counters. Chuck Musciano has written an elegant C-language CGI program that can maintain a counts database for an arbitrarily large number of different HTML documents. Conversely, Ken Roberts has written an extremely simple perl CGI script that is included using a parsed HTML document, but that can be used by only a single document. The details (and/or source code) can be found, respectively, at the URLs:

```
http://melmac.corp.harris.com/access_counts.html
```

`http://www.best.com/~kroberts/acc_kntr.html`

CONVERT UNIX MAN PAGES TO HTML

There are several utilities for dynamically converting UNIX man pages into HTML documents. These allow for remote access to UNIX system manuals, and provides a model of how large collections of data can be dynamically integrated into a Web site.

MAN2HTML

Man2html is a perl program by Earl Hood that can read UNIX man pages, in formatted nroff form only, and produce HTML as output. Although you can do this on a per-file basis, man2html is designed to be used in a CGI program; instructions are included with the distribution on how to do this, along with an example man.cgi script. This gives WWW clients access to all your UNIX online documentation. You can also configure man2html to include hypertext links to other man pages related to the one you are reading. In addition, man2html supports the `man -k keyword` man page search facility.

Additional information about man2html is found at the URL:

`http://www.oac.uci.edu/indiv/ehood/man2html.doc.html`

Man2html was written by Earl Hood.

BBC_MAN2HTML

Bbc_man2html.pl is a perl program for distributing UNIX man pages via a World Wide Web server. Bbc_man2html.pl uses the **ISINDEX** element to prompt for a particular man page—the user enters the desired man page title in the query box. At present `man -k keyword` searching is not implemented. Bbc_man2html.pl uses the RosettaMan program (discussed below) to format the man pages into HTML, so you also need this program.

Bbc_man2html.pl is available at:

`ftp://src.doc.ic.ac.uk/computing/information-systems/www/tools/translators/`

Bbc_man2html.pl was written by Brooks Cutter.

ROSETTAMAN: UNIX MAN PAGE TO HTML

RosettaMan is a filter for UNIX-style manual pages. It takes as input man pages formatted for a variety of UNIX flavors (not just [tn]roff source) and produces as output a variety of file formats. RosettaMan is a tcl script and requires the interpreters that come with the tcl distribution.

The RosettaMan archive can be found at:

```
ftp://ftp.cs.berkeley.edu/ucb/people/phelps/tcltk/rman.tar.Z
```

RosettaMan is copyrighted by T. A. Phelps.

GENERAL-PURPOSE CGI LIBRARIES

One of the most tedious aspects of writing a CGI program is parsing the environment variables, command-line arguments, or standard input data to the program. These data are encoded using the URL syntax, so that a gateway program must first decode the information before it can be used. There are currently several packages that can help in this process, by providing a library of routines for doing these basic tasks. This section briefly describes these packages.

CGIC—AN ANSII C LIBRARY FOR CGI PROGRAMMING

Thomas Boutell, the provider of many useful Web resources, has made available his cgic C library. Cgic contains routines for parsing **FORM** data, correcting for well-known browser errors, and contains stable exception and error handling. There is also a debugging mode, useful when developing new CGI applications. There are also routines to handle the more standard **FORM** data types, such as bounds checking and multiple-choice selection.

Additional information about cgic, including downloading instructions, can be found at:

```
http://sunsite.unc.edu/boutell/cgic/cgic1.tar.Z
```

The cgic package is being developed by Thomas Boutell.

EIT CGI LIBRARY

Enterprise Integration Technologies has made available a library of C functions that are extremely useful in constructing CGI programs. Included are routines for parsing input from **FORM** or **ISINDEX** queries, routines for generating MIME response headers, and much more. Details about the different available functions are found at

```
http://wsk.eit.com/wsk/dist/doc/libcgi/libcgi.html
```

while the source code and executable libraries are available from

    http://wsk.eit.com/wsk/dist/

in subdirectories corresponding to your operating system, and below that in the subdirectories named *libcgi*. For example, if you are using the IRIX operating system, the libcgi material is at:

    http://wsk.eit.com/wsk/dist/irix/libcgi/

If you don't find your operating system in this list, just go to one of the other directories and download source code.

UNCGI

Uncgi is a useful front-end package that handles parsing for you. Uncgi decodes all the **FORM** fields and places them in environment variables. Uncgi then calls your processing program (C, perl, or whatever), passing to it these environment variables. Note that this may be a problem if the string being passed in an environment variable becomes too large, since some systems place limits on the size of environment variables.

Additional information about uncgi, including downloading instructions, is available at:

    http://www.hyperion.com/~koreth/uncgi.html

Uncgi is written by Steven Grimm.

LIBWWW-PERL—LIBRARY
FOR GENERAL WEB APPLICATIONS

Libwww-perl is a library package of perl (Version 4) functions that provides a useful API for writing Web applications. This is an excellent, general-purpose perl library, designed for a variety of Web applications, both on the client and server side. This package is highly recommended to any serious Web programmers. Note, however, that libwww-perl was *not* designed specifically for CGI programming, so that it is not ideal for CGI applications.

Additional information about libwww-perl, including downloading instructions and copyright information, is available at:

    http://www.ics.uci.edu/pub/websoft/libwww-perl/

The libwww-perl library is written by Roy Fielding, of the University of California at Irvine.

DATABASE CGI GATEWAY PROGRAMS

Needless to say, there is great interest in using the World Wide Web as a front end to sophisticated database packages. This requires the construction of gateway programs to connect the **FORM** or **ISINDEX**-based query input mechanisms of the WWW with the backend SQL (or other) mechanisms used by databases such as Sybase, ORACLE, and WAIS. The following is a list of current efforts at constructing these interfaces, including instructions on how to obtain more information. All these packages will require customization to your particular database requirements; nevertheless, they provide a powerful starting point for integrating WWW applications with your database technologies.

If you are currently using a commercial database product, then you should also contact your vendor; because of the growth of the Web, several database companies have developed gateway tools for interfacing their products with **ISINDEX** and **FORM**s-based queries.

WAIS GATEWAYS

WAIS, for Wide Area Information Servers, is an extremely popular Internet network publishing and textual database system. WAIS is designed as a client/server system, with WAIS clients able to interrogate WAIS databases using a well-defined protocol. This protocol is supported by a number of WWW clients, so that it is often possible to directly interrogate a WAIS server by constructing a URL (with appropriate query strings) that points to that WAIS server.

However, many clients still do not support the WAIS protocol, and in many cases this direct method is not ideal for accessing WAIS servers. Often it is easier to interact with a **FORM** interface designed to construct WAIS queries in a manner more convenient to the user. For these reasons, there are currently several gateway programs that allow non-WAIS-capable clients to access a WAIS server, and that allow for sophisticated **FORM**s interfaces to WAIS servers. The following is a list of some of the server-side CGI packages designed to accomplish these tasks.

BASIC WAIS

The NCSA HTTP server distribution comes with several small CGI programs, including wais.pl, a small perl program written by Tony Sanders. Wais.pl uses the **ISINDEX** mechanism to obtain a query string from the user, passes this string to a local WAIS database query engine (waisq), and returns the results to the user as an HTML document. This is a simple and easy-to-understand perl script that has served as the basis for a number of other WAIS gateway programs.

Wais.pl is available at the NCSA gateway program archive:

```
ftp://ftp.ncsa.uiuc.edu/Web/httpd/Unix/ncsa_httpd/cgi/wais.tar.Z
```

SON OF WAIS

Son-of-wais.pl is a perl script based on the original wais.pl package from NCSA. Son-of-wais.pl adds nice formatting of the returned data and more complete instructions for the user. The perl package is available at:

```
http://dewey.lib.ncsu.edu/staff/morgan/son-of-wais.html
```

(the perl code is part of the HTML document). Son-of-wais.pl was written by Eric Lease Morgan of North Carolina State University Libraries. Eric does point out that the package kidofwais.pl (described in the next section) is a significant improvement upon son-of-wais.pl.

KIDOFWAIS

Kidofwais.pl is another perl script WAIS gateway program based on wais.pl, but with significant functionality improvements over both wais.pl and son-of-wais.pl. Kidofwais.pl also uses the **ISINDEX** query interface, but allows for pattern searches (`astro*` matches any word beginning with "astro") as well as complex Boolean searches. The program returns search results complete with useful information about the resulting items, such as document type and length. In addition, when the documents are retrieved, the search string is highlighted in boldface, for easier location and identification.

Additional information is available at:

```
http://www.cso.uiuc.edu/grady.html
```

which includes pointers to the perl packages you will need (kidofwais.pl and print_hit_bold.pl) and to other documents with additional information on installing and configuring the package. Kidofwais.pl was written by Michael Grady.

SFGATE

SFgate is another perl-based WAIS gateway program but is distinctly different from wais.pl or its derivatives. SFgate does not access a server-side WAIS query engine. Instead WAIS client software is built into SFgate, so that it can itself query any Internet-accessible WAIS database. In addition, SFgate supports a **FORMs** query interface, so that the user can select various data-bases (searching several at the same time) and enter complex query information into text input boxes. You can also create customized **FORMs** interfaces, to make it easier for your users to access the database.

SFgate is designed to work well with freeWAIS-sf servers. FreeWAIS-sf is a WAIS variant, modified, among other things, to allow for structured fields. Information about freeWAIS-sf can be found (in LaTeX and texinfo format) at:

```
http://ls6-www.informatik.uni-dortmund.de/freeWAIS-sf/
```

while additional information about SFgate is available from:

```
http://ls6-www.informatik.uni-dortmund.de/SFgate/SFgate.html
```

which includes directions to the most recent source code for the package. SFgate was written by Ulrich Pfeifer.

WAISGATE

WAIS Inc. has developed a WAIS-to-Web gateway program called WAISgate. Source code for this gateway is not available, but the gateway is accessible, for free, on the main WAIS server at *www.wais.com*. Additional information about WAISgate can be found at this site, through the URL

```
http://www.wais.com/waisgate-announce.html
```

WWWWAIS

WWWWAIS is a small ANSI C program that acts as gateway between waisq and waissearch (the WAIS programs that search WAIS indexes) and a **FORMs**-capable World Wide Web browser. WWWWAIS allows for cus-tomized **FORMs** interfaces and a database access control mechanism (restrict-ing access to certain Internet domains), and lets users choose from among multiple searchable databases. As with the previously mentioned packages, WWWWAIS returns the search results as a hypertext document.

Additional information about WWWWAIS can be found at:

```
http://www.eit.com/software/wwwwais/wwwwais.html
```

while the source code and support files are available from:

```
ftp://ftp.eit.com/pub/web.software/wwwwais/
```

Get the **README** file first to find out what you need. WWWWAIS was writ-ten by Kevin Hughes of Enterprise Integration Technologies.

GATEWAYS TO STRUCTURED QUERY LANGUAGE (SQL) DATABASES

There are also several gateway packages for linking the World Wide Web to commercial database packages such as ORACLE or Sybase. Listed here are some of these efforts. If you have a commercial database product, you should consult your vendor to find out if they provide or know of similar software.

GSQL-ORACLE BACKEND

GSQL-Oracle Backend is a CGI program for linking WWW applications to an ORACLE database, using either **ISINDEX** or **FORMs** interfaces. GSQL-Oracle Backend is written in PRO-C, the C language development environment for ORACLE, so you need this development option to compile GSQL-Oracle Backend. The package comes complete with installation instructions, and should compile easily on most UNIX machines.

Additional information about GSQL-Oracle Backend is available at:

```
ftp://ftp.cc.gatech.edu/pub/gvu/www/pitkow/gsql-oracle/oracle-backend.html
```

while an archive of the package is available from:

```
ftp://ftp.cc.gatech.edu/pub/gvu/www/pitkow/gsql-oracle/gsql-oracle.tar
```

GSQL-Oracle Backend was written by James Pitkow of the Graphics, Visualization, and Usability Center at the Georgia Institute of Technology. For further information, see:

```
http://www.cc.gatech.edu/gvu/
```

WEB/GENERA

Web/Genera is a software tool set for the integration of Sybase databases into the World Wide Web. Web/Genera can be used to retrofit a Web front end (**FORM** or **ISINDEX**) to an existing Sybase database, or to create customized interfaces. To use Web/Genera, you write a specification of the Sybase database and of the desired appearance of its contents on the Web, using a simple high-level schema notation. Various Web/Genera programs process this description file to generate SQL commands and formatting instructions, which together extract objects from your database and format them into HTML. You don't have to write a single line of code to do this, and need only learn how to describe the database using the Genera schema notation, which is generally easy to use (well, that's what the documentation says).

Genera supports URLs linked to specific database objects, as well as powerful **FORMs**-based relational query construction. You can also use Genera to generate full-text searches of Sybase databases, via Web/WAIS and Gopher/WAIS interfaces.

Additional information about Web/Genera, including links to the most recent version of the package and substantial documentation, can be found at:

```
http://gdbdoc.gdb.org/letovsky/genera/general.html
```

Web/Genera was developed by Stanley Letovsky, under work supported by National Science Foundation grant BIR-9201652. It is freely available to the public.

WDB—A WEB INTERFACE TO SYBASE

WDB is a CGI package similar to Web/Genera and also based on perl and sybperl. Like Web/Genera, WDB allows you to use high-level description files to specify the structure of the database and the format of the responses, so that you can construct a generic WWW-Sybase interface without writing a single line of code. Notable is the ability to turn data from the database into hypertext links, so that it is possible to access any database element directly via a URL.

Additional information about WDB, including a list of required software and pointers to the source code archive, is found at:

```
http://arch-http.hq.eso.org/bfrasmus/wdb/wdb.html
```

WDB was written by Bo Frese Rasmussen of the European Southern Observatory.

GSQL GATEWAY

GSQL is a C program invoked from the HTTP server via a shell script. GSQL is a simple gateway to Sybase or other SQL databases. It parses an SQL-specification file (called a *PROC* file) to create an HTML **FORM,** and uses the user **FORM** input to call the database back-end program to process the SQL query. Search query results are then returned to the client. The PROC file maps components of the SQL string to widgets (fields, buttons, pull-down menus, etc.) for user input or selection. Substantial documentation on GSQL, and on the construction of PROC files, can be found at:

```
http://www.ncsa.uiuc.edu/SDG/People/jason/pub/gsql/starthere.html
```

The source code for GSQL can be found at:

```
http://base.ncsa.uiuc.edu:1234/gsqlsrc/gsql.tar
```

GSQL was written by Jason Ng of NCSA.

HTORACLE

HTOracle was one of the first database gateway programs developed for the WWW. HTOracle is a small package of programs, written in Pro-C and C, that takes **ISINDEX**-style queries and passes them to an ORACLE database as an SQL SELECT statement, and then returns the results to the client as a plain-text table. Documentation on the package is sketchy, but what there is can be found at

```
http://www.w3.org/hypertext/WWW/RDBGate/ArthurNotes.html
```

while pointers to the various source-code components are at:

```
http://www.w3.org/hypertext/WWW/RDBGate/Implementation.html
```

The HTOracle code has formed the basis for a number of other database gateways, including OraPlex. HTOracle was written by Arthur Secret of CERN.

ORAPLEX

OraPlex is an adaptation of the HTOracle database gateway program. Originally designed for integration with the Plexus server, OraPlex is now available as a CGI-compliant package, so that it can be used with other CGI-compliant servers. To use OraPlex, you need a local ORACLE database and oraperl, a perl package written by Kevin Stock that is designed for accessing ORACLE databases.

The oraperl package is found in the directory:

```
ftp://ftp.demon.co.uk/pub/perl/db/oraperl
```

The original Plexus-only OraPlex programs are found in the directory

```
http://moulon.inra.fr/oracle/
```

under the names *oraplex_pl.html* and *oracle_search.html*, while the newer CGI-compliant package is found at:

```
ftp://moulon.inra.fr/pub/www-oracle
```

The C language version of the database gateway package that uses the standard CGI interface and that can run under any server is discussed at:

```
http://moulon.inra.fr/oracle/www_oracle_eng.html.
```

```
http://moulon.inra.fr/oracle/www_oraperl_eng.html
```

Documentation in French is available at:

```
http://moulon.inra.fr/oracle/www_oraperl.html
```

```
http://moulon.inra.fr/oracle/www_oracle.html
```

OraPlex was written by Guy Decoux of the Institut National de la Recherche Agronomique.

MACINTOSH SEARCH TOOLS: TR-WWW

TR-WWW is a Macintosh-based search engine, and works only with the MacHTTP and Star Nine servers. TR-WWW provides a **FORMs**-based interface to a search engine that dynamically searches (using Boolean searches) server document collections consisting of HTML, plain text, or Microsoft Word files. The documents do not have to be preindexed, as TR-WWW can index the documents in real time. TR-WWW is thus ideal for searching rapidly evolving collections of documents. Search results can be reviewed (as HTML documents) sorted by keyword or by WAIS-style relevance ranked results.

Additional information about TR-WWW is found at:

```
http://www.monash.edu.au/tr-www.html
```

which includes links to further documentation and archives of the software package.

REFERENCES

General starting point for CGI resource discovery

The Yahoo site has additional, and usually up-to-date, pointers to resources, and to platform-specific (Mac, PC, Amiga, etc.) material.

```
http://www.yahoo.com/text/Computers_and_Internet/Internet/World_Wide_Web/
CGI___Common_Gateway_Interface/
```

Online CGI and FORM tutorials

```
http://agora.leeds.ac.uk/nik/Cgi/start.html
```

```
http://blackcat.brynmawr.edu/~nswoboda/prog-html.html
```

```
http://www.catt.ncsu.edu/~bex/tutor/index.html
```

FORM/Gateway tutorials

```
http://www.webcom.com/~webcom/html/tutor/forms/intro.html
```

```
http://robot0.ge.uiuc.edu/~carlosp/cs317/cft.html
```

CGI programmer's reference

```
http://www.best.com/~hedlund/cgi-faq/
```

CGI program archive sites

```
http://www.oac.uci.edu/indiv/ehood/perlWWW/
```

```
ftp://ftp.ncsa.uiuc.edu/Web/httpd/Unix/ncsa_httpd/cgi/
```

```
http://128.172.69.106:8080/cgi-bin/cgis.html
```

```
ftp://ftp.rz.uni-karlsruhe.de/pub/net/www/tools/cgi-src/
```

```
http://web.sau.edu/~mkruse/www/scripts/
```

```
http://pubweb.nexor.co.uk/public/perl/contrib/lib/CGI
```

```
http://www.bio.cam.ac.uk/web/form.html
```

Program libraries for gateway program developers

Perl libraries:

```
http://www.bio.cam.ac.uk/web/form.html
```

```
http://ftp.ncsa.uiuc.edu/Web/httpd/ncsa_httpd/cgi/cgi-lib.pl.Z
```

```
http://www-genome.wi.mit.edu/ftp/pub/software/WWW/cgi_docs.html
```

(Perl Version 5)

C libraries:

```
http://sunsite.unc.edu/boutell/cgic/cgic.html
```

```
http://wsk.eit.com/wsk/dist/doc/libcgi/libcgi.html
```

Special utilities

CGI-Wrap—secure user access to CGIs with httpd:

```
ftp://pluto.cc.umr.edu/pub/cgiwrap/
```

Database-Web gateway references:

Information about setting up WAIS gateways:

```
http://wintermute.ncsa.uiuc.edu:8080/wais-tutorial/wais.html
```

```
http://wintermute.ncsa.uiuc.edu:8080/wais-tutorial/wais-and-http.html
```

Some examples of useful WAIS gateway programs:

```
http://www.eit.com/software/wwwwais/wwwwais.html
```

```
http://www.cis.ohio-state.edu/hypertext/faq/usenet/wais-faq/
getting-started/faq.html
```

Sites for additional database–Web gateway information:

```
http://www.cs.vu.nl/~anne007/waissearch/pointers.html
```

```
http://www-rlg.stanford.edu/home/jpl/websearch.html
```

```
http://cgsc.biology.yale.edu/dbgw.html
```

```
http://oneworld.wa.com/htmldev/devpage/dev-page3.html
```

```
http://www.w3.org/hypertext/WWW/RDBGate/Overview.html
```

HTML AND WEB

UTILITIES AND TOOLS

This chapter examines tools useful in developing and maintaining Web document collections. The first section looks at the use of images in HTML documents, and discusses image formats and image processing tools, as well as the active imagemap facility. The next section looks at HTML utility programs; such tools can, for example, help you convert specially formatted documents (such as mail archives) into HTML document collections; generate an HTML Table of Contents from a collection of HTML documents; create a graphical map of the links within a collection of documents; or check your HTML documents for invalid hypertext references. The chapter concludes with a discussion of Web indexing tools and *robots*—these are search engine/database combinations that allow for automated indexing of documents spanning multiple sites. This latter section overlaps somewhat with the discussion of database programs at the end of Chapter 9, so if this section is of particular interest, you should look to Chapter 9 for additional inspiration.

IMAGES IN HTML DOCUMENTS

Inlined images, included using the tag `<IMG SRC="image_url">`, are one of the most exciting features of HTML, allowing the communication of important graphical information, as well as the creation of documents with colorful, visual appeal. However, as an author you should always think about clients who will be visiting your pages using text-only browsers, or with image loading disabled—these visitors will not see the images, so you must always design your pages to be understandable in their absence. So—use the **ALT** attribute to provide a text alternative!

Although most browsers support multiple image formats, there are only three formats that are universally acceptable. These are the GIF format images (GIF87 and GIF89), X-Bitmaps, and X-Pixelmaps. The different image types can usually be inferred by the filename suffix: GIF image files usually have the suffix *.gif*, X-Bitmaps the suffix *.xbm,* and X-Pixelmaps the suffix *.xpm*. A fourth format, JPEG, is also now widely supported. JPEG image files usually have the filename extension *.jpg* or *.jpeg*. This format is supported by almost all newer browsers, but is not supported by older versions of Mosaic or MacWeb. A fifth format, PNG, for Portable Network Graphics (with filename extension *.png*), is becoming common, but is at present not widely supported by Web browsers. Like GIF, the PNG format allows for transparency, interlacing, and image compression, the latter using a nonproprietary compression algorithm. PNG also supports greater color depth than GIF, as well as features for color and gamma correction. Browser developers are already working to include support for the PNG format in their products.

X-BITMAP IMAGE FORMAT

X-Bitmaps are a common format on UNIX workstations, and are often found in image and icon libraries. An X-Bitmap assigns a single bit to each image pixel and therefore supports only black-and-white images. Simple bitmaps can be useful, however, as most browsers treat the white portion as *transparent*— the black part of the image is displayed in black, while the white background transparently takes on the color of the underlying window. This permits attractive black icons, since the surrounding background box is invisible to the user. However, X-Bitmaps are inefficient at storing images, and are uncommon outside the UNIX environment. As we shall see, the GIF format is a better choice in most cases.

X-PIXELMAP IMAGE FORMAT

X-Pixelmaps are similar to X-Bitmaps but assign 8 bits to each pixel, as opposed to only 2. This format can support images with 256 distinct colors. The main drawback of X-Pixelmaps (like X-Bitmaps) is size: X-Pixelmaps are an inefficient way of storing image information and tend to be very large. In general, you should convert X-Bitmaps and X-Pixelmaps to GIF format images whenever possible.

JPEG IMAGE FORMAT

The JPEG (for Joint Photographic Experts Group) image format was designed expressly for storing photographic images in a compact digital format. The JPEG compression algorithm includes sophisticated techniques for *lossy* image compression (the more compression, the poorer the quality of the stored image), and can support more than 256 colors in an image file, which is necessary for storing high-quality images. In general, the JPEG format is better than the GIF format at storing photographic images, both in terms of image quality and image file size, while the GIF format is better for images containing few colors and with large single-colored regions, as is common in buttons, logos, clip art, and so on. You should be aware that some browsers currently cannot display inlined JPEG image files.

GIF IMAGE FORMAT

GIF is the most common image format in World Wide Web applications. This format can store black-and-white, grayscale, or color images, although it is limited to a maximum of 256 colors (or shades of gray) per image. The GIF format encodes the image information using a *color indexing* scheme. When you create a GIF image, the software takes the raw image data, uses an image analysis algorithm to find the set of 256 (or fewer) colors that best describe the color content of the image, and creates a *color table* mapping these colors onto integers ranging from 0 to 255. This color table can be optimized for each image. For example, if a picture is of a red sunset, this table will contain mostly reds, whereas if it is a picture of a forest, it will be mostly greens. The software then examines each pixel in the original image, finds the color in the color table that is closest to the actual color, and assigns the corresponding color index value to this pixel. The resulting GIF image file consists of an array of these *color indexes* plus a *color map* table that maps each of the 256 indexes onto the chosen color. This technique can yield a breathtakingly successful rendering of the original image, even though only 256 distinct colors are used.

The GIF format also stores the images in a compressed format, which is particularly effective for images containing large single-color regions, such as icons or logos. This means that a GIF format version of a logo can be wonderfully small, and hence quickly delivered over a network. This compression is not, however, very efficient with photographic images, where there are no large single-color regions, and where the image is highly irregular. In these cases, a JPEG format image will most likely be smaller, and of better quality, than the corresponding GIF image.

There are two versions of the GIF format: GIF87 and GIF89. The GIF89 format is more sophisticated than GIF87, and in particular allows you to make one of the colors in the image *transparent*. This is equivalent to the transparency of the white portion of an X-Bitmap image. The use and creation of transparent GIFs are described a bit later on.

REDUCING GIF IMAGE SIZE: THE COLOR MAP

Color image files are much bigger than black-and-white image files, since they contain a lot more information: up to 8 bits of information per pixel, as opposed to only one bit per pixel for black-and-white. Also, images that contain more colors are often bigger than those that contain only a few colors, even if they are physically the same size. This is because the GIF format is clever enough to know, if an image has only 8 colors instead of 256, that it needs fewer bits per pixel to map each color properly. (In addition reducing the number of colors often makes it easier to compress the image, further reducing image size.) Thus, if you want to make your image files small, which is often desired on the World Wide Web, use as few colors as possible. You can use image-processing programs such as Adobe Photoshop, Paintshop Pro (a shareware program for Windows PCs), Lview Pro (another shareware program for PCs), Graphic Converter (a shareware program for the Macintosh), or the pbmplus or ImageMagick packages (shareware programs for UNIX workstations) to reduce the number of colors in the image. Other packages offer similar functionality.

The limited graphical display capabilities of many current computers is another reason to reduce the size of image color maps. Most computers are equipped with graphics cards capable of simultaneously displaying only 256 colors. A WWW browser will therefore have no trouble displaying a single 256-color GIF image. However, there will clearly be problems if it tries to simultaneously present two 256-color GIF images, each with its own color map. Clearly both color maps cannot be used, since this requires as many as 512 colors, and not 256. Most browsers try to *dither* the color—that is, they try to find an average color map that is acceptable to both images. This often fails miserably, resulting in very poor quality color for both images.

You can alleviate this problem in two ways: by ensuring that the images you have created for simultaneous display use the same color map, or by limiting each image to at most 40 or 50 colors. The former option is useful, but difficult to implement. The second option can be accomplished using image processing programs such as the ones listed earlier. Almost all of them allow you to reduce the size of the color table, and at the same time dither the remaining colors to optimize the quality of the image. This technique allows you to simultaneously display four or five images before you "run out" of space in the color map. It also has the side-effect of reducing the size of the image files, which is a nice bonus.

REDUCING IMAGE SIZE: RESCALING IMAGES

There are other image processing ideas to consider. For example, you may want to reduce the size of an image, either because the original is just too big, or because you want to create a small icon of the image and link it to the bigger version. You can create reduced image sizes with a variety of programs, including the ones listed above.

When you *shrink* an image you may want to *smooth* it at the same time. Smoothing reduces edge sharpness created by the size reduction process. Some programs do this automatically, while others let you turn smoothing on and off. Note that you want to smooth during the size reduction and not after, since once the image is shrunk, smoothing simply blurs what's left.

INTERLACED GIF IMAGES

The GIF format stores images as a sequence of thin (1 pixel high) horizontal strips. Usually these are stored one after the other, so that when you receive an image file on your browser, you receive the first (top) strip, followed by the second, the third, and so on. If your browser displays the image as it is being downloaded, the image then appears to "wipe" in, starting at the top and wiping downwards.

As you have certainly noticed, this does not always happen. Sometimes the image opens rather like a venetian blind—a rough outline of the image appears first, and detail is gradually added. This occurs due to a special GIF feature called *interlacing*. With interlaced GIF images, the strips are stored in nonconsecutive order. For example, the strips might be stored in the order 1, 11, 21, 31, 41, and so on, followed by 2, 12, 22, and so on. A rough outline of the image is obtained from the first batch of slices, while subsequent batches fill in the gaps and refine the image. In the end, both kinds of images take the same amount of time to arrive, but to the user the presentation of an interlaced image is much more appealing, since the basic outline of the entire image appears more quickly. Thus, it is often a good idea to select the interlaced GIF format.

Most standard image processing programs, including those mentioned at the beginning of this section, are capable of producing interlaced GIFs. The image processing tool GIFtool, described later in this chapter, can add interlacing to your GIF images should your other graphics tools not be able to do so.

TRANSPARENT GIF IMAGES

Unlike X-Bitmaps, GIF images have no implicit transparent color. This is inconvenient if the image is simply a black-and-white logo, a colored bullet on a plain background, or an equation to be presented inline with the text. Fortunately, the GIF89 format allows you to declare one of the color indexes as transparent, giving the same transparency features that black-and-white X-Bitmaps have. To enable transparency, you must find the color index value corresponding to the color you want to make transparent (usually the background), and then use a program to modify the image file and make this color index transparent. Several ways to do this are outlined below.

TRANSPARENCY (MACINTOSH)

Aaron Giles of Cornell University Medical College has developed an elegant and useful program called **transparency**. This simple, graphically oriented program allows you to easily edit GIF images and make one of the colors transparent.

You operate **transparency** either by dragging a file to the transparency icon or by double-clicking on the transparency icon and opening the desired GIF image file. To select the transparency color, you simply place the mouse pointer inside the image and hold down the mouse button. You are presented with the color palette for the image, and can select the color you wish to make transparent by putting the mouse pointer over the desired color and releasing the button. You can choose to have no transparent color by selecting the "NONE" bar at the top of the palette. Upon releasing the mouse button, there is a short pause, after which the image is redrawn with the selected color rendered transparently. You now select the "Save as GIF89..." menu from the pull-down File menu to save the newly transparent version.

Transparency is available at a number of anonymous FTP sites, including:

```
ftp://ftp.med.cornell.edu/pub/aarong/transparency/
```

The program is found in a file named *transparency*sit.hqx*, where the star represents the version number. Additional information about **transparency** can be found at:

```
http://www.med.cornell.edu/~giles/projects.html
```

GIFTRANS (UNIX AND PC-DOS)

Giftrans is a simple C-language program, written by Andreas Ley, that can convert any GIF file into the GIF89 format, making one of the colors transparent in the process. **Giftrans** is available in source code (for compilation on any platform, but most specifically for UNIX workstations) and as an executable program for PCs running DOS. **Giftrans** is a command-line program, and does not need Windows to run. If you have the correct information, you can run **giftrans** from a simple text terminal.

Typically, **giftrans** is used as follows:

```
giftrans -t xx image.gif > transparent_image.gif
```

which translates the file *image.gif* into *transparent_image.gif* and makes the color labeled by xx transparent. There are several ways of labeling the color, the most common being:

- Specify the absolute RGB value for the color (as a 24-bit RGB value). For example, the command

```
giftrans -t #ffffff image.gif > transparent_image.gif
```

makes the color white transparent (ffffff is the RGB code for white).

- Specify the color index value. For example, the command

```
giftrans -t 21 image.gif > transparent_image.gif
```

makes the color found in color index 21 transparent.

How do you find the color index or RGB value of the color you want transparent? To find this information, you need a graphics program that can tell you the color indexes or RGB values for a given pixel. Several shareware graphics programs can do this—**xv** is a common UNIX program suitable for this task. With **xv**, you load the image file, place the mouse over the desired color, and depress the left mouse button. This gives the mouse coordinates with respect to the upper left-hand corner of the image, plus color information for the pixel. This is presented in the following manner:

```
132, 34  5 = 203, 203, 203 (0, 1, 79 HSV)
```

The first two numbers are the x and y coordinates of the pixel. The number just before the equals sign is the color index, while the next three numbers are the RGB values for this color (in decimal numbers). The three numbers in brackets are an alternative color coding scheme.

To make this color transparent, you turn to **giftrans**. You have two ways to make the above color transparent—using the color index:

```
giftrans -t 5 image.gif > transparent_image.gif
```

or the RGB value:

```
giftrans -t #cbcbcb image.gif > transparent_image.gif
```

where cb is the hexadecimal code for the decimal number 203. If you run **giftrans** without any arguments, the program prints out a list of possible arguments and their meanings.

Giftrans is available from a number of anonymous FTP sites. Its original home is:

```
ftp://ftp.rz.uni-karlsruhe.de/pub/net/www/tools/
```

The file *giftrans.exe* is the DOS executable version, while *giftrans.c* is C source code (you will also need *getopt.c* if compiling on a PC), and *giftrans.1* is the UNIX-style manual page.

The program **xv** is available from many anonymous FTP sites. You will need both a C compiler and the standard X11 libraries to compile **xv** on your machine. **Xv** is available at:

```
ftp://ftp.cis.upenn.edu/pub/xv/xv-3.10a.tar.Z
```

GIFTOOL (UNIX)

GIFtool is a multipurpose GIF manipulation program that allows you to add interlacing or transparency to a GIF format image. **GIFtool** can be used in batch mode, so you can batch-convert a number of files at the same time. The source code for **GIFtool** is available, as are precompiled binaries for several platforms. Additional information about **GIFtool**, including directions to the source and binaries, is found at:

```
http://www.homepages.com/tools/
```

PHOTOSHOP TRANSPARENT GIF PLUG-IN

Oddly enough, commercial programs such as **Photoshop** and **CorelDRAW!** cannot write out transparent GIF images. Fortunately, Adobe provides a plug-in module for **Photoshop** that allows the package to write out transparent GIFs. This plug-in can be obtained from the Adobe home page, at

```
http://www.adobe.com/
```

If you use other commercial packages, such as **CorelDRAW!**, you should consult with the company to find if there is a comparable utility.

ACTIVE IMAGES

Active images, clickable images—whatever they are called, you have certainly seen them, and would love to have them. Making an image an active image means that users can click their mouse pointer on top of the image and have different things happen, depending on where they clicked. For example, the active image could be a city map, such that clicking on different locations returns information about particular buildings, transportation routes, or historic monuments.

Active images require special features on both the client and the HTTP server. First, the client must be able to measure the coordinates of the mouse pointer when the user clicks on the active image, and must be configured to send this information to an HTTP server gateway program for interpretation and action. Second, there must be a gateway program on the server capable of interpreting this coordinate data. Third, there must be a database on the server relating, for each image, the click coordinates to the appropriate action. This means you must sit down with your image file, mark out the desired regions, link these regions to particular URLs, and store this information in a file that can be read by the gateway program. This procedure is described below.

ALLOWED FORMATS FOR ACTIVE IMAGES

You must use the GIF format for active images. Several browsers cannot measure image coordinates for X-Bitmaps or JPEG images, so that these formats will not work. You can use the various image processing programs mentioned previously to convert images into the required format.

THINGS TO THINK ABOUT BEFORE STARTING

Before you get carried away with active images, stop and think about your audience. First recall that many users will not be able to view your active images, because their browser does not support that capability (rare, but still possible); because they are using a text-only browser, such as lynx (quite common); or because they have disabled image loading because of a slow network connection (also common). Consequently, you should make the images as small as possible, and should try to provide a text-only way of accessing the same data. For example, your active image document can have a line of text explaining what the image does and offering a hypertext link to a document providing a text-only approach to the same information. In particular, any active image element should have an **ALT** text string that explains the purpose of the active image, and that tells the user what to do if the image is not visible.

MAKING AN IMAGE ACTIVE

In HTML you include an image within a document using the **IMG** element, for example:

```
<IMG SRC="image.gif" ALT="[The author, and a Large, Hairy Llama]">
```

This image is passive, and just sits there. As discussed in Chapters 1 and 4, you can turn this image into a hypertext link by putting it inside an anchor element, for example:

```
<A HREF="http://some.site.edu/linked_doc.html">

    <IMG SRC="image.gif" ALT="[The author, and a Large, Hairy Llama]">

</A>
```

Now, when you click on the image, you are linked to the indicated document. In a sense this is an active image, but the action is restricted to a single function.

To make an image fully active, you must do two things. First, you must add the **ISMAP** attribute to the **IMG** element, which tells the browser that this is an active image. Second, you must surround the **IMG** element with a hypertext anchor that points to the gateway program that can process the image coordinate data. Thus, the HTML markup for an active image is:

```
<A HREF="http://some.site.edu/cgi-bin/imagemap/my_database"><IMG

      SRC="image.gif"

      ALT="[The author, and a Large, Hairy Llama - an ACTIVE image ]"

      ISMAP ></A>
```

which tells the browser that this is an active image and that, when a user clicks inside the image, the coordinates of the click should be sent to the gateway program *imagemap* at the given URL. The coordinate information is sent to this URL using the HTTP GET method. The HTTP request header sent to the server looks like:

```
GET /cgi-bin/imagemap/my_database?x,y HTTP/1.0
```

where x and y are the *integer pixel coordinates* of the mouse pointer measured from the *upper left-hand corner* of the image.

Note that the path *my_database* is appended to the end of this URL. As discussed in Chapters 6 and 8, URLs that point to gateway programs are treated in a special way, and any directory-like information appended to the URL after the program name (like *my_database*) is treated as "extra path" information, and is passed as a parameter to the gateway program. In this example, *my_database* is additional path information used by *imagemap* to find the *imagemap database* for this particular image. This allows the *imagemap* program to be used with any number of active images, each image having its own personalized database.

Imagemap is an actual CGI program for handling active image data, and is distributed with the current NCSA HTTPD server. An older version of this program is also available and has similar, if somewhat more limited, functionality. Should you currently be using the older version, the newer and more flexible version is available at:

```
http://hoohoo.ncsa.uiuc.edu/docs/setup/admin/imagemap.txt
```

Imagemap is a CGI-compliant C-language program, and can be used on any HTTP server supporting the CGI specification. The remainder of this discussion centers on using the newer **imagemap** program and on creating the associated databases. Additional online documentation, including interactive examples, can be found at:

```
http://hoohoo.ncsa.uiuc.edu/docs/setup/admin/NewImagemap.html
```

INSTALLING IMAGEMAP

If you are installing the **imagemap** program, or are replacing your old version, you simply download the file

    http://hoohoo.ncsa.uiuc.edu/docs/setup/admin/imagemap.txt

rename it *imagemap.c,* and compile with your C compiler (note that the program requires the CGI-utility package *utils.c,* which comes with the NCSA HTTPD server distribution). You then install the resulting *imagemap* executable in your server's CGI program directory. On NCSA servers, this is usually *cgi-bin,* located in the directory structure containing the server executable, server support directories, and configuration files. (This is *not* the directory that contains the HTML and other documents you make available via the server.) Once installed, the program is accessible through URLs such as

    http://some.site.edu/cgi-bin/imagemap

where the *cgi-bin* directory is a *virtual* name used by the server to reference the directory containing CGI programs. Check your server configuration files to verify that this name is correct.

CREATING THE IMAGE DATABASE

The imagemap database file relates a region of the image with a URL to be accessed when a user clicks inside that region. You can specify regions as circles, rectangles, polygons, or points. You can include comments in these map database files by placing a hash character (#) as the first character in the line. Figure 10.1 shows a simple map file, named *blobby.map.*

This file declares that clicks within the circle centered at coordinates 50,20 (and with an edge at 50,30) are linked to the designated URL, and makes similar declarations for a rectangle (indicated by rect) and a polygon (indicated by poly). These coordinates are measured in pixels from the upper left-hand

■■■■■ **Figure 10.1** The example imagemap map database file *blobby.map.*

```
# Imagemap file for blobby.gif

circle   /dir1/blob2/his_head.html       50,20 50,30

rect     /dir1/blob2/his_left_foot.html  25,78 40,85

poly     /dir1/blob2/his_body.html       45,38 35,50 40,72 50,75 60,72 65,50 55,38

default  /cgi-bin/nph-no_op.sh
```

corner of the image. The "default" method indicates the URL to access if the user clicks in places not falling inside any of the mapped regions.

The general form of a map file entry is

```
method   URL   x1,y1 x2,y2 ... xn,yn
```

where `method` specifies the manner in which the region is being specified (`circle`, `rect`, `poly`, `point`, or `default`); `URL` is the URL to be accessed if the click occurs inside this region; and `xn` and `yn` are the integer coordinates of a point, measured from the upper left-hand corner of the image. These coordinates are measured in pixels, so you will need some way of measuring the pixel coordinates in an image. Tools for doing this are presented later.

Note that mapped regions can overlap. The **imagemap** program reads the map file from the beginning of the file, so that if a click occurs at a point lying within two mapped regions, the program takes the first one it encounters.

The URLs specified in a map file can be complete URLs, or partial URLs of the form

```
/path/stuff/file
```

which references a file or gateway program relative to the HTTP server *document directory*. With the NCSA, Apache, and certain other servers, you can also use the form

```
/~user/stuff/file
```

where `user` is the name of a user on the system. This references a file or gateway program relative to the user's personal HTML area.

The following is a list of the different methods for declaring active regions and the parameters required for these methods:

`circle` *URL* *center edgepoint* This maps the region inside the indicated circle to the given URL. Two coordinate pairs are required: one for the circle `center` (xc,yc) and the other for an `edgepoint` (xe,ye) lying on the edge of the circle. An example entry is

```
circle  /path/file.html  50,40  20,30
```

`point` *URL* *x,y* This declares a specific *point* in an image as active. When you click on the image, and the click is not inside a circle, rectangle, or polygon, the **imagemap** program locates the point closest to the coordinates of the click and accesses the indicated URL.

poly   *URL*   *x1,y1 x2,y2, ... xn,yn* This maps the region inside the indicated polygon to the given URL. Each coordinate pair represents a vertex of the polygon. You should make sure that the line segments do not cross one another (no bow ties!). The polygon is automatically closed by linking the last point x1,y1 to the first coordinate x1,y1. The current NCSA program limits you to, at most, 100 corners in a given polygon.

rect   *URL*   *upper_left_corner lower_left_corner* This maps the region inside a rectangle to the given URL. The coordinates of the upper-left and lower-right corners of the rectangle are required, in that order. For example:

```
rect    /path/file2.html 20,20  40,50
```

default   *URL*   This URL is accessed if the click did not lie inside any other region. This is never accessed if you define a point, since a clicked location will always be *closest* to a defined point—even if it's the only point!

REFERENCING THE DATABASE

Now that you have a database—for example the *blobby.map* database of Figure 10.1—where should you put it, and how do you reference it? This database can go anywhere you can put regular HTML documents or data files; you indicate its location to the **imagemap** program via the extra path information in the URL. For example, let us suppose that the HTTP server document directory is */u/Web* and that the collection of documents and images related to blobby is found in the directory */u/Web/weird/blobby*. A possible choice is to put the map file in the same directory as the image, so that the absolute path for the map file is */u/Web/weird/blobby/blobby.map*. You would access this map file from the **imagemap** program by writing, in your HTML document

```
<A HREF="http://some.site.edu/cgi-bin/imagemap/weird/blobby/blobby.map">

   <IMG SRC="blobby.gif" ISMAP>

</A>
```

where *some.site.edu* is the site containing all these documents. Note that the path to the *blobby.map* file, relative to the document directory of the HTTP server (*/u/Web*), has been added to the imagemap URL. The string

`/weird/blobby/blobby.map` is passed to the **imagemap** program, and is used by **imagemap** to locate the database *blobby.map.*

With the NCSA Apache, Netscape Netsite, and some other servers, this method is not restricted to the regular document directory. If a user has created a personal HTML directory, he or she can place map files in this directory and access the maps, using URLs such as

```
<A HREF="http://some.site.edu/cgi-bin/imagemap/~user/path/blobby.map">

<IMG SRC="blobby.gif" ISMAP>

</A>
```

where user is the username of the person with the personal public HTML directory and *path/blobby.map* is the path leading to the map file from the root of his or her personal document directory.

GETTING A CLICK TO DO NOTHING

Sometimes, you want a click to do nothing. For example, your image could be a map of buildings, but you don't want anything to happen when the user clicks on nonmapped objects, like roads or trees. In this case, the ideal result is for the client to retain the current document on the browser window screen. This can be accomplished by linking the `default` method in your imagemap file to a server script that returns an appropriate server response message to the client. In Figure 10.1, the `default` method references the script *nph-no_op.sh,* which does exactly this. This script contains four simple lines:

```
#!/bin/sh

echo "HTTP/1.0 204 No response — server CGI-script output"

echo "Content-type: text/plain"

echo "Server: $SERVER_SOFTWARE"

echo
```

Output from a script with the *nph-* prefix is sent directly to the client without being parsed by the server (see Chapter 8 for more information about *nonparsed header* gateway programs). This script sends the HTTP status code 204, which tells the client that there is no server message and that the client should retain the current document.

Tools for Generating Imagemap Files

Generating a map file is not difficult and only requires some concentration, a piece of paper, and an image viewing program that gives the pixel coordinates of the mouse pointer. The generic UNIX program for this purpose is **xv** (found at many anonymous FTP sites by searching for the string xv-3.00 or xv-3.10). You load the image into **xv**, locate the coordinates, and type the numbers into a map file. A similar procedure can be followed with typical Macintosh or PC image editing programs.

Of course, this is much easier if you have a graphical tool for editing images and automatically generating the map files. Thomas Boutell has satisfied this need with his program **mapedit**, which allows you to read the GIF image into a resizable window; use the mouse to draw circles, rectangles, and polygons on top; and specify a URL for each of the marked regions. You can also insert comments, which is important if you want to understand the content of the map file at a later date.

Mapedit is available for both UNIX systems and PCs running Windows. Both versions are found at:

    ftp://sunsite.unc.edu/pub/packages/infosystems/WWW/tools/mapedit

The PC version comes as a *zip* archive containing the executable program, support files, and documentation, while the UNIX version comes as a compressed tar file (the current version is in the file *mapedit1.1.2.tar.Z*). The UNIX package must be compiled for your system. You will need an ANSI-C compiler, the X-Windows libraries at level X11R5 or higher, the X11 **imake** utility (usually a part of the X distribution), and the X11 Athena widget set. Compilation instructions come with the installation kit. Additional information about **mapedit** can be found at:

    http://sunsite.unc.edu/boutell/mapedit/mapedit.html

There are, of course, other programs that can help you create imagemap database files. The shareware program **WebMap** fulfills this role for Macintosh users, while for Windows users there are the programs **Map This** and **Web Hotspots**. Information about these three packages can be found, respectively, at:

    http://www.city.net/cnx/software/webmap.html

    http://galadriel.ecaetc.ohio-state.edu/tc/mt/

    http://www.hooked.net/users/1auto/hotspots.html

OTHER SERVER IMAGEMAP GATEWAY PROGRAMS

The CERN HTTP server comes with its own image-mapping gateway program, which uses a technique somewhat different from that of the NCSA **imagemap** routine—consult the CERN server documentation for more information. There are also a few other image-mapping CGI programs. **Mac-ImageMap,** for example, provides image-mapping capabilities for the Macintosh **WebSTAR** (formerly MacHTTP) server, using the same mapping mechanism as the NCSA imagemap program. The program **glorglox**, on the other hand, takes a completely different route, and maps individual pixels onto URLs. Others programs are available; you should inquire at standard archive sites, such as Yahoo, for information about other tools. However, as a document creator your best bet is to stick with the CERN or NCSA default image-mapping programs, since these are well tested and widely available.

Information about **Mac-ImageMap** can be found at

```
http://weyl.zib-berlin.de/imagemap/Mac-ImageMap.html
```

while the details of **glorglox** are available at

```
http://www.uunet.ca/~tomr/glorglox/
```

IMAGE ICON ARCHIVE SITES

There are several sites on the World Wide Web that maintain extensive archives of publicly accessible images and icons. These are useful places to find icons for your own documents. Here are some of the more popular icon archive sites:

```
http://www-ns.rutgers.edu/doc-images/
```

```
http://www.mindspring.com/~guild/graphics/graphics.html
```

```
http://www.dsv.su.se/~matti-hu/archive.html
```

```
http://www.cli.di.unipi.it/iconbrowser/icons.html
```

Mirrors at:

```
http://www.link.it:8000/iconbrowser/
```

```
http://sunsite.unc.edu/gio/iconbrowser/
```

```
http://www.cit.gu.edu.au/~anthony/icons/index.html
```

Mirrors at:

```
http://bsdi.com/icons/AIcons/
```

```
http://www.hlt.uni-duisburg.de/AIcons/

http://www.ircam.fr/images/archives/

http://www.netspace.org/icons/AIcons/
```
```
http://hobbes.nmsu.edu/multimedia/icons/

http://www.eecs.wsu.edu/~rkinion/lines/lines.html

http://white.nosc.mil/images.html
```

Lists of other image archive sites are at:

```
http://www.yahoo.com/World_Wide_Web/Programming/Icons/

http://oneworld.wa.com/htmldev/devpage/dev-page3.html#doc-i

http://www.cs.yale.edu/homes/sjl/clipart.html
```

HTML UTILITY PROGRAMS

There are several small utility programs useful in managing collections of HTML documents. Most are perl programs, and should run on any computer that has perl. In general, these programs were developed on UNIX workstations.

CURL

Curl is an HTML document management tool that automatically creates links between HTML documents. **Curl** constructs links based on information maintained, by the document author, in a special *contents* file. This information lists the names of each of the HTML documents as well as the relationships between them. **Curl** takes this information and modifies each document to create the necessary links to its neighbors, parents, starting page, and so on. **Curl** can generate several different types of contents lists, which are in turn automatically inserted into automatically generated contents pages.

Additional information about **Curl**, including instructions about how this ANSI-C program can be obtained, are available at

```
http://munkora.cs.mu.oz.au/~ad/curl-announce.html
```

Curl is being developed by Andrew Davidson of the Department of Computer Science at the University of Melbourne in Australia.

DTD2HTML

Dtd2html is a perl program that takes an SGML Document Type Definition file (DTD) and generates a collection of HTML documents explaining the structural relationship among the elements defined in the DTD, complete with hypertext links between the documents in the collection. This package will be useful if you are interested in learning more about the HTML DTD.

Dtd2html was written by Earl Hood. More information about **dtd2html** is available at:

```
http://www.oac.uci.edu/indiv/ehood/dtd2html.doc.html
```

HTML TABLE CONVERTER

As mentioned in Chapters 2 and 4, HTML 2.0 does not contain elements for creating structured tables, although such elements are defined in HTML 3 and are currently implemented on some (but not all) browsers.

The transition from the **TABLE**-less world of today to the **TABLE**-full world of tomorrow is made somewhat easier by a small perl program created by Brooks Cutter. This program accepts documents containing HTML 3 **TABLE** elements, and formats the table portions (where possible) into an appropriate plain-text table, enclosing the table between <PRE> and </PRE> tags. Using this package, you can in principle write your documents using the **TABLE** elements and then quickly convert them into a form acceptable to today's browsers. Then, when browsers mature to the point of handling tables, you will already have tables in the correct format.

A caveat, however—this package dates from mid-1994, and the table specification has changed somewhat since then. This package may, therefore, not properly convert tables constructed using the current specification. You may consequently need to modify this program to get it to work properly with advanced tables.

The package (a UNIX shell archive) is available at:

```
ftp://sunsite.unc.edu/pub/packages/infosystems/WWW/tools/html+tables.shar
```

HYPERMAIL

Hypermail is a C-language program that takes a file of mail messages, in UNIX mailbox format, and generates a set of cross-referenced HTML documents. **Hypermail** converts each letter in the mailbox into a separate HTML file, with links to other, related articles. It also converts e-mail addresses, and hypertext anchors in the original letters, into HTML hypertext links. **Hypermail** archives can be incrementally updated, which significantly eases the periodic updating of hypermail archives.

Detailed information about **Hypermail** can be found at:

    http://www.eit.com/software/hypermail/hypermail.html

The program itself is available from:

    http://www.eit.com/software/hypermail/

The current C-language version of **Hypermail** was written by Kevin Hughes of Enterprise Integration Technologies Inc.

INDEX MAKER

Index Maker is a shareware perl program for maintaining an indexed list of selected WWW sites. The indexing requires active input on the part of the person registering new URLs, which makes this tool distinct from, and perhaps less glamorous than, the robot-based indexing tools discussed later in this chapter. At the same time, **Index Maker** can be very useful for constructing personal indexes, or special-purpose indexes, where active participation of the users can readily keep the index accurate and up-to-date.

Additional information about **Index Maker** can be found at:

    http://web.sau.edu/~mkruse/www/scripts/index2.html

Index Maker is being developed by Matt Kruse.

MHonArc: Mail to HTML Archive

MHonArc is a perl package for converting Internet mail messages, both plain text and MIME encoded, into HTML documents. This can be extremely useful, for example, if you are archiving electronic mail messages or newsgroup postings and want to make them available on the WWW. The package uses the letter's subject line for the HTML **TITLE** and as an **H1** heading in the HTML version of the letter, and converts relational headers such as *References* or *In-Reply-To* into the appropriate hypertext links, if possible.

MHonArc can also sort letters according to their topical thread and connect them together with *Next* and *Previous* hypertext links. In addition, **MHonArc** creates an index of the letters or articles, and creates a link from each converted letter to this index.

The home page for **MHonArc** is:

```
http://www.oac.uci.edu/indiv/ehood/mhonarc.doc.html
```

This contains directions for obtaining the most recent version of **MHonArc** and pointers to extensive documentation. The author is Earl Hood.

MOMSPIDER

The Multi-Owner Maintenance spider, or **MOMspider**, is a Web-roaming *robot*, designed to help in maintaining distributed collections of HTML documents. **MOMspider** traverses a list of webs, and constructs an index of the collection, recording the attributes and connections of the web within a special HTML map document. **MOMspider** can be used to report changes in web layout, to report linking and other problems, and to generate an overview of a large web collection. Since **MOMspider** explores links dynamically and autonomously, it is formally a *robot*, and obeys the *robot exclusion policy*. Robots and the exclusion policy are discussed in the concluding section of this chapter.

Additional information about **MOMspider**, including instructions as to where to obtain the perl source code, can be found at:

```
http://www.ics.uci.edu/WebSoft/MOMspider/
```

MOMspider was written by Roy Fielding, of the Department of Information and Computer Science at the University of California, Irvine.

HTMLTOC: TABLE OF CONTENTS GENERATOR

Htmltoc is a perl program that can automatically generate a table of contents (ToC) for a single HTML document, or for a collection of related documents. **Htmltoc** uses the HTML **H1–H6** headings to locate sections within a single document, and uses the order of the heading (**H1, H2,** and so on) to determine the hierarchical relationship of the ToC. This, among many other features, can be significantly customized.

When **htmltoc** creates a table of contents, it creates hypertext links from the table of contents to the documents themselves. It does this by editing the original documents and adding the appropriate hypertext anchors. The original documents are backed up during this process, so that you can recover the original material without difficulty.

Additional documentation on **htmltoc**, including directions for obtaining the most recent version, can be found at:

```
http://www.oac.uci.edu/indiv/ehood/htmltoc.doc.html
```

Htmltoc was written by Earl Hood.

TREELINK

Treelink, written in **tk** and **tcl,** is a package that draws a hypergraph of the hypertext links, starting from a given hypertext document. **Treelink** analyzes the connections and draws a treelike graph until it reaches a certain predefined depth (number of links). This graph often gives useful insights into the connection and arrangement of links to a particular document.

Additional information about **Treelink,** including instructions as to where to obtain the source code, can be found at:

```
http://aorta.tat.physik.uni-tuebingen.de/~gaier/treelink/
```

Treelink was written by Karsten Gaier.

WEBCOPY

WebCopy is a perl program that retrieves a specified HTTP URL. There are many control switches that permit recursive retrieval of documents (but only from the same server—**WebCopy** will *not* retrieve documents from domain names other than the one specified in the initial URL) and the retrieval of included inline image files. **WebCopy** does not comply with the *robot exclusion standard* (see the end of this chapter), since it is largely intended for retrieving a single document, or a small number of documents.

Additional information about **WebCopy,** as well as directions for obtaining the perl source, are found at:

```
http://www.inf.utfsm.cl/~vparada/webcopy.html
```

WebCopy was written by Victor Parada.

WEBLINKER

WebLinker is a tool, developed at CERN, to help manage distributed collections of Web documents. **WebLinker** makes use of the concept of Local Resource Names, or *LRNs,* a naming scheme developed for local Web documents. The **WebLinker** (and **WebMaker**—see Chapter 11) developers argue that LRNs, combined with **WebLinker,** can significantly simplify the management of large document collections.

Additional information on **WebLinker,** and on Local Resource Names, can be found at:

```
http://www.cern.ch/WebLinker/
```

WebLinker is currently being developed by the Harlequin Group, Ltd. Inquiries should be addressed to *web@harlequin.com.*

WEBXREF

Webxref is a perl program that verifies hypertext links between documents, starting from an indicated HTML file. This is a relatively new tool, and has not been widely used to date. Additional information about **Webxref,** as well as directions for obtaining the perl source, are found at:

```
http://www.sara.nl/cgi-bin/rick_acc_webxref
```

Webxref was written by Rick Jansen.

WEB INDEXING TOOLS

One common demand is for a Web index—after all, it is fine knowing that there is useful information out there, and quite another actually trying to find it. A growing number of tools have been developed to address this issue. These tools provide mechanisms for indexing document collections, and for making these indexes accessible over the Web. In some cases, these tools have been used to provide global Web indexes (such as the Lycos search engine, at `http://www.lycos.com`), but they are often also appropriate for indexing local collections. For example, these tools could be used to index all servers at a particular university, to provide a local, searchable index of university resources.

The following sections review briefly some of these tools, but you are referred to the sites themselves for details.

ALIWEB

ALIWeb is a Web indexing tool that indexes only those sites that want to be indexed. If a site wishes to be indexed by ALIWeb, the site administrator contacts the ALIWeb server, and registers his or her site with the ALIWeb system, using a **FORM** interface. In addition, the site administrator must construct a specially formatted index file for his or her site, and place this in a location accessible to ALIWeb. The ALIWeb data-collection robot then automatically visits the site and retrieves the index file, which is used to generate the ALIWeb index.

Additional information about ALIWeb is available at

    http://web.nexor.co.uk/public/aliweb/doc/introduction.html

HARVEST

Harvest is the newest, and perhaps most exciting, of the Web indexing and information discovery tools. The product of the Internet Research Task Force Research Group on Resource Discovery (IRTF-RD), based at the University of Colorado at Boulder, Harvest is a collection of tools for gathering, organizing, and indexing resources, combined with utilities that allow this information to be replicated and distributed among a number of different sites. Harvest contains a number of improvements upon previous Web indexing tools, such as Lycos, ALIWeb, or WWW Worm, and is currently the tool of choice for those interested in setting up a local Web indexing system. It even has its own newsgroup!

Additional information about Harvest can be found at:

    http://harvest.cs.colorado.edu/harvest/

LYCOS

The Lycos indexing system, a product of the Computer Science faculty of Carnegie Mellon University, utilizes a Web *robot* that wanders the Web and retrieves documents, which are subsequently indexed by the Lycos search engine. The search engine provides a number of ways of searching through the database, and has become one of the most widely used global search tools on the Web.

Additional information about the Lycos system can be found at:

    http://lycos.cs.cmu.edu/

THE WWW WORM

The World Wide Web Worm is one of the oldest of the Web indexing systems. The WWWW uses a Web-wandering robot that autonomously extracts and indexes Web documents, but it also allows users to register their own URLs using a fill-in **FORM**. The current index contains over 3 million URLs, making it one of the more complete indexes of the Web.

Additional information about the World Wide Web Worm is found at:

    http://www.cs.colorado.edu/home/mcbryan/WWWW.html

The World Wide Web Worm was developed by Oliver McBryan of the University of Colorado at Boulder.

ROBOTS, WANDERERS, AND SPIDERS

In the World Wide Web, *robots*, *wanderers*, and *spiders* are essentially synonyms, and indicate programs that automatically traverse the Web, successively retrieving HTML documents and then accessing the links contained within those documents. They are usually autonomous programs, in that they access links according to their programming, and without human intervention. There are many uses for such programs. The programs range from web-mapping and link-verifying programs such as **MOMspider** and **link_verifier,** to programs that retrieve Web documents and generate searchable Web indexes, such as ALIweb, Harvest, and Lycos. Indeed, if it were not for robots, it would now be almost impossible to find anything on the Web, given the millions upon millions of resources that are now available.

However, sometimes a Web site administrator wants to keep robots away from certain collections of documents, perhaps because the documents are only temporary, and so should not be indexed, or perhaps because the documents are internal resources that should not be indexed outside of the site. Alternatively, a server may be heavily loaded with users, in which case you don't want your service to human customers slowed by a bunch of eager little robots, happily grabbing all your documents as fast as they can.

Martijn Koster has developed a convention whereby a server administrator can tell robots whether or not they are welcome to access the server and, if they are welcome, which files and directories they should avoid. This information is stored in the file *robots.txt*, which must always be available at the site URL:

```
http://domain.name/robots.txt
```

An example is `http://www.hprc.utoronto.ca/robots.txt` which "protects" the Web server used by the author. Robots that comply with the *robot exclusion standard* check this file as soon as they arrive at a site, and use the data in the file to determine if they are welcome, and, if so, where they are welcome. An example *robots.txt* file is

```
User-Agent: *              # Applies to all robots

Disallow:   /localweb/docs/   # local web documents

Disallow: /tmp/            # Temporary Files
```

which tells *all* Web robots that they should avoid the indicated directories.

Additional information about robots and the construction of *robots.txt* files is available at:

http://web.nexor.co.uk/mak/doc/robots/robots.html

REFERENCES

Issues in computer graphics

http://www.cs.cmu.edu/afs/cs.cmu.edu/user/rwb/www/gamma.html

http://www.inforamp.net/~poynton/Poynton-articles.html

ftp://ftp.inforamp.net/pub/users/poynton/doc/colour/

Online transparent GIF tutorial

http://melmac.corp.harris.com/transparent_images.html

Online imagemaps tutorial

http://www.webcom.com/~webcom/html/tutor/imagemaps.html

11

WEB DEVELOPER
RESOURCES

This chapter briefly reviews software resources useful to a Web developer. The first section looks at HTML editors and document translators: document translators are utilities that can batch convert files from another format, such as LaTeX, Frame MIF, or RTF into HTML, or vice versa. The second section briefly discusses Web browsers and browser helper applications—recall that you should always preview your Web projects on multiple browsers to ensure that your documents are understandable on these different platforms. The final section discusses HTTP servers, and outlines the issues to think about when setting up a Web site.

In all three sections, references to up-to-date, online software directory sites are provided. These sites contain brief descriptions of most editors, document translators, browsers, browser helper applications, and HTTP servers, complete with pointers to the packages themselves. You should consult these directory sites to find out what's currently available, and to obtain up-to-date information on individual packages.

HTML EDITORS AND DOCUMENT TRANSLATORS

This section reviews tools for creating HTML documents. The first part describes editors specifically designed for writing HTML documents, while the second part looks at document translators/converters. The latter are programs designed to convert from a document format such as WordPerfect, FrameMaker, or LaTeX, into HTML, and vice versa. The division is somewhat arbitrary, since the combination of a document processing system and a good HTML conversion program is often ideal for preparing HTML documents. Keep this in mind if you are looking for a tool related to a particular document processing system and do not see what you are looking for in the section on editors.

The third part of this section lists HTML validation tools. These are programs that can check an HTML document for correct HTML syntax and commands, and check that the hypertext links reference valid URLs. These tools are very useful, as most HTML editors do not check HTML syntax or the validity of the URLs. HTML syntax validation tools use the SGML *Document Type Definition (DTD)* for HTML, so that you also need the HTML DTD file. Included are suggestions of where to find these DTDs, and a brief description of the validation process. Hypertext link validation tools were also discussed at the end of Chapter 10—look there also, as the entries are not duplicated here.

The descriptions in this chapter include pointers to additional documentation on each package, along with directions for obtaining the software. These pointers can also be used to obtain the current status of a particular package.

The collection of tools is constantly growing and evolving, so this chapter is certainly incomplete. Links to the resources listed in this chapter are maintained at the following Web site:

```
http://www.hprc.utoronto.ca/HTMLdocs/tools_home.html
```

This site also contains references to other Web sites maintaining comparable lists of editors, document translation programs, and other development utilities. These lists are more up-to-date than a printed book, but less current than the material available through the various newsgroups. For up-to-date additions, you should browse the USENET newsgroups *comp.infosytems.www.users, comp.infosystems.www.misc*, and *comp.infosystems.www.authoring.misc*.

HTML EDITORS

This section reviews HTML editors. Each editor is described briefly but with sufficient detail that you can see how it works and get an idea of its strengths and weaknesses. However, nothing is better than trying it out, and you are encouraged to do so!

At the beginning of each description, you will find the editor name and a list of supported platforms (PC, Macintosh, or UNIX). The description also notes if the product is commercial software or shareware, and briefly describes the overall layout and operation of the program. Also mentioned are known problems with the current versions of these editors. You should regard this information as an aid in using these editors and not as a judgment on the packages, since I have not tested the packages in equal detail. No attempt is made to describe the relative ease of use, as in general they all seem easy to use and straightforward to learn. Each description includes a list of URLs pointing to additional information about the editor, and to actual locations of the editor, if available in this way.

Some of these packages are advertised as What-You-See-Is-What-You-Get (*WYSIWYG*) HTML editors. In the World WideWeb, this is a misleading term, since each Web browser will display the same HTML document in a different way, ranging from the graphical rendering of browsers such as MacWeb and Mosaic to the text-only rendering of lynx. This does not mean that WYSIWYG capabilities are bad—they can be useful to give an idea of what the document can look like. However, the actual display on real browsers may be quite different from the editor's rendition. The only effective way to verify the clarity of your document design is to preview your documents on a few different browsers and adjust the design to ensure that the important information is clearly presented by all of them. This may sound like a lot of work, but after going through this procedure a few times you will quickly develop a feeling for the types of document design that are universally successful, regardless of the browser.

Since writing HTML documents requires only the standard printable ASCII characters, you can prepare and edit HTML documents using a plain-text editor. For example, if you are using a PC you can use the **EDIT** program that comes with DOS, or the **Notepad** editor that comes with Windows. If you are using a Macintosh you can use the **TeachText** text editor (limited to files smaller than 20,000 characters) or freeware editors such as **BBEdit-Lite**. On UNIX machines you can use the ever-present editor **vi** or more sophisticated editors such as **emacs** or **epoch**.

WINDOWS EDITORS

4W Publisher

Formerly known as **Web Builder,** this is not an HTML editor per se, but is useful for building main menus and keyword indexes for a large number of complex HTML documents. For more information, see the **4W Publisher** home page at:

```
http://www.infoanalytic.com/webbldr/index.html
```

AmiWeb (Ami Pro Add-on)

The **AmiWeb** home page, including links to the current version of the software, can be found at:

```
http://www.cs.nott.ac.uk/~sbx/amiweb.html
```

CU_HTML.DOT (Word 2.0 and 6.0 Add-on)

CU_HTML.DOT is a Microsoft Word 2.0 and 6.0 for Windows document template that adds to the Word editor a selection of special HTML styles, plus a macro for converting Word documents prepared using these HTML styles into an HTML document.

Full documentation, in HTML format, is available at the **CU_HTML.DOT** home page:

```
http://www.cuhk.hk/csc/cu_html/cu_html.htm
```

The ZIP file containing the template itself and hypertext documentation is found at:

```
ftp://ftp.cuhk.hk/pub/www/windows/util/
```

GT_HTML.DOT (Word 2.0 and 6.0 Add-on)

This is another package of Microsoft Word for Windows macros. Additional information is available at:

```
http://www.gatech.edu/word_html/release.htm
```

HotDog Web Editor

According to frequenters of the *comp.infosystems.www.authoring.html* hierarchy, **HotDog** has become one of the most popular HTML editors for Windows. **HotDog Professional** is in development. The **HotDog** home page, including a link to a 30-day evaluation copy of the software, is at:

```
http://www.sausage.com
```

HoTMetaL and HoTMetaL Pro

HoTMetaL is a shareware HTML editor from SoftQuad Inc. **HoTMetaL** is one of their many SGML products. You can obtain the program from any one of the following mirror sites at this URL:

```
http://www.sq.com/products/hotmetal/hm-ftp.htm
```

HoTMetaL Pro is the commercially supported version of the editor, available for Windows, SunOS, and MacOS. It includes many additional features. For a comprehensive features list, see:

```
http://www.sq.com/products/hotmetal/hmp-org.htm
```

For more information on **HoTMetaL** and other HTML and SGML publishing products by SoftQuad, see their home page at:

```
http://www.sq.com
```

or the **HoTMetaL FAQ**:

```
ftp://ftp.cs.concordia.ca/pub/www/Tools/Editors/SoftQuad/hotmetal/FAQ
```

You can also contact SoftQuad by phone (416-239-4801) or e-mail *hotmetal@sq.com*.

HTML Assistant

HTML Assistant is a Windows text editor with extensions to assist in creating HTML hypertext documents. **HTML Assistant Pro** has additional features. Information about **HTML Assistant** and **HTML Assistant Pro**, and links to downloadable demonstration versions, are found, respectively, at the URLs:

```
http://cs.dal.ca/ftp/htmlasst/htmlafaq.html
```

```
http://fox.nstn.ca/~harawitz/htmlpro1.html
```

HTML Author

HTML Author is a freeware HTML editor for Windows. A home page for **HTML Author**, including links to the software and online documentation, can be found at:

```
http://www.salford.ac.uk/docs/depts/iti/homepage.html
```

HTML Converter (Word 6.0 Add-on)

This is a Word 6.0 for Windows package that converts a text file into HTML. For information, see the Hype Media's UK home page at:

```
http://www.netkonect.co.uk/hype/index.html
```

HTML Easy Pro!

HTML Easy Pro! is another simple-to-use HTML editor. A home page with a demonstration of some of the extended features of **HTML Easy Pro!**, plus a link to the software, can be found at:

```
http://www.seed.net.tw/~milkylin/htmleasy.html
```

H.T.M.L. Handler

This is a free multiple document editor for Windows. For information, including a screen shot, see the **H.T.M.L. Handler** home page at:

```
http://www.umn.edu/nlhome/m447/reinb001/hthand.html
```

HTML Writer

HTML Writer is a powerful yet easy-to-use HTML editor for Windows. Information, including a tips and tricks guide and instructions on how to subscribe to the **HTML Writer** mailing list, is available at the **HTML Writer** home page:

```
http://lal.cs.byu.edu/people/nosack/index.html
```

HTMLed

HTMLed is a customizable text-mode HTML editor. A **Pro** version of **HTMLed**, which has many enhancements, is also available. For more information about **HTMLed** and **HTMLed Pro**, respectively, including links and information to obtain the packages, see the following URLs:

```
http://www.ist.ca/htmled/
```

```
http://www.ist.ca/htmledpro/
```

Hypertext Master

This is a full-featured HTML editor for Windows. More information on the software, and a link to the software itself, can be found at:

```
http://www.tcp.co.uk/~bob866/hyper.html
```

InContext Spider

The **Spider** editor, from InContext Systems, is a fine SGML-based editor with a number of useful features. More information on InContext and the **Spider** editor, including instructions for obtaining a demonstration version, can be found at:

```
http://www.incontext.ca/demo/icspeval.html
```

Internet Assistant for Word (Word 6.0 Add-on)

This was designed by Microsoft as an extension for HTML authoring. Additional information about **Internet Assistant** can be found at the URL:

```
http://www.microsoft.com/MSOffice/Word/ia/default.htm
```

while the package itself is found at:

```
ftp://ftp.microsoft.com/deskapps/word/winword-public/ia/README.TXT
```

```
ftp://ftp.microsoft.com/deskapps/word/winword-public/ia/wordia.exe
```

<Live Markup>

<Live Markup> is another feature-rich WYSIWYG HTML editor for Windows. The enhanced version, **<Live Markup>PRO**, has added features. More information, including information on how to obtain, register, and upgrade the software, can be found at:

```
http://www.mediatec.com/mediatech/index.html
```

NaviPress

NaviPress, by Navisoft, features an easy-to-use menu-, dialog-, and palette-based WYSIWYG interface for creating, editing, and formatting Web pages. For more information, including a technical overview, documentation, and links for downloading the software, see the **NaviPress** home page at:

```
http://www.navisoft.com/products/press/press.html
```

TILE (Lotus Notes Add-on)

TILE (Tool for Internet/Lotus Exchange) is an application for creating professional World Wide Web documents from Lotus Notes databases. A number of Internet directories have been created with **TILE**, and are listed at:

```
http://tile.net/
```

The **TILE** home page, including specifications and feature lists for the package, is at:

```
http://tile.net/tile/info/index.html
```

Web Publisher

This product is billed as an automated HTML production tool. Examples of its features, as well as instructions for obtaining the software, can be found at:

```
http://www.skisoft.com/skisoft/
```

Web Spinner

Web Spinner is another Windows-based HTML editor. *Win32s* is required, and can be obtained along with the editor itself from the **Web Spinner** home page:

```
http://www.execpc.com/~flfsoft/webspn.html
```

WebAuthor (Word 6.0 Add-on)

WebAuthor is Quarterdeck's HTML authoring package. For information, see the **WebAuthor** home page at:

```
http://www.qdeck.com/webauthor/fact.html
```

WordPerfect Internet Publisher (WordPerfect 6.1 Add-on)

Internet Publisher contains everything a WordPerfect 6.1 user needs to create HTML documents. For information, see the **WordPerfect Internet Publisher** home page and white paper at:

```
http://wp.novell.com/elecpub/intpub.htm
```

Macintosh Editors

Alpha

The **Alpha** text editor provides a comprehensive HTML mode for creating and editing HTML documents. The **Alpha** home page, which includes links to the software, is found at:

```
http://www.cs.umd.edu/~keleher/alpha.html
```

BBEdit HTML Extensions

BBEdit is a popular Macintosh text editor that comes in two versions: the freeware program **BBEdit-Lite** and the full-blown commercial package **BBEdit 3.5**. The **BBEdit** editor is a product of Bare Bones Software (*bbsw@netcom.com*). The **BBEdit-Lite** freeware version is available via anonymous FTP from various sites, including:

```
ftp://ftp.std.com/pub/bbedit/
```

More information can be found at the **BBEdit** home page at:

```
http://northshore.shore.net/~quantum/BBEdit.html
```

Extensions Package 1   This macro package creates extension menus for all standard formatting commands. Information is available at:

```
http://www.uji.es/bbedit-html-extensions.html
```

The macros themselves are found at either of the following sites (the first is the home location):

```
ftp://ftp.uji.es/pub/mac/util/bbedit-html-ext.sea.hqx
```

```
ftp://sumex-aim.stanford.edu/info-mac/bbedit-html-ext-b3.hqx
```

This package was developed by Carles Bellver.

EXTENSIONS PACKAGE 2   This package lacks support for some elements, but does have other utilities. Information about this package is found at:

```
http://www.york.ac.uk/~ld11/BBEditTools.html
```

while the macros themselves are at:

```
ftp://ftp.york.ac.uk/pub/users/ld11/BBEdit_HTML_Tools.sea.hqx
```

Arachnid

Arachnid, by Second Look Computing, is a winner of the 1995 Apple Enterprise Award in the Publishing for Government, Business, and Education category. It is a free, full-featured product. To keep abreast of this quickly developing product, or to obtain a copy, visit the **Arachnid** home page at:

```
http://sec-look.uiowa.edu/about/projects/arachnid-page.html
```

HTML.edit

HTML.edit is a stand-alone HyperCard 2.2 application (you do not need your own HyperCard to run the program). Information about **HTML.edit**, including instructions on how and where to obtain the software, can be found at:

```
http://ogopogo.nttc.edu/tools/HTMLedit/HTMLedit.html
```

HTML Editor

HTML Editor is a shareware program. Registered users receive free electronic updates. Information can be found at:

```
http://dragon.acadiau.ca/~giles/HTML_Editor/Documentation.html
```

HTML-HyperEditor

This is a HyperCard stack—you must have HyperCard 2.2 installed on your machine. More information on this product can be found at:

```
http://balder.syo.lu.se/Editor/HTML-HyperEditor.html
```

HTML Grinder

HTML Grinder, by Matterform Media, is a *modular* editor for the Mac. The HTML Grinder home page containing feedback, tips, and download links can be found at:

    http://www.matterform.com/mf/grinder/htmlgrinder.html

HTML Web Weaver

HTML Web Weaver is a popular Macintosh text-based shareware editor. Information on how to obtain a copy of the HTML Web Weaver or an alpha release of the forthcoming World Wide Web Weaver for Macintosh can be found at:

    http://137.143.111.3/web.weaver/about.html

HTML Writer

HTML Writer is an HTML editor for the Macintosh written in SuperCard. Unfortunately, the author is no longer updating this product. The home page is:

    http://www.uwtc.washington.edu/JonWiederspan/HTMLEditor.html

NaviPress

NaviPress, by Navisoft, is a combination browser and editor. More information on NaviPress and NaviServer can be found at:

    http://www.navisoft.com/products/press/press.htm

S.H.E.

S.H.E., for Simple HTML Editor, is a text-mode editor written as a HyperCard stack—HyperCard is required to run this program. Additional information about S.H.E. is found at:

    http://dewey.lib.ncsu.edu/staff/morgan/simple.html

while the HyperCard stack can be obtained at:

    ftp://ftp.lib.ncsu.edu/pub/software/mac/simple-http-editor.hqx

OS/2 EDITORS

Boxer

Although Boxer is not an HTML editor per se, it is popularly known as an "OS/2 Must-Have Utility." Boxer can be downloaded directly from:

```
ftp://ftp.hobbes.nmsu.edu/os2/editors/boxos2_X.zip
```

where X is the version number (currently 7).

HTML Generator

HTML Generator is a basic text-based HTML editor for OS/2. The package is available for download from:

```
ftp://ftp.leo.org/pub/comp/os/os2/editors/htmlg102.zip
```

HTML Wizard

HTML Wizard is a popular, well-designed, and full-featured HTML editor for OS/2. The package is available for download from the Hobbes FTP site at:

```
ftp://hobbes.nmsu.edu/os2/editors/htmlwiz.zip
```

SpHyDir

SpHyDir (Structured Professional Hypertext Directory Manager) is a professional, object-oriented tool capable of building complex HTML documents for the Web. An informative home page can be found at:

```
http://pclt.cis.yale.edu/pclt/sphydir/sphydir.htm
```

WebWriter/2

WebWriter/2 can serve as a source viewer and editor. This package is available for download from the Hobbes FTP archive at:

```
ftp://hobbes.nmsu.edu/os2/editors/ww2_09b2.zip
```

UNIX Editors

A.S.H.E.

A.S.H.E. (A Simple HTML Editor) is a shareware HTML editor written using C, Motif, and the NCSA HTML Widget set. Links to a README file and the most recent source are at:

```
ftp://ftp.cs.rpi.edu/pub/puninj/ASHE/
```

and a presentation on **A.S.H.E.** made to the Second WWW Conference in Chicago can be found, in slide-show format, at:

```
http://www.cs.rpi.edu/~puninj/TALK/head.html
```

Emacs

The **emacs** editor, a product of the Free Software Foundation, is one of the most popular UNIX text editors. (The first package was written by Marc

Andreessen, then of NCSA.) The name of this lisp program is **html-mode.el** and it is available, for example, from:

```
ftp://ftp.std.com/customers2/src/network/WWW/w3/extras/
```

Html-helper-mode is a more recent and fully featured **emacs** macro package. Information about **html-helper-mode,** including links to the software and related files, is found at:

```
http://www.santafe.edu/~nelson/hhm-beta/
```

HoTMetaL

HoTMetaL by SoftQuad Inc. is a freeware HTML editor for Sun SPARCs running X11 or OpenWindows, and PCs running Windows. The commercial version is **HoTMetaL Pro.** For more information on these and other specialized SGML products, see the SoftQuad, Inc. home page at:

```
http://www.sq.com/
```

NaviPress

NaviPress by Navisoft removes the necessity for manual editing of HTML. For more information, including a technical overview and documentation, see the **NaviPress** home page at:

```
http://www.navisoft.com/products/press/press.htm
```

Phoenix

Phoenix is a popular X-Windows-based editor. More on **Phoenix,** including installation and usage instructions, and links to the source code, can be found at the home page:

```
http://www.bsd.uchicago.edu/ftp/pub/phoenix/README.html
```

tkHTML

Information about **tkHTML** is found at:

```
http://www.ssc.com/~roland/tkHTML/tkHTML.html
```

The program itself is available from:

```
ftp://ftp.u.washington.edu/public/roland/tkHTML/
```

tkWWW

tkWWW is actually a UNIX WWW *browser* but also supports document editing. Two sources of information on this product's editing features are as follows:

```
http://uu-gna.mit.edu:8001/tk-www/help/overview.html
```

```
http://www.osf.org/ri/hci_papers/tkwww.html
```

WebMagic Author

WebMagic Author is part of SGI's WebForce Software Environment. The **WebMagic Author** home page, including information on how to obtain a copy of the software, can be found at:

```
http://www.sgi.com/Products/WebFORCE/WebForceSoft.html
```

WYSIWYG HTML Editor

WYSIWYG HTML Editor is a UNIX HTML text editor. More information on this software is found at:

```
http://web.cs.city.ac.uk/homes/njw/htmltext/htmltext.html
```

NɛXT Editors

NeXTStep HTML-Editor

NeXTStep HTML-Editor is a graphical HTML editor for NeXT workstations. Information about the editor is rather scant, but some can be found at the Scholarly Communications Project:

```
http://scholar.lib.vt.edu/jpowell.html
```

while the program itself is available at:

```
ftp://borg.lib.vt.edu/pub/next/
```

WebPages

Created by IT Solutions, **WebPages** is a commercial Web publishing package for NeXTStep. More information, including design model samples, is found at the **WebPages** home page:

```
http://www.its.com/products/WebPages.htmld/
```

DOCUMENT CONVERTERS

Often you have a number of preexisting files that you would like to convert to HTML format. Alternatively, you may already be using a document preparation program such as LaTeX, Scribe, or FrameMaker and would like to be able to continue using these tools and convert the resulting documents into HTML. These are jobs for a document translator or converter—a program that can take your document in its original format and convert it to a close equivalent in HTML.

There are several packages that have been written to accomplish this task, including some powerful commercial products. As mentioned earlier, these conversions may not be ideal, since there is often no direct match between print markup languages and HTML. Consequently you may have to edit the resulting HTML documents to add elements that could not be translated, and so on. Nevertheless, editing a largely correct document is a much easier task than typing the whole thing in from scratch.

There are also several packages that can convert from HTML to another markup language more appropriate for printing. This is very useful for preparing printed versions of HTML documents for reading away from a computer. Some packages (such as **latex2html** and **WebMaker**) allow you to prepare parent manuscripts containing alternative blocks of markup: one block for printing and another for HTML. This is very useful for preparing documents that read well in either presentation format.

Many of these packages are script programs, often written in perl. Thus these programs require that you have perl or another appropriate interpreter on your machine.

A list of the resources given in this section is maintained at the Web site:

    http://www.hprc.utoronto.ca/HTMLdocs/tools_home.html

Other useful lists of translators and filters are found at:

    ftp://ftp.isri.unlv.edu/pub/mirror/infosystems/WWW/tools/translators/

    http://www.yahoo.com/Computers_and_Internet/Internet/World_Wide_Web/HTML_Converters/

    http://www.w3.org/hypertext/WWW/Tools/

    http://union.ncsa.uiuc.edu/HyperNews/get/www/html/converters.html

The programs are listed in alphabetical order. You are most likely interested in matching a document format or program name to a particular tool. Table 11.1 matches conversion programs to standard word processor names and document formats—this is a good place to start, if you know the data format you wish to convert to HTML.

ASC2HTML (UNIX)

asc2html.pl is a perl script for converting plain ASCII files into HTML.

asc2html can be found at:

    ftp://ftp.isri.unlv.edu/pub/mirror/infosystems/WWW/tools/translators/

asc2html was written by Oscar Nierstrasz of the University of Geneva, Switzerland.

▬▬▬ **Table 11.1** Conversion Programs for Different Document Formats

Format	Program
Excel Spreadsheet	XL2HTML.XLS, XLTOHTML
FrameMaker	Cyberleaf, frame2html, mif2html, miftran, MifMucker, WebMaker
Interleaf	Cyberleaf, TagWrite
LaTeX/tex	hyperlatex, latex2html, tex2rtf
Microsoft Word	TagWrite, Cyberleaf
nroff/troff	mm2html, ms2html
Plain text	asc2html, charconv, HTML Markup, HTML Markdown, striphtml, TagWrite, txt2html, WEBIT
PostScript	ps2html
QuarkXPress	BeyondPress
Rich Text Format (RTF)	HLPDK, rtftohtml, RTFTOHTM, TagWrite, tex2rtf
Scribe	scribe2html
SGML (other than HTML)	TagWrite
Texinfo	texi2html
UNIX mail file	Hypermail
UNIX man pages	RosettaMan
Ventura Publisher (Corel)	TagWrite
WordPerfect	Cyberleaf, TagWrite, WPTOHTML, WP2X

BEYONDPRESS (MACINTOSH)

BeyondPress, a product of Astrobyte Online, is a commercial package for converting QuarkXPress documents into HTML. The **BeyondPress** home page is at:

```
http://www.astrobyte.com/Astrobyte/BeyondPressInfo.html
```

CHARCONV (UNIX)

Charconv is a program filter (written in ANSI-C) that can transform one encoding of an extended character set into another. **Charconv** is available at:

```
ftp://ftp.isri.unlv.edu/pub/mirror/infosystems/WWW/tools/translators/
charconv/charconv.tar.gz
```

CYBERLEAF (UNIX)

Cyberleaf is a full commercial document conversion package from Interleaf Inc. (*i-direct@ileaf.com*). An informative home page including screen shots, a **Cyberleaf** FAQ, and instructions for obtaining the software can be found at:

```
http://www.ileaf.com/ip.html
```

FRAME2HTML (UNIX)

Frame2html is a collection of programs to facilitate the conversion of FrameMaker documents and books to HTML. The **frame2html** package is available at:

```
ftp://ftp.isri.unlv.edu/pub/mirror/infosystems/WWW/tools/translators/
```

HLPDK (WINDOWS)

HLPDK is a Windows software package for developing online hypertext help documentation. A shareware version of **HLPDK** is available at:

```
ftp://garbo.uwasa.fi/pc/programming
```

in the files *hdk115a.zip*, *hdk115b.zip*, and *hdk115l.zip*. There is also a professional, supported version. For additional information, contact Ron Loewy (*rloewy@panix.com*).

HTML MARKDOWN AND
HTML MARKUP (MACINTOSH)

HTML Markdown is a utility that quickly and conveniently strips tags from an HTML document. **HTML Markup** is the converse. The home pages for these products can be found, respectively, at:

```
http://htc.rit.edu/markdown.html
```

```
http://htc.rit.edu/klephacks/markup.html
```

HYPERLATEX (UNIX)

Hyperlatex is a package that lets you use a subset of the LaTeX language to prepare documents in HTML. Additional information about **hyperlatex** can be found at:

```
http://www.cs.ruu.nl/people/otfried/html/hyperlatex.html
```

while the source for the program is available at:

```
ftp://ftp.cs.ruu.nl/pub/SGI/IPE/Hyperlatex-1.3.tar.gz
```

LATEX2HTML (UNIX)

Latex2html is a powerful perl package that can translate LaTeX documents into corresponding HTML. **Latex2html** requires several additional packages to function properly, as explained in the **latex2html** documentation, which is found at:

    http://cbl.leeds.ac.uk/nikos/tex2html/doc/latex2html/node1.html

MifMucker (UNIX)

MifMucker is a perl script front end for passing FrameMaker documents through a series of processing filters. More information on how to obtain and use this package is available at:

    http://www.oac.uci.edu/indiv/ehood/mifmucker.doc.html

Miftran (UNIX)

Miftran is a general-purpose MIF (FrameMaker's Maker Interchange Format) translation program. The **Miftran** source along with a helpful README file can be found at:

    ftp://ftp.alumni.caltech.edu/pub/mcbeath/web/miftran/

Mm2html (UNIX)

Mm2html.pl is a perl script that converts nroff documents, written using the "mm" macros, into HTML.

Mm2html can be found at:

    ftp://cs.ucl.ac.uk/darpa/mm2html/

Ms2html (UNIX)

Ms2html.pl is a perl script that converts an annotated text file into the corresponding HTML markup. **Ms2html.pl** can be found at:

    http://iamwww.unibe.ch/~scg/Src/Scripts/ms2html

You need the files *ms2html.pl, button.pl,* and *url.pl.*

Ps2html (UNIX)

Ps2html is a perl package that converts arbitrary PostScript text to HTML. Additional information about **ps2html** can be found at

    ftp://bradley.bradley.edu/pub/guru/ps2html/home.html

while the package itself can be obtained from:

    ftp://bradley.bradley.edu/pub/guru/ps2html/v2/ps2html-v2.tar

RosettaMan (UNIX)

RosettaMan is a filter for UNIX-style manual pages. The **RosettaMan** archive can be found at:

```
ftp://ftp.cs.berkeley.edu/ucb/people/phelps/tcl/rman.tar.Z
```

rtftohtml (Macintosh, UNIX)

rtftohtml is a program that converts Microsoft Rich Text Format (RTF) documents into their HTML equivalents. Additional information about **rtftohtml** can be found at:

```
ftp://ftp.cray.com/src/WWWstuff/RTF/
```

Executable binaries are provided for Sun and Macintosh platforms. These are found at:

```
ftp://ftp.cray.com/src/WWWstuff/RTF/latest/binaries/
```

while the source code is available at:

```
ftp://ftp.cray.com/src/WWWstuff/RTF/latest/src/unix.tar
```

RTFTOHTM (Windows)

RTFTOHTM is a Word 2.0 for Windows extension package that converts RTF documents to HTML. **RTFTOHTM** can be found at:

```
ftp://oak.oakland.edu/SimTel/win3/winword/html090.zip
```

(or higher numbers for more recent revisions).

Scribe2html (UNIX)

Scribe is a document markup and production system, similar to markup languages like [t/n]roff or LaTeX. The Scribe2html conversion package is free and is available at:

```
ftp://gatekeeper.dec.com/pub/DEC/NSL/www/
```

stripsgml (UNIX)

stripsgml is a small perl program that strips SGML markup (including HTML) from a text document to create a plain-text version. **stripsgml** is available at:

```
http://www.oac.uci.edu/indiv/ehood/perlSGML.html
```

TagWrite (Windows)

TagWrite is a commercial document conversion tool produced by Zandar Corp. For more information (including pricing), you should contact Zandar (phone: 802-889-1058).

Tex2RTF (UNIX)

Tex2RTF is a utility for converting from a simple LaTeX subset to HTML, RTF, and Windows Help RTF formats. Information on the different versions can be found at:

`http://www.aiai.ed.ac.uk/~jacs/tex2rtf.html`

TEXI2HTML (UNIX)

Texi2html is a perl script that converts texinfo-format files to HTML. More information on this products is available at:

`http://wwwcn1.cern.ch/dci/texi2html/`

Texi2html can be obtained at:

`ftp://ftp.isri.unlv.edu/pub/mirror/infosystems/WWW/tools/translators/texi2html/`

TXT2HTML (UNIX) (BY SETH GOLLUB)

This program is a perl script that takes in a standard text file and writes out HTML. The product's home page, including a before-and-after conversion example, is found at:

`http://www.cs.wustl.edu/~seth/txt2html/`

TXT2HTML (UNIX)
(SAME NAME, DIFFERENT PROGRAM)

This is another perl script that converts a plain-text document into HTML. Although development of this **txt2html** was recently discontinued, the home page for the package, with instructions on downloading and using the software, can still be found at:

`http://homepage.seas.upenn.edu/~mengwong/txt2html.html`

WEBIT (UNIX)

This perl script takes an innovative approach to text-HTML conversion, and is a functional and elegant alternative to full-blown HTML editors. The WEBIT home page can be found at:

`http://futures.wharton.upenn.edu/~attau791/webit.html`

WebMaker (UNIX)

WebMaker is a package for creating FrameMaker documents and converting them to HTML. Information about **WebMaker**, including information about how to obtain the package, can be found at:

```
http://www.cern.ch/WebMaker/WebMaker.html
```

or by writing *(webmaker@cern.ch.)*.

WPTOHTML (DOS)

This is a WordPerfect macro package for converting WordPerfect 5.1 for DOS and WordPerfect 6.0 for DOS files into HTML. The macro packages are available at:

```
ftp://oak.oakland.edu/SimTel/msdos/wordperf/
```

in the files *wpt60d10.zip* (for WordPerfect 6.0) and *wpt50d10.zip* (for WordPerfect 5.1).

WP2X (DOS, UNIX)

WP2X is a C-language program for converting WordPerfect 5.1 files into other formats, including HTML. Information can be found at:

```
http://www.milkyway.com/People/Michael_Richardson/wp2x.html
```

XL2HTML.XLS (Macintosh, Windows)

This is a Visual BASIC macro for Microsoft Excel 5.0. The product's home page can be found at:

```
http://rs712b.gsfc.nasa.goc/704/dgd/xl2html.html
```

XLTOHTML (Macintosh)

This is an AppleScript program that converts Excel 4.05 or 5.0 for Mac spreadsheets into HTML 3.0 tables. The home page for this product, including links to the source, can be found at:

```
http://www.rhodes.edu/software/readme.html
```

HTML VERIFIERS

More and more commercial HTML editors have some sort of HTML validation built in. However, for the rest of us, there are several simple stand-alone tools for checking the validity of HTML elements in a document. These often use the HTML Document Type Definition (DTD) file as the definition of the HTML syntax, so you will require this file to use these tools. The "official" home of HTML information (including DTDs) is:

```
http://www.w3.org/hypertext/WWW/MarkUp/MarkUp.html
```

and you will find the "official" HTML 2.0 DTD at:

```
http://www.w3.org/hypertext/WWW/MarkUp/html-spec/html-pubtext.html
```

A collection of HTML DTDs, including those for HTML 3 and the Netscape HTML extensions, can be obtained from:

```
http://www.halsoft.com/html/
```

New DTD files will appear with each revision of the language. To test your documents' compatibility with this new standard you need only download the revised DTD and plug it into your verification program.

▮▮▮▮▮ TIP

Why Validate?

Why bother validating your HTML as long as the rendered result looks good, you may ask? Looks can be deceiving. For a brief discussion of the virtues of validating your HTML, see:

```
http://www.earth.com/bad-style/why-validate.html
```

SGMLS (DOS, UNIX)

sgmls is an SGML syntax-checking program. This program takes as input an SGML file and checks the document structure against the relevant document type definition (DTD). URLs pointing to the current HTML DTD are listed at the beginning of this section and in the "References" section at the end of Chapter 4. As output, the program prints a list of syntax errors and the line number at which the errors occurred.

As an example, consider the file *test.html* shown in Figure 11.1.

▮▮▮▮▮ Figure 11.1 Example HTML document *test.html*.

```html
<HTML>
<HEAD>
<TITLE> <em> Instructional </em>and Research Computing Home Page</TITLE>
</HEAD>
<BODY>


<h1> Instructional and Research Computing </H1>
<hr>
This is the Instructional and Research Computing Group <B>(IRC)</B>
```

```
World Wide Web home page. If you get lost try the

<a href="big%20dog.html"> big dog help </a> or

<a href="http://www.university.ca/</a>home.html"> right here </a>

<hr>

<oL>

<LI> consulting services in <A HREF="InsT/intro.html"> instructional

technology and applications</A>

applications</A>.<P>


</ol>

<HR>


</BODY>

</HTML>
```

The following command on a UNIX computer will validate the file *test.html*—note how the DTD is specified in the command line:

```
sgmls -s html.dtd test.html
```

On a PC running DOS, the command is:

```
sgmls.exe -s html.dtd test.html
```

Often the DTD comes in two parts: the DTD itself, plus a second file called the SGML *declaration*, often with a name like *html.decl*. You need both these files for **sgmls** to work. You can either append them together (*html.decl* first, followed by *html.dtd*), or pass them as subsequent arguments, as in:

```
sgmls -s html.decl html.dtd test.html
```

The output lists the errors and the line numbers at which they occurred. Figure 11.2 shows the **sgmls** output for the file in Figure 11.1.

Figure 11.2 Sgmls error output after parsing *test.html* (shown in Figure 11.1).

```
sgmls: SGML error at test.html, line 3 at ">":

EM end-tag ignored: doesn't end any open element (current is TITLE)
```

```
sgmls: SGML error at test.html, line 3 at ">":

Bad end-tag in R/CDATA element; treated as short (no GI) end-tag

sgmls: SGML error at test.html, line 3 at "d":

HEAD end-tag implied by data; not minimizable

sgmls: SGML error at test.html, line 3 at ">":

TITLE end-tag ignored: doesn't end any open element (current is HTML)

sgmls: SGML error at test.html, line 4 at ">":

HEAD end-tag ignored: doesn't end any open element (current is HTML)

sgmls: SGML error at test.html, line 21 at ">":

A end-tag ignored: doesn't end any open element (current is OL)
```

The errors at line 3 are due to the illegal character markup inside the **TITLE** element. The subsequent errors at lines 3 and 4 are a result of this same mistake. The error at line 21 is a very typical error: the file has a duplicate </A> ending tag.

Where do you find **sgmls**? It is a public domain package, and can be found at many anonymous FTP sites including:

```
ftp://jclark.com/pub/sgmls/
```

The source code archive is in the files *sgmls*.tar.Z,* while the PC executables are in the files *sgmls*.zip* (where * is a version number).

Sgmls was written by James Clark *(jjc@jclark.com)*.

HALSOFT HTML VALIDATION SITE

If you want to check your files but do not feel comfortable downloading the **sgmls** package, you can use it remotely instead—the **Halsoft Validation Site** provides this service, over the Web, to the general public.

The Halsoft validator checks either an entire document currently in place at a specific URL (you use a fill-in **FORM** to tell the validator the URL of the document), or a small sample of HTML, which you send to the validator, using a fill-in **FORM**. There are options for selecting "strictness" of the validation, and for specifying the version of HTML you wish to check against—thus you can check for valid Netscape enhancements, or even for valid documents containing Java **APP** tags. The validator returns a list of all the errors. For more information (and to try it out), visit the **Halsoft** site at:

http://www.halsoft.com/html-val-svc/

<HTMLCHEK>

This validator will check either HTML 2.0 or HTML 3.0 files for syntax errors, including local link verification, and generates simple reference-dependency maps. The program requires the awk or perl interpreter to run, and will do so on any platform for which either is available. Depending on the situation, **<htmlchek>** can be more or less strict than the HTML 2.0 DTD, and will report stylistic problems as well as true errors. More information can be found at:

http://uts.cc.utexas.edu/~churchh/htmlchek.html

WEBLINT

Designed to pick "fluff" off Web pages, **Weblint** is a perl script written by Neil Bowers *(neilb@khoros.unm.edu)* that checks basic structure and identifies the following errors: unknown elements, unknown tag context, overlapped elements, illegally nested elements, mismatched opening and closing tags, unclosed elements, unpaired quotes, and unexpected heading order. HTML 3.0 elements such as **TABLE, MATH,** and **FIG** are supported. The **Weblint** home page, including links to obtain the software, is found at:

http://www.unipress.com/weblint/

LINK VERIFIERS

Sgmls verifies that your HTML tags are correctly placed, but cannot ensure that the hypertext links go to valid locations. To check hypertext links you need a "link verifier." This is a program that reads your document, extracts the hypertext links, and tests the validity of the URLs. Note that some link checkers were discussed at the end of Chapter 10—please look there also, should this topic be of interest.

LINKCHECK

Linkcheck is a perl program designed to run on UNIX machines, but it may run on other platforms, given some work.

Linkcheck checks **gopher, ftp,** and **http** URLs in a document. It cannot check other URLs such as **mailto, wais, telnet, rlogin,** or **tn3270. Linkcheck** tests **gopher** URLs by fully accessing the indicated URL, which can be slow if the URL links to a large file. It tests **ftp** URLs by listing directory contents rather than fetching the document, which is a lot nicer. **Http** URLs are checked by using the HTTP HEAD method, which is just as nice. If the HEAD method access fails, **linkcheck** tries the GET method (some servers do not understand the HTTP HEAD method).

Linkcheck does have difficulties with relative URLs. You need to specify the URL of the directory *containing* the file to allow checking of relative URLs, so the document must be in an HTTP server-accessible directory. This makes it impossible to check the file prior to placing it on the server. In addition, **linkcheck** cannot validate partial URLs containing relative paths; any URL starting with the string . . / is labeled invalid.

Linkcheck is available from:

```
ftp://ftp.math.psu.edu/pub/sibley/
```

You need the files *linkcheck, about.linkcheck* (documentation for the package), *ftpcheck* (for checking FTP links), and *mconnect.pl*. **Linkcheck** requires a program called **mconnect**, which allows an interactive connection with a remote mailer program. If your system does not have **mconnect**, you can use the **mconnect.pl** perl program instead.

If you require **mconnect.pl**, you will also need two additional perl packages: **sock.pl** and **telnet.pl**. These are found at:

```
ftp://anubis.ac.hmc.edu/pub/perl/scripts/netstuff/sock.pl.gz
```

```
ftp://ftp.cis.ufl.edu/pub/perl/scripts/telnet.shar.gz
```

If you use **ftpcheck**, you also need the auxiliary **ftplib.pl** library. This can be found at:

```
ftp://ftp.cis.ufl.edu/pub/perl/scripts/ftplib.pl
```

LVRFY

lvrfy is a script that verifies all the internal links by starting with one page and parsing all the hyperlinks, including images, and then recursively checking all the links. **lvrfy** is a regular shell script—it assumes that **sed, awk, csh, touch,** and **rm** are in your path. One drawback of this verifier is its speed, which averages 7.5 seconds per file; and there are a number of other small bugs that may manifest themselves if the HTML itself has not been verified. The **lvrfy** home page can be found at:

```
http://www.cs.dartmouth.edu/~crow/lvrfy.html
```

VERIFY_LINKS

Verify_links is a **FORMs**-based CGI program for validating hypertext links in an HTML document. **Verify_links** is limited to verifying **http** URLs and cannot check FTP, Gopher, telnet, and other links. In this respect it is not as useful as **linkcheck**. However, it is more reliable than **linkcheck** in validating **http** URLs, and, in particular, local or relative URLs. It also can check POST actions to a limited degree, and will "push the buttons" in a **FORM** to verify the existence of the attached CGI program. Like **linkcheck**, **verify_links** attempts to use network-friendly requests such as the HTTP HEAD request to minimize the load on the network, and only falls back to full file retrieval if this fails.

Additional information about **verify_links** can be found at:

```
http://wsk.eit.com/wsk/dist/doc/admin/webtest/verify_links.html
```

Verify_links is a product of Enterprise Integration Technologies.

WEBXREF

This is a perl program for generating a list of cross-references from an HTML document, and from the HTML documents linked to that document. The output includes a list of all referenced HTML files, directories, images, URLs (**http, mailto, news, ftp, telnet, gopher**), CGI scripts, and named anchors. Additionally, files, directories, and anchors that are not found or are unreadable are also listed. Currently, **Webxref** does not support anchors that are split across line breaks. Future features may include checking of external URLs and an "avoid" mode to disable checking of certain links. The **Webxref** home page can be found at:

```
http://www.sara.nl/cgi-bin/rick_acc_webxref
```

WEB BROWSERS AND HELPER APPLICATIONS

There are literally dozens of different Web browsers, available for UNIX, VAX/VMS, and NeXT workstations, PCs running DOS, Windows, or OS/2, Macintoshes, and Amigas (the Web is *not* just Netscape!). Almost all of these browsers are freely available over the Internet, complete with online documentation at the browser developer's Web site. Links to most of these sites, along with brief product descriptions, can be found at the following reference sites (it is the author's privilege to list his own site first):

```
http://www.hprc.utoronto.ca/HTMLdocs/tools_home.html
```

```
http://www.w3.org/hypertext/WWW/Clients.html
```

```
http://www.stars.com/Vlib/Users/Browsers.html
```

```
http://www.yahoo.com/Computers--and--Internet/Internet/World_
Wide_Web/Browsers/
```

These sites also list helper applications, which you will need for viewing or playing nonstandard data types, such as audio and video files, or Adobe PDF files.

To keep even more up-to-date, you can monitor the various newsgroups devoted to Web browsers (the different Web newsgroups were listed in the "References" section of Chapter 1). Announcements about new browsers or other tools will appear in the newsgroups before appearing in organized lists.

In some cases you may find that a program is no longer available at the site indicated in the above reference sites. In this case you should use archie to locate an alternative site. The archie client program is available for almost all computer platforms and is available for downloading from many anonymous FTP sites. A detailed description on using archie to search for programs is given in Appendix C, along with instructions for obtaining an archie client.

NETWORKING SOFTWARE— CONNECTING TO THE NETWORK

Running any browser requires an Internet connection, either an ethernet (or other) card connecting your computer to a local network, or a telephone dial-up SLIP or PPP network link. In both cases, you also need software that allows your computer to "talk" to the connection using TCP/IP. That means you must install TCP/IP networking software. Some free TCP/IP software is available on the Internet, but you really do need to understand what you are doing to set this up properly. There are also a number of commercial packages that provide TCP/IP functionality, at modest cost. I advise you to consult your local computer shop if you are uncomfortable with installing these packages.

PCs running DOS or Windows 3.1 can obtain essentially free TCP/IP software by installing the **trumpet winsock** package. This is found at many FTP sites; the following site is generally kept up-to-date:

```
ftp://papa.indstate.edu/winsock-1/winsock/
```

A handy troubleshooting reference can be found at:

    http://www.webcom.com/~llarrow/trouble.html

A word of warning: There is also a USENET newsreader program named **trumpet,** so be careful not to get the two mixed up.

If you are running a Windows 3.1 application, you will also need the Windows *WINSOCK.DLL* program library. This is a package of routines that act as an interface between your Windows application (such as Mosaic) and the actual TCP/IP software. This library is free and comes as part of the **trumpet winsock** distribution. Many browser distributions also include this library.

If you are running OS/2 Warp, then the required TCP/IP software should be integrated with the system. The system is less clear with Windows 95, but there also the system should come with networking support. In either case, check with your computer shop, just to make sure.

If you have a Macintosh, you also need appropriate SLIP, PPP, and TCP/IP software to run these browsers. All Macintosh browsers require at least System 7, and you will also need MacTCP 2.0.2 (and preferably 2.0.4) to provide the TCP/IP software. There is also a MacPPP package for PPP support. You should contact your local Macintosh software outlet to obtain these packages.

These issues do not come up on UNIX, VAX/VMS, or NeXT platforms, as these systems come with Internet networking built in.

HTTP SERVERS AND SERVER UTILITIES

So you are thinking of setting up your own server. You have a connection to the Internet (hopefully a fast one!) and perhaps a computer. Now you want to get some server software and get things running. At this stage a little advance planning can help you avoid much future grief. The following guidelines should help you decide which platform and server to choose. But—be sure to do a little Web surfing, to make sure the material presented here is up-to-date. The sites listed at the end of this section can help you obtain up-to-date information on just about every available Web server.

BASIC SERVER ISSUES

The assumption is that you want to set up a reliable server and that you are not doing this just for fun (although fun should be a component in this process). You then need a server that is fast, easy to maintain, and reliable (the machine does not crash), since you want it to run 24 hours a day—recall that your server can be accessed at any hour, day or night, from around the world. Given these criteria, there are a number of options available. In order of decreasing desirability these are: (1) UNIX, VMS, Windows NT, (2) OS/2 or Novell servers, and (3) other platform servers.

For commercial applications, you will also be interested in data encryption. In general, data passing over the Internet can be easily intercepted and read, which is not a pleasant thought should you be transmitting confidential documents or financial information such as credit card numbers. If you intend to request such information of your site visitors, you will want to obtain a commercial server that supports data encryption technology. Currently, the Netscape **Netsite Commerce** server is the only widely used server that supports data encryption, using the *Secure Sockets Layer* (SSL) encryption technology (discussed in Chapter 7). Encryption only works if the technology is also built into the browser, and Netscape includes SSL support in their Navigator line of browsers. Since the Netscape Navigator is the most popular browser on the Web, the **Commerce Server** is currently the best way to connect securely with the largest possible audience.

Other commercial servers such as **Website** (Windows NT), **OpenMarket Webserver** (UNIX), **WebSTAR** (Macintosh), and **Edime Webware** (Novell) plan to include or already include support for SSL or other encryption technology.

UNIX SERVERS

The consensus among WWW administrators is that a UNIX machine, combined with a commercial or well-supported noncommercial server (for example Netscape Netsite, Apache, CERN, or NCSA servers) is an ideal package for distributing hypertext materials. There are several reasons for this choice. First, the UNIX operating system is designed to run many simultaneous processes (multitasking), so that a well-designed UNIX server can almost effortlessly respond to many simultaneous HTTP service requests. Also, UNIX is designed to isolate the server and user processes from the management level of the operating system, which ensures reliable operation even under heavy loads. Last, many of the original server packages (Netscape Netsite, CERN, NCSA, Apache, and others) were originally written for UNIX machines.

The noncommercial packages are freely available, with precompiled executable versions often available for UNIX computers from Sun, Hewlett-Packard, Silicon Graphics, and others. Also, the source code is usually publicly available, so you can download and compile it yourself.

If you use a UNIX server, but use machines such as Macintoshes or PCs for your document development, you can make the server filesystems accessible to these machines by remote-mounting the HTTP server directories on the PCs or Macintoshes. For example, **PC-NFS** allows PCs to mount UNIX filesystems, while **CAP** (Columbia AppleTalk Protocol) allows similar access for a Macintosh. Setting up a development environment such as this requires some thought, as you must take into account the peculiarities of each of the systems (for example, PCs only allow eight-character filenames and three-character filename extensions), but in general this networked approach is useful in integrating a WWW development environment into a heterogeneous collection of computers.

Setting up a UNIX server need not be expensive. Although buying a machine from a vendor such as Sun or Hewlett-Packard is one option, you can also purchase a standard PC clone and install the freeware UNIX clone **linux** or **bsd386**. The NCSA and Apache servers have been successfully ported to linux, so that you can set up a linux-based HTTP server for little more than the cost of a PC. However, there are currently no commercial server packages for **linux**, although the **CyberPlus** server, designed expressly for **linux**, is under development. In general, if you need commercial server software, first determine your requirements; second, determine the server packages that meet these requirements; and third, find an appropriate, supported platform and operating system.

The downside of the UNIX approach is complexity. UNIX is a sophisticated operating system and can be difficult to learn and manage. If you do not have someone in your organization familiar with UNIX, then you should consider hiring someone who is; learning UNIX and installing an HTTP server are *not* things you want to be doing at the same time!

VMS SERVERS

The VMS operating system, which runs on VAX and some DEC ALPHA machines, is a multitasking operating system like UNIX that can also efficiently support server software such as an HTTP server. There are, however, few HTTP server packages for VMS, and they currently do not support commercial features such as data encryption.

WINDOWS NT OR OS/2

Windows NT and OS/2 are the next-best choice for hosting an HTTP server. Both Microsoft's Windows NT and IBM's OS/2 efficiently run simultaneous processes and also carefully separate user processes (such as an HTTP server) from the management level of the operating system. These systems are also generally easier to configure than a UNIX system, in particular for those coming from a PC background (this may be more the author's perspective than fact!). It is certainly true, though, that both OS/2 and Windows NT are easily integrated into PC networks, since this was a major goal of their system designs. In addition, several Windows NT–based servers now support data encryption technologies, making these platforms viable tools for commercial server activities.

NOVELL

Novell machines are dedicated servers, so it is no surprise that there are now HTTP servers expressly designed for Novell. This is also a viable option, should you wish to serve out documents from your fileserver. The **Edime Webware** server also supports SSL data encryption.

WINDOWS OR MACINTOSH

There are a number of packages available for PCs running Windows 3.x or Windows 95, and for Macintoshes. Several of these are quite full-featured. The Windows or Macintosh option is at the bottom of the list because of the limitations of the operating systems. DOS, Windows 3.x (and, to some degree, Windows 95), and the Macintosh System 7 operating systems are not designed for multitasking, nor are they designed to safely separate the management level of the operating system from user processes. The first limitation means that it is difficult to write an efficient HTTP server—in general these servers quickly bog down when the number of HTTP requests grows large. The second limitation is the reason PC and Macintosh computers often crash while running innocuous programs like spreadsheets or word processing programs (or HTTP servers!). For a Macintosh or PC user this is an irritation. For World Wide Web users trying to access your now "dead" server, this is a major annoyance.

If you are going to use a Windows or Macintosh HTTP server for serious dissemination of material on the Web, you should dedicate a machine specifically to that task. This means not letting anyone use it to do other tasks, since extra user programs significantly increase the risk of a system crash. In addition you will want to regularly test that the system is "alive." This is true of any server but even more so for platforms where crashes are common. Nothing will impress prospective clients or customers less than a fancy service that does not work properly.

BEHIND A FIREWALL?

Lastly, just a reminder that if you are behind a firewall and want to both run a server and access the outside world, then you need the CERN HTTP, Netscape Netsite Proxy, or the **Commerce Builder** server. These are three of the handful of servers that provide the *proxy support* you need.

SERVER SOFTWARE

New servers are constantly being launched on the market, and new features are constantly being added to current software. The Yahoo site maintains a relatively current listing of server software, and you are encouraged to look there for updates. This information can be obtained at:

```
http://www.yahoo.com/text/Computers_and_Internet/Internet/World_Wide_Web/HTTP/Servers/
```

You should also glance at the URL:

```
http://www.proper.com/www/servers-chart.html
```

which contains a nice (and regularly updated) features summary for several of the more popular HTTP servers.

REAL-WORLD

EXAMPLES

Chapter 12 is a change of pace from the rest of the book. This chapter contains *examples* of World Wide Web sites, demonstrating the types of presentations that can be accomplished on the Web, and also illustrating aspects of the Web collection design process. These examples cover areas ranging from scientific research to comic strips. I asked the authors of these collections to themselves write brief descriptions of their sites and of the design issues they found important in developing these materials. For this second edition, several of these authors have had a chance to reflect upon the changes that have taken place "on the Web" over the last year, with illuminating results. I encourage you to read these brief descriptions and intelligent observations. I also encourage you to visit their sites, and compare the current versions of their sites and HTML documents with the figures in this chapter, which capture how these sites looked less than a year ago. I can guarantee that you will find the exercise useful, as it demonstrates both how the Web has changed, and how well-designed Web collections can evolve easily with these changes.

ELECTRONIC E-PRINT SERVERS

http://xxx.lanl.gov/

Paul Ginsparg
Los Alamos National Laboratories
http://xxx.lanl.gov/pg.html

The Los Alamos National Laboratory e-Print server is an automated archive for electronic communication of research information. In many fields of physics e-Print servers have become the primary means of communicating ongoing research work, since they are inexpensive, democratic (anyone with Internet access can access the work), and fast. There are currently eight different physics e-Print databases, archiving several tens of thousands of electronic articles. These articles are all written in TeX or LaTeX, which has become the text formatting language of choice in the physics community.

E-Print articles are submitted by electronic mail to an archive site, using a special electronic letter format containing both the article itself and an abstract. An automatic program running at the archive site (rather like a LISTSERV program) automatically unpacks the letter and archives the abstract and the full article, and adds both to a searchable database.

Originally this archive was only accessible by e-mail, so that accessing the archive required sending an e-mail letter containing search and command strings (such as "find all papers by Jones written this year"). The results of the search were then mailed back to the person who sent the request. This access method still works, but has been largely supplanted by a more efficient World Wide Web search interface. Submission of articles, however, still must be done by electronic mail.

Figure 12.1 shows the home page for the Los Alamos e-Print server. Note that it allows for both **FORMs** and non-**FORMs** access to the database. When the project started, the **FORMs** element didn't exist. While everyone should in principle now have access to a **FORMs**-compliant client, the lower-end clients are frequently painful to use (the more sophisticated the use of a graphical interface, the harder it is to duplicate in a terminal mode). Therefore, the site was deliberately designed so that everything possible from the **FORM** page is also possible via ordinary pages. Note that the button that leads to the **FORM** interface is itself a **FORM**, so it only functions for clients that understand **FORMs**.

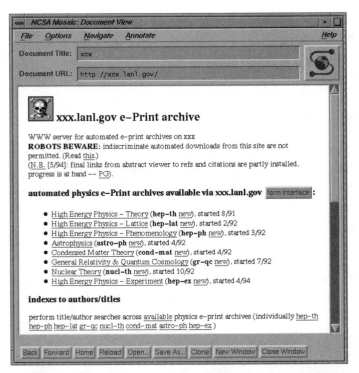

▬▬▬▬ **Figure 12.1** The home page for the Los Alamos e-Print server.

The home page is designed to put near the top things people access most frequently, so that you only need to scroll down for secondary information. Since this was an overlay to a preexisting database, already divided into separate "archives" corresponding to different subfields of physics, it was natural to branch from the home page to a separate page for each of the archives. On the other hand, it was important to avoid the common error of slavishly reproducing exactly the functionality familiar from the previous interface.

In particular I wanted the "new" link to daily abstract listings to be immediately accessible, in order to convey the ease with which these listings could be obtained, and to eventually help people move away from the less-efficient e-mail interface.

The home page is one of the few static HTML documents in the entire interface—the rest of the pages are generated by CGI scripts, and all the HTML is added dynamically at request time to the preexisting plain-text files used by the e-mail interface. This has two advantages: (1) only a single set of files has to be maintained for both formats, and (2) any change in the interface (e.g., a new link on an abstract page) can be made globally by changing a single script. In the next revision even this front page will be generated by a gateway to make it easier to maintain and update.

The skull icon was originally put in as a joke during testing (it was grabbed from the "kill process" button on the processes panel from NeXTStep—a 2-bit monochrome image, colorized using **xv**). It was originally there to evoke the skull that appears together with "xxx" on bottles of poison, but later came to symbolize the death-defying survival of the system in the absence of funding support.

Figure 12.2 shows a typical **FORM** page. The **FORM** page is generated by a script that knows where you came from (the default selectors are "hep-th" from the front page, but if you come from the "cond-mat" page they would be "cond-mat"). This page contains four different archive selectors in the four different **FORM**s. It is unfortunate that I had to use separate archive selectors,

■■■■■ **Figure 12.2** The HTML **FORM** database interface.

due to the limitations of the original NCSA **FORM**s implementation—a **FORM** could have only a single Submit button, so that different actions from different **FORM** Submit buttons were not possible. I chose not to use horizontal line `<hr>` elements between the separate **FORM**s, since that stretched things out vertically and sometimes required users to scroll to see the full **FORM**.

Mosaic for X-Windows Version 2.5 does allow multiple Submit buttons supporting different actions from within a single **FORM,** but it will be some time before all browsers upgrade to this feature (see the "Update" at the end of this section for updated information on this feature).

The basic methods of obtaining information from the e-mail interface—FIND, LIST, GET, and HELP—are also the basic functionalities in the **FORM** interface, except that GET is restricted to GET ABSTRACT. This allows the user to read the abstract and then decide if he or she wants to download the full article, and ensures that large file downloads are not made inadvertently.

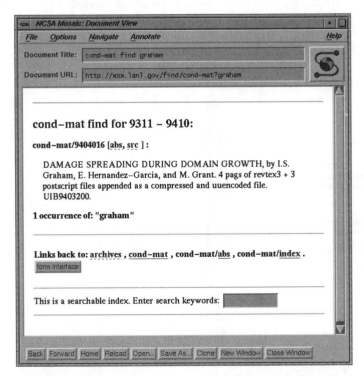

▬▬▬▬ **Figure 12.3** Result of searching with the bottom form from Figure 12.2 for the name "graham."

The "Find" and "Listings" commands use the same output as the e-mail interface, except that the document is piped through **sed** (the UNIX stream editor) to automatically reformat the text and to pattern match appearances of the form "arch-ive/9401001," converting them to hypertext anchors in the displayed document. The result of a "Find" is shown in Figure 12.3, searched from the past year's articles containing the name "graham."

Clicking on the "abs" anchor downloads the article abstract. This is shown in Figure 12.4.

The "abs" script just pipes the conventional e-mail abstract (in this case, *cond-mat/papers/9404/9404016.abs*) through **sed** to reformat the document, maintaining the basic feel of the plain-text abstract but changing the title to a header, and of course adding the hypertext link to the source.

The document source interface is similar to the e-mail interface, but takes advantage of HTTP's ability to transmit binary data files. Thus the returned articles are sent in compressed formats when possible, significantly reducing the sizes of the transmitted data—most clients read the HTTP content-encoding MIME header and automatically uncompress the data upon receipt. In

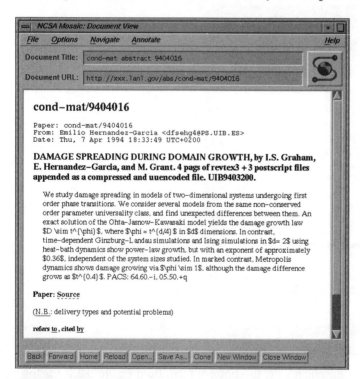

■■■■ Figure 12.4 Abstract for the article found in Figure 12.3.

contrast, the e-mail interface requires uncompressed and specially coded data to ensure safe communication of the document.

One overall design choice was to keep the URL names as simple and logical as possible, using the NCSA HTTP ScriptAlias feature. For example, articles, abstracts, and gateway programs are referenced via directory and filenames such as */list/hep-th/9401, /abs/hep-th/9401001, /find/hep-th?, /e-print/hep-th/9401001,* and so on. Since the entire package is generated by scripts, the leading field is "aliased" to the appropriate script, which parses the rest of the URL to determine archive and other information on which to operate.

UPDATE: OCTOBER 1995

The electronic print server has evolved significantly over the past year. There are now 16 different physics groups, as opposed to eight, and the system is now being used in several other fields, including computation and linguistics, mathematics, economics, earth sciences, and Bayesian analysis. All the scripts have been rewritten in perl, which gives more control over all aspects of the output. In addition, the **FORM**s interfaces were revamped to take advantage of multiple Submit buttons in the same **FORM**. A few browsers (particularly lynx, but also older versions of common browsers) do not support multiple Submit buttons, so the perl gateway programs that generate **FORM**s check the *HTTP_USER_AGENT* environment variable and serve out the old version of the **FORM** to those older clients.

In addition, the underlying database has been revamped—the documents are now indexed using the glimpse database, which allows for Boolean and approximate searches. Last, the package can dynamically generate PostScript (and PDF) on-the-fly from the underling TeX source, using special buttons on the abstract pages labeled "PS."

Thus, although the functionality is the same, the whole system has been improved and enhanced. You will get a good impression of the changes by visiting the URL listed at the beginning of this section, and comparing the screen captures (from the old version) with the newer documents.

ONCOLINK

http://cancer.med.upenn.edu/

E. Loren Buhle, Jr., Ph.D.
219 Scottdale Road
Lansdowne, PA 19050
(e-mail: *buhle@mscf.med.upenn.edu*)

Phone: 610-622-4293
Fax: 610-622-1343

INTRODUCTION

OncoLink was launched on the Internet on March 7, 1994, to provide comprehensive and timely information regarding cancer to an audience ranging from practicing clinicians to newly diagnosed patients to the "worried well" population who live in fear of cancer. Since one in three Americans will be diagnosed with cancer in his or her lifetime, I created OncoLink as an experiment to see if anyone would care, and if they did care, how they would use such a repository of information. The information on OncoLink ranges from methods of diagnosis and types of treatment of cancer, to information about the psychosocial elements a patient and his/her family may experience throughout the cancer experience.

The material on OncoLink must be traversed with ease, regardless of topic or educational background of the user. OncoLink users range from those with no prior knowledge of biology to practicing clinical oncologists. The material on OncoLink must be both comprehensive and easy to navigate. Thus many of the documents have extensive hypertext links to allow inexperienced users to learn as they go, while not encumbering more experienced users. Some of the material on OncoLink is explicit, such as the stereotactic radiosurgical approach to brain tumors. Other material deals with more amorphous issues such as "Quality of Life" and "Death and Dying." The home page of OncoLink, as of August 1994, is shown in Figures 12.5 and 12.6.

Figure 12.5 HTML document of OncoLink home page. (This file has been truncated to save space.)

```
<HTML>

<HEAD>

<TITLE>Welcome to OncoLink</TITLE>

<LINK REV="MADE" HREF="mailto:buhle@xrt.upenn.edu">

</HEAD>

<BODY>

<H2>Welcome to OncoLink</H2>

<H1><img alt="Oncolink logo" src="/I/docs/images/oncolnk2.gif">

<A HREF="/s/sounds/welcome.au">

<img alt="" src="/I/docs/images/www/sound.xbm"></A></H1>

<p>
```

```
<H2>The University of Pennsylvania Multimedia Oncology Resource</H2>

<HR>

<A HREF="/0h/stuff/upmc">

<img alt="Info about Penn" src="/I/docs/images/penn1.gif"></A>

<A HREF="/I/docs/images/child.gif">

<img alt="Children's artwork" src="/I/docs/images/child_sm.gif"></A>

This artwork was donated by a pediatric cancer patient and <b>will change

</b>at frequent intervals!

<i>(Click here to see the gallery of children's artwork)</i>

<A HREF="/0h/docs/images/child/gallery1">

<i>in Part 1</I></A> or <A HREF="/0h/docs/images/child/gallery2"><i>Part
2</i></A><p>

<HR>

<img src="/I/docs/images/light_bulb.gif">

<A HREF="/1s/stuff/latest_stuff">

What's <i>NEW </i> on OncoLink?</A><p>

<img src="/I/docs/images/question.gif">

<A HREF="/7wc/stuff/search_wais/OncoLink.inv">

<b>WAIS Search</b> of OncoLink</A> or a <A

HREF="/7g/stuff/search_dir1"><b>single-word SEARCH</b></A> of OncoLink.<p>

<img alt="" src="/I/docs/images/news1.gif">

<A HREF="/1s/buhle/cancer_news">

CANCER news, warnings, etc.</A>

<P>

<HR><img alt="" src="/I/docs/images/menat.gif">

<i>This cancer information resource is under continuous development.

OncoLink is best used with a World Wide Web client (e.g. Mosaic, lynx,

etc.), but can also be reached via a gopher server, using

port 80.</i><BR><b>October has been designated as Breast Cancer

Month in the United States of America and Canada.</b><p>
```

```
<HR>

.

.

.

<b>OncoLink</b> was awarded the International

<b>Best of the Web '94

Award</b> for <b>Best Professional Service</b>. To see the other award

winners, please

<A HREF="http://wings.buffalo.edu/contest/awards/index.html">click

here</A>.

 Thank you for your support and we look forward

to making this resource even more valuable!

</BODY>

</HTML>
```

THE ONCOLINK IMPLEMENTATION

When OncoLink was launched, it was implemented using the GN server on a DEC 3000-800 computer running the OSF/1 operating system. The GN server allows rapid dissemination of hypertext and plain-text information to World Wide Web and Gopher clients, respectively. The GN server software was initially selected on the basis of its simplicity of design, high speed of the software, high security of the implementation, and the ability to service both Gopher and the World Wide Web. The GN server software was felt to be the most secure WWW server, in that the resources served to the client must be defined within the server in a predetermined menu file. The documents served by the GN server have been readily ported to other WWW servers, including both the CERN and NCSA HTTP servers, WN (the HTTP-only replacement for GN), and the Netscape Commerce server. For political reasons, OncoLink has been moved to a DECstation 5000/125 running the NCSA HTTP server.

The OncoLink home page (Figures 12.5 and 12.6) is accessed by World Wide Web clients at the Uniform Research Locator:

> http://cancer.med.upenn.edu/

It can also be accessed from a Gopher client via the command:

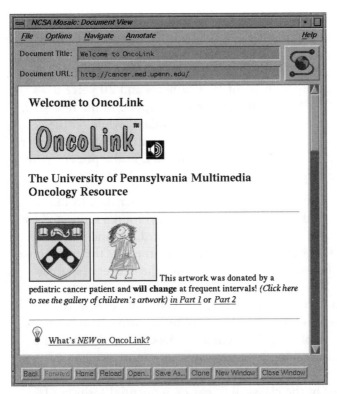

Figure 12.6 Home page to the OncoLink Resource site.

```
gopher cancer.med.upenn.edu
```

The name `cancer.med.upenn.edu` is an alias for an actual numerical Internet (IP) address of a machine on the Internet. Should OncoLink move to another machine, the name `cancer.med.upenn.edu` will remain the same and the alias will be changed in the Internet name server tables to reflect the transition.

In order to track usage patterns, GN generates a detailed log of all access transactions. This log is a very important and powerful aspect of information publishing via the Internet, providing valuable feedback to OncoLink's maintainer. In addition to providing an insight into OncoLink's most popular resources, the time between hypertext key requests and the path between the selection of one key and the next hypertext key gives an insight into the information sought, the portions of the document read, and the time the requester spent on each section of the document. Studying this log also revealed how many requests were from (a) graphical WWW clients, (b) text-based hypertext-capable WWW clients, and (c) Gopher clients.

USE OF ONCOLINK

OncoLink was released on the Internet as a WWW and Gopher server in the evening of March 7, 1994. In the first year of operation OncoLink logged over a million transactions, from more than 130 countries. Over this year, the shift of users went from approximately 80 percent WWW users and 20 percent Gopher users to 95 percent WWW and only 5 percent Gopher. In the first year, the bulk of the WWW activity occurred during the weekdays, while on the weekends a large majority of users accessed OncoLink via the available Gopher clients on America Online and other commercial providers. In the present year (1995), WWW services have proliferated and largely replaced Gopher.

In December 1994 OncoLink averaged over 20,000 "hits" per day, from around the world. GN logged the IP address, time, and resource requested by each client "hit," thus letting us monitor the user of OncoLink and watch how documents were read. Gopher access could be discerned by the selection of the non-HTML files. In the early days of OncoLink, the cancer resources served by Gopher and WWW were essentially identical, the Gopher resources lacking only the multimedia and the hypertext. As OncoLink developed, the Gopher menus were extended to allow access to contents formerly only available within the hypertext keys of HTML documents. Documents such as the "Pediatric Oncology Case of the Month" progressed in a more nonlinear direction, requiring access to hypertext keys to access the treatment given, and so on. While still represented in the classical linear or sequential fashion of printed literature (i.e., the entire document is laid out in a chronological sequence), the "Case of the Month" remains the most popularly requested document. An example of a "Case of the Month" is shown in Figure 12.7.

A critical element to disseminating information on the Internet is to listen to the user and generate a flexible and intuitive interface that accommodates the user's needs. OncoLink began with discrete menus defining specialties within the practice of oncology (cancer) treatment. Thus, there were menus pertaining to Pediatric Oncology, Gynecologic Oncology, Medical Oncology, Surgical Oncology, and Radiation Oncology. Our users quickly requested a "disease-oriented" selection of menus, as a breast cancer patient would not necessarily know which menu item to select first. We rapidly discovered a certain class of OncoLink users rarely used the menus at all, preferring to move from document to document via the hypertext links, reading a very small portion of the documents they accessed. When we analyzed the server log files to look at what portions of the document the users read, we realized there was a very tight focus on information sought. Thus, some users browsed the many items on OncoLink, while others focused their attention very sharply on certain pieces of information.

World Wide Web documents accessed from icons of images for hypertext keys were more apt to be selected than merely hypertext documents. Using several pediatric oncology "Case of the Month" presentations, where the user is led from the initial presentation of the patient through the patient's treatment (Figure 12.7), we recorded the sequence of hypertext selections of a given user (tracked by following an IP address in a contiguous chunk of time). While physicians usually selected the hypertext keys in the order of their presentation, the completeness of the selection was higher when the hypertext anchors were miniaturized icons of the full-size figure. In documents targeting patients, iconic hypertext keys for procedures were often selected over text-based hypertext keys.

OncoLink must also allow inexperienced users, who are not exactly sure what their questions are, to make use of the many navigational aids and find what they are looking for in the OncoLink resources. One of the design criteria behind OncoLink is to allow users to find something relevant to their queries

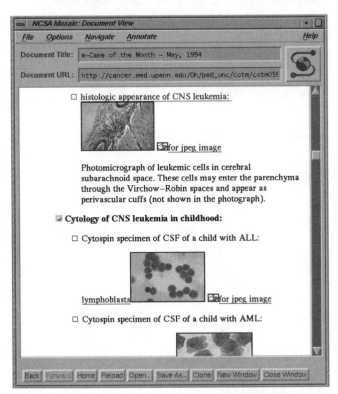

Figure 12.7 "Case of the Month" page. This is a detailed scientific document of a particular cancer case, including hypertext links to related documents and to full-scale images of the scientific versions and figures.

within five minutes of their first interaction with OncoLink. By using the search mode (Figure 12.8), a user can rapidly examine pertinent articles contained anywhere on OncoLink.

A variety of search engines have been employed on OncoLink. All of the search engines were "full-text" searches, reviewing query terms throughout the entire resource base at OncoLink. The first search engine (grep) employed an exact search on targets consisting of single words. This was suitable when OncoLink was very small, but when OncoLink grew to over 6,000 documents and 20,000 accesses per day across 800 Mbytes of information (December 1994), this type of search engine was completely impractical.

The WAIS search engine was subsequently employed to allow multiple search terms, with support for Boolean searching using AND and OR relationships (e.g., "tamoxifen AND breast"). Figure 12.8 shows the interface to this search tool, while Figure 12.9 shows the results of a search for "tamoxifen AND breast." A review of the log files, however, revealed that many users mis-

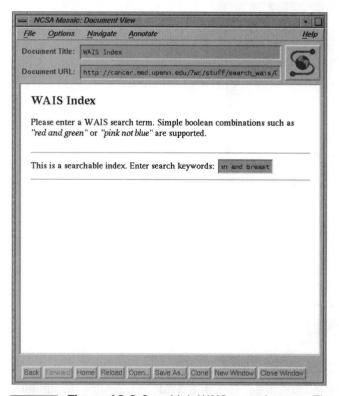

■■■■■ **Figure 12.8** OncoLink WAIS search page. The documents at OncoLink are indexed by a WAIS database. These can be searched to find useful documents. In this case the search is for "Tamoxifen" and "breast."

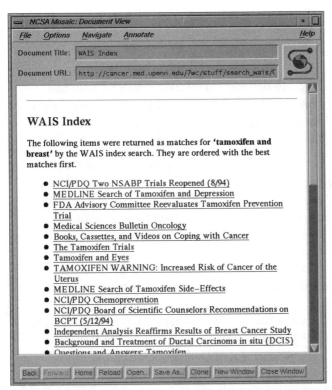

Figure 12.9 OncoLink WAIS search results. The documents listed contain information related to "Tamoxifen" and "breast." Clicking on the highlighted text downloads the document for viewing. This list is created by a "gateway" program that sorts the search results and inserts the hypertext links.

spelled the target words, requiring the addition of a phonics algorithm to the WAIS search engine to be more forgiving in finding the requested information. This modified WAIS engine used an inverted search index computed at 3 A.M. each morning. Searching the inverted index was very fast, and most queries were completed in less than five seconds. Unfortunately, the WAIS implementation seemed to miss resources about 10 percent of the time.

The most recent system employs the Glimpse engine, created at the University of Arizona. This engine enjoys many of the same features as WAIS, but is much easier to deploy and maintain.

The ability to use search tools was codified into previously "static" links to provide "dynamic" links. An example of a simple dynamic link would be a request for "All the recent papers on breast cancer" from the National Institute of Cancer. The result of this hypertext selected query would be different from month to month. A more complicated example is the selection of the hypertext link "taxol." OncoLink has dozens of different articles discussing taxol. Is the user interested in the isolation of taxol from the yew tree, the patient side-effects of taxol, clinical protocols using taxol, the molecular action of taxol, or the organic synthesis of taxol? A static link to only the side-effects of taxol addresses only some of the issues. If the server tracks the type of documents requested on OncoLink, it may be able to steer patient-oriented articles to the patient, clinical articles to the oncologist, and so on.

OncoLink strives to present "one-stop shopping" for people involved with cancer. Clearly, all the knowledge of cancer will never be stored on OncoLink. Much of the information on cancer will be shared elsewhere on the Internet. The ability to reproducibly find this information, as well as to monitor issues of concern to OncoLink's users (and of concern to the Internet cancer population in general), is an area for future work using active and passive computer agents. Active agents, also called knowbots and World Wide Web Worms (WWWW), are useful for indexing the contents of other information services on the Internet. Passive agents, also called sentries, can monitor the USENET newsgroups, Internet listservs, and other forums of electronic cancer information (e.g., CompuServe's CANCER forum). Other areas of active research focus on including interactive sessions on OncoLink, much like the multi-threaded bulletin board services found on CompuServe, with the direction of evolving to the interactive television marketplace.

OncoLink was a success due to both the quality of the content provided and the Internet's ability to make the information readily accessible. OncoLink made information on cancer, whether it be text-, image-, or multimedia-based, available to the consumer at any time of the day or night, anywhere in the world.

UPDATE: OCTOBER 1995

The creator of OncoLink has since left the University of Pennsylvania, and is actively developing and encouraging the use of patient-oriented health care information resources throughout the world.

VIEWS OF THE SOLAR SYSTEM

```
http://www.c3.lanl.gov/~cjhamil/SolarSystem/homepage.html
```
Calvin J. Hamilton

Los Alamos National Laboratory
Mail Stop 3265
Los Alamos, NM 87545

BACKGROUND

While browsing the Internet during the fall of 1993 I ran across some images of planets in our solar system, which sparked in me a latent interest in astronomy. I subscribed to *sci.astro* and related astronomy USENET newsgroups and, after a short time, found the major Internet repositories of deep space and solar system images.

I found many nice images, but the selection was not very complete. In particular, there were very few images of Pluto, Uranus, Mercury, and the satellites of the planets. Some of the images were well done; others were only a sloppy scan of a photograph. I could also tell that many of the images had been subsampled or reduced in size from the original data that were available.

It is understandable why larger images were not provided on the Internet. Large images require a lot of disc space, and individuals who want to download them to their personal computers may not have the ability to handle or view such large files. However, I considered the selection and resolution of images unacceptable. I had seen very high quality photographs in books about astronomy, and I wanted those images, in high-quality formats, to be available to the public via the Internet.

I located the raw image data taken by the Voyager and Viking spacecraft, which, at the time, was located at the anonymous FTP site `explorer.arc.nasa.gov`—a similar resource can still be found at

    http://cdwings.jpl.nasa.gov/PDS/public/jukebox.html

but, without a lot of image processing, these images displayed poorly on a computer. Using my image processing background, I began filtering and enhancing the raw data and produced some high-resolution image mosaics and image files that displayed well on an 8-bit color computer monitor (recall that an 8-bit monitor can only display 256 different colors at the same time).

At about this same time I was introduced to NCSA Mosaic and the World Wide Web. I could see that this would be an ideal way to make my images available to the public. Although I did not know it, this was the beginning of "Views of the Solar System" (Figure 12.10). I started by making an HTML document for each planet, with links to my images and NASA's Jet Propulsion

Laboratory (JPL/NASA) images. Then I decided that it would be nice to have some statistical information about each planet (Figure 12.11). I went to the library, located some books on astronomy, and added a few selected statistics to each of the planetary pages. By this time I had become fascinated with the solar system and with astronomy. Every couple of weeks I checked out a stack of astronomy-related books. After reading these books, I decided to include a short description of each of the planets. I also found that there was a significant amount of information available from JPL and NASA over the Internet. I incorporated this information into the tour.

As time went on I decided to add separate WWW pages for each planetary satellite for which I had an image. In my free time I would process new images and add them to my pages. Often I would look through the astronomy books I had checked out from the library, and when I found an image I liked, I would locate the raw Voyager/Viking data and process it to give computer images of quality comparable to those found in the book. I subsequently added sections on asteroids, comets, meteoroids, and the history of space exploration.

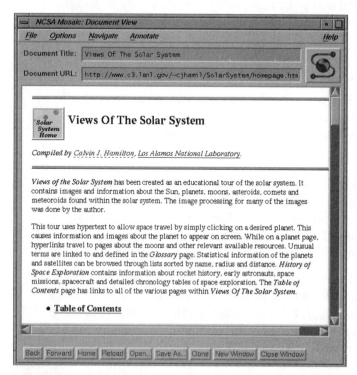

Figure 12.10 Top of the home page for "Views of the Solar System."

During the past year, and since the first publication of *The HTML Sourcebook*, "Views of the Solar System" has grown from 200 megabytes to more than 800 megabytes. Over 400 megabytes of digitized video clips have been added. These videos clips were taken from the NASA Apollo mission and planetary exploration video series. During the past year, NASA has placed a significant amount of new raw image data online for Internet access. I have used these data to completely update the images on the Mercury page and have added images to numerous other pages. Over 200 megabytes of images have been added throughout the entire tour. Earth was expanded to include sections on "Earth from Space", "Clouds from Space," "Terrestrial Impact Craters," and "Terrestrial Volcanoes." The Moon page was updated to include comprehensive Apollo Landing mission summaries. Similar updates were made to Venus and Mars. Over 190 pages of information can be browsed on "Views of the Solar System."

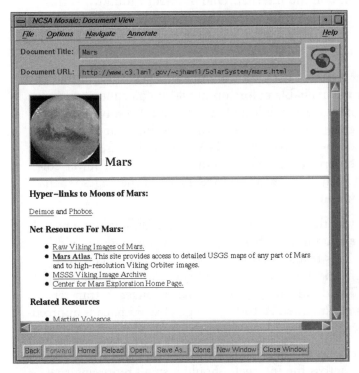

■■■■■ **Figure 12.11** Top of the home page for the planet Mars. The document contains several icons of Mars images, along with details about the Martian surface, atmosphere, and so on.

"Views of the Solar System" continues to grow. It has the greatest variety of solar system images and information on the Internet, and provides a large selection of images of planetary moons that can only be found at this site. It is being used by schools all over the world, and was published on CD-ROM by the German *CHIP* magazine. I have had numerous individuals contact me about using bits and pieces of the tour. I am currently in the process of preparing "Views of the Solar System" for publication within the United States.

One problem I have been faced with is the volume of accesses that I receive each week—approximately 80,000 hits as of mid-summer 1995. I have set up several mirror sites throughout the world to help relieve the load on the Los Alamos server.

HTML ISSUES

When I started writing HTML pages, my biggest obstacle was finding proper documentation. I eventually found that the best way to learn the HTML syntax was to look at examples on the Internet. One problem I found was that my Mosaic browser overlooked certain errors that other browsers did not. I only found out about these problems when someone on the Internet was kind enough to point them out.

Since "Views of the Solar System" uses a lot of inline images, I found that certain pages used up all of the available colors on my 8-bit color monitor and that as a result some of the images didn't look good at all. I resolved this problem by using image color compression software developed at Los Alamos National Laboratories. Whenever I found an HTML page that used too many colors, I compressed the colors in the images so that they used far fewer colors, typically 128. This greatly improved the appearance of the pages when displaying on 8-bit color monitors.

Another important issue was the size of the inline images. On my home page I used 72 × 72 pixel images and on my other pages I chose a maximum width and height of 150 pixels. This tends to be a little bit larger than images on many sites on the Internet. The advantage of the larger inline image is that the details are much clearer. The disadvantage is that it takes longer to transfer these large images across the Internet. A 150 × 150 pixel GIF image is approximately 12,000 bytes, whereas a 72 × 72 pixel image is only about 2,700 bytes.

I also had to decide what types of image files and formats to use when transferring noninlined images across the Internet. Should a small representative image be returned, or the best image available? I chose the latter option. In certain cases I have very large mosaics, in which case I provide a small and a large version of the same image (Figure 12.12). I also avoid lossy compression methods such as JPEG, unless I receive the raw image in that format. The JPEG lousy image compression technique tends to leave the image with unsightly blocks scattered throughout the image. Once lossy compression is used, further image processing or enhancement is useless. I save all 8-bit images in GIF format and 24-bit images in TIFF format.

Until recently I used the HTML <HR> tag for separator bars dividing document sections. I now use a three-dimensional-looking bar (a GIF image) as a separator. This bar uses three colors and takes up 579 bytes. I tried separators with a rainbow appearance, but they required too many colors; I needed these colors for the actual images instead.

I organized "Views of the Solar System" somewhat like a book. The home page is like an introduction, with links to the major portions of the tour. The home page also contains links to educational and other space-related resources. Organizationally the home page links to a cover page, a Table of Contents

▬▬▬▬ **Figure 12.12** Detail from the Mars page. Clicking on the face of Mars downloads the larger GIF image of the same feature.

page, and chapters on our solar system, each planet, asteroids, comets, meteoroids, and the history of space exploration. Each planet page has further links to the planet's satellites and other related resources. Many of the terms used in "Views of the Solar System" are linked to an extensive glossary page. There is also a section on people who have made a contribution to the understanding of the world and universe we live in.

SUMMARY

I am not a astronomy professional, but during the last year I have read many books and have learned much about our solar system. Perhaps this demonstrates that you don't have to be an expert in a particular field to make a significant contribution. If time and money permit I would enjoy making continual improvement to this tour. "Views of the Solar System" has been an evolving and somewhat experimental project that I hope will continue to be educational and beneficial for others.

NETBOY—"CHOICE OF AN ONLINE GENERATION"

http://netboy.com

Stafford Huyle
e-mail: *netboy@interaccess.com*

I had been looking for a way to publish a comic years before I came into contact with the Web. I spent all my time in school drawing cars and spaceships, while my teachers sneered that my work wasn't "real art." I knew that the standard was to get a little strip going in a free edition of some college rag, and nurture it for years while praying that it would be noticed. This wasn't the way for me; it was just not dynamic enough.

In my job as the marketing director for InterAccess, a Chicago-based Internet provider, I thought a lot about the possibilities of self-publishing on the Net. There was a tremendously intelligent audience out there, hungry for good entertainment. I knew that I should approach them. At the time, however, there was no way to distribute a comic effectively.

When I discovered the Web, I realized that it was a very promising forum. I felt that it was the up-and-coming interface with the Net—yet there was so little of interest on it! I wanted to read a comic that was cool enough to joke about the standard knowledge that all onliners have. It didn't exist, so I decided to create it. NetBoy is the first Internet-topical comic.

Between my own experiences online and behind the scenes at InterAccess, I observed a lot of funny stuff. I also had the resources to produce a comic—a scanner, technical help, and a company willing to give my comic a chance. If I were producing this alone, it could get quite expensive because of the amount of traffic moving through the site. However, I have worked out a reciprocal arrangement with InterAccess. They feel that the publicity that they get from NetBoy's success is a good reward for assisting me in getting the comic out.

I played with different styles and felt that a black-and-white stick figure column would serve several purposes. It would play with the fact that the delivery medium was colorful. It would be easy to download. It would be simple for me to draw, so I could keep my day job. It seemed pleasingly goofy to me that my technological heroes were mere stick figures. Finally, the medium meant that I could choose any size and format.

I draw the comic by hand, as it gives the best control. Once it is scanned in, all the touch-ups and lettering are done in Photoshop with a custom font. For file formats, I chose GIF over JPEG because of the inline capability. Format is very important. You must plan your readers' traffic well in advance.

I created a beta in May 1994 to get a feel for my capabilities and audience. I experimented for a couple of months; the current version of NetBoy debuted on July 1, 1994. The home page for NetBoy is shown in Figure 12.13.

The goal of NetBoy is really to create a hip place to be online. There is the comic, but there are also back issues, feedback, N-Mart, contests, and links to other comic pages. It's paying off; NetBoy has been growing with the Web. In just the first three months, readership went from 500 per month to over 90,000. Over a million people have read it now, and the audience is growing by 20 percent a month. This is thanks to enthusiastic word of mouth, comics being tacked up in computer labs, links from many pages, and media coverage.

Of course I do all this for free, but I have been thinking of ways to make money from my project. For a time, I flirted with the idea of offering a paid daily subscription to NetBoy via e-mail as a MIME-encoded document, but I realized that this move would greatly restrict my readership (even though I had planned to keep the large Saturday editions free). I am now taking the Microsoft approach—making NetBoy the standard against which all others are judged (and copied). I know that I can build up a loyal readership by giving readers a strong product for free.

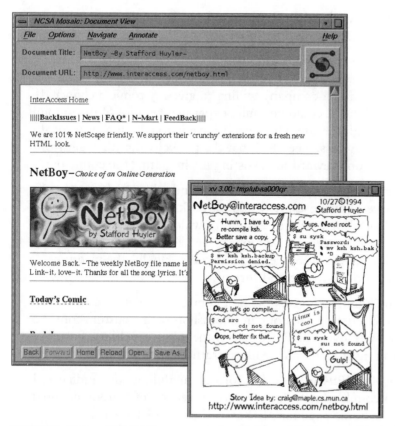

████████ **Figure 12.13** Home page for NetBoy. Clicking on "Today's Comic" downloaded the displayed GIF image. This image is new every day.

With this readership growing every day, I feel the future is in merchandising. Because so many people are reading NetBoy, there is a growing market for NetBoy books, mugs, etc. I have already done a good business selling NetBoy T-shirts (Figure 12.14).

My advice to anyone else starting out would be to learn good HTML and provide a solid service. If you do a weekly or daily, keep it up religiously. If the competition is 100 percent reliable in their new pages and you're not, then you may lose.

With strong perl programming skills, you can create forms to monitor reader feedback, which is most helpful. You can see what's working and what's not—everything from a certain vein of humor to the layout of the page.

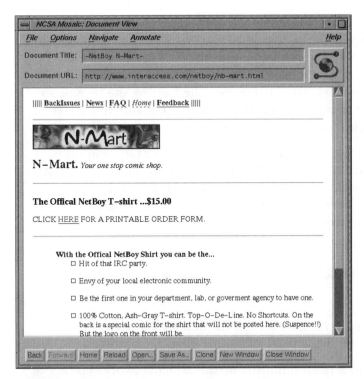

Figure 12.14 Want to buy a NetBoy T-shirt? This is the page to look at.

Another pointer is that you should give your feature a consistent name each day it is released. For example, I call each new comic "today-netboy.gif." This way readers can link the GIF image into their own home pages. People want their reading delivered with a minimum of fuss.

The Web is the most effective publishing medium that I have ever encountered. I am very pleased with it, and if I had to do it again, I would only have started sooner.

UPDATE: OCTOBER 1995

NetBoy is an Intertainment network that debuted in July 1994, with a weekly 12-panel comic strip. That strip—*netboy@interaccess.com*—grew to cult status on the Internet in about six months, grabbing media attention and turning NetBoy into an Internet celebrity.

THE PAST

The NetBoy site became one of the first generation of Web entertainment, and helped pioneer personal Web publishing with fresh and fun content. NetBoy reached the peak of its cult personality by October 1994, appearing in four national newspapers as well as *Wired* magazine. The NetBoy site became so popular that the site had to go on hiatus for a few months until a new network could be put in place to handle the access load.

The second NetBoy site was then built, offering daily entertainment summaries. It was featured in an article in *People Magazine* in July 1995, which brought even more interest, and which has propelled me into expanding NetBoy into a more full-featured multimedia experience, offering much more than just a weekly comic strip.

THE PRESENT

The third generation of *NetBoy.com* is currently under production.

THE FUTURE

Along the lines of a television studio/station, the new *NetBoy.com* Intertainment site will offer many types of cutting-edge digital diversions.

The Web is changing into a full multimedia *broadcasting* network. Just a year ago we had just a few pictures—now there are pictures, real-time audio, and platform-independent applications (e.g., Java) that interact with the user and with Internet documents. The tools for the artist are now in place.

See ya online.

SAN FRANCISCO RESERVATIONS' WORLD WIDE WEB PAGE

http://www.hotelres.com/

Eric J. Fraser
Programmer/Analyst
University of California
Computer Science Division
(e-mail: *fraser@CS.Berkeley.EDU*)

INTRODUCTION

San Francisco Reservations (SFR) is a central hotel reservations agency serving the San Francisco Bay area. SFR agents reserve hotel rooms at volume discount rates and monitor seasonal specials and promotions, passing on the savings to the public. Before the WWW page was set up, business was handled by a toll-free telephone number and by fax. While much of the business infrastructure was done on computers (a UNIX network), there was no previous need for an Internet connection.

In June of 1994, at an informal dinner party, a discussion began on ways to improve the computing environment at SFR. On that day's front page of the Business section of the *New York Times*, there was an article about a florist that had set up a WWW page:

```
http://florist.com:1080/flowers/bf1006.html
```

We decided that the Net had definitely "gone commercial" and that if a florist shop could make it on the Internet, then surely SFR should have a place as well.

In the following month, the details were worked out on how much it would cost to get an Internet connection, on which local service provider to use, whether to get a dedicated SLIP-type connection or a dedicated digital line, and what additional hardware might be needed. After much boring deliberation, it was decided that SFR would get a dedicated frame-relay (56 kbps) connection to a small co-op style Internet provider, and to use one of the already owned 486 machines, running linux.

SFR's WWW server was up and operational in the beginning of September 1994. Even before we announced the page to the relevant newsgroups, users were accessing the documents. As it went, first someone logged in from Stanford, then from Japan, and then from Australia, all within an hour. It was very exciting to see that quick a response. Since that day the number of people accessing the page has grown quite rapidly. On average there are around 150 users per day, more than we expected in our first month.

WHY ON THE WORLD WIDE WEB?

Designing a system using HTML/HTTP seemed like the natural choice for SFR. In fact it was decided that it was the only way to go in connecting to the Internet. Some of the deciding factors were:

- speed with which HTML/HTTP was becoming the standard of information servers
- ease of programming
- availability of easy-to-use browsers, including Mosaic, lynx, and tkwww
- nonintrusive nature
- support for graphics, sounds, MPEG movies
- CGI and **FORMs** capabilities

The foremost appeal of WWW is its widespread use. WWW is rapidly becoming the standard for information servers around the world, replacing the text-only Gopher servers. SFR's hope was to allow access to the greatest number of people. WWW seemed to be the proper choice.

Another advantage is that the WWW offers a way that people can do business in a nonintrusive manner on the Internet. Unlike mailing lists and postings to USENET newsgroups, which take up disc space and network bandwidth on computers where it is unwanted, the WWW gives users the ability to browse only those remote servers that they choose. SFR is generally perceived as a service-oriented business, since clients are not charged for making reservations. The notion of invasive business is not as relevant to SFR as it may be to someone selling life insurance, for instance, but it is still in any company's best interest to play by the rules of the Internet.

The most desirable quality of HTML and the World Wide Web, for someone creating pages, is that it gives you the ability to copy something you like and use it as a model. Browsers such as Mosaic allow users to view the source code of the document they are presently looking at. By piecing together ideas from several different pages, you can quickly get something presentable up and running. In the creation of SFR's pages, many ideas were found in other documents.

Mosaic has become the WWW viewer of choice. There are, however, several others that are available, giving users the ability to view the same information in several different ways. Lynx allows users to get a text-only view of WWW. This is quite useful to those who do not have a fast connection or for those who do not have an IP address (or TIA).

In addition, the glory of sight and sound is available to those who have a fast connection. HTML offers an easy way to include graphics, sounds, and

MPEG movies with the documents. As you will see in the following screen-captures, the ability to display images was a key design element in SFR's WWW pages.

Finally, HTML includes CGI and HTML **FORM**s capability (although not all viewers support this). These give HTML the flexibility and power to handle almost any task. If a script can be written that sends output to standard output, then it can be incorporated into an HTTP server as a CGI program and be accessed from your HTML documents. There are several cases where SFR's WWW page requires this sort of flexibility, including the ability to check availability of all hotels for any given day, the ability to search hotel lists for those that match specific criteria, and the ability to process reservation requests.

DESIGNING THE WWW PAGE

━━━ **Figure 12.15** HTML document for the San Francisco Reservations' home page.

```
<title> San Francisco Reservations</title>


<img src="sfrheader.gif" ALT="SAN FRANCISCO RESERVATIONS">
<hr>


Welcome to <b>San Francisco Reservations</b>' (SFR) World Wide Web

page!  This service provides hotel reservations in the San Francisco

area at no cost to the user.  SFR rates are, in most cases, the lowest

rates available.  Feel free to browse around and send us

<A href="/feedback.html">

    <img align=top src="icons/email.gif" ALT="[e-mail]">

</a>

if you have any questions or concerns.


<h2>Search San Francisco Hotel List by:</h2>
```

```
<A href="/srchloc.html">
<img src="icons/srchloc.gif" ALT="[Hotel Location]"></a>
<A href="/srchprice.html">
<img src="icons/srchprice.gif" ALT="[Hotel Price]"></a>
<A href="/srchtype.html">
<img src="icons/srchtype.gif" ALT="[Hotel Type]"></a>
<A href="/srchkey.html">
<img src="icons/srchkey.gif" ALT="[Key Word]"></a>


<h2>Other Information</h2>


<A href="/sfrinfo.html">
<img align=middle src="icons/sfrinfo.gif" ALT="[Help]"></a>
For more information about San Francisco Reservations. <br>
<A href="/availability.html">
<img align=middle src="icons/availability.gif" ALT="[Availability]"></a>
Examine hotel availability.<br>
<A href="/otherwww.html">
<img align=middle src="icons/otherwww.gif" ALT="[Elsewhere]"></a>
Other points of interest on the World Wide Web.<br>


<hr>


<b>San Francisco Reservations</b><br>
22 Second Street, 4th Floor<br>
San Francisco, California 94105<br>
<img src="icons/phone_num.gif" ALT="(800) 677-1550 or (415) 227-1500">
<address>sfr@hotelres.com</address>
```

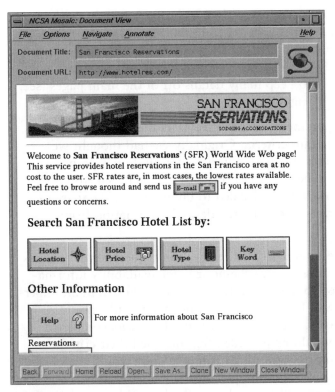

Figure 12.16 Home page for San Francisco Reservations.

The overall design goal for San Francisco Reservations' World Wide Web page was to create an easy-to-use system that would give users the ability to virtually browse through hotels before making a reservation: trying to describe in words the way a hotel lobby looks or feels is a difficult thing to do. Given this desire, there were other important considerations.

First of all, information should be clear and concise. The most important place for this is the home page (Figures 12.15 and 12.16). Here it should be clear to the user what exists on the server. For the design of SFR's page we asked ourselves the following two questions: "What do users know when they get here?" and "What do they want to find out now that they are here?" This helped shape the notion of having several search paths for finding hotels: by hotel location, price, type, and keyword (if the user has a specific hotel in mind). To maintain conciseness, depth was always chosen before breadth whenever possible. By this I mean it is better to have a single link to a page listing other WWW pages than to list all the pages on the front page (which I have seen done on several pages). Also, we included a help button in as many places as possible, allowing us to keep many details off of the main pages (see, for example, the home page in Figure 12.16).

One of SFR's key design requirements was to give users the ability to get partial lists of hotels based on certain criteria. Originally we had thought we would build static lists of hotels for these criteria: after all, hotels do not change their location, name, type, or prices very often. For the sake of longevity and robustness, however, we decided to build a single database of hotel data and write perl scripts to extract the desired information from this database.

Similarly, we needed to have a standardized reservation request form for users to complete, plus the ability to get up-to-the-hour hotel availability information. Perl scripts were written to handle these situations, although in an imperfect manner. Availability of San Francisco hotels can change suddenly, especially in high tourist season. We had hoped that when users completed their search of hotels, a list would be provided that matched their criteria along with the availability information for each hotel. Users would then be restricted from submitting a reservation request for any hotel that was not available. We determined, empirically, that this method could be ineffective, since hotels could quickly become unavailable during the time the user was browsing the "available" hotels list. We maneuvered around this problem by checking availability only at the time a user is ready to make a reservation. However, it is rather inconvenient to find a few hotels that you like only to discover one-by-one that they are sold out. To handle this, we allow the user to view all hotel availability for an entire month when a hotel is deemed sold out (we also have a link to this information on the home page, for those who know exactly what days they are to be in San Francisco).

Inline images in HTML pages should be small, should have a minimal number of colors, and should be used sparingly. While it was important for SFR to have a flashy WWW server, it was realized early on that there is a beauty-versus-usability trade-off, and that usability is far more important. Receiving large pictures over busy networks will test the patience of any user. After all, there are thousands of other pages the user could be looking at instead of waiting for your GIF image to arrive. In SFR's case the details about each hotel include pictures of sample hotel rooms, exterior photographs, hotel lobbies, and local area maps that the user might wish to view (Figures 12.17 and 12.18). We made these available without sacrificing usability by making a small-sized copy of the image (an "icon") and linking the small image to the full-sized version. By doing so, we made it possible for users to get an idea of what the picture is like from the small version; if they are interested in seeing the details, they can click on the image. Here is some example HTML code of this:

```
<A HREF="majes_l.gif">

<IMG ALIGN=middle SRC="majes_l_small.gif">

lobby photo</A>
```

Finally, if the user is interested in making a reservation, he or she can click the "Submit Reservation Request" button. This returns the **FORM** shown in Figures 12.19 and 12.20, which can be used to check room availability. Subsequent **FORM**s allow a user to actually make the reservation, should rooms be available.

A final constraint was to make our server both Mosaic- and lynx-friendly. Many WWW servers cater to only one or the other. Mosaic users love all kinds of graphical buttons, big pictures, and clickable imagemaps. Lynx users, however, cannot see the pictures and are sometimes left helpless as to what to do. For example, SFR's home page uses clickable graphic buttons for the different search paths, with descriptions of each button on the button itself. Mosaic users will see the nice descriptive button (e.g., Hotel Location), while if you are not careful, lynx users will only see the text string "[IMAGE]". To solve this problem, the "**ALT**" attribute should be used. Here is an example:

```
<A HREF="/srchloc.html">

<IMG SRC="srchloc.gif" ALT="[Hotel Location]">

</A>
```

With the ALT command lynx users will see "[Hotel Location]" in place of the image, providing a useful and aesthetically pleasing page to view. In general, it is good practice to view each page in several formats before you are done. You should also realize that there are many people using Mosaic who have the inline image loading turned off. Try this out. SFR is still working on how to make this look nice.

■■■■■ **Figure 12.17** HTML document for the Cartwright Hotel page.

```
<title>Cartwright Hotel</title>


<h1>Cartwright Hotel</h1>
524 Sutter Street /Powell<br>
San Francisco, CA 94102
<br>
        <FORM METHOD="POST" ACTION="/cgi-bin/hoteldates.pl">
        <input type="hidden" name="H_code" value="'CARTWRIGHT HOTEL'">
        <input TYPE="submit" value="Submit Reservation Request"><p>

    <A href="cartw_l.gif">
    <img align=middle src="cartw_l_small.gif">
    lobby photo</a>


    <A href="cartw_r.gif">
    <img align=middle src="cartw_r_small.gif">
    sample room photo</a>


    <A href="cartw_m.gif">
    <img align=middle src="cartw_m_small.gif">
    local area map</a><br>


<hr>
<pre>           1994 Published Rates  |   SFR Value Rates (based
                          |on availability)

=====================================================================
                              |  (4/1-10/31/94)  (11/1-12/31/94)
  Dbl. 1-2 Pers.     $119/$129 |  1-2 Pers. $79   1-2 Pers. $69
```

```
    Queen 1-2 Pers.    $119/$129   |   1-2 Pers. $79    1-2 Pers. $69

    2 Twin 1-2 Pers.   $119/$129   |   1-2 Pers. $79    1-2 Pers. $69

    Extra Pers.        $ 12/$ 12   |             $12              $12


    Children 12 yrs. & under Free</pre>
<hr>


    <img align=middle src="../icons/question.gif">
    What are<A href="../sfrvaluerates.html"> SFR Value Rates</a>?<p>


<b>Check In</b>: [Open] <b>Check Out</b>: [1:00pm]<br>
<b>Accepted Credit Cards</b>: [AX, MC, Visa,
                              Diners, Discover, JCB].<p>


<em>                         Credit Card Required to Guarantee
                             Arrival.  To Change or Cancel a
                             Reservation, Notify Us 48 hrs Prior to
                             Date of Arrival to Avoid a Charge.
</em>
<pre>  [N] Airport Shuttle

  [Y] Parking [$12 self-parking nearby]

  [Y] Restaurant [Teddy's 7am-11am Bkfst]

  [N] Room Service

  [Y] Continental Bkfst [$5]

  [N] In-Room Movies

  [N] VCR

  [N] View

  [N] Fireplace

  [N] Air Conditioning
```

```
     [Y]  Roll Away/Crib [$10/Free]

     [Y]  Suites [1 Bedroom]

     [N]  Kitchen

     [N]  Handicap

     [N]  Business Center

     [N]  Pool

     [N]  Fitness Center

     [N]  Pets</pre>
```

Neighborhood: Comfortable downtown location. 1 1/2 blocks from Union
Square, 1/2 block to Cable Car.

Lobby: Light, bright lobby with overstuffed sofas and chairs.
Reading room/library adjacent. Traditional style decor.

Guest Rooms: 114 small homey rooms and suites, fresh flowers, reading
pillows, clock radios.

Suites: 1 bedrooms done with antiques.

Services: Personalized service, meeting facilities available.
Turndown service.

FINAL NOTES

The creation of SFR's WWW page was completed in about a month. It was decided that it should be "finished" before it was officially announced, so that it could be thoroughly tested. We have found, however, that it is a continually changing project. By allowing users to send us feedback, we have received sev-

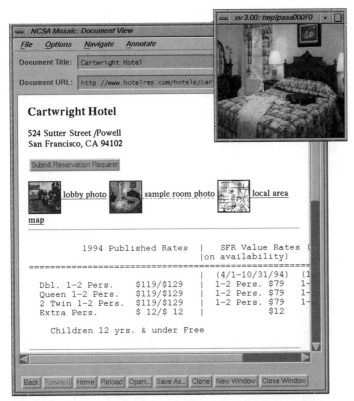

Figure 12.18 Typical page describing a San Francisco hotel. Clicking on the image icons yields larger, more detailed images of the hotel or of the rooms, as shown in the inset. Note the use of the **FORM**s "hidden" **INPUT** element.

eral suggestions that have shaped the way the pages look. The helpful and supportive atmosphere on the Internet is a vital resource that is invaluable.

UPDATE: OCTOBER 1995

Almost a year has passed since writing the description of the San Francisco Reservations' (SFR) WWW page (http://www.hotelres.com/) for the first edition of this book. SFR's page has proven to be a commercial success, and is now receiving over ten times more access hits than a year ago. The original page design is still in place, with only minor periodic changes to keep hotel information current.

Looking back, I would probably have spent more time integrating the system with other applications within the computing environment at SFR. In

Figure 12.19 Reservations and availability HTML document. This page was generated by the server-side perl script **_hoteldates.pl_**. Note the use of the **FORM**s `<input type="hidden"...>` element to store the name of the hotel. This is how the server-side script knows what hotel is being considered.

```
<html><head>

<title>Travel Dates</title>

</head>

<body>

<h1><img src="../icons/box.gif" ALT="">Travel Dates

<img src="../icons/box.gif" ALT=""></h1>

<b>Hotel:</b> 'CARTWRIGHT HOTEL'

<p>In order for us to determine the availability of this hotel, please

fill out the following information.  If you are making a reservation for

tonight, please call us at (800) 677-1550 or (415) 227-1500 so that we

can be sure that your request is processed in time.  Our hours are 7am

to 11pm Pacific Standard Time, seven days a week.

<FORM METHOD="POST" ACTION="/cgi-bin/grind.pl">

<hr>Enter Dates in the form: MM/DD/YY

<p>Arrival Date:      <input NAME="Arrdate" SIZE="8">

<p>Number of Nights: <input NAME="Night_stay" SIZE="2">

<p><hr>

<input TYPE="submit" value="check availability">

<input TYPE="reset" value="clear">

<p><pre>


</pre>

<input type= "hidden" name="H_code" value="'CARTWRIGHT HOTEL'">

</FORM>

<p> Generated by: <var>/home/http/cgi-bin/hoteldates.pl</var><br>
```

```
Date: 8:51:49 PST on Wed 19 Oct 94.<p>

</body>

</html>
```

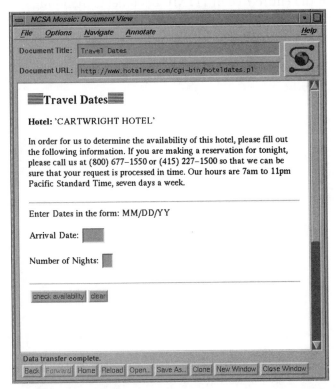

Figure 12.20 Reservations and availability query page for the Cartwright Hotel. This is accessed by clicking on the "Submit Reservation Request" page shown in Figure 12.18.

particular, several large databases of hotel and travel information already exist on a separate machine. Instead of maintaining HTML pages separately, I would have generated all hotel HTML code "on the fly," using SQL calls from the HTTP server. While this would be somewhat slower than serving documents directly, the system is more reliable and easier to maintain—that is, when hotel rates change in the database, they are automatically changed in the Web information.

The concept of dynamic HTML code can be pushed even further. In the original design, all of the search and hotel selection capabilities were generated dynamically by CGI programs. The advantage to this is that I can then change only a few lines of code and the changes occur in several places. Some commercial sites now do this with the entire tree of HTML documents, handling everything from the creation of header/footer information to the creation of GIF and JPEG images.

CHARACTERS AND COMPUTER CHARACTER SETS

A computer character set is simply an agreed-upon relationship between computer binary codes and a set of letters or graphical characters. Since almost all computers use the byte (8 bits) as the basic storage unit, standard character sets are often designed so that a single 8-bit byte stores a single character. Since there are 8 bits in a byte, each byte can represent 256 possible characters ($256=2^8$). Any agreed-upon relationship between these binary codes and a set of characters is called an 8-bit character set.

THE ISO LATIN-1 CHARACTER SET

Character sets are useful only if they are commonly understood—that way I can write a document using a character set and send it to you, knowing that you can turn that digital information back into the characters I intended. Character sets for international use are specified by the International Standards Organization (ISO). The ISO has specified several different character sets that fit inside 8-bit characters. For World Wide Web applications, the default set of printable characters is the ISO Latin-1 (also known as ISO 8859-1) character set—the complete set of these printable characters is shown in Table A.1. The first 128 characters in this character set are equivalent to the 128 characters of the US-ASCII (also known as ISO 646) character set. US-ASCII is known as a 7-bit character set, since it consists of only 128 characters and can be represented using just seven bits (2^7). Of these 128 characters, 32 are special characters for controlling printing devices and communications lines.[1] These characters are not printable, and are indicated in Table A.1 by two- or three-letter character sequences that mnemonically designate their function. For example, NUL is a null character, BEL is the bell character (rings a bell), CR is carriage return, BS is the backspace character, and so on. In addition, Table A.1 indicates the space character (decimal 32) with the symbol SP, as otherwise this would be invisible. Some of the important control characters, and their meanings, are:

Character Code	Meaning	Decimal
NUL	Null character	00
BS	Backspace	08
HT	Tab	09
LF	Line Feed/New Line (also NL)	10
CR	Carriage Return	13
SP	Space character	32
DEL	Delete	127

There are 128 additional characters in the 8-bit character set. The first 32 are undefined control characters, marked in Table A.1 by a double dash "--". The remaining characters are the ISO Latin-1 printable characters, and consist of many of the accented and other special characters commonly used in western European languages.

URL CHARACTER ENCODINGS

As discussed in Chapter 4, any 8-bit character can be represented in a URL by an *indirect reference* or encoding. Thus, any ISO Latin-1 character can be represented by the special character sequence

```
%xx
```

---

1 Formally these control characters are not ISO Latin-1 characters, but are part of another ISO specification, which defines byte codes for special data line control characters.

where *xx* is the *hexadecimal* or *hex* code corresponding to the character. Table A.1 shows both the decimal and hexadecimal codes for all the ISO Latin-1 and control characters. As an example the URL *encoding* for the percent character itself is:

```
%25
```

since the percent character is character 37 (hexadecimal 25) in the character set.

HTML CHARACTER AND ENTITY REFERENCES

In HTML, any ISO Latin-1 can be represented by either a *character reference* or an *entity reference*. A character reference represents each character through its *decimal* code. Thus, the character reference for a capital U with an umlaut (Ü) is

```
&#220;
```

since this is character 220 in the ISO Latin-1 character set. Numerical references are awkward and difficult to remember (and also depend on which character set you are using), so HTML also allows *entity references* for some of these characters. For example, the entity reference for a capital U with an umlaut (Ü) is

```
&Uuml;
```

Table A.1 lists the entity references, where defined, for the characters in the ISO Latin-1 character set, along with each character's decimal and hexadecimal character reference codes. Some of the entity reference names were only recently added, as part of the HTML 2.0 specifications, and are supported by few browsers. These names are italicized and slightly indented to distinguish them from the more commonly supported values. To ensure that your documents are properly viewed by most browsers, you should instead use character references for these particular characters.

In HTML, the four ASCII characters (>), (<), ("), and (&) have special meanings. Therefore, to display them in text as ordinary characters, you must use character or entity references, both of which are given in Table A.1. For example, the entity reference for the less than sign is <.

Figures A.1 and A.2 show the use of entity references in an HTML document. Figure A.1 uses the entity references that have long been employed in HTML documents, along with the newer references introduced in HTML 2.0—in fact, the document in Figure A.1 can be used to test a browser's capability to interpret these entity references. The newer references are not understood by some Web browsers. Thus, it is best to use character references until these entity definitions are more widely adopted.

Not all computers use the ISO Latin-1 character set. UNIX computers and PCs running Windows use the ISO Latin-1 character set by default, while PCs running DOS and Macintoshes do not, although the first 128 characters of the Macintosh and DOS characters sets are the US-ASCII characters. You must therefore take care on these platforms when preparing documents for use on the World Wide Web—it is always safe to use the character or entity references mechanisms for non-ASCII characters.

REFERENCE CAVEATS

Formally, the semicolon is not always necessary in character or entity references, and it can in principle be omitted if this will not confuse the parsing of the entity or character reference. For example, `&Uuml is an...` is an acceptable entity reference, but `&Uumlis an` is not. As a document author, it is always best to include the semicolon, as some browsers do not understand entity references when the semicolon is absent.

Also, the ampersand character indicates the start of a reference only when it is followed by an ASCII letter character (e.g., `&a..` to start an entity reference), or by the hash character plus a digit (e.g., `&#2..` to start a character reference). If both of these are absent, the ampersand is treated as a regular character. To be safe, however, it is best to use the ampersand character's character or entity reference if you wish it displayed as a character.

CHARACTER SETS AND MIME TYPES

The MIME protocol includes a "charset" definition for indicating the character set used to encode a particular document. The general mechanism would be to use a content-type header of the form

```
Content-type: text/subtype; charset=character_set
```

where *character_set* is the character set used for the subsequent data. The World Wide Web assumes the type `ISO-8859-1` in the absence of any other specification. The MIME standard supports over a dozen different charset values, but these are not currently supported by Web applications. Such support will soon be necessary for a truly multilingual World Wide Web.

FUTURE WEB CHARACTER SETS

The ISO Latin-1 character set imposes obvious limitations on the characters allowed in HTML documents, and makes it impossible to represent many of the world's common languages. The basic problem is the use of 8-bit character codes, as the 256 characters allowed by an 8-bit code are clearly insufficient. Although there are 8-bit character sets developed for different language sets (ISO 8859-2, 8859-3, and so on) this is not an ideal solution, since it leads to a multitude of different character sets, while the 8-bit limit makes encoding of languages such as Chinese or Japanese extremely difficult. In addition, many machines employ different character sets to represent the same characters, or support only a limited collection of character sets, making universal transport of digital documents quite difficult.

The long-term solution is to switch to a universal 16- or 32-bit character set. Long-word character sets can support many more characters in an internally consistent manner, and can provide the cross-platform compatibility essential for universal document transport. Current efforts are focused on the extended character set ISO 10646. This is a 16-bit character set, designed to be upward-compatible with ISO 646 (the ASCII character set) and ISO 8859-1. The ISO 10646 character set consists of a collection of 256-character character sets. Each of these different character sets is indexed by the first byte in a 16-bit word, while the second byte references the character of the indicated set. Thus, ISO 10646 is often described as a collection of 256 different 256-character character sets (for a total of 65,536 characters), each set lying in its own plane.

ISO 10646 is compatible with ISO 8859-1, in that the first 256-character set in ISO 10646 is equivalent to ISO 8859-1. Thus the hexadecimal byte codes for the letter "k" in the two character sets are:

ISO 10646	ISO 8859-1
00 6b	6b

where the first "plane" of characters in ISO 10646 is referenced by the null leading byte (note how byte *order* is also important). Web applications that read a document coded in ISO 10646 would simply ignore the null characters and interpret the document as containing standard ISO 8859-1 characters. Unfortunately, this does not work with current browsers.

In addition, there are several 8-bit encodings of the ISO 10646 character set, in which special 8-bit *control codes* are used to switch between different planes of the 16-bit character set. However, there are several such encodings, each optimized for different purposes. A browser must be designed to understand these different encodings if it is to understand documents encoded in these character sets. At present, very few browsers have this capability.

The debate over the appropriate universal character set continues, and to date no final decision has been made. There are literally dozens of competing character sets, each with strengths and weaknesses, and with its own collection of enthusiastic, if not rabid, supporters. The references at the end of this appendix provide some starting points, should you wish to delve deeper into this frustratingly complex, yet extremely important issue.

■■■■■■ **Table A.1** ISO Latin-1 characters and control characters, showing decimal codes, hexadecimal codes, and currently supported and proposed HTML entity references. Most proposed entity reference names, shown in italics, are not supported by current browsers (see Figure A.1). In these cases you should use character references.

Character	Decimal	Hex	Entity Reference	Character	Decimal	Hex	Entity Reference
NUL	0	0		SOH	1	1	
STX	2	2		ETX	3	3	
EOT	4	4		ENQ	5	5	
ACK	6	6		BEL	7	7	
BS	8	8		HT	9	9	
LF	10	a		VT	11	b	
NP	12	c		CR	13	d	
SO	14	e		SI	15	f	
DLE	16	10		DC1	17	11	
DC2	18	12		DC3	19	13	
DC4	20	14		NAK	21	15	
SYN	22	16		ETB	23	17	
CAN	24	18		EM	25	19	
SUB	26	1a		ESC	27	1b	

▬▬▬▬ **Table A.1** Continued

Character	Decimal	Hex	Entity Reference	Character	Decimal	Hex	Entity Reference
FS	28	1c		GS	29	1d	
RS	30	1e		US	31	1f	
SP	32	20		!	33	21	
"	34	22	&quot;	#	35	23	
$	36	24		%	37	25	
&	38	26	&amp;	'	39	27	
(	40	28		)	41	29	
*	42	2a		+	43	2b	
,	44	2c		-	45	2d	
.	46	2e		/	47	2f	
0	48	30		1	49	31	
2	50	32		3	51	33	
4	52	34		5	53	35	
6	54	36		7	55	37	
8	56	38		9	57	39	
:	58	3a		;	59	3b	
<	60	3c	&lt;	=	61	3d	
>	62	3e	&gt;	?	63	3f	
@	64	40		A	65	41	
B	66	42		C	67	43	
D	68	44		E	69	45	
F	70	46		G	71	47	
H	72	48		I	73	49	
J	74	4a		K	75	4b	
L	76	4c		M	77	4d	
N	78	4e		O	79	4f	
P	80	50		Q	81	51	
R	82	52		S	83	53	

Table A.1 Continued

Character	Decimal	Hex	Entity Reference	Character	Decimal	Hex	Entity Reference
T	84	54		U	85	55	
V	86	56		W	87	57	
X	88	58		Y	89	59	
Z	90	5a		[	91	5b	
\	92	5c		]	93	5d	
^	94	5e		_	95	5f	
`	96	60		a	97	61	
b	98	62		c	99	63	
d	100	64		e	101	65	
f	102	66		g	103	67	
h	104	68		i	105	69	
j	106	6a		k	107	6b	
l	108	6c		m	109	6d	
n	110	6e		o	111	6f	
p	112	70		q	113	71	
r	114	72		s	115	73	
t	116	74		u	117	75	
v	118	76		w	119	77	
x	120	78		y	121	79	
z	122	7a		{	123	7b	
|	124	7c		}	125	7d	
~	126	7e		DEL	127	7f	
—	128	80		—	129	81	
—	130	82		—	131	83	
—	132	84		—	133	85	
—	134	86		—	135	87	
—	136	88		—	137	89	
—	138	8a		—	139	8b	
—	140	8c		—	141	8d	

■■■■■■ **Table A.1** Continued

Character	Decimal	Hex	Entity Reference	Character	Decimal	Hex	Entity Reference
—	142	8e		—	143	8f	
—	144	90		—	145	91	
—	146	92		—	147	93	
—	148	94		—	149	95	
—	150	96		—	151	97	
—	152	98		—	153	99	
—	154	9a		—	155	9b	
—	156	9c		—	157	9d	
—	158	9e		—	159	9f	
	160	a0		¡	161	a1	&iexcl;
¢	162	a2	&cent;	£	163	a3	&pound;
¤	164	a4	&curren;	¥	165	a5	&yen;
¦	166	a6	&brvbar;	§	167	a7	&sect;
¨	168	a8	&uml;	©	169	a9	&copy;
ª	170	aa	&ordf;	«	171	ab	&laqno;
¬	172	ac	&not;	–	173	ad	&shy;
®	174	ae	&reg;	¯	175	af	&hibar
°	176	b0	&deg;	±	177	b1	&plusmn;
2	178	b2	&sup2;	3	179	b3	&sup3;
´	180	b4	&acute;	µ	181	b5	&micro;
¶	182	b6	&para;	·	183	b7	&middot;
,	184	b8	&cedil;	1	185	b9	&sup1;
º	186	ba	&ordm;	»	187	bb	&raquo;
¼	188	bc	&frac14;	½	189	bd	&frac12;
¾	190	be	&frac34;	¿	191	bf	&iquest;
À	192	c0	&Agrave;	Á	193	c1	&Aacute;
Â	194	c2	&Acirc;	Ã	195	c3	&Atilde;
Ä	196	c4	&Auml;	Å	197	c5	&Aring;
Æ	198	c6	&AElig;	Ç	199	c7	&Ccedil;

■■■■■■ **Table A.1** Continued

Character	Decimal	Hex	Entity Reference	Character	Decimal	Hex	Entity Reference
È	200	c8	&Egrave;	É	201	c9	&Eacute;
Ê	202	ca	&Ecirc;	Ë	203	cb	&Euml;
Ì	204	cc	&Igrave;	Í	205	cd	&Iacute;
Î	206	ce	&Icirc;	Ï	207	cf	&Iuml;
Ð	208	d0	*Ð*	Ñ	209	d1	&Ntilde;
Ò	210	d2	&Ograve;	Ó	211	d3	&Oacute;
Ô	212	d4	&Ocirc;	Õ	213	d5	&Otilde;
Ö	214	d6	&Ouml;	×	215	d7	*×*
Ø	216	d8	&Oslash;	Ù	217	d9	&Ugrave;
Ú	218	da	&Uacute;	Û	219	db	&Ucirc;
Ü	220	dc	&Uuml;	Ý	221	dd	&Yacute;
Þ	222	de	&THORN;	ß	223	df	&szlig;
à	224	e0	&agrave;	á	225	e1	&aacute;
â	226	e2	&acirc;	ã	227	e3	&atilde;
ä	228	e4	&auml;	å	229	e5	&aring;
æ	230	e6	&aelig;	ç	231	e7	&ccedil;
è	232	e8	&egrave;	é	233	e9	&eacute;
ê	234	ea	&ecirc;	ë	235	eb	&euml;
ì	236	ec	&igrave;	í	237	ed	&iacute;
î	238	ee	&icirc;	ï	239	ef	&iuml;
ð	240	f0	&eth;	ñ	241	f1	&ntilde;
ò	242	f2	&ograve;	ó	243	f3	&oacute;
ô	244	f4	&ocirc;	õ	245	f5	&otilde;
ö	246	f6	&ouml;	÷	247	f7	*÷*
ø	248	f8	&oslash;	ù	249	f9	&ugrave;
ú	250	fa	&uacute;	û	251	fb	&ucirc;
ü	252	fc	&uuml;	ý	253	fd	&yacute;
þ	254	fe	&thorn;	ÿ	255	ff	&yuml;

██████████ **Figure A.1** Listing of the HTML document *en_test.html*, showing all currently defined and proposed HTML entity references. This document can be used to test your browser's support of these entity names.

```
<html>

<head>

<title> Appendix A: Entity References </title>

</head>

<body>

<h1 align=center> Appendix A — Entity References </h1>

<PRE>

<B>"Special" Character References</B>


&amp;lt;        -   &lt;        &amp;gt;        -     &gt;

&amp;amp;       -   &amp;       &amp;quot;      -     &quot;


<B>HTML 2.0 Standard Entity References </B>


&amp;AElig;     -   &AElig;     &amp;Aacute;    -   &Aacute;   &amp;Acirc;    -   &Acirc;

&amp;Agrave;    -   &Agrave;    &amp;Aring;     -   &Aring;    &amp;Atilde;   -   &Atilde;

&amp;Auml;      -   &Auml;      &amp;Ccedil;    -   &Ccedil;   &amp;ETH;      -   &ETH;

&amp;Eacute;    -   &Eacute;    &amp;Ecirc;     -   &Ecirc;    &amp;Egrave;   -   &Egrave;

&amp;Euml;      -   &Euml;      &amp;Iacute;    -   &Iacute;   &amp;Icirc;    -   &Icirc;

&amp;Igrave;    -   &Igrave;    &amp;Iuml;      -   &Iuml;     &amp;Ntilde;   -   &Ntilde;

&amp;Oacute;    -   &Oacute;    &amp;Ocirc;     -   &Ocirc;    &amp;Ograve;   -   &Ograve;

&amp;Oslash;    -   &Oslash;    &amp;Otilde;    -   &Otilde;   &amp;Ouml;     -   &Ouml;

&amp;THORN;     -   &THORN;     &amp;Uacute;    -   &Uacute;   &amp;Ucirc;    -   &Ucirc;

&amp;Ugrave;    -   &Ugrave;    &amp;Uuml;      -   &Uuml;     &amp;Yacute;   -   &Yacute;
```

```
&amp;aacute;   -   &aacute;    &amp;acirc;    -   &acirc;    &amp;aelig;   -   &aelig;

&amp;agrave;   -   &agrave;    &amp;aring;    -   &aring;    &amp;atilde;  -   &atilde;

&amp;auml;     -   &auml;      &amp;ccedil;   -   &ccedil;   &amp;eacute;  -   &eacute;

&amp;ecirc;    -   &ecirc;     &amp;egrave;   -   &egrave;   &amp;eth;     -   &eth;

&amp;euml;     -   &euml;      &amp;iacute;   -   &iacute;   &amp;icirc;   -   &icirc;

&amp;igrave;   -   &igrave;    &amp;iuml;     -   &iuml;     &amp;ntilde;  -   &ntilde;

&amp;oacute;   -   &oacute;    &amp;ocirc;    -   &ocirc;    &amp;ograve;  -   &ograve;

&amp;oslash;   -   &oslash;    &amp;otilde;   -   &otilde;   &amp;ouml;    -   &ouml;

&amp;szlig;    -   &szlig;     &amp;thorn;    -   &thorn;    &amp;uacute;  -   &uacute;

&amp;ucirc;    -   &ucirc;     &amp;ugrave;   -   &ugrave;   &amp;uuml;    -   &uuml;

&amp;yacute;   -   &yacute;    &amp;yuml;     -   &yuml;


<B>Proposed Entity References </B>


      -          &amp;iexcl;    -   &iexcl;    &amp;pound;   -   &pound;

&amp;curren;   -   &curren;    &amp;yen;      -   &yen;      &amp;brvbar;  -   &brvbar;

&amp;sect;     -   &sect;      &amp;uml;      -   &uml;      &amp;copy;    -   &copy;

&amp;ordf;     -   &ordf;      &amp;laquo;    -   &laquo;    &amp;not;     -   &not;

&amp;shy;      -   &shy;       &amp;reg;      -   &reg;      &amp;hibar;   -   &hibar;

&amp;deg;      -   &deg;       &amp;plusmn;   -   &plusmn;   &amp;sup2;    -   &sup2;

&amp;sup3;     -   &sup3;      &amp;acute;    -   &acute;    &amp;micro;   -   &micro;

&amp;para;     -   &para;      &amp;middot;   -   &middot;   &amp;cedil;   -   &cedil;

&amp;sup1;     -   &sup1;      &amp;ordm;     -   &ordm;     &amp;raquo;   -   &raquo;

&amp;frac14;   -   &frac14;    &amp;frac12;   -   &frac12;   &amp;frac34;  -   &frac34;

&amp;iquest;   -   &iquest;

</PRE>

</body>

</html>
```

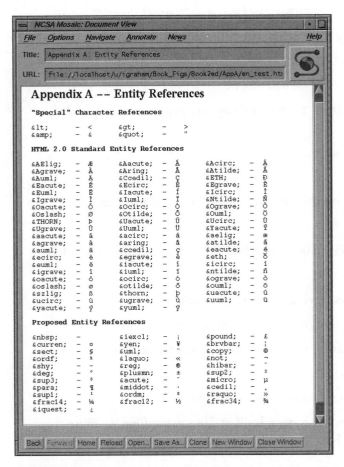

Figure A.2 Mosaic for X-Windows Version 2.6 rendering of the HTML document listed in Figure A.1.

REFERENCES

General information about character sets on the Internet and World Wide Web

http://www.echo.lu/impact/oii/chars.html

ftp://ds.internic.net/rfc/rfc1345.txt

http://www.ebt.com:8080/docs/multilingual-www.html

http://www.w3.org/hypertext/WWW/International/Overview

`http://www.w3.org/hypertext/WWW/MarkUp/html-spec/charset-harmful.html`

Draft specification for integrating internationalization into the Web

`http://www.alis.com:8085/ietf/html/`

(Look for files with names like `draft-ietf-html-i18n...`)

Detailed discussion of ISO 8859-1, and of designing programs for a multilingual environment

`ftp://ftp.vlsivie.tuwien.ac.at/pub/8bit/FAQ-ISO-8859-1`

`ftp://ftp.vlsivie.tuwien.ac.at/pub/8bit/ISO-programming`

List of character sets in use on the Internet, and associated problems

`ftp://ftp.isi.edu/in-notes/iana/assignments/character-sets`

UNICODE character sets (ISO 10646 is related to this character set model)

`http://www.stonehand.com/unicode.html`

List of ISO 10646 characters, giving their byte encodings

`ftp://ftp.ifi.uio.no/pub/SGML/CHARSET/ISO10646-1%3A1993.L3`

Introduction to SGML declarations, and SGML character set issues

`http://www.sil.org/sgml/wlw11.html`

`http://www.sgmlopen.org/sgml/docs/ercs/ercs-home.html`

And if you want to read a book, have a look at *Understanding Japanese Information Processing*, by Ken Lunde (O'Reilly & Associates, Inc., 1993).

MULTIPURPOSE INTERNET MAIL EXTENSIONS (MIME)

MIME, for Multipurpose Internet Mail Extensions, is an extension to the traditional Internet mail protocol that allows for the communication of multimedia electronic mail. The original Internet mail protocol, defined in the document RFC 822, was designed with simple ASCII text messages in mind—the protocol defined a mail message as a block of text, preceded by specially defined header information specifying routing information about the message (where it is from, who it is to, who copies were sent to, etc.), and the characters (basically, ASCII) allowed in Internet mail messages. However, the protocol said little about the format of the message *content*. At the time (which was not that long ago!), most electronic mail messages were plain-text files, so that concerns about other formats were unwarranted.

Today, however, there is enormous demand for sophisticated electronic mail that allows delivery of messages containing many components, such as a Rich Text or HTML text documents, image files, sound, and even video data. Such messages can easily be communicated by mail only if all mail programs and mail servers share a standard for constructing, encoding, and transporting such complex, possibly multipart, messages.

The MIME protocol is designed to provide this common standard. MIME provides an open protocol for multimedia/multipart mail messages as an extension upon the original RFC 822 mail protocol: MIME defines how to code the content, while RFC 822 specifies how to package the message and get it to its destination. MIME defines several new document headers that specify such things as the nature of a message (multipart or single part), how the message parts are separated, the data content of each part, and the encoding scheme used to encode each part. This is, of course, an overly simplified description of the MIME protocol, and for further details, you are referred to the relevant documentation (RFC 1521). The following sections summarize the features that are most important for Web applications.

THE MIME CONTENT-TYPE

Of primary interest to us is the MIME content-type header. This should already be familiar to you, since it is the header used to indicate the content of files being transferred using the HTTP protocol. Whenever you request a document from an HTTP server, the server must first determine the type of the document and send the appropriate content-type header ahead of it. For example, if an AIFF data file is being returned, the server must send back the content-type header:

```
Content-type: audio/aiff
```

Similarly, when a client uses the POST method to send data to a server, the data is preceded by a content-type header that tells the server the format of the data arriving. The only currently defined type for posted **FORM** data is:

```
Content-type: application/x-www-form-urlencoded
```

(see Chapters 6 and 8).

How do content-type headers work? Each header has a minimum of two parts, giving the data *type* and *subtype*, using the format:

```
Content-type: type/subtype
```

Type can be any of image, audio, text, video, application, multipart, message, and extension-token (these names, like the string `"content-type"`, are case-insensitive). The meanings of the first four are obvious, and indicate the overall type of the data. The `application` type is for other data (perhaps binary) that need to be processed in a special way. This could be a program to run, or perhaps a PostScript document to be executed by a PostScript previewer. `Multipart` indicates a message containing more than one part, while `message` refers to an old-fashioned RFC 822 message body. `Extension-token` is any name beginning with `X-`, and refers to experimental data types. This allows you to create special MIME types and not conflict with established types.

Subtype gives the specifics of the content. Thus, `text/html` means a text file that is an HTML document, `application/postscript` means a PostScript file to be run through a PostScript interpreter, and so on. There are lots of content-types: Table B.1 lists the ones most important in WWW applications. Subtypes can also be experimental extension types, such as the `x-www-form-urlencoded` subtype shown previously.

When looking at Table B.1, keep in mind that because of the flexibility of the HTTP client/server interaction, there are many content-types used by WWW applications that are not commonly used in electronic mail messages.

CHARACTER SET
SPECIFICATIONS FOR TEXT TYPES

Any text content-type (that is, `text/*`) can in principle (see the NOTE below!) take an optional parameter, `charset`, which is used to specify the character set used in the text document—it's no good receiving a text document file if you don't know the relationship between the bytes you receive and the characters intended. The general format for including this parameter is

```
Content-Type: text/subtype; charset=char_set_name
```

where *subtype* is the text subtype (commonly `html` or `plain` in Web applications), and *char_set_name* is the name of the character set with which the document is encoded. Note how the semicolon (`;`) is used to separate the type/subtype field from the `charset` parameter. Some of the possible values are `US-ASCII`, `ISO-8859-1` (ISO Latin-1), `ISO-8859-2`, . . . up to `ISO-8859-9`. The nine ISO sets are the 8-bit Latin character sets defined by the ISO. Web applications assume the ISO Latin-1 character set by default, so you usually do not need the `charset` parameter. There is currently much discussion on upgrading the Web to support character sets such as `ISO-10646-1` (a 16-bit character set), or Japanese character sets such as `ISO-2022-JP`, but as yet no clear consensus. Currently, very few computers support these larger, more versatile character sets, and without this support, their use is not practical. (See Appendix A.)

■■■ **NOTE**

At present, most Web applications ignore `charset` specifications, and assume that text documents are encoded with the ISO Latin-1 character set.

■■■

HTML-LEVEL SPECIFICATION

The text/html MIME type, at least in Web applications, can take the additional optional parameter `version`. This specifies the level or version of the HTML language used by the document. For example,

```
Content-type: text/html; version=2.0
```

indicates that the data are written using the HTML 2.0 specification.

MULTIPART MESSAGES

One special content-type defined as part of the MIME mail protocol is the multipart/mixed. This type specifies a message that contains several message parts, all contained within a single message called a multipart/mixed message. The *boundary* between the parts is specified by a special *boundary* parameter, which must be set with the content-type header. The general form is:

```
Content-Type: multipart/mixed; boundary=randomstring
```

where `randomstring` is a random character string used to separate the message parts. Message parts are denoted by a line containing the string `--randomstring` (the boundary string preceded by two dash characters). This, in turn, is followed by the content-type declaration for the part—the content-type declaration must be followed by a blank line, containing only a CRLF pair, to indicate the end of the headers and the start of the data. The end of one part of the data, and the beginning of the subsequent part, is indicated by another string `--randomstring`. The end of the last part, and the end of the message, is indicated by the special string `--randomstring--`. Here is a simple outline:

```
MIME-Version: 1.0

Content-type: multipart/mixed; boundary=23xx1211


—23xx1211

Content-type: text/html


.... html document data  ....

—23xx1211

Content-type: audio/aiff


..... audio data ....

—23xx1211—
```

This simple example leaves a great deal out, but gives the general idea of the approach. The message contains two parts: a text file in HTML format, and an audio file in AIFF format. The MIME "multipart" message indicates that there is more than one component to the message, and specifies the string used to divide the message parts.

This multipart model is employed in Netscape's experimental MIME type `multipart/x-mixed-replace`, discussed at the beginning of Chapter 9. The multipart specification is also critical to the `multipart/form-data` type being developed to support the downloading of complex **FORM** data, including client-side data files, to servers. This type is discussed, in detail, in the final reference given at the end of this appendix.

HOW DOES THE SERVER DETERMINE CONTENT-TYPE?

For the server to be able to send a content-type header, it must somehow know what a document contains. The convention is to use the filename extension, or suffix, to indicate the content type. Thus, files with the extension *.mpeg* are assumed to be MPEG movies, while files with the *.html* extension are assumed to be HTML documents, and so on. On PC servers, these names are shortened to three letters, for example, *.mpg* for MPEG movies and *.htm*

for HTML documents. You can specify more than one extension for each type
if that is more convenient. When you place a document on a server, you must
be sure to give it the filename extension matching the content of your file. At
the same time, you must be sure to update your server's database relating
filename extensions to MIME types, if you add a previously unknown type.

If the server does not know the type of a file, it assumes a default content-
type, often `text/plain`.

HOW DOES THE CLIENT
DETERMINE CONTENT-TYPE?

If a client receives a file from a Gopher or HTTP server, it reads the content-
type from information sent by the server: HTTP servers send a content-type
header, while Gopher servers have another mechanism for indicating the data
content. With FTP or local file access, this support is not available, and the
client must itself be able to determine the file content. Again, this is done by
the filename extension, so that a Web client must also have a database matching filename extensions to data types.

The location of this database varies from client to client, but in all cases it
involves matching a filename extension to a MIME type/subtype. For example, with Mosaic for X-Windows or Netscape for X-Windows (and, in fact,
for most UNIX browsers), the database is found in a file called *mime.types*,
which is often found in the directory */usr/local/lib/mosaic* (your mileage may
vary). You can also place a copy in your own home directory, which overrides
this default. With Windows applications, the settings are usually part of the
applications INI file. For example, with WinMosaic the database is contained
in the *MOSAIC.INI* file (which you sometimes must edit by hand), while with
Netscape, the data is contained in the file *NETSCAPE.INI*, which can easily be
modified from within Netscape using the "Preferences..." item under the pull-
down "Options" menu. Most Macintosh applications store configuration
information, including the names of helper applications, in a preferences files
kept in the Macintosh Applications Preferences folder. In almost all cases,
these settings can be configured from the browser using pull-down menus
while running the browser.

▬▬▬▬ **Table B.1** MIME Content-Types Commonly Used in the World Wide Web, Showing Corresponding Filename Extensions and Data Types

MIME Type/Subtype	Typical Filename Extensions	Description of Data Content
message/rfc822	mime	MIME message
application/postscript	ai eps ps	PostScript
application/rtf	rtf	MS Rich Text Format
application/x-tex	tex	Tex/LaTeX
application/x-texinfo	texinfo texi	TexInfo format
application/x-troff	t tr roff	troff document
application/x-troff-man	man	troff with MAN macros
application/x-troff-me	me	troff with ME macros
application/x-troff-ms	ms	troff with MS macros
application/x-gtar	gtar	gnu tar format
application/x-tar	tar	4.3BSD tar format
application/x-ustar	ustar	POSIX tar format
application/x-bcpio	bcpio	Old CPIO format
application/x-cpio	cpio	POSIX CPIO format
application/x-shar	shar	UNIX sh shell archive
application/x-pdf	pdf	Adobe Acrobat pdf format
application/zip	zip	Pkzipped files
application/mac-binhex40	hqx	Macintosh binhexed archives
application/x-stuffit	sit sea	Macintosh Stuffit archive
application/macwriteii	??	MacWrite file
application/msword	??	MS word document
application/octet-stream	tar dump readme	tar, binary dump, trick extension to force a save to disc
application/octet-stream	bin uu	binary, UUencoded
application/octet-stream	exe	PC executable
application/x-dvi	dvi	TeX dvi format file
application/x-wais-source	src wsrc	WAIS "sources"

■■■■■■ **Table B.1** Continued

MIME Type/Subtype	Typical Filename Extensions	Description of Data Content
application/hdf	hdf	NCSA HDF data format
audio/basic	au snd	"basic" SUN audio— 8-bit u-law PCM encoding
audio/x-aiff	aif aiff aifc	Macintosh audio format
audio/x-wav	wav	Microsoft audio format
image/gif	gif	GIF format
image/xbm	xbm	X-Bitmap
image/xpm	xpm	X-Pixelmap
image/ief	ief	Image Exchange Format
image/jpeg	jpeg jpg jpe	JPEG image
image/tiff	tiff tif	TIFF image
image/rgb	rgb	RGB image
image/x-xwindowdump	xwd	X Windowdump image
image/x-pict	pict	Macintosh PICT image
text/html	html htm	HTML document
text/plain	txt	plain text
text/plain	c c++ pl cc h	program listing
text/x-setext	etx	Structure enhanced text
text/richtext	(*undefined*)	Enriched Text
video/mpeg	mpeg mpg mpe	MPEG Movie
video/quicktime	qt mov	Macintosh QuickTime
video/x-msvideo	avi	Microsoft video format
video/x-sgi-movie	movie	SGI movie format
multipart/mixed	(*usually e-mail*)	Mail messages with multiple parts

■■■■■ **Table B.1** Continued

MIME Type/Subtype	Typical Filename Extensions	Description of Data Content
Special HTTP/WWW types		
multipart/x-mixed-replace		See Chapter 9 (Netscape extension)
multipart/form-data		See Chapter 9 and Appendix B
application/x-www-form-urlencoded		See Chapter 6
application/x-www-local-exec		See Chapter 9

REFERENCES

The Internet Mail Protocol is defined in RFC 822, at:

```
ftp://ds.internic.net/rfc/rfc822.txt
```

(The site `ds.internic.net` is an archive site for *all* Internet RFC documents.)

MIME is defined in RFC 1521, at:

```
http://www.ncsa.uiuc.edu/SDG/Software/Mosaic/Docs/rfc1521.txt
```

```
http://www.oac.uci.edu/indiv/ehood/MIME/MIME.html
```

```
ftp://ds.internic.net/rfc/rfc1521.txt
```

Introductory documentation on MIME, in PostScript (`.ps`) or plain text (`.txt`), is available at:

```
ftp://ftp.uu.net/networking/mail/mime/mime.ps
```

```
ftp://ftp.uu.net/networking/mail/mime/mime.txt
```

A definitive list of registered MIME types is found at:

```
ftp://ftp.isi.edu/in-notes/iana/assignments/media-types/
```

The proposed `multipart/form-data` MIME content-type is discussed in the draft proposal:

```
ftp://ds.internic.net/internet-drafts/draft-ietf-html-fileupload-*.txt
```

where the asterisk is the (changing) document version number. Look for the most recent (highest numbered) version.

FINDING SOFTWARE

USING ARCHIE

Most of the software mentioned in this book is freely available on the Internet, and we have included URLs pointing to typical sites archiving the executable versions or source codes for these programs. However, you may find that a program has moved and is no longer available at the indicated location. In this case you should not panic, but should use archie to locate an alternative archive site.

STANDARD ARCHIE

Archie clients (the software you run on your own PC or workstation) are available for almost all computer platforms. DOS, UNIX, NeXT, and VMS versions can be found at:

```
ftp://ftp.cs.widener.edu/pub/archie/
```

Versions compiled for particular operating systems are indicated by the filename, for example, *archie-dos.zip* for PCs running DOS and *archie-vms.com* for VAX/VMS computers. The source code itself is found in the file *archie-1.4.1.tar.Z*. The source code compiles simply and easily on most UNIX workstations. Other sites containing archie are:

```
ftp://ftp.unipg.it/pub/unix/infosys/archie/
```

```
ftp://unix.hensa.ac.uk/pub/uunet/networking/info-service/archie/clients/
```

```
ftp://ftp.mr.net/pub/Info/archie/clients/
```

This command-line archie client works identically on DOS, UNIX, or VAX/VMS computers: You control the program through a series of command-line options you type after the name of the program, and archie prints the results of the search to the screen. Most often you will want to make a *case-insensitive substring* search for filenames that contain the substring of characters that you type in. In this case you give archie a character substring contained in the name of the package or program you are looking for: giving a case-insensitive substring, and not the entire name, makes allowances for changing version numbers, possible changes in capitalization, and site-to-site variations in the name. For example if you are looking for the program **WinWeb** you would type, at the command line prompt:

```
archie -s WinWeb
```

The string -s indicates a case-insensitive substring search, so that archie will return all file or directory names containing the pattern WinWeb anywhere in the name, and with any combination of upper- and lowercase letters. Here is just part of the output from the above search:

```
Host ftp.einet.net

        Location: /einet/pc/winweb

              FILE -rw-rw-rw-     424263  Aug 10 10:21  winweb.zip
```

This gives the Internet domain name where the package was located (*ftp.einet.net*), the directory on this server that contains the file (*/einet/pc/winweb*), and the name of the file found (*winweb.zip*). You can then use anonymous FTP to access this site, or just use your WWW browser, pointing it to the URL:

```
ftp://ftp.einet.net/einet/pc/winweb/winweb.zip
```

Your archie client gets the information about file locations from an archie *server*. Each archie client has a built-in server name that it uses by default. Sometimes this server is busy, and does not return a prompt response. You can select another server using the command-line option -h. For example,

```
archie -h archie.sura.net -s winweb
```

means to search for the substring winweb on the alternate server
archie.sura.net. Typing the command:

```
archie -L
```

gives a short list of archie servers known by your archie client. Here it a typical example:

```
archie.ans.net (USA [NY])

archie.rutgers.edu (USA [NJ])

archie.sura.net (USA [MD])

archie.unl.edu (USA [NE])

archie.mcgill.ca (Canada)

archie.funet.fi (Finland/Mainland Europe)

archie.au (Australia)

archie.doc.ic.ac.uk (Great Britain/Ireland)

  * archie.rutgers.edu is the default archie server.

  * For the most up-to-date list, write to an archie server and give it the command

    'servers'.
```

Each archie server maintains and generates its own databases of files and their
locations, so different archie servers do not contain the same information.
Therefore, if one machine does not give you a useful response, it is a good
idea to try another.

ARCHIE FOR MACINTOSHES

Macintosh users have access to an elegant shareware program called **anarchie**.
Anarchie combines archie searches with an FTP retrieval package for retrieving files from the returned list. To do an archie search with anarchie, first
select "Archie..." from the pull-down "File..." menu. Then select the archie
server you want, type the search string into the "Find:" box, select the type of
search to use, and press the "Find" button to start the search. Anarchie then
displays a small window telling you it is working, and even gives an estimate
of the time required to complete the search. You can even start up multiple
parallel archie searches and simultaneously look for the desired files on several

archie servers. When finished, anarchie produces a window containing the list of successful results. Double-clicking on an item in this list starts up an FTP connection to the relevant site and automatically downloads the file to your computer.

Anarchie is available at many sites, including:

```
ftp://ftp.cac.psu.edu/pub/mac/comm/anarchie/Anarchie-121.hqx

ftp://sumex-aim.stanford.edu/info-mac/comm/net/anarchie-110.hqx

ftp://sics.se/pub/info-mac/comm/net/anarchie-110.hqx
```

DOWNLOADING FILES USING FTP

If you have a WWW browser, you can just type in the URLs to access files: browsers come with the FTP protocol built in. Thus to access the file *winweb.zip* from the server *ftp.einet.net* in the directory */einet/pc/winweb,* you would type in the URL:

```
ftp://ftp.einet.net/einet/pc/winweb/winweb.zip
```

If you leave out the filename, that is:

```
ftp://ftp.einet.net/einet/pc/winweb/
```

you get a contents listing for the directory */einet/pc/winweb/.* You can then click on the file you want to download.

Sometimes this procedure doesn't work, and you get a terse message stating that the browser was "unable to connect to the URL." This often means that the server you are trying to connect to already has too many people making FTP connections, and has refused you access. To test this, you can make the FTP access the old-fashioned way, by running a stand-alone FTP program. Recall that, after making the FTP connection, you log in as user *anonymous*, and give your *e-mail address* as a password. At this point the FTP server may refuse your connection: most FTP servers place a limit on the number of people who can simultaneously access the server, and if the server is already full, your connection will be refused. But, at least now you know the problem.

Here is an example FTP session on a UNIX computer to the site *ftp.einet.net* (the string green:~> is the command-line prompt). I am trying to get the *winweb.zip* program I found with the earlier archie search. My own input is in boldface, while the computer response is in regular font. Commentary is added in italics.

```
green:~> ftp ftp.einet.net    (start ftp, pointing to the desired Domain name)

Connected to ftp.einet.net.

220 ftp.einet.net FTP server (Version 6.42 Wed Jul 6 12:37:10 CDT 1994) ready.

Name (ftp.einet.net:igraham): anonymous

331 Send e-mail address as password (for example: joe@green.utirc.utoronto.ca).

Password:   (type in your e-mail address—it will not be visible)

230-

230- Welcome to the EINet public FTP server.  For information about

230- EINet, send e-mail to einet-info@einet.net.

230-

230- If you encounter any unusual problems, please report them via e-mail

230- to ftp@ftp.einet.net.  If your client hangs on multi-line responses,

230- please try using a dash (-) as the first character of your user name.

230- This will turn off the continuation messages that may be confusing

230- your client.

230-

230- All connections and transfers are logged.

230-

230-

230 Anonymous login ok; access restrictions apply.

Remote system type is UNIX.

Using binary mode to transfer files.

ftp> cd /einet/pc/winweb    (change into the directory containing what we want)

250 CWD command successful.
```

```
ftp> ls     (list the directory contents, just to see what's there)

total 1888

drwxr-xr-x   2 6522      2000          512 Aug  1 19:43 debug

drwxr-xr-x   2 6522      2000          512 Aug 19 15:36 parts

 rw-r--r--   1 6522      2000        22022 Jul 27 14:39 pkunzip.exe

 rw-r--r--   1 6522      2000       245756 Jul 27 14:40 vbrun300.zip

 rw-r--r--   1 6522      2000         7680 Aug  2 15:26 winvoke.wri

 rw-r--r--   1 6522      2000       596336 Sep 28 19:15 winweb.zip

 rw-r--r--   1 6522      2000       596336 Sep 28 19:15 winweb1.00A2.1.zip

 rw-r--r--   1 6522      2000       424263 Jul 26 19:50 winweb1.00A2.zip

226 Transfer complete.

ftp> bin     (set FTP session to binary mode to transfer zip files or programs)

200 Type set to I.

ftp>

get winweb.zip          (get the file from the server)

200 PORT command successful.

150 Opening BINARY mode data connection for winweb.zip (596336 bytes).

596336 bytes received in 122.55 seconds (4.75 Kbytes/s)

ftp> quit               (we're finished, so quit)

221 Goodbye.

green:~>
```

In this session, the command bin was used to set *binary* transfer mode. This is needed for transferring binary data (such as images, movies, or sound files), compressed, program, or archive files. If you are transferring plain text files, such as README files or **.txt* files, you should type the letter a to select *ascii* mode. *Do not* use ascii mode for programs, archives, images, or wordprocessor files (such as Word or WordPerfect documents). Ascii mode "corrects" for the fact that different computers use different characters to mark the end of a line of text. This "correction" will corrupt these other file formats.

VIRUS PROTECTION

Anytime you download programs from the Internet onto PCs, Macintoshes, or Amigas, you run the risk of importing a computer virus. You must be very cautious about this. You should make sure that you have virus detection software on your computer, that you use it to check files that you download, and that you keep the software up to date; computer viruses are evolving almost as fast as the World Wide Web. To date there have been few cases in which WWW software has been contaminated by a virus, but this is no reason to relax. Computer viruses are a major problem, and you should always be on guard.

"LISTENING" AND "TALKING" AT A TCP/IP PORT

This appendix contains the source code for the programs **listen.c.** and **back-talk.c**. **Listen.c** is a simple program that *listens* at a TCP/IP port and prints to the screen (or terminal) any characters received at the port. This program was used to observe the data that WWW client browsers send to HTTP servers. **Backtalk.c** , like **listen**, prints to the terminal any characters received at the port, but also allows you to type characters to the terminal that are sent on to the remote program that is *talking* to that port. Thus, **backtalk** can act like a simpleminded HTTP server—or rather, *you* and **backtalk** can act like a simpleminded server, since you have to type by hand all the server response headers that a server would return to a client. Note that **Ctrl-D** indicates the end of a transmission (without terminating the program), so you end your typed message with this character. **Ctrl-C** both ends the transmission and kills **backtalk**.

Listen and **backtalk** were written for UNIX machines, particularly for DECstations running the operating system Ultrix 4.3A. Some work may be needed to port these programs to System V–based machines. Porting to PCs or Macintoshes may require a bit more work.

To run either program, you simply type the program name at the shell prompt. Listen (or backtalk) then prints the port number it is listening at, and goes silent. Here is typical output:

```
% listen

listening on 2055
```

At this point, any data sent to port 2055 on this computer will be printed on the screen just below the string `listening on 2055`. With backtalk, any characters you type to the screen will be sent to the remote client process attached to this port. You terminate either program by typing **Ctrl-C**.

Backtalk and listen were both written by Norman Wilson of the High Performance Research Computing Group at the University of Toronto.

PROGRAM LISTING FOR LISTEN.C

```c
#include <stdio.h>

#include <sys/socket.h>

#include <netinet/in.h>

main(argc, argv)

int argc;

char **argv;

{

        int verbose;

        int lfd, sfd;

        struct sockaddr_in myaddr, claddr;

        struct in_addr ia;

        int inane;

        int pid;

        verbose = 0;

        if (argc > 1 && strcmp(argv[1], "-v") == 0) {

                verbose = 1;

                argc--;
```

```
        argv++;
}

if ((lfd = socket(AF_INET, SOCK_STREAM, 0)) < 0) {

        perror("socket");

        exit(1);

}

myaddr.sin_family = AF_INET;

myaddr.sin_port = 0;

myaddr.sin_addr.s_addr = INADDR_ANY;

if (bind(lfd, &myaddr, sizeof(myaddr)) < 0) {

        perror("bind");

        exit(1);

}

inane = sizeof(myaddr);

if (getsockname(lfd, &myaddr, &inane) < 0) {

        perror("getsockname");

        exit(1);

}

if (listen(lfd, 5) < 0) {

        perror("listen");

        exit(1);

}

fprintf(stderr, "listening on %d\n", ntohs(myaddr.sin_port));

fflush(stdout);

while (inane = sizeof(claddr), (sfd = accept(lfd, &claddr, &inane)) >= 0) {

        if ((pid = fork()) < 0)

                perror("fork");

        else if (pid == 0)
```

```
                    copydata(sfd, verbose);

            /* else parent */

            close(sfd);

            if (verbose)

                    fprintf(stderr, "accept %s:%d, pid %d\n",

                            inet_ntoa(claddr.sin_addr), ntohs(claddr.sin_port),
    pid);

        }

        exit(0);

    }

    copydata(fd, verbose)

    int fd;

    int verbose;

    {

        char buf[200];

        int mypid;

        FILE *fp;

        mypid = getpid();

        if ((fp = fdopen(fd, "r")) == NULL) {

            fprintf(stderr, "%d: can't fdopen\n", mypid);

            exit(1);

        }

        while (fgets(buf, sizeof(buf), fp)) {

            if (verbose)

                printf("%d: ", mypid);

            fputs(buf, stdout);

            fflush(stdout);

        }

        exit(0);

    }
```

PROGRAM LISTING FOR BACKTALK.C

```c
#include <stdio.h>

#include <sys/signal.h>

#include <sys/socket.h>

#include <netinet/in.h>


main(argc, argv)

int argc;

char **argv;

{

    int verbose;

    int lfd, sfd;

    struct sockaddr_in myaddr, claddr;

    struct in_addr ia;

    int inane;

    int pid;

    FILE *sfp;


    verbose = 0;

    if (argc > 1 && strcmp(argv[1], "-v") == 0) {

        verbose = 1;

        argc--;

        argv++;

    }

    if ((lfd = socket(AF_INET, SOCK_STREAM, 0)) < 0) {

        perror("socket");

        exit(1);

    }

    myaddr.sin_family = AF_INET;
```

```
myaddr.sin_port = 0;

myaddr.sin_addr.s_addr = INADDR_ANY;

if (bind(lfd, &myaddr, sizeof(myaddr)) < 0) {

    perror("bind");

    exit(1);

}

inane = sizeof(myaddr);

if (getsockname(lfd, &myaddr, &inane) < 0) {

    perror("getsockname");

    exit(1);

}

if (listen(lfd, 5) < 0) {

    perror("listen");

    exit(1);

}

fprintf(stderr, "listening on %d\n", ntohs(myaddr.sin_port));

fflush(stdout);

while (inane = sizeof(claddr), (sfd = accept(lfd, &claddr, &inane)) >= 0) {

    if ((pid = fork()) < 0) {

        perror("fork");

        continue;

    }

    if (pid == 0) {        /* child: copy in */

        if ((sfp = fdopen(sfd, "r")) == NULL) {

            fprintf(stderr, "child can't fdopen connection for reading\n");

            exit(1);

        }

        copydata(sfp, stdout, verbose);
```

```
                    exit(0);

            } else {            /* parent: copy out */
                if (verbose)
                    fprintf(stderr, "accept %s:%d, pid %d\n",
                            inet_ntoa(claddr.sin_addr),
                            ntohs(claddr.sin_port), pid);
                if ((sfp = fdopen(sfd, "w")) == NULL) {
                    fprintf(stderr, "parent can't fdopen connection for writing\n");
                    continue;      /* leave child running */
                }
                copydata(stdin, sfp, 0);
                fclose(sfp);
                kill(pid, SIGTERM);     /* kill child, so connection closes */
                clearerr(stdin);     /* clear EOF flag */
            }
            close(sfd);
        }
        exit(0);
}


copydata(frfp, tofp, verbose)
FILE *frfp, *tofp;
int verbose;
{
        char buf[200];
        int mypid;

        mypid = getpid();
```

```
        while (fgets(buf, sizeof(buf), frfp)) {
            if (verbose)
                fprintf(tofp, "%d: ", mypid);
            if (fputs(buf, tofp) == EOF
            || fflush(tofp) == EOF) {
                perror("write");
                break;
            }
        }
    }
```

TAGS FOR

IDENTIFYING

LANGUAGES—RFC 1766

Tags for identifying languages on the Internet are specified by the Internet RFC 1766. This specification is built upon the ISO standards for language codes (ISO 639) and country codes (ISO 3166), with extensions for situations not covered by the ISO standards.

In general, a language tag takes the following form:

```
lang-subtag-subtg2...
```

Where *lang* is a string of *case-insensitive* ASCII letters (a–z) that specifies the language, and *subtag* is an (optional) extension that defines a subgroup of that language (there can be multiple subtags, separated by successive dashes). Each string can be at most eight characters, with the prefix x- indicating a value defined for private use. Although uppercase letters are allowed, their use is discouraged, particularly in the lang tag.

Lang If the lang tag has only two characters, then these characters refer to the language specified in the ISO 639 language codes (see below). Thus fr refers to the French language, while ja refers to Japanese. The only other possibilities at present are private language codes, beginning with the prefix x-.

Subtag The subtag(s) can refer to variants of a language, usually through the two-letter *national variant* codes specified in ISO 3166 (e.g., fr-CA for Canadian French), but also through dialects (e.g., en-cockney), or even physical script variations appropriate to a language. National variant subtags are traditionally written in uppercase, although this is not required.

Here are some simple examples:

en-US	American English
en-cockney	Cockney dialect of English
x-romulan	Romulan language
ar-EG	Egyptian Arabic
fr	French (generic)

The ISO 639 language and ISO 3166 country codes are summarized in the next sections.

Note that in Web applications, you can use a language code without a country code. This implies generic settings appropriate to the language.

There are currently few Web applications that make use of language code information.

ISO 639 LANGUAGE CODES

Table E.1 contains the two-letter language codes from the ISO 639 international standard. In applications, these two-letter codes are represented by case-insensitive ASCII character codes.

In the World Wide Web, language codes are used to select between special native language symbols, such as punctuation marks, currency, numerical notation (e.g., commas instead of periods as the decimal separator), text direction (left to right or right to left), and so on. The use of these codes is discussed in Chapter 5. Note that these language codes are *not related* to the character set used by an HTML document.

ISO 3166 COUNTRY CODES

In addition to codes for the world's languages, the ISO has also specified two-letter codes for the different countries of the world. These are summarized in the ISO 3166 two-letter country-code standard, summarized in Table E.2. As with the language codes, the country codes are case-insensitive.

You may notice that these are also the country codes used by the Internet domain name scheme for indicating the country domain of an Internet address. Absent from this list are the nonnational names commonly used in domain naming schemes, such as ARPA (old-style Arpanet—obsolete), COM (Commercial), EDU (Educational), GOV (Government), INT (International), MIL (U.S. Military), NATO (for NATO, soon to be obsolete), NET (Network), and ORG (Nonprofit organization).

■■■■ **Table E.1** Two-letter ISO 639 Language Codes

Code	Language	Code	Language
aa	Afar	ab	Abkhazian
af	Afrikaans	am	Amharic
ar	Arabic	as	Assamese
ay	Aymara	az	Azerbaijani
ba	Bashkir	be	Byelorussian
bg	Bulgarian	bh	Bihari
bi	Bislama	bn	Bengali; Bangla
bo	Tibetan	br	Breton
ca	Catalan	co	Corsican
cs	Czech	cy	Welsh
da	Danish	de	German
dz	Bhutani	el	Greek
en	English	eo	Esperanto
es	Spanish	et	Estonian
eu	Basque	fa	Persian
fi	Finnish	fj	Fiji

■■■■ Table E.1 Continued

Code	Language	Code	Language
fo	Faeroese	fr	French
fy	Frisian	ga	Irish
gd	Scots, Gaelic	gl	Galician
gn	Guarani	gu	Gujarati
he	Hebrew	ha	Hausa
hi	Hindi	hr	Croatian
hu	Hungarian	hy	Armenian
ia	Interlingua	id	Indonesian
ie	Interlingue	ik	Inupiak
in	Indonesian	is	Icelandic
it	Italian	iu	Inuktitut
iw	Hebrew (obsolete)	ja	Japanese
ji	Yiddish (obsolete)	jw	Javanese
ka	Georgian	kk	Kazakh
kl	Greenlandic	km	Cambodian
kn	Kannada	ko	Korean
ks	Kashmiri	ku	Kurdish
ky	Kirghiz	la	Latin
ln	Lingala	lo	Laothian
lt	Lithuanian	lv	Latvian, Lettish
mg	Malagasy	mi	Maori
mk	Macedonian	ml	Malayalan
mn	Mongolian	mo	Moldavian
mr	Marathi	ms	Malay
mt	Maltese	my	Burmese
na	Nauru	ne	Nepali
nl	Dutch	no	Norwegian
oc	Occitan	om	(Afan), Oromo

■■■ **Table E.1** Continued

Code	Language	Code	Language
or	Oriya	pa	Punjabi
pl	Polish	ps	Pashto, Pushto
pt	Portuguese	qu	Quechua
rm	Rhaeto-Romance	rn	Kirundi
ro	Romanian	ru	Russian
rw	Kinyarwanda	sa	Sanskrit
sd	Sindhi	sg	Sangro
sh	Serbo-Croatian	si	Singhalese
sk	Slovak	sl	Slovenian
sm	Samoan	sn	Shona
so	Somali	sq	Albanian
sr	Serbian	ss	Siswati
st	Sesotho	su	Sundanese
sv	Swedish	sw	Swahili
ta	Tamil	te	Tegulu
tg	Tajik	th	Thai
ti	Tigrinya	tk	Turkmen
tl	Tagalog	tn	Setswana
to	Tonga	tr	Turkish
ts	Tsonga	tt	Tatar
tw	Twi	ug	Uigur
uk	Ukrainian	ur	Urdu
uz	Uzbek	vi	Vietnamese
vo	Volapuk	wo	Wolof
xh	Xhosa	y	Yiddish
yo	Yoruba	za	Zuang
zh	Chinese	zu	Zulu

Table E.2 Two-letter Country Codes, from ISO 3166

Code	Country	Code	Country
AD	Andorra	AE	United Arab Emirates
AF	Afghanistan	AG	Antigua and Barbuda
AI	Anguilla	AL	Albania
AM	Armenia	AN	Netherland Antilles
AO	Angola	AQ	Antarctica
AR	Argentina	AS	American Samoa
AT	Austria	AU	Australia
AW	Aruba	AZ	Azerbaijan
BA	Bosnia-Herzegovina	BB	Barbados
BD	Bangladesh	BE	Belgium
BF	Burkina Faso	BG	Bulgaria
BH	Bahrain	BI	Burundi
BJ	Benin	BM	Bermuda
BN	Brunei Darussalam	BO	Bolivia
BR	Brazil	BS	Bahamas
BT	Bhutan	BV	Bouvet Island
BW	Botswana	BY	Belarus
BZ	Belize	CA	Canada
CC	Cocos (Keeling)	CF	Central African Republic
CG	Congo	CH	Switzerland
CI	Ivory Coast	CK	Cook Islands
CL	Chile	CM	Cameroon
CN	China	CO	Colombia
CR	Costa Rica	CS	Czechoslovakia (obsolete)
CU	Cuba	CV	Cape Verde
CX	Christmas Island	CY	Cyprus
CZ	Czech Republic	DE	Germany
DJ	Djibouti	DK	Denmark

████ **Table E.2** Continued

Code	Country	Code	Country
DM	Dominica	DO	Dominican Republic
DZ	Algeria	EC	Ecuador
EE	Estonia	EG	Egypt
EH	Western Sahara	ER	Eritrea
ES	Spain	ET	Ethiopia
FI	Finland	FJ	Fiji
FK	Falkland Isl. (Malvinas)	FM	Micronesia
FO	Faroe Islands	FR	France
FX	France (Europe only)	GA	Gabon
GB	Great Britain (U.K.)	GD	Grenada
GE	Georgia	GF	Guyana (Fr.)
GH	Ghana	GI	Gibraltar
GL	Greenland	GM	Gambia
GN	Guinea	GP	Guadeloupe (Fr.)
GQ	Equatorial Guinea	GR	Greece
GS	South Georgia & South Sandwich Islands	GT	Guatemala
GU	Guam (U.S.)	GW	Guinea Bissau
GY	Guyana	HK	Hong Kong
HM	Heard & McDonald Islands	HN	Honduras
HR	Croatia	HT	Haiti
HU	Hungary	ID	Indonesia
IE	Ireland	IL	Israel
IN	India	IO	British Indian Ocean Terr.
IQ	Iraq	IR	Iran
IS	Iceland	IT	Italy
JM	Jamaica	JO	Jordan
JP	Japan	KE	Kenya
KG	Kyrgyz Republic	KH	Cambodia

Table E.2 Continued

Code	Country	Code	Country
KI	Kiribati	KM	Comoros
KN	St. Kitts Nevis Anguilla	KP	Korea (North)
KR	Korea (South)	KW	Kuwait
KY	Cayman Islands	KZ	Kazachstan
LA	Laos	LB	Lebanon
LC	Saint Lucia	LI	Liechtenstein
LK	Sri Lanka	LR	Liberia
LS	Lesotho	LT	Lithuania
LU	Luxembourg	LV	Latvia
LY	Libya	MA	Morocco
MC	Monaco	MD	Moldova
MG	Madagascar	MH	Marshall Islands
MK	Macedonia (prev. Yug.)	ML	Mali
MM	Myanmar	MN	Mongolia
MO	Macau	MP	Northern Mariana Islands
MQ	Martinique (Fr.)	MR	Mauritania
MS	Montserrat	MT	Malta
MU	Mauritius	MV	Maldives
MW	Malawi	MX	Mexico
MY	Malaysia	MZ	Mozambique
NA	Namibia	NC	New Caledonia (Fr.)
NE	Niger	NF	Norfolk Island
NG	Nigeria	NI	Nicaragua
NL	Netherlands	NO	Norway
NP	Nepal	NR	Nauru
NU	Niue	NZ	New Zealand
OM	Oman	PA	Panama

███████ **Table E.2** Continued

Code	Country	Code	Country
PE	Peru	PF	Polynesia (Fr.)
PG	Papua New Guinea	PH	Philippines
PK	Pakistan	PL	Poland
PM	St. Pierre & Miquelon	PN	Pitcairn
PR	Puerto Rico (U.S.)	PT	Portugal
PW	Palau	PY	Paraguay
QA	Qatar	RE	Reunion (Fr.)
RO	Romania	RU	Russian Federation
RW	Rwanda	SA	Saudi Arabia
SB	Solomon Islands	SC	Seychelles
SD	Sudan	SE	Sweden
SG	Singapore	SH	St. Helena
SI	Slovenia	SJ	Svalbard & Jan Mayen Islands
SK	Slovakia (Slovak Republic)	SL	Sierra Leone
SM	San Marino	SN	Senegal
SO	Somalia	SR	Suriname
ST	St. Tome and Principe	SU	Soviet Union (obsolete?)
SV	El Salvador	SY	Syria
SZ	Swaziland	TC	Turks & Caicos Islands
TD	Chad	TF	French Southern Territory
TG	Togo	TH	Thailand
TJ	Tadjikistan	TK	Tokelau
TM	Turkmenistan	TN	Tunisia
TO	Tonga	TP	East Timor
TR	Turkey	TT	Trinidad & Tobago
TV	Tuvalu	TW	Taiwan
TZ	Tanzania	UA	Ukraine
UG	Uganda	UK	United Kingdom

■■■■■■■ **Table E.2** Continued

Code	Country	Code	Country
UM	U.S. Minor outlying islands	US	United States
UY	Uruguay	UZ	Uzbekistan
VA	Vatican City State	VC	St. Vincent & Grenadines
VE	Venezuela	VG	Virgin Islands (GB)
VI	Virgin Islands (U.S.)	VN	Vietnam
VU	Vanuatu	WF	Wallis & Futuna Islands
WS	Samoa	YE	Yemen
YT	Mayotte	YU	Yugoslavia (obsolete?)
ZA	South Africa	ZM	Zambia
ZR	Zaire	ZW	Zimbabwe

REFERENCES

Tags for the identification of languages on the Internet (**RFC 1766**):

http://ds.internic.net/RFC/rfc1766.txt

The ISO 639 Language Codes: Standards Document: ISO 639:1988 (E/F)

The International Organization for Standardization, 1st edition, 1988. Prepared by ISO/TC 37—Terminology (principles and coordination).

An unofficial summary of the codes can be found at:

http://www.stonehand.com/unicode/standard/iso639.html

The Registry agency for ISO language codes is:

International Information Centre for Terminology (Infoterm)
P.O. Box 130
A-1021 Wien
Austria
Phone: +43 1 26 75 35 Ext. 312
Fax: +43 1 216 32 72

ISO 3166 Country Codes: Standards Document: ISO 3166:1988 (E/F)

An unofficial summary of the codes can be found at:

ftp://ftp.isi.edu/in-notes/iana/assignments/country-codes

The official Registry agency for ISO country codes is:

ISO 3166 Maintenance Agency Secretariat
c/o DIN Deutches Institut für Normung
Burggrafenstrasse 6
Postfach 1107
D-10787 Berlin
Germany
Phone: +49 30 26 01 320
Fax: +49 30 26 01 231

REL AND REV
ATTRIBUTES FOR
HYPERTEXT
RELATIONSHIPS

A standard hypertext anchor can link two documents or resources together, but does not provide any explanation of the reason behind the link. This is sometimes a problem for a person reading HTML documents, as they cannot tell the important navigation links from the unimportant ones. This is even more of a problem for a person attempting to manage a large collection of interlinked documents, as this manager has no way of structuring or prioritizing the links, so as to get a feel for the overall structure and organization of the collection.

Fortunately HTML anchor elements can take the attributes **REL** and **REV**, which are used to define the relationships between the linked resources. However, this is only useful if there are universally understood values for **REL** and **REV,** as otherwise different authors will use different values, so that documents labeled with **REL** and **REV** cannot be shared or intelligently combined. This appendix provides a list of some commonly accepted **REL** and **REV** values, and their meanings. The references at the end of the chapter provide links to working documents that are constantly updating this list, and upon which this appendix was based.

ANCHOR AND LINK ELEMENTS

In HTML, links between a document and other Internet-accessible resources are usually indicated by **A**, or *anchor* elements, which were discussed in detail in Chapters 2 and 4. (For this discussion, we are ignoring hypertext links implied by **SRC** attributes to **IMG** [or other] elements, which also indicate a form of hypertext relationship.) Through the **HREF** attribute, the **A** element can indicate a link *from* the anchored location in the document *to* another Internet-accessible resource. At the same time, the **NAME** attribute allows an anchor element to be labeled as the possible *destination of* a hypertext link. (In HTML 3, the **ID** attribute serves the same purpose, and can also appear in a number of elements other than **A**.)

LINK elements in the **HEAD** of a document can, as discussed in Chapter 4, be used to describe hypertextual *relationships* between two documents, or between a document and another Internet-accessible resource. For example, the element

```
<LINK REL="author" HREF="mailto:igraham@flober.rodent.edu">
```

indicates a relationship between the current document and the indicated URL—in this case, that the object at the end of the link bears, in some way, on the author of the document containing the **LINK** element. The *meaning* of this relationship is defined by the value assigned to the attribute **REL** or, alternatively, **REV**. The purpose of **REL** and **REV** is to assign meaning to a hypertext relationship, so that **REL** and **REV** are allowed attributes for both **LINK** and **A** elements. However, since **LINK** indicates a *relationship* between resources, it must always have a **REL** or **REV** attribute to describe that relationship. The possible types of relationships are almost limitless. Commonly accepted values are described in this appendix.

MEANING OF A
HYPERTEXT LINK—REL AND REV

As just noted, the **LINK** element is only meaningful if the *relationship* between the two resources is specified as part of the element. For example, the element

```
<LINK HREF="http://bla.bla.edu/junk.html">
```

is meaningless, since it says nothing about the relationship between the two resources. As discussed in Chapter 4, the *meaning* of the hypertext relationship between a document and the resource to which it is linked is indicated by the attributes **REL** and **REV**. **REL** specifies the relationship of the *destination* of the hypertext link to the *start* of the link. Thus, **REL**="previous" indicates that the linked resource is the previous document, relative to the current one, in a logical, author-specified sequence. **REV**, on the other hand, indicates the relationship of the *current* document to the *destination* of the link. Thus, **REV**="previous" indicates that the current document is the previous document, relative to the linked document, in a logical author-specified sequence.

REL and **REV** are often, but not always, the converse of one another. The importance of having both terms will be evident from the examples given later in this appendix.

The values assigned to **REL** and **REV** are sequences of *name tokens*. As mentioned in Chapter 4, name tokens are case-insensitive strings that can contain any ASCII letter (a-z, A-Z) or number (0-9), plus the dash (-) or period (.) characters, but nothing else. They must also begin with a letter. Multiple values can be assigned to a single **REL** or **REV** attribute, simply by separating the values by whitespace, and enclosing the collection of values in double quotes. Thus,

```
REL="contents  previous"
```

indicates that the linked document is both a table of contents related to the current document, and the previous document in an author-defined sequence of documents.

BROWSER INTERPRETATION
OF LINK ELEMENTS

Unlike **A**, **LINK** is not specifically designed to be an active anchor, although it may be used by a browser to customize the user interface, so as to indicate important, related documents. At present, most Web browsers ignore **LINK** elements. However, browsers currently under development will reconfigure the user interface to include buttons linked to resources indicated by certain **LINK**s. For example, **LINK** elements with **REL/REV** values of "previous" and "next" may produce customized button bars on graphical browsers, allowing the user to click on the buttons and link directly to the next and previous documents of the author-specified sequence. Similar features may result from **LINK**s to indexes, table of contents pages, and so on.

This functionality is only possible if there are well-understood meanings for the **REL** and **REV** values, so that the browser can unambiguously know the intent of the document author. The **REL/REV** values specified in this appendix help to provide this set of standard values and meanings.

REL AND REV IN A ELEMENTS

It is clear that **REL** and **REV** are essential for **LINK** elements—without such values, a **LINK** has no useful meaning. At the same time, **REL** and **REV** can be extremely useful with **A** anchors, since they provide useful information about the nature of the link. Browsers may use this information to render a link differently, or to behave differently. For example, clicking on the following anchor

```
<A HREF="/cgi-bin/lin.pl" REL="glossary">reference material</A>
```

might cause the browser to spawn a second window containing the glossary document, as opposed to replacing the currently displayed material.

Perhaps more importantly, **REL** and **REV** attributes provide information needed by site managers when trying to understand the overall organization of a large document collection. Information about the relationships defined by the links or anchors, such as "next", "previous", "index", or "glossary", make it much easier to categorize and organize the collection, and to provide an overview of the collection's structure. Link information can also be valuable to a Web browser, which can use the information to provide navigational aids for a document collection, since the relationship values allow for the differentiation of important navigational nodes from navigationally less-important references.

DEFINED RELATIONSHIPS FOR REL AND REV

The currently accepted values for **REL** and **REV** and their meanings, as given here, are taken from a discussion paper, written by Murray Maloney, on hypertext links and **REL/REV** values in HTML. This document is available at the URLs listed in the "References" section at the end of this appendix.

The relationships are divided into five broad categories. *Navigational* values define links to or from documents or other tools that are useful in navigating through a collection of documents. *Sequential* values define a preferred or logical sequence between documents. Such a sequence is usually defined by the author. *Hierarchical* values define hierarchical relationships between documents. *Related document* values define related documents, such as bibliography or citation lists. Finally, *meta* values define links to meta-information, such as author and copyright.

NAVIGATION VALUES

Navigational values define relationships to (or from) documents designed to assist a user in navigating through a document collection. Possible values are `"content"` (table of contents), `"index"` (an index), and `"navigate"` (a navigational aid).

contents (or toc)—Identifies a relationship with table of contents.

> **REL**=`"contents"`—The target document is a table of contents relevant to the current document.

> **REV**=`"contents"`— The current document is a table of contents relevant to the linked document.

Examples:

```
<A REL="contents" HREF="htmlindex.html">table of contents</A>

<LINK REL="contents" HREF="htmlindex.html">

<LINK REV="contents" REL="glossary" HREF="refs/glossary.html">
```

The first two links indicate that the target document is the table of contents relevant to the current document. The third example states that the current document is a table of contents relevant to the linked document, and also states that the linked document is a glossary relevant to the current document.

index—Identifies a relationship with an index.

> **REL**=`"index"`— The target document is an index related to the current document.

> **REV**=`"index"`— The current document is an index related to the linked document.

Example:

```
<LINK REL="index" HREF="/cgi-bin/indx_srch.pl">
```

This indicates that the linked resource is an index relevant to the current document. In this example, the resource is a gateway program, which could be a gateway to a searchable index of the document collection containing the current document.

navigate—Identifies a relationship with a navigational aid. A navigational aid can consist of a partial table of contents, a clickable document map, or some other resource.

REL=`"navigate"`—The link is *to* a navigational aid relevant to the current document.

REV=`"navigate"`—The current document is a navigational aid related to the linked document.

SEQUENCE VALUES

Often, a collection of hypertext documents is presented as a sequence of documents, rather like a printed book. In this case, there are obvious first and last documents, as well as obvious next and previous pages. Relationships with these documents are indicated by the values `"begin"`, `"end"`, `"next"`, and `"previous"`.

begin (or *first*)—Identifies a relationship with the author-defined start of a sequence of documents.

REL=`"begin"` —The link is *to* the start of the author-defined sequence of documents, of which the current document is part.

REV=`"begin"`—The link is *from* the start of the author-defined sequence; that is, the current document is the start of the sequence.

Examples:

```
[ <A REL="begin"    HREF="intro.html">Start</A> ]

[ <A REL="previous" HREF="doc2_1.html">Prev</A> ]

[ <A REL="next"     HREF="doc2_3.html">Next</A> ]

[ <A REL="end"      HREF="biblio.html">End</A> ]

 - - -

[ <A REL="contents" HREF="htmlindex.html"><EM>ToC</EM></A> ]

{ <A REL="index"    HREF="/cgi-bin/indx.pl"><EM>Index</EM></A> ]
```

This example uses all the attribute values defined in this section to construct a navigational button bar containing the words *Start*, *Prev*, *Next*, and *End*. Each of these words is in turn linked to the starting, previous, next, and end documents of the document collection. There are also links to the table of contents (*ToC*) and *Index*.

end (or *last*)—Identifies a relationship with the author-defined end of a sequence of documents.

 REL=`"end"`—The link is *to* the end of the author-defined sequence of documents, of which the current document is part.

 REV=`"end"`—The link is *from* the end of the author-defined sequence; that is, the current document is the end of the sequence.

next— Identifies a relationship with the next or subsequent document in an author-defined sequence of documents. An obvious analogy is the next page of a printed book.

 REL=`"next"`—The link is *to* the next document in a linear document sequence.

 REV=`"next"`—The link is *from* the next document in the document sequence; the current document is the next document relative to the linked document.

previous—Identifies a relationship with the previous document in an author-defined sequence of documents. An obvious analogy is the previous page of a printed book.

 REL=`"previous"`—The link is *to* the previous document in a linear document sequence.

 REV=`"previous"`—The link is *from* the previous document in the document sequence; the current document is the previous document relative to the linked document.

HIERARCHY VALUES

Often a collection of documents can be described hierarchically. Possible relationships are then `"parent"` (the top of the local branch in the hierarchy), `"child"` (a subordinate document), `"sibling"` (a document of equivalent level in the hierarchy), and `"top"` (the top or root document of the hierarchy).

child—Identifies a relationship with a subordinate relationship, or subdocument. This is much like saying that a file is subordinate to the directory in which it is contained.

REL=`"child"`—The link is *to* a subdocument, or child document, of the current document.

REV=`"child"`—The current document is a child, or subdocument, of the linked document.

Example:

```
<LINK REV="child next" HREF="dlooble.html">
```

This indicates that the current document is the child of the document *dlooble.html*, and is also the next document following *dlooble.html* in the author-defined logical document sequence.

parent—Identifies a relationship with a superior element in the hierarchy. This is not the inverse of a child, since a parent can have more than one child.

REL=`"parent"`—The link is *to* the parent document of the current document.

REV=`"parent"`—The current document is the parent of the linked document.

sibling—Identifies a relationship with a sibling, or equivalent document, in the hierarchy. A given document can have any number of siblings.

REL=`"sibling"`—The link is *to* a sibling of the current document; that is, the current document and linked document have a common parent.

REV=`"sibling"`—The link is *from* a sibling of the current document; that is, the current document and linked document have a common parent.

top (or *origin*)—Indicates a relationship with the top of a logical or hierarchical tree of which the current document is a part.

REL=`"top"`—The link is *to* the logical top node of the document hierarchy containing the current document.

REV=`"top"`—The link is *from* the top of the logical document hierarchy containing the linked document.

Example:

```
<A REL="parent top" HREF="intro.html">Introduction</A>
```

This link is to a document that is the parent of the current document, as well as the top of the hierarchical tree containing the current document.

RELATIONAL VALUES

Relational values indicate documents that have well-understood contextual relationships to a collection of documents. Examples are glossaries, bibliographies, lists of definitions, and so on. Possible values are `"biblioentry"` (a bibliographic entry), `"bibliography"` (a bibliography), `"citation"` (for a bibliographic citation), `"definition"` (for the definition of a word or term), and `"glossary"` (for a glossary).

biblioentry—Identifies a relationship with a bibliographic entry—typically used within an **A** element to indicate a link to a bibliographic entry related to a citation.

> **REL**=`"biblioentry"`—The link is to a bibliographic entry related to the current document: the anchor may contain a citation, the link being to the appropriate bibliographic entry.

> **REV**=`"biblioentry"`—The link is from a bibliographic entry related to the document to which the link is directed. This usage would be extremely uncommon.

Example:

```
<A REL="biblioentry" HREF="bib.html#ISG"></CITE>The HTML Sourcebook</CITE></A>
```

This link is to a bibliographic entry relevant to the citation *The HTML Sourcebook*.

bibliography—Indicates a relationship with a bibliography. A bibliography may simply be a document containing bibliographic entries, or it might be a queryable bibliographic database.

> **REL**=`"bibliography"`—The link is to a bibliography related to the current document.

> **REV**=`"bibliography"`—The link is from a bibliography to a document for which the bibliography is relevant.

Example:

```
<LINK REL="bibliography" REV="top" HREF="/refs/biblio.html">
```

The linked document is a bibliography relevant to the current document, and the current document is also the top of a hierarchical document collection containing the bibliography.

citation—Indicates a relationship with a bibliographic citation.

REL=`"citation"`—The link is to a bibliographic citation, in which case the anchor may be a bibliographic entry.

REV=`"citation"`—The anchored text in the current document is a citation related to the linked document or resource. Since the anchored text is a citation, it should also be placed inside **CITE**.

Examples (from Murray Maloney's discussion paper):

```
... as described by Tim Berners-Lee [ <A REL="citation" HREF="#TBL">1</A> ]

...

... is described in Tim Berners-Lee's

<CITE>

   <A NAME="TBL" REV="citation" HREF="./biblio/TBL.html">The

   Hypertext Markup Language</A>

</CITE>
```

The first example shows a link to a citation, while the second shows a link from a citation to additional information relevant to the citation.

definition—Indicates a relationship with a definition of a word or term. A definition would most typically be specified as part of an **A**, as it is specific to a word or term, and not generic to a document.

REL=`"definition"`—The link is to the definition of the text contained within the anchor element.

REV=`"definition"`—The current document, or the anchor within the current document, contains the definition associated with the term targeted by the hypertext link. This form would rarely be used.

Examples:

```
<A REL="definition" HREF="/cgi-bin/defns.pl#cgi">CGI</A>

<A REL="definition" HREF="glossary.html#cgi">CGI</A>
```

These indicate links to resources containing definitions of the term, in the first case via a gateway program, in the second via a glossary document containing **NAME**-anchored term definitions.

glossary—Indicates a relationship with a glossary document, or with a query interface to a glossary.

REL=`"glossary"`—The link is to a glossary or glossary query interface that contains glossary information relevant to the current document.

REV=`"glossary"`—The current document is a glossary or glossary query interface relevant to the linked document.

Example:

```
<LINK REL="glossary" HREF="glossary.html">
```

The linked document *glossary.html* is a glossary related to the current document.

META-INFORMATIONAL VALUES

Meta-informational values describe relationships with documents that contain information *about* the document collection, but that are not explicitly part of the collection. Accepted values are `"author"` (the document author), `"copyright"` (copyright information), `"disclaimer"` (a legal disclaimer), `"editor"` (the editor[s] of the document), `"meta"` (a meta-document containing meta-information relevant to the current document), `"publisher"` (the document publisher), and `"trademark"` (trademark notice or related information).

author — Indicates a relationship with the author of a document.

REL=`"author"`—The link is *to* the author (for example, via a **mailto** URL), or to information about the author.

REV=`"author"`—The current document contains information about the author of the linked document.

Example:

```
<LINK REV="made" REL="author" HREF="mailto:isq@fe.fi.fo.fum.org">
```

The destination of the link is the author of the current document (the link lets you send him or her mail); at the same time, the target of the link "made" the current document.

copyright — Indicates a relationship with copyright information relevant to a document.

REL=`"copyright"`—The link is *to* a document containing copyright information relevant to the current document.

REV=`"copyright"`—The current document contains copyright information appropriate to the linked document.

Example:

```
<LINK REL="copyright" HREF="copy_info.html">
```

The destination of the link contains copyright information relevant to the current document.

disclaimer — Indicates a relationship with a legal disclaimer associated with a document.

REL=`"disclaimer"`—The link is *to* a document containing a legal disclaimer relevant to the current document.

REV=`"disclaimer"`—The current document contains a legal disclaimer relevant to the linked document.

editor — Indicates a relationship with information about the editor (or editors) of the document.

REL=`"editor"`—The link is *to* the editor(s) (for example, a **mailto** URL), or to information about the editor(s).

REV=`"editor"`—The current document contains information about the editor(s) of the document.

meta — Indicates a relationship with a node containing diverse meta- (**LINK**, **META,** or other) information relevant to a document.

REL=`"meta"`—The link is *to* a document containing meta-information about the current document.

REV=`"meta"`—The current document contains meta-information relevant to the linked document.

publisher — Indicates a relationship with information about the publisher (or publishers) of a document.

REL=`"publisher"`—The link is *to* the publisher(s) (for example, via a **mailto** URL), or to information about the publisher(s).

REV=`"publisher"`—The current document contains information about the publisher(s) of the linked document.

trademark — Indicates trademark information relevant to a document.

REL=`"trademark"`—The link is *to* trademark information relevant to the current document.

REV=`"trademark"`—The current document contains trademark information relevant to the linked document.

LEGACY VALUES

Some simple **REL/REV** values are already in use. These are:

made — Defines a relationship with the creator of a document.

REV=`"made"`—Indicates that the current document was created by the user referenced by the indicated URL.

Examples:

```
<LINK REV="made" HREF="mailto:igraham@foo.bar.edu">
```

```
<LINK REV="made" HREF="http://home.edu/igraham/home.html">
```

These links indicate that the current document was created by the person referenced at the indicated URL.

CLASS ATTRIBUTES AND OTHER EXTENSIONS

The list of **REL** and **REV** values will grow as uses are found for new relationship values. Murray Maloney's discussion paper reviews some other, proposed, values. In HTML 3, both **LINK** and **A** can take a **CLASS** attribute, which leads to the possibility of selecting certain relationships according to their class. For example, multiple author-defined navigation sequences could be defined, according to the **CLASS**, via:

```
<LINK REL="next" CLASS="beginner" HREF="...">
```

```
<LINK REL="next" CLASS="expert" HREF="...">
```

which could permit selecting alternate paths through the collection, depending on the experience of the user. Alternatively,

```
<LINK REL="next" CLASS="path-A" HREF="...">

<LINK REL="next" CLASS="path-B" HREF="...">
```

could allow exploration of the same set of documents using alternate exploratory paths. This is not currently possible, as it requires an implementation of **CLASS**, along with well-defined values and meanings for a set of **CLASS** values.

REFERENCES

A general discussion of hypertext links and of **REL** and **REV** values is found in the HTML 2.0 and HTML 3 references listed in Chapters 4 and 5. Murray Maloney's discussion paper presents a more detailed treatment of these issues, as well as a complete list of generally accepted, and proposed, **REL** and **REV** values. This document can be found at:

http://www.sq.com/papers/Relationships.html

http://ogopogo.nttc.edu/tools/html/mmaloney_links.html

agent   A program that can travel over the Internet and access remote resources for you, on your behalf. A proper agent should be able to run on remote machines and travel freely from machine to machine. The Java language shows promise for permitting safe agents, since the Java interpreter does not let *Java applets* harm the computers they contact.

anchor   The location of a hypertext link in a document. An anchor can be either the start of a hypertext link or the destination of a hypertext link.

anonymous FTP   Computers can run a special server known as an anonymous FTP server, which permit guests to log in on the computer and access public resources. In general, when you log in to an FTP site as user *anonymous*, you (or your browser) use your e-mail address for the password string.

applet   A program that can be *downloaded* over a network and activated on the user's computer. To do this safely, you must have a safe way of running applets. The Java language offers this possibility.

archie   A system that automatically generates and maintains a contents database for anonymous FTP servers. An archie server accesses information from FTP servers and archives the directory listings. An archie client can access these databases and search for programs or files matching a particular name.

archive file   A single file that contains a collection of different files and/or directories. Archive files are often used to transport collections of files across the Internet, since you can transport a large collection in a single archive file. UNIX archives have the extension *.tar* (for **T**ape **AR**chive). PKZIP is often used to create archives on DOS computers (suffix *.zip*), while Stuffit is often used to create Macintosh archives (suffixes *.sea* or *.sit*). **PKZIP** and **Stuffit** archives are also *compressed*.

ASCII   American Standard Code for Information Interchange, a 7-bit character code capable of representing 128 characters. Many of these characters are special control characters used in communications control, and are not printable.

attribute   A quantity that defines a special property of an HTML element. Attributes are specified within the start tag. For example, <IMG SRC="image.gif"> means that the element **IMG** has an attribute **SRC,** which is assigned the indicated value.

browser   Any program used to view material prepared for the World Wide Web. **Mosaic, MacWeb,** and **lynx** are examples of browsers. Browsers are able to interpret URLs and HTML markup and also understand several Internet protocols, such as HTTP, FTP, and Gopher.

CERN   Centre Européen pour la Récherche Nucleaire, a large physics particle-accelerator laboratory located near Geneva, on the French-Swiss border. The World Wide Web originated here, largely due to the efforts of Tim Berners-Lee.

CGI   Common Gateway Interface, the specification for how an HTTP server should communicate with server gateway programs. Most servers support the CGI specification.

client   A program used to extract information from a server. For example, a browser such as **MacWeb** is a client that can access data from HTTP (and other) servers.

compressed   Many files on the Internet are compressed—this reduces the space taken up by a file and makes transmitting it over the Internet faster. The user must then have a program to decompress the file.

CRLF   The combination of carriage-return (CR) and linefeed (LF) characters. This combination is used by several Internet protocols, including HTTP, to denote the end of a line.

CSO   Computing Services Office, a system that allows you to search for student and/or faculty names at a school or university. It is one approach at trying to make a "white pages" for Internet e-mail addresses.

CWIS   Campus Wide Information Systems, electronic systems for distributing campus information, which first became common with central university **Gopher** servers.

dial-up connection   The action of using a telephone and modem to connect to a remote computer. Dial-up connections are slow compared with direct connections.

domain name   A computer on the Internet can have a *domain name* that is mapped onto its formal numeric Internet (IP) address. Domain names allow you to reference Internet sites without having to know the numerical addresses.

download   Transfer of a file from a remote computer to a local computer.

DTD   Document Type Definition. An SGML document type definition is a specific description of a markup language. This description is written as a plain text file, often with the filename extension *.dtd*. The HyperText Markup Language (HTML) has its own Document Type Definition file, often called *html.dtd*.

e-mail   Electronic mail.

element (HTML)   The basic unit of an HTML document. HTML documents use start and stop *tags* to define structural elements in the document. These elements are arranged hierarchically, to define the overall document structure. The name of the element is given in the tag, and indicates the meaning associated with the block. Some elements are *empty*, since they don't affect a block. Elements that have content are also often called *containers*.

end tag   A markup tag that denotes the end of an *element*.

firewall   A *firewall* is used to separate a local network from the outside world. In general a local network is connected to the outside world by a "gateway" computer. This gateway machine can be converted into a firewall by installing special software that does not let unauthorized TCP/IP packets pass from inside to outside and vice versa. You can give users on the local network, and "inside" the firewall, access to the outside world using the **SOCKS** package or by installing the CERN HTTP *proxy server* on the firewall machine.

fragment identifier   A text string included via a **NAME** attribute in an A element, that can be used to reference the **NAMEd** location —thus the word *fragment*, since it references just a fragment of the document.

FTP   File Transfer Protocol is an Internet client-server protocol for transferring files between computers.

GIF   GIF, for Graphics Interchange Format, is a format for storing image files. It is one of only three formats that can appear inline in an HTML document, the other two being X-Bitmaps and X-Pixelmaps.

Gopher   A protocol for distributed information delivery commonly used in distributed information systems. Gopher clients give you access to this information. Gopher is a menu-based delivery system and does not have hypertext capabilities.

header   The leading part of a data message. Thus HTTP messages are sent with an HTTP *header* preceding the actual communicated data.

helper application   A program launched or used by a browser (such as **Mosaic** or **MacWeb**) to process files that the browser cannot handle internally. Thus users have helpers to view JPEG images or play sound files, and also to uncompress compressed files or unstuff archives.

hits   In database searches, the number of documents that resulted from the search; for servers, the number of document requests being served by the server.

home page   The introductory page for a World Wide Web site. A home page usually provides an introduction to the site, along with hypertext links to local resources.

HTML   HyperText Markup Language, a markup language defined by an SGML Document Type Definition (DTD). To a document writer, HTML is simply a collection of tags used to mark blocks of text and assign them special meanings.

hyperlink   See hypertext link.

hypertext   Any document that contains *hypertext links* to other documents. HTML documents are almost always hypertext documents.

hypertext link   A hypertext relationship between two anchors, leading from the *head* to the *tai*. n the Web, this is usually a link from one hypertext document to another. Linking points are associated with **anchors**.

IETF   Internet Engineering Task Force, a collection of task forces at work on developing standards for Internet protocols and architectures. There are IETF groups working on such issues as URLs, HTTP, and HTML.

inline image   An image that is merged with the displayed text. Placing images in this manner is often described as "inlining" the images.

Internet   You mean you don't know? The Internet is the worldwide network of computers communicating via the TCP/IP protocols.

Internet provider   The company from whom you purchase your Internet connectivity. This could either be a dedicated connection (for example, a telephone connection that stays open twenty-four hours a day) or a dial-up connection. Usually you run software such as PPP or SLIP to allow Internet connectivity across the line.

Internet resources   The collection of data, documents, and databases available on the Internet.

IP address   The numerical Internet protocol address of a computer on the Internet. Every computer on the Internet has a unique numerical address.

ISO   International Standards Organization, an international organization responsible for setting international standards, such as the ISO Latin-1 character set.

ISO Latin-1   An 8-bit character code developed by the International Standards Organization. An 8-bit code contains 256 different characters. In the ISO Latin-1 code, the first 128 characters are the equivalent to the 128 characters of the US-ASCII character set (also called the ISO 646 character set). The remaining 128 characters consist of control characters and a large collection of accented and other characters commonly used in European languages.

Java   A programming language, developed by Sun Microsystems, designed specifically for use in *applet* and *agent* applications. Java programs can only run under a Java interpreter, which is designed to eliminate the risk of a rogue Java applet damaging the local computer.

JPEG   From Joint Photographic Experts Group, JPEG is an image format. In general JPEG allows for higher quality images than GIF. Browsers cannot display JPEG images inline, and instead must display them using *helper* programs.

kerberos   A network authentication system, based on the key distribution model. It allows machines communicating over networks to prove their identity to each other through a trusted third party. It also prevents eavesdropping or replay attacks (recording and retrying encryption keys "snooped" off the network), through support for a variety of data encryption schemes.

LAN   Local Area Network.

link   See hypertext link.

linux   A freeware clone of UNIX for 386-based PC computers. Linux consists of the linux kernel (core operating system), originally written by Linus Torvalds, along with utility programs developed by the Free Software Foundation and others. Since PC hardware is inexpensive and linux is essentially free, the combination of the two is a practical way of developing inexpensive and reliable HTTP service.

listserv   An automated electronic mailing list, managed by a **listserv** program. Listervs are commonly used by discussion groups.

Lynx   A very popular character-mode (text-only) World Wide Web browser.

MIME   Multipurpose Internet Mail Extensions, a scheme for allowing electronic mail messages to contain mixed media (sound, video, image, and text). The World Wide Web uses the MIME content-type to specify the type of data contained in a file or being sent from an HTTP server to a client.

Mosaic   A graphical browser for the World Wide Web, developed at NCSA. There are also several commercial versions of Mosaic.

MPEG   MPEG, which stands for Motion Picture Experts Group, is a common video file compression method.

multimedia   A mixture of media—text, audio, and video—under the control of a computer. The World Wide Web is a form of multimedia.

nameserver   A computer (and a program on the computer) that translates domain names into the proper numeric IP address (or vice versa).

NCSA   National Center for Supercomputing Applications. The NCSA is situated at the Urbana-Champaign campus of the University of Illinois. The NCSA software development team developed the Mosaic and NCSA HTTPD server programs.

NNTP   Network News Transfer Protocol, used for communicating USENET articles across the Internet.

packet   A small package of data. The TCP/IP Internet protocol breaks messages up into packets, and sends each packet independently to the message destination. The protocol ensures that there is no error in transmission and that the entire message arrives.

partial URL   A location scheme containing only partial information about the resource location. To access the resource, a client program must construct a full URL, based on the partial URL. It does so by assuming that all the information not found in the partial URL is the same as that used when the client accessed the document containing the partial URL reference. A partial URL is often also called a *relative URL*, since the location of the linked resource is determined *relative* to the location of the document containing the partial URL.

PEM   Privacy Enhanced Mail, a special mail protocol that provides encryption of mail message content.

perl   Practical Extraction and Reporting Language, a scripting language written by Larry Wall. Because powerful data and text manipulation programs can be written quickly and easily using perl, it has become a popular language for writing CGI applications.

PGP   An acronym for Pretty Good Privacy, this is a publicly available encryption scheme that uses the "public key" approach—
messages are encrypted using a "public" key, but can only be decrypted by a "private" key, retained by the intended recipient of the message.

port number   Any Internet application communicates at a particular port number specific to the application. For example FTP, HTTP, Gopher, and telnet are all assigned unique port numbers so that the computer knows what to do when contacted at a particular port. There are accepted standard numbers for these ports so that computers know which port to connect to for a particular service. For example, Gopher servers generally "talk" at port 70, while HTTP servers generally "talk" at port 80. These default values can be overridden in a URL.

PPP   Point-to-Point Protocol is a communications protocol that allows you to turn a dial-up telephone connection into a point-to-point Internet connection. This is commonly used to run WWW browsers over a phone line.

provider   See *Internet provider*.

protocol   In computer networks, a protocol is simply an agreed convention for inter-computer communication. Thus the TCP/IP protocol defines how messages are passed on the Internet, while the FTP protocol, which is built using the TCP/IP protocol, defines how FTP messages should be sent and received.

Proxy server   A server that acts as an intermediary between your computer and the computer you want to access. Thus if you make a request for a resource from computer "A," this request is directed to a proxy server, which makes the request, gets the response from computer "A," and then forwards the response to you. Proxy servers are useful for accessing World Wide Web resources from inside a *firewall*.

relative URL   See partial URL.

RFC   An *RFC*, or Request For Comments, is a document, written by groups or individuals involved in Internet development, that describes agreed-upon standards or proposes new standards for Internet protocols. For example, the rules for electronic mail message composition are specified in the document RFC 822.

robots   On the World Wide Web, a program that autonomously searches through trees of hypertext documents, retrieving files for indexing (or other purposes). Also called *worm*.

router   A computer that determines, on a local basis, which route packets will take en route to their destination.

RSA   A common, commercial public-key encryption technology, owned by RSA Data Security Inc. RSA Inc. also holds several patents on public-key encryption in general, so that popular publicly available encryption tools, such as PGP and PEM, infringe on the RSA patents. PGP and PEM therefore cannot be used in commercial products without licensing approval of RSA Inc.

server   A program, running on a networked computer, that responds to requests from client programs running on other networked computers. The server and client communicate using a client-server *protocol*.

SGML   Standard Generalized Markup Language, a standard for describing markup languages. HTML is defined as an instance of SGML.

shell   The UNIX *shell* is the program that interprets the commands typed at the terminal. A shell can also be used to run simple script programs called *shell scripts*. There are several different shells, with slightly different commands and syntax. The most common are the Bourne shell (**sh**), the C shell (**csh**), and the Korn shell (**ksh**).

SLIP   Serial Line Internet Protocol is a communications protocol that allows you to turn a dial-up telephone connection into an Internet connection. SLIP can be used to run WWW browsers over a phone line, but is less stable than a PPP connection.

SMTP   Simple Mail Transfer Protocol, the standard by which electronic mail messages are communicated over the Internet.

SOCKS   A software package that allows hosts inside a firewall to communicate with the outside world. To allow access to the outside world, a secure network must run a SOCKS server on its gateway/firewall machine, and all its networking software must be configured to talk to the SOCKS server. SOCKS is a proxy server without the special caching capabilities of the CERN HTTP server.

start tag (HTML)   A markup tag that denotes the start of an *element*.

tag (HTML)   HTML marks documents using *tags*. A tag is simply typed text surrounded by the less than and greater than signs, for example: <TAG>. An *end tag* has a slash in front of the tag name, such as </TAG>.

tar   An acronym for tape **ar**chiver, *tar* is a program (and file format) commonly used on UNIX systems for archiving and transporting large collections of files and/or directories.

TCP/IP   Transmission Control Protocol/Internet Protocol, the basic communication protocol that is the foundation of the Internet. All the other protocols, such as HTTP, FTP, and Gopher, are built on top of TCP/IP.

telnet   A terminal emulation protocol that allows you to make a terminal connection to other computers on the Internet. This requires that you run a telnet client on your computer and connect to a telnet server on the other machine.

TIA   *TIA* (The Internet Adapter) is a program that you can run on a dial-in UNIX account and that allows you to create a SLIP-like connection between your home computer and the dial-in site. TIA is useful if you have a UNIX account with a company that does not provide PPP or SLIP service.

TIFF   TIFF, for Tag Image File Format, is a graphic file format developed by Aldus Corporation. TIFF is the standard format of many graphics and desktop publishing programs.

tn3270   A variant of *telnet* that emulates the behavior of IBM model 3270 display terminals.

UNIX   An operating system, commonly used on the backbone machines on the Internet. Most Web servers are run under the UNIX operating system.

URC   URC (Uniform Resource Characteristics) is an as-yet unspecified format for representing aggregate information about a resource or collection of resources.

URI   Uniform Resource Identifier, the generic term for a coded string that identifies a (typically Internet) resource. There are currently two practical examples of URIs, namely Uniform Resource Locators (*URLs*) and relative URLs.

URL   Uniform Resource Locator, the scheme used to address Internet resources on the World Wide Web. A URL specifies the protocol, domain name/IP address, port number, path, and resource details needed to access a resource from a particular machine. Partial (sometimes called relative) URLs are an associated scheme that specify a location relative to the location of a document or resource containing the URL reference.

URN   URNs or Uniform Resource Names, are as yet undefined, but are the holy grail of addressing, as a file would retain the same URN, regardless of which computer the file resided on.

USENET   The Internet's worldwide bulletin board system, consisting of over 4,000 topical discussion groups, called newsgroups. The newsgroups related to the World Wide Web were mentioned at the end of Chapter 1. USENET postings are distributed around the world using the *WWTP* protocol.

viewer   A program launched by a browser (such as Mosaic or MacWeb) to view files that the browser cannot handle internally. Thus you have viewers for JPEG images, sound files, and MPEG movies. Viewers are also often called *helpers* or *helper applications*.

visit   When you access a World Wide Web document you are said to be *visiting* the site.

VMS   An operating system that runs on Digital Equipment Corporation VAX (and some Alpha-based) computers.

whitespace   Any combination of space or tab characters that separate two characters or two character strings.

WAIS   Short for Wide Area Information Servers, a system and protocol for Internet-accessible databases. The WAIS protocol is based on the *Z39.50* protocol.

WAN   Wide Area Network.

worm   On the Web, a worm is synonymous with a robot (see robots). Alternatively, a computer program that can make copies of itself.

WWW   The World Wide Web. Also called the Web or W^3.

Z39.50   A protocol for expressing search information, allowing remote searching of databases. Many library systems support the Z39.50 protocol.

INDEX

A

A (anchor) element, 25
description of, 186-92
HREF attribute, 186, 188
ID attribute (HTML 3), 258
METHODS attribute, 191
NAME attribute, 74-75, 186, 188-89, 258
in PRE element, 186
REL and REV attributes, 102, 189-90, 658, 660
spaces in, 25
TARGET attribute (Netscape), 144, 191-92
TITLE attribute, 190-91
URN attribute, 190
ABBREV element (HTML 3), 308
ABOVE element (HTML 3), 324, 331-32
accents, for mathematical symbols, 329
ACCEPT attribute, INPUT element (HTML 3), 281
Accept-Charset field (HTTP), 408
Accept-Encoding field (HTTP), 408-9
Accept field (HTTP), 384-85, 407
Accept-language field (HTTP), 409
ACRONYM element (HTML 3), 308
ACTION attribute, FORM element, 158-59
active images, 515-23
allowed formats for, 515-16
considerations before using, 516
getting a click to do nothing, 521
imagemap program and, 517-21
making an image active, 516-17
ADDRESS element, 40, 46, 153
ALIGN attribute
ARRAY element (HTML 3), 328
in BODY-content elements (HTML 3), 259-60
CAPTION element (HTML 3), 218, 274
elements that can use, 260
FIG element (HTML 3), 266, 272
Hn (H1-H6) and P elements, 81, 171
HR element (Netscape), 172
IMG element, 21, 81-83, 193, 194-95
INPUT element, 164
INPUT element (HTML 3), 281
MARQUEE element (Microsoft Internet Explorer), 243
P element (HTML 3), 181, 184-85

TAB element (HTML 3), 304-5
TABLE element (HTML 3), 294
for TABLE elements (HTML 3), 86-88, 291
TD element (HTML 3), 221
TEXTAREA element (HTML 3), 282
TH element (HTML 3), 220
TR element (HTML 3), 219
alignment
of images, 81-85
ALIWeb, 529-30
Allow field (HTTP), 410
Alpha HTML editor, 540
ALT attribute, IMG element, 21-22, 111, 193, 194
AmiWeb, 536
anarchie, 631-32
anchor element. *See* A (anchor) element
animation techniques
client pull, 452-53
server push, 453-62
Apache server, 386, 405-7, 417
APIs (application programming interfaces), gateway, 449-50
APPLET element (Netscape), 226, 234-35
Arachnid, 541
Archie, finding software using, 629-32
AREA element, description of, 198-201
Arena browser, 247-48
ARRAY element (HTML 3), 327-28, 335-36
asc2html, 546
A.S.H.E., 543
ATOP element (HTML 3), 324, 333
attributes, 5-6, 131-32.
See also specific attributes
case sensitivity of, 134
literal strings and, 134
unknown, 135-36
values assigned to, 134, 139
audio snippets, inline, BGSOUND element (Microsoft Internet Explorer), 244
AU element (HTML 3), 308
authentication, 397-400, 416
Authorization field (HTTP), 409
author name, 308
AUTH_TYPE environment variable, 436
AXIS attribute, TD element (HTML 3), 300

B

BACKGROUND attribute, BODY element (HTML 3), 88, 151
backgrounds, 88
browsers not capable of rendering, 89
backtalk program, 381, 637
program listing for, 641-44
BANNER element (HTML 3), 263
BAR element (HTML 3), 329, 330
BASE element, 142
description of, 143-44
TARGET attribute (Netscape), 144
BASEFONT element (Netscape), 232
Basic authentication scheme, 397-400, 416
bbc_man2html.pl, 495
BBEdit, 540-41
BEHAVIOR attribute, MARQUEE element (Microsoft Internet Explorer), 243
B element
description of, 209
for mathematical expressions (HTML 3), 329
BELOW element (HTML3), 324
BELOW element (HTML 3), 332
BeyondPress, 547
BGCOLOR attribute
BODY element (Netscape), 152
MARQUEE element (Microsoft Internet Explorer), 243
TD element (Microsoft Internet Explorer), 222
TH element (Microsoft Internet Explorer), 220
BGPROPERTIES attribute, BODY element (Microsoft Internet Explorer), 152
BGSOUND element (Microsoft Internet Explorer), 244
BIG element, 225
BIG element (HTML 3 and Netscape), 310
blank lines, 12
BLINK element, 136
BLINK element (Netscape), 233-34
BLOCKQUOTE (BQ) element, 80, 153, 157-58, 310
in HTML 3, 263-64
BODY-content elements, in HTML 3, 140, 257-86
ALIGN attribute, 259-60
BANNER, 263
BLOCKQUOTE (BQ), 263-64
CAPTION, 273-74

677